Ancient Greek Music

Ancient Greek Music

M. L. WEST

CLARENDON PRESS · OXFORD

Oxford University Press, Walton Street, Oxford OX2 6DP
Oxford New York Toronto
Delhi Bombay Calcutta Madras Karachi
Kuala Lumpur Singapore Hong Kong Tokyo
Nairobi Dar es Salaam Cape Town
Melbourne Auckland Madrid
and associated companies in
Berlin Ibadan

Oxford is a trade mark of Oxford University Press

Published in the United States
by Oxford University Press Inc., New York

First issued as a Clarendon Paperback 1994

British Library Cataloguing in Publication Data
Data available

Library of Congress Cataloging in Publication Data
West, M. L. (Martin Litchfield), 1937–
Ancient Greek music / M.L. West.
Includes bibliographical references and index.
1. Music, Greek and Roman. I. Title.
ML169.W5 1992 780'.938—dc20 91–5170
ISBN 0–19–814897–6
ISBN 0–19–814975–1 (Pbk)

3 5 7 9 10 8 6 4

Typeset by Joshua Associates Ltd, Oxford
Printed in Great Britain on acid-free paper by
Biddles Ltd., Guildford and King's Lynn

PREFACE

M Y interest in the subject goes back to my second year as an under-graduate, when, browsing in J. U. Powell's corpus of fragments of Hellenistic verse, *Collectanea Alexandrina*, I was surprised to come upon several pages of music. They revealed themselves to be transcriptions of the two Delphic Paeans which are our most sub-stantial specimens of ancient melody. I committed one of them to memory, and the next spring, when I went to Greece for the first time, on arriving at Delphi I sang it at the top of my voice in the ruins of the sanctuary where it had had its première 2,084 springs pre-viously. My two travelling companions distanced themselves some-what. A little later, as we examined the stone on which the text is inscribed, one of them stumbled against it, and it nearly crashed from its moorings and shattered. (I married her all the same.)

In the hope that the book may be of interest not only to classicists but also to musicologists, and indeed anyone with an interest in the history of music, I have tried to avoid allusions that might be unintel-ligible to one or the other group. There are bound to be mentions of ancient authors, places, and institutions that will be unfamiliar to non-classicists, but where I have left them unelucidated they should be inessential to the argument. Reference works such as *The Oxford Classical Dictionary* or Mrs M. Howatson's *Oxford Companion to Classical Literature* will assist in most cases. All quotations from ancient sources are given in translation, and any Greek words appear in transliteration. Almost no musical knowledge is presup-posed.

I am indebted to Dr A. C. Baines, the former Curator of the Bate Collection of Historical Wind Instruments at Oxford, for encourage-ment and advice on various questions that arose in connection with Chapter 4; to Dr Günter Poethke of the Ägyptisches Museum in Berlin for important information concerning the musical papyrus that resides there; to Stephanie West for examining the same and answering a series of my queries about its text; to Professor W. G. Arnott, Professor Sir John Boardman, Professor J. N. Coldstream, Dr P. A. Hansen, Dr J. G. F. Hind, and Dr B. B. Rasmussen (Curator of Classical Antiquities in the National Museum of Denmark) for help with various questions; to Professor A. D. Trendall for permission to reproduce a plate from his book *Early South Italian Vase Painting*, published by Philipp von Zabern of Mainz, 1974; and to authorities of the following institutions for photographs and permissions: the Allard Pierson Museum, Amsterdam; the National Museum of Greece; the British School at Athens; Münzen und Medaillen AG, Basle; the Antikenmuseum and Staatliche Museen, Berlin; the Indiana University Art Museum, Bloomington; the Museum of Fine Arts, Boston; the Musées Royaux d'Art et d'Histoire, Brussels; the National Museum of Denmark; the Ruhrland Museum, Essen; the Museo Archeologico Etrusco, Florence; the Archaeological Museum, Heraklion; the British Museum; the Staatliche Antikensammlungen, Munich; the Museo Nazionale and Biblioteca Nazionale, Naples; the Metropolitan Museum, New York; the Musée du Louvre, Paris; the Museo della Villa Giulia, Rome. My thanks to them all; and, very far from least, to the production staff of the Oxford University Press for the effort they have devoted to a rather demanding book.

M.L.W.

All Souls College, Oxford
January 1992

CONTENTS

LIST OF PLATES

LIST OF FIGURES

ABBREVIATIONS

Ancient authors, text collections, periodicals, encyclopaedias

So far as possible I have used the same abbreviations as *The Oxford Classical Dictionary* (2nd edn., 1970). Note in addition:

Anon. Bellerm.	Anonymus Bellermanni.
CEG	P. A. Hansen, *Carmina Epigraphica Graeca*, i–ii (Berlin and New York, 1983–9).
Cleon.	Cleonides, *Introduction to Harmonics*, cited by Jan's page.
FGE	D. L. Page, *Further Greek Epigrams* (Cambridge, 1981).
GP	A. S. F. Gow and D. L. Page, *The Greek Anthology: The Garland of Philip* (Cambridge, 1968).
HE	A. S. F. Gow and D. L. Page, *The Greek Anthology: Hellenistic Epigrams* (Cambridge, 1965).
Mart. Cap.	Martianus Capella, *De nuptiis Philologiae et Mercurii*.
MGG	*Die Musik in Geschichte und Gegenwart* (Allgemeine Enzyklopädie der Musik, Kassel, 1949–79).
NG	*The New Grove Dictionary of Music and Musicians*, ed. S. Sadie (London, 1980).
Nicom. *Ench.*	Nicomachus, *Enchiridion*, cited by Jan's page.
Philod. *Mus.*	Philodemus, *On Music*.
PMG	*Poetae Melici Graeci*, ed. D. L. Page (Oxford, 1962).
Psell. *De trag.*	Michael Psellus, excerpt on tragedy, ed. R. Browning, in Γέρας: *Studies presented to G. Thomson* (Prague, 1963).
RE	Pauly–Wissowa, *Real-Encyclopädie der classischen Altertumswissenschaft* (Stuttgart, 1894–1980).
Sammelbuch	F. Preisigke and others, *Sammelbuch griechischer Urkunden aus Ägypten* (Strasburg etc., 1915–).

SLG	*Supplementum Lyricis Graecis*, ed. D. L. Page (Oxford, 1974).
Supp. Hell.	*Supplementum Hellenisticum*, ed. H. Lloyd-Jones and P. J. Parsons (Berlin and New York, 1983).
TrGF	*Tragicorum Graecorum Fragmenta*, ed. B. Snell and others (Göttingen, 1971–).
ZPE	*Zeitschrift für Papyrologie und Epigraphik*.

Modern authors cited by name alone or with abbreviated title

Aign, B., *Die Musikinstrumente des ägäischen Raumes bis um 700 vor Christus* (Frankfurt am Main, 1963).

Baines, A., *Bagpipes* (Oxford (Pitt Rivers Museum), 1960; revised edn., 1979).

—— *Brass* = *Brass Instruments* (London, 1976).

—— *Woodwind* = *Woodwind Instruments and their History*, 3rd edn. (London, 1967).

Barker, A., *GMW* = *Greek Musical Writings* (Cambridge, 1984–9).

Becker, H., *Zur Entwicklungsgeschichte der antiken und mittelalter-lichen Rohrblattinstrumente* (Hamburg, 1966).

Behn, F., *Musikleben im Altertum und frühen Mittelalter* (Stuttgart, 1954).

Burkert, W., *LS* = *Lore and Science in Ancient Pythagoreanism* (Cambridge, Mass., 1972).

Chailley, J., *La Musique grecque antique* (Paris, 1979).

Gentili, B., and Pretagostini, R. (eds.), *La Musica in Grecia* (Rome and Bari, 1988).

Georgiades, T., *Der griechische Rhythmus* (Hamburg, 1949).

Gevaert, F. A., *Histoire et théorie de la musique de l'antiquité* (Ghent, 1875–81).

Howard, A. A., 'The Aulos or Tibia', *Harv. Stud.* 4 (1893), 1–63.

Kaimio, M., *Characterization of Sound in Early Greek Literature* (*Commentationes Humanarum Litterarum*, 53, Helsinki, 1977).

Kunst, J., *Ethno-musicology*, 3rd edn. (The Hague, 1959).

Maas, M., and Snyder, J. McI., *Stringed Instruments of Ancient Greece* (New Haven and London, 1989).

Merriam, A. P., *The Anthropology of Music* (Northwestern University Press, 1964).

Nettl, B., *FTM* = *Folk and Traditional Music of the Western Continents*, 2nd edn. (Englewood Cliffs, NJ, 1973).

Neubecker, A. J., *Altgriechische Musik* (Darmstadt, 1977).

Pack, R. A., *The Greek and Latin Literary Texts from Greco-Roman Egypt*, 2nd edn. (Ann Arbor, Mich., 1965).

Paquette, D., *L'Instrument de musique dans la céramique de la Grèce antique* (Paris, 1984).

Pearson, L., *Aristoxenus, Elementa Rhythmica* (Oxford, 1990).

Pickard-Cambridge, A. W., *DFA* [2] = *The Dramatic Festivals of Athens*, 2nd edn. revised by J. Gould and D. M. Lewis (Oxford, 1968).

— *DTC* [2] = *Dithyramb, Tragedy, and Comedy*, 2nd edn. revised by T. B. L. Webster (Oxford, 1962).

Pöhlmann, E., *Beiträge* = *Beiträge zur antiken und neueren Musikgeschichte* (Frankfurt am Main, 1988).

— *DAM* = *Denkmäler altgriechischer Musik* (Nuremberg, 1970).

Reinach, T., 'Tibia', in C. Daremberg and E. Saglio, *Dictionnaire des antiquités grecques et romaines*, v (1919), 300–32.

Rimmer, Joan, *Ancient Musical Instruments of Western Asia in the British Museum* (London, 1969).

Sachs, C., *HMI* = *The History of Musical Instruments* (New York, 1940).

— *RT* = *Rhythm and Tempo* (New York, 1953).

— *WM* = *The Wellsprings of Music* (The Hague, 1962).

Schlesinger, Kathleen, *The Greek Aulos* (London, 1939).

Sifakis, G. M., *Studies in the History of Hellenistic Drama* (London, 1967).

Thesleff, H., *The Pythagorean Texts of the Hellenistic Period* (Åbo, 1965).

Webster, T. B. L., *The Greek Chorus* (London, 1970).

Wegner, M., *Bilder* = *Griechenland* (*Musikgeschichte in Bildern*, ii. 4, Leipzig, 1963).

— *Musikleben* = *Das Musikleben der Griechen* (Berlin, 1949).

— *Musik und Tanz* (*Archaeologia Homerica*, U, Göttingen, 1968).

Welch, C., *Six Lectures on the Recorder* (London, 1911).

Wille, G., *Musica Romana: Die Bedeutung der Musik im Leben der Römer* (Amsterdam, 1967).

Winnington-Ingram, R. P., *Mode in Ancient Greek Music* (Cambridge, 1936).

Introduction

MUSIC, Musik, musique, musica, muzsika, muzyka, musiikki, müzik, miwsig: the world owes the word to the Greeks. Melody, harmony, symphony, polyphony: these too. Orchestra, organ, chorus, chord, tone, baritone, tonic, diatonic, diapason, chromatic, rhythm, syncopation: all from Greek. Ancient Greek culture was permeated with music. Probably no other people in history has made more frequent reference to music and musical activity in its literature and art.

Yet the subject is practically ignored by nearly all who study that culture or teach about it. Sometimes its very existence seems to be barely acknowledged. In a justly celebrated book on the Lesbian poets we read that it is a natural assumption that all or almost all Sappho's poems 'were recited by herself informally to her companions'.[1] The isles of Greece, the isles of Greece, where burning Sappho loved and *recited*? In that generally admirable volume *The Oxford History of the Classical World* (1986) we look in vain for a section on Greek music. The subject is indeed touched on in connection with lyric poetry, but in the briefest terms. Many similar cases could be cited.

The most pervasive sign of the average classicist's unconcern with the realities of music is the ubiquitous rendering of *aulos*, a reed-blown instrument, by 'flute'. There was a time when it was legitimate, because the classification of instruments had not been thought out scientifically and it was quite customary to speak of a 'flute family' that included the reed-blown instruments.[2] But that tolerant era is long past, and now the only excuse for calling an aulos a flute is that given by Dr Johnson when asked why he defined 'pastern' as the knee of a horse: 'Ignorance, madam, pure ignorance.' Yet countless literary scholars and even archaeologists persist in this deplorable habit, deaf to all protests from the enlightened. One might as well call the *syrinx* a mouth organ. Those who rely on the standard

---

[1] D. L. Page, *Sappho and Alcaeus* (Oxford, 1955), 119. His emphasis is on 'informally', as opposed to a formal or ceremonial setting.　　　[2] See Becker, 36–8.

Greek–English lexicon are not well served in this matter: 'flute' appears erroneously in at least seventy articles.

But the malady extends to other instruments too. Even so eminent a musicologist as Dr Egon Wellesz, in his *History of Byzantine Music and Hymnography*, besides calling *auloi* flutes, renders *kitharai* as 'zithers'. In the New English Bible, supposedly an effort of the most authoritative and up-to-date scholarship, not only are *auloi* constantly 'flutes' but in the Book of Revelation *kitharai* are 'harps' and *kitharōidoi* 'harpers'. The Jerusalem Bible commits the same errors, only more consistently.[3] Meanwhile *pēktis*, which in the classical period does mean a harp, is variously rendered by different scholars as a 'lyre' or a 'lute'.[4]

It must be allowed that those wishing to inform themselves about Greek music have not found things made particularly easy for them. Accounts of the subject in English have been few and far between. They have tended to be of the highest scholarly accomplishment, but daunting to the uninitiated inquirer, who has soon found himself floundering among disjunct enharmonic tetrachords and Mixolydian/Hypoaeolian/Hyperphrygian transposition-keys, and has halted before a long table of notes with prodigious names like *paranētē diezeugmenōn* and *tritē hyperbolaiōn*. Little wonder if he has cried out, like Thomas Morley's Philomathes, 'heere is a Table in deede contayning more than ever I meane to beate my brayns about'.[5]

Well, he will eventually come upon such horrors in this book too; they are unfortunately necessary. But I scheme to lead him to them so gently and persuasively that by the time they rear up before him they will not seem so formidable after all. I am particularly well qualified to attempt this, being wholly without musical training. I have to take these things slowly to make them clear to myself.

I try to explain everything from the ground up, desiring the book to be accessible to anyone who knows roughly what an octave is. To the reader whose musical theory is at or near this minimum level I say with Epicurus, 'I congratulate you on coming to philosophy untainted by any education.' As for those who have left this state of innocence behind, I trust they will bear patiently with explanations

---

[3] Likewise H. W. Parke, *Festivals of the Athenians* (London, 1977), 35.
[4] Webster, 93, and others; J. E. Powell, *Lexicon to Herodotus* (Cambridge, 1938), 305.
[5] T. Morley, *A plaine and easie introduction to practicall musicke* (London, 1597), 34.

of things that to them are elementary. They may occasionally find
that their learning is a treacherous light. Some, for instance, who are
familiar with the terms chromatic and enharmonic as they are used
in connection with Western music will be unprepared for the fact
that they mean something different in Greek. And some who are
sure they know what the Dorian or the Lydian mode is may be dis-
concerted to discover that in Antiquity it was nothing of the kind.

Apart from petty snares like these, there is a general danger of coming to ancient Greek music with preconceptions formed by Western
musical culture. Some nineteenth-century investigators fell prey to
such preconceptions to a degree that looks grotesque from this distance. Can we do better? Yes, we can; in particular, because of the
great advances made by ethnomusicology in the present century, and
the general widening of musical horizons. The concert-going or radio-
listening public nowadays wanders in a landscape that extends not
from Bach to Brahms but from Gregorian chant to gamelan and
gagaku. Ancient Greek music is not part of our local, West European,
post-Renaissance tradition, but it *is* part of world music, and it needs
to be seen in ethnological perspective. Musical instruments and
melodic styles have histories that extend over millennia and across
geographical zones far larger than the territories of a single nation. At
various points it will be appropriate to refer to comparative material
from the ancient Near East or from more recent musical cultures in
the Balkans, Africa, or elsewhere. There may even be mention of
'primitive' music, which I hope will be taken in the right spirit. It is not a
question of setting the Greeks on the level of what used to be called
'savages'. The fact is that their music is better understood by putting it
in the broad category of ethnic music, extending down to the most
primitive and limited manifestations of the melodic instinct, than by
looking in it for the workings of supposedly natural and universal
principles which are actually abstracted from German music of the
eighteenth and nineteenth centuries, as was once the approach.[6]

[6] From the writings of Rudolph Westphal: (1) 'The rhythm of ancient music is so
essentially one with the rhythm of modern composers that without detailed knowledge of the rhythmic forms used by these, and in particular without detailed apprecia-
tion of the rhythms of the great J. S. Bach, the necessary parallels were lacking which
alone enabled the material transmitted by the Greek rhythmicians to be correctly
understood' (*Die Musik des griechischen Alterthumes nach den alten Quellen neu
bearbeitet* (Leipzig, 1883), 5). (2) 'The Greeks' non-diatonic music that admits intervals smaller than a semitone, which are wholly foreign to the modern art, will probably, alas, remain for ever an enigma to scholarship' (*Griechische Harmonik und
Melopoeie*, 3rd edn. (Leipzig, 1886), ix).

Source material

How do we know anything about ancient music? The evidence can be summarized under five heads.

First, there is the evidence of archaeology and art. We have some remains of actual instruments, mainly pipes, but only, of course, their less perishable parts. There are also models of instruments, made for votive or other purposes, and figurines, statues, and reliefs representing men, women, or deities playing instruments. Above all, there are large numbers of vase-paintings, particularly from Athens in the sixth and fifth centuries BC and from Greek South Italy in the fourth. They have much to tell us not only about forms of instruments but also about performing techniques and contexts. They can even tell us something about singing. Other forms of pictorial art, such as engraved gems, frescos, and mosaics, contribute additional information for later periods.

Secondly there are the innumerable references to music and music-making scattered through Greek literature from the eighth century BC onwards. The lyric and comic poets are especially rich in them. We are fortunate in the fact that many musical references by lost authors of these categories and by out-of-the-way historians and antiquarians were collected and quoted by Athenaeus of Naucratis (AD *c.* 200) in his *Deipnosophistai*, a lengthy work in dialogue form in which all aspects of the Classical supper-party and symposium are eruditely discussed and illustrated. Athenaeus' dull-witted contemporary and fellow citizen Pollux is also of importance as a compiler of Classical terminology, catalogued in the manner of Roget's *Thesaurus* with no discussion and only sporadic citation of sources. Latin authors provide further useful material, in so far as they reflect Greek sources or allude to current Greek or common Graeco-Roman musical practice.

As a third category we may distinguish specialist writing on music. This supplies us with much information of a technical nature on which other authors are largely silent. Of especial importance is Aristoxenus of Tarentum, a pupil of Aristotle. A number of his many works were to do with music in one aspect or another. Nearly all of them are lost, regrettably, though valuable fragments are preserved by Athenaeus and others. What has survived in a more continuous state consists of a few pages from his *Elements of Rhythm* and three books of *Harmonics*, the first of which represents a different treatise from the rest;

the third book breaks off in mid-argument.[7] Aristoxenus' harmonic theory was highly influential, and it is regurgitated in several works written probably between the second and fifth centuries AD, where lost portions of Aristoxenus' exposition are also reflected. These works are the *Introductions to Harmonics* of Cleonides and Gaudentius, the *Introductions to Music* of Bacchius and Alypius, and the much longer and more wide-ranging work *On Music* by Aristides Quintilianus. Cleonides' lucid handbook, formerly misattributed to Euclid, is the most purely Aristoxenian.

Other works of about Aristoxenus' time or soon after it are the *Sectio Canonis* or *Division of the kanōn*, which may be a genuine work of Euclid's, and the (pseudo-)Aristotelian *Problems*. The *Problems* are a collection of about 900 scientific questions in the form 'Why is it that . . .' with reasoned suggestions for answers, arranged under thirty-eight headings and put together in the Peripatetic school. Two of the sections, the eleventh and nineteenth, are concerned with matters of acoustics and harmony respectively. The *Sectio Canonis* is a short treatment of harmony from the mathematical angle, the *kanōn* being the graduated rule of a monochord which gives out different notes according to the length of the resonating section of the string. This approach is also represented in several works of the first half of the second century AD: Theon of Smyrna's *Explanation of Mathematical Matters for Readers of Plato*, Nicomachus of Gerasa's *Harmonic Handbook*, and, much more important, the *Harmonics* of Ptolemy. In the third century the Neoplatonist Porphyry wrote a commentary on Ptolemy's work. This too contains some useful matter.

The Epicurean philosopher Philodemus (first century BC) wrote a work on music which is partially preserved; it is a polemic against the view that music has ethical effects on the listener. Sextus Empiricus (AD *c.* 200) argues similarly in his essay *Against the Musicians*, which forms the sixth book of his *Against the Scientists*. The dialogue *On Music* which comes down to us as a work of Plutarch's, but is certainly not by him, is a source of unique value for the early history of Greek music, or at least for what was believed about it in the Classical period. Though itself late—perhaps of about Athenaeus' time—it cites excellent Classical authorities such as Glaucus of Rhegium

---

[7] 'Harmonics', in ancient terminology, is the science dealing with the ordered arrangement of notes in scales and the relationships between scales. It was not concerned like modern harmonic theory with chords and chord-successions.

(*c.* 400 BC, author of a book *On the Ancient Poets and Musicians*), Heraclides Ponticus (mid-fourth century BC), and Aristoxenus (lost writings), and it paraphrases substantial excerpts from them in undigested form.

There are other, still later sources that preserve valuable nuggets of information derived from Classical historians of music. There is the *Chrestomathy* of the fifth-century Neoplatonist Proclus, a history of poetry of which half survives in an epitome by Photius; and a brief discussion of tragedy by Michael Psellus (eleventh century), not published until 1963.[8] Many elements of Greek theory were taken over by the Arab writers on music, the most important of whom is Abū n-Naṣr Muḥammad ibn Muḥammad ibn Tarḫān ibn ʾUzlaǵ al-Fārābī, popularly known as Al-Fārābī (*c.* 870–950).[9]

Two Latin authors occasionally cited are Martianus Capella (early fifth century) and Boethius (early sixth century). Martianus' *De nuptiis Philologiae et Mercurii* is a survey of the liberal arts. The treatment of music, which occupies the ninth book, is based primarily on Aristides Quintilianus. Boethius too is writing a compendium of the subject as one branch of the higher learning among others. His main authorities are Nicomachus, Cleonides, and Ptolemy. Though he has little of independent value for our inquiry, he is of great historical significance as the point of departure for medieval theorists.

Finally a mention must be made of the so-called Anonymus Bellermanni, the notional author (or, according to the latest editor, three authors) of a scrappy collection of material on music, transmitted in a number of Byzantine manuscripts and first published by F. Bellermann in 1841. It is drawn to a marked extent from Aristoxenus and Aristides Quintilianus, but contains some valuable matter not found elsewhere, including half a dozen little instrumental tunes and exercises.[10]

---

[8] By R. Browning in Γέρας: *Studies presented to G. Thomson* (Prague, 1963), 67 ff.

[9] His *Grand Book of Music* (*Kitābu l-Mūsīqī al-Kabīr*) is translated by R. D'Erlanger in *La Musique arabe*, i (Paris, 1930).

[10] D. Najock, *Anonyma de musica scripta Bellermanniana* (Leipzig, 1975). —The above brief survey is not intended to be a comprehensive catalogue of all who wrote on music, but merely to introduce the names of the main ones whom the reader will find referred to in the book. For a fuller review see Neubecker, 16–38. Of the authors and works I have mentioned, the following are translated, with excellent introductions and notes, in Barker, *GMW*: the pseudo-Aristotelian *Problems* (selection), Aristoxenus, Euclid, Nicomachus, Ptolemy, pseudo-Plutarch, Athenaeus (selection), Aristides Quintilianus.

The fourth category of evidence consists of non-literary documents, especially inscriptions, occasionally also papyri. These may record, for example, the hiring of musicians of some particular sort, the conferment of honours on some virtuoso, the establishment of musical subjects in a school curriculum, or the musical contests held at some festival and the prizes assigned to each.

The fifth category consists of actual musical scores. From at least the fourth century BC the Greeks had a system of notation, or rather two parallel systems, one used for vocal, the other for instrumental music. They were probably known to few outside specialist circles, but occasionally it was thought worth while, when the text of a song was displayed on an inscription, to furnish it with its notes, and in rather more cases we find papyrus fragments bearing notation. These usually seem to be remnants not of scores of some single continuous composition but of miscellanies of excerpts, perhaps to serve as items in some recitalist's programme, or as exercises or examples in a lesson. Exceptionally, a few specimens of ancient melody survived into a medieval manuscript tradition. Besides the instance of the Anonymus Bellermanni mentioned above, we have a coherent group of poems associated with the Cretan musician Mesomedes (early second century AD), the first four of which have managed to retain the melodic notation which originally seems to have adorned them all.[11]

These four pieces, published by V. Galilei in 1581, were the only specimens of ancient music known until 1841, when they were joined by the Bellermann tunes. Towards the end of the nineteenth century the corpus began to expand. A little song carved on a tombstone, found in 1883, was followed by a papyrus fragment with some lines from a Euripidean chorus (1891) and by two more extensive texts of paeans inscribed at Delphi (1893). Since then only a couple more inscriptions have turned up (1945, 1980), but papyrus fragments have accrued steadily (1918, 1922, 1931, 1955, 1959, 1962, 1965, 1966, 1973, 1976, 1986; publication of several others is in hand). We can reasonably hope for more in years to come. But it will be disappointing if they are all as wretchedly brief and lacunose as the ones we have.

[11] Athanasius Kircher's claim in his *Musurgia Universalis* (Rome, 1650) to have discovered settings of the first few lines of Pindar's First Pythian Ode and of a verse and a half of Gregory Nazianzen in old MSS in a Sicilian monastery is no longer believed by anyone. On these and other unauthentic fragments see Pöhlmann, *DAM* 43–52.

Two of our fragments preserve music from the end of the fifth century BC, in both cases from choruses of Euripides. In a few other instances the music cannot be later than the third century BC and might be earlier. But the bulk of our material is either late Hellenistic or from the Roman period. It tells us a certain amount about the music of those times, but not much about that of the Classical age.

A catalogue of the surviving musical documents, with transcriptions of the better-preserved items, will be found in Chapter 10. Citations of them elsewhere are accompanied by a bold-face numeral referring to the catalogue.

Musical preliminaries

C D E F G A B C

Here is an excerpt from a piano keyboard. It covers an octave, from one C to the next. The adjacent octaves would look exactly the same: the octave is a repeating structure.

Why does the octave enjoy this status? Why are two notes an octave apart both called C, as if they were the same? It is because notes separated by this interval blend supremely well together, so that when they are sounded simultaneously one is hardly aware that they are not the same. Because of their affinity, a scale begun on one of them achieves a sense of completeness when it reaches the other. Many melodies take an octave for their compass for the sake of this sense of wholeness.

There is a physical reason for the consonance of notes at the octave. They travel on sound-waves whose vibration-frequencies stand in the simple ratio 2 : 1, the rapider one corresponding to the higher note.[12] This means that there is a constant coincidence of wave-peaks, every peak of the slower wave matching every second peak of the faster one. The more regularly such agreement occurs, the better the blend perceived between two sounds.

Taking the white and black notes of the keyboard without distinction, we see that they divide the octave into twelve equal steps of a

---

[12] The same ratio will apply to the lengths of vibrating strings, provided that they are of the same material, thickness, and tension: a string that is just half the length of another—or a single string stopped at its mid-point—will give out a note an octave higher.

semitone. We will leave aside the question why it is divided into twelve steps rather than some other number. But given that it is so divided, why does the keyboard not look like this:

—with the notes lettered from A to L? Why the distinction between white and black keys, with the white ones looking as if they are trying to squeeze the black ones out? The answer—or part of the answer— is that our music, on the whole, is based on scales that go by tonal rather than semitonal steps. It is much more convenient for the fingers to make these steps by striking adjacent keys than to have to keep omitting alternate ones.

Very well, then, why is the keyboard not like this:

—with six white notes alternating with six black ones? Why is it seven and five, in an asymmetrical arrangement, so that the white notes are not always a tone apart but, at two points (E–F and B–C), only a semitone?

Answer: it is a consequence of the outstanding importance in melody and harmony of the two most consonant intervals after the octave, the ones corresponding to the vibration-ratios 3 : 2 and 4 : 3, in which, while not every peak of the lower note's wave coincides with one of the higher note's, every second or third one does. These intervals are the ones we know respectively as the fifth and the fourth.[13] Added together, they make exactly an octave; the mathematical aspect of this is that $\frac{3}{2} \times \frac{4}{3} = \frac{2}{1}$, since adding two intervals corresponds to multiplying their ratios.

Because of the musical importance of these two intervals, there is

[13] The fifth is what you get if you start from C (or any other white note except B) and, counting that as no. 1, go up to white note no. 5; the fourth is what you start on a white note (other than F) and go up to no. 4. Other intervals (third, sixth, eleventh, etc.) are named on the same principle. They are of the major type (major third, etc.) when equivalent to the span from C to the relevant white note, minor when one semitone less. Thus C to A, or D to B, is a major sixth (nine semitones), E to C is a minor one (eight semitones).

very strong reason to divide our octave into fourth + fifth (C–F–C) or fifth + fourth (C–G–C), or both at once (C–F–G–C). This is the most natural and fundamental principle of division of the octave, and any other principle that is applied must be subordinated to it. Now, if we make a division into twelve semitone steps, a fourth will correspond to five steps and a fifth to seven. But if the keyboard were laid out as above, with an unvarying alternation of white and black notes, then either a fourth or a fifth taken from a white note would land us on a black note, whereas the purpose of distinguishing white and black is to line up the notes of our basic melodic scale on the whites. The asymmetric grouping achieves this aim.

To reach the fourth we take two melodic steps of a tone and one of a semitone (not necessarily in that order); for a fifth, it is three tones and a semitone. But why have we made our characteristic melodic step the tone, a unit that does not fit a whole number of times into either fourth or fifth? Where does this unit come from?

The answer is that it appears in the first instance as the difference between the fourth and the fifth. If you construct a fourth and a fifth up from C (or what comes to the same thing, a fifth up from the lower C and another down from the upper one), you get two notes (F and G) between which this new interval of a tone is automatically born. It corresponds to the ratio $9 : 8$ ($\frac{3}{2} \div \frac{4}{3} = \frac{9}{8}$). And it easily reproduces itself. If you have the skeleton structure C–F–G–C, and you take a fourth down from G and a fifth back up, you make C–D–F–G–A–C. Repeat the operation from A, and you have C–D–E–F–G–A–B–C: all of the white notes. Repeat it again from B, and you start filling in the black notes. Soon your keyboard is complete. Further cycles of fourths and fifths will only make the same notes recur.

However, by their third appearance, if your fourth and fifths have been perfectly true ones, and you have a reasonable ear, it will be starting to become apparent that something is amiss. Your notes are now about a quarter of a tone out of tune. The longer you go on re-inventing them, the worse it gets. The reason is that the apparently coherent system has a hidden flaw, a design fault. When you take two $9 : 8$ tonal bites out of a fourth (C–F, or G–C), what is left (E–F, B–C) is not a true semitone but something slightly smaller, actually 12 per cent smaller. The inaccuracy perpetuates and compounds itself. None of the black notes constructed as above will divide the tones into equal halves. The second time round the inequality will be greater.

So working with true 3 : 2 fifths, 4 : 3 fourths, and 9 : 8 tones does not produce a system that will stand up to much to-ing and fro-ing, or a division of the octave into twelve equal semitones, five in the fourth and seven in the fifth. That is achieved by fudging, otherwise known as Equal Temperament. The semitones *are* made equal, and the fourths and fifths allowed to become slightly impure. This compromise between the laws of nature and the needs of art has developed since the sixteenth century, being essential for music in which modulation between different keys is a regular resource.

The Greeks understood that the size of intervals is determined by numerical ratios; some of them, remarkably, came close to a correct physical explanation.[14] A number of authors describe or prescribe tunings for musical scales in terms of ratios. They all take it as axiomatic that the octave is 2 : 1, the fifth 3 : 2, and the fourth 4 : 3. There is no question of adjusting these intervals to conform with other requirements.

When it comes to the subdivisions of the fourth, they offer a variety of different formulae. From this and other evidence we know that Greek music used many intervals that cannot be adequately expressed by talking of semitones, tones, major thirds, etc. Nor is it helpful to leave them as ratios. If two notes are stated to be related in the ratio 32 : 27, not many people will get any impression of what sort of interval is meant.

We shall therefore make use of the cent system invented by the tone-deaf philologist, mathematician, and musicologist A. J. Ellis (1814–90). On this system the octave is divided into 1,200 cents, 100 for each semitone of the equal-tempered scale. Any interval, however unconventional, can be accurately expressed and comprehended by the use of this form of measurement. For example, the 32 : 27 interval converts into 294 cents, from which we can see at once that we are talking of an interval of the order of $1\frac{1}{2}$ tones.[15]

The cent system has the further advantage that the sum of two or more intervals can be determined simply by adding the cent numbers instead of multiplying ratios or fractions. For example, the true

---

[14] See ps.-Arist. *Pr.* 19. 39 and *De audibilibus* 803ᵇ34–804ᵃ8, and especially Euc. *Sect. Can.* pp. 148–9 Jan with Barker's notes in *GMW* ii. 35 n. 29, 95, 107, 192f.; Burkert, *LS* 379–83.

[15] The actual conversion from ratios to cents involves either a calculation using logarithms or consultation of a cent table. I have used the one published by E. M. von Hornbostel, *Zeitschrift für Physik* 6 (1921), 29ff., reproduced in Kunst, fig. 61. For further explanation see Kunst, 4–9; Sachs, *WM* 23–8.

fifth and fourth equal 702 and 498 cents (as against 700 and 500 in
the tempered scale). The 9 : 8 tone by which the fifth exceeds the
fourth is (702 − 498 =) 204. It is easy to work out that when two
such tones are marked off within a fourth, the residue is an interval of
90 cents, a little less than half a tone.

Intervals are a matter of relative pitch. The absolute pitch of a
piece of ancient music cannot be established exactly, and anyway it
may have differed in different performances. But we can make a
good guess at it by comparing the compass of the widest-ranging
vocal compositions with the natural range of the male voice. This is
explained more fully in Chapter 9. Many pieces lie in the tenor range,
and in transcriptions of them it is most convenient to use the treble
(G) clef with an '8' under the clef-sign to show that it is transposed an

octave lower: ♪ = middle C. Transcription exactly at the best-

guess pitch would sometimes involve key-signatures with several
sharps or flats. In the interests of easier reading I have avoided this
by shifting to a nearby pitch (never more than a tone away from the
best-guess pitch) so that no more than one sharp or flat is required,
adding the annotation 'original a tone (semitone) lower (higher)'.[16]
Similarly, in discussing abstract scales or the scales of particular
compositions I treat them so far as possible as being in the 'natural'
key, that is, the one in which their notes appear as white notes.

Notes of a specific octave are designated by italic letters and differentiated according to the following convention:

C to *B* is the octave below the one below middle C.
c to *b* is the octave below middle C.
c′ to *b′* is the octave from middle C upwards.
c″ to *b″* is the next above that.

Besides the standard inflection-signs, ♯ sharp, ♭ flat, and ♮ natural,[17] it
will sometimes be necessary to employ symbols to specify that a note
is raised or lowered by something less than a semitone. For this I use
the self-explanatory signs ↑ and ↓. Where the interval is to be defined
more precisely, a cent number is appended to them. Thus $e{\uparrow}^{40}$ will
signify '*e* sharpened by about 40 cents'.

I think we can now proceed.

---

[16] In this I follow the recommendation of Sachs, *WM* 31.
[17] Double sharps and double flats will not be required.

1

Music in Greek Life

Beyond the North Wind there lies a paradise that no traveller can reach either by land or by sea. It is the country of the Hyperboreans, that blessed people whom Apollo loves and with whom he spends the winter months of every year. Untouched by illness or old age, in perpetual peace and ease, they adorn their heads with bright wreaths and spend their days in cheerful feasting,

> and the Muse, in accord with their ways,
> does not forsake that land: dance-choruses of girls
> are everywhere, and the assertive voices
> of lyres and resounding shawms are ever astir.

So the young Pindar imagined an ideal society; and in another song he described how the virtuous dead enjoy amenities far superior to those of the dim and eerie Homeric Hades, in a fragrant city set amid flowery meadows, forests, and amiable rivers, where they amuse themselves as they will,

> some with horses and exercise, some with board-games,
> some with lyres: in full blossom
> their thriving fortune stands.[1]

Pindar was a professional musician. But most Greeks, we may be sure, would have agreed with him in putting music high on the list of requisites for the good life. Music, song, and dance were seen as being, together with orderly sacrifices to the gods and athletic facilities for men, the most characteristic manifestations of a civilized community in peacetime.[2] The grimness of war is expressed by calling it 'danceless, lyreless, generating tears'.[3] Words like 'lyreless'

---

[1] Pind. *Pyth.* 10. 37 ff.; fr. 129. 6 f.
[2] Cf. *Od.* 8 (the Phaeacians, esp. ll. 97–103, 246–53); *Hymn. Hom.* 30. 7–16; 'Theog.' 757–64, 773–9, 789–94; Bacchyl. fr. 4. 61–80; Aesch. *Supp.* 667–97; Pind. *Pyth.* 5. 66; Ar. *Ran.* 729; Pl. *Leg.* 803 e.
[3] Aesch. *Supp.* 681, cf. Eur. *Phoen.* 784–91.

are similarly used to convey the joylessness of death and other miseries.[4]

Of course, Greek music was not always merry. It could be used for lamentation or gloomy foreboding, pessimistic reflection or the narration of horrific myths. But such was the general association of music-making with festive and joyful occasions that Sappho could reprimand her daughter, who was grieving over some loss, saying

> In a house of the Muses' servants it's not right
> for there to be lament . . . it would not befit us.

Conversely, when Admetus goes into mourning for his wife, he orders that neither lyre nor pipe is to be heard in the town for twelve months.[5] Music is constantly associated with the idea of celebration. When we are visited by great good fortune or achieve some special success, our thoughts turn towards champagne: the Greek's turned towards singing and dancing.[6] Aeschylus can even say, of the Erinyes' control over men's fortunes, that 'to some they give songs, to others a life dimmed with tears', where 'songs' is shorthand for 'good fortune'.[7]

Public festivals

When he thought of music and song as a feature of well-ordered city life, the Greek thought above all of the music and song associated with the public worship of the gods. Many of the regular local festivals, held annually or in some cases at longer intervals, had musical events or at least musical elements in them: singing processions, choral dances, sacrifices accompanied by ritual hymns.

Those participating in the ceremony often made their approach to the central location, a shrine or altar, in a formal and showy procession, in which there might be a singing chorus or choruses, sometimes dancing as they sang, or with separate dancers, instrumental accompaniment being usually provided by a piper. Such processions are attested in literary sources for various festivals, for example the Panathenaea, Oschophoria, and City Dionysia at Athens and the Daphnephoria at Thebes, and they are depicted on a number of

[4] Soph. *OC* 1222 etc.; J. Diggle, *PCPS* 20 (1974), 11; Barker, *GMW* i. 69–73; Maas–Snyder, 80, 229 n. 6.

[5] Sappho fr. 150; Eur. *Alc.* 430 f.; cf. Apollod. *Bibl.* 3. 15. 7.

[6] Cf. Aesch. *Ag.* 23, 31, Soph. *Trach.* 205–20, Eur. *Erechtheus* fr. 65. 5–10 Austin, *El.* 859–79, *Tro.* 325–41, 542–7, *HF* 761–97.

[7] *Eum.* 954.

Archaic vases. The processional song, *prosodion*, was recognized by the ancients as a particular category of choral lyric, to which great poets such as Pindar and Bacchylides made contributions. What may be the oldest surviving fragment of Greek lyric verse comes from a processional composed for a Messenian contingent going to sacrifice on Delos.[8] A number of eighth- and early seventh-century vases show processions or processional dances, apparently of a ritual nature, accompanied by the lyre, the pipes, or both.[9]

The central sacrifice and the preparation of the meat for the sacrificial feast were carried out with a musician in attendance, again usually a piper; the absence of pipes is one of the things that Herodotus finds noteworthy in Persian sacrifices.[10] In some cults there were traditional hymns, invocations, or formulae sung round the altar. Then came the feast, a joyful occasion in which music might play a further part.

We often hear of choruses of men, boys, or girls in connection with festivals, and we often see them represented in art.[11] The two most widely recognized species of cultic song were the paean and the dithyramb. The paean, which might be anything from a brief solemnity consisting of little more than the formula *Iē Paian*, *Iē Paian*, sung in unison, to a long and elaborate song like the Paeans of Pindar, was particularly often heard, and in one form or another it was something that every man on occasion joined in singing. It had a firm place in private social life as an auspicious thing to sing after a dinner, at the beginning of a symposium, or in a wedding procession. It was frequently sung by soldiers or sailors at moments of exaltation, whether going into battle, or during it, or returning from it in triumph. There were many public festivals at which the paean had its place as a holy song, for example the Panathenaea at Athens, the Theoxenia at Delphi, the Hyakinthia and the Gymnopaidiai at Sparta. It could also be sung *ad hoc* as a civic response to some exceptional event, either as a prayer for deliverance from danger or

---

[8] *PMG* 696. It is ascribed to Eumelus, sometime before 735 BC. This may be too early—it is doubtful whether Delos enjoyed such national importance in the 8th c.— but the fragment may go back to the time of the Messenian revolt from Sparta, *c.*660.

[9] See Pl. 2; Maas–Snyder, 11, 19–23 figs. 5*b*, 7*a*, 10–13; 48 fig. 13*a*.

[10] J. Quasten, *Musik und Gesang in den Kulten der heidnischen Antike und christlicher Frühzeit* (*Liturgiegeschichtl. Quellen und Forschungen* 25, Münster, 1930), 6–9, 42 f.; Hdt. 1. 132. 1; Men. *Dyscolus* 432; Apollod. *Bibl.* 3. 15. 7. Evidence from vase paintings: Wegner, *Musikleben*, 97 f., 191.

[11] See generally Webster.

as a thanksgiving if the danger was averted.[12] It had many different manifestations. While most often addressed to Apollo (with whom the originally independent divine saviour Paiā(wō)n was commonly identified), it could on occasion be addressed to other gods, or even to powerful men, in whom salvation lay. Though usually sung in chorus, it could be sung by a soloist. It might be delivered by voices alone, or accompanied by the lyre or the pipes, according to circumstances. It might take the form of a dancing processional,[13] but more often it was performed dancing on the spot or standing still.[14]

The dithyramb, although in principle dedicated to a god, Dionysus, has an altogether less holy feel to it, and in many cases it appears to have become virtually secularized. It is first mentioned by Archilochus as the 'lovely song of lord Dionysus' that the wine-blitzed reveller may begin and his companions take up. This sounds like a spontaneous act of merrymaking that might break out on any night of the week. But normally we hear of dithyrambs only as institutionalized festival events. What form they took in the Archaic period is a matter for conjecture. It is certainly tempting to suppose that at least some of the various costumed groups of dancers who appear in archaic vase-painting from several regions, some of them crowned with ivy and accompanied by a piper, were performers of dithyrambs.[15] By the late sixth century BC, if not before, the composition of dithyrambs for city festivals had been taken up by leading musicians such as Lasus and Simonides. The dithyramb now was both a spectacle and a sophisticated art form, no mere alcoholic knees-up (if that is what it had been formerly) but a genre as articulate and intellectually demanding as any other put before the public. The Athenians seem to have had a fair appetite for them: the spectator at the City Dionysia in the spring could see as many as twenty, presented by men's and boys' choruses from each of the ten official tribes, with prizes awarded for the best. Each chorus was fifty strong,

---

[12] Deliverance from plague: *Il.* 1. 472–4 (after), Soph. *OT* 5, 186 (before). A total eclipse: Pind. *Paean* 9. An earthquake: Xen. *Hell.* 4. 7. 4. Aristoxenus (fr. 117) recorded an occasion when, to cure an outbreak of craziness among the women of Locri and Rhegium, the oracle demanded the singing of twelve paeans a day for sixty days, 'which resulted in the appearance of many paean-writers in Italy'.

[13] *Hymn. Hom. Ap.* 514 ff.

[14] On the paean generally see H. W. Smyth, *Greek Melic Poets* (London, 1904), pp. xxxvi–xlii; L. Deubner, *Neue Jahrb.* 22 (1919), 385–406; A. von Blumenthal, *RE* xviii. 2340–62.

[15] See Pl. 3; Pickard-Cambridge, *DTC*² 80, 96, 100 f.; Webster, 17, 26, 29 f., etc.

dancing in circular formation with its piper in the middle. Thus every year a thousand citizens performed in dithyrambs at that festival.

This was by no means the only occasion in the Athenian calendar for male choruses to perform. They are attested for the Anthesteria (February–March), Thargelia (May–June), Panathenaea (July–August), Hephaestea and Promethia (date uncertain), and there were also the dramatic contests at the winter Lenaea and the City Dionysia, in which choral song and dance, and also lyric dialogue between actor and chorus (and, after Aeschylus, solo arias), had an established place. This musical element was by no means merely incidental to classical drama, but an important factor in its total impact. Aeschylus' older contemporary Phrynichus was remembered with affection two generations after his death not for the power of his plots but for the sweetness of his melodies and the resourcefulness of his choreography. Aristophanes in his critique of Aeschylus and Euripides in his *Frogs* devotes special attention to their music. Some of the Athenian survivors of the military disaster at Syracuse in 413 BC are said to have obtained food and water because they were able to sing portions of Euripides, and there is a story of the choral entry from his *Electra* being sung by a man at a dinner of Peloponnesian generals in 404.[16]

Girls' choruses could also provide a public spectacle. Homer tells of a girl who aroused the lust of Hermes as he saw her singing and dancing in a chorus in honour of Artemis.[17] At Sparta in the late seventh century there were festivals at which girls sang beautiful songs composed for them by Alcman. In the best-preserved specimen of these so-called *partheneia*, the religious ceremonies are mentioned only briefly; the main emphasis falls on the chorus-members themselves, their finery, and their girlish feelings. About three generations later the author of the Delian Hymn to Apollo describes the god's festival on Delos, to which people bring their families from all over Ionia. There is boxing, dancing, song, and best of all is the chorus of local maidens, who sing hymns to Apollo, Artemis, and Leto, and also heroic myths.[18] At Delphi too, the other great national centre of Apolline cult, there was a girls' chorus to sing his praises.[19]

[16] Plut. *Nicias* 29. 4, *Lys.* 15. 4. G. Arrighetti, *Satiro, Vita di Euripide* (Pisa, 1964), 143, suggests Philochorus as Plutarch's source.

[17] *Il.* 16. 182f.

[18] *Hymn. Hom. Ap.* 146–64; cf. Eur. *Hec.* 463, *HF* 687. Girls' choruses sent to Delos from the Cyclades: Strab. 10. 5. 2 p. 485.

[19] *Hymn. Hom.* 27. 11–20, Pind. *Paean* 2. 97, 6. 16.

At Thebes there was one that performed at a nocturnal festival of the
Mother of the Gods.[20] We saw that Pindar imagined the Hyperboreans as comfortably provided with girls' choruses. He himself,
like Simonides and Bacchylides, composed *partheneia*, perhaps for
more than one city.[21] The fact that the most eminent poets applied
themselves to such business, or were commissioned for it, shows the
importance attached to attaining the highest artistic quality in these
girls' choral performances.

In general, the music and dancing associated with religious
ceremonies were designed above all to give pleasure to the on-
lookers. Only at the climactic moment of sacrifice did a solemn or
reverential mood prevail. For the rest, the atmosphere was festive. In
480 BC a Megarian poet prayed to Apollo to keep the Persians away
from his city,

> so the people in good cheer
> when spring arrives may bring you splendid hecatombs,
> delighting in the banquet and the lyre
> and paean-dances round your altar, and glad cries.[22]

Not everything had to be subordinated to the god's needs. A paean
or dithyramb might contain much that had little relevance to the
deity being honoured. And with a crowd gathered in holiday spirits,
it is not surprising that the musical entertainments sometimes pro-
liferated. The rhapsodes who were skilled in the singing of Homer
and other epic narrative would naturally be attracted to the scene
and eager to earn money by performing; a prefatory hymn to the god
of the festival would be sufficient accommodation to the occasion.
The same applies, more or less, to those who practised the more distinctly musical arts of singing to or playing the kithara or the pipes.
There were current in Antiquity a number of citharodes' prefatory
hymns,[23] collectively ascribed to the famous seventh-century cithar-

---

[20] Pind. *Pyth.* 3. 78.

[21] It should be noted that the term *partheneion*, which merely indicates that the
performers were girls but says nothing about the occasion, may overlap with such
terms as *prosodion* and paean.

[22] 'Theog.' 776–9. The poet may be the Philiadas of Megara who composed an
epitaph for the men from Thespiae who fell at Thermopylae (D. L. Page, *Epigram-
matica Graeca* (Oxford, 1975), 40).

[23] A citharode is one who sings accompanying himself on the kithara, whereas a
citharist is one who simply plays the instrument. Similarly an aulode sings to pipe
accompaniment, an aulete plays the pipes.

ode Terpander, just as the rhapsodes' hymns came to be collectively ascribed to Homer. They were presumably for festival use.

Offering prizes for the best singer or instrumentalist was a natural development. Already in the late eighth century, at the funeral games held in honour of the Chalcidian king Amphidamas, there was a contest for performers of hexameter song, which Hesiod won.[24] In one of the shorter 'Homeric' hymns the poet prays to Aphrodite for 'victory in this competition'.[25] At Athens, probably from about 525 BC, relays of rhapsodes were organized into performing the complete *Iliad* and *Odyssey* at the Great Panathenaea held every four years.[26] Before that, no doubt, they had performed portions of these and other epics haphazardly, though on a competitive basis.[27] In the fifth century there were competitions for rhapsodes at the festival of Asclepius at Epidaurus.[28] There must have been many opportunities for hearing epic song other than at festivals, but festivals will have been a common setting.

In the seventh century, competitions for citharodes are attested for the octennial Pythian festival at Delphi and for the Karneia at Sparta. We know that competitors came from far and wide. Early in the sixth century the Pythian festival was augmented by further musical events. These too attracted performers, and a public, from many parts of Greece. Twenty years later the Panathenaea at Athens underwent a similar reorganization. There too citharodes, aulodes, and auletes competed for prizes; the vase-painters depict them standing in turn on a podium before a seated judge.[29]

This section may be concluded with a short account of the musical elements in three major festivals, two Athenian and one Laconian.

First, the City Dionysia of Athens, which has already been mentioned more than once. As a preliminary, the statue of Dionysus was taken out to a suburb so that the god's mythical entry into Athens

[24] Hes. *Op.* 654–9.

[25] *Hymn. Hom.* 6. 19. In the preceding lines he has described Aphrodite's occupation of Cyprus, and we may guess that the occasion of the hymn was one of the Cyprian festivals of Aphrodite, such as the panegyris at Old Paphos (Strab. 14. 6. 3 p. 683; M. P. Nilsson, *Griechische Feste* (Leipzig, 1906), 364 f.).

[26] Pl. *Hipparch.* 228 b, Lycurg. *Leoc.* 102.

[27] Cf. J. A. Davison, *JHS* 78 (1958), 38 f. = *From Archilochus to Pindar* (London, 1968), 58–60.

[28] Pl. *Ion* 530 a.

[29] See Pl. 4; Wegner, *Musikleben*, 108 f., 189 f., 211, and pl. 7*a*, *b*, 18; Davison, *JHS* 78 (1958), 37, 42, and 82 (1962), 141 f. = *From Archilochus to Pindar*, 55 f., 64–8.

from the north-west could be re-enacted, and while it was there, a sacrifice took place and a hymn was sung. When the statue had returned to its normal place, the festival proper began with a grand procession to the holy precinct where the sacrifices were to be made. The procession called at various altars in the city, including that of the Twelve Gods in the Agora, and dancing choruses performed at each one. Either in this procession or in a separate 'revel' later in the day, huge wooden phalli were carried along, and lusty songs addressed to them, a practice also observed in other Greek Dionysiac cults. Also on this day, it is assumed, the twenty dithyrambic choruses performed their pieces. The next three or four days were filled with the dramatic performances. In the last quarter of the fifth century the pattern was that on each of three days a tragic poet produced three tragedies and a satyr-play, and a comic poet one comedy: a daily progress from the sublime to the ridiculous.[30]

At the Great Panathenaea, choruses of young men and women sang paeans and danced through the first night on the Acropolis. We hear of 'ring-choruses' (the term normally used at Athens in connection with dithyrambs), and of dances in armour by men and by boys. At dawn a great procession set out bearing a new robe for Athena's statue. The sheep and cattle to be sacrificed were conducted by the religious officials, and after them came a band of citharists and auletes playing in concert at the head of the rest of the crowd of participants (Pl. 5). After the offerings had been made and everyone had feasted on the meat, the musical and athletic contests must have got under way. Altogether the festival lasted four days. The citharodic, aulodic, and auletic performances could perhaps have been completed in a single day, or part of one. The rhapsodes' recitals of the entire *Iliad* and *Odyssey*, on the other hand, must have extended over more or less the whole period of the festival.[31]

The Laconian Hyakinthia occupied three days in early summer. The first was a day of mourning for the death of Hyakinthos, and for this reason the sacrifice was not accompanied by the usual music. On the second day, however, the mood was very different. The whole of Sparta attended to watch a splendid display. A chorus of boys sang a paean to Apollo, probably marching or prancing along, as we are told that they had their tunics tucked up and that the rhythm was

---

[30] L. Deubner, *Attische Feste* (Berlin, 1932), 138–42; Pickard-Cambridge, *DFA*[2] 57 ff.; H. W. Parke, *Festivals of the Athenians* (London, 1977), 125–36.

[31] For the Panathenaea see Deubner, op. cit. 22–35; Parke, op. cit. 33–50.

anapaestic, which is typical of marches. They were accompanied by an aulete, but they also carried lyres and swept across the strings with their plectrums. Following a parade of riders on horses with richly ornamented trappings, further massed choirs of young men appeared and sang songs by older Spartan poets, accompanied on the aulos, while at the same time dancers performed the appropriate traditional movements. There were also processions of girls in brightly painted wagons, and enough animals were sacrificed for all the citizens not only to eat well themselves but also to treat their slaves and their friends.[32] Other sources refer to a paean sung by men as an important feature of the festival, and to women's choruses dancing at night.[33]

Private ceremonial

From state festivals we turn to ceremonies or celebrations that arise from private events (weddings, funerals, etc.) but are also to some extent in the public domain; they spill out of the house, as it were, and involve the whole neighbourhood.

One of the principal episodes in a Greek wedding was the convey- ance of the bride by the groom from her father's house to her new home. They rode in a wagon, accompanied by all their friends and well-wishers, who waved torches and sang a hymenaeum, while others danced or played instruments. Homer describes such a pro- cession in his account of the shield of Achilles:

> They were conducting brides from their chambers by torchlight
> through the city, and the hymenaeal rang loud;
> young male dancers spun about, and among them
> auloi and lyres sang out, while the women
> standing in their doorways admired it all.[34]

In an imitation of the passage a sixth-century poet adds dancing choruses and singing to panpipes; there are women dancing to lyres, besides a rout of young men led by a piper.[35] But it is Sappho who gives the vividest account of such a scene in her poem on the wedding of Hector and Andromache. As Hector brings his bride into Troy, everyone takes to chariots and mule-cars to accom- pany him.

[32] Polycrates, *FGrH* 588 F 1 (probably late Hellenistic period).
[33] Xen. *Ages.* 2. 17; Eur. *Hel.* 1465 ff.; Hieron. *Adv. Iovinian.* 1. 308 M.; Nilsson (as n. 25), 137.
[34] *Il.* 18. 492–6.   [35] Ps.-Hes. *Sc.* 272–85.

> Lyres, melodious shawms, and the clatter of castanets
> blended there, and the voices of girls in the holy song;
> up to heaven the glorious clamour arose . . .

There is drinking in the streets, a riot of incenses and perfumes; matrons ululate, while the men sing a paean that incorporates a celebration of the bridal couple.[36]

After the newly-weds had gone in for the night, the singing continued outside the closed door. Pindar refers to the songs that unmarried girls sing in the evening for their friend, the bride, and several fragments of them occur among the remains of Sappho's work. One of these fragments implies that the epithalamia went on throughout the night.[37]

Another, rarer occasion for personal celebration was provided by victory in a sporting event, especially if it was at one of the prestigious festivals such as the Olympic, Pythian, Isthmian, or Nemean Games. The Epinician Odes of Pindar and Bacchylides (and fragments of some by Simonides) show us what fine and elaborate songs a wealthy victor might commission. The less wealthy, no doubt, also made merry with such music as they could command. The victor's friends might sing in his honour on the very day of the victory, as they dined and drank in the evening.[38] When he returned to his home, a less impromptu celebration awaited him, with a chorus of local young men[39] performing another, perhaps longer song in a festive setting—an *enkōmion*—at his house, or in front of it,[40] or at some public altar where he was sacrificing. People beyond his immediate circle might well take an interest, as his success brought glory on the whole town. As with wedding songs, we hear of lyres and pipes providing accompaniment jointly.[41]

---

[36] Sappho fr. 44. Cf. also Pind. *Pyth.* 3. 88 ff., Aesch. *Ag.* 705–8, Soph. *Ant.* 813–15 with Jebb's note, Eur. *Tro.* 308–41, *HF* 10–12, *IA* 1036–57, Ar. *Pax* 1316–66, *Av.* 1728–65, *Thesm.* 1034 f., Catull. 61. 123, and for vase-paintings Wegner, *Musikleben* 95, 191.

[37] Sappho frs. 30, 104–17; Pind. *Pyth.* 3. 17–19. Later literary compositions based on the epithalamion are Theoc. *Id.* 18 (where the girls sing in the evening and say they will return at dawn; cf. Aesch. fr. 43); Catull. 62. Cf. also Ap. Rhod. *Argon.* 4. 1160, Procl. ap. Phot. *Bibl.* 321 a 17; H. W. Smyth, *Greek Melic Poets*, pp. cxii–cxx; P. Maas, *RE* ix. 130–4; E. Contiades-Tsitsoni, *Hymenaios und Epithalamion* (Stuttgart, 1990).

[38] Cf. Pind. *Nem.* 6. 37 f. Bacchylides' short Odes 2 and 7 were composed in these circumstances.

[39] Pind. *Ol.* 6. 87, *Pyth.* 10. 55, *Nem.* 2. 24, 3. 4, 66, *Isthm.* 8. 1; Bacchyl. 11. 10.

[40] Bacchyl. 6. 14.   [41] See p. 346.

Funerals too impinged on the community, especially in the eighth and seventh centuries, when it seems to have been a matter of prestige for the most prominent families to convey their dead to the pyre in ostentatious style, with the largest possible number of mourners following the bier, wailing and tearing their hair and garments. Before setting out on this last journey, the deceased had been washed, anointed, dressed in clean clothes, and laid out for a day or longer in his house or sometimes outside it. Here his relatives, particularly the women, bewailed him, and in certain cases, it seems, laments were sung by trained threnodists brought in from outside.[42] There is little literary evidence for singing (as distinct from wailing) during the funeral procession, but a black-figure cup of the late seventh century and a somewhat later terracotta plaque show it accompanied by a piper, and in the fourth century Plato mentions a practice of hiring foreign singers who escort the dead with music of a Carian character. For the funeral procession of the courtesan Pythionice her lover Harpalus engaged a large professional choir and band.[43] Another black-figure cup shows the procession approaching the tomb, where a praying woman and a piper are waiting.[44] Prepared dirges might be sung at the tomb, if not at the time of burial, on subsequent days of commemoration when offerings were made to the dead, or when another member of the family was brought to a nearby resting-place. From Solon's time onwards we hear of laws passed in various cities to curb the extravagance and demonstrativeness of funerals. At Ioulis in the island of Ceos and at Delphi they included a stipulation that the funeral procession should be silent. Lamentation at the tomb was restricted, and at Athens 'composed dirges' were forbidden, in other words, one might give vent to spontaneous expressions of grief for one's own kin but not

---

[42] *Il.* 24. 719–76, *Od.* 24. 43–64, Aesch. *Pers.* 935–40, *Sept.* [861 ff.], Pl. *Leg.* 947 bc; E. Reiner, *Die rituelle Totenklage der Griechen* (Stuttgart and Berlin, 1938), 61–70; M. Alexiou, *The Ritual Lament in Greek Tradition* (Cambridge, 1974), 5 f., 11–14, 27–9, 39–42; E. Vermeule, *Aspects of Death in Early Greek Art and Poetry* (Berkeley and LA, 1979), 14–17; R. Garland, *The Greek Way of Death* (London, 1985), 23–31. On a Corinthian hydria of *c.* 560 (Louvre E 643; Wegner, *Bilder*, 41) one of the Nereids mourning Achilles as he lies on his bier holds a lyre in one hand.

[43] Paris 355, *CVA* France 10 (Bibl. Nat. 2) pl. 71, 73; Pl. *Leg.* 800 e with schol., cf. Hsch. κ 824; Posidonius, *FGrH* 87 F 14 = fr. 168 Theiler. In Aesch. *Sept.* 915–21 the funeral procession for Oedipus' sons is characterized by crying or lamenting, and likewise in the spurious ending (1058–67); *thrēnos* in 1064 does not necessarily signify a song by Antigone.

[44] Paris 353, *CVA* loc. cit. pl. 71–2.

make it into an art form.[45] In some other places, however, wealthy families instituted commemorative dirges. At Corinth the noble Bacchius' Megarian wife was lamented annually by a chorus of fifty young men and girls sent from Megara.[46] Sophocles represents Clytaemestra as having decreed monthly sacrifices and choral performances in commemoration of Agamemnon.[47] The Cypriot prince Nicocles honoured his dead father with 'choruses and music' as well as with athletic contests and horse and naval races.[48] At Megalopolis Philopoemen was honoured following his death in 182 BC with annual sacrifices and encomia sung by the young.[49] Dirges commissioned from such poets as Simonides and Pindar achieved literary currency. We know nothing of the circumstances in which they were performed; they may have been either semi-public or purely domestic occasions.

Domestic and personal music-making

In the society portrayed in the Homeric poems it is music and song that provide the normal entertainment of the household, especially epic song of the type practised by Homer himself. The bards Phemius and Demodocus are attached to the kings' mansions in Ithaca and Scheria respectively, and they are called upon to play their lyres and sing of the deeds of men while the company eats and drinks and listens.[50] Odysseus considers that there is no greater pleasure than that of sitting at a feast, well supplied with food and wine, and listening to a bard.[51] These singers also provide music for dancing,[52] and in one episode Demodocus gives an outdoor performance either after or simultaneously with a dance by a group of boys.[53] The Trojans and their allies, settled round their camp-fires for the night, divert themselves with auloi and panpipes.[54] Under the

---

[45] F. Sokolowski, *Lois sacrées des cités grecques* (Paris, 1969), nos. 77C15 (Delphi), 97A11 (Ioulis); Plut. *Sol.* 21. 5; Alexiou, op. cit. 14–23; Garland, op. cit. 21f.

[46] *Anecd. Bekk.* 281. 26, cf. Zenobius (vulg.) 5.8 in Leutsch–Schneidewin, *Corpus Paroemiographorum Graecorum*, i. 117.   [47] *El.* 277–81.

[48] Isoc. 9. 1.   [49] Diod. 29. 21.

[50] *Od.* 1. 150–5, 325–422; 8. 43–108, 471–541; 17. 261–71, 358–60; 22. 330–56; cf. Stesichorus, *SLG* 148. 3–4. The lyre is called 'dinner's companion', *Od.* 8. 99, 17. 271.

[51] *Od.* 9. 5–11.

[52] *Od.* 1. 152, 421; 4. 17–19; 23. 133–47.

[53] *Od.* 8. 250–369; see J. B. Hainsworth's notes on 254 and 256–384 in A. Heubeck and others, *A Commentary on Homer's Odyssey*, i (Oxford, 1988), 362.

[54] *Il.* 10. 13.

influence of wine, it is remarked, even a very sensible man will sing, dance, chuckle, and say indiscreet things.[55] The gods too are imagined as diverting themselves with music in their more carefree moments on Olympus. Apollo plays the lyre, the Muses sing, and sometimes other gods and goddesses dance.[56]

Much of the elegiac and lyric poetry of the seventh, sixth, and fifth centuries was composed to be sung at the symposium, the post-prandial drinking-party at which, in aristocratic circles, the men of the house relaxed with their friends. They took it in turns to sing whatever they cared to: a little hymn to a god, a piece of political comment or exhortation, reflections on the joys of wine or the pains of love, moral advice, humorous abuse. At the end of the evening the merry guests were liable to carouse through the streets, still singing and dancing, and pay further visits on acquaintances.

So far as we can tell, pieces in elegiac metre were sung with a piper (male or female) providing the accompaniment, while those in more elaborate metres were accompanied by the singer himself on a lyre or less often a harp. A creative poet would keep producing new songs; others would repeat old ones. Theognis promises his friend Cyrnus that he has made his name immortal:

> You'll be at every dinner, every feast,
> and many a man will have you on his lips,
> and lovely lads accompanied by alto pipes
> will sing of you in voices sweet and clear.[57]

Thus Theognis confidently expects that his own songs to Cyrnus will circulate widely at symposia, far into the future. Certainly at Athens in the fifth century symposiasts regularly sang songs or excerpts from 'classic' poets—Alcman, Alcaeus, Stesichorus, Anacreon, Simonides, Phrynichus, Pindar, and others—including pieces originally composed for quite other purposes.[58]

The ability to play the lyre was not uncommon among the archaic

---

[55] *Od.* 14. 463–6, cf. 1. 421, 17. 605, 18. 304, *Hymn. Hom. Merc.* 56.

[56] *Il.* 1. 603–4, Hes. *Th.* 36–52, ps.-Hes. *Sc.* 201–6, *Hymn. Hom. Ap.* 186–206, *Titanomachia* fr. 6 Bernabé = 5 Davies, Pind. *Pyth.* 1. 1–12, Hermippus fr. 31 K.–A.

[57] Theog. 239–43.

[58] See Pl. 6; Ar. *Nub.* 1354 ff., fr. 235, Eup. frs. 148, 395, Timaeus, *FGrH* 566 F 32; R. Reitzenstein, *Epigramm und Skolion* (Giessen, 1893), 24–33. On the symposium generally as a setting for the performance of song see my *Studies in Greek Elegy and Iambus* (Berlin and New York, 1974), 11–17; W. Rösler, *Dichter und Gruppe* (Munich, 1980), 37 ff., 87 f., 94 f., 98 ff.; E. L. Bowie, *JHS* 106 (1986), 13–21; O. Murray (ed.), *Sympotica* (Oxford, 1990).

nobility. Achilles and Paris are represented in the *Iliad* as able to play it; so could several of Pindar's patrons.[59] Themistocles was looked down upon for being unable either to play the lyre or to sing.[60] Cimon, though he could sing quite adequately, was also said (by a hostile writer) to have lacked musical education,[61] and in the 420s 'he doesn't know how to play the lyre' was equivalent to 'he hasn't had a good education'.[62] Socrates was taking lessons in the lyre at an advanced age.[63]

The fact that not everyone could play the lyre is reflected in the procedure followed at the Athenian symposium of this period, about which we have fairly detailed information. When dinner was over, libations were poured; the third libation was to Zeus Saviour, and at this everyone joined in singing a paean. Then the drinking began. A branch of bay or myrtle was passed round, and each guest as he received it was expected to sing or recite something, or continue the item begun by the previous singer. A hired piper provided the necessary accompaniments. Afterwards those who had the skill sang songs to the lyre.[64]

By the end of the century, however, fashions were changing. Young men scandalized their elders by reciting speeches from decadent modern dramas instead of drawing on the traditional repertoire, or they rejected altogether the idea of doing a party piece. Some hosts relied on hired dancing girls, acrobats, and instrumentalists to entertain their guests, while others, disdaining such floor-shows, contented themselves with their own intellectual conversation.[65]

If the men's symposium was the main occasion for domestic music-making, we should not overlook the existence of other, less conspicuous ones. While the men made merry, the women of the household stayed in their own quarters, but likely enough they were singing too. Agathon's guests at the party described by Plato decide

[59] *Il.* 3. 54, 9. 186; the Cyrenaean exile Damophilus, Pind. *Pyth.* 4. 295; Timocritus of Aegina, *Nem.* 4. 14; perhaps Hiero, *Ol.* 1. 16; Arcesilaus, *Pyth.* 5. 114.

[60] Ion of Chios, *FGrH* 392 F 13 (Plut. *Cim.* 9. 1, *Them.* 2. 4, Cic. *Tusc.* 1. 4).

[61] Stesimbrotus, *FGrH* 107 F 4; for his singing, Ion, loc. cit.

[62] Ar. *Vesp.* 959, 989, cf. *Eq.* 188f., 985ff. (of Cleon), Eup. fr. 208.

[63] Pl. *Euthydemus* 272c, cf. *Menex.* 236a.

[64] Dicaearchus frs. 88–9 Wehrli and other sources; see Reitzenstein (as n. 58), ch. 1; F. Wehrli, *Die Schule des Aristoteles*, i (Basle, 1944), 69–71.

[65] Ar. *Nub.* 1354ff., Eup. frs. 148, 398, Ephippus fr. 16, Antiphanes fr. 85; Pl. *Prt.* 347d, *Symp.* 176e, Xen. *Symp.* 2. 1–3. 1, 7. 2–5, 9. 2–7, Hippolochus (*c.* 300 BC) ap. Ath. 129a, d; Reitzenstein, op. cit. 30ff.

to dispense with their piper's services and 'let her go and pipe to herself or, if she likes, to the women inside'.[66] Vase-painters often show scenes from the women's room with various instruments being played (Pl. 7). In an earlier generation Sappho and her friends made music in festive privacy, with flower garlands, scented unguents, and soft couches, just as happily as any male gathering.

Women also sang to relieve the monotony of work. Calypso and Circe in the *Odyssey* sing at their looms, and there are later references besides to singing while weaving.[67] Women sang while grinding corn or pounding things in mortars.[68] Mothers and nurses sang lullabies to babies.[69] Wool-workers too had their own songs.[70]

Men engaged in solitary occupations, or insufficiently occupied, likewise sought solace in music. Achilles, having ceased to take part in the fighting at Troy, passes the time singing and playing the lyre in Patroclus' company. The young Anchises, alone at the ranch-house, wanders about playing the lyre, quite loudly. Vase-painters (if not epic poets before them) imagine Paris as having been playing the lyre to himself when the three goddesses arrived to ask his opinion of their beauty, and likewise Aegisthus when Orestes burst in to kill him.[71] The patient watchman in *Agamemnon* warbles to himself in order to stay awake. Aristophanes compares Aeschylus' songs (as parodied by 'Euripides') to those of a rope-maker. The comic poet Crates may have referred to songs of bath-attendants.[72] Herdsmen sang and played the panpipes.[73] Singing-contests between them were no doubt an established custom long before Theocritus gave it literary status in his bucolic Idylls.

Children's songs must not go unmentioned. Some of the games that children played involved verses or ditties that accompanied particular actions. Several are quoted by late antiquarian writers, and

---

[66] Pl. *Symp.* 176e.

[67] *Od.* 5. 61; 10. 221, 254, Eur. *IA* 788, Epicharmus fr. (spur.) 14.

[68] Ar. *Nub.* 1358, *PMG* 869, Ar. Byz. fr. 340A Slater (*himaios*); Ar. fr. 352, Phrynichus Comicus fr. 14, Nicochares fr. 9, Nicophon fr. 8; Tryphon fr. 113 Velsen ap. Ath. 618d.

[69] Pl. *Leg.* 790de, Theoc. *Id.* 24. 7–9, Chrysippus, *SVF* iii. 184. 8, Ath. 618e, Sext. Emp. *Math.* 6. 32, Hsch. s.v. *baukalân*.

[70] Tryphon, loc. cit.

[71] *Il.* 9. 186, *Hymn. Hom. Ven.* 80; Maas–Snyder, 52 fig. 16, 104 fig. 9, 137 fig. 17.

[72] Aesch. *Ag.* 16, cf. Ar. *Nub.* 721; Ar. *Ran.* 1297; Crates fr. 42 (but see below, n. 77).

[73] *Il.* 18. 526, Epicharmus frs. 4, 105(?), ps.-Aesch. *PV* 574, Soph. fr. 281a, Eur. *Alc.* 577, *IA* 576, ps.-Eur. *Rhes.* 553, Pl. *Resp.* 399d, Philoxenus, *PMG* 819; see R. Seaford's note on Eur. *Cyc.* 41–81.

although there is no guarantee that they go back to the Classical period, we can hardly suppose that nothing of the kind then existed. The ball-game that Nausicaa plays with her young friends in the *Odyssey* seems to have been combined with a song and dance. Aristophanes refers to a little verse that children chanted, while clapping their hands, if a cloud passed over the sun.[74] In certain places there were longer songs that children sang on a particular day of the year, when they went round from house to house asking for gifts of food.[75]

Music accompanying activity

The Greeks well understood the value of music as an adjunct to work and bodily movement, especially to that which is of a repetitive or rhythmical character. It stimulates the spirits and it assists in maintaining the rate of achievement and, where necessary, in synchronizing everyone's efforts. The songs of the wool-workers and the rope-makers have been mentioned, and the women's grinding and pounding songs. There is a terracotta model from Thebes, dating from the sixth century BC, which shows a group of women kneading dough, probably in a bakery, with a piper playing a suitable strain to them.[76]

The comic poet Teleclides mentioned a song sung by hired labourers as they went to work in the fields—perhaps at harvest time, when extra hands are particularly needed. There was a traditional reapers' song called the *Lityerses*, referred to by Menander and others. Theocritus gives what purports to be a version of it, and also speaks of a girl piper playing for the reapers as they work.[77] Another such traditional song was the *Linos*, performed at the time of the vintage. Homer describes it as a processional sung by a boy to the lyre, as young people of both sexes, carrying the baskets of grapes,

---

[74] *PMG* 852, 861, 875, 876; *Od.* 6. 101; Ar. fr. 404.

[75] Hom. *Epigr.* 15 (Samos), *PMG* 848 (Rhodes), and other material collected in Ath. 359 d–360 d. The custom has survived in Greece and has many parallels in other lands; cf. A. Dieterich, *Kleine Schriften* (Leipzig and Berlin, 1911), 324–52; Jacoby on *FGrH* 526 F 1; S. Baud-Bovy, *Byzantina-Metabyzantina* 1 (1946), 23–32, and *Revue de musicologie* 54 (1968), 8–10; K. Meuli, *Gesammelte Schriften*, i (Basle and Stuttgart, 1975), 33–68.

[76] See Pl. 8.

[77] Teleclides fr. 8; Men. *Carchedonius* fr. 3 Sandbach; Theoc. *Id.* 10. 16, 41, with Gow's note. Pollux 4. 55, however, says that the *Lityerses* was sung at threshing-floors. The singing bath-attendants of Crates (above, n. 72) are perhaps a scribal error for gleaners (*balaneōn*: *kalameōn*).

pranced along behind with answering cries.[78] We hear also of pipe music and song accompanying the treading of the grapes.[79]

Pipers might on occasion assist at major building works. Lysander assembled as many girl pipers as he could get hold of to play as the walls of defeated Athens were destroyed.[80] When the city of Messene was built in 369 BC, the walls (which are still to be seen) went up to the accompaniment of pipe music.[81] One of the Ptolemies, perhaps Philopator (reigned 225–205 BC), is recorded as having had pipers play to invigorate workmen who were toiling to drag a large ship to the water.[82]

On board ship a piper could perform a useful service in helping to keep the rowers in time, as well as in keeping them cheerful, and he was a regular member of an Athenian trireme's crew. When Alcibiades returned from exile in 408 BC, he did so in style, with a well-known tragic actor as his boatswain and the champion aulete Chrysogonus setting the stroke for his rowers.[83]

Men marching into battle might also find music beneficial to their morale and to the unity of their rhythm. Homer mentions nothing of the kind, but Corinthian vase-painters of the seventh century show a piper accompanying lines of warriors into the fight, and in the fifth century and later many authors attest this as the regular usage of the Spartan army.[84] Thucydides describes the Spartans advancing to

[78] *Il.* 18. 561–72; cf. Hes. fr. 305, *PMG* 880, Hdt. 2. 79.

[79] Callixenus, *FGrH* 627 F 2 p. 170. 11 J., Poll. 4. 55; cf. Philod. *Mus.* 4. 5 p. 47 Neubecker; *Sammelbuch* 5810 (an aulete's contract dated AD 322); Longus, *Daphnis and Chloe* 2. 36; *Anacreontea* 59. 8; Arethas' scholium on Clem. *Protr.*, i. 297. 4 Stählin. An Egyptian relief of the early 3rd millennium shows two men clapping out a rhythm with sticks as the vintagers tread grapes.

[80] Xen. *Hell.* 2. 2. 23, elaborated by Plut. *Lys.* 15. 5. Plutarch took the music to be celebratory, but it may at the same time have been 'music while you work'.

[81] Paus. 4. 27. 7.

[82] Diogenes of Seleucia ap. Philod. *Mus.* p. 34 van Krevelen = 195 Rispoli, cf. p. 154 Kr. = 47 Neubecker; E. K. Borthwick, *BICS* 35 (1988), 91–3. Callixenus, describing what may be the same launching, speaks only of shouts and trumpet signals (*FGrH* 627 F 1 p. 162. 29 J.).

[83] Duris, *FGrH* 76 F 70. Other references: Ar. *Ach.* 554, Eur. *Tro.* 126, *IG* 2². 1951. 100, Dem. *De Cor.* 129, Philod. *Mus.* 4 pp. 47, 48 Neubecker, Poll. 1. 96, 4. 56, 71. Eur. *IT* 1125 substitutes a panpiper.

[84] See Pl. 9; J. Salmon, *JHS* 97 (1977), 89 f.; Epicharmus fr. 75 (with schol. Pind. *Pyth.* 2. 127), Thuc. 5. 70, Xen. *Lac. Pol.* 13. 7–8, Arist. fr. 244, Polyb. 4. 20. 6, Plut. *Lyc.* 21. 4, 22. 4–5, etc. The Cretans marched to pipe and lyre (Ephorus, *FGrH* 70 F 149 p. 88. 29 J., cf. Polyb. loc. cit., Gell. *NA* 1. 11. 6, ps.-Plut. *De mus.* 1140c, Ath. 517a, 627d). Herodotus (1. 17. 1) describes Alyattes' Lydian army marching to the motley sound of auloi, panpipes, and harps. See further W. K. Pritchett, *Ancient Greek Military Practices*, i (Berkeley and LA, 1971), 105–8.

battle 'slowly, to the music of many pipers, as is their established custom, not for religious reasons but so that their approach should be even and rhythmical and their line not broken, as tends to happen with large forces as they come forward'. Plutarch develops the picture further:

When their battle-line was ready drawn up, with the enemy looking on, the king would slaughter the nanny-goat, giving the word for everyone to put on wreaths and telling the pipers to pipe the Castor tune, while he gave the lead in the marching paean. It was a solemn and terrifying sight to see them, stepping in time to the pipe, with no split in their line and no disturbance in their spirits, calmly and cheerfully following the music into mortal danger.

Not only communal but also individual exertions might take their tempo from the pipe. Hipponax, in a satirical song addressed to an emaciated glutton, recommends him to drink medicine, but first to strip and do physical exercises 'while Kikon plays you Kodalos' air'.[85] It was common to have a piper in attendance while training for, or sometimes competing in, athletic events of several kinds. Many sixth- and fifth-century vase-paintings bear witness to this, most frequently in connection with the long jump or with throwing the discus or javelin. We are told that for the long jump in the Olympic pentathlon the 'Pythian melody' was played, apparently by the aulete who had won the prize for piping at the Pythian Games two years previously.[86] Philostratus says that the purpose was to give the jumper an additional stimulus. Other authors refer to piping as an accompaniment to boxing and (at a certain Argive festival) to wrestling.[87]

---

[85] Fr. 118c; my *Studies in Greek Elegy and Iambus*, 147f.

[86] See Pl. 10; Paus. 5. 7. 10, 17. 10; 6. 14. 10; cf. Diogenes of Seleucia, *SVF* iii. 225. 31 (who also mentions the discus (?) and shadow-boxing), ps.-Plut. *De mus.* 1140d, Philostr. *De gymnastica* 55.

[87] Epicharmus fr. 210; Paus. 5. 17. 10 (the chest of Cypselus); ps.-Plut. *De mus.* 1140c. The Etruscans are said to have had it for boxing, and also for flogging slaves and kneading dough (Alcimus, *FGrH* 560 F 3, Arist. fr. 608, Eratosth. *FGrH* 241 F 4; for kneading, cf. above, p. 28). See further Wegner, *Musikleben*, 101f., 192–4 (list of vases) and pl. 5a; H. A. Harris, *Greek Athletes and Athletics* (London, 1964), 81, 84, and pl. 7, 12*b*; J. Jüthner, *Philostratos über Gymnastik* (Leipzig and Berlin, 1909), 301, and *Die athletischen Leibesübungen der Griechen*, ii(1) (*Sitz. Wien* 249. 2, 1968), 163 Abb. 36, 174 Abb. 48, 220, 341, and pl. 46a, 52, 55b, 60, 90, 94*b*.

Music's potency

The Greeks were familiar with the idea that music can alter the disposition of those who hear it. They acknowledged its power to soothe, to console, to distract, to cheer, to excite, to inflame, to madden. They had definite theories, which will be described in a later chapter, about the various moral and emotional effects of different musical modes and rhythms. There are stories of music being employed deliberately to manipulate people's moods. It is said that when Sparta was in a state of unrest in the first half of the seventh century BC, an oracle recommended sending for 'the Lesbian singer': Terpander was invited to come, and his singing restored the city to good order. Similar achievements are attributed to Thaletas and Stesichorus.[88] Pythagoras is supposed to have noticed, while out star-gazing one night in Tauromenium, a young man who, carried away by love, jealousy, copious drink, and Phrygian pipe-music, was preparing to set fire to his mistress's door; the sage calmed him by persuading the piper to play a more dignified melody.[89]

None of these episodes can be taken as historical, but the idea that music might achieve such results certainly enjoyed some currency. The Pythagoreans in particular claimed to have developed (or rather to have inherited from Pythagoras) a science of musical psychotherapy and a daily programme of songs and lyre pieces that made them bright and alert when they got up, and when they went to bed purged them of all the day's cares and prepared them for agreeable and prophetic dreams.[90] We also hear of a painter who found that a citharode's singing enabled him to achieve a likeness.[91]

A more primitive stratum of belief is reflected in the use of music

---

[88] Arist. fr. 545, Diod. 8. 28, ps.-Plut. *De mus.* 1146b, *Suda* iii. 370. 10, etc.; Plut. *Lyc.* 4. 3; Philod. *Mus.* p. 42 Kr. = 221 Rispoli, 182 Kr. = 65 Neubecker (*PMG* 281 c, d).

[89] Cic. *De consiliis suis* fr. 3 p. 339 Müller, Sext. Emp. *Math.* 6. 8, Iambl. *De vita Pythagorica* 112. A like story is told of Damon in Galen, *De placitis Hippocratis et Platonis* 9.5, Mart. Cap. 9. 926.

[90] Aristox. frs. 26, 121, Quint. *Inst.* 9. 4. 12, Dio Chrys. *Or.* 32. 57 (i. 283. 24 Arnim), Plut. *De Is. et Os.* 384a, Aristid. Quint. 2. 19 p. 91. 27, Porph. *Vita Pythagorae* 30, 32f., Iambl. *De vita Pythagorica* 64f., 110f., 164, 224, Mart. Cap. 9. 923. Cf. Pl. *Ti.* 47d, Xenocrates ap. Mart. Cap. 9. 926, Chamaeleon fr. 6 Giordano, Aristox. fr. 6; E. R. Dodds, *The Greeks and the Irrational* (Berkeley and LA, 1951), 80.

[91] Diogenes of Seleucia, *SVF* iii. 227. 19 (Philod. *Mus.* 4 pp. 48f. Neubecker). Perhaps the reference is to Parrhasius, who is reported to have sung while painting (Theophr. fr. 79 W. with Ael. *VH* 9. 11).

as a means of countering physical ills. This is music as magic, as one among the various mysterious special techniques at the disposal of the shaman or seer.[92] In historical Greek medicine it played no part: regular doctors relied on physical measures such as exercise, baths, diet, drugs, or surgery. But it survived in the 'fringe medicine' of quacks and old women, religious healers and purveyors of esoteric lore. We may distinguish three manifestations of it: incantations; paeans and purificatory songs; and music supposed to be efficacious by virtue of its intrinsic musical properties.

With incantations the music (if any) is of little importance; what matters is the correct wording. In one passage of Homer (but not in others) the binding of a wound is complemented by an incantation to stop the bleeding, and Pindar represents Asclepius as using incantations among other methods of healing.[93] In the case of the so-called 'sacred disease', epilepsy, the superstitious were especially ready to turn to those who used such measures.[94] Pythagoras is said to have employed 'incantations and spells' as well as pure music in healing the sick.[95] Midwives used them, together with potions, to induce and facilitate labour.[96] Of course, incantations had a role in various kinds of magic, not just in healing. We hear of them in connection with influencing the winds,[97] putting someone under a spell,[98] compelling someone to fall in love,[99] purifying houses and livestock.[100]

The paean has already been considered in a wider context (p. 15).

---

[92] Cf. F. Densmore, 'The Use of Music in the Treatment of the Sick by American Indians', *Musical Quarterly* 13 (1927), 555 ff.; A. Machabey, 'La Musique et la médecine', *Polyphonie* 1950 nos. 7/8, 40 ff.; D. M. Schullian and M. Schoen, *Music and Medicine* (New York, 1948). David delivered Saul from an evil spirit by playing his lyre (not harp): 1 Sam. 16: 23.

[93] *Od.* 19. 457; Pind. *Pyth.* 3. 51.

[94] Hippoc. *De morbo sacro* 1. 12, 39, Dem. |25|. 80.

[95] Porph. *Vita Pythagorae* 30, 33, Iambl. *De vita Pythagorica* 164.

[96] Pl. *Tht.* 149 cd.

[97] Aesch. *Ag.* 1418, a metaphor implying a reality.

[98] Aesch. *Eum.* 306 ff., Pl. *Resp.* 364 c, *Leg.* 933 a.

[99] Eur. *Hipp.* 478, Xen. *Mem.* 2. 6. 10.

[100] Pl. *Resp.* 364 b, Theophr. *Hist. Pl.* 9. 10. 4. Often they are a metaphor for 'charming' someone by persuasion: Pind. *Pyth.* 4. 217, ps.-Aesch. *PV* 173, etc. For some other Classical references to incantations see Pind. *Nem.* 8. 49, Aesch. *Ag.* 1021, *Eum.* 649, Soph. *Trach.* 1000, *Aj.* 582, Eur. *Alc.* 967, *Cyc.* 646, Ar. *Ran.* 1033, Pl. *Chrm.* 155 e, *Euthydemus* 290 a, *Resp.* 426 b, *Symp.* 202 e. Euripides (*Alc.*) and Plato (*Chrm.* 156 a) refer to their being written down for exact transmission, which underlines the overriding importance of the wording. See further L. Edelstein, *Ancient Medicine* (Baltimore, 1967), 235–9.

It is associated with the idea of purification from injurious elements. A seventh-century Cretan composer of paeans, Thaletas or Thales of Gortyn, is said to have gone to Sparta in accordance with an oracle (the story is parallel to the one about Terpander mentioned above) and delivered the city from a plague by means of his music.[101] We are told that Pythagoras used to sing paeans of Thaletas to the lyre to put his disciples in a serene state of mind, and that he had certain 'paeonic' or healing songs with which he cured bodily sicknesses.[102]

Other passages suggest that this Pythagoras (who is a projection of the notions and ideals of some later Pythagoreans) owed the efficacy of his musical therapies to the judicious selection and arrangement of appropriate modes, scales, and rhythms. Some of them were wordless melodies on the lyre.[103] In this case it was clearly the music itself, independently of any associated text, that was regarded as potent.

According to some writers the Pythagoreans much preferred the lyre to the pipes, which they considered crude and vulgar.[104] The magical power of the lyre was, after all, reflected in the myths of Amphion, whose music charmed the stones to assemble themselves into walls for Thebes, and Orpheus, who not only shifted rocks and trees but even overcame the stern powers of the underworld and brought his wife back from the dead. Later Pythagoreans, in the Hellenistic period, appear to have tried to emulate Orpheus by using lyre music to liberate souls from the bonds of death.[105] But in general it was the pipe that was considered the instrument with the greatest power to produce strange effects. To 'pipe on' someone meant metaphorically to bewitch or put a spell on him.[106] Some held that certain kinds of pipe music were effective in treating physical ailments, including fainting, epilepsy, sciatica, and even snake-bites.[107]

---

[101] Pratinas, *PMG* 713 (iii).

[102] Porph. *Vita Pythagorae* 32, 33; cf. Iambl. *De vita Pythagorica* 110.

[103] Porph. 30, Iambl. 64 f., 164.

[104] Aristid. Quint. 2. 19 p. 91. 28, Iambl. 111. But Ath. 184 e says many Pythagoreans practised the art of piping, including Euphranor, Archytas, and Philolaus, the first two of whom even wrote books about it. Aristoxenus (fr. 95) looked down on pipes and panpipes as being too easy to learn.

[105] M. L. West, *The Orphic Poems* (Oxford, 1983), 29–32.

[106] *Kataulein*, Eur. *HF* 871, Pl. *Resp.* 411 a, *Leg.* 790 e. Piping and dancing in cures for madness: ibid. 791 a.

[107] Theophr. frs. 87–8; ps.-Democr. B 300. 7. On some modern studies of physiological responses to music see Merriam, 111–14.

Music and the citizen

We have seen that music in one form or another impinged on everyone in Greek society. There was no one who was not exposed to it,
and no one who did not think that it was in principle a good thing,
even if he deplored particular styles. In the earlier period, down to
the fifth century BC, the level of participation in music-making was
relatively high, and we cannot always draw a clear line between the
professional and the amateur.

As regards participation there were, at the most basic level, verses
and formulae that everyone sang as part of a crowd, like the paean in
battle or after dinner and the hymenaeal refrain at wedding processions. From time to time one might be called upon to perform in a
chorus at a festival or a private celebration. It has been mentioned
that at the City Dionysia in fifth-century Athens 500 men and 500
boys were required for the dithyrambic contest alone, not to
mention those who made up the tragic and comic choruses. Good
singers must have been more sought after than bad; yet we hear that
some were drafted who could not sing and had to keep silent.[108] At
the symposium, until the late fifth century, one was expected to sing
something, and few were unable to meet the challenge.

The ability to play an instrument was naturally more restricted,
but it was not restricted to professionals. As we saw, Homer represents Achilles and Paris as able to handle a lyre; so could men like
Alcaeus, Damophilus, and perhaps Hiero and Arcesilaus. It was not
a rare accomplishment among upper-class Athenians in the fifth
century. In the earlier part of the century, according to Aristotle,
many of them also learned something of the pipes, though this instrument then fell out of favour.[109]

When we speak of professionals, it is worth making a distinction
between those who possessed a special expertise and held an
audience by virtue of their individual talent and those who merely
provided a routine service. In the first category we must begin by
mentioning the Homeric singer, who earned his keep by performing

---

[108] See below, p. 47. On the selection of choruses see Pickard-Cambridge, *DFA*[2]
76 f.

[109] Arist. *Pol.* 1341a26–39. Alcibiades is said to have taken the lead in rejecting it
(Pamphila ap. Gell. *NA* 15. 17, Plut. *Alc.* 2. 5–7, cf. ps.-Pl. *Alc. I* 106 e; Duris, *FGrH*
76 F 29, on the other hand, says that Alcibiades learned the art from the virtuoso
Pronomus). Callias and Critias are notable Athenians of the period who did learn it
(Chamaeleon fr. 5 Giordano).

regularly at a particular house, or travelled from one community to another in search of patronage. Later there were the citharodes and auletes who performed at festivals and competed for prizes there. We cannot tell how many of them depended on their art for a livelihood, but they certainly developed a more than ordinary skill, and from time to time they introduced refinements in the construction of their instruments or in the techniques of playing them. Then there were the poet-composers like Simonides, Bacchylides, and Pindar, who created songs for a fee for patrons in various parts of the Greek world. The other category, that of those who provided a routine service, is represented by the professional mourners who sometimes appeared at funerals, and by the pipers, male or female, who played accompaniments for other people to sing to, for instance at the symposium. They were commonly slaves or hirelings, sometimes of foreign origin.

The former class of professional naturally enjoyed a rather higher status than the latter. Homer represents the epic singer as someone worthy of esteem and respect from everyone; like the seer, the healer, or the carpenter, he is welcome in a new place because of the special skill that he exercises for the public's benefit.[110] The provision of valuable prizes for singers and instrumentalists at games presupposes that they are not people to be looked down upon. The victorious aulete in the Pythian Games of 490 BC, Midas of Acragas, was able to commission a celebratory ode from Pindar. Pindar himself obviously reckons to be a man of high standing, a friend of kings and tyrants, able to address them on equal terms. Later, virtuoso citharodes and auletes enjoyed great public acclaim, and were sometimes commemorated by public or private monuments.[111]

But their exceptional technical ability displayed itself in musical innovations that, while delighting the ear of the crowd, displeased many educated critics who had been taught an older set of rules.[112] And this new music was beyond the reach of amateur players, who were left with a static repertory that to many sounded increasingly old-fashioned. The result was a decline in private music-making, a greater tendency to leave it to the professionals, and the emergence of a snobbish feeling that it was after all not an altogether worthy

---

[110] *Od.* 8. 479, 17. 382–6, cf. 22. 345f.
[111] Cf. e.g. Pliny, *HN* 35. 109 (Telestes), Ath. 19b (Archelaus), Paus. 9. 12. 5 (Pronomus).
[112] See Ar. *Nub.* 961–72, Pl. *Leg.* 658e–659c, 700a–701a.

pursuit for an enlightened man—except perhaps when he was drinking and having a little fun.[113]

Music teaching

Songs that are popular in the society in which one moves are easily
picked up without formal instruction. Playing an instrument is more
difficult. It may sometimes happen that someone who happens to
have an instrument available can master its technique just by playing
with it, but normally some tuition is necessary. The great majority of
those who played in ancient Greece will have learned from someone
else. Informal tuition from a friend, a relative, or a benevolent expert
might be available at any time. In the Archaic period this was
perhaps the only kind of instruction that existed. But by the beginning of the fifth century, at least at Athens, there was an organized
system of musical education.

The qualification 'at least at Athens' is to be emphasized. We must
always remember that in early Greece different communities had
very different cultural traditions and institutions. They all liked the
lyre and the pipes, but in the Archaic age there may have been plenty
of people able to play these instruments without there having to be
any systematic arrangements for teaching them to the young. What
did call for some organization was the training of choruses to sing
and dance at the many festivals and other occasions when choral
performances were expected. In some of the Dorian states, in particular, choral training was institutionalized. In Crete boys were
drafted into 'herds' and subjected to a disciplined regimen directed
towards making them hardy men and tough fighters. As part of this
they learned dances in armour and the singing of paeans.[114] At
Sparta there were similar arrangements. In the fragments of Alcman
we can see that the girls who sang his songs were under the guidance
of a chorus-manager (*chorāgos*) and taught to revere her and obey
her like a helmsman. Perhaps she was responsible for teaching them
more than song and dance. Sappho, who presided over a 'house of
the Muses' servants', was certainly understood by later generations
to have been a music-teacher and chorus-leader to whom people
sent their daughters for some sort of education. She must have been
practised at writing, to judge by the preservation (in antiquity) of ten
volumes of her poetry, and it is possible that she taught this art to her

[113] Arist. *Pol.* 1339ᵃ33–b10.
[114] Ephorus, *FGrH* 70 F 149. 16, cf. Pl. *Leg.* 660b.

juniors. At Syracuse in the early fifth century the *chorāgos* taught letters as well as music, and the verb *chorāgein* stood for 'school' teaching generally.[115]

At Athens choruses were formed anew for each event, and if the composition to be performed was an original one, as was often the case, the composer normally took over the training of the singers. The chorus, therefore, did not make a suitably stable institution for a programme of education. For this, boys were sent to a 'lyre-man' (*kitharistēs*) and a physical trainer (*paidotribēs*). The lyre-man taught them to sing and play songs from the established repertory. He sometimes taught reading and writing too.[116] But before long we find the teacher of letters (*grammatistēs*) established as a separate figure beside the music teacher. He made the boys read and learn passages from Homer and other improving poets, while the music teacher drilled them in the works of the lyricists.[117]

Vase-paintings give us some vivid glimpses into the Athenian school of the early Classical age. The finest and best-known is a cup by Duris dating from the 480s. It shows lessons in music and letters taking place in the same house (Pl. 11). On one side of the cup a teacher and pupil sit facing one another on stools, each fingering a lyre. Another teacher (or rather the same one in a different lesson) is shown seated on a chair holding a papyrus roll, on which an epic verse can be read, and the pupil stands before him to recite. The slave who has brought the boy to school sits at the back and watches. On the other side we see a younger, perhaps subordinate teacher, and again two distinct lessons. In one the teacher plays the pipes while the pupil, standing, prepares to sing. In the other the teacher is writing or correcting something in an exercise book made of waxed wooden tablets strung together, and the boy is again standing in front of him with the slave in attendance. In another scene, on a water-jar of the second quarter of the fifth century attributed to the Agrigento

---

[115] Alcm. *PMG* 1. 43–101, cf. 10b; Sappho fr. 150, *SLG* 261a, *Anth. Pal.* 9. 189, Philostr. *VA* 1. 30, *Imag.* 2. 1, *Suda* iv. 323. 8; Epicharmus frs. 13, 104, Sophron fr. 155.

[116] Ar. *Eq.* 986ff., *Nub.* 963ff., Eup. fr. 17. Plato, *Cri.* 50d, speaks as if it were a legal requirement to have one's son educated in music and gymnastics, but perhaps the passage should not be taken literally.

[117] Pl. *Prt.* 325d–326c, cf. 312b, *Clitophon* 407bc, *Alc. I* 106e, *Leg.* 812b, Xen. *Lac. Pol.* 2. 1. According to Aristotle (*Pol.* 1339ᵇ2) there was no similar formal teaching of music at Sparta. But Chamaeleon (fr. 5 Giordano) claims that everyone there learned the pipes, as also at Thebes and in his own town of Heraclea on the Black Sea.

Painter, the instructor sings to the lyre, while his teenage pupil accompanies the melody on pipes. Other young men holding instruments are standing awaiting their turns. One of them is passing the time of day with what looks like a leopard cub; there is also a dog in the room, and a small child squatting on the floor sucking its thumb.[118]

Conclusion

On this homely note we may bring our survey to a close. It is not intended to be exhaustive or encyclopaedic, but simply to give an idea of the many and various ways in which music played a part in the life of ancient Greece, so that the more detailed data to be presented in the following chapters may be seen against this general background. The picture has been deliberately limited to the Archaic and Classical periods (eighth to fourth centuries), in order to maintain a semblance of coherence. Some account of later developments will be supplied in the final chapter.

---

[118] Duris cup: Berlin F 2285. Agrigento Painter: London E 171 (Wegner, *Musikleben*, pl. 13; Paquette, 171 pl. viib, misidentified in the caption). Other school scenes are listed by E. Pöhlmann, *Würzburger Jahrbücher* 14 (1988), 15–19.

2

The Voice

By far the greater part of Greek music—as of ethnic music overall—
consisted of song, either solo or choral. Instruments were sometimes
played on their own, but mostly they served to accompany the
human voice. There normally was such accompaniment (except
when someone was singing to entertain himself while doing something else), but its role was subordinate. A choir of many voices was
not balanced by an equivalent band of instrumentalists; very often a
single piper supplied the accompaniment, even for a chorus of fifty,
as in the Athenian dithyramb. According to a writer of the Aristotelian school, we enjoy listening to a singer more when he sings to
an aulos or a lyre, not because of the additional sonority but because
it helps to define the tune. It is not better with more instruments,
because that tends to obscure the song.[1] Another tells us that the
aulos is better than the lyre for singing to, because it blends better
with the voice and covers the singer's mistakes, whereas the lyre
shows them up.[2]

One can do other things melodically with the voice besides singing. One can hum, yodel, imitate bird or animal cries, or croon word-
lessly. The Greeks, however, did not exploit these possibilities for
musical purposes.[3] Nor did they have songs composed partly or
wholly of nonsense syllables, as some peoples do. On the contrary,
their songs (so far as our knowledge goes) were settings of
thoroughly articulate, often highly sophisticated poetic texts, with
little verbal repetition. Hence it was important that the words should
be clearly heard and not submerged in instrumental sound. Lasus of
Hermione, the first poet known to have interested himself in musical
theory, composed at least two pieces in which he contrived to avoid

---

[1] Ps.-Arist. *Pr.* 19. 9.   [2] Ibid. 19. 43.
[3] Aristophanes may emphasize the identity of bird or frog singers by incorporating
appropriate calls in their songs (*Av.* 227 ff., *Ran.* 209 ff.), but these songs are predominantly in Greek; he is not producing anything in the manner of Janequin's *Chant
des oyseaux*.

the sound *s*—one of the commonest sounds in the Greek language—
and his reason is said to have been that it was 'harsh and unsuitable
for the aulos', meaning presumably that it did not in his opinion
sound distinctly against the aulos accompaniment.[4]

Besides singing, there was a technique of reciting verse with
instrumental accompaniment. This was called *parakatalogē* ('parallel recital'). Its invention is attributed to Archilochus, which implies
that it was used (or believed to have been used) in the performance
of the Ionian iambus.[5] It was also used in drama: we cannot always be
sure in which passages, but probably (*a*) where the metre is anapaestic of the non-lyric ('marching') type, as for example in many choral
entries and exits; (*b*) where iambic trimeter or dactylic hexameter
lines in the Attic dialect (i.e. without the Doric colouring typical of
tragic song) occur in a lyric context; (*c*) in some scenes composed in
trochaic or iambic tetrameters.[6] One would guess that the verses
were recited in a more stylized manner when accompanied by music
than in ordinary dialogue scenes. Perhaps 'chanted' would be an
appropriate term.[7] The instrumentalist—an aulete in the case of
drama—must have followed the same metrical pattern, but what
kind of melodic line he pursued it is impossible to say.[8]

Choruses were either male (men or boys) or female. There is some
early evidence for mixed dancing,[9] but not for men and women singing in unison.[10] Men's and boys' choruses too were usually separate,
though we do hear of men and boys singing together, an octave
apart.[11] As it is common in many cultures for different voices to sing

---

[4] Ath. 455 c (Heraclid. Pont. fr. 161, *PMG* 702 and 704); 467 a (Aristox. fr. 87).

[5] Ps.-Plut. *De mus.* 1141 a.

[6] See Pickard-Cambridge, *DFA*[2] 156–65, who collects the ancient evidence and
discusses at length the question of the use of *parakatalogē* in drama; also A. W.
Gomme and F. H. Sandbach, *A Commentary on Menander* (Oxford, 1973), 37; my
Greek Metre (Oxford, 1982), 77–9, 98.

[7] Aristid. Quint. p. 6. 3 ff. speaks of a type of delivery used in reading poetry,
intermediate between ordinary speech and song. Cf. Nicom. *Ench.* p. 239. 13–17.

[8] Pickard-Cambridge's statement (157) that the accompaniment was on higher
notes than the recitation is based on a misconception, not peculiar to him, about the
phrase *hypo tēn ōidēn*; see p. 206 below, n. 41. In any case, in the sentence in question
the author is no longer speaking about *parakatalogē*. One source, Psell. *De trag.* 9,
recognizes a kind of 'exclamation' (*anaboēma*) in tragedy that is intermediate
between singing and recital but almost belongs in the sung category.

[9] Webster, 5 f., 46–8.

[10] References to this appear in later sources: ps.-Arist. *Mund.* 399ᵃ16 (late Hellenistic), Sen. *Ep.* 84. 9 (copied by Macrob. *Sat.* praef. 9).

[11] Aristox. fr. 99 (Pind. fr. 125); ps.-Arist. *Pr.* 19. 39 a.

in parallel at the interval of a fifth, a fourth, a third, or even a second,[12] it is worth noting that the octave parallelism is the only one recognized in the Greek sources and the existence of others is denied.[13]

Choruses varied considerably in size. A male chorus of seven sang at the Nemean Games at some period.[14] The Muses, sometimes represented as singing together, are nine in number, which may or may not reflect an institution of earthly choirs of this size.[15] Alcman's first Partheneion was sung by a choir of ten girls, while another Spartan festival, celebrating the wedding of Helen, involved a choir of twelve, at least in the third century BC.[16] The choruses of tragedy had twelve members in Aeschylus' time, but subsequently fifteen; those of comedy had twenty-four, and those of the dithyramb fifty. A boys' chorus of thirty-five used to go from Messina to participate in a festival at Rhegium.[17] Herodotus mentions a chorus of a hundred young men sent to Delphi by the Chians about 500 BC.[18] This is far the largest we hear of in the Classical period. However, at the wedding-feast of a Macedonian grandee about 300 BC a choir of a hundred sang a hymenaeum, while in the grand procession laid on by Ptolemy II at Alexandria, designed to be the greatest show on earth, one of the lesser attractions (preceded by a series of floats full of statues of gods and kings, and followed by 2,000 heavily decorated bulls) was a choir of 600 men, accompanied by thirty citharists.[19] Not that huge choirs were *de rigueur* in the Hellenistic age. An inscription relating to the Delphic Soteria in the year 257/6(?) BC lists men's and boys' choruses consisting of no more than five (professional) singers, and comic choruses of seven. A little over a century later a comedy was put on at Delphi with a chorus of four.[20]

What kind of sound did the Greek singer seek to produce? According to Curt Sachs,[21]

Nowhere outside the modern West do people sing with a voice for which we have coined the honorific title of 'natural' . . . to the western ear, all oriental

---

[12] See Sachs, *WM* 177–81.   [13] Ps.-Arist. *Pr.* 19. 17–18.
[14] Or perhaps at the Pythian, since there may be a gap in the text: Hyg. *Fab.* 273. 7.
[15] See my note on Hes. *Th.* 60. A late inscription from Magnesia on the Maeander attests boys' and girls' choirs of nine each in the local cult of Zeus Sosipolis. Cf. also the Hellenistic verses in *POxy*. 8 (Powell, *Coll. Alex.* 186. 9).
[16] Alcm. *PMG* 1. 99; Theoc. *Id.* 18. 4.
[17] Paus. 5. 25. 2.   [18] Hdt. 6. 27. 2.
[19] Hippolochus ap. Ath. 130a; Callixenus, *FGrH* 627 F 2. 33 (Ath. 201f).
[20] *SIG* 424; 690. Cf. Sifakis, 71–4, 85.   [21] *WM* 85.

and primitive singing is unnatural and seasoned with strange, unwonted mannerisms.

However, I suspect that this statement reflects a somewhat excessive reaction to the Europocentric outlook of older writers. Singing styles the world over have since been analysed in great detail by the American musicologist Alan Lomax. He finds that they characterize large geographical and historical regions, zones thousands of miles broad and millennia deep. He claims to establish that they show a marked correlation with features of social organization, especially with the type of economy, male dominance, and the repression of female sexuality.[22] The variables include vocal width and tension, raspiness, gutturality, tremolo, nasality, emphasis, tempo, volume, pitch level in relation to the singer's natural range, amount and type of ornamentation, strictness of intonation and rhythm, precision of enunciation, and, where there are several voices, the degree of blending.

The commendatory adjective most regularly applied to the singing voice in Greek is *ligys* or *ligyros*. It is also applied to the lyre, the aulos, panpipes, bird-calls, the stridulation of cicadas, the wind, people weeping, a smooth-tongued orator, and to pliant, swishy things such as whips and the tails of hounds. A scientific writer defines the *ligyrā* voice as one that is 'refined and concentrated, like those of cicadas, grasshoppers, and nightingales, and in general all those voices that are refined and have no alien noise accompanying them: it is not a matter of volume, or of low, relaxed tone, or of contact between sounds, but rather of high tone, refinement, and precision'.[23] We had better not try to extract too much from this. The Greek singer fairly certainly did not endeavour to sound like a grasshopper, though a symposiast does apologize for not being able to 'sing *liga*, like a nightingale', because he was carousing the previous night too.[24] The essential quality expressed by *ligys* seems to be clarity and purity of sound, free from roughness or huskiness.

Other indications are consistent with this. Aeschylus imagines Iphigeneia singing the paean for her father's dinner guests 'virginal, pure-voiced'. Aristophanes' Hoopoe praises the 'clean' sound of the

---

[22] A. Lomax, *Folk Song Style and Culture* (Washington, DC, 1968). Cf. Kunst, 12 with literature; Nettl, *FTM* 19, 47f.; Sachs, *WM* 85–91; W. Wiora, *Ergebnisse und Aufgaben vergleichender Musikforschung* (Darmstadt, 1975), 44f.

[23] Ps.-Arist. *De audibilibus* 804a21.

[24] 'Theog.' 939f.

nightingale's lament and her 'liquid' melody.[25] A fine singing voice is also characterized as 'sweet', 'like honey', or as 'lily-white'. Again, these expressions suggest that it was a smooth, pure tone that was most admired.

Singers practised before breakfast, we are told, because the voice is impaired by food; the windpipe is roughened by it, as after a fever. Intoxication is also said to lead to failure of the voice.[26] Plato refers to choirs dieting and fasting when in training for competitions.[27] One of Antiphon's speeches was written for a man who found himself accused of murder because a boy who was being trained at his house to sing in a chorus had died after drinking a potion to improve his voice. We know no further details of the misadventure, but singers who take potions presumably do so for the sake of a more melli-fluous tone and to prevent hoarseness. In a comic fragment a citharode declares that washing his throat down with the sticky parts of a conger eel will strengthen his breath and voice.[28] When Nero was learning citharody, he

omitted nothing that that type of artist did for the sake of conserving or developing the voice: he would lie with a lead sheet on his chest, purge himself with enemas and emetics, and abstain from eating obstructive fruits and foods.

Presently he resolved to perform in public, 'although his voice was slight and husky'.[29] Finally, the romance-writer Longus, in the second century AD, completes his picture of a rustic wedding by saying that the attendant countryfolk sang the hymenaeum 'in a harsh, rough voice, as if they were breaking up the soil with forks, not singing a wedding-song'.[30] Thus the style of the educated singer is defined by its antithesis.

The notes of the song were attacked cleanly, without swooping or sliding from one to the next. This, according to Aristoxenus, is what differentiates song from speech.

In conversation we avoid bringing the voice to a standstill at a particular pitch, unless we are forced to it by emotion, but in singing, on the contrary, we avoid continuous sliding up and down, and pursue stationary pitch as far as possible. The more we make each note single, static, and unchanging, the

---

[25] Aesch. *Ag.* 245; Ar. *Av.* 213 f.; cf. Kaimio, 202.
[26] Ps.-Arist. *Pr.* 11. 22; 11. 46.
[27] *Leg.* 665 e.   [28] Clearchus Comicus fr. 2.
[29] Suet. *Ner.* 20.   [30] *Daphnis and Chloe* 4. 40. 2.

more correct the melody is perceived as being.... The voice has to pass imperceptibly across the interval as it ascends or descends, and render the notes bounding the interval so that they are distinct and stationary.[31]

Song was expected to be loud and clear. Circe's whole curtilage reverberates as she sings at her loom; the earth resounds to the Muses' song as they make their way to Olympus, and when they are there, it echoes round the mountain's peak and the homes of the gods; the songs of the Trojan girls at Hector's wedding rise to the sky. Pausanias tells us that the mythical Eleuther failed to win the Pythian contest for a hymn to Apollo, although he sang 'loud and agreeably', because the hymn he performed was not his own.[32] Pindar is said to have employed someone else to teach his chorus because his own voice was 'thin'.[33] While symposiasts sang from their couches, people singing seriously before an audience or in lessons stood up straight, so that there was no constriction of the chest.[34] Vase-painters show mouths well open. Citharodes, aulodes, and other standing singers often have their heads thrown back as they sing, as if to project the sound as far as possible. Some of them perhaps over-did it, for Timotheus in the epilogue to his *Persians* criticizes 'out-of-date music-spoilers, maulers of songs', who sing in stentorian voices like town criers.[35] Perhaps what he is objecting to is not volume in itself but a shouting instead of a singing tone. But perhaps the New Music of the late fifth century BC, of which Timotheus was a leading representative, was finding new artistic possibilities in dynamic restraint. The dramatists of the time occasionally composed lyric dialogues that had to be sung softly so as not to wake a character who was asleep.[36]

One feature associated with the New Music is a tendency to orna-mentation. This is something which by its nature tends to be restricted to solo singing, and it was in solo, not choral singing that

[31] Aristox. *Harm.* 1. 9–10. Cf. Theophr. fr. 89. 13 (Barker, *GMW* ii. 117), Nicom. *Ench.* 2 p. 238. 16 ff.

[32] *Od.* 10. 227, Hes. *Th.* 42, 69, Sappho fr. 44. 26, cf. *Hymn. Hom.* 19. 21, Ar. *Av.* 216, 776–80; Kaimio, 138 n. 383, 237; Paus. 10. 7. 3.

[33] Schol. Pind. *Ol.* 6. 148 a, 149 a.

[34] Wegner, *Musikleben* 70 f.

[35] *PMG* 791. 216–20. A later citharode performing this very work of Timotheus' in 207 BC impressed the crowd with the *lamprotēs* of his voice (Plut. *Phil.* 11. 4); the word can be translated 'splendour' or 'magnificence'. There is a wholly unreliable story that Terpander choked to death when someone threw a fig into his wide-open mouth as he was singing (Tryphon, *Anth. Pal.* 9. 488; *FGE* 99–101).

[36] Eur. *HF* 1042 ff., *Or.* 136 ff., Soph. *Phil.* 843 ff.

the New Music specialized. It is not possible to say much on the subject here: in the ancients' critical remarks about this music it is difficult to distinguish between melodic complexity and ornamentation in performance, and between instrumental and vocal antics. We shall go into more detail in Chapter 7. But there seems to have been occasional employment of ornaments for expressive effect. Euripides, as parodied by Aristophanes,[37] uses some sort of trill or turn on the first syllable of the verb 'twirl', to give musical expression to its meaning. The practice seems to have been contained within fairly narrow limits at this period, while certain of the later musical texts show it being used a little more extensively. The implication of Aristophanes' satire is that it was a novelty. We get the impression that older music was sung in a straightforward way, voice matching instrument note for note, without noticeable decorative embellishments.

In choral singing a good blend of voices was admired. The Muses sing 'with voices coinciding', and Alcman pretends that his choir's voice is a single Muse or Siren voice.[38] Seneca, apparently using a Greek philosopher's example, speaks of how all the voices in a choir blend into one and are not heard individually.[39]

All in all, the indications are that early Greek singing style was not characterized by any special mannerisms. Clarity and purity of tone, resonance, and coincidence with the accompaniment were the virtues commended. So far as we can see, it was much like that 'natural' mode of singing which Sachs finds only in the modern West.

However, there may have been special styles associated with certain songs of foreign provenance, or with certain religious contexts. The boy who sings the *Linos* in Homer (cf. above, p. 28) is described as singing it in a 'slender' voice. One might suppose this to be merely because of his youth, except that an ancient commentator states that the *Linos* is 'a song of lament which is sung in an attenuated voice'.[40] Perhaps he is inventing an explanation of Homer's phrase, but it looks more like a genuine piece of learning. It is particularly interesting that a constricted vocal style, employed by a solo performer with poorly co-ordinated antiphonal responses from a chorus, has been identified by Lomax as part of a distinctive pattern

---

[37] *Ran.* 1314, 1348.
[38] Hes. *Th.* 39; Alcm. *PMG* 30.
[39] *Ep.* 84. 9; cf. ps.-Arist. *Mund.* 399[a]16.
[40] *Il.* 18. 570 with schol. b (p. 558. 44 Erbse) = *PMG* 880.

typical of the area of 'Old High Culture' extending from North Africa
across Asia to Malaysia; he specifically mentions harvest songs as
traditional manifestations of this style. And Herodotus states that
the *Linos*, under different names, was widely sung in the Near East,
including Cyprus, Phoenicia, and Egypt.[41]

Prophets apparently used a peculiar screaming voice for deliver-
ing prophecies, though whether this should be included under
singing is doubtful.[42] Mention should also be made of what has been
claimed as evidence for the use of a special technique at the fifth-
century symposium. Two vase-paintings depict singers with their
open right hands held near their right ears, as if to hear better.
According to the interpretation of D. Gerhardt, what they are
actually doing is pressing their thumb against their larynx in order to
produce a tremolo effect or glottal shake, a practice alive today in
parts of the Middle East.[43]

Finally, it may be instructive to note some of the difficulties that
the average non-professional singer sometimes encountered. Not all
types of composition were within his competence; it is observable in
tragedy that singing parts are reserved for certain actors, not
required of all. Singing in a high register was felt to be difficult, but on
the other hand we hear that people tended to sing sharp rather than
flat.[44] They also had trouble with the note *parhypatē*, located just a
semitone or less from the bottom of the scale, perhaps because of a
tendency to slip to the tonically more important bottom note, or to
hold further off it.[45] Choruses perhaps did not rehearse as long or as
efficiently as they do for a modern concert. At any rate they
depended a good deal on their leader. 'You know, of course,' says
Demosthenes, 'that if one takes away the leader, the rest of the
chorus is done for.'[46] He gave the lead and did his best to keep his

[41] Lomax, op. cit. (as n. 22), 97; Hdt. 2. 79.

[42] Poets use the verbs *klazō* and *laskō* in this connection, both applicable *inter alia*
to screaming birds or howling dogs; and also verbs more generally expressing loud
cries, like *iācheō*, *eporthiazō*.

[43] Red-figure stamnos, *CVA* Italia 27 Villa Giulia III. 1c pl. 11. 5; red-figure cup,
Munich 371; Wegner, *Musikleben*, 69f. and pl. 30*b*. In an Egyptian tomb painting of
the 12th Dynasty a man is shown singing with his left hand against his left ear. A
related technique appears to be attested on a relief of Ashurbanipal from Nineveh
(BM 124802), where a woman singer in a procession of Elamite musicians is pressing
or gently beating the left side of her throat with the extended fingers of her right hand
(Rimmer, 37 and pl. xiv*b*).

[44] Ps.-Arist. *Pr.* 19. 37; 19. 26, 46.

[45] Ibid. 19. 3–4 with von Jan's notes.

[46] *Meid.* 60.

fellows to the correct rhythm, which they managed better when there were more of them.[47] Care had to be taken to place the singers in the chorus according to their individual competence.[48] The leader's place was in the middle, while at the edges there might be two or three who could not sing at all, and who kept mum.[49]

[47] Ps.-Arist. *Pr.* 19. 22, 45, *Mund.* 399ᵃ15, Dio Chrys. *Or.* 56. 4 (ii. 122. 1 Arnim), Ael. *NA* 15. 5.

[48] Pl. *Euthydemus* 279 c, Xen. *Ages.* 2. 17, ps.-Plut. *Apophthegmata Laconica* 208 d, 219 e; but it is not always clear to what extent dancing ability was the deciding factor.

[49] *Mesochoros*, *Fouilles de Delphes* iii. 1. 219, Plin. *Ep.* 2. 14. 6; Men. fr. 153 Koerte. A word meaning 'liking to stand at the edge of the chorus' is attested for Alcman (*PMG* 32). Cf. ps.-Plut., op. cit. 219 e.

3

Stringed Instruments

The problem of classifying the musical instruments of the world's peoples on scientific principles has long exercised musicologists. The most influential system is the one devised by E. M. von Hornbostel and C. Sachs, which operates with four main categories (and many subdivisions): idiophones (that is, instruments made from sonorous materials that will yield a sound simply by being struck, shaken, rubbed, etc.), aerophones, membranophones, and chordophones.[1] For our purposes, however, the familiar layman's classification into stringed, wind, and percussion instruments will serve perfectly well. It corresponds, incidentally, to a classification recognized by some ancient writers.[2]

The stringed instruments of the ancient world were played by plucking with the fingers, striking with a plectrum, or a combination of both. (Bowed instruments did not appear until the Middle Ages.) The purpose in each case was to make tuned strings vibrate and to amplify these vibrations to a reasonable level of audibility by transmitting them to a resonant soundbox.

The standard stringed instruments in Greece at all periods were lyres of various forms. From at least the end of the seventh century BC there were also some harps, and from the second half of the fourth century BC some lutes. The defining features of a lyre are that it has two arms projecting from the body and linked by a crossbar or yoke; the strings extend from the crossbar over an open space and then over a bridge on the front soundboard to a fastening at the base. In

[1] *Zeitschrift für Ethnologie*, 46 (1914), 553–90; Sachs, *HMI* 454–67; K. Wachsmann in *NG* ix. 237–45.

[2] Ath. 636c, Nicom. *Ench.* 2 p. 240. 22 J., Cassiod. *Mus.* 6. 1209c. More often we find a simple dichotomy of strung and blown (Aristox. fr. 95, Aristocles ap. Ath. 174c, Manilius *Astr.* 5. 331, Poll. 4. 58f., Aristid. Quint. p. 85. 3ff., *al.*), percussion instruments being either left out of account or grouped with stringed instruments as 'struck'. Certain late sources make the human voice a third category beside blown and struck instruments (Augustine, *In Psalm.* 150. 8, *De doctr. Christ.* 2. 17. 27; Isid. *Orig.* 3. 20–2). Anon. Bellerm. 17 has blown, strung, and 'bare' (*psīla*), the last category including both the voice and such things as musical jars.

Greek lyres the strings are of equal length. In a harp, on the other hand, the strings are attached to an arched or angled neck fixed at one end of the soundbox, and they meet the soundboard at an oblique angle. They lie in a plane perpendicular to the soundboard, not parallel as in the case of the lyre, and they are of conspicuously differing lengths. In a lute the relation of the strings to the soundbox is similar to that in a lyre, but instead of the two arms and crossbar there is a single extended neck along which the strings run and against which they are pressed to shorten the vibrating length and obtain different notes.

Lyres, harps, and lutes were all in use in Mesopotamia well before 2000 BC, and widely established in west Asia and the eastern Mediterranean in the second millennium. The Greek instruments have their own features and history, but they are visibly related to oriental models.

LYRES

The lyre makes its first appearance in a pavement graffito at Megiddo, Israel, dated to about 3100 BC. From early in the third millennium it is attested for the Sumerians, as a massive instrument with up to eleven strings. Similar lyres are represented in artefacts of the Hittite Old Kingdom in the first half of the second millennium. A lighter, more portable version was developed by the western Semites and spread to Babylonia and Egypt.[3]

These oriental lyres had a more or less rectangular soundbox and were often asymmetrical, with one arm longer than the other, a slanting crossbar, and strings of unequal length. The lyres depicted in Minoan and Mycenaean art, on the other hand, are symmetrical and have a round base. The number of strings, where determinable, is usually seven or eight, though the lyre depicted in a fresco from the palace at Pylos has only five, and one vase sherd from Tiryns shows only three. In some cases, including one of the earliest representations, a Middle Minoan II sealstone from Knossos (c. 1900–1700 BC), we can see that the player supported the lyre against himself by means of a sling attached to the further arm of the instrument and looped round his left wrist, and that he used a plectrum attached by a

---

[3] See B. Bayer, *The Material Relics of Music in Ancient Palestine and its Environs: An Archaeological Inventory* (Tel Aviv, 1963), 26 f.; Sachs, *HMI*; Rimmer; *NG* under Anatolia, Egypt, Mesopotamia, and Lyre.

cord to the centre of the base of the soundbox. All these features recur in lyres of the Archaic period, and argue some continuity of tradition.[4]

The lyre is the only stringed instrument attested for the Minoan and Mycenaean civilizations, and this seems to foreshadow its dominance in Classical Greece, where only the pipes approach it in importance, and all other instruments are of marginal significance. As between lyre and pipes, it was the lyre that in general enjoyed the greater prestige. It was the only instrument regularly played by an Olympian god (Apollo) and appreciated by the other gods. Aristoxenus and the other writers on harmony have lyre music primarily in view.

The Greek lyres are of several distinct types, which may be classified as follows:

A. Box lyres
   1. Round-based ('phorminx', 'cradle kithara')
   2. Square-based, standard type ('concert kithara')
   3. Square- or round-based, horn-armed ('Thracian kithara')
   4. Rectangular ('Italiote kithara')
B. Bowl lyres
   1. Standard type ('lyra', 'chelys')
   2. Long-armed ('barbitos')

The box lyres or kitharas have a more substantial sound-chest than the others, built out of wood. They are altogether more elaborately crafted and obviously more expensive. These—in particular the A2 type—were the instruments used by the professional musician in public performance. The bowl lyres, with a soundbox generally made out of a tortoise shell, must have had a less powerful sound, and they were what was used in domestic settings, at the symposium, and in the Athenian schoolroom.

Before going into further detail, I must say something about nomenclature. The Greek words *phorminx*, *kitharis* or *kitharā*, *lyrā*, *chelys*, and *barbitos* overlap in usage. Homer uses only *phorminx* and *kitharis*, both of the same instrument, which was probably a round-based box lyre.[5] *Lyrā* appears from Archilochus on, and the

   [4] Wegner, *Musik und Tanz*, 26 f.; C. W. Blegen, *AJArch.* 60 (1956), 96, pl. 41 (Pylos fresco); Maas–Snyder 2–3, 7–8, 16–18 (figs.).
   [5] *Phorminx*, his usual word, looks ancient; *-inx* is an old suffix, and the verb *phormizō* appears to be an old derivative (from *phorming-yō). *Kitharis* is assumed to be a loan-word from a non-Greek language, but its source has not been traced. (The

poet of the Homeric Hymn to Hermes applies all three words, as well as *chelys* ('tortoise'), to the bowl lyre that Hermes makes from a tortoise shell. In an Attic vase-painting of the earlier sixth century BC[6] a tortoise-shell lyre is labelled LYRA. Pindar uses both *phorminx* and *lyrā* of his own instrument, which was probably a box lyre (of whatever shape). Other poets too seem to use the terms interchangeably.[7] *Barbitos* (in late Greek also *barbiton*) stands apart: it is relatively rare, and when it is used in the Classical period it seems to refer specifically to the long-armed bowl lyre. Fourth-century writers distinguish *kitharā*, *lyrā*, and *barbitos* as different instruments.[8] They do not mention *phorminx*, which had probably been a strictly poetic word for a considerable time. There is no doubt that by *kitharā* they mean the box lyre, as used by citharodes in vase paintings, and by *lyrā* the ordinary bowl lyre. In what follows I shall use 'lyra' in this specific sense while continuing to use 'lyre' in the generic sense.

Box lyres (kitharas)

After the Mycenaean period there is very little evidence until the mid-eighth century, when scenes of human activity came back into artistic fashion in Greece. A Cypriote pot of the eleventh century and another of c. 800 show round-based kitharas with three and four strings respectively. In a third Cypriote representation of c. 850 the base is somewhat pointed, though it is a rounded point; again there are three strings.[9]

In late Geometric art (mid-eighth to early seventh century) lyres appear more frequently.[10] They are nearly all box lyres, and predominantly round-based, though a few have a pointed base. The

same is true of *lyrā*.) It may be a modification of *kitharos*, which appears in medical writing with the sense 'thorax', but which may originally have been a word denoting some sort of foreign-made chest. The form *kitharā* appeared early in the 5th c., no doubt by analogy with *lyrā*, and soon prevailed over *kitharis*.

[6] Munich 2243, Maas–Snyder, 48 fig. 12.

[7] 'Theog.' 761, 778/792, Simon. *PMG* 511 fr. 1a. 5, Aesch. *Supp.* 697, *Eum.* 332, Bacchyl. 1. 1, 4. 7, 14. 13, Ar. *Av.* 219, *Thesm.* 327, Eur. *Phoen.* 822/5, etc. See Maas–Snyder, 79 f.

[8] Pl. *Resp.* 399d; Arist. *Pol.* 1341[a]19/40; Aristox. fr. 102 (who opines that Homer's *kitharis* was a *lyrā* and not a *kitharā*); Anaxilas fr. 15 K.–A. Later writers also distinguish *kitharā* from *lyrā*, e.g. Ptol. *Harm.* 1. 16, 2. 16, Paus. 5. 14. 8, Aristid. Quint. pp. 85. 8/14, 91. 2/5, 92. 11.

[9] All illustrated in Maas–Snyder, 19; my Pl. 12.

[10] For detailed surveys see Wegner, *Musik und Tanz*, 3–16; Maas–Snyder, 11–23.

upper edge of the soundbox is sometimes straight, so that the face of
the box is roughly semicircular, but more often it is scooped out, in
some cases so deeply that the box appears reduced to a crescent-
shaped tube little if at all wider than the arms. The scooped-out
shapes resemble those of most Minoan and Mycenaean representations, though in a little bronze model from the twelfth century the
concavity is so shallow that it approximates to the half-moon shape.
However, the eighth-century representations, like the earlier Cypriote ones, diverge consistently from the Mycenaean ones in regard
to the number of strings. They normally show three or four, exceptionally two or five. Against some dozens of these we can set only
one example from the middle of the century that may have seven or
eight strings,[11] and one from the end of the century that probably had
six or seven in its complete state.[12]

The reliability of artistic representations in this matter is obviously
limited, especially when they are as crude or stylized as those of the
late Geometric. Some scholars take the view that seven was the
standard number of strings throughout, and that we should not infer
from the artefacts the currency of a three- or four-stringed lyre.[13]
Certainly in some cases we may say that a painter or the maker of a
small model had room for only three or four strings in the space
available, given the thickness of his brush-strokes or the metal
strands he could make. But in other cases more strings could easily
have been accommodated; and in view of the quantity of the
evidence, besides the existence of a literary tradition that Terpander
increased the number of the lyre's strings from four to seven,[14] it
seems reasonable to accept that a round-based kithara with only
four strings may have been in general use in the eighth century.[15]

This would have been the *phorminx* with which the epic singer

---

[11] Athens 14447. Wegner, *Bilder*, 26, states that the original has five strings (and
so in *Musik und Tanz*, 14 f., 73), but the photographs there and in Paquette 89 seem to
show seven (as Paquette says, p. 88) or eight (as he says on p. 86).

[12] Athens, sherd from the Argive Heraion, the earliest clear example of a kithara
with a flat base.

[13] H. Abert, *RE* xiii. 2481 f., iA. 1761; Maas–Snyder, 8 f., 11, 203.

[14] See below, p. 330.

[15] Perhaps some had only three, but as between three and four the artistic evidence
does not have the same probative value as it has between four and seven, and we
should expect there to be a standard number corresponding to the requirements of a
particular type of singing. In these conclusions I follow L. Deubner, *MDAI*(A) 54
(1929), 194–200 and *Phil. Wochenschr.* 50 (1930), 1566 f.; Wegner, *Musik und
Tanz*, 3–16.

accompanied himself. One or two of the representations actually show a seated player who might be taken for such a performer.[16] The majority, however, show the player standing and accompanying male, female, or mixed groups of dancers. The instrument appears quite large, often large enough to reach from the player's waist to the top of his head. Perhaps its size owes something to artistic licence, but the kitharas of sixth- and fifth-century painting on the whole maintain a similar height in relation to their players.

In the seventh century seven-stringed kitharas begin to appear more regularly. Some of them are still round-based and not noticeably different in design from the eighth-century models, apart from the greater number of strings. Some, however, represent a distinctly different design. They are flat-bottomed, and their arms are more obviously composite: the lower sections, rising from and continuing the soundbox, curve round towards each other, while the upper sections, which carry the crossbar, are straight and parallel. In the finest example, engraved on a piece of bronze armour from towards the end of the century,[17] the insides of the lower arms are carved into elaborate volutes. What we see here is closely similar to the standard kithara of the Classical period as depicted on very many Attic and Italian vases. When pseudo-Plutarch tells us[18] that the form of the kithara was established in the time of Kepion, a pupil of Terpander, it was no doubt the Classical kithara that his source had in mind. The association of its design with a citharode of the earlier seventh century is consistent enough with the evidence of art for us to suspect that Kepion's name was preserved by a genuine tradition among citharodes, though his subordination to the famous Terpander might well be a secondary construction. And if one genuine tradition about innovation in kithara design survived from that time, we have the more reason to attach weight to the tradition of an earlier four-stringed lyre.

The Athenian vase-painters render the curlicues on the inner arms of the kithara in a very detailed and consistent way (Pl. 14): they no longer look like mere ornamentation, but like some kind of mechanism for releasing or adjusting the tension of the arms. This is

[16] Especially a Cretan bronze figurine of the late eighth century, Heraklion 2064 (Pl. 13); cf. J. N. Coldstream, *Geometric Greece* (London, 1977), 284, 'a seated minstrel singing to a four-stringed lyre'.
[17] Said to be in a private collection on Zacynthus; illustrated in Wegner, *Bilder*, 45; Aign, 238; Maas–Snyder, 45.
[18] *De mus.* 1133 c.

how Sachs interprets them,[19] and D. Paquette has offered a detailed explanation.[20] What remains puzzling, if this view is correct, is the way in which the design of the functional device seems to be pre-figured in the purely ornamental intricacies of the older kithara. In fact there was a long tradition, going back to Minoan and Egyptian models, of volutes, zigzags, or other complications in the arms of the box lyre below the crossbar. Whether they had any structural purpose is not clear.[21]

The great majority of representations of the kithara give us only a full frontal or (less often) a full dorsal view, and do not allow us to form any idea of the depth of the soundbox. However, reliefs from the Sicyonian Treasury at Delphi and the Parthenon, and a red-figure vase showing a kithara from the side, together with one or two other scraps of evidence, indicate that the back of the soundbox had quite a bulge or hump, especially towards the top, and that there was a ridge running down the bulge to the base.[22] The soundbox, in other words, seems to have been shaped something like the stern half of a rowing boat with the hull folded up to seal the front and the top covered over with a deck, the whole thing standing on its end.

The square-based kithara in this classic form was the instrument of the professional citharode who competed at the Pythian, Pan-athenaic, and other contests, or put on public performances of his own. The vase-painters also supply it to the citharodes' patron deity, Apollo, while other gods such as Hermes and Dionysus play simpler kinds of lyre (see below). Aristotle speaks of the kithara as a 'professional' (*technikon*) instrument, unsuitable for general educational use.[23] The citharode emphasized that he was a man apart by wearing an especially fine costume: an ankle-length, richly ornamented or

---

[19] *HMI* 130, 'an ingeniously made, and artistically carved, lever which lifted the crossbar, thus tightening all the strings at once. This invention had a forerunner, how-ever; as early as the fifteenth century B.C., Egyptian lyres had movable arms which, piercing the body, could be pushed upward at will by the player's knee or chest.' Like-wise J. W. Schottländer (unpublished dissertation cited by Neubecker 73); B. Lawer-gren, *Imago Musicae* 1 (1984), 150, 'drawn details suggest hinges, springs, and other movable parts'. For slackening lyre-strings when not in use cf. Plut. *De educandis liberis*, 9 c.

[20] Paquette, 91, 95 f., 241–3.

[21] According to Wegner, *Musikleben*, 32 f. and *Musik und Tanz*, 7, 8, it was advantageous to prevent the vibrations from the strings reaching the soundbox from the crossbar, via the arms, and interfering with the resonances set up directly through the bridge.

[22] See R. A. Higgins and R. P. Winnington-Ingram, *JHS* 85 (1965), 69 f.; Maas–Snyder, 33, 65.   [23] *Pol.* 1341ᵃ18.

pleated robe, a decorated mantle, and a gold wreath on his head.[24] His kithara might have gilded arms and be inlaid with carved ivory, or (at least at a later period) set with jewels and precious stones. Sometimes he suspended from it a length of embroidered cloth, a practice inspired by oriental pomp.[25]

The round-based kithara continues to appear on the vases of the Classical period.[26] However, after about 600 BC it is less common than the square-based type; after about 530 we find it only in Dionysiac and carousal scenes; and after about 500 it is played only by women or by Muses. By the fourth century it has practically disappeared.[27] Evidently it was disdained by professionals—it is not furnished with the tension levers (if that is what they are) of the citharode's instrument[28]—while symposiasts and other amateurs came to prefer the lighter bowl lyres, the lyra and barbitos, leaving their old kitharas for the women.

Two other forms of kithara must be mentioned. One of them appears in a number of fifth-century vase paintings, in most cases in the hands of one of the legendary Thracian singers, Orpheus or Thamyras. Hence it has been called the 'Thamyras kithara' or 'Thracian kithara'.[29] Its base can be either round or squared off with deeply fluted corners. The top edge of the soundbox is a convex arc, with no extensions towards the arms, which are thin and willowy, somewhat like those of the barbitos, but conspicuously ribbed, and describing a different curve. The round-based version, which has an

---

[24] See Pl. 14. Cf. Hdt. 1. 24. 4–6, Plato Com. fr. 10, Aelius Dionysius ε 58, Poll. 10. 190; for a later period, *Rhet. Her.* 4. 47 with Lucian, *Ind.* 8–10, Ov. *Met.* 11. 165–7; M. Bieber, *JDAI* 32 (1917), 65 f.; Maas–Snyder, 58.

[25] Gilded arms: Soph. fr. 244. Ivory: Ar. *Av.* 218; Maas–Snyder, 35. Amber? Ar. *Eq.* 532. Ivory facings are already Mycenaean (Maas–Snyder, 8). Lyres found in Sumerian royal tombs were cased or decorated with gold or silver and adorned with semi-precious stones. We recall Achilles' fine ornamented lyre with its silver crossbar (*Il.* 9. 187; cf. Pind. *Pyth.* 4. 296). For bejewelled kitharas in the later Graeco-Roman world cf. Ovid, *Rhet. Her.*, and Lucian, locc. citt.; Juv. 6. 382. For the patterned cloth hanging see Maas–Snyder, 32–4, 68. 7th-c. Assyrian reliefs show harpists with decorative woven cloths hanging from the base of their instrument.

[26] See Pl. 15. In this context it is often called a phorminx (although there is no evidence that this name was ever used by the Greeks to distinguish it from the square-based kithara), or by others a 'cradle kithara'.

[27] Maas–Snyder, 29 f., 139–45, 170.

[28] B. Lawergren, however, suggests that its arms were hinged and could be pushed sideways to alter the tension of the strings (*Imago Musicae*, 1 (1984), 171).

[29] See Pl. 16; Maas–Snyder, 145–7. Others have suggested 'horned kithara' or 'cithare-lyre'. The lyre held by Musaeus in New York 37.11.23, which Maas–Snyder include under this type, seems to me to be a standard kithara.

oval outline, seems to have an early cognate in a curious lyre depicted on a sherd from Old Smyrna, dating from the first half of the seventh century, though here the soundbox appears very small.[30]

The other type is a later development, appearing in South Italian vase-painting after about 360 BC. It has been called the 'Italiote kithara'. It differs from all previous Greek lyres in having a rectangular soundbox and (as its arms are straight, continuing the lines of the sides of the soundbox) a rectangular shape overall.[31] Lyres of a similar shape had long been current among the western Semites and in Egypt,[32] and it may be that the Italiote model, which breaks so markedly with Greek tradition, was an import from the Levant.

Bowl lyres (*lyra and barbitos*)

We pass now to the bowl lyres. These did not require the services of a skilled cabinet-maker for their construction, and although at Athens and elsewhere they were turned out by professional instrument-builders, they could in principle be put together by anyone—a lonely herdsman, for example. It was the herdsman's god, Hermes, who was supposed to have invented the lyra. The fourth Homeric Hymn describes how he constructed it from materials that lay naturally to hand in his rural environment. He scraped out a tortoise's shell, drilled holes in it, and fitted some lengths of cane into them. He stretched a piece of hide across the open side. Then he attached arms and a crossbar, and strung the frame with seven strings of sheep-gut.[33]

Words for 'tortoise' (*chelys, chelunnā*) sometimes stand for 'lyre' in poetry. The size and markings of shells depicted in art indicate that the tortoise used was the *testudo marginata*, whose carapace nowadays grows to between nine and twelve inches in length and four to five in depth.[34] The arms may sometimes have been made

[30] Maas–Snyder, 42 fig. 1.

[31] See Pl. 17; A. M. Di Giulio in Gentili–Pretagostini, 117–19; Maas–Snyder, 175–8, 192–3.

[32] See M. Wegner, *Die Musikinstrumente des alten Orients* (Münster, 1950), pl. 8*a* (Asiatic Bedouin in an Egyptian painting from the early 2nd millennium) and 5*b* (Assyrian relief from Zenjirli, 8th c.); Aign, 164f. (North Syrian seals, 8th–7th c.), 314 (N. Syrian grave stele, 8th c.), 160 (Egyptian silver bowl from Cyprus, 7th c.); *NG* vi. 73 (Egyptian steatite bowl, 6th–5th c.).

[33] *Hymn. Hom. Merc.* 41–54. Cf. Soph. *Ichneutae*, 298–320, 374–5, and for other versions of the myth T. Hägg, *Symb. Osl.* 64 (1989), 36–73.

[34] H. D. Roberts, *World Archaeology*, 12 (1981), 303; Maas–Snyder, 95. Remains found at Bassae (Arcadia) and other sites, however, are from shells only 15–18 cm. long: P. Courbin, *BCH* Supp. 6 (1980), 93–114 (*testudo hermanni hermanni*);

from animal horns or ivory, but the usual material will have been wood.[35] They were held fast against the upper rim of the shell by being jammed under one of the cane spars, which in the case of one of the Argive lyres (sixth–fifth century) formed two arches intersecting at right angles and oriented on the major and minor axes of the shell's ellipse.[36] Strings were of twisted sheep's gut, of sinew, or perhaps sometimes of flax.[37]

The lyra is not seen in any Minoan or Mycenaean representations so far known. Fragments of drilled tortoise shell found at a Late Bronze Age site on Melos have been interpreted as lyra remnants, though other explanations are possible.[38] Artistic representations appear from about the end of the eighth century onward and become frequent from the sixth.[39] The lyra appears in many contexts: dances, sacrifices, processions, symposia; domestic, school, and mythological scenes. Apollo or the Muses sometimes have it instead of the kithara. It may be played by men, women, or children. It is the ordinary instrument of the non-professional.

The barbitos differs from the normal lyra most obviously in the form of its arms. They are distinctly longer, and instead of having a gentle regular inward curve they are straight as they rise from the soundbox, diverging, until at a certain distance they bend decisively towards each other (and forward, as appears from a side view on one vase[40]) and then turn upwards again at a sharp right angle, the last sections being parallel and carrying the crossbar. The length of its strings would indicate that the barbitos had a deeper pitch and a

P. Phaklaris, Ἀρχαιολογικὸν Δελτίον 32 (1977), 218–33; Maas–Snyder, 94. Paus. 8. 54. 7 says that tortoises very suitable for lyres lived on Mt. Parthenion in the Argolid, but were deemed sacred to Pan and jealously guarded by the locals.

[35] Philostr. *Imag.* 1. 10. 1–2 describes Hermes making them from goat-horns. See also below, p. 59, on the *phoinix*. Ivory: *PMG* 900, *IG* 1³. 343. 29, 2². 1388. 80 (ivory lyres for festival use), cf. Philostr. loc. cit. A gilt lyre, *IG* 1³. 343. 29. The Elgin lyre in the British Museum had arms of sycamore. Unspecified wooden parts of the lyre are mentioned by Pl. *Phd.* 86b, Philostr. loc. cit. (box-wood). Theophr. *Hist. Pl.* 5. 7. 6 says that holm-oak is good for the crosspieces of lyres and harps.

[36] Soph. fr. 36 implies that without its cane a lyre collapses. See Roberts (as n. 34), 308f.; Courbin (as n. 34), 96ff.

[37] H. Abert, *RE* iA. 1762; Hägg (as n. 33), 59. On technicalities of manufacture see further P. Phaklaris (as n. 34); P. Courbin (as n. 34); H. D. Roberts (as n. 34), 303–12; Paquette, 145–71; A. Bélis, *BCH* 109 (1985), 201–20; Maas–Snyder, 94–8.

[38] C. Renfrew, *The Archaeology of Cult: The Sanctuary at Phylakopi* (London, 1985), 325f.; alternative explanations in Hägg (as n. 33), 63 n. 102. The Egyptians made soundboxes for lutes out of small tortoise shells (Hägg, 55 with literature).

[39] See Pl. 18; Paquette, 145ff.; Maas–Snyder, 36–9, 48–52, 81–94, 100–12, 178–80, 194.   [40] Brussels A 3091; Maas–Snyder, 125 and 138 fig. 22.

softer tone than the lyra, and this is confirmed by ancient statements.[41] Although seven is the commonest number of strings shown
in the vase-paintings, as we might expect, there are enough well-
executed examples with only five or six to suggest the possibility that
the barbitos was sometimes so strung.[42]

The barbitos is first mentioned by Anacreon, though Sappho and
Alcaeus referred to an instrument called *barmos* which some
ancient scholars took to be the same.[43] It appears in Attic art rather
suddenly in the last quarter of the sixth century, and fades away in
the second half of the fifth. The attractive suggestion has been made
that it was brought to Athens by Anacreon when he moved there
from Samos.[44] Certainly it is associated with him both by the vase-
painters and in later literary allusions.[45] It is nearly always depicted
in the context of the symposium or associated revelry and amorous-
ness, or in the hands of Dionysus and his entourage. It evidently
enjoyed a great vogue in certain elegant Athenian drinking circles in
the late sixth and early fifth centuries. The comic poet Magnes probably made fun of them in his lost play *The Barbitos-players*. Aeschylus may have provided Dionysus with a barbitos in his *Edonoi*.[46]
Pindar, Bacchylides, and Euripides mention it, but only in connection with private festivity.[47]

---

[41] Pind. fr. 125, who speculates that its invention was inspired by the octave-
doubling (in the bass?) of the deep Lydian harp; ps.-Arist. *De audibilibus* 803ᵃ34,
schol. Eur. *Alc.* 345, *Etymologicum Genuinum* β 38, *al.*

[42] See Maas–Snyder, 124.

[43] Anac. *PMG* 472, Sappho 176, Alc. 70. 4. 5th-cent. vase-painters at Athens
depict Sappho playing a barbitos (Pl. 19). Cf. Hor. *Carm.* 1. 1. 34. The form *barōmos*
attributed to Sappho in Ath. 182 f. is probably a corruption, cf. 636 c and Alc. loc. cit.;
while the Aeolic *barmitos* cited by the *Etymologicum Genuinum* β 38 = *Etym.
Magn.* 188. 21 may be an accidental and spurious product of an effort to use *barmos*
in support of the alleged etymology of *barbitos* from *barymitos* 'with deep-toned
threads'. *Barmos* may have some distant kinship with *phorminx*, and *barbitos* with
Middle Persian *barbaṭ* 'short-necked lute'.

[44] Maas–Snyder, 40, 113, 118 f., 127. A similar instrument is represented on an
East Greek sealstone a little earlier than the first Attic pictures (Maas–Snyder, 39, 52
fig. 18).

[45] Critias fr. 8. 4 Diehl, 'Simon.' *Epigr.* 67 Page, Neanthes, *FGrH* 84 F 5 (Anacreon
as inventor of the barbitos), Antip. Sid. *HE* 273, Anon. *Anth. Pal.* 7. 23 b, *Anacreontea* 15. 34; Wegner, *Musikleben*, 44 f.; Maas–Snyder, 118–20.

[46] See the parody at Ar. *Thesm.* 136 f.

[47] Pind. frs. 124 d, 125; Bacchyl. frs. 20 ʙ 1, 20 c 2 (*Enkomia*); Eur. *Alc.* 345, *Cyc.*
40. Theoc. *Id.* 16. 45 perhaps echoes an *Enkomion* of Simonides for the Scopadae
rather than the 'Epinicia and Laments' to which the scholiast refers; see Simon. fr.
eleg. 29. 3 West². Proclus in Phot. *Bibl.* 321 a mentions the barbitos as the instrument
for singing skolia to at drinking-parties.

After about 440 BC the barbitos is less often depicted, and by 400 it has disappeared from Attic vases, though it may still be found here and there in Apulian and Etruscan art of the first half of the fourth century.[48] A poet of the Middle Comedy portrayed an instrument-maker (apparently Doric-speaking) whose products still included barbitoi, but Aristotle regards them as *passé*. Dionysius of Halicarnassus, three centuries later, notes that they are no longer in use among the Greeks, though the Romans use them in all their old sacrificial rituals.[49]

Lyres of unknown type

We know the names of a number of other lyre-type instruments that cannot be defined more closely. There was one called *phoinīx* or *phoinīkion*, presumably of Phoenician provenance, first mentioned by Alcaeus. Herodotus remarks that the horns of the Libyan antelope are used for the arms of the *phoinīx*, which suggests Carthage as one place of manufacture. Aristoxenus knew it as a foreign instrument. A passage in the Aristotelian *Problems* shows that it could (and did) play octave concords.[50] We also hear in later sources of a *lyrophoinīx* or *lyrophoinīkion*, which must have been something between a *phoinīx* and an ordinary lyra.[51]

Pollux mentions a variety of kithara called *Pȳthikon* or *daktylikon*, used for instrumental playing without song.[52] This type of performance was a special accomplishment of certain virtuosi—the music must have been comparatively elaborate (below, p. 69)—and it is understandable that they were fussy about their instruments. The name *daktylikon*, 'finger-lyre', perhaps refers to its being played

[48] Maas–Snyder, 127, 170.

[49] Anaxilas fr. 15, Arist. *Pol.* 1341ᵃ39, Dion. Hal. *Ant. Rom.* 7. 72. 5. *Barbitos* continues as a poetic word for 'lyre' in later Anacreontic verse and in epigram.

[50] Alc. p. 507 Voigt = fr. 424 A Campbell (cf. *ZPE* 80 (1990), 7); Hdt. 4. 192. 1; Aristox. fr. 97; ps.-Arist. *Pr.* 19. 14. The Persian king may have had a player attached to his court, if that is what *phoinīkistēs* means at Xen. *An.* 1. 2. 20. Ephorus, *FGrH* 70 F 4 and Skamon, *FGrH* 476 F 4 said that the instrument was a Phoenician invention (cf. Phot., *Etym. Magn.* 797. 21), but Semos (*FGrH* 396 F 1) claimed that it got its name from the palm-tree (*phoinīx*) of his native Delos, from which its shoulders were made. Pollux 4. 59 and Isidore *Orig.* 3. 22. 3 list it among other types of lyre and harp. The lexicographer Cyril (N. Naoumides, *GRBS* 9 (1968), 272) takes it to be a harp, harps being well known for playing in octaves, but the mentions of its arms and shoulders show that this is wrong. I do not know what led LSJ to say that it was like a guitar.

[51] Juba, *FGrH* 275 F 15 (Syrian origin) and 84; Poll. 4. 59; Hsch. ('a type of kithara').   [52] Poll. 4. 66.

with all ten fingers instead of five plus a plectrum. The alternative name, *Pȳthikon*, is unambiguous: the instrument was to be heard at the great Pythian musical contests, where prizes for songless kithara-playing are said to have been introduced in 558 BC.[53] But 'Pythian kithara-playing' became a recognized art form that could be displayed anywhere. In 97 BC a 'Pythian citharist' is listed among the great band of Athenian musicians who made the pilgrimage to Delphi; he may well have used the *Pȳthikon* mentioned by Pollux. A third-century AD inscription from Mt. Helicon records prizewinners in a series of contests, one of which was for a 'Pythian citharist'.[54]

The *pentachordon*, a Scythian product strung with five thongs of raw oxhide and played with a goat's-hoof plectrum,[55] sounds an altogether more primitive object than any we have been discussing, but perhaps it had charms beyond our imagining.

The *skindapsos* or *kindapsos* is described as four-stringed, lyre-like, with arms made from springy willow(?) branches. It was apparently plucked with the fingers but also strummed, and it was derided as a silly instrument.[56] Aristoxenus listed it as of foreign provenance, and Aelian makes it Indian.[57]

The *spādīx*, not mentioned before the Imperial age, was a lyre-type instrument with louche associations.[58] The *byrtē* and the *psaltinx* are recorded in lexica with the bare explanations 'lyre' and 'kithara' respectively. The name *psaltinx*, a pretty coinage, implies that plucking the strings, as opposed to damping or strumming them, had a larger role with this instrument than with most lyres.[59] In the interests of completeness I should perhaps mention *kinyrā*, which is the Greek rendering of the Hebrew *kinnôr* (Septuagint, Josephus) and has no existence as a Greek instrument.[60]

---

[53] Paus. 10. 7. 7, cf. Strab. 9. 3. 10.

[54] *SIG* 711 L 32; *IG* 7. 1776. 19 f.; cf. *PMichigan* 4682 (O. Pearl, *Illinois Classical Studies* 3 (1978), 132–9.   [55] Poll. 4. 60.

[56] Anaxilas fr. 15, Matron, *Supp. Hell.* 539, Theopompus of Colophon, *Supp. Hell.* 765, Timon, *Supp. Hell.* 812. 3, Hsch. ε 1411–12; below, p. 67 n. 86.

[57] Aristox. fr. 97, Ael. *NA* 12. 44. Named after an Indian tribe, the Kindapsoi: *Etym. Gen.* = *Magn.* 514. 34, cf. Hsch. κ 2730. It is sometimes supposed that the *skindapsos* was a lute, but the only argument offered is the number of strings (R. A. Higgins and R. P. Winnington-Ingram, *JHS* 85 (1965), 66 f.).

[58] Quint. *Inst.* 1. 10. 31, Poll. 4. 59, Nicom. p. 243. 12, Λέξεις Ἡροδότου 180 p. 229 Rosén, Hsch. σ 1376. The name means 'palm-frond' or 'broken-off bough'.

[59] *Psallō* 'pluck a string', *psaltos* 'plucked'; *-inx* on the model of *phorminx* (if not of wind instruments such as *sȳrinx*, *salpinx*, *phōtinx*).

[60] J. P. Brown, *Journal of Semitic Studies* 10 (1965), 207 f. See also below, p. 226, on Pythagoras of Zacynthus' triple lyre.

Stringing and tuning

In all the Greek lyres we know about, the strings were secured to a brace ('tailpiece' would be the technical word) at the base of the soundbox and then passed over a bridge (*magas* or *magadion*) which held them off the soundbox while transmitting their vibrations to it. At the far end they were attached to the crossbar, and it was here that the tension was adjusted.

There was more than one method of attachment. The Mycenaean lyre of which some bits were retrieved from a beehive tomb at Menidi in Attica had holes drilled in its yoke, probably for fixed (not rotating) pegs round which the strings were secured. One or two early Archaic and even Classical representations have been interpreted as showing fixed pegs,[61] but this is uncertain. What clearly was common, from the seventh century on, was winding the string round the yoke and binding in some kind of solid piece that the player could push up or down to adjust the tension. Sometimes it seems to have been a straight slip of wood or some other hard material. This is the same means of tuning as was used for the early Mesopotamian lyres. Often, however, the vase-painters depict a series of globules above and below the yoke. These have been taken as the ends of 8-shaped pieces,[62] but some of the representations are very difficult to reconcile with this interpretation. They seem rather to be beads tied on the strings.[63] From the sixth century we also find examples of a method used in Mesopotamia and Egypt in the New Kingdom and still employed in East Africa. The strings are wound on the crossbar over strips of cloth, leather, or other material, which sometimes appear as quite bulky bundles. To tune the instrument the player encircled the binding with his thumb and one or two fingers and rotated it on the crossbar.[64] In other cases again, especially with lyras, the strings appear simply to be tied round the crossbar with no

---

[61] E. Pöhlmann in *Serta Indogermanica* (Festschrift G. Neumann, Innsbruck, 1982), 307; Paquette, 97.

[62] Pöhlmann, op. cit. 308f.; cf. H. Roberts (as n. 34), 307f.; Maas–Snyder, 98.

[63] See esp. Paquette, 105 C3, 107 C6, 115 C21, 117 C28, 121 C36, 137 Cb7, 151 L2, 153 L4, 159 L20, 167 L36–7.

[64] See Pl. 20; Rimmer, 14f.; Aign, 290; Maas–Snyder, 2, 6, 7, etc.; Paquette, 96, 248f.; *NG* xi. 397f. Many vase-paintings show lyres being tuned; see H. Roberts in T. C. Mitchell (ed.), *Music and Civilisation* (*British Museum Yearbook* 4, 1980), 49 with n. 31; Paquette, 119, 121, 125, 127, 137, 157, 161, 163, 167, 169, 179, 185; Maas–Snyder, 72, 77, 111.

underlay and no lever.[65] In two fourth-century Italian paintings and on the Boston Throne the strings are attached to rings which encircle the yoke and have projecting lugs above and below to facilitate adjustment.[66] Finally, from the second century BC there is evidence for tuning-pegs of the modern sort that could be twisted in the yoke.[67]

Number of strings

The question of the scales to which the lyre was tuned will be addressed in a later chapter. But while we are considering the physical features of the instrument, there is more to be said about the number of its strings. What we have seen so far is that the standard number from the seventh century onward, as in the Minoan and Mycenaean era, was seven, but that there is fairly abundant evidence for round-based box lyres with only three or four strings in and before the eighth century, and that some barbitoi may have had five or six.

The frequency with which vase-painters depict precisely seven strings shows that they often took care over the matter and counted. But we cannot expect them to do so invariably, and when they depict more or less than seven we must clearly be very cautious about taking them literally. On the other hand we should not make it an article of faith that seven is the only possible number. If we find six or eight strings represented, it may very well mean nothing. But when we find nine, ten, or eleven, this is not so easy to dismiss as mere carelessness. A nine-stringed lyra appears as early as *c.*560,[68] and there are about five more instances in the Classical period; in the fourth century there are several round-based and Italiote kitharas with nine strings. Those cited in Table 3.1 are even better provided, and a number of further examples occur in later reliefs and Roman wall-paintings.[69]

[65]   e.g. Paquette, 129 pl. v*b*, 163 L27, 179 B8.

[66]   See Paquette, 119 C30, 161 L26; A. Bélis, *BCH* 109 (1985), 209.

[67]   Pöhlmann (as n. 61), 310 f.; Bélis, 217. Pöhlmann interprets Pherecrates fr. 155. 14–16 as evidence that the 5th-c. citharode Phrynis invented this method of tuning, and he finds an allusion to it also in Pl. *Resp.* 531 b. Both passages, however, are to be otherwise explained; see pp. 225, 360.

[68]   Corinthian hydria, Paris E643; Maas–Snyder, 38, 51 fig. 15*a*.

[69]   O. J. Gombosi, *Tonarten und Stimmungen der antiken Musik* (Copenhagen, 1939), 72 f. A grave stele from Crisa (E. Braun, *Ann. Ist.* (1855), 63 pl. 16; T. Schreiber, *Atlas of Classical Antiquities* (London, 1895), i. 89. 8) shows a kithara with nineteen strings.

TABLE 3.1. *Evidence from vase-painting for lyres with more than 9 strings*

Approximate date	Vase	Lyre type	No. of strings
480	St. Petersburg 674	round-based kithara	11
440–430	Harvard 1925.30.42	round-based kithara	10
440–430	Ferrara VT T617	square-based kithara	11
420–410	Ruvo, Jatta 1538	Thracian kithara	10
420–410	Ruvo, Jatta 1093	lyra	10
360–350	Naples 1762 inv. 82110	square-based kithara	11
350	Fenicia collection[70]	square-based kithara	10
350	Berlin Antiqu. 8519 (bronze mirror)	lyra	12
325	Warsaw 138485	Italiote kithara	10
300	Tübingen 1671 F37	Italiote kithara	12

Literary evidence, some of it contemporary, confirms that from the middle of the fifth century certain provocative citharodes were adding extra strings to their instruments. Aristophanes alludes to a new music that rejoices in having gone beyond the monotony of seven notes; Ion of Chios, who died in 422, wrote a poem acclaiming the novelty of an eleven-stringed lyre; Pherecrates speaks of Timotheus raping Music with his dozen strings; Timotheus himself glories in having brought forth a kithara with 'eleven-note measures and rhythms'.[71] Later writers produce various conflicting lists of who first added the eighth string, who the ninth, who the tenth, and so on.[72] Some of the names are unknown to us and may be legendary, but from the ones we recognize it is evident that the increase beyond

---

[70] M. Jatta, *Mon. Ant.* 16 (1906), tav. 3.

[71] Ar. fr. 467, Ion fr. 32 West, Pherecr. fr. 155. 25, Timoth. *PMG* 791. 229. The interpretation of the last passage is contested. Whatever it is that Timotheus had eleven of, he says that Terpander had ten, which was itself an advance over the original lyre of Orpheus. A reference to nine-string melodies by the early comic poet Chionides (fr. 4) is probably to harp music; see below, p. 349.

[72] U. von Wilamowitz-Moellendorff, *Timotheos* (Leipzig, 1903), 74; Gombosi, op. cit. 64f. According to Nicomachus, p. 274. 6 J., the number eventually reached eighteen.

seven strings was generally thought to have begun in the mid-fifth century or a little earlier. Simonides (*c.*556–468) is named for the eighth, Phrynis (*c.*490–420) for the eighth and ninth, Timotheus for the eighth and ninth, or the ninth only, or the tenth and eleventh, or the eleventh only. Ion's poem gives a definite *terminus ante quem* for an eleven-stringed lyre. Beyond that we cannot establish anything much in detail, but it is clear that a few citharodes were performing with more strings than the usual seven. This was something limited to exceptional virtuosi: it did not bring about a general change of practice, and it is not surprising that comparatively few vase-paintings reflect it. It remains uncertain what weight we should attach to the isolated portrayals of a nine-stringed lyra in the mid-sixth century and an eleven-stringed kithara in the early fifth.

Order of strings

Although it is not universally true that lyre strings are arranged in order of pitch, it is virtually certain that this was the case with Greek lyres. The notes of the standard octave were named after the corresponding strings of the lyre: bottom, alongside-bottom, third, alongside-middle, middle, forefinger, alongside-uppermost, uppermost, the adjectives taking the feminine form to agree with an understood *chordē* 'string'. 'Bottom' was the highest in pitch and 'uppermost' the lowest: the terms do not refer directly to pitch,[73] but to the position of the strings on a lyre held tilted away from the body (see below). The strings nearest to the player, therefore, played the lower notes. This is confirmed by the fact that the 'forefinger' note is in the lower part of the scale, and by the explicit testimony of Plutarch.[74] The asymmetrical lyres of the west Semitic peoples had the same arrangement, the longer string being nearer the player.

Playing technique

Lyres may be played while sitting, standing, walking (for example in a sacrificial procession), or dancing (especially in a group). The professional citharode gave his performances standing on a podium. The player held the instrument against the left side of his body, with

[73] The Greeks did not as a rule speak of 'high' and 'low' pitch, but of 'piercing' (*oxys*) and 'heavy' (*barys*). There are, however, instances of higher/lower notes being called 'above'/'below' (*anō/katō*): ps.-Arist. *Pr.* 19. 3, 37, 47. Cf. Barker, *GMW* ii. 385.

[74] *Quaest. Plat.* 1008 e. Cf. Anon. Bellerm. 86–7 ('outward', 'inward', of rising/falling note-pairs).

his left hand coming at the strings from one side through the frame and his right hand from the other. The kithara was generally held upright or with only a slight tilt towards or away from the player; the lyra and barbitos were more often tilted away from him, sometimes as far as the horizontal. He supported the instrument by means of a strap or sling looped round his left wrist and attached to the further arm of the lyre. This feature can already be seen in Minoan and Mycenaean representations.[75] It limited the movement of the left hand and thus the spacing of the strings.

The hands' business is depicted in a very consistent fashion, again from Minoan times on. The fingers of the left hand pressed or plucked individual strings; the right hand swept across all the strings with a plectrum.[76] The same technique was employed in the west Semitic area and Egypt, and it is still in use among the lyre-playing peoples of east Africa.[77] The plectrum, which was attached by a cord to the base of the lyre, had a comfortable handle and a short, pointed blade of ivory, horn, bone, or wood.[78]

Let us try to be more precise about the role of the left hand, and the relation between its operations and those of the plectrum.

The vase-painters, especially after the archaic period, show us a great variety of left hand positions in as detailed and realistic a fashion as we could expect. Unfortunately they cannot often make it clear which of the fingers behind the strings (or less often in front of them, when the instrument is shown from the back) are actually in contact with them, and they cannot give us cinematographic pictures. In the majority of cases the fingers are fairly straight and

[75] Maas–Snyder, 3, 7, 16 fig. 2a, 17 fig. 3a, etc. It is clearly visible ibid. 45 fig. 8 (late 7th c.), 77 fig. 15 (*c.*520), 102 fig. 6, 111 fig. 26 and 28, 130 figs. 3–4 (6th–5th c.); Paquette, 85 pl. iv*a*–*b*, 104 C3, 115 C24–25, 119 C33, 125 C44, 143 pl. vi*b*, 151 L2, 155 L11, 157 L13, 179 B7, 181 B11, 185 B20.

[76] Exceptions are very rare. The early Cretan 'minstrel' (above, n. 16) seems to have no plectrum; and in the latter part of the 4th c. we find three Italiote kitharas being plucked with both hands like a harp (Paquette, 107 C6, 115 C22, 23). It may be significant that one of them has ten strings and another nine. Cf. p. 70.

[77] Cf. Sachs, *HMI* 79, 101, 107f., 132f.; Aign, 223–5; Paquette, 248; Maas–Snyder, 3, 8, 12, 34, 63f., 68, 92f., 122f., 142, 146, 177; *NG* vi. 271f., xviii. 331.

[78] *IG* 2². 1388. 80, Pl. *Leg.* 795 a, Arist. fr. 269, Verg. *Aen.* 6. 647, (ps.-)Tib. 3. 4. 39, etc.; cf. Headlam on Herod. 6. 51. Apollo of course has a golden one (*Hymn. Hom. Ap.* 185, Pind. *Nem.* 5. 24, Eur. *HF* 351). Fragments of ivory plectra have been found at Mycenae and Menidi (Bronze Age) and Sparta (Archaic): see Maas–Snyder, 8, 37, 48 fig. 13d. Homer's failure to mention the plectrum encouraged the fallacious theory (*Suda* iv. 323. 10) that it was invented by Sappho, who does refer to it (fr. 99. 5 L.–P., see *ZPE* 80 (1990) 1f.).

slightly spread. Sometimes some or all of them are bent forwards, or curled right over so that the nails are towards the strings. Sometimes the thumb is bent across the palm, or out away from it. Sometimes the player is clearly pulling at a string with a finger and thumb. Sometimes his fingers are contorted in some quite complicated manœuvre. The right hand is usually holding the plectrum well beyond the strings, as if it has completed a vigorous outward sweep.[79]

One function of the left hand was certainly to pluck individual strings. The indications in the paintings are confirmed by literary references to 'plucking' in lyre-playing.[80] But it is widely held that the left hand also served to modify the sounds produced by the plectrum, by damping certain strings and perhaps also by touching them lightly as they vibrated, so shortening the vibrating length and raising the note.

As regards the latter possibility, the fact that the hand is trapped in its wrist sling means that it could not move up and down the strings (as can a violinist's hand, for example): there was only one short section of each string, somewhere near the middle, that it could reach. So the only effect that could have been produced by stopping with fingers of the left hand would have been to raise notes by large intervals of the order of an octave. This does seem to have been done by some virtuoso citharists as a special effect (below, p. 69), but it would not have served any purpose, so far as we can tell, in the ordinary rendering of Greek melodies.[81]

The idea of damping is more plausible as a regular part of lyre-playing. It was advocated by C. Saint-Saëns (the composer), who

[79] See H. Roberts (as n. 64), 44 ff.; Maas–Snyder, 34, 63 f., 92 f., 122 f., 142, 146, 177.

[80] Ion fr. 32. 3 W.; Ar. *Eq.* 522 (if the allusion is to Magnes' *Barbitos-players*); Pl. *Lysis* 209 b, 'and I imagine that when you pick up the lyre, your father and mother don't stop you tuning any strings you like either up or down, and plucking them and striking them with the plectrum'; with explicit reference to the left hand, Apul. *Flor.* 15, Philostr. *Imag.* 1. 10. 4, Philostr. Jun. *Imag.* 7. 3, ps.-Asc. *Verr.* 2. 1. 53 (ii. 237. 1 Stangl).

[81] Stopping with the right hand, or pressing the plectrum on a string at a point below the bridge to increase its tension and raise its pitch, are also unlikely except possibly as virtuoso tricks. See R. P. Winnington-Ingram, *CR* 2 (1952), 34 f. and *CQ* 6 (1956), 183–6, against Sachs and Gombosi; J. M. Barbour, *Jour. Am. Musicol. Soc.* 13 (1960), 13–15; H. Roberts (as n. 64), 49–52. Paquette (whose interpretations of the vase-paintings often seem over-subtle or arbitrary) still believes in such a use of the plectrum, and he reproduces a detail from a 4th-c. Lucanian amphora (Louvre K 526) where it does appear to be pushed under the strings of a kithara. Perhaps this is a representation of virtuoso playing of that period (the lyre has nine strings); or perhaps the artist is simply incompetent (the player has two left thumbs).

drew attention to the fact that some African lyres are played in this way, by rhythmic strumming with a plectrum and by damping all the strings that are not required to ring out.[82] But this strumming sometimes alternates with plucking; and so it must have been in Greece (whether or not the strumming was combined with damping), as we have seen that plucking was certainly of some importance, and it would not make sense to pluck simultaneously with the sweeps of the plectrum. Virgil implies an alternation when he describes the playing of Orpheus in Elysium: 'now he strikes them (the seven strings) with his fingers, now with his ivory plectrum'.[83] Ptolemy, listing the finest effects of lyre-playing that cannot be reproduced on the monochord, mentions among them the simultaneous striking of more than one note (with the plectrum), and 'plucking in addition' (*epipsalmos*, perhaps of decorative notes subsidiary to the main melody).[84]

Ancient sources make it clear that when a singer was accompanied by the lyre—the usual role of the instrument—its basic function was to duplicate the sung melody. From the latter part of the fifth century on, some divergent or additional notes were played as well, but the earlier practice is reported to have been simple unison.[85] We should naturally suppose that it was the plucking fingers that picked out the melody, and that the plectrum-strums came mainly where the voice paused. This is confirmed by the passage of Aristophanes where Euripides, wishing to imitate a citharode without actually having a kithara to hand, does so by adding *phlatto-thratto-phlatto-thrat* after each line of song,[86] and by Apuleius' description of a statue of a youth playing a kithara: 'his left

---

[82] C. Saint-Saëns in Lavignac's *Encyclopédie de la musique*, i (Paris 1913), 538–40; Sachs, *HMI* 132f.; G. A. Plumley, *El Tanbur* (Cambridge, 1976); *NG* vi. 271f., xviii. 331. It should be pointed out that damping the strings does not reduce them to silence but gives their sound a dull, dead quality.

[83] *Aen.* 6. 647. Other Latin poets transfer the epithet 'ivory' to the player's fingers (Prop. 2. 1. 9) or thumb (Stat. *Silv.* 5. 5. 31). Does this refer to a practice of attaching picks to the individual fingers? Mention of the thumb is frequent after Ovid (*Am.* 2. 4. 27, *Met.* 5. 339, 10. 145, 11. 170; Tib. 2. 5. 3; Pers. 6. 5; Venantius Fortunatus 7. 1. 1); Martial 14. 167 recommends a plectrum for avoiding a blistered thumb.

[84] *Harm.* 2. 12 p. 67. 5; see Barker, *GMW* ii. 341.

[85] Ps.-Plut. *De mus.* 1141b, cf. Pl. *Leg.* 812de; ps.-Arist. *Pr.* 19. 9, 43 (above, p. 39 n. 1).

[86] *Ran.* 1281ff. Other verbal imitations of the plectrum-stroke are *threttanelo* (Ar. *Plut.* 290); *tēnella* in the traditional acclamation of a victor, *tēnella kallinīke*, where the loud stroke across the lyre-strings served as a cue, just like our 'hip-hip' before 'hooray!'; and *blityri* in the saying *blityri kai skindapsos*, 'blityri and delyrium', meaning 'idle nonsense'.

hand, fingers apart, sets the strings going, while the right hand moves the plectrum towards the kithara as if ready to strike it when the voice has paused in its song'.[87]

The strumming compensated for the temporary absence of the voice by its loudness. Apart from the fact that all the strings were sounding together (even if some of them were damped), a plectrum in itself produces a stronger and sharper sound than do bare fingers; and it appears to have been employed energetically. Lucian gives us a satirical account of a bad citharode who attacks his instrument with such force that he breaks three strings at once.[88] The strums might come thick and fast, as in the music that Epicharmus describes being provided by an expert citharist for dances in honour of Semele.[89] In the dances depicted on certain works of art where the dancers themselves carry and apparently play kitharas,[90] it may be that they did not do much more than strum, with a piper providing the continuo. We have evidence that this is how it was with the boys' chorus at the Spartan Hyakinthia (above, p. 21).

In such circumstances as those, with lyres serving chiefly to punctuate the pipe music with joyous peals of string sound, it may not have mattered if all the strums were alike. In serious playing, however, we should certainly expect some variety to be sought: at the least, some differentiation between non-cadential and cadential pauses, between mere suspensions of the melodic line and places where it reached some kind of completion. This is where damping with fingers of the left hand would come in—damping various selections of strings to allow different notes to dominate the tone cluster at different moments.

One text distinctly suggests the use of this technique. Quintilian, to illustrate the point that the human mind can attend to several things

---

[87] *Flor.* 15. Cf. also Lygdamus (Tibullus 3) 4. 41, *digiti cum uoce locuti*. On the other hand Lucian, *Imag.* 14, praising the playing of Panthea of Smyrna, speaks of her exact rhythm, 'the kithara singing in unison and the plectrum synchronized with her tongue'.

[88] *Ind.* 9. For another story about a citharode breaking a string during a contest see Strab. 6. 1. 9 (Timaeus, *FGrH* 566 F 43, Conon, *FGrH* 26 F 1. 5, *Anth. Pal.* 9. 584. 4, etc.). By contrast, the citharists of Aspendos in Pamphylia were proverbial for playing in an introvert way, as if only to themselves, without the grand flourishes with the plectrum (Cic. *Verr.* 2. 1. 53 with schol. Bob. and ps.-Asc. ad loc., Zeno Myndius ap. Zenobium Athoum 3. 161 = vulg. 2. 30; Crusius, *RE* ii. 1724).

[89] Epicharmus fr. 109 Kaibel.

[90] e.g. on a sarcophagus from Capua of the first half of the 6th c. (Maas–Snyder, 44 fig. 5*a*), and the Attic red-figure vase New York 25.78.66 (Pl. 16).

simultaneously, refers to the citharodes. At the same time as they are recalling the words and music from their memories, they are thinking about the sound of their voice and the melodic line, they are tapping out the rhythm with one foot, and they are sweeping across some strings with the right hand while the left pulls, restrains (i.e. damps?), or presents others.[91] Quintilian is speaking of citharodes and of the Imperial age. But there is no particular reason to think that he is speaking of the special technical tricks developed by a few exceptional virtuosi. What he describes may have been the normal strumming technique on all types of Greek lyre from the beginning. It is consistent with our expectations of variety in the strumming, and with the evidence of the vase-paintings. When a player is shown on the vases as pulling a string between finger and thumb, we may wonder whether he is not retracting it from the plectrum's path (Quintilian's *trahunt*) rather than plucking it, for which a single fingertip must normally have sufficed.

When the Athenian schoolboy learned to play the lyre, then, I suppose him to have been taught (*a*) songs by the famous lyricists, Alcaeus, Anacreon, and others, (*b*) how to pick out the melodies with his left hand as he sang them, and (*c*) how to punctuate them with appropriate strums, damping or pulling back particular strings with his left hand while striking across with the plectrum held in his right.

It remains to speak of the use of the kithara as a solo instrument, not accompanying song. Greek writers call this 'bare lyre-playing', *psīlē kitharisis*, and treat it as something of a special art. It is said to have been invented by one Aristonicus of Argos, a resident of Corcyra, and to have been introduced to the Pythian festival in 558 BC.[92] There were also prizes for it at the Panathenaea in the Classical period.[93] We hear of particular performers who advanced the art. Lysander of Sicyon, perhaps in the early fifth century, was credited with increasing the power and duration of the notes, achieving fine 'colourings', and evoking a sort of echo at the upper octave called 'whistling', presumably by the technique described above, p. 66. Stratonicus of Athens in the early fourth century was the first to play solos on a kithara of more than seven strings.[94] At some stage a

---

[91] *Inst.* 1. 12. 3 *alios neruos dextrá percurrunt, alios laeuá trahunt, continent, praebent.* Cf. E. K. Borthwick, *CQ* 9 (1959), 26 f.

[92] Menaechmus, *FGrH* 131 F 5; Paus. 10. 7. 7, cf. above, p. 60.

[93] *IG* 2². 2311. 15 (= *SIG* 1055), early 4th c.   [94] See pp. 341, 368.

special form of kithara came into use for solo performances at the great festivals, the *Pȳthikon*, which has been mentioned earlier.

The 'psilocitharist' clearly did more than simply render songs without words. It must have been a more elaborate style of playing, involving a greater density of notes, more agile fingering, and the display of varied tonal effects. Plato dismisses it, together with solo piping, as a tasteless and meaningless stunt that seeks to astonish by speed, accuracy, and the production of bestial noises.[95] Some performers, if not all, may have abandoned the plectrum to give themselves the full use of their ten fingers. It has been noted that the Italiote kithara is sometimes depicted being played in this way, and it was suggested as an explanation of the fact that the *Pȳthikon* was also called *daktylikon*. Ammonius defines the citharist as one who 'only plucks the strings' as opposed to the citharode who 'also sings'.[96]

HARPS

The defining features of a harp have been described on p. 49. It is among the most ancient of stringed instruments, being derived directly from the primitive musical bow. The oldest type, the arched harp, retained something of the bow's basic form: the soundbox was prolonged into a curved neck that formed an arch with it, and the strings were strung across this arch. Arched harps were in use among the Sumerians from 3400 BC or earlier, and among the Egyptians by the twenty-sixth century. After about 2000 BC they were displaced in Mesopotamia by the angular harp, in which the neck was jointed to the soundbox at a right angle or (later) an acute angle. This type too reached Egypt after a few centuries. It is depicted in a Cypriote representation of the mid-second millennium, and two more of the twelfth century.[97]

In view of this diffusion, we might have expected to find the harp well established in the Aegean area in the Bronze and early Iron Ages. In fact evidence for its presence is exceedingly scarce before about 600 BC. From the pre-Greek Cycladic culture of the third millennium (*c.* 2800–2300) we have a number of small marble models of seated male musicians playing angular harps. These are

---

[95] *Leg.* 669e–670a.   [96] *Diff.* 271.
[97] London 1920.12–20.1 and 1946.10–7.1; Aign, 60, 62; Rimmer, 22; H. Catling, *Cypriot Bronzework in the Mycenaean World* (Oxford, 1964), pl. 34–5.

the oldest examples of frame harps; that is, they have the angled structure of soundbox and neck strengthened by the addition of a 'front pillar' which joins the extremities and completes the triangle.[98] A similar instrument may be represented on certain Cretan seals of the Middle Minoan II period (*c.*1900–1700), but the shape is so distorted by the format that one cannot be sure that a lyre is not meant.[99] For the next thousand years we draw a complete blank; and then there is only a single vase-painting from a late eighth-century Attic grave, showing a figure holding a crudely-drawn instrument that is most naturally interpreted as a triangular frame harp, though again some have taken it as a lyre.[100]

Otherwise harps do not appear in Greek art until the second half of the fifth century. However, there are earlier references in poetry. The author of the burlesque poem *Margites* attributed to Homer, as well as Sappho, Alcaeus, Anacreon, and Pindar, all know an instrument called *pāktis* (Lesbian, Doric) or *pēktis* (Ionic–Attic). Taking their mentions together with those in other Classical writers, we gather that it was a plucked chordophone with many strings, characterized by the playing of octave concords, or the echoing of the melody at octave intervals, and strongly associated with the Lydians.[101] This must be a harp. It might well have come to the East Greeks from Lydia, though the name *pēktis* is a Greek formation.[102]

In Attic vase-painting after about 450 BC we find angular harps of three different designs, almost always played by women (Pl. 21 and 22). One is an open-sided harp (i.e. with no front pillar), with a soundbox that arches round and grows more capacious towards the end opposite the neck, so that the long strings transmit their vibrations to the area of greatest resonance. It is played with the neck horizontal at the bottom, on the player's left knee, while the

---

[98] Aign, 29–32; Maas–Snyder, 1, 15 fig. 1.
[99] Aign, 35–6, 39–40.   [100] Athens 784; Aign, 95.
[101] *Margites*, *POxy.* 3964; Sappho 22. 11, 156, Alc. 36. 5, Anac. *PMG* 373, 386, Pind. fr. 125, Soph. fr. 412, Hdt. 1. 17. 1, Ar. *Thesm.* 1217, Telestes, *PMG* 810. 4, Diogenes, *TrGF* 45 F 1, Pl. *Resp.* 399c.
[102] From *pēktos* 'joined', applied in Homer to things made by a joiner (a plough, a timber building); Sophocles (fr. 238) uses it of lyres. In Hellenistic verse and later literary language *pēktis* itself is often used for 'lyre', its proper meaning forgotten. Later still it is used of panpipes (Anon. Bucol. (*Bucolici Graeci*, p. 168 Gow) 11 and 63; Heliodorus 4. 17. 1; Agathias, *Anth. Pal.* 16. 244; Cometas, *Anth. Pal.* 9. 586. 5; cf. Aristid. Quint. p. 58. 13, Hsch.), while Hesychius and Photius also record an interpretation as 'lute' (probably the source of J. E. Powell's error in his *Lexicon to Herodotus* s.v.).

soundbox rises up next to her body and arches away from it; the strings are vertical, the longest ones being furthest from her. The second type is similar except that it is a frame harp, having a front pillar. The third is markedly different. It is again a frame harp with the neck at the bottom and vertical stringing, but the soundbox is straight, spindle-shaped (widest in the middle, tapering to the ends), and usually on the far side from the player.[103] This type, sometimes called 'spindle harp', is rarely seen after the end of the fifth century.[104]

Besides *pēktis*, Attic writers refer to the *trigōnos* or *trigōnon* ('triangular'), which is evidently not a synonym of *pēktis*.[105] As the 'spindle harp' is aggressively triangular and the other types are not, it is assumed that the name *trigōnos* belongs to it. *Pēktis* probably covered both of the other two, which differ from each other only in the matter of the pillar. If so, it is a reasonable inference that the harp of Sappho and Alcaeus had an affinity with the Attic types with arching soundbox held next to the player. The one without the pillar is closer to oriental models and no doubt the earlier.[106]

It is generally believed that another early Greek name for a harp was *magadis*. The word, which must be a derivative of *magas* 'bridge (of a lyre)', appears in a quotation from Alcman, where its meaning

---

[103] This playing position is quite exceptional from an ethnographic point of view, to go by the distribution table in *NG* viii. 215.

[104] For the artistic material see R. Herbig, *MDAI*(A) 54 (1929) 164–93; Wegner, *Musikleben*, 203–5; Paquette, 194–201; Maas–Snyder, 151–4, 161, 163–4, 181–3, 195–7.

[105] Soph. frs. 239, 412, Eup. frs. 88. 2, 148. 4, Ar. fr. 255, Pherecr. fr. 47, Plato Com. fr. 71. 13, Theopomp. Com. fr. 50, Diogenes, *TrGF* 45 F 1. 9, Pl. *Resp.* 399c, Arist. *Pol.* 1341ª41, Aristox. fr. 97. The masculine form *trigōnos* is the older. Sophocles calls it Phrygian, but Diogenes has it in a Lydian context with the *pēktis*, and Photius (α 2956–7 = *Anecd. Bekk.* 452–3) attributes its invention to Tyrrhenos of Lydia. Juba, *FGrH* 275 F 15, makes it Syrian, while Ptolemy, *Harm.* 3. 7, speaks of contemporary Alexandrian *trigōna*. It is described by Aelian (ap. Porph. in Ptol. *Harm.* p. 34. 30) as having strings of equal thickness but graded in length, the longest being furthest out.

[106] All the ancient oriental harps are pillarless. On the 7th-c. Assyrian reliefs from Nineveh we see open angular harps with from eighteen to twenty vertical strings, held the same way round as the Attic *pēktis* (Rimmer, pl. x, xii, xiii). Their soundboxes curve forward only slightly, if at all, but otherwise they are quite similar to the Greek instrument. An older version, with only seven strings and a very bulky soundbox, is represented on a clay plaque from Eshnunna of the early 2nd millennium (*NG* viii. 192, fig. 5). Cognates can be traced across Persia and Central Asia to the Far East. The soundbox of the *pēktis* in S. Italian vase-painting is often adorned with a series of raised crests along the outer edge. This is presumably the type of harp designated by the name *pēlēx*, which normally means 'crested helmet' or 'serpent's crest' (Poll. 4. 61); see Pl. 17.

cannot be determined, and then in a corrupt fragment of Anacreon in connection with the plucking of a twenty-stringed instrument.[107] The instrument is doubtless a harp, but it is not clear that *magadis* is its name; it may well mean simply 'octave concord', as this sense is found elsewhere, and the verb *magadizō* means not 'play a harp' but 'produce an (octave) concord'.[108] We have seen that Anacreon elsewhere calls his harp a *pēktis*. There is only one unambiguous classical reference to the *magadis* as an instrument, and even that is not above suspicion.[109] The word was not current in the spoken language in this sense. A series of later scholars and antiquarians, beginning with Aristoxenus, recognized it as an instrument, but were undecided as to whether it was a harp or an aulos, and if it was a harp, whether or not it was the same as the *pēktis*. Clearly they had no direct knowledge of an instrument called *magadis*: their views were based on interpretations of the literary references noted above.[110]

The vase-painters give harps varying numbers of strings, from nine up to twenty or so. (One sealstone shows about thirty-two.) Of course, artists are limited by their medium, and they did not necessarily make a scrupulous count. But the figures agree well with literary evidence. We have Anacreon's authority for a twenty-stringer, and that of an early comic poet for a nine-stringer.[111] The *trigōnos* on the vases seems usually to have more strings than the *pēktis*, and a higher ratio between the lengths of the longest and shortest string (4 : 1 or more). We cannot safely base calculations on apparent measurements of this kind in works of art, but as no Greek music involved a division of the octave into more than seven steps, we can say that all these harps would have had a range of more than an octave, and Anacreon's twenty-stringer would have spanned nearly three octaves at the least, perhaps more.

[107] Alcm. *PMG* 101, Anac. *PMG* 374.

[108] Diogenes, *TrGF* 45 F 1. 10 (the Lydian *pēktis*), Xen. *An.* 7. 3. 32 (trumpets), Anaxandrides fr. 36 K.–A. (metaphorical), Theophilus fr. 7. 2 (singing, metaphorical), ps.-Arist. *Pr.* 19. 18, 39b, Philochorus, *FGrH* 328 F 23 (an octave echo on the kithara, cf. above, p. 69, and Hsch. μ 4). This may be the sense also in Telestes, *PMG* 808. 2 and Cantharus fr. 12. Ion, *TrGF* 19 F 23 apparently refers to a Lydian magadis-aulos, which puzzled ancient scholars; if the verse is not corrupt (cf. *BICS* 30 (1983), 79), it presumably refers to an aulos on which concords were played.

[109] Soph. fr. 238; the word is scanned abnormally and might be an intrusive gloss. If it is original, we cannot tell what kind of instrument is meant.

[110] Aristox. frs. 97–9, Menaechmus, *FGrH* 131 F 4, and various others collected in Ath. 634c–7a; Hsch., Phot. The above paragraph was written before I saw A. Barker's paper in Gentili–Pretagostini, 96–107; he comes to similarly sceptical conclusions. [111] Chionides fr. 4. Cf. below, p. 77, on the *enneachordon*.

Greek melody, however, being overwhelmingly vocal and so normally constrained by the natural compass of the voice, may be supposed to have moved within much narrower limits, even in purely instrumental compositions; after all, the common instruments, the lyres and pipes, had a range matched to that of the voice. The extra capacity of the harp was probably used not to accommodate a peculiar style of harp melody that meandered up and down across two or three octaves, but—in the main, at least—for that doubling or answering of the basic melody in the upper or lower octave which we hear of in connection with this instrument.[112]

Harps had similar tuning arrangements to lyres, the tension of the strings being adjusted at the neck by means of bandages, beads, or rings.[113] Sometimes the neck of the *pēktis* was raised off the player's thigh by a parallel bar below it, to protect the tuning from disturbance by contact. The strings were plucked with both hands; only exceptionally was a plectrum used.[114] The female harpists who might be hired for parties were called *psaltriai*, literally 'pluckers'.[115] In the later fourth century *psaltērion*, 'plucking instrument', emerged as the ordinary generic word for the harp.

There is no special word for someone who sings to the harp (like *kitharōidos*, *lyrōidos*, *aulōidos*), and it is sometimes held that the instrument was not used to accompany the voice. Literary evidence, however, proves that it sometimes was, and while most harpists in art seem to have their mouths closed, there is at least one apparent exception.[116] The fifth-century comic poets associate the harp with

[112] Anac., Diogenes, above, n. 101; cf. Pind. fr. 125, Phrynichus, *TrGF* 3 F 11, Soph. fr. 412. Aristox. *Harm.* 1. 20 gives two and a half octaves as the maximum range of any one voice or instrument; but it is possible that he is leaving harps out of account.

[113] See R. Herbig, *MDAI*(A) 54 (1929), facing p. 168; 180–3 figs. 6–10; and his somewhat agnostic discussion, pp. 184–6.

[114] The evidence of art agrees with that of literary references, where plucking is often emphasized, and with the statement of Aristox. fr. 99. Only on two 4th-c. Italian vases is a plectrum shown (Paquette, 187 pl. viiia, 201 H14). In Mesopotamia there was a type of horizontal harp that was played with a plectrum, like a lyre, but vertical harps were played with the fingers alone, as also elsewhere in the ancient Near East.

[115] Ion, *TrGF* 19 F 22 (Lydian setting), Eubulus, *Psaltria* (title), Pl. *Prt.* 347 d, Theopomp. *FGrH* 115 F 213, Men. fr. 264, Arist. *Ath. Pol.* 50. 2 (distinguished from *kitharistriai*, as the respective verbs are distinguished, Hdt. 1. 155. 4, *SIG* 578. 15 ff. (Teos, 2nd c. BC), 959. 10 (Chios), Nic. Dam. *FGrH* 90 F 4 p. 334. 7 J.). There is a story that the Spartans fined a visiting harpist 'because he plays (*kitharizei*) with his fingers' (ps.Plut. *Apophthegmata Laconica* 233 f.).

[116] Sappho 21, 22?, Phrynichus, *TrGF* 3 F 11 (oriental setting), Ion, *TrGF* 19 F 22 (Lydian), Eup. fr. 148, Plato Com. fr. 71. 14; New York 07.286.35 (Paquette, 195 H2).

sensual, erotic, and adulterous songs,[117] and in general it appears in contexts of love and pleasure, from Sappho's time on. Anacreon speaks of a boy carrying one in a dance, but its usual place is the banqueting-room or the boudoir, and its players, in the Classical period, are nearly always women.[118] Later we hear of male exponents who gave solo recitals or taught the young.[119]

The sambȳkē

We come next to the instrument which is usually called *sambȳkē* (Latin *sambūca*), but in the earliest references *iambȳkē* and in two late lexica *zambȳkē*; the variations probably represent different renderings of a foreign word that began with a sound like *zh*.[120] Some Hellenistic antiquarians assumed the *iambȳkē* to be something different from the *sambȳkē*, and speculated that it used to accompany the singing of *iamboi*.[121] But its associations in Eupolis are just those of the *sambȳkē* later, and *iamboi* have nothing to do with it.

The instrument had short strings and a high register.[122] We have an idea of its form, because there was a kind of Roman siege engine that presented a similar appearance and was named after it. It was for scaling a wall where the approach was by water. A broad, covered stairway was mounted on the prows of two ships lashed together, projecting out to the front, and it was raised into position by means of cables which passed over pulleys high on the masts and were

---

[117] Chionides fr. 4; Eup. and Plato Com. locc. citt. These two speak of the *trigōnos*, and Aristotle distinguishes this from the *pēktis* as being more voluptuous (*Pol.* 1341ᵃ40).

[118] Anac. *PMG* 386; Wegner, *Musikleben* 50f., 92; Maas–Snyder, 147–54, 181–2.

[119] Recitalists: Alcidamas(?) in *PHib.* 13. 7, 25, Machon 104ff., *IG* 11. 105, 120 (Delos, 284, 236 BC; in the latter, two *psaltai* perform *meta prosōidiou*, 'with accompanying song'), Plut. *Quomodo adul.* 67f, Chares, *FGrH* 125 F 4, etc. Teachers: Men. fr. 430a Koerte, *SIG* 578. 15 (Teos, 2nd c. BC).

[120] *Iamb-* Eup. fr. 148.4, and manuscript variation points to this in Arist. *Pol.* 1341ᵃ41; *zamb-* Hsch., Phot. It is listed as a foreign import by Aristox. fr. 97, Juba, *FGrH* 275 F 15(?), Strab. 10.3.17. *Sammû* is a Babylonian type of lyre. A similar fluctuation between s- and z- occurs in the name of the Thracian deity Salmoxis/Zalmoxis. Neanthes, *FGrH* 84 F 5 (cf. *Suda* ii. 607. 19), claimed that the *sambȳkē* was invented by Ibycus. This might mean that Ibycus provided the first mention of it in literature, but it may be merely an attempt to derive *iambȳkē* from *Ibykos*, just as Semus, *FGrH* 396 F 1, postulated an inventor Sambyx to avoid the assumption of foreign origin.   [121] Phillis ap. Ath. 636b, Hsch., Phot., *Suda*.

[122] Ath. 633f; Aristid. Quint. p. 85. 10, who comments on its feminine and ignoble sound.

hauled upon from the rear decks. 'And the contrivance is suitably so named, because when it is raised the combined shape of the ship and the stairway resembles a *sambȳkē*.'[123] The *sambȳkē*, then, had a more or less boat-shaped soundbox and a neck that rose from one end of it at an angle approaching the vertical. Its strings—whether or not the ships' cables contributed to the likeness—must have run diagonally from the neck to the face of the soundbox.

This can only be a form of the primitive arched harp (p. 70). Anyone who glances at the illustrations in *The New Grove*, xii. 196–7 (Sumerian, 3400–2400 BC), vi. 74 (Egyptian, *c.*1567–1320 BC), viii. 191 (Indian, AD *c.*320–500), 192 and 213 (modern African), and iii. 481–2 (Burmese), will see at once what kind of instrument the ship and stairway contrivance was named after. It is a design that has survived with little variation for some 5,000 years.

In Greek and Roman art it is elusive. But there is one representation on an Athenian vase of the second quarter of the fifth century,[124] and another on a Roman fresco from Stabiae, now in the Naples Museum. The Greek example has a soundbox like that of a lyra, made from a tortoise shell with a hide stretched over it.[125] Five strings can be seen. There is a bridge on the soundbox like that of a lyra, but this may be a mistake of the painter in treating an unfamiliar instrument; he seems to be in some doubt as to how the strings are attached. The player, who is not actually playing but standing idle while a friend plays the pipes, holds a plectrum in her right hand. The *sambȳkē* in the Roman painting is made of wood and has about seven strings.[126]

Eupolis couples the *iambȳkē* with the *trigōnos* as the appropriate instruments for adulterers to serenade their mistresses and entice them out. *Sambȳkē* and *trigōnos* are often mentioned together.[127]

[123] Polyb. 8. 4. 2–11, cf. Andreas, *FGrH* 571 F 1, Plut. *Marc.* 15. 5, and others cited by Ath. 634 a; Festus (Paulus) p. 434 f. L., Vegetius 4. 21.

[124] See Pl. 23; white-ground lekythos, Brussels A 1020. Paquette, 194 (on his fig. H3), correctly interprets it as an arched harp and refers to African parallels, but he fails to identify it as the *sambȳkē*. (The identification is suggested by R. A. Higgins and R. P. Winnington-Ingram, *JHS* 85 (1965), 67 n. 34.) Maas–Snyder, 95 f., 110 fig. 23, erroneously take it to be a lyra seen sideways on. It is clear that it has a single neck, not two arms.

[125] Exactly the same is true of many Ugandan harps: *NG* viii. 214.

[126] The early Hellenistic explorer Pythagoras recognized the *sambȳkē* in a four-stringed instrument that he saw in use among the Nubian Troglodytes of coastal Sudan and also among the Parthians (Ath. 633 f).

[127] Eup. fr. 148. 4, Arist. *Pol.* 1341a41, Aristox. fr. 97, Phillis ap. Ath. 636 b, Plut. *De tribus reipublicae generibus* 827 a.

Occasionally, it seems, they were confused, the name *sambȳkē* being applied to the triangular harp.[128] *Sambȳkē* certainly remained much the more familiar word, and it retained its image of sensuality and low hedonism. The hired girls who played it were themselves called *sambȳkai*, or *sambȳkistriai*, and we hear of them from about 300 BC in contexts of mild debauchery.[129] In the early second century BC they were introduced to Rome, scandalizing the straight-laced.[130] The *trigōnos* could be described, not much later, as more or less obsolete, though we hear of it again as an Alexandrian instrument in the second century AD.[131]

Harps(?) of unknown type

In his list of instruments of foreign origin, between harps and lutes, Aristoxenus includes the *klepsiambos*. Pollux too lists it among stringed instruments. But we can say nothing more about it, except that it was no longer current by the time of Apollodorus, in the mid-second century BC.[132]

In the same context Aristoxenus mentioned 'the so-called *enneachordon*' ('nine-stringer'); this too was obsolete in Apollodorus' day. It may have been a harp but, if so, we cannot say why it was distinguished from other harps by a special name.[133]

The *nablas* or *nabla* was a Phoenician harp that arrived in Greece about the end of the fourth century BC. Its sound is described as 'throaty'. It was played without a plectrum, and was regarded as suitable for merrymaking.[134]

---

[128] Euphorion (ap. Ath. 635 a/f) apparently considered the *sambȳkē* as a many-stringed instrument adapted from the older *magadis*, and Vitruvius 6. 1. 5 (following Posidonius fr. 71 Theiler?) applies the name to the triangular vertical frame harp; likewise Aelian ap. Porph. in Ptol. *Harm.* p. 34.30 D. In the *Suda* (ii. 607. 19, iv. 317. 22) it is explained as 'a type of triangular kithara'.

[129] Philemon fr. 45. 5, Plaut. *Stich.* 381 (after Menander), Hippolochus ap. Ath. 129a (Rhodian *sambȳkistriai* in diaphanous dresses), *PHib.* 270. 1, Polyb. 5. 37. 10, 8. 6. 6.

[130] Livy 39. 6. 8 (187 BC), Scipio Aemilianus *Orat.* fr. 20 Malc., Plut. *Ant.* 9. 8, Pers. 5. 95, Juv. 3. 63 f.?, Arn. *Adv. Nat.* 2. 42, S.H.A. *Hadr.* 26. 4, Mart. Cap. 9. 924.

[131] Apollodorus, *FGrH* 244 F 219; Ptol. *Harm.* 3. 7, Ath. 183e.

[132] Aristox. fr. 97, Phillis ap. Ath. 636b (from Aristox.), Poll. 4. 59, Apollodorus, *FGrH* 244 F 219. According to Hesychius certain songs of Alcman were also known as *klepsiamboi* (*PMG* 161d). Pollux also mentions a *pariambos*, and Ath. 183c apparently takes *pariambides* to be musical instruments in Epicharmus fr. 109; but that is a misunderstanding.

[133] Aristox., Phillis, Apollodorus, locc. citt. For nine-stringed harps cf. above, p. 73; for lyres, pp. 62 f.

[134] Philemon fr. 45, Sopatros frs. 10 and 16 Kaibel, Euphorion ap. Ath. 182e, Strab. 10. 3. 17, Ov. *Ars Am.* 3. 327, Clem. *Strom.* 1. 16. 74, Manetho 4. 185, Hsch.

The *heptagōnon* mentioned by Aristotle[135] as a hedonistic instrument (like the *trigōnon* and *iambӯkē*) is something of a mystery. It may have been another type of harp, to judge from the context, but it is hard to conceive of a harp with seven corners.

Finally, for the sake of completeness, I refer to the *Indica* which appears in a very late and indiscriminate list of stringed instruments that must go back to an older Greek or Latin source.[136] It was apparently a harp or lyre set up on a stand, or large enough to stand on the ground, as it was 'struck' by two players at once.[137]

ZITHERS

Pollux lists a *simikon* (or according to two manuscripts *simikion*), which had thirty-five strings, and an *epigoneion*, which had forty. These figures are far higher than seems to have been usual for Greek harps, and Sachs suggested that the instruments in question were in fact board zithers, that is, that the strings were strung horizontally across the surface of a broad soundbox that extended under their whole length. That the *epigoneion* was originally played in a horizontal position is suggested by Juba's statement that 'it has now been modified into an upright *psaltērion*' while retaining its original name. Three later Roman sarcophagi do carry representations in relief of a relatively small upright zither with eight to ten strings.[138]

The original *epigoneion* and the *simikon* may have been designed not for musical performance but for the academic study of intervals and scale-divisions. The first was named after Epigonus, a Sicyonian musician of (perhaps) the late sixth century, and he also gave his

The name corresponds to the Hebrew *nēḇel*; the Jewish instrument, according to Josephus (*AJ* 7. 306), had twelve strings. See Sachs, *HMI* 115–17; É. Masson, *Recherches sur les plus anciens emprunts sémitiques en grec* (Paris, 1967), 67–9; A. Sendrey, *Music in Ancient Israel* (London, 1969), 278–89.

[135] *Pol.* 1341ª41.

[136] Isid. *Orig.* 3. 22. 3.

[137] A nine-stringed lyre mounted on a pedestal and plucked by two players, one standing on each side, is seen on a relief from Amarna. Another with eight strings, very tall, is also represented. (N. de G. Davies, *The Rock Tombs of El Amarna*, iii (1905), pl. v, vii; Behn 65 and pl. 38, figs. 86–7.) A standing lyre played by two people is also seen on a Hittite vase from Inandyk in the Ankara museum.

[138] Poll. 4. 59, Juba, *FGrH* 275 F 84; Varro, *Sat. Men.* 352?; Sachs, *HMI* 137 and pl. viiib facing p. 144. An *epigoneion psaltērion* is perhaps mentioned in Ath. 456d (Chamaeleon fr. 42 Giordano; MSS. *epitonion*). *Psaltērion* usually means a harp, but could in principle apply to any plucked instrument. In the Middle Ages zithers received the name *psalterium*, our 'psaltery'.

name to a school of harmonic theorists.[139] We also hear of a fifth-century harmonic theorist called Simos, and it is a natural guess that the *simikon* was named after him.[140] Aristoxenus criticizes some of his predecessors for dividing the octave into twenty-four quarter-tones in their search for the common basis of the various heptatonic modal scales. Perhaps, then, the *epigoneion* and *simikon* were board zithers devised in order to experiment with and demonstrate such analyses, and tuned not modally but with the smallest possible intervals between each successive pair of strings. The span of an octave and a fourth, divided into quarter-tones, would yield just thirty-five notes, the number of the *simikon*'s strings. When, some centuries later, performing zithers arrived, the name *epigoneion* was transferred to them.[141]

LUTES

The lute first appeared in Mesopotamia towards the end of the third millennium, and before the middle of the second it spread, together with other west Semitic instruments, to the Hittite and Egyptian kingdoms. A female lutenist in a transparent dress, clearly of Egyptian inspiration, is depicted on a faience bowl of *c.*1400–1200 BC found in Cyprus.[142] But the instrument does not seem to have reached the Greek world until well into the fourth century BC.

There are about a dozen representations of it in Greek art between about 330 and 200, mostly terracottas.[143] In one type, seen in three instances, the soundbox has straight edges, converging slightly towards the neck, and a vaulted back with a central spine and triangular base. The neck is clearly demarcated from the soundbox, and up to twice its length. The more common type has a rounded soundbox which tapers into the neck without any obvious dividing

---

[139] Aristox. *Harm.* 1. 3. See p. 225. A similar suggestion about the *epigoneion* was made by Gevaert, ii. 247 f.

[140] Duris, *FGrH* 76 F 23.

[141] Upright zithers are represented on a fragment of a bronze situla from west Iran, dating from the early 2nd millennium (Rimmer, 26 f. and pl. vii *b*).

[142] J. L. Myres, *Handbook of the Cesnola Collection* (New York, 1914), 273 f. no. 1574; Aign, 61.

[143] Listed and discussed by R. A. Higgins and R. P. Winnington-Ingram, *JHS* 85 (1965), 62–71 with pl. xvi–xvii; cf. Wegner, *Bilder*, 106 f.; Paquette, 192 f., 200 f.; Maas–Snyder, 185 f., 197 f. figs. 18–19. Remains of a lute were discovered in the early years of the 19th c. in a woman's grave by the road from Athens to Eleusis; see Pöhlmann, *Beiträge*, 99–107.

line (Pl. 24). Only one example gives an indication of the number of
strings: it had four, or perhaps five.

The player is normally a woman (or Muse), or else an Eros. The
lute is held horizontally with the neck to the player's left. The player
stops the strings against the neck with the fingers of the left hand to
shorten their vibrating length and raise the note to the required pitch.
One representation indicates the presence of frets on the neck for
the exact attainment of particular notes. The right hand uses a
plectrum in some instances (as was customary with the lutes of the
Near East), but in other cases the fingers pluck the strings.

The earliest literary allusion to lutes is perhaps to be found in the
comic poet Anaxilas, sometimes in the mid-fourth century. In his
play *The Lyre-maker*, the catalogue of this craftsman's products
includes the *trichordos*, 'three-stringer'. An instrument with so few
strings—at that date—is likely to be one so designed that the strings
can be stopped in order to yield more notes, and that is likely to be a
lute. According to Pollux, the *trichordon* (*sic*) was invented by the
Assyrians, who gave it the name *pandoura*.[144] He also refers to a
monochordon invented by the Arabs. The ancient oriental lutes
were indeed of one, two, or three strings.

The name *pandoura* (or *pandouros, phandouros, pandouris,
pandourion*; Latin *pandura*) established itself as the usual one; it is
first attested (but of a Nubian instrument) about 270 BC.[145] Nicomachus identifies it with the monochord used by Pythagoreans for
acoustic research, which suggests that he, like Pollux, knew of one-
stringed lutes.[146]

---

[144] Anaxilas fr. 15, Poll., 4. 60. Clement, *Strom.* 1. 76. 5, ascribes 'the *trichordon*'
to the Phrygian Agnis (= Hyagnis), but it is not certain whether an instrument is meant
here (see p. 173 n. 43). *Pandoura* may ultimately (it has been conjectured) derive,
through Semitic intermediaries, from Sumerian *pan-tur* 'little bow'. See however
É. Masson (as n. 134), 91. It may also be related to *tanbur(a), tambura* and similar
forms, which occur widely in eastern Europe, the Middle East, and central Asia as
names of lute-type instruments.

[145] Pythagoras (the explorer) ap. Ath. 183f; then Euphorion ap. Ath. ibid. and
182e, Protagorides, *FGrH* 853 F 2, Varro *Ling.* 8. 61, Mart. Cap. 9. 906, 924 (where
Egyptian origin is assumed; from Varro, *De novem disciplinis?*), S.H.A. *Heliogab.* 32.
8, Luxorius *Anth. Lat.* 371. 3, *MAMA* iii. 24.

[146] p. 243. 14 J. The monochord, in which the pitch was varied not by stopping the
string against frets but by moving a bridge under it, was not well suited to serve as a
performing instrument. Ptolemy, *Harm.* 2. 12, discusses its shortcomings in this role.

4

Wind and Percussion

Wind instruments—at any rate, those that chiefly concern us—work by setting up vibrations in air that is enclosed in a pipe or pipes. You cannot achieve this simply by blowing into the pipe. There are essentially three things you can do. You can blow sideways across the air column—across the end of the pipe, or across a hole in its side. This is the principle of the flute.[1] Or you can blow down the pipe with your mouth shut. The breath bursting out sets your lips vibrating against each other, and these vibrations are imparted to the air column. This is the principle of the trumpet and the horn. Or you can have a mouthpiece containing a vibrating reed that sets the air going. This is the principle of the clarinet and the oboe.

All three types of instrument were known to the Greeks, but those of the third type, known generically as *auloi*, were much the most important.

AULOI

Aulos is a native word meaning basically 'tube' or 'duct'. The musical aulos was a pipe with finger-holes and a reed mouthpiece. The player almost always played two of them at once, one with each hand, so we shall often refer to auloi in the plural.[2]

This practice of playing pipes in pairs was universal in the ancient Near East. We have a pair of silver pipes from Ur dating from about 2600 BC, now in the University Museum at Philadelphia, and paired pipes are depicted on later Mesopotamian and Egyptian monuments. Some Egyptian instruments have survived. A figurine from the small Cycladic island of Keros, dating from the middle part of the

---

[1] The recorder and the tin whistle are examples of 'fipple' flutes, in which the player has the illusion of blowing down the pipe but in fact the specially designed mouthpiece sends his breath obliquely across the main air column and up a flue.

[2] It is curious that Greek writers never seem to use the dual form *aulō*, as might be expected in the Attic dialect with objects so obviously making a pair.

third millennium, represents a man playing a pair of pipes. The
Minoans also knew them, as we can see from their appearance in a
sacrificial scene on the Hagia Triadha sarcophagus.[3]

It is not clear how early they became established in Greece itself.
No Mycenaean representations are known. The earliest evidence
dates from the end of the eighth century.[4] In the Homeric poems the
instrument is mentioned only twice: once as being played round the
camp fires of the Trojans and their allies, and once in a description of
wedding festivities.[5] It is remarkable that Homer says nothing of
auloi in a whole series of contexts in which they were regularly used
later: paeans, dirges, sacrifices, marching to battle, rowing, feasting,
dancing. It has been argued that this must be due to deliberate exclusion of an instrument regarded as lacking in dignity.[6] It may be so,
but the suspicion must remain that the pipes were only introduced
(or reintroduced) to Greece at a comparatively late date, perhaps
from Asia Minor or Syria.[7]

Organological classification

The grievous error of calling the aulos a flute has been sufficiently
castigated in the Introduction. What, then, should it be called? 'Pipe'
is unobjectionable but uninformative. 'Double reed pipe' may be
thought better, but the phrase is fraught with ambiguity and may
mislead the innocent. It is not automatically clear whether 'reed pipe'
means a pipe made from a hollow reed or a pipe equipped with a
vibrating reed; and incidentally, this so-called 'reed' in the mouthpiece is not necessarily made of reed. Again, it is not clear, unless a
hyphen is inserted, whether 'double' applies to the reed or to the
pipe. For reed mouthpieces fall into two categories, generally known
as single reed and double reed. In the single-reed type, a cut is made

---

[3] Sachs, *HMI* 72 f., 91 f., 98–100, 119 f.; Rimmer, 34–6 and pl. xii–xiii; Aign, 34,
47; *NG* vi. 71–4, xii. 197–200; Paquette, 23.

[4] Wegner, *Musik und Tanz*, 21 f.

[5] *Il.* 10. 13, 18. 495. Book 10 is generally agreed to be an addition to the original
Iliad. Some rhapsode also added auloi to the dance illustrated on Achilles' shield (*Il.*
18. 606 a in *PBerol.* 9774).

[6] H. Huchzermeyer, *Aulos und Kithara in der griechischen Musik bis zum Ausgang
der klassischen Zeit* (Emsdetten, 1931), 32–4.

[7] Several representations are known from the eastern Mediterranean area *c.* 800–
700: a Phrygian figurine with a double(?) hornpipe, BM 134975 (Rimmer, 28 f. and
pl. viii c; on hornpipes see later); a Cypriote bronze cup showing an oriental ritual procession (Aign, 64); a relief from Karatepe (Aign, 175; *NG* i. 389). There is also a Sardinian figurine of the 8th or 7th c. (*NG* vi. 314).

down the side of a cane or straw (the top end of which is stopped), so as to create a narrow blade or tongue which, when excited by blowing, will beat against the opening that it covers. In the other type, the mouthpiece terminates in two thin blades that beat against each other; they can be, and in antiquity were, made simply by flattening the end of a hollow stem. In both types of mouthpiece the beating part is completely enclosed by the player's mouth.

In the Hornbostel–Sachs classification system this distinction between single-reed and double-reed instruments is treated as fundamental, the former being classified as clarinets and the latter as oboes. Some musicologists, however, maintain that the more significant distinction to be made is between pipes of conical bore (widening from mouthpiece end to exit) and those of cylindrical bore (equal diameter throughout).[8] The modern clarinet is cylindrical, the oboe conical. The difference is acoustically important, because in response to overblowing[9] a conical pipe raises its note by an octave, whereas a cylindrical one raises it by a twelfth (octave plus fifth).

The numerous preserved specimens and fragments of Greek auloi[10] are all cylindrical, and the vast majority of artistic representations are of cylindrical pipes, though a small number appear distinctly conical.[11] The variation may not have been of any practical significance, since overblowing was probably not a part of normal playing technique. (I shall return to this point.) Some instruments were made out of bones and might have had a naturally conical exterior form for this reason, though the bone auloi we have are mostly polished down to cylindrical shape.

As to mouthpieces, it looks as if both the double and the single reed were known, further confusing the question of whether to put the aulos in the oboe or the clarinet category. However, in the Classical period the evidence points to general use of the double reed. The material remains tell us nothing, their mouthpieces having all perished. Pictorial representations are equally unhelpful when the auloi are shown being played, as the reeds are hidden in the player's mouth. But sometimes the whole instrument is visible, and then, as a

---

[8] Cf. J. MacGillivray in *Music Libraries and Instruments* (Cambridge, 1959); Becker, 31–4; Rimmer, 35.

[9] When the blowing force increases beyond a certain point, the pitch suddenly shoots up into a higher register. See below, p. 101.

[10] The pre-Hellenistic examples are listed below, p. 97.

[11] e.g. Paquette, 41 A12, 47 A24, 101 fig. 15, 185 B23; see Howard, 3f., 22; Reinach, 'Tibia', 303; Becker, 49f.

rule, its tip seems either to taper down to a fine point or to be splayed from a ligatured waist into a triangular or fan shape.[12] These must be double reeds, seen either sideways on or from above. The shape resembles preserved specimens from Ptolemaic Egypt.[13] In certain cases we see other conformations, difficult to interpret. But it is hard to find any clear example of a single-reed mouthpiece in Greek art.

Literary references point the same way. Theophrastus gives an account of the plant used for making aulos reeds, and of how it was prepared and cut. He calls the manufactured article either a 'tongue' or a *zeugos*, which implies a matching pair of things working together—not the separate mouthpieces of a pair of auloi, but the twin blades of the double-reed mouthpiece. He refers to the 'mouth' of the tongue being at the point where the reed-stem was cut in two, and to the advantage of this mouth closing up naturally, or (for a more elaborate style of piping) of the tongue being flexible enough to 'take down-bends'. All this seems to make sense only in terms of the double reed.[14] Other writers allude to techniques of squeezing the mouthpiece with the lips or pressing it against the (upper?) teeth, to modify the tone or the pitch.[15] It was possible for the 'tongue' to break off and stick to the player's palate.[16] Again, the double-reed mouthpiece seems to be presupposed. A double-reed mouthpiece affords far more scope for the control and nuancing of pitch than any single-reed one, as well as greater dynamic range.[17]

The single-reed or clarinet mouthpiece was known to other ancient peoples,[18] and I should not venture to assert that it was not known to the Greeks. But the evidence of both art and literature indicates that it was the double reed that was standard in the Classical period. Under the Hornbostel–Sachs system, therefore, the

[12] See Paquette, 24 fig. 3, 43 A13, 47 A28, 49 A30, 53 A40–1, 55 A45, A47–8, 57 A49–51, 59 A55; Wegner, *Musikleben*, pl. 11; id., *Bilder*, 47 (= Paquette, 11 pl. 1*b*); my Pl. 17 and 21.

[13] Brussels Conservatoire Museum; Baines, *Woodwind*, 193 fig. 41. The ligature 'was presumably put on the young plant while it was growing' (ibid. 192).

[14] Theophr. *Hist. Pl.* 4. 11. 1–7. The passage is translated with excellent notes by Barker, *GMW* i. 186–9, cf. ii. 103. Becker, 51–62 argues unconvincingly that it refers to single-reed mouthpieces. On aulos reeds and their provenance see also Pind. *Pyth.* 12. 26 with schol. 44a, fr. 70, Eur. fr. 100 Austin, schol. Eur. *Or.* 147, Strab. 12. 8. 15 p. 578.

[15] Ps.-Arist. *De audibilibus* 801ᵇ37, 804ᵃ12; Hsch. o 98.

[16] Schol. Pind. *Pyth.* inscr.

[17] Baines, *Woodwind*, 199.

[18] At any rate the Egyptians (Sachs, *HMI* 91 f.; *NG* vi. 71, 74) and Etruscans (Becker, 59 fig. 8: tomba Francesca Giustiniani).

aulos should be classified as an oboe. Those who regard the form of the bore as the decisive criterion will seek a different term.[19]

It must be admitted that 'oboe-girl' is less evocative than the 'flute-girl' to which classicists have been accustomed, and that when it is a question of translating Greek poetry 'oboe' is likely to sound odd. For the latter case I favour 'pipe' or 'shawm'.[20] I have found no very satisfactory solution to the girl problem.

Parts and accessories

The stem of the mouthpiece reed fitted into a bulbous section of pipe. Vase-paintings (Pl. 25) often show two of these bulbs, one socketed into the other, or occasionally, as it appears, even three. In other instances the instrument has continuous straight outlines but is crossed by bands at the corresponding places, indicating joints between separate pieces. From the surviving remains we know that the hole through the bulbs was narrow and cylindrical: it did not open out into a chamber, and the outer rotundity must have been merely ornamental. The player may have been able to modify the pitch of the instrument by adjusting the joints, or by varying the number of segments. In certain cases there was an open cup before the first bulb, forming a rest for the player's lips, and corresponding to the 'pirouette' of the later European shawm.

The terms *holmos* (connoting a smoothly rounded object) and *hypholmion* (what goes under the *holmos*) apparently referred to these parts of the aulos. Probably the *holmos* was the bulb and the *hypholmion* the open cup into which the reed was fitted.[21]

Three of the preserved aulos bulbs have a small hole bored into them from the side. There has been speculation as to whether this had some acoustic role. In one case, however, there are indications that the hole held a rivet of some kind. Perhaps a pin was pushed through it into the reed stem to hold the latter securely in place.[22]

---

[19] Becker's 'euthyphone' (cylindrical) and 'enclinophone' (conical) cannot be called felicitous.

[20] Some musicologists do use 'shawm' in the generic sense of double-reed pipe, while others reserve it for particular species (see *NG* xv. 665). The word derives from *calamus*.

[21] Eup. fr. 289 (someone complaining of *holmoi* that give out a snoring or wheezing sound), Pherecr. fr. 276, Poll. 4.70, Ptol. *Harm.* p. 9. 3; Hsch. '*hypholmion*: part of the aulos near the mouth, or the tongues' (or 'where the tongues are'); cf. Howard, 28 f.; Schlesinger, 70 f.

[22] See Howard, 32–5; N. B. Bodley, *AJArch.* 50 (1946), 225; *Délos* xviii. 813; J. G. Landels, *Hesp.* 33 (1964), 394 and *BSA* 63 (1968), 232, 234.

Some authors mention a part called the *sȳrinx* which could be bent either up or down to raise the pitch of the instrument above its normal range.[23] This recalls what Theophrastus says about the reed 'taking down-bends'. But the *sȳrinx* cannot be either the reed or the main pipe, because we hear of a conservative aulete in the fourth century BC who, disdaining the special effects that *sȳringes* could produce, would not let the makers put them on his auloi.[24] They were therefore a refinement not essential to the playing of the instrument, though customary by the fourth century. The name implies a tube of some kind, and a grammatical source defines the *sȳrinx* as 'the hole' of musical pipes.[25] Perhaps it was a special form of connector between the reed and the main pipe. But there is nothing that can be identified with it among the remains of later auloi. We shall return to the problem later.

The main pipe was made of reed, bone (especially the tibia of a deer), ivory, wood, or metal; or bone or wood encased in metal. In the surviving examples (none of which is of reed) it is usually constructed from two or more sections socketed together. The bore was quite narrow, generally about 8–10 mm. The Classical aulos normally had five finger-holes; the second (counting from the mouthpiece end) was on the underside of the pipe, for the thumb, and might be slightly displaced to left or right away from the hand, according to whether the aulos was the left or right member of its pair. The location of the thumb-hole in the second position (instead of in the first, as in the modern recorder) is characteristic of Near Eastern and Asiatic reed instruments in general today.[26] Sometimes there was a sixth hole lower down the pipe which was not fingered but functioned as a vent and (unless plugged) limited the effective acoustic length of the pipe.[27]

---

[23] Aristox. *Harm.* 1. 21, ps.-Arist. *De audibilibus* 804ᵃ14, Plut. *Non posse vivi* 1096b.

[24] Ps.-Plut. *De mus.* 1138a. Also ps.-Aristotle distinguishes between squeezing the *zeugē* (the reeds) and bending the *sȳringes* down.

[25] Hdn. i. 44. 5 Lentz (*Epimerismi, Anecd. Ox.* ii. 409. 23; *Etym. Magn.* 736. 28).

[26] Baines, *Woodwind*, 202f.

[27] Cf. Baines, *Bagpipes*, 22, 'Vent holes are common in reed instruments. . . . Their function is complex. Partly it is to equalize the tone of the lowest note with that of the others; partly it may be to permit a considerable extension of the tube-length to serve the purpose of an acoustic resonator; and partly it is to provide a means of tuning the lowest note (by plugging or partially plugging a vent hole).' P. R. Olsen, *Dansk Årbog for Musikforskning* 1966/7 (1968), 3–9, describes a pair of bone auloi acquired by auction, each with five holes of which the third and fifth are on the under side. The

The Theban virtuoso Pronomus (*c*. 400 BC) is credited with the invention of auloi on which several different modal scales could be played, previous auletes having had to keep a set of different instruments for this purpose.[28] The improvement was no doubt achieved by means of rotatable collars which enabled holes to be opened or closed. This meant that auloi could be given a larger number of holes, from which the player could select the ones he needed for a particular scale. Some late auloi found at Meroe, Pompeii, and elsewhere were of this type. They had anything up to twenty-four holes, closed by collars which had hook-shaped levers on them for easier operation. Some of the holes were smaller than others, and often the small ones were on the side of the pipe. Certain holes were elongated, narrower at one end, and presumably the corresponding collar could be adjusted to expose either the wider or the narrower part of the opening.[29] In Roman art we often see instruments with short subsidiary tubes rising like chimneys from several of their holes. They were apparently mounted on the rotating collars and could probably be alternated with ordinary holes; they could have had the effect of lowering the note, probably by a semitone.[30] Another type of mechanism is represented in a bronze model aulos (presumably a votive offering) found at Pergamum, perhaps of the second century BC. Here the two lowest holes were opened or closed not by rotating collars but by half-collars that were pushed down by rods, which had buttons on them at the top end.[31]

At its lower end the pipe sometimes opened out a little, or terminated in a definite flare or bell, for the better projection of low notes. This feature is quite prominent in many Archaic representations.[32] It virtually disappears from Attic art after about 520 BC, but

arrangement is quite incredible, and the finger-holes are too high up the instrument. Presumably the auloi were found in pieces and incorrectly restored.

[28] Paus. 9. 12. 5, cf. Ath. 631 e.

[29] See Howard, 5–8, 48–51; Reinach, 'Tibia', 308; T. L. Southgate, *JHS* 35 (1915), 14 f., 20; Schlesinger, 74–9. According to Poll. 4. 80 it was Diodorus of Thebes (5th c.?) who first increased the number of the aulos' holes 'by opening up lateral paths for the air-stream'. Plutarch, *Comp. Ar. et Men.* 853 e, alludes to the production of loud and remarkable effects by 'pulling back the *pantrēton*' ('all-perforated').

[30] See Gevaert, ii. 296; Howard, 8–11; Reinach, 'Tibia', 308 f.; Schlesinger, pl. 14 facing p. 110. They may be what are called *bombȳkes* ('bass-pipes') in Plut. *Quaest. conv.* 713 a and Arcadius p. 188. 12 Barker. In earlier writers the word applies to the lowest part of the main pipe, or its lowest note, or to a particular variety of aulos.

[31] See Fig. 4. 1; A. Conze, *Berl. Abh.* 1902(1), 7 f. and pl. 1; Behn 101 f.

[32] e.g. Wegner, *Bilder*, 39, 65, 71, 75; Paquette, 39 A1, 47 A24–5, 49 A29.

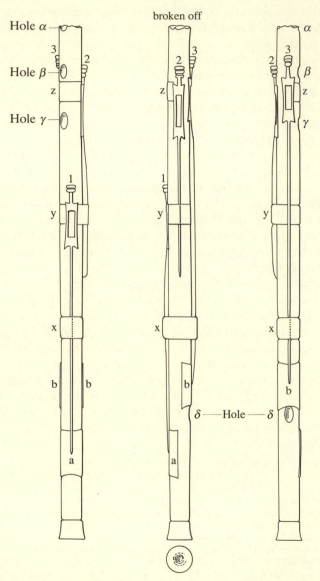

Fɪɢ. 4.1. Bronze model aulos from Pergamum. Second century ʙᴄ (?) (*Abhandl. preuss. Akad.* 1902(1).)

remains in Etruscan and South Italian. In auloi with a vent-hole below the finger-holes, the last section of the pipe would play little part in the production of sound and a bell would serve no real purpose.

The aulete sometimes wore a special kind of strap, called a *phorbeiā* ('halter'), that went across his mouth (with a hole, or two holes, for the pipes) and round the back of his head, usually with a second strap going over the top of his head to prevent the first one from slipping down. The device first appears in south Anatolian art about 700 BC, and in Greek not long afterwards.[33] Its purpose was to support the player's lips and cheeks and to take some of the strain involved in blowing. It is worn especially by professionals giving displays, and hardly ever by women, who presumably played in a less strenuous style.[34]

When not in use, auloi were kept in a skin bag (*sybēnē*) with two compartments and a strap to hang it up by. Attached to it was a small box (*glōttokomeion*) for the easily damaged reeds.[35] There may also have been protective caps that could be put over the reeds when they were in place on the instrument.[36]

Sizes and species

Aristoxenus, in a monograph on the boring of auloi, said that there were five kinds of aulos: *parthenioi, paidikoi, kitharistērioi, teleioi*, and *hyperteleioi*, literally 'girl-type, boy-type, lyre-playing-type, grown-up, hyper-grown-up', or less literally 'soprano, treble, tenor, baritone, bass'. Elsewhere he mentions the *parthenioi* and *hyperteleioi* as having the highest and lowest registers respectively, the total range from the top note of the former to the bottom note of the latter being something over three octaves.[37] Aristotle also knows this

[33] See Pl. 25. Karatepe relief, Aign, 175, *NG*, i. 388; bronze figurine of a trumpeter from Mylasa, Caria, Aign, 78, cf. 183, *NG* i. 390f.; Spartan figurines in R. M. Dawkins, *The Sanctuary of Artemis Orthia at Sparta* (London, 1929); the Chigi vase, Pl. 9. In Attic vase-painting it is often shown being worn. On a Lucanian bowl (Taranto 8263, Paquette, 59 A55) we see one dangling from an aulete's hand.

[34] Cf. Becker, 121ff.; D. M. MacDowell on Ar. *Vesp.* 582.

[35] Paquette, 32, 47 A28, 49 A30, 55 A43, etc. A *sybēnē* of ivory with gold appliqué is mentioned in a list of temple property from 422/1 BC (*IG* 1³. 351. 18). Later terms are *aulothēkē* and *aulodokē*. One of box-wood is mentioned by Leonidas, *HE* 2234.

[36] A few of the later vase-paintings (after 450) can be so interpreted (see Paquette, 59 A55, 129 pl. vα, 185 B23) and one of the Pompeian auloi may have such a cover (Reinach, 'Tibia', 307 figs. 6949–51; Behn, 108 and fig. 141).

[37] Aristox. fr. 101 and *Harm.* 1. 20f.

classification, and confirms that the *parthenioi* were higher than the *paidikoi*.[38] According to Pollux, the five sorts were used to accompany girls' dances, boys' singing, kithara-playing, paeans, and men's choruses respectively, but this is clearly not a complete account and it may be based on antiquarian speculation rather than on Classical authority.[39]

Pitch is not determined solely by length of pipe, but we may assume that these different auloi did differ in length, the lowest in pitch being the longest. In artistic representations we can certainly see some variation in length (as measured, for example, against the player's forearm), but we cannot demarcate one category from another;[40] it is comparatively seldom that we can feel sure that the artist intended to depict shorter or longer pipes than the average. Two definitely short pairs appear on non-Attic vases, in both cases with a female player.[41] The length suggested is about 20–25 cm. (8–10 inches). The two Archaic auloi from Ephesus were probably about this size when complete. Most instruments look at least half as long again, and some twice as long. Apart from the Ephesian ones, the surviving auloi, where complete enough to be measured, are of 30 cm. upward, the longest being the elaborate instruments from Pompeii (49–57 cm.). Pausanias mentions a statue of the famous Argive aulete Sakadas with a pair of auloi as tall as himself. Auloi that might be so described can be found in Roman art.[42]

Several other terms designating aulos types occur in Classical literature before Aristotle and Aristoxenus. Anacreon and Aeschylus know 'half-hole' ones (*hēmiopoi*), which later interpreters equated with *paidikoi*. Aeschylus also equipped the followers of Dionysus with *bombȳkes*, presumably pipes with a low register.[43] Herodotus describes Alyattes' Lydian army marching upon Miletus to the accompaniment of 'panpipes, harps, and aulos both women's and men's'. This sounds like a distinction between smaller/higher and larger/deeper, and in fact Athenaeus equates 'men's pipes' with the two lowest of Aristoxenus' types, the *teleioi* and *hyperteleioi*.[44]

[38] *HA* 581b10. Cf. also ps.-Arist. *De audibilibus* 804ᵃ11, Ath. 176 f.

[39] Poll. 4. 81.   [40] As attempted by Paquette, 25.

[41] Paquette, 49 A29 (Clazomenian, early 6th c.) and 39 A2 (Boeotian, *c.* 430).

[42] Paus. 9. 30. 2; Reinach, 'Tibia', 305 n. 3 and fig. 6944. Hesychius gives *Sakadeion* as a musical instrument: was the name given to these extra long auloi?

[43] Anacr. *PMG* 375, Aesch. fr. 91, Ath. 182 c, Hsch.; Aesch. fr. 57. 3, cf. Poll. 4. 82, Hsch., and above, n. 30.

[44] Hdt. 1. 17. 1, Ath. 176 f. For similar distinctions of male and female instruments in other cultures see Sachs, *HMI* 53; *WM* 97–9; Kunst, 52.

The 'Lydian magadis-aulos' of Ion of Chios was mentioned in the previous chapter. Possibly it consisted of an unequal pairing of 'male' and 'female' pipes designed to sound an octave apart.[45]

Unequal pipes of a special kind called 'Phrygian' or *elymoi* make more persistent appearances in the Greek world. Their characteristic feature was that one of the pair, normally the left one, was a horn-pipe, having a cow-horn attached to the end of the pipe and curving upwards from it. They first appear accompanying a Minoan sacrifice, on the Hagia Triadha sarcophagus, and then in an eighth-century bronze figurine from Asia Minor, where the player wears a Phrygian hat.[46] They are not depicted in extant Greek art, but according to Pausanias they were represented on the Chest of Cypselus at Olympia. There are sporadic references to them in pre-Hellenistic literature, especially as an oriental instrument.[47] Later they came to be seen and heard more regularly, especially in connection with the cult of the Great Mother and at Rome. In about 245 BC a Greek official in an Egyptian town was making arrangements for a party, and wrote to a colleague, 'Make every effort to send me the aulete Petōus with both his Phrygian and his other pipes.' An epigram of uncertain date celebrates a cabaret dancer who performed wild dances to the torches of Cybele, excited by the horn-pipe.[48] The Phrygian pipes played an important role in music for the Roman stage, as we know from the scholia to Terence, and they often appear in Roman art.[49] They are said to have been made of box-wood,[50] and to have had a narrower bore and a much deeper pitch than Greek pipes.[51] Latin poets describe their sound as

[45] Cf. above, p. 73 n. 108, and Poll. 4. 80, 'the "marital piping" consisted of two auloi of different sizes, suggesting a concord, but also the importance of the man being the greater', with Plut. *Coniugalia praecepta* 139 cd.

[46] Cf. above, n. 3; Rimmer, 28 f. and pl. viiic; A. Bélis, *Rev. Arch.* (1986), 21–40.

[47] Paus. 5. 17. 9; Archil. fr. 269, Soph. frs. 450 and 644 (both in Asiatic settings), Eur. *Bacch.* 127 (Phrygian pipes in Cretan Rhea-cult), *IA* 576 (Phrygian), Callias fr. 23, Cratinus Junior fr. 3 (Cyprus).

[48] *PHib.* 54. 2; Thyillus *Anth. Pal.* 7. 223 (*FGE* 96 f.). Cf. also Lucr. 2. 619 f., Catull. 63. 22, 64. 263 f., Varro *Sat. Men.* 131, Verg. *Aen.* 11. 737, Hor. *Carm.* 1. 18. 13, Tib. 2. 1. 86, Ov. *Met.* 3. 533, 4. 392, *Fast.* 4. 181, 190, *Pont.* 1. 1. 39, Philip *Anth. Pal.* 6. 94. 3 (*GP* 2722), Stat. *Theb.* 6. 120–2, Lucian *Podagra* 33, Nonnus *Dion.* 43. 71, 45. 43.   [49] See Howard, 35–8, 42–3; Wille, 169–71.

[50] Poll. 4. 74, cf. Verg. *Aen.* 9. 619, Ov. *Met.* 14. 537, *Pont.* 1. 1. 45, *Ciris* 166, Sen. *Agamemnon* 689, Stat. *Theb.* 5. 94, etc. But Philip and Thyillus locc. citt. speak of lotus, and Varro of bone.

[51] Aelian ap. Porph. in Ptol. *Harm.* p. 34. 15. For the deep sound cf. also *Anth. Pal.* 6. 51. 5 (*HE* 3836), Ath. 185 a, Aristid. Quint. p. 121. 14, Catull. 63. 22, 64. 263, Stat. *Theb.* 6. 120.

raucous.[52] Varro is quoted for the rather puzzling statement that the right-hand pipe had one hole and the left-hand pipe two, one of which produced a high note and the other a low one. Virgil too speaks of a 'two-hole melody', and 'two-holed pipes' are mentioned by Athenaeus immediately after Phrygian ones.[53] I suspect that these were not pipes with only two finger-holes, but pipes with two parallel tubes of different length or bore, both played with the left hand, while the right hand played a separate single-bore pipe; the longer of the left-hand pipes would serve to provide a deep drone. This is the arrangement found in the Sardinian *launeddas*, in which musicologists have recognized a unique survival from antiquity. It is a triple clarinet with a shorter pipe played by the right hand and two longer ones, bound together, by the left, the longer of these two being a bass drone.[54] The launeddas has no horn, but most of the hornpipes found in Europe and north Africa have two pipes bound together so that one finger closes holes in both at once, and the instrument represented in the eighth-century BC Phrygian figurine mentioned above appears to have been of this type.[55] It does not seem, in view of the evidence of art, that this was the only or even the usual form of the Phrygian pipes, but it may have been one variety.

From the fourth century BC we hear of a small pipe called *gingros*, *gingrās*, *gingriās*, or *gingrainos*, of Phoenician or Carian origin. It is described as being a hand's span in length, high-pitched and plaintive, and used in teaching beginners.[56] Another variant of the name is *ginglaros*, which according to Pollux is a small Egyptian aulos suitable for playing as a single pipe.[57] This suggests that it had enough holes to occupy both hands. The practice of playing a single pipe (*monaulos*), though rare, had been known since the Archaic age. It is attested by early figurines from Sparta, and by occasional literary references.[58] The pipe that was so played was at least in some

---

[52] Lucr. 2. 619, Catull. 64. 263 f., Ov. *Fast.* 4. 190, Sen. *Agam.* 689, Val. Flacc. 2. 583, etc. Aristid. Quint. p. 85. 4, however, characterizes it as 'feminine, wailing, mournful'. Cf. Acro on Hor. *Carm.* 4. 15. 30.

[53] Verg. *Aen.* 9. 618, Varro ap. Serv. ad loc. (fr. 283 Funaioli), discussed by Howard, 47; Ath. 176 f, cf. Poll. 4. 77.

[54] See Paquette, 237 f.; *NG* ix. 390.

[55] See *NG* viii. 719 f.; Rimmer, 29.

[56] Xenophon(?), Antiphanes and others cited by Ath. 174 f–175 b; cf. Athenion fr. 1. 31, Poll. 4. 76, Hsch.; *gingrina*, Festus (Paulus) p. 95 M.

[57] Poll. 4. 82; *ginglarion*, *Anecd. Bekk.* 88. 4.

[58] H. Hofmann, *Arch. Anz.* 1904. 57 (9th–8th c., unknown provenance, not certainly Greek; Aign, 87); A. J. B. Wace, *BSA* 15 (1908/9), 137, and in R. M.

cases made of reed or straw, and among the Doric-speakers of south Italy called *tītyrinos*.[59] In Theocritus we hear of the 'straw pipe' as a rustic instrument inferior to the panpipe.[60]

From the fourth century again there is evidence for a type of single pipe with its mouthpiece at the side instead of on the end. It may have been called a *plagiaulos* ('transverse pipe'), though this term seems usually to denote the flute (below, p. 113). The reed was fitted into a short tube that slanted into the main pipe, the upper end of which was closed. There are two surviving examples in the British Museum, and a few artistic representations.[61]

Various further names of aulos types are recorded in later sources. Some of them may be equivalent to types already discussed. For example, auloi called 'medium-sized' (*mesokopoi*) presumably correspond to one of Aristoxenus' categories. There are *Pỹthikoi* which are identified as *teleioi*: this was the type used for elaborate instrumental solos at the Pythian Games and elsewhere.[62] No doubt it was equipped with every available technical resource—side-holes, collars, and so forth. It is contrasted with the 'choral' aulos, which had a propensity for higher notes and was used for accompanying dithyrambic and other choral song.[63] This was perhaps identical with

---

Dawkins, *The Sanctuary of Artemis Orthia*, 262, 269, 273 fig. 126j, 276, pl. CLXXXIII, CLXXXIX 13, CXCVI 22 (7th c.; Aign, 245ff.); Soph. fr. 241, Anaxandrides frs. 19, 52, Araros fr. 13, Sopatros fr. 2 Kaib., Hedylus, *HE* 1877, Posidonius fr. 86 Th., Protagorides, *FGrH* 853 F 2 (all in Ath. 175e–176d); Poll. 4. 75, Pliny, *HN* 7. 204, Mart. 14. 63.

[59] Anaxandrides fr. 52, Hedylus loc. cit.; Artemidorus ap. Ath. 182d, Amerias ibid. 176c, Hsch. s.v.

[60] *Id.* 5. 7, cf. 6. 43, 20. 29, Verg. *Ecl.* 3. 27. See Welch, 272–89; Schlesinger, 45f.

[61] Ps.-Arist. *De audibilibus* 801b32ff. (reed mouthpiece, softer tone than the ordinary aulos). The references to the *plagiaulos* are collected in notes 144–5 below. Surviving specimens and art: Howard 16f., 55–8; T. L. Southgate, *JHS* 35 (1915), 16; Schlesinger, 78f.; Wegner, *Bilder*, 57; Paquette, 26.

[62] Compare the application of the same designation to a type of lyre, pp. 59f.

[63] Poll. 4. 81, Aristid. Quint. p. 85. 6–8. In Roman comedy, according to Suet. fr. 12 Reiff., the choral pipes accompanied a chorus, the *pythaulicae* a solo song. *Pỹthaulēs* and *choraulēs* are the two principal kinds of aulete who perform at public games in the imperial period: Varro, *Sat. Men.* 561, Strab. 17. 1. 11 p. 796, *SIG* 795A. 3 (*c.* AD 29), Sen. *Ep.* 76. 4, Petron. *Sat.* 53, 69, Pliny, *HN* 37. 6, Juv. 6. 77, Mart. 5. 56. 9, 6. 39. 19, 11. 75. 3, Suet. *Ner.* 54, *Galba* 12. 3, Apul. *Met.* 8. 26, Plut. *Ant.* 24. 2, Lucillius, *Anth. Pal.* 11. 11. 1, schol. Ar. *Av.* 858, Hyg. *Fab.* 273. 7, etc.; *IG* 5. 1. 758, 7. 1773. 18, 27, 1776. 17, 21 (the choral aulete is here called *kyklios*, i.e. dithyrambic, cf. *PMichigan* 4682 published by O. Pearl, *Illinois Classical Studies* 3 (1978), 132–9, and Hsch. s.v. *kyklioi auloi*); 14. 737, 2499, *CIG* 1720, 2758, *BCH* 18 (1894) 98 no. 15; Latin inscriptions in Wille 321f.

the 'tragic' aulos,[64] while a 'theatrical' aulos used for solo pieces cannot be distinguished from the *Pȳthikos*.[65] 'Underhole' and 'side-hole' pipes (*hypotrētoi, paratrētoi*), if not the same again, must at any rate be instruments of the more elaborate sort.[66] 'Convivial' pipes (*paroinioi*), described as small and of equal size, would be the common type used at the Archaic and Classical symposium.[67] There is also mention of 'spondaic' pipes, which were long and suitable for solemn hymns and libations.[68] They would have needed to produce a deep and stately sound, but not a large number of different notes. Then there were 'marching' auloi (*embatērioi*) for processions, and 'finger' auloi (*daktylikoi*) for dance-songs.[69] Another type was named because of its stocky shape *skytaliās* or *skytalion*, 'walking-stick'.[70] We also hear of a high-pitched Libyan 'horse-herding' pipe (*hippophorbos*), made of bay-wood, and of others called *Athena*, *idouthoi, mardos, batnos* (Messenian), *katamphōtoi*, and *tyrikiloi* (made of reed).[71]

Aulos scales

Many attempts have been made to infer, from the disposition of holes in surviving specimens of ancient auloi, the notes and intervals that they were designed to play. This is not a hopeless enterprise, but the prospects of achieving valid results are limited by a number of factors. In principle, the opening or closing of different holes by the fingers changes the note by varying the length of the resonating air column, which more or less ceases to resonate at the first open hole from the mouthpiece. The intervals between different notes will

---

[64] Mentioned together with *kitharistērioi* and with *lȳsiōidikoi* by Ath. 182c, who cites Ephorus (*FGrH* 70 F 3) and two specialist writers on auloi as his authorities. The *lȳsiōidikoi* were named after a sort of Hellenistic cabaret act, for which see p. 378.

[65] Poll. 4. 82, *hypotheātroi auloi*.

[66] Ath. 176f, Poll. 4. 77(?), 81 ('suitable to dirges, blowing high and slow').

[67] Poll. 4. 80. For their relatively small size cf. Theog. 241, Anac. *PMG* 375 with Ath. 182c, and the adoption of the *gingras* by symposiasts as attested by Amphis fr. 14 K.–A. However, the auloi depicted in sympotic scenes on vases do not seem particularly small.

[68] Poll. 4. 81, cf. 'Marius Victorinus' (Aphthonius), *Gramm. Lat.* vi. 44. 22. Their player was called a *spondaulēs* (inscriptions; cf. Cic. *De Or.* 2. 193(?), Diom. *Gramm. Lat.* i. 476. 9 ff.)

[69] Ath. 176f, Poll. 4. 82; cf. the kithara called *daktylikon*, p. 59.

[70] Juba, *FGrH* 275 F 81, equates this with the Phrygian *elymos*; this is plausible inasmuch as walking-sticks often had a curving handle, like the curving horn on the end of the Phrygian pipe. Poll. 4. 82 (cf. Hsch.) simply says that the *skytalion* was small.   [71] Poll. 4. 77, Hdn. i. 142. 22 L., Hsch.

correspond (again, in principle) to the ratios between the resonating lengths, measured from the tip of the reed to the opening at which the air-stream escapes from the pipe. The instrument will produce its lowest note with all finger-holes closed so that the whole length of the pipe (assuming that there are no vent-holes) is functioning. Opening a hole half way down raises the note by an octave. Opening one two thirds of the way down raises it by a fifth. And so on. So without knowing the absolute pitch at which a pipe played, we can in theory determine the relative pitches of its notes by measuring to each hole. We could do this even if the bottom end of the pipe were broken off and lost. But it would be essential to have the mouthpiece and reed intact.

Unfortunately in the case of Greek auloi we never do have the reed, and we have to guess how far it stuck out from its holder. In any case the exact intonation of a given hole is also affected by its size—a larger hole gives a higher note than a smaller one in the same position—and by its internal contours. In the early aulos the holes were of equal size, but in at least one (undated) case it can be seen that a hole has been 'tuned' by undercutting its rim.[72] The player could also vary the pitch by covering a greater or smaller portion of the hole (half-stopping or quarter-stopping), or by cross-fingering, that is, by closing holes below the one that is 'speaking'.[73] According to Proclus, 'they say that each aulos-hole yields three notes at least, and more if the side-holes are opened too'.[74] Apart from fingering techniques, the player could also modify the pitch by altering the position of his lips on the reed. In addition to the devices mentioned earlier (pp. 84, 86 f.), we hear that he could make the note higher by widening the angle between his two auloi; here too a change of lip position must have been the effective factor.[75] We hear also that those who blow with warmer breath and project it in a steady, sighing manner produce a lower sound.[76]

---

[72] J. G. Landels, *Hesp.* 33 (1964), 395.

[73] This lowers the pitch slightly. See Schlesinger, 245 ff. Achilles Tatius 8. 6. 6 speaks of the aulete closing off all the holes except one. Classical vase-paintings indicate a greater variety of technique, including some cross-fingering; see below, n. 91. Cf. also Aelian ap. Porph. in Ptol. *Harm.* p. 34. 27 with Barker, *GMW* ii. 232 n. 102.

[74] Commentary on Pl. *Alc.*, iii. 41 Cousin. The 'side-holes' are a feature of the later aulos, cf. p. 87.

[75] Aristox. *Harm.* 2. 42, Plut. *Non posse vivi* 1096 b.

[76] Arist. *Gen. An.* 788ª20, *Pr.* 11. 13.

So in practice the player could adjust each note to suit himself.
This is what Plato means when he says that playing the auloi is a
matter of aiming at each note by practised guesswork, and that it
involves a great deal of imprecision and little that is fixed and reliable.[77] Aristoxenus writes:

> It is not because the aulos has bore-holes and cavities and so forth that it
> plays fourths or fifths or octaves in true accord or gives each of the other
> intervals its due size, but because of skilful operation, partly by the hands,
> partly by the other parts with which the player has the power to raise or lower
> pitch. For although all the holes etc. are provided, none the less auletes
> mostly miss the proper intonation, for all their taking the pipes away (from
> each other?) and setting them parallel, blowing harder or less hard, and
> modifying other factors. . . . Just as there is no attunement in strings unless
> one applies skill and tunes them, so there is none in bore-holes unless skilful
> operation brings them into tune. That no instrument tunes itself, but that its
> tuning must be ruled by the ear, clearly needs no proof, because it is
> obvious. . . . (The aulos) is particularly variable both in respect of its manu-
> facture and its operation and its intrinsic nature.[78]

Ethnomusicologists have found that in most pipes in most countries the spacing of finger-holes is not calculated so as to produce a
rational series of intervals but is governed by the principle of equi-
distance. Either all holes are equidistant, or there are two groups of
equidistant holes, one for each hand. This does not give rise to equal
musical intervals, which require increments of length that are in a
geometrical, not an arithmetical progression. Some correction of
notes may be made by adjusting the sizes or contours of holes, but
for the rest it is taken for granted that the player will make the necessary corrections by such techniques as have been mentioned
above.[79]

Kathleen Schlesinger wrote a massive, a terrifying book, *The
Greek Aulos*, based on the belief that Greek pipes too had equidistant finger-holes. She was untroubled by the fact that this is not
true of the only surviving classical auloi that she studied, the two
Elgin auloi in the British Museum. Nor is it true of auloi from Sparta,
Ephesus, and Locri, which had been published before she wrote but
to which she paid no attention; nor is it true of others which have

---

[77] *Phlb.* 56 a.
[78] *Harm.* 2. 42–3. Cf. also Ptol. *Harm.* 1. 8 p. 17. 3 ff.
[79] Cf. E. M. von Hornbostel in *Festschrift Wilhelm Schmidt* (Vienna, 1928); Sachs,
HMI 181 f.

been published since. Often the inequality of the spacing is so marked that it can only be intentional. But can we discover the intention?

There is reason to believe that pipes incorporated certain basic intervals as a matter of design. A passage in Aristoxenus suggests that auloi were commonly bored to give successive intervals of $\frac{3}{4}$ tone, $\frac{3}{4}$ tone, tone, and then again $\frac{3}{4}$, $\frac{3}{4}$; the sequence $\frac{3}{4} + \frac{3}{4} + 1$ makes up the interval of a fourth. A slightly later Peripatetic writer observes that in auloi the length-ratio 2 : 1 corresponds to the octave interval and that 'the aulos-borers take it so'.[80] He is writing at a time of more sophisticated auloi than those of the Classical period; but we also hear that before Pronomus' invention of collars the aulete needed a different pair of auloi for each mode, which certainly implies that an aulos' holes should contain some clues to its intended scale.

According to the unanimous testimony of all the ancient writers on music, the interval of the fourth was basic to the structure of every modal scale. We should therefore expect that an aulos would normally have at least one pair of holes yielding notes a fourth apart, in other words at distances from the reed-tip in the ratio 4 : 3. As has been said, we never know just where the reed-tip was. But it is sometimes possible to estimate it closely enough to identify the relevant holes. Once that is done, it becomes possible to determine intervals for the other holes. This is the approach which J. G. Landels has fruitfully followed in his analyses of the Brauron and Reading auloi, and it can be extended to several others.[81]

Here is a list of extant auloi and aulos fragments from the Archaic and Classical periods.

1. Thirteen bone fragments from Sparta, *c.*650–600 BC. R. M. Dawkins, *The Sanctuary of Artemis Orthia at Sparta* (London, 1929), 236 f. and pl. CLXI–II.
2. Two little girls' auloi from Ephesus, *c.*600–550. D. G. Hogarth, *Excavations at Ephesus: The Archaic Artemisia* (London, 1908), 194 and pl. XXXVII 12; T. J. Dunbabin (ed.), *Perachora: The Sanctuaries of Hera Akraia and Limenia,* ii (Oxford, 1962), 448 f. British Museum, GR 1907.12–1.423.

---

[80] Aristox. *Harm.* 2. 37; ps.-Arist. *Pr.* 19. 23. Ptolemy, on the other hand, implies that aulos-makers work by trial and error (*Harm.* 2. 12 p. 66. 32).

[81] R. J. Letters's attempt to do this, however (*CQ* 19 (1969), 266–8) makes some improbable assumptions about mouthpiece-extrusions, especially with the Elgin auloi, and yields dubious results.

3. Aulos section from Lindos, before 525. C. Blinkenberg, *Lindos: Fouilles de l'Acropole* 1902–1914. 1. *Les Petits Objets* (Berlin, 1931), 153–5 and pl. 16.

4. Many fragments from Perachora, archaic? T. J. Dunbabin (as above), 448–51 and pl. 190.

5. Aulos from Brauron, Attica, sixth–fifth century. J. G. Landels, *BSA* 58 (1963), 116–19.

6. Fragments from the Athenian Acropolis, before 480? Athens, National Museum 7207–9, unpublished.

7. Aulos section from the Athenian Agora, mid-fifth century. C. Boulter, *Hesperia* 22 (1953), 114 and pl. 41.

8. Various fragments from the Athenian Agora, fifth century BC to first century AD. J. G. Landels, *Hesperia* 33 (1964), 392–400, fig. 1 and pl. 70.

9. Bone fragment from Aegina, fifth century? A. Furtwängler, *Aegina: Das Heiligtum der Aphaia* (Munich, 1906), 429 fig. 337.

10. Bone aulos from Corinth, fifth century. G. R. Davidson, *Corinth: Result of Excavations*, xii. *The Minor Objects* (Princeton, NJ, 1952), 196 f., fig. 30 and pl. 90.

11. Part of bone aulos from Locri, south Italy, not later than fifth century. *Notizie degli Scavi* (1917), 104.

12. Two wooden auloi (the Elgin auloi), fifth century? K. Schlesinger, *The Greek Aulos* (London, 1939), 411–20 and pl. 17. British Museum, GR 1816.6–10.502.

13. Well-preserved aulos (the Reading aulos), probably from Asia Minor, probably not before fourth century. J. G. Landels, *BSA* 63 (1968), 231–8; my Pl. 26.

14. Pair of wooden auloi, late fourth century? A. Bélis, *BCH* 108 (1984), 111–22. Paris, Louvre E 10962a, b.

15. Pair of auloi, unknown date and provenance. P. R. Olsen, *Dansk Årbog for Musikforskning* 1966–7 (1968), 3–9. Copenhagen, National Museum, inv. 14411–12.

The Brauron aulos has six holes, which we designate (counting from the mouthpiece end) as I, T (thumb-hole on the under side), II, III, IV, V; the last is a vent, sounding the lowest playable note. The upper part of the pipe is lost, but if one assumes its length to have been such that the holes T and IV sounded notes a fourth apart, one finds that the intervals I–T and IV–V both come out at very close to a tone, 196 and 194 cents respectively. The fourth T–IV is made up of intervals of 171, 155, and 172 cents (from top to bottom).

Similar calculations for other six-hole auloi yield results as shown in Table 4. 1. We seem to have a fairly consistent pattern here of a

Table 4.1. *Intervals on 6-hole auloi (cents)*

	I	T	II	III	IV	V
Ephesus A	162	152	193	153	149	
B	149	161	163	174	153	
Perachora	lost	172	168	158	163	
Locri	198	178	161	159	213	
Corinth	202	164	175	159	223	

498

scale extending over a major sixth in the scheme tone + fourth + tone, the fourth being subdivided into three roughly equal steps of rather less than a tone. One of the little Ephesian auloi shows a pattern matching the $\frac{3}{4}, \frac{3}{4}, 1, \frac{3}{4}, \frac{3}{4}$ tone series mentioned by Aristoxenus.

However, the two Elgin auloi do not fit this scheme. The whole of the main tube of each is preserved with one bulb, and it is clear that even with one or two more bulbs they cannot have been long enough to make the T–IV interval as small as a fourth. If fourths are to be found on these pipes, the most plausible places seem to be T–III on pipe A and I–II on pipe B, with one extra bulb in each case and cent-counts as in Table 4.2. A. C. Baines, experimenting with a replica of pipe A, with a reed extrusion of 5.5 cm. from the bulb, was able to obtain a good pentatonic scale, *a c' d' f'* (or *e'*) *g' a'*.[82]

Table 4.2. *Intervals on the two Elgin auloi*

	I	T	II	III	IV	V
A	277	271	227	210	227	
B	289	209	193	183	253	

[82] Baines, *Woodwind*, 200.

The Reading aulos (Pl. 26) has only five holes, and would produce its lowest note with all of them closed and the full length of the pipe resonating. The mouthpiece end is well preserved apart from the actual reed, the extrusion of which can be gauged within fairly narrow limits. The intervals work out quite satisfactorily (Table 4.3).

TABLE 4.3. *Intervals on the Reading aulos*

I	T	II	III	IV	End
236	202	140	156	498	
		498			

Both T–IV and IV–End give perfect fourths, while the top note is a rather wide tone[83] above T and a fraction over an octave above the bottom note. The T–IV fourth is made up of $\frac{3}{4} + \frac{3}{4} + 1$ tone intervals (in ascending order).

The two Copenhagen pipes also have five holes, but until it has been established how they should be assembled (it is possible that each contains sections belonging to the other) it will not be profitable to attempt an analysis. But it is clear that, like the Elgin auloi, they had hole-arrays which were out of phase, beginning and ending lower down one pipe than the other.

The same is true of the Louvre auloi. These must have had closure collars, since one of them has nine holes and the other seven. With a 3.3 cm. reed extrusion in each case we obtain the sets of intervals shown in Table 4.4. The total length of the two pipes is the same, 41 cm., and Mme Bélis is no doubt correct in her assumption that they were played as a pair.[84] She identifies the one with the greater number of holes as the one played by the right hand. It looks as if it

[83] Very close to a 'septimal' tone, i.e. the interval produced by the ratio 8 : 7 (231 cents).

[84] We cannot be certain that this is true of the Elgin and Copenhagen auloi, which are slightly unequal in length. Two pipes of the Classical period found together might represent members of a set playing different modes rather than a pair to be played in tandem.

TABLE 4.4. *Intervals on the Louvre auloi*

	I	T	II	III	IV	V	VI	VII	VIII	End
b	231	132	170	196	228	95	183	239	360	
			498			506				
a	250	180	109	178	206	90				284
				493						

had an upper register (holes I–IV) in which the thumb played a part, and a lower one (IV–VII, with I–III shut off and VIII as a vent; or V–VIII?) in which it merely supported the pipe, each register covering a fourth plus a septimal tone. Holes III–VIII are about level with holes I–V on the other pipe.

Overblowing

So far we have considered only the instrument's 'fundamental' notes, that is, those produced by the air column vibrating as an integral whole from reed to aperture. Another set of notes, 'harmonics', can sometimes be elicited from pipes by 'overblowing', a trick that causes the air column to break up into two, three, or more equal parts, resonating at twice, thrice (etc.) the frequency of the whole. With modern wind instruments overblowing is a normal part of playing technique, greatly extending the compass of the instrument. But was it so in Antiquity?

It certainly does not seem to have been commonplace. There are no clear references to the effect in ancient writers; and it is not used by those peoples who still employ reed-blown pipes in pairs. There is a good reason for this. Manipulating a reed mouthpiece so as to produce harmonics as desired is something calling for great skill. To achieve them and control them on two mouthpieces simultaneously would be particularly difficult.[85] There would also be the problem of a sizeable gap between the fundamental and harmonic registers, because a cylindrical pipe normally overblows to the third harmonic, that is, at tripled frequency, an octave and a fifth above the

[85] Schlesinger, 67.

fundamental. As the fundamental scale on the earlier aulos does not seem to have exceeded an octave or so, there would be a gap of a fifth between the highest fundamental and the lowest harmonic. The harmonics therefore could not conveniently serve to extend the melodic range upwards, but only to provide some sort of high echo effect in regions where a singing voice would find it hard to follow. Further, Aristoxenus' statement that to span three octaves you would need to go from the highest note of the soprano aulos to the lowest note of the bass one rather implies that each instrument had a range of an octave or thereabouts, the bass being some two octaves below the soprano. If harmonics had been in regular use, the tenor and bass auloi should have comfortably covered three octaves between them.[86]

On the other hand we must reckon with the possibility—some might say likelihood—that virtuosi did employ overblowing to increase the range of effects in instrumental solos. Aristoxenus adds to the remark just cited, as if by way of an afterthought, 'yes, and when the *sȳrinx* is pulled down, the highest note of him who *sȳrittei* (whistles, or plays the *sȳrinx*), compared with the lowest of him who *aulei*, would exceed the stated limit'. I have already mentioned this and other passages referring to the mysterious *sȳrinx* that raised the pitch of an aulos. Most of them do not make it clear whether the rise is of the order of a tone or of more than an octave. But Aristoxenus could be understood as referring to a quite distinct high register, to play in which was called *sȳrittein* as opposed to the *aulein* of ordinary piping. 'Whistling', *sȳrigmos*, was a traditional element in the programme pieces performed at the Pythian auletic contest; it represented the dying hisses of the serpent shot by Apollo.[87] The same term was applied to a special effect on the kithara which sounds as if it was an octave harmonic (above, p. 69). This all suits the idea of overblowing being used by experts for certain purposes. Yet it seems that it required a special feature incorporated in the auloi. One thinks of the 'speaker hole' of modern woodwind instruments, a very small hole strategically placed on the tube, which, when opened by means of a key, facilitates the production of harmonics.[88] If this is

[86] Aristox. *Harm.* 1. 20; Becker, 74, cf. 51.

[87] Xen. *Symp.* 6. 5, Strab. 9. 3. 10 p. 421. The Megarian aulete Telephanes, who disliked the *sȳrinx* and would not have it on his pipes, stayed out of the Pythian contest for this reason in particular (ps.-Plut. *De mus.* 1138a).

[88] Howard, 30–5, interprets the *sȳrinx* in this way. The small holes found in some aulos bulbs (p. 85) do not seem to be suitably situated to serve as speakers.

what the *syrinx* was, its 'pulling' or 'bending' down or up would refer to the operation of its closing mechanism, and the apparent connection with the bending down of the reed, as mentioned by Theophrastus (above, p. 84), would be illusory.

The relation of the two pipes

It was, as we have said, the almost invariable ancient practice to play auloi in pairs. What was the point of this, and what was the relation between the two pipes?

Paired pipes are still widely used in the Balkans and across the Islamic countries from Egypt to the Far East, though they are almost always fixed together side by side so that the fingers can cover holes in both pipes at once, something never seen with Greek auloi. 'Frequently one of the two pipes has fewer holes than the other, to provide for all kinds of accompaniment from a plain drone to ingenious harmonic and rhythmic counterpoints.'[89] In Antiquity too there may have been variety. We should not take it for granted that one single form of relationship between the pipes persisted unchanged through centuries in the course of which the aulos itself evolved considerably and skilled players were ever striving to impress the public with new feats of virtuosity.

In Archaic and Classical art the two pipes are constantly shown as equal in length.[90] Moreover, the player's hands are regularly at equal distances along each pipe, generally between half-way and three-quarters of the way down, and the fingers of each hand are doing identical things.[91] On a fifth-century vase where the holes on the two pipes are clearly represented, no difference in their number or spacing can be made out.[92] All this suggests that both pipes played in the same register and (to a large extent, at least) the same melody.

The fragment of vocal score that we have for Euripides' *Orestes* contains a certain number of instrumental notes referring to the aulos accompaniment. They mostly occur singly, suggesting that

[89] A. C. Baines in A. Baines (ed.), *Musical Instruments Through the Ages* (Harmondsworth, 1961), 224.

[90] An oinochoe by the Nicosthenes Painter, Paris, Cabinet des Médailles 258 (Paquette, 41 A10, *c.*520 BC) forms an apparent exception, with the left-hand pipe seemingly about 15% longer than the right-hand. But possibly it is meant to be a pipe of equal length held at a lower angle.

[91] See e.g. Paquette, 21 pl. II*b* (all holes covered), 45 A21 (all uncovered), A22 (middle and fourth fingers down, index and little fingers up), 53 A38 (little fingers under the pipes).

[92] London E 53 (Paquette, 45 A19).

there was just one note for the auloi to play. But at two places a pair of notes is given, a fourth apart. They may be meant to sound successively; but I am inclined to interpret them as representing a divergence of the two pipes (see below, p. 207). Certainly Theophrastus in his account of reed-making appears to reckon with some differentiation of function between the pipes. He specifies that the reeds for a pair of auloi must be cut from the same section of the cane if they are to sound in accord, but also that the lower part of the section will make the reed for the left-hand pipe and the upper part, which will not be quite so hard, the reed for the right-hand pipe.[93] The two then are not identical, though they must blend well. Aristoxenus remarks that in listening to an aulete 'one can judge whether his auloi are in concord or not, and whether their discourse is clear-cut'. Unfortunately we cannot tell whether with 'concord' he is thinking only of unison or also of concordant intervals such as the fourth; and whether by 'discourse' (*dialektos*) he means to suggest a dialogue between the two pipes.[94]

Archaeological evidence from the fourth century gives us something more definite. The Louvre auloi, which have every appearance of forming a pair, differ, as we have seen, in the number and placing of their holes. The one with the fewer holes has them lower down the pipe than the other. On a Campanian wine-jug Marsyas is shown holding a pair of pipes in his left hand; the hand hides all but two holes on one pipe and all but one on the other, but it is obvious that the disposition of holes is different. If he is holding the left pipe on the left of the right pipe, it is the left pipe that has the lowest hole.[95]

In the first century BC Varro illustrates the relationship between pastorality and agriculture by the image of the pipes which are related but distinct, the right-hand pipe 'singing' the melody, the other supporting it. Agriculture corresponds to the latter, being 'inferior' in respect of antiquity, just as the left-hand pipe is 'lower' with respect to the holes of the right-hand pipe. Varro cites Dicaearchus for the subordinate position of agriculture, but unfortunately it is unclear whether the image of the pipes goes back to Dicaearchus.[96] With a Roman author there is a greater risk that he is talking about

[93] *Hist. Pl.* 4. 11. 7.
[94] Aristox. in ps.-Plut. *De mus.* 1144 e. For *dialektos* cf. 1138b (also from Aristoxenus); Arist. *De An.* 420[b]8; Phot. *Lex.* s.v. *niglareuōn*.
[95] Adolphseck 165 (Paquette, 45 A20).
[96] Varro, *Rust.* 1. 2. 15 f.; Dicaearchus fr. 51 W.

the Phrygian auloi, where it is clear that the two pipes had differentiated roles.[97]

Auloi in performance

The instrument had quite a penetrating tone, to judge by the ability of a single pair of auloi to accompany a choir of up to fifty men. The larger sizes must have had a fairly deep voice in view of the narrowness of the bore. Aristophanes represents the sound of piping by *mümü*, *mümü*, and likens it to the buzzing of wasps.[98] 'Buzzing' (*bombos*, *bombȳx*) is associated particularly with the lowest notes. There was in fact a particular manner of playing called 'wasping' (*sphēkismos*) in reference to this effect.[99] Playing in a high register could be characterized as 'screeching', or as 'squawking like geese'.[100] Pollux provides a list of adjectives applicable to piping: they include strong, intense, forceful; sweet-breathed, pure-toned (*ligyros*, cf. p. 42); wailing, enticing, lamenting.[101]

The aulos was noted for its ability to express and to arouse different emotions. The old aulos-tunes attributed to Olympus, even if badly played, according to Plato, have the power to possess the hearer with frenzy and mark him out as being in need of religious purification.[102] Aristotle calls the aulos 'orgiastic', i.e. conducive to religious frenzy, and it is regularly mentioned (together with drums) in connection with Bacchic, Corybantic, and suchlike ecstatic cults.[103] We hear of a man whom the sound of auloi at the symposium always affected with panic.[104] 'Longinus' speaks of the aulos sending

[97] See above, pp. 91 f.; also Apul. *Flor.* 3 (Hyagnis the first to play two pipes instead of one, separating the hands and making a musical blend of high and low, *acuto tinnitu et graui bombo*, with the left and right hole-arrays); Festus p. 109. 13 M. (unequal pipes with a different number of holes).

[98] *Eq.* 10, *Ach.* 864–6; cf. Pl. *Cri.* 54 d. In Pl. *Cra.* 417 e, when Socrates produces the hypothetical word from which he wants to derive *blaberon*, '*boulapteroun*', Hermogenes comments that it sounds like an imitation of the aulos prelude of the *nomos of Athena*.

[99] Hsch.

[100] Hsch. s.v. *krizei*; Diphilus fr. 78. Cf. Festus (Paulus) p. 95 M., '*gingrire* properly refers to the noise made by geese; hence a certain type of small pipes is called *gingrinae*'.

[101] Poll. 4. 72, cf. 73.

[102] Pl. *Symp.* 215 c, cf. *Minos* 318 b.

[103] Arist. *Pol.* 1341ᵃ21; Aesch. fr. 57, Eur. *Hel.* 1351, *Bacch.* 127 (Phrygian pipes), Men. *Theophoroumene* 27 f., etc.; cf. p. 91. Those possessed by Corybantic madness think they hear aulos music (Pl. *Cri.* 54 d; cf. Galen vii. 60 f. K., Aëtius *Iatrica* 6. 8).

[104] 'Hippoc.' *Epidemics* 5. 81.

the listeners out of their minds and setting their feet tapping to the rhythm.[105] But it can also fill the soul with calm if it is played soberly and sweetly.[106] The expert aulete can provide whatever is wanted: he can assuage grief, enhance joy, inflame the lover, exalt the devout.[107]

The vase-painters often give an indication of the effort required to blow the two pipes, by showing the player's cheeks bulging; we have mentioned the use of a device for relieving the cheek muscles of some of this strain. When the instrument fell out of favour in certain Athenian circles in the second half of the fifth century, the tale was invented that Athena herself had thrown it away after she realized how it distorted her features.[108] But there were some who were able to blow strongly while maintaining facial composure.[109] Such was the famous Theban Pronomus, who charmed audiences exceedingly by his facial expression and the whole movement of his body as he played.[110]

This use of body movement to add expressiveness to the performance is said to have been started by a Sicilian aulete, Andron of Catana, and then to have been taken up by Cleolas of Thebes. It was evidently common in the fourth century. Aristotle speaks disparagingly of hack players who roll about if there is reference to a discus, or grab at the chorus-leader if the music is depicting the monster Scylla, as if the audience would not otherwise get the point.[111] As with the kithara, this was an age of showmanship.

We do not know whether Greek pipers employed the technique known as circular breathing, whereby the player breathes in through the nose while continuing to expel air from the reservoir in his mouth and is thus able to sustain an unbroken stream of sound. This is practised by the launeddas-players of Sardinia and the reed-pipers of the Near East, as well as by some Western instrumentalists.[112] It may perhaps have been known in Antiquity as an Arab accomplishment, since the Greeks had a proverbial expression 'an Arabian aulete', applicable to people who chattered on without ever paus-

---

[105] *Subl.* 39. 2.

[106] Plut. *Quaest. conv.* 713 a.

[107] Philostr. *VA* 5. 21. 2–3. Cf. Plut. *Quaest. conv.* 657 a; above, pp. 31, 33.

[108] Melanippides, *PMG* 758, contradicted by Telestes, *PMG* 805. Alcibiades is also said to have rejected the aulos for this among other reasons (Plut. *Alc.* 2. 5).

[109] Poll. 4. 68–9, cf. Philostr. *VA* 5. 21. 4.

[110] See Pl. 27; Paus. 9. 12. 6.

[111] Theophr. fr. 92 W.; Xen. *Symp.* 6. 4; Arist. *Poet.* 1461ᵇ30. So too in a later age, Epiphanius, *Panarion* 25. 4. 10 (i. 272 Holl).

[112] Sachs, *HMI* 91, 248.

ing.[113] However, it is not clear whether the reference is to piping without breath-pauses or just to piping that goes on for hours.[114] Some of the sources that cite the phrase also quote a verse from some comic poet,

> He charges a drachma to pipe, and four to stop.

The bagpipe

One instrument that does play without breath-pauses is the bagpipe, developed from the old reed-blown pipe by the addition of a bag made from the whole skin of a small animal or the bladder of a larger one. This serves as an air reservoir supplying a constant flow of wind. The bag is kept inflated either by a blowpipe or by bellows; the player holds it under his arm and squeezes it to maintain the air pressure. Most bagpipes have two, three, or four sounding pipes, each equipped with its own reed. One of these (or sometimes two) is the 'chanter' or melody pipe which the player fingers, while the others are drones emitting a single continuous note.[115]

The instrument is found over a large area that covers the whole of Europe, western Asia as far as India, and parts of north and east Africa, with many regional variations. It must certainly have had a wide distribution by the early Middle Ages. In Antiquity, however, it is only scantily documented, and it cannot be said to have played any significant part in the history of Greek music. It may not have appeared at all before the second century BC, and even after that it is doubtful how often it was seen. It seems to have been in the main an instrument of low-class urban mendicants and mountebanks, at first from the Near East.[116] The antiquarian writers of the late second century AD, Athenaeus and Pollux, who are so industrious in listing all the different types of auloi and other instruments that they can find in previous literature, say nothing of the bagpipe. But we know it existed in the Mediterranean world before their time.

Perhaps the first clear evidence for it is provided by a Hellenistic

---

[113] First alluded to by Cantharus fr. 1, where Kassel and Austin cite other testimonia.

[114] The last movement of Holst's *Beni Mora* suite commemorates the composer's experience of hearing an Arab in Algeria playing the same phrase on a bamboo flute for over two hours non-stop.

[115] See in general Baines, *Bagpipes*, and in A. Baines (ed.), *Musical Instruments Through the Ages*, 224–7; F. Collinson, *The Bagpipe* (London, 1975); *NG* ii. 19–32.

[116] Cf. Baines, *Bagpipes*, 66 f.

gem depicting an elderly satyr who sits in a pose recalling Rodin's *Thinker*. Behind him is a tree, from which hang a panpipe and a bag-pipe. The latter has two chanters and a bass drone, all flared at the end. It looks as if this may have been a mouth-blown bagpipe, but the inflating arrangements are not clear.[117]

Then there are three figurines from late Ptolemaic Egypt, each depicting a man in Syrian dress who is playing or preparing to play two (if not three) instruments at once. In his left hand he holds a pan-pipe. Under his left arm he holds an inflated skin bag, into the end of which is fixed a pipe that extends to his right hand. In at least one of the figurines the pipe is clearly marked with finger-holes. In another—the only one where the feet are not broken off—the man's right foot presses down on a clapper, or more probably a bellows supplying the bag with air. In this figurine he is assisted by a naked boy or dwarf, who also treads down on the pedal while at the same time clashing a small pair of cymbals together.[118] The bagpipe repre-sented in these models is of a very basic design, inflated by bellows, not by a blowpipe, and with a single exit-pipe which could function either as a chanter or as a drone accompanying the melody of the panpipe. It can be compared in the latter respect with the native Indian bagpipe, which has only one exit-pipe, the finger-holes of which are often stopped up with wax so that it becomes a drone accompanying another instrument. The Indian bagpipe, however, is mouth-blown. Bellows-blown bagpipes are most characteristic of eastern Europe, though also found in France, northern England and lowland Scotland, and Ireland.

Nero, ever eager to display his artistic talents, performed publicly on a bagpipe, rather to the amusement of his empire. Dio Chryso-stom refers to his competence at piping both with his mouth (that is, with ordinary auloi) and by the method of putting a bag under his arm to avoid the uncomely distortion of the face that normal piping involves. Clearly his bagpipe, like that of the Syrian one-man band,

---

[117] See Pl. 28; J. Boardman, *Engraved Gems: The Ionides Collection* (London, 1968), 21 f., 93, and pl. 16; *Antiquity* 43 (1969), pl. xlv *b*. Professor Boardman tells me that the gem is 'more likely to be earlier than the first century BC than not', but that these gems are 'horribly difficult to date'.

[118] This one is illustrated in Sachs, *HMI*, facing p. 144, though he (143) erro-neously took the bag to be joined up with the panpipe to make a sort of organ; and in Baines, *Bagpipes*, 65; Collinson, *The Bagpipe*, facing p. 28; all three in H. Hickmann, *Musikgeschichte in Bildern*, ii. 1: *Ägypten* (Leipzig, 1961), 95, and in *Antiquity* 43 (1969), pl. xliv–xlv, where there is also a possible fourth example from Roman Gloucester (Collinson, *Antiquity* 43, 305–8).

was bellows-operated. Dio does not seem to know a name for the instrument; but both a Greek and a Latin word for a bagpiper were current in Italy.[119] In the following century a papyrus fragment from the Arsinoite nome of Egypt unexpectedly presents no less than nine bagpipers in a list of musicians (all pipers of various kinds) and others.[120]

A much earlier allusion to a Greek bagpipe has been suspected in a passage of Aristophanes' *Lysistrata*, where a Spartan character calls to an attendant to take up the 'puffers' (*phūsātēria*) so that he can sing and perform one of his native dances. An Athenian endorses the appeal, saying 'Yes, yes, take up the *phūsallides*'. The first word could refer equally well to ordinary blown pipes or to bellows, while the second is elsewhere used of puffed-up things such as foam bubbles, and would seem more appropriate to something visibly swelling when inflated than to plain auloi. On the other hand, if some sort of Spartan bagpipe is meant, it is hard to see why *phūsallis*, which would denote the bag, is in the plural.[121]

REEDLESS PIPES

The panpipe

The panpipe consists of a set of tubes of reed or other material, with no finger-holes but each having a different resonating length and so yielding a different note, all fastened together side by side. They are stopped up at the lower end (at least in Europe) and played by blowing across the open upper end. The Greek name for the instrument is *sȳrinx*, a term which we have already met with a different connotation in connection with the aulos. Since it basically means

[119] *Ascaules, CIL* 4.636 (graffito in a Pompeian brothel) and Mart. 10.3.8; *utricularius*, Suet. *Ner.* 54. The Dio passage is *Or.* 71.9 (ii. 184.3 Arnim). Galen iv. 459 K. speaks of 'blowing *askoi* (skin bags)'.

[120] G. A. Petropoulos, *Papyri Societatis Archaeologicae Atheniensis* i (1939), no. 43 verso (AD 131–2).

[121] Ar. *Lys.* 1242–6. There is nothing at all to be said for seeing a reference to Theban bagpipes in another Aristophanic passage, *Ach.* 863 (Bergler, van Leeuwen). A 5 cm. tube, tapered at one end, with a bore reducing from 12 to 8 mm., found at Ephesus and dating from before 550, was described by D. G. Hogarth as 'mouthpiece of bagpipe(?)' (*Excavations at Ephesus: The Archaic Artemisia*, 194 and pl. xxxvii), but nothing seems to point particularly to this identification. Ps.-Arist. *Pr.* 19.50 remarks that an inflated skin bag will sound an octave lower than another of half the size; but the reference is more likely to drumming than to bagpiping.

'tube', we might expect the plural *sȳringes* as the name of the pan-pipe, and this is in fact found down to the end of the fifth century.[122]

The panpipe is a very simple instrument with a wide distribution, from central Europe across Asia to Melanesia and western Latin America. It was certainly invented at a very early epoch. Bone tubes from European sites of the Upper Palaeolithic period have been interpreted as belonging to panpipes, and the instrument is perhaps to be recognized in an object held by a man participating in a ritual hunters' dance in a wall painting at Çatal Hüyük in eastern Anatolia, dated to the fifty-ninth century BC.[123] It is represented among the Cycladic figurines of the third millennium, and specimens made from bird bones, dating from around 2000, have been found at Mariupol in the southern Ukraine and elsewhere in the former Soviet Union.[124] It is not attested for the high civilizations of the Near East; perhaps they had discarded it in favour of their more developed wind instruments. But it was current in the first millennium BC not only in Greece but in north Syria, the Balkans, north-eastern Europe, and Italy.[125]

In Greece it had a rather lowly status, appearing most often as the characteristic instrument of herdsmen and herdsmen's gods.[126] We hear of it also in other (mythical) contexts of spontaneous popular music-making: by the camp-fires of the Trojans and their allies, on shipboard, or at weddings, in each case together with auloi.[127] In the Archaic period, at least, it might sometimes be set beside the lyre and the aulos as a representative of musical activity, even among the gods. On the François Vase the Muse Calliope herself plays a panpipe as the gods arrive for the wedding of Peleus and Thetis.[128]

[122] *Hymn. Hom. Merc.* 512(?), Eur. *Ion* 498, *IA* 1038; the singular first unequivocally in Ion, *TrGF* 19 F 45, Soph. *Phil.* 213, Eur. *Or.* 145, *IA* 1085.

[123] *NG* vi. 312; J. Mellaart, *Anatolian Studies* 16 (1966), 189 and pl. LXI*a*.

[124] Paquette, 63 fig. 9; A. Häusler, *Acta Musicologica* 32 (1960), 153–5; Aign, 298.

[125] 8th-c. shaman's grave in Poland, *NG* vi. 313; Syrian relief, *c*.700?, *NG* i. 391; bronze urns from the Illyrian Hallstatt culture, 6th–5th c., *NG* xiv. 159 and 160 fig. 2; Etruscan monuments. At a later period Pollux (4. 77) associates the panpipe with the (continental) Celts and Britons.

[126] *Il.* 18. 526, ps.-Aesch. *PV* 574, Ion, *TrGF* 19 F 45, Eur. *Alc.* 576, *Phaethon* 71, *IA* 576, 1085, Pl. *Resp.* 399 d, Aristox. fr. 95, etc. Invented by Hermes, *Hymn. Hom. Merc.* 511 f.; played by Pan, *Hymn. Hom. Pan.* 15, Eur. *El.* 702 f., *Ion* 498, *Bacch.* 952, etc.; by Silenus, Pl. *Symp.* 215 b.

[127] *Il.* 10. 13, 18. 606 a (interpolated, *PBerol.* 9774); Eur. *Tro.* 127, *IT* 1125; ps.-Hes. *Sc.* 278, Eur. *IA* 1038.

[128] This is also the wedding Euripides is referring to in *IA* 1038: behind both, perhaps, lies the epic account in the *Cypria*.

The sixth-century statue of Apollo on Delos held the three Graces in one of his hands, and they were equipped, one with a lyre, one with a panpipe, and one with auloi.[129] These three instruments are said to have accompanied the ceremonial bringing of sacred objects to Delos from the Hyperboreans; and in the Ephesian cult of Artemis, too, the panpipe may have become established in the ritual.[130] In Athenian life, however, the panpipe seems to have played almost no part. It is seldom represented in Attic vase-painting, and never (so far as I know) in scenes from real life. It is more popular with the fourth-century Italian painters, but usually in the hands of Pan, Silenus, etc. In the later poets and novelists it is often brought in as a picturesque feature of bucolic and other rustic settings.

The number of tubes shown in art varies between three and nine in the Archaic period, four and ten in the Classical period, and four and eighteen in the Hellenistic period. Two Greek sources mention a panpipe with nine 'voices', while seven is the conventional number in Latin verse.[131] The Classical Greek panpipe had a rectangular shape, all the tubes being cut to the same length and then blocked with wax to the depth necessary to give the required notes.[132] This is also the shape represented in the early Cycladic figurine and in the Syrian relief mentioned above. The Hallstatt and Etruscan representations, on the other hand, show the tubes graded in length, and in the later Hellenistic period this became the usual form of the Greek as of the Roman instrument.[133]

The pipes are regularly described as being stuck together with wax. The assembly was reinforced by a cloth binding or a wooden frame or spars.[134] Sometimes, at least in the Hellenistic and Roman ages, panpipes were made from a solid block of wood, ivory, or other

[129] Ps.-Plut. *De mus.* 1136 a; cf. Frazer on Paus. 9. 35. 3.

[130] Ps.-Plut. *De mus.* 1136 ab; Call. *Dian.* 243.

[131] Ps.-Theoc. *Id.* 8. 18, cf. Gow ad loc.; Longus, *Daphnis and Chloe* 1. 15; Verg. *Ecl.* 2. 36, Ov. *Met.* 2. 682, Calp. 4. 45.

[132] See Pl. 29; ps.-Arist. *Pr.* 19. 23; ps.-Theoc. *Id.* 8. 19 with schol.; A. Furtwängler, *Kleine Schriften*, i (Munich, 1912), 157 f.; G. Haas, *Die Syrinx in der griechischen Bildkunst* (Vienna, 1985).

[133] Ps.-Theoc. *Syrinx*, Poll. 4. 69, Achilles Tatius 8. 6. 4; Verg. *Ecl.* 2. 36, Ov. *Met.* 1. 711, etc.; A. S. F. Gow, *Journ. Phil.* 33 (1913–14), 135 f. and *Theocritus* (Cambridge, 1952), ii. 554. There is one isolated example of the graded type from the Classical period (Louvre CA 1959, *c.* 460 BC; Haas, op. cit. fig. 94). For examples of other, irregular shapes see Reinach in Dar.–Sag. iv. 1598; Haas, op. cit. The name *pteron* 'wing' given to a blown instrument by Anon. Bellerm. 17 must refer to an asymmetrical panpipe, the shape of which Poll. 4. 69 likens to a bird's wing.

[134] Poll. 4. 69, Hsch. s.v. *plastinx*; Reinach, loc. cit. 1596 f.; Paquette, 63 f.

material, with bored holes.[135] Certain vase-paintings show the top edge of each tube scooped out to a cup shape as seen from back and front.[136]

The player held the instrument in both hands, moving it from side to side as he blew across the tops of the pipes. The method of playing naturally favoured gliding up and down the scale, as it was more difficult to dart between non-adjacent notes than in the case of the lyre or aulos. Nevertheless, we do hear in one passage how the player 'jumps from one note to another, wherever the construction of the music summons him'.[137] The instrument was quite small, and played in a high register. When it accompanied a singer, it did so in a higher octave.[138] Aristotle, however, was acquainted with its use as a solo instrument. Despite its general neglect in polite society, there appear to have been a few executants who cultivated it for public display. A Hellenistic inscription from Magnesia, specifying arrangements for the festival of Zeus the City Saviour, prescribes that an aulete, a panpiper (*sȳristēs*), and a citharist are to be laid on to entertain the crowd.[139]

The flute

The flute, like the panpipe, dates from time immemorial. Bone pipes with one or more finger-holes are known from palaeolithic, mesolithic, and neolithic sites.[140] Among the ancient civilizations of the Near East, however, the flute was prominent only in Egypt; there are Sumerian and Akkadian representations, but they are rare.[141] The Egyptian (and Mesopotamian) flute was long and narrow, made of cane or metal, with from three to eight finger-holes towards the lower end. Although held sideways, to the player's left, it was end-blown, not side-blown; that is, the flautist blew across the open end of the tube (as with the panpipe), not across a hole in the side.[142]

In Greece the flute is not attested before the Hellenistic age, and

[135] Reinach, loc. cit.
[136] Paquette, 61 pl. III, 64. This is one of various rim shapes found among the world's flute-type instruments; see *NG* vi. 664, and below, p. 113. It occurs in the Romanian panpipe; see Welch, 270.
[137] Achilles Tatius 8. 6. 6.   [138] Ps.-Arist. *Pr.* 19. 14.
[139] Arist. *Poet.* 1447ª26; *SIG* 589. 46 (196 BC). (It is possible, however, that the *sȳristēs* could be a flautist; see below.) Cf. also Diod. 17. 72. 5 (Alexander at Persepolis); *SIG* 1257 (Ephesus, 1st c. AD); Lucian *Syr. D.* 43; Chariton 6. 2. 4; John Chrysostom, *Homil. 37 in Matth.*, *Bibl. Patr.* i. 523.
[140] Baines, *Woodwind*, 171 f.; *NG* vi. 312 f.
[141] Sachs, *HMI* 71 f.; Rimmer, 19.   [142] Sachs, *HMI* 90; *NG* vi. 71–4.

then but seldom. Occasionally a distinction is made between the 'multiple-stem *sȳrinx*' (i.e. panpipe) and a 'single-stem *sȳrinx*', which must be a flute with finger-holes.[143] 'Single-stem *sȳrinx*' is given in lexica as a meaning of the word *ȳnx*, which must accordingly have been one sort of flute. *Iynx* is also the name of a bird, the wryneck, whose call is said to imitate 'the transverse aulos': this presumably refers to a flute, not to the instrument described on p. 93, and where *plagios aulos* or *plagiaulos* appears as the source of a soft wind-like sound, or as a rustic instrument in settings appropriate for the panpipe, we must again interpret it as a flute.[144] Another term that probably designates a flute is *phōtinx*, which Hesychius rather wildly defines as 'a *sȳrinx*, a transverse aulos, like a sort of trumpet' (because blown without a reed?). The *phōtinx* was current at Alexandria, and the word perhaps incorporates an Egyptian root with the Greek suffix -*inx* on the analogy of *sȳrinx et al.*[145]

Representations in art show that there was both an end-blown and a side-blown flute.[146] A specimen of the latter type, found at Halicarnassus, is preserved in the British Museum. It has a scooped mouthpiece raised slightly from the side of the tube. A replica was found to have a soft, cooing tone.[147]

The pitch pipe

A lexical source records that a chorus-trainer might give his choir their starting note 'by piping on the so-called *epitonion*'.[148] This is

[143] Euphorion ap. Ath. 184a (Hermes as inventor, or alternatively certain Thracians).

[144] *Iynx*: *Anecd. Bekk.* 265. 21 = *Etym. Magn.* 480. 1; Ael. *NA* 6. 19. The melodious soughing of the wind in the trees of the Isles of the Blest likened to 'the calm piping of transverse auloi': Lucian, *Ver. Hist.* 2. 5. Rustic: ps.-Theoc. *Id.* 20. 29, Bion fr. 10. 7 Gow, Philodemus *Anth. Pal.* 11. 34. 5 = *GP* 3292, Longus 1. 4. 3, 4. 26. 2, Heliodorus 5. 14. 2; invented by Midas, Pliny *HN* 7. 204.

[145] Earliest attestation Posidonius fr. 86 Th.; invented by Osiris, Juba, *FGrH* 275 F 16 ('the *plagiaulos* called *phōtinx*'); Alexandrian, Ath. 175f ('the *phōtinx* aulos'); made of lotus-wood, ibid. 182d (cf. Poll. 4. 74, Libyan *plagiaulos* = lotus-wood aulos); used in enticing crabs from their lairs, Plut. *De soll. an.* 961e, Ael. *NA* 6. 31; grouped with *plagiaulos* but distinct from it, Nicom. p. 243. 16. Apuleius, *Met.* 11. 9, describes pipers in the worship of Sarapis who play an *obliquus calamus* that extends past their ear. The 'Libyan lotus' that appears several times in Euripides is merely a poetic equivalent of the aulos.

[146] See Howard, 14f.

[147] C. T. Newton, *A History of Discoveries at Halicarnassus, Cnidus, and Branchidæ*, ii. 1 (London, 1862), 339; Welch, 248f. Now BM 1976. 1–4.2.

[148] *Etymologicum Gudianum* cod. z s.v. *apotomon*, p. 177. 12 de Stefani. The name is formed from *tonos* 'pitch'.

likely to have been a reedless pipe, since the pitch of a reed pipe would be more liable to inconstancy. If it was the same as the *tonarium* on which C. Gracchus had a slave quietly give him appropriate pitch levels while he was orating,[149] it could sound different notes. It was presumably a kind of flute.

The organ

The organ was invented by the brilliant engineer Ctesibius, who worked in Alexandria in the time of Ptolemy II.[150] His wife may have given recitals on it.[151] Apart from that, we do not know by what stages it achieved popularity. But from the first century BC it does begin to appear as an instrument with some currency, and it enjoyed great favour at Rome and in the imperial provinces. It was usually known as the *hydraulis*, *hydraulos*, or *hydraulikon organon* ('hydraulic instrument').[152]

Our knowledge of its construction is derived mainly from detailed descriptions by Heron of Alexandria and (a more advanced model) Vitruvius. There are over two dozen artistic representations, which give us a good idea of its external appearance. And we have all the metal parts from a small organ which was presented to the fire brigade at Aquincum near Budapest in AD 228 and which met its end when, sadly, their premises burned down.[153]

Sound production was through a set of bronze pipes, graded in length as in the late Hellenistic panpipe and standing upright over the keyboard. Their tops are usually shown as making a straight diagonal line, but occasionally describe an upward curve. In most representations the longer pipes are to the player's left. In many organs of the Roman period there were several ranks of pipes. Vitruvius appears to speak of organs with four, six, or eight ranks. The

---

[149] Cic. *De Or.* 3. 225, Quint. *Inst.* 1. 10. 27.

[150] No credence can be given to the attribution to a later barber of the same name (Aristocles ap. Ath. 174b–e). See K. Tittel, *RE* ix. 63–7; J. Perrot, *L'Orgue de ses origines hellénistiques à la fin du XIIIe siècle* (Paris, 1965), 26–32.

[151] If it is legitimate to transfer to Ctesibius the engineer what Aristocles said of Ctesibius the barber, that he taught his wife Thais to play the instrument.

[152] Two 3rd-c. sources abbreviate it to *hydra*, while from the 4th c. on it is sometimes called simply *organum*. Pollux 4. 70 for some unexplained reason calls it the 'Etruscan aulos'.

[153] Heron, *Pneumatica* 1. 42, Vitr. 10. 8; H. Degering, *Die Orgel: ihre Erfindung und ihre Geschichte bis zur Karolingerzeit* (Münster, 1905), 67–86 and plates; Perrot, op. cit. 103–40; W. Walcker-Mayer, *Die römische Orgel von Aquincum* (Stuttgart, 1970); M. Kaba, same title (*Musicologia Hungarica* n.f. 6, Kassel, Basle, and London, 1980).

Aquincum organ had four ranks, with thirteen pipes in each; the pipes of one rank were open at the top, the rest stopped. Each rank could be closed off separately by means of sliding shutters operated from the side. The function of the different ranks is debated. Some think that they were tuned to different modal scales, since some sources refer to the organ's ability to play in various modes.[154] In some cases the ranks may have played in different registers: the stopped pipes of the Aquincum organ would have given notes an octave lower than open ones of the same length and diameter, and in a lamp from Carthage modelled in the form of an organ the front rank has about half and the second rank two-thirds of the height of the third, suggesting registers an octave and a fifth higher.[155]

Organ pipes seem usually to have had flues, not reeds. This is true of the Aquincum organ's pipes, and flues are often represented in the works of art. It was, after all, the panpipe that provided the obvious model for the array of tuned pipes, and Philo of Byzantium, a pupil of Ctesibius, refers to his organ as 'the panpipe that is played with the hands, which we call *hydraulis*'.[156] On the other hand, Vitruvius speaks of the pipes as having *lingulae*, 'tongues', which should mean 'reeds', and it is perfectly plausible that reed pipes were sometimes used.[157]

Under the pipes there were perforated sliders operated by the keyboard, and under them a horizontal wind canal (one for each rank of pipes). When a key was depressed, a slider was pushed into position so as to release pressurized air from the wind canal into the pipe. When the key was released, a spring pulled the slider back again and shut off the air.

The wind canals were supplied from a dome-shaped chamber lower down. The upper part of the dome contained air which was being pumped in through another duct. The lower part contained water which was admitted at the base from a surrounding cistern.

---

[154] Tert. *De Anim.* 14. 4, Anon. Bellerm. 28. Cf. Walcker-Mayer, op. cit. 54–79; *NG* viii. 834, xiii. 725.

[155] Perrot, op. cit., pl. xi.6, xii, and p. 131.

[156] *Belopoïika* 61 (*Berl. Abh.* 1918 no. 16, 66).

[157] Vitr. 10. 8. 4. However, Simpl. *in Phys.* p. 681. 7 (*Comm. in Arist. Graeca*, ix) refers to the organ as having 'tongues' of trumpets or auloi fitted into the holes of the casing; trumpets do not have reeds, so the meaning here is presumably just 'mouthpieces' (cf. Heron *Pneum.* 1. 16, Poll. 4. 85). Nothing can be inferred from the fact that organ pipes are called *auloi*, and that the verb *aulein* is several times used of the organ's sound by Constantine Porphyrogenitus (*De Caerimoniis* 1. 5, 44; 2. 48, 50, 73, 79).

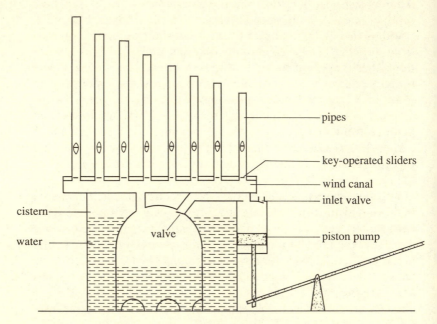

pipes

key-operated sliders

wind canal

inlet valve

cistern

water

valve

piston pump

FIG. 4.2. Hydrostatic organ

The water level in the cistern was higher than that in the dome, and therefore the water in the dome exerted a constant upward pressure on the air above it. In this way the intermittent inflow of air from the pump was converted into a steady flow up to the wind canals and pipes. (A valve prevented its return up the duct leading from the pump.)

The air pump was itself a revolutionary invention of Ctesibius', with practical applications that have been exploited ever since. It consisted of a piston in a cylindrical chamber at the side of the cistern, and it was operated by a long lever supported on a pivot. (In the later organ there were two pumps, one at each side.) The organist had a young assistant to work the lever up and down. The cistern was housed in a handsome cabinet, generally square or hexagonal in plan, up to a metre high, rather less in diameter but mounted on a broader platform for stability. In most cases the standing player could see comfortably over the top of the pipes. From the fourth century AD, however, some taller organs are depicted.[158]

The player used both hands,[159] and we can assume that he often allowed two or more pipes to speak at once. There is some evidence for the use of octave or other concordant chords on the organ,[160] and it may be that some instruments were designed to play in parallel fifths or octaves by having ranks of pipes tuned at these intervals apart.[161] With more than one rank in play, pressing one key would automatically produce a chord.

Certainly the sounds of the organ were considered to be highly agreeable.[162] The Romans, at least, were also impressed by its loudness. Seneca groups it with horns and trumpets as producing a louder sound than the human mouth can. Nero, who was greatly interested in the organ and had ambitions to perform on it before the public, is said to have sent an urgent summons to his Privy Council in the night, only to announce that he had discovered a way to make the organ sound both louder and more harmonious.[163]

One development that increased the instrument's power—we cannot say whether it had anything to do with Nero, but it came not later than the second century, and must have been due to someone familiar with the bagpipe—was the elimination of the water tank in favour of a wind bag inflated by bellows and compressed to force air out to the pipes.[164] This made for a much lighter and more easily transportable instrument, not prone to plumbing problems (corrosion, leaks, freezing), and yet capable of producing a stronger head of air. Pollux characterizes the bellows organ as smaller than the

[158] For further mechanical details and diagrams see Perrot, op. cit. 49–70; Peter Williams, *A New History of the Organ* (London and Boston, 1980), 22–8; *NG* viii. 833f., xiii. 711–13, 725f.

[159] Cf. Philo of Byzantium, *Belopoiika* 61, Tert. *De Bapt.* 8. 1, Julian, *Anth. Pal.* 9. 365. 6; often suggested by artistic evidence, though the player is generally hidden below the shoulders.

[160] Ath. 174b, August. *Enarratio in Psalmos* 150. 7, Prudent. *Apotheosis* 389.

[161] Cf. above on the lamp from Carthage.

[162] Cic. *Tusc.* 3. 43 (a base pleasure); Vitr. 10. 7. 4; Pliny *HN* 9. 24 (the favourite instrument of dolphins); Ath. 174a (the erudite diners hear the sounds of an organ coming from a neighbour's); Theodoretus in *PG* lxxxiii. 589a; Cassiod. *in Psalmos* 150. 4 (*PL* lxx. 1053a).

[163] Sen. *QNat.* 2. 6. 5, Suet. *Ner.* 41, 54; Cass. Dio 63. 26. 4.

[164] The replacement of Ctesibius' plunger pump by bellows is actually independent of the replacement of the water tank by a wind bag. It is quite likely that some water organs were operated by bellows; the pumps were more difficult to make and to maintain.

hydrostatic type,[165] and the little Aquincum organ seems to have operated without water, since no trace of a cistern was found. By the fourth century, however, more massive bag organs were being built. The emperor Julian describes one in an epigram: it has a 'cavern' of oxhide, and the organist's young assistants 'squeeze out' the music by 'dancing', whether on the wind bag or on the bellows.[166] Ammianus Marcellinus writes of the construction of carriage-sized organs and lyres; Claudian of the organ's countless voices and thunderous tones.[167] Finally we hear of the organ having a wind chest made from two elephant hides and being fed by twelve bellows, producing a roar like thunder that could be heard more than a mile away.[168]

The hydrostatic organ was ousted by the pneumatic type; it was the latter that returned to western Europe from Byzantium in the eighth century and evolved by degrees into the modern organ.[169] But Ctesibius' basic conception—the provision of a continuous wind supply to an array of tuned pipes, controlled from a keyboard—remains unchanged to this day.

The trumpet

It is by courtesy that we give attention to this instrument, as it was not used for musical purposes but only for giving signals, especially for battle and in certain ritual and ceremonial contexts.

The Greek trumpet (*salpinx*) consisted of a fairly long, straight tube of narrow, cylindrical bore, ending in a prominent tulip-shaped bell. It was generally of bronze, with (according to Pollux) a bone mouthpiece. Vase-paintings suggest a length of 80 to 120 cm. The trumpeter usually holds the instrument in one hand and plants the other hand on his hip or the side of his rib-cage. He is not infrequently shown wearing a *phorbeiā* (cf. p. 89).[170] This device, as

---

[165] Poll. 4. 70.

[166] *Anth. Pal.* 9. 365 (misinterpreted by Nonnus, *Dion.* 3. 236–8, as if the 'dancing' were that of the player's fingers). Theodoretus (*PG* lxxxiii. 589b) also refers to the wind bag being 'squeezed out' by human feet, and this is depicted on the obelisk set up in 390 by Theodosius in the Hippodrome at Constantinople: the bag trails out of the organ along the ground, and two children are standing on it (Perrot, op. cit. 112 and pl. iv). Cf. also the illustration from a 12th-c. MS in St John's College, Cambridge, Perrot, 349f. and pl. xxv. 3.   [167] Amm. Marc. 14. 6. 18, Claud. *Carm.* 17. 316–19.

[168] Ps.-Hieron. *Ep.* 23. 1 (*PL* xxx. 213b); Perrot, op. cit. 192f. with the MS illustration pl. xxii. 2.

[169] Cf. Degering and Perrot (as n. 153); Tittel, *RE* ix. 73, 77; *NG* viii. 835, xiii. 724–7.

[170] See Pl. 30; Paquette 74–83; Poll. 4. 85. The 7th-c. Aristonothus crater (Paquette, 79 T8) appears to show a trumpet of exceptional length, at least 150 cm.,

we have mentioned, is first attested in south Anatolia. The Anatolian trumpet, however, like the Mesopotamian, seems to have been of conical form.[171] The Greek trumpet more resembles the Egyptian, which was cylindrical with a conical bell.[172] The Greeks themselves considered the instrument to be an Etruscan invention.[173] Aristarchus, the great Alexandrian scholar, observed that Homer's heroes never employ the trumpet, although the poet himself knows it and makes use of it in a simile.[174] This does indeed suggest that the conventions of epic battle narrative were formed at a time when the trumpet was not yet in common use.

Its loudness made the trumpet ideal for giving signals at a distance or to a large crowd. It could summon people to assembly,[175] start a chariot race,[176] co-ordinate the efforts of men launching a big ship or struggling with a heavy siege engine.[177] It could give signals for various other things.[178] But what is most often mentioned is its giving the signal to attack on the field of battle.[179] So regular is this association that trumpets are thought of as becoming redundant in peacetime.[180] However, they did have a role in certain cults. A black-figure lekythos shows a trumpeter heading a sacrificial procession, and later inscriptions from several places refer in this connection to the 'holy trumpeter'.[181] The Argives summoned Dionysus out of the water with small trumpets.[182]

---

but it may be out of proportion. An ivory trumpet of nearly this length, with a funnel-shaped bronze bell, is preserved in the Boston Museum of Fine Arts; it was presumably made for ceremonial purposes, and its date is unknown. See L. D. Caskey, *AJArch.* 41 (1937), 525–7.

[171] See Rimmer, 29 f., 37 f. and pl. viiib, xvi; *NG* i. 388, 391 f.

[172] H. Hickmann, *La Trompette dans l'Égypte ancienne* (Cairo, 1946).

[173] Aesch. *Eum.* 567, Soph. *Aj.* 17 with schol., schol. *Il.* 18. 219, Poll. 4. 85, etc.

[174] *Il.* 18. 219 with schol. [175] Aesch. loc. cit., cf. Bacchyl. 18. 3.

[176] Black-figure pot lid, Louvre 182; Soph. *El.* 711; cf. Paus. 6. 13. 9.

[177] Callixenus, *FGrH* 627 F 1 p. 162. 29 J.; Ath. 415 a. A relief from the palace of Sennacherib (705–681 bc) shows an army of men hauling and levering along a colossal stone bull, with four trumpeters giving signals to synchronize them (BM 124820; Rimmer, 38).

[178] Ar. *Ach.* 1001, Eur. *Tro.* 1267, Thuc. 6. 32. 1, Xen. *Hipparchicus* 3. 12. At Macedon it announced the last course of dinner (Hippolochus ap. Ath. 130 b).

[179] Ibycus(?) *SLG* 166. 6, Simon. fr. eleg. 7. 4 West², Aesch. *Pers.* 395, *Sept.* 394, Soph. *Aj.* 291, etc. When ps.-Arist. *De audibilibus* 803ᵃ25 refers to trumpets being played at low volume by revellers on their way to visit friends after parties, we should probably not think of 'serenades' (Maux, *RE* iA. 2010) but of a mock assault.

[180] Aesch. fr. 451 n. 9, Bacchyl. fr. 4. 75, Ar. *Pax* 1240.

[181] London B 648; *hierosalpinktēs*, see LSJ. Cf. Poll. 4. 86–7; L. Ziehen, *Hermes* 66 (1931), 231 ff. [182] Socrates, *FGrH* 310 F 2 with Jacoby.

Besides the fundamental note of the pipe, which from its length would have lain somewhere in the range *c* to *g*, the ancient trumpeter would certainly have been accustomed to produce one or two (if not more) of the higher notes of the harmonic series.[183] His trumpet-calls could thus be differentiated not only by rhythmic but also by melodic pattern. Bacchylides speaks of the trumpet 'shrieking out the song of war'. An early fifth-century painting of a trumpeting Amazon is surrounded by the meaningless syllables TOTĒ TOTOTE, which apparently represent her fanfare.[184] Ennius famously rendered the trumpet's alarum as *taratantara*, which at least suggests a definite rhythmic figure and, to a specialist, a technique of tonguing.[185] A trumpeter also knew how to 'sound the retreat', and according to later authorities there were distinct trumpet-calls for various commands that might be given.[186] Plutarch tells of a Roman barber who had a jay that was an excellent mimic of all it heard. One day some trumpeters performed outside, whereupon the jay fell into complete silence. Some conjectured that it had been poisoned by a rival barber, others that it had been deafened by the trumpets and had lost its voice together with its hearing. But after a period of meditation the bird suddenly burst out in a perfect imitation of the trumpets, singing 'their tunes with all their punctuations, modulations, and note-patterns'.[187]

From the fourth century on we find records of competitions for trumpeters at games. We do not know by what criteria they were judged. The chief one may have been simply volume, as apparently in the parallel contests for town criers.[188] Seventeen prizes in the late fourth century were accumulated by Herodorus of Megara, a man of

---

[183] Cf. p. 101; Baines, *Brass*, 27–31.

[184] Bacchyl. 18. 3; 'a song not of the lyre', Arist. *Rh.* 1408ᵃ9; Antip. Sid. *HE* 178. The painting is a black-figure epinetron by the Sappho Painter, Eleusis 907. A. Bélis, *BCH* 108 (1984), 99–109, makes a bold attempt to identify the notes; she relies on the use of similar syllables in the 'solmization' system attested at a much later period (below, p. 265).

[185] Ennius, *Ann.* 451 Skutsch, with his note, p. 608; Baines, *Brass* 63; P. Bate in *NG* xix. 60, '*Tonguing*. In playing mouth-blown wind instruments, the technique by which detached notes, or the first notes of phrases, are given a clean start. . . . In playing the flute or cup-mouthpiece instruments [this would probably include the Classical trumpet. MLW] the tongue is placed against the palate behind the upper teeth [and withdrawn sharply]. The movement is similar to that employed in forming the consonant "T".'

[186] Thuc. 5. 10. 3, Xen. *An.* 4. 4. 22, Poll. 4. 86, Aristid. Quint. p. 62. 11–19; later historians cited by Reinach in Dar.–Sag. v. 525. Cf. also Tymnes, *HE* 3603.

[187] *De soll. an.* 973 b–e.   [188] Cf. Poll. 4. 91.

heroic frame and appetite who wore a lion-skin, slept on a bear-skin, could sound two trumpets at once, and blew so loudly that it was painful to be in the vicinity.[189] Other champions are said to have been audible at a distance of fifty stades, that is, some nine or ten kilometres.[190]

Conchs and horns

Certain sea shells and animal horns require only the making of a mouth-hole to become natural trumpets, and they have been put to this use from the earliest times. The most suitable kinds of shell are the triton ('trumpet shell'), the cassis ('helmet shell'), and the strombus ('true conch').[191] Side-blown triton shells had a role in Minoan cult.[192] In Classical Greek literature shell trumpets are occasionally mentioned as being used by common people, especially rustics, for attracting the attention of neighbours, etc.[193] They are also attributed to sea deities such as Tritons and Nereids, and to some foreign peoples not civilized enough to have war trumpets.[194] We hear too of children blowing through limpets and mussels.[195]

The cow-horn (*keras*) likewise served as a poor man's trumpet.[196] Its wide conical bore gave it a softer-edged tone than the cylindrical trumpet. The author of the Aristotelian *De audibilibus* comments on its acoustic properties, and recommends baking the horn to improve its sonority.[197] But it could not rival the *salpinx* for loudness, which was what the Greeks most wanted from these signalling instruments, and they saw no point in imitating the shape in metal.

---

[189] Ath. 414f–415a, Poll. 4. 89.

[190] Poll. 4. 88.

[191] Baines, *Brass*, 42–4.

[192] M. P. Nilsson, *The Minoan-Mycenaean Religion*, 2nd edn. (Lund, 1950), 153 f.; Aign, 49.

[193] Archil. fr. 214, 'Theog.' 1229 f. (a party guest summoned home), Eur. *IT* 303, Theoc. *Id.* 9. 25 with Gow, Plut. *Quaest. conv.* 713 b, Naumachius 62 f. Heitsch.

[194] Moschus, *Europa* 123 f., etc., and art from the 4th c.; Theoc. *Id.* 22. 75, Lycoph. *Alex.* 250, Sext. Emp. *Math.* 6. 24, Heliodorus 9. 17. 1 (cf. *CQ* 40 (1990) 287). On a late 6th-c. cup by the Nicosthenes Painter (Castle Ashby 57; Paquette, 83 T15) a conch is blown by a young man who holds a spear and walks between a winged horse and a fully equipped hoplite.

[195] Alc. 359 (cf. *ZPE* 80 (1990) 6), Dicaearchus fr. 99 W.

[196] Xen. *An.* 2. 2. 4; 7. 3. 32 (Thracian); Polyb. 26. 1. 4; vase-paintings in Paquette, 72 f.; in general, Baines, *Brass*, 44–8.

[197] *De audibilibus* 802ª17 ff., ᵇ1 ff., 803ª33. Cf. Baines, 44, 'an animal horn is prepared for blowing by first removing the bony core with hot water or simply leaving the horn exposed to the air and flies'.

The bull-roarer

Our final 'wind' instrument, the only one that is not blown, has even less in the way of musical credentials than the cow-horn and the conch. It is what is known to anthropologists as the bull-roarer, and to the Greeks as the *rhombos*. It consists of a shaped piece of wood whirled round on the end of a string to produce a demonic roaring noise, and it is widely used in primitive initiation ceremonies.[198] In Greece it was used in some mystery cults, especially those of Dionysus and Cybele, in association with drums and cymbals.[199] It also had magical uses, and it could be a child's toy.[200]

PERCUSSION

Percussion instruments played a comparatively slight part in ancient Greek music. It is important to distinguish between two categories of percussion. On the one hand there are instruments whose function is to provide a sharply defined rhythm; these are essentially clappers with a dry, non-resonant sound. On the other hand there are those whose function is to make an exciting noise, like drums, cymbals, and jingles. The first category did have a limited role in support of the auloi and the lyre, but the second was restricted to orgiastic cults.

Clappers

An ancient urge drives men to respond to music and song with bodily movement, and to accentuate the rhythm by stamping, clapping the hands, or slapping the buttocks or some other fleshy area. Clappers of inanimate material, widely found in early cultures, represent an extension of these natural means of beating time.[201] The most primitive type consists simply of sticks beaten together. Hinged clappers that could be operated with one hand are attested from the early third millennium in Sumer, and were used by dancing-girls both there and subsequently in Egypt.[202]

[198] *NG* iii. 450–1; I have cited other literature in *The Orphic Poems*, 157 n. 59.
[199] Aesch. fr. 57. 8f., Eur. *Hel.* 1362, Eup. fr. 83, Flaccus(?) *Anth. Pal.* 6. 165 (*FGE* 167); Diogenes, *TrGF* 45 F 1, Ap. Rhod. *Argon.* 1. 1139, Philod. *Mus.* p. 106 Kr.
[200] Ar. fr. 315, Theoc. *Id.* 2. 30 with Gow, Leonidas, *HE* 2248; *The Orphic Poems* 157.
[201] Sachs, *HMI* 25f., *WM* 112f.; Kunst, 50–2; *NG* iv. 427f.
[202] *NG* vi. 72f., xii. 197.

Dancing accompanied by hand-clapping and by a lyre-player or aulete is represented on a number of late eighth- and early seventh-century vase-paintings, and also described in a passage of the *Odyssey*.[203] There were dances of singing choruses in which the feet stamped energetically enough to produce a 'lovely thumping'; and a little later, Archaic vases show us lively dancers who slap their thighs, bellies, or other parts.[204]

Clappers or castanets (*krotala* or *krembala*) made from two short lengths of wood strung together are probably to be recognized on two Late Geometric vases. Here they are held by men, but in later times they are mostly a property of women, who are frequently shown dancing with them in Classical vase-painting, a pair in each hand, while someone else plays a lyre or auloi.[205] Sappho imagines the wedding procession of Hector and Andromache as being surrounded by a happy mixture of pipe, lyre, and castanets. It is in popular, festive music-making that they have their place, not in the theatre, in professional contests, or in cult.[206]

The implements depicted in art are rather larger than modern castanets, and can hardly have been used at such a high rate of striking. They appear to be about 12–15 cm. in length, wider at the head than at the hinge, sometimes with a right-angled projection back from the head. It may be that the pairs held in the two hands were differentiated in sound. We also hear of clacking shells or earthenware pieces together, without a lyre, as a vulgar method of accompanying a song.[207]

Auletes sometimes wore a special shoe, called *kroupeza*, with a

---

[203] *Od.* 8. 377–80; Wegner, *Musik und Tanz*, 23f.; Webster, 7, 9f., 50. Later we hear of clapping only occasionally, in popular contexts, as *Carm. Pop. PMG* 876b (above, p. 28), Autocrates fr. 1. 5, Plut. *Quaest. conv.* 623b, Lucian, *Ver. Hist.* 2. 5, Clem. *Paedagogus* 3. 11. 80. 4; Gregory of Nazianzus, *Or.* 5. 35 (*PG* xxxv. 709 a), *Ep.* 232 (*PG* xxxvii. 376a), *Carm.* 2. 1. 88. 88 (*PG* xxxvii. 1438a); Orph. *Argon.* 440; perhaps *Anacreontea* 49. 8, 59. 7. In Theophr. *Char.* 19. 10 Diels, clapping along with the piper is cited as an example of boorish behaviour.

[204] Hes. *Th.* 70, cf. 8, *Il.* 18. 571, *Hymn. Hom. Ap.* 516; Webster, 15, 21, 24.

[205] See Pl. 31; Aign 94; Wegner, *Musik und Tanz*, 24; *Musikleben*, 62f., 93, 212–14 and pl. 28; *Bilder*, 50f., 97, 99; Paquette, 203–9.

[206] Sappho 44. 25, Dicaearchus fr. 60 W., Meleager, *HE* 4361, ps.-Verg. *Copa* 2. In several passages where *krotala* are mentioned in connection with the worship of Cybele or Bacchus I take them to be a special type which I discuss below together with cymbals.

[207] Ar. *Ran.* 1305 with schol., Hermippus fr. 31, Phrynichus, *Praep. Soph.* 79. 6 de Borries, Eust. *Il.* 838. 23, 1327. 24. Photius s.v. *krembaliazein* mentions ivory clackers.

clapper attached to the sole so that they could beat time audibly for a chorus while they piped.[208]

Drums, cymbals, and cymbal-clappers

The drum known to the Greeks (*tympanon*, in poetry also *typanon*) was not a kettledrum, as lexica and commentators often state, but a shallow frame drum or tambour of modest size (Pl. 32). The skin was stretched over a circular open frame of 30–50 cm. diameter; probably the back as well as the front was covered, but only one side was struck. The drum was held upright in the left hand and smitten with the fingertips or knuckles of the right. In some fourth-century representations there is a short handle attached to the frame.

The South Italian vases of that time sometimes show a drum of a more elaborate structure, with a smaller but wider circular frame inside the larger, so that from a raised central area the skin slopes away to the rim. The inner and outer areas no doubt gave a different sound.[209]

The drum is not definitely attested in Greek literature or art before the fifth century BC, unless the fourteenth Homeric Hymn is earlier than that. It was certainly imported from the Orient, where drums of similar form had been in constant use from about 2000 BC.[210] In Greece as in the East, the instrument was played predominantly by women; men involved with it were liable to be considered effeminate.[211] It appears almost exclusively in connection with orgiastic cults such as those of the Great Mother, Dionysus Baccheus, and Sabazius.[212]

---

[208] Cratinus fr. 77, Paus. Att. κ 48, Poll. 7. 87, 10. 153, schol. Aeschin. 1. 126 (who calls it *bātalos*); cf. Alcidamas(?) in *PHib.* 13. 29 f., Lucian, *Salt.* 10, Suet. *Calig.* 54. See Pl. 27 (Pronomus); Wegner, *Bilder*, 55; A. Bélis, *BCH* 112 (1988), 323–39. There is evidence that the Hittites had known a similar device (*NG* i. 392).

[209] Sachs, *HMI* 148 f.; Wegner, *Musikleben*, 64–6; Paquette, 206, 209–13.

[210] Neo-Sumerian and Old Babylonian: Sachs, *HMI* 76; Rimmer, 23 f. and pl. VI; *NG* xii. 197. Egyptian (New Kingdom): Sachs, 97; *NG* vi. 72 and 73 fig. 4. Assyrian, Syro-Phoenician: Rimmer pl. VII, IX; *NG* i. 388 f. Jewish: Sachs, 108 f. *Ty(m)panon* may have a connection with the Hebrew name of the instrument, *tōp* (Aramaic *tuppa*): É. Masson, *Recherches sur les plus anciens emprunts sémitiques en grec*, 94 f.

[211] Eup. fr. 88; *PHib.* 54. 11 (cf. above, p. 91), 'and send me Zenobius the effeminate with his drum, cymbals, and clappers, as the women need him for their sacrifice'; Demetr. *Eloc.* 97.

[212] *Hymn. Hom.* 14. 3, Pind. fr. 70b. 9, Aesch. fr. 57. 10, Hdt. 4. 76. 4, Eur. *HF* 889, *Hel.* 1347, *Bacch.* 59, 124, 156, 513, *Cyc.* 65, 205, fr. 586, Ar. *Vesp.* 119, *Lys.* 3, 388, Diogenes, *TrGF* 45 F 1. 3, Dem. *De Cor.* 284, Men. *Theophoroumene?* p. 146 Sandbach (OCT), Dioscorides *HE* 1623 ff., etc. In vase-painting the drum does not appear before the second half of the 5th c., and then usually in the hands of Bacchants.

The same is true of cymbals (*kymbala*), and of a special type of clapper with bronze heads, both of which are often mentioned in association with drums.[213] Cymbals again are of oriental origin, and they were known in Minoan Crete.[214] They appear in Greek art from perhaps the seventh century, certainly the sixth, and specimens survive from several sites.[215] They are smaller than modern concert cymbals, not more than 18 cm. in diameter. They have the form of a cup surrounded by a flat rim. At the back they have either a metal ring through which the middle finger could be inserted or a hole through which a thong could be tied.

The *krotala* or *krembala* mentioned together with drums, or in the context of religious music, are sometimes said to be of bronze,[216] and appear to be distinct from the normal castanets used by dancing-girls. One might suppose them to be the same as *kymbala*, except that both are occasionally named together.[217] They are probably little cymbals mounted on clappers, or rather on the flexible prongs of a split cane which only had to be shaken to and fro to make them clash together. Such an instrument certainly existed in the Roman imperial period, in Coptic Egypt, and in Sassanid Persia, and it is also known from Burma.[218] The same meaning, I believe, should be assigned to the term *rhoptra*, which is used of a Bacchic musical

For a doubtful drummer in a Laconian figurine of the first half of the 6th c. see Aign, 249. On drums in South Italian art see A. M. Di Giulio in Gentili–Pretagostini 109–13.

[213] *Hymn. Hom.*, Pind., Aesch., Eur. *Hel.*, *Cyc.* 205, Men., Diogenes, as in n. 212; ps.-Arist. *Mir. Ausc.* 838^{b}34–839^{a}1; *PHib.* loc. cit.; Philip, *Anth. Pal.* 6. 94, etc. The clash of metal was held to have apotropaic properties; see Gow on Theoc. *Id.* 2. 36, adding Apollodorus, *FGrH* 244 F 110, who tells of a gong used by the priest of Kore at Athens on the occasion of her descent to Hades. M. A. Schatkin, *Jahrbuch für Antike und Christentum* 21 (1978), 147–72, assembles much material on gongs and bells in ancient cult and magic.

[214] Old Babylonian: Rimmer, 25, 47. Assyrian: Rimmer, 39f., 47, pl. xxi; *NG* xii. 198, 199 fig. 5. Jewish: Sachs, *HMI* 121f. Minoan: Aign, 51. The Egyptians do not seem to have had cymbals until Ptolemaic times.

[215] First on an amphora fragment from Delos and in a 6th-c. Laconian bronze statuette of a girl. Aign, 99f., 249f.; Wegner, *Musikleben*, 63f., 214; *Bilder*, 60f.; Paquette, 212f.

[216] Eur. *Cyc.* 205, Anon. *PMG* 955, Call. fr. 761, Antip. Sid. *HE* 597.

[217] *PHib.* and ps.-Arist. locc. citt.

[218] Rimmer, 41 figs. 11–12; Sachs, *HMI* 103f., 123 (where he interprets one of the Biblical cymbal types, the *məṣiltayim*, as this sort of clapper); Behn 50, 78, and figs. 70, 106. The making of *krotala* from a split cane is attested by schol. Ar. *Nub.* 260. The J. Paul Getty Museum possesses an example of a similar instrument in which the cymbals slide on a rod fixed between the prongs of a bronze fork: see M. Jentoft-Nilsen, *Getty Mus. Jour.* 11 (1983), 157f.

instrument in a number of post-Classical texts. *Rhoptra* are said to be of bronze, and Nonnus says explicitly that they are shaken, that they clap, and that they have two pieces of bronze yoked together.[219] Since *rhoptron* elsewhere denotes hinged things that come down with a bang (the bar of a trap, or a door-knocker), it would be very appropriately applied to cymbal-clappers of the sort described above.

Rattles and jingles

Our concern being with music, it is not necessary to discuss every kind of noise-making device. We need not linger over bells, which, as in the Near East, were used mainly as horse trappings, or over bird-scarers, or children's rattles.[220] We must, however, take note of certain items which, while perhaps intrinsically no more musical than those, were used, or may have been used, in a musical context.

In several eighth-century women's tombs in Greek South Italy remains have been found of a small instrument consisting of two parallel bronze bars linked by between ten and fifteen wooden spars, each of which was loosely encased in a delicate, flexible coil of bronze wire. Shaking or picking at the instrument would cause the coils to tinkle together. The best-preserved example, with fifteen coils, is from a tomb which also contained a set of sixteen equal tube-chimes and a set of thin metal discs, graded in size, which presumably also belonged to some sort of jingling device.[221] The instrument with coils seems closely related to an object represented on an eighth-century Phoenician or Syrian ivory box from Nimrud, in the British Museum. Musicians in procession towards a goddess are playing double pipes, a small round frame drum, and rectangular box-like instruments crossed by a row of bars, which they hold

[219] Orph. fr. 105b, 152, Flaccus *Anth. Pal.* 6. 165. 3 (*FGE* p. 47), Cornutus, *Theol. Graec.* p. 59. 22 L., Lucian, *Podagra* 36, Agathias, *Anth. Pal.* 6. 74. 7; Nonnus, *Dion.* 9. 116 f., 14. 348, 17. 344, 46. 120, 47. 731, etc.

[220] Bells: Rimmer, 37–9, ps.-Eur. *Rhes.* 308; also in shields, Aesch. *Sept.* 386, Soph. fr. 859; in sentry-relays, Thuc. 4. 135, Ar. *Av.* 842, 1160; on certain priestly costumes, Plut. *Quaest. conv.* 672a, cf. Dem. 25. 90. Bird-scarer (of bronze, used by Heracles to banish the Stymphalian birds): Pisander fr. 4 Bern. = 5 D., Pherec. *FGrH* 3 F 72, Hellanicus, *FGrH* 4 F 104, Ap. Rhod. *Argon.* 2. 1055. Children's rattles: Arist. *Pol.* 1340b26 (a superior model invented by Archytas), Leonidas, *HE* 2246, Plut. *Quaest. conv.* 714e.

[221] P. Zancani Montuoro, *Atti e memorie della Società Magna Grecia* 15–17 (1974–6) 27–42 and pl. ix–xvi.

vertically by the top corner and touch or sweep with the right hand.[222]

What seems to be a later cognate of the same instrument starts to appear on Apulian vases about 360 BC, and is then seen on several hundred of them. They show an object that resembles a small ladder, except that the rungs (six to twenty in number) are two or three times too close together, and each rung has a blobby excrescence in the middle. The thing is mainly associated with women, Aphrodite, and Eros. It is perhaps 60 cm. long by 18 cm. wide. It is clearly some sort of musical instrument: in several cases it appears beside lyres and harps, and in one painting a woman, seated and facing another woman who dances, is holding it up by one corner with her left hand while touching the 'rungs' with her right, which is spread out with fingers extended.[223] It is as if she were sweeping across strings, but they cannot be strings: they are too short, they are all the same length, they have the attachments in the middle, and there is no sign of a soundbox. Perplexed scholars have often called the instrument a xylophone. But a xylophone would have bars graded in length to give different notes, and it would need to be struck with a hammer, not riffled over with the bare fingers. Others use the designation 'Apulian sistrum', which is more appropriate. *Sistrum* (Greek *seistron*) means a rattle,[224] and the problematic object can only have given voice by rattling or jingling. Presumably the 'rungs' of the

[222] British Museum 118179; R. D. Barnett, *The Nimrud Ivories* (London, 1957), 78–9, 191, pl. 16–17; Rimmer, 40, pl. vɪɪb; Aign 158; Zancani Montuoro 34f. and pl. xɪv. It had usually been taken as a small zither (Sachs, *HMI* 118; Rimmer), but on a rectangular zither we should expect to see the strings parallel to the long axis, not at right angles to it. The same instrument is represented in two or three terracottas from Kharayeb (Lebanon) of about the 3rd c. BC (M. H. Chéhab, *Bull. Mus. Beyrouth* 10 (1951–2), 38; 11 (1953–4), pl. xɪɪɪ–xɪɪɪɪ). A 5th-c. inscribed bone tablet from the Orphic community in Olbia has on its verso a curious design which could be taken as a drawing of the instrument under discussion; see my *The Orphic Poems*, 17 and 19.

[223] See Pl. 33; Wegner, *Musikleben*, 66f., 229, pl. 24; *Bilder*, 110f.; G. Schneider-Herrmann in *Festoen, Festschrift A. Zadoks-Josephus Jitta* (Leiden, 1976), 517–26 and *Bulletin Antieke Beschaving* 52–3 (1977–8), 265f.; A. D. Trendall and A. Cambitoglou, *The Red-Figured Vases of Apulia*, i (Oxford, 1978), 315f.; E. Keuls, *AJArch.* 83 (1979), 476f.; Paquette, 206, 214f.; Maas–Snyder, 190 fig. 2b, 196 fig. 16; A. M. Di Giulio in Gentili–Pretagostini, 113–17. I mention as a curiosity J. G. Landels's suggestion in *CR* 29 (1979), 132 that the object is 'a knitting machine or a hair-waver'.

[224] It is applied especially to the rattle traditionally used in the Egyptian cult of Isis, which consisted of a metal frame on a handle with loose rods crossing it. See Sachs, *HMI* 69f., 89f.; Dar.–Sag. iv. 1355–7; *NG* xvii. 354.

ladder rotated freely and loosely round internal rods, and the contraption had some specially pleasant sound quality.

In fact it corresponds very well to an instrument described by Pollux under the name *psithyrā*, which means 'rustle':

The *psithyrā* is an African invention, in particular of the Troglodytes, and its shape is rectangular. (Some think it is the same as what is called the *askaros*.) It consisted of a rectangular frame a cubit long, with bobbins drawn through it; these, when rotated, made a noise similar to a *krotalon*.[225]

The reference to the Troglodytes must derive from the Hellenistic explorer Pythagoras.[226] He must have seen something similar among the Nubians of coastal Sudan.

Tuned percussion arrays

The idea of lining up a set of objects, each of which would give out a different note when struck, so that tunes could be played on them, was exploited by a few isolated individuals from time to time, but it never took root. Mention has been made of the graded set of metal discs from an early south Italian grave. A tradition of metal chimes may have persisted in that part of the world. About 500 BC Hippasus of Metapontum is said to have used bronze discs of different thicknesses to demonstrate concordant intervals, and a century later Glaucus of Rhegium cultivated the art of playing tuned discs.[227]

Another harmonic theorist, Lasus of Hermione, is said to have operated with vessels part-filled with liquid.[228] One Diocles (perhaps the writer on music who was the father of the sophist Alcidamas) is credited with inventing the art of playing tunes on a set of dishes, which he hit with a stick. Allusions to this form of entertainment, however, are very rare.[229]

---

[225] Poll. 4. 60. Cf. Hsch. s.v. *askaroi*: 'a kind of shoes or sandals; or, as some say, *krotala*'.

[226] Cf. above, pp. 76 n. 126, 80 n. 145.

[227] Below, p. 234 n. 38.

[228] Theon Smyrn. p. 59. 7 ff.

[229] *Suda* ii. 104. 5, cf. Kassel–Austin, *Poetae Comici Graeci*, v. 18; Anon. Bellerm. 18; Jo. Philoponus, *Comm. in Arist. Graeca* xv. 358. 13.

5

Rhythm and Tempo

It is conventional, in writing about ancient Greek music, to voice a lament that 'the music itself' is almost entirely lost. So far as its melodic lines are concerned, this is true: we have only a few dozen specimens to represent a thousand years' music, and of these few dozen, most are tattered fragments with scarcely a line complete, and nearly all are from compositions of post-Classical date. Of music from before the last decade of the fifth century BC we have not a single note.

On the other hand there is quite a considerable amount of music from the Archaic and Classical periods of which we can claim to know the rhythms, with at least a fair approximation to the truth. We should count ourselves fortunate that it is this way round. There would be little satisfaction to be had from knowing the ups and downs of the melodies if we had no idea of the rhythms that gave them shape. For rhythm is the vital soul of music. The Greeks acknowledged its fundamental role.

Melody in itself is lax and inert, but when combined with rhythm it becomes hard-edged and active.[1]

Notes as such, because of the lack of differentiation in their movement, leave the interweaving of the melody obscure and confuse the mind: it is the elements of rhythm that make clear the character of the melody.[2]

Some of the ancients described rhythm as male, melody as female, on the grounds that melody is inactive and without form, playing the part of matter because of its capacity for opposite qualifications, while rhythm moulds it and moves it in a determinate order, playing the part of the maker in relation to the thing made.[3]

---

[1] Ps.-Arist. *Pr.* 19. 49.
[2] Aristid. Quint. p. 31. 10–13, trans. Barker, *GMW* ii. 434.
[3] Ibid. p. 40. 20–5, trans. Barker, *GMW* ii. 445. The theory alluded to was probably Peripatetic; see Barker's n.

Imagine, if someone sang or played the most beautiful melody but paid no heed to the rhythm, is it conceivable that anyone would tolerate such music-making?[4]

We can claim knowledge of the rhythms of ancient music because there is good reason to believe that they are reflected with reasonable fidelity in the metres of those verse texts which we know to have been sung (and in many cases danced). The metres are quantitative, based on patterns of long and short syllables which must correspond to patterns of long and short notes. The repetitive nature of these patterns usually makes their rhythmical character obvious; and when we find them built up into extended complex sequences which are repeated entire from one strophe to another, this can only be understood as a discipline imposed by the rhythm of music that was itself repeated. As A. M. Dale puts it, 'every Greek poet was his own composer, and no poet would write words in elaborate metrical schemes merely to annihilate and overlay these by a different musical rhythm'.[5] In the surviving fragments of poetic texts furnished with musical notation, the note values are commonly left unspecified, and this is because they were felt to be sufficiently indicated by the metre of the words. When they are specified, they confirm the presumption that short syllables are set on short notes and long syllables on long notes.

It was a feature of the ancient Greek language that the distinction between short and long syllables was clear-cut. All verse metre was based on this binary opposition, whether it was spoken verse or sung. Even in prose oratory the interplay of long and short syllables automatically yielded rhythmic patterns, which the orator was advised to be careful about; the inadvertent production of a verse occasionally aroused the audience to jocularity.[6] It was only natural that this opposition of long and short, being built into the words themselves, should be maintained in vocal music. And as a general rule it remained a *binary* opposition, between two note values of which one had twice the duration of the other. The evidence for this is of several kinds:

[4] Dion. Hal. *Dem.* 48 (i. 233. 19 U.–R.); cf. *Comp.* 56 (ii. 39. 13), 'I have observed the same thing happening with regard to rhythm—everyone complaining and being discontented if somebody played an instrument or danced or sang in uneven time and destroyed the rhythm.'

[5] *Collected Papers* (Cambridge, 1969), 161.

[6] Cf. the *Oxford Classical Dictionary*, 2nd edn., s.v. Prose-rhythm (W. H. Shewring and K. J. Dover).

1. The interchangeability, in many metres, of a long syllable with two shorts.

2. The application in musical texts of the symbol $-$, which we know signified a 'diseme', a doubling of the normal 'monoseme' short note, to notes on which a long syllable was sung.

3. The proportional ratios assigned by Aristotle, Aristoxenus, and other writers on rhythm to the constituent parts of various types of 'foot': $- \cup \cup$ (dactyl) $= 1 : 1$, $\cup -$ (iambus) $= 1 : 2$, $- \cup \cup \cup$ (paeon) $= 2 : 3$, etc.[7]

In some circumstances, as we shall see later, a long syllable might be given a value equivalent to three shorts (triseme), or even four (tetraseme). But where this happens, it is as a variation of a rhythmic pattern that is clearly defined by longs and shorts of the usual $2 : 1$ ratio. These always predominate.

The Greek composer of vocal music, then, used only a small number of different note values: in most cases only two, one twice the length of the other—we will represent them as ♩ and ♪—corresponding to the opposition of long and short syllables. When he divided a long syllable between notes, it was normally between two notes of the shorter value. His rhythmic system was 'additive', built up from units of fixed size, as opposed to the 'divisive' principle of Western music in which the constant is a measure of time (a bar) that may be divided into fractions of many different sizes.[8] The modern composer has great freedom of choice in the matter of how much time he allots to each syllable of his text. From the words

> It's a long way to Tipperary,
> it's a long way to go:
> it's a long way to Tipperary,
> to the sweetest girl I know,

there is no way of discovering that the relative values of the notes are 1, 1, 2, 3, 1, 1, 1, 2, 4; 1, 1, 2, 4, 2, 6; 1, 1, 2, 3, 1, 1, 1, 2, 4; 1, 1, 2, 2, 2, 2, 8. But with an ancient Greek text the limits of uncertainty are much narrower. Often there is no uncertainty at all. For example, in Anacreon's little song beginning

---

[7] Arist. *Rh.* 1409[a]4, Aristox. *Rhythm.* 2. 30 Pearson, Quint. *Inst.* 9. 4. 46–7, Aristid. Quint. 1. 15–17 p. 35. 3 ff., schol. Heph. p. 109. 14 ff., Anon. Ambros. 14 (Studemund, *Anecdota Varia* (Berlin, 1886), 227. 6 ff.), 'Marius Victorinus' (Aphthonius) in *Gramm. Lat.* vi. 40. 23 ff., 42. 7 ff., etc.

[8] On these concepts see Georgiades 21–50; Sachs, *RT* 90–5, 131.

Polioi men hēmin ēdē
krotaphoi karē te leukon

(*PMG* 395), we can at once read off the note values (1, 1, 2, 1, 2, 1, 2, 2; 1, 1, 2, 1, 2, 1, 2, 2; etc.), seize the simple rhythmical scheme governing them, and recognize it as a common one for which we have a name. In fact we have names for most kinds of rhythm and rhythmical scheme that we encounter, because it is a characteristic of Greek verse and song that they are based on a limited number of metrical types. We can assume that each metre corresponds to a particular rhythm, even if the exact rhythmic interpretation of the metrical data may be subject to doubt at some points.

There are certain authors who speak of the natural quantities of syllables being sometimes distorted in the interests of rhythm. Plato insists that in his ideal republic melody and rhythm must follow the words, not vice versa, implying that it is not always that way round in contemporary music.[9] According to Dionysius of Halicarnassus,

> Prose diction does not violate or change round the quantities of any word, but keeps the long and short syllables just as they have been handed down naturally; but music and rhythm alter them, diminishing or increasing them, so that often they turn into their opposites, for they do not regulate their time-values by the syllables but the syllables by the time-values.[10]

Fortunately the musical fragments that we have provide an antidote to this alarming statement. They show us long syllables being occasionally protracted to the value of three or (in the later texts) four shorts. In a papyrus of the first or second century AD we find one example of a short closed syllable (final -*on*) being treated as long within the verse, and there are two or three instances of this happening at verse-end.[11] We do not find any case of a long syllable being shortened.[12] So it is safe to say that the distortions that Dionysius

---

[9] *Resp.* 398 d, 400 a, d.

[10] *Comp.* 64 (ii. 42. 15 U.–R.); similarly Longinus, *Proleg. in Heph.* p. 83. 14 Consbruch, Anon. Ambros. p. 231. 28 Stud., 'Mar. Vict.' (Aphth.) in *Gramm. Lat.* vi. 42. 3 (from a common source, cf. R. Westphal, *Griechische Rhythmik* (Leipzig, 1885), 210).

[11] **30** *POsl.* 1413 a 4; at verse-end, ibid. 18, **29** *POxy.* 2436 ii 4, **31** *PMichigan* 2958.13. More surprising lengthenings of what should be short syllables occur in **51** *POxy.* 1786; but this Christian hymn dates from a time when Greek had lost the original opposition of long and short syllables, and knowledge of the 'correct' quantities had ceased to be general.

[12] Perhaps what Dionysius has in mind is epic correption, the shortening of a long vowel or diphthong at the end of a word when another vowel follows at the beginning

refers to can only have been prevalent to a very limited extent, and perhaps only at a late period, since Plato's remarks are quite unspecific and do not go so far as to imply actual reversals of syllabic values. Even where these phenomena occur, they are not likely to mislead us, because they stand out as anomalies in a rhythmic scheme that is otherwise clear and regular.

Beating time: 'Bars'

The ancients were well acquainted with the practice of beating time to music. In the previous chapter we have mentioned clapping and body-slapping in some Archaic dance, clappers and castanets, and the aulete's clapper-shoe. An essayist of the early fourth century BC speaks of lecturers on music who sing and play pieces for comparative purposes, beating out the rhythms on the 'little board' beneath their feet. Quintilian describes the citharode marking time with his foot as he plays, and elsewhere he refers to rhythm being measured out by foot-tapping or finger-snapping.[13] It was also measured out by bodily movement whenever people marched or danced to music.

 From the second half of the fifth century BC, if not earlier, it was customary to divide each measure into 'up' and 'down' segments (*anō, katō*), later called 'lift' and 'step' (*arsis, basis*) or 'lift' and 'placement' (*arsis, thesis*), corresponding to the raising and lowering of the foot.[14] These segments were not necessarily equal in length. When they were unequal, the 'down' part of the measure—the thesis, to use what became the established term—was usually the longer. Theoreticians classified rhythms according to the ratio between the segments (1 : 1, 1 : 2, etc.). Their writings provide us with a quantity of information on how the division was made in the case of various

of the next word. But that phenomenon has its origin in the spoken language; see my *Greek Metre*, 11 f.

[13] Alcidamas(?) in *PHib.* 13. 29 ff., Quint. *Inst.* 1. 12. 3, 9. 4. 51, 55. Cf. also Simias, *Egg* 10–12; Cic. *Orat.* 198; Caesius Bassus ap. Rufinum, *Gramm. Lat.* vi. 555. 24; Terentianus Maurus 2254 f.; 'Mar. Vict.' (Aphth.), *Gramm. Lat.* vi. 40. 15, 44. 4; Philostr. *Imag.* 1. 10. 4; Philostr. Jun. *Imag.* 7. 3; Gregory of Nyssa, *Contra Eunomium* 1. 17.

[14] *Anō/katō*: Damon ap. Pl. *Resp.* 400b, ps.-Hippoc. *De Victu* 1. 18. 3, Aristox. *Rhythm.* 2. 17, 20, 25, 29. *Arsis/basis*: Aristox. *Rhythm.* 2. 20, 21, Psell. *Intro. Rhythm.* 8, 12. *Arsis/thesis*: Herophilus T 183 von Staden (pp. 354 f., cf. 276–82, 392 f.), Aristid. Quint. p. 31. 9 ff., Bacchius, *Harm.* 98, 101, Excerpta Neapol. p. 414. 8 Jan = 28. 14 Pearson, Anon. Bellerm. 1, 3, Anon. Ambros. pp. 225. 16, 227. 10 ff. Stud., etc. This pair of terms probably goes back to a Peripatetic source, cf. ps.-Arist. *Pr.* 5. 41.

rhythms, and we can supplement it from indications in the musical texts, where the arsis is often marked by dots above the note-symbols. This evidence will be cited later when particular rhythms are discussed.

There is an obvious analogy betwen these 'feet', as Greek writers call them, with their arsis and thesis, and the 'bars' with up-beats and down-beats by which most Western music of recent centuries is conventionally measured out. In transcribing the ancient musical documents into modern notation it will be convenient to treat the 'feet' as bars and to place bar-lines accordingly. But it is important to note certain differences between these Greek bars and those to which the modern musician is accustomed. He will think of a bar as containing a certain number of beats (two, three, four, or whatever) which are equally spaced and which do not necessarily coincide with the start of a note; and he will think of the first one as being the down-beat, perhaps associated with some kind of accent. In the Greek method of beating time, the beat-cycle is constituted from elements which may be of unequal duration, and are practically always coextensive with a note or a group of notes; the down portion may follow the up portion rather than precede it. Where it does follow it, it might seem appropriate to shift our bar-lines so that the down-beat comes at the beginning of a bar, as in Example 5.1. But this prejudices the ques-

Ex. 5.1

tion whether the ancient down-beat had any kind of accentual significance; it makes what are certainly four measures into more than four; and it obscures the identity of the units perceived by the ancients. It is surely preferable to mark out the measures which they recognized as such, when we can identify them. We must just bear in mind that this demarcation does not carry any implication of a dynamic accent at any particular point.[15] There is no reason why we

[15] Jaap Kunst, after recommending ethnomusicologists transcribing exotic melodies to use bar-lines 'for the sake of legibility . . . where the rhythm seems to call for' them, observes 'No doubt one will frequently feel, when tackling the same phonogram some days later, an inclination to distribute the bar-lines differently. The reason for this is the fact that accentuation in the music of many exotic peoples is

should not inscribe a time-signature in the modern style when and as appropriate.

It is important to realize that the bar in this music is created by a particular repeating note-pattern, or by a set of note-patterns recognized as equivalent variants of one another. It is not to be thought of (as in Western music) as an abstract receptacle that may be filled by any combination of notes. This is another aspect of the difference between additive and divisive rhythm. So, once the note-pattern changes, the bar-length and time-signature may well change too. In some Greek music the note-pattern did not change, and the rhythm was straightforward and uniform throughout. But in other cases the rhythms were much more flexible and varied, representable only by changing time-signatures and bar-lengths.

In what follows, we shall first review six basic types of rhythmic movement, and then try to say something of the varieties of their combination.

Dactylic and anapaestic

The dactylic hexameter (– ∪ ∪ – ∪ ∪ – ∪ ∪ – ∪ ∪ – ∪ ∪ – –) was one of the commonest Greek metres throughout Antiquity. In Homer's time epic poetry in this metre was sung to the lyre. Certain features of the versification, and explicit testimony from Dionysius of Halicarnassus, indicate that the ratio of the long to the short notes in such singing was less than the standard 2 : 1, probably more like 5 : 3, but not precisely measurable. This no doubt reflects the ratio between long and short syllables in ordinary speech, as against the precise mathematical ratio generally imposed by musical rhythm, especially when music is accompanied by bodily movement.[16] Dionysius says that there was also a foot of the form ∪ ∪ – which had the same

---

much weaker than that in Western music; in some cases this accentuation is put into it by the investigator, because we Westerners seem to feel the need of making what is heard more comprehensible by "phrasing" it in some way or other.' (Kunst, 40.)

[16] Dion. Hal. *Comp.* 109 (ii. 71. 10 U.–R.), citing specialist rhythmicians, cf. 144 (ii. 93. 15); my *Greek Metre*, 20 f., 36–9. In his classic study *Hungarian Folk Music* (Oxford, 1931), 9, Béla Bartók distinguishes two forms of rhythm used in Hungarian songs: 'tempo giusto', i.e. strict rhythm, deriving from rhythmical motions such as work and dancing, and 'parlando-rubato', independent of corporal movement and based on the rhythm of the words. The Greek evidence points to an analogous distinction. The connection between musical rhythm and bodily movement is made by Pl. *Phlb.* 17 d, ps.-Arist. *Pr.* 19. 38; cf. Aristox. *Rhythm.* 2. 9, Bacchius, *Harm.* 93, Aristid. Quint. 1. 13.

irrational rhythm. The rhythmicians called it 'cyclic', and distinguished it from the ordinary anapaest. A lyric fragment quoted to
exemplify it looks as if it may come from Stesichorus. It would be
understandable if Stesichorus, whose lengthy narrative songs were
very epic in character, and who made much use of $-\cup\cup-\cup\cup\ldots$
and $\cup\cup-\cup\cup-\cup\cup\ldots$ sequences, gave these metres the same
rhythmic values as the Homeric singers employed.[17]

It may be that dactyls sometimes had this rhythm even in dramatic
song in the late fifth century, as there are certain cases where $-\cup\cup$
and $\cup\cup\cup$ seem to be treated as almost equivalent, which is easier to
understand if $-\cup\cup$ was something like ♪ ♫ than if it was ♩ ♫.[18]

In other cases, no doubt, dactyls had the rationalized rhythm
𝄴♩ ♫ . The rhythmicians in fact adopted 'dactylic' as a generic term
for all kinds of foot in which thesis and arsis were of equal duration.
In the case of the dactyl the long note was the thesis and the two short
ones made up the arsis.[19] As in epic verse, the arsis could sometimes
be filled by one long syllable instead of two short ones, though this
was done much more sparingly in lyric song than in epic. Presumably
such a long syllable was sometimes divided between two notes of the
melody. It was quite exceptional for the thesis-long to be divided
between two short syllables.

When a sequence of dactyls continued up to a pause or a break in
the melodic flow, it ended with a bar of the form |♩ ♩ | or |♩ ♪𝄽‖ or
|♩ 𝄽‖ .

Anapaests in the classical period are especially associated with
parading choruses, who chanted verse in this metre with an aulete
playing an accompaniment. In tragedy there were also some anapaestic songs, mainly for soloists, but again tending to go with entries
and perambulations. It was the natural metre for marching to. The
unit of composition is practically always the two-foot measure corre-
sponding to a double pace: |𝄴♫ ♩ ⋮ ♫ ♩ |. The short notes formed
the arsis and the long one the thesis. Substitution of a long for two
shorts and vice versa is frequent, but generally so managed (at any rate

---

[17] Dion. Hal. ibid.; *PMG* 1027 e (misprinted).
[18] See my *Greek Metre*, 131 f., and cf. Dion. Hal.'s comment on *Od.* 11. 598 in
Comp. 144 (ii. 93. 15 f. U.–R.), that the dactyls in the line 'have irrational syllables
mixed in with them, so that some of them do not differ much from trochees'.
[19] Cf. Damon ap. Pl. *Resp.* 400 b, Aristox. *Rhythm.* 2. 30, Aristid. Quint. 1. 15, etc.

in the recited type) as to avoid having four consecutive short notes. A
pause was always marked in the recited type, and often in the sung
type, by a bar of the form |♫♩ ♩ 𝄽 ‖ or |♫♩ ♪𝄾𝄽 ‖ . We have a late
musical setting of an anapaestic passage in **30** *POsl.* 1413; there are
pauses at three places, and in each case the expected crotchet rest is
notated. Two other anapaestic pieces, **34** *POxy.* 3704 and **51** *POxy.*
1786, show a different technique, no doubt of late origin, in which
some bars begin with rests, |𝄾 ♩ ♩ ♩ | or |𝄾 ♩ ♫♩ | .

Iambic, choriambic, trochaic

The name *iambos* was applied by the metricians to the foot ∪ −, and
the rhythmicians took 'iambic' as the generic name for measures in
which the ratio of arsis and thesis was 1 : 2. But in all the 'iambic'
verse with which we are familiar the unit of measurement is not the
single foot ∪ − but the so-called metron ∪ − ∪ − with its several
variants. Thus the very common verse of the pattern ⏔ − ∪ − ⏔ − ∪ −
⏔ − ∪ − was always called an iambic trimeter, not a hexameter.[20] In
musical terms this basic measure appears as a bar |𝄢 ♪♩ ♪♩ | . The
first ♪♩ formed the thesis and the second ♪♩ the arsis.[21] As the thesis
and arsis were of equal duration, the measure fell into the rhythmicians' 'dactylic' category, not the 'iambic', and they in fact called it
an 'iambic dactyl'.[22]

In spoken verse in iambic metre, the first position of each metron
could be occupied by a long or a short syllable indifferently
(× − ∪ −). In sung verse too a long syllable was sometimes admitted
in that place, but less often than in spoken verse, since it put more of
a strain on the relatively strict rhythm of musical performance. It
meant that the first short note of the bar had to be lengthened somewhat, presumably at the expense of the following long note, which
nevertheless had to remain long enough to carry its own long syllable. If absolute regularity of beat was maintained, the rhythm of

[20] Already in Hdt. 1. 12. 2, cf. 1. 174. 5.
[21] Aristid. Quint. p. 38. 5; so marked in musical texts, **15** Song of Seikilos, **23**
Anon. Bellerm. 97, **29** *POxy.* 2436 ii. 6–8, **31** *POsl.* 1413 a. 19; but the other way
round, **28** Anon. Bellerm. 104.
[22] *Daktylos kat' iambon, POxy.* 2687 ii 3, Aristid. Quint. loc. cit. The rhythmicians' terminology here differs strikingly from that of the metricians, who called the
measure an iambic dipody or tautopody, or a diiambus (Heph. p. 12. 7, 14. 2, etc.;
Anon. Ambros. p. 229. 9 Stud.).

such a bar would have approximated to |♫ ♩. ♪♩ | . Aristoxenus, however, while assigning to the first note a value intermediate between a normal long and short, seems to have left the second with its regular length.[23] It is worth noting that in such cases the 'irrational' long syllable normally belonged to the same word (or closely connected word-group) as the syllable immediately following it, as if that made it easier to squeeze. In what follows I shall use the symbol ♦ for a note that may be either ♩ or ♪. When it appears in a timed bar, it will usually represent a note that should be short to fit the measure but in fact is sometimes long.

Other variants of the iambic metron do not involve this problem of irrational note-values. Either or both of the long notes could be divided into two short ones, giving |♫♫ ♪♩| or |♪♩ ♫♫| or |♫♫ ♫♫|, except that at the end of a series, if there was a pause or any interruption of the rhythmic flow, the last long note could not be divided.[24] Division of long notes could be combined with the irrational long at the beginning of the metron: |♩ ♫ ♪♩| or |♩♩ ♫♫| or |♩ ♫♫♫|.

Another set of forms was produced by amalgamating ♪♩ into a single triseme note in either half of the metron, giving |♩. ♪♩ | or |♪♩ ♩. | or |♩. ♩. |. In the Archaic period the first of these seems to have been confined to the beginning of a sequence, and the other two to the end. From the time of Simonides we find them being used more freely, in choral lyric and tragedy, though not much in comedy. At any rate, we find the syllabic sequences − ᴗ −, ᴗ − −, and − − being used among ordinary iambic metra as if they were equivalent to them; occasionally, particularly in Bacchylides, − ᴗ − or ᴗ − − in one strophe corresponds to ᴗ − ᴗ − at the same place in another. The assumption that triseme notes are involved in such cases is confirmed by the fragments

---

[23] So I infer from his remarks about the 'irrational *choreios*' (*Rhythm.* 2. 20), a foot in which the thesis was equivalent to two short notes and the arsis to between one and two. From Aristid. Quint. p. 37. 24 ff. we learn that 'irrational *choreios*' covered both − ᴗᴗ (for ᴗ −) in iambic rhythm and ᴗᴗ − (for − ᴗ) in trochaic. Cf. also Bacchius 101 (− − with irrational arsis and long thesis); Gevaert, ii. 52–6.

[24] It might, however, be replaced by a short note plus a compensatory rest. This phenomenon, known to modern metricians as *brevis in longo* at period-end, occurs in nearly every type of metre and composition, and will be taken for granted in the following pages.

of a rhythmician's treatise preserved in a papyrus, and by the notation in two later musical texts.[25]

In certain instances it appears necessary to suppose that a long syllable/note was prolonged to a triseme across the bar-line. Where the syllabic sequence is ◡ – ◡ ◡ ◡ – ◡ –, it divides cleanly between two bars, |♪♩ ♫♫|♩. ♪♩ |. On the other hand, where we find ◡ – ◡ – ◡ ◡ –, it can only be |♪♩ ♪♩ |♪♫ ♪♩ |. The Attic poets seem to have preferred the latter type.[26]

Transposition of the first two note-values of the standard metron produces the so-called choriamb, |♩ ♪♪♩ |. This is quite often found in association with other iambic forms, and in Anacreon, Aristophanes, and Sophocles we even encounter response between × – ◡ – in one strophe and – ◡ ◡ – in another, in verses composed from measures of both kinds.[27] This kind of equivalence, based on the convertibility of short–long and long–short, is familiar to us particularly from Scottish airs, for instance, as illustrated in Example 5.2. Musicians know the accented short note followed by a longer one as the Scotch snap.[28]

Ex. 5.2

| Gin a body meet a body | \|2/4 ♫ ♫. \| ♫ ♫. \| |
| comin' through the rye, | \| ♫. ♫ \| ♩ \| |

Ilka lassie has her laddie:	| ♫ ♫. | ♫ ♫. |
nane, they say, hae I,	| ♫ ♫ | ♩. ♪|
yet a' the lads they smile at me	| ♫ ♫ | ♫ ♫|
when comin' through the rye.	| ♫. ♫ | ♩ ‖

Trochaic rhythm is the converse of iambic, with a basic model |♩ ♪♩ ♪|, an irrational long admitted in the last place instead of

[25] *POxy.* 2687 (Pearson, *Aristoxenus: Elementa Rhythmica*, 36 ff.); **15** Seikilos, **29** *POxy.* 2436.
[26] See *ZPE* 37 (1980), 148.
[27] My *Greek Metre*, 57 f., 105.
[28] Cf. Georgiades, 83–6 (modern Greek folk music); Bartók, *Hungarian Folk Music*, examples no. 62, 130, 283.

the first, and other variants corresponding to those of iambic: |♫♩♩ ♪|, |♩. ♩ ♪|, etc. Again, the first half of the bar was taken as the thesis and the second half as the arsis.[29]

However, a trochaic sequence, when continued to a pause, almost always ends |♩ ♪♩ 𝄽|, that is, with an iambic close, and from one point of view trochaic rhythm is identical with iambic, only with the bar-lines shifted one place to the right, or, to put it in ancient terms, with the feet or metra differently demarcated. It was natural to adopt this alternative segmentation when the sequence began − ∪ − × . . ., even if it was to end . . . × − ∪ −. In beginning so, composers were seeking a different effect from that of × − ∪ −: a more 'downhill' effect, which they often emphasized by means of word-ends coinciding with the trochaic bar-lines. It was felt as a running or tripping rhythm, and the name 'trochaic' expresses this.[30]

Paeonic

The third rhythmic genus recognized by Aristotle and Aristoxenus is the paeonic, in which the thesis and arsis are in the durational ratio 2 : 3. This is quintuple time, something not very familiar in Western music but well known in the folk music of Eastern Europe and elsewhere.[31]

In the Archaic and Classical periods this rhythm was normally expressed in the note-patterns |⅝♩ ♪♩| and |♩ ♫♩|, rarely|♫♩♩ |. According to Aristides Quintilianus the first long note constituted the thesis and the rest of the foot the arsis. Others, however, divide − ∪ : −, and say that either part may be the thesis.[32] Paeonic rhythm was associated with an energetic form of dance, and while we have

[29] According to Aristid. Quint. p. 38. 4. But in **47** *POxy.* 3162 it was apparently marked the other way round.

[30] Damon ap. Pl. *Resp.* 400b, cf. Ion, *TrGF* 19 F 42, Arist. *Rh.* 1408ᵇ36, Anon. Ambros. p. 223. 2 ff. Stud., etc.

[31] Finns, Tatars, Turks, Hungarians, Bulgarians, Russians, Basques; in modern Greek song, Georgiades 21–5, 80–2, 161; S. Baud-Bovy, *La Chanson populaire grecque du Dodécanèse* (Paris, 1935); *Essai sur la chanson populaire grecque* (Nauplia, 1983), 5 f.; cf. Sachs, *RT* 93 f., 126. Russian composers have sometimes used this type of rhythm in concert music, for example Tchaikovsky in the second movement of his *Pathétique* symphony and Rachmaninov in his tone poem *The Isle of the Dead*. For other occasional examples in the Western musical tradition see Sachs, 340–4; *NG* xv. 512f.

[32] Aristid. Quint. p. 37. 6; Anon. Ambros. p. 227. 12 Stud.; 'Mar. Vict.' (Aphth.) *Gramm. Lat.* vi. 41. 2.

sporadic examples in Alcman, Bacchylides, and tragedy,[33] it was mainly used in Old Comedy. Aristophanes particularly liked four-bar verses of the form | ♩ ♫ | ♩ ♫ | ♩ ♫ | ♩ ♪♩ ‖. As in all other Greek rhythms, we observe that the final note before a pause must either be long or, if short, coupled with a rest to make up the value of a long. The paeonic series therefore may end with | ♩ ♪♩ ‖ or | ♩ ♫ 𝄾 ‖ (or, in Alcman, | ♩ ♩. ‖) but not with | ♩ ♫ ‖ .[34]

A peculiarity of this rhythm as it appears in Aristophanes is the freedom with which paeonic feet of the form – ◡ ◡ ◡ can alternate with, or even respond antistrophically with, trochaic metra (– ◡ – ◡̆).[35] The same ambiguity besets the term 'Cretic', which the comic poets apparently associate both with paeonic and with trochaic dance-rhythm.[36] The metricians apply it to the foot – ◡ –,[37] whereas the rhythmicians assign it to the trochaic measure |⅝ ♩ ♪♩ ♪| .[38] It seems that there was a type of music and dance, believed to be of Cretan origin, or especially characteristic of Crete, in which there was a certain fluidity as between the two rhythms. A similar fluidity has been noted in certain modern Greek dance-songs, the same song being rendered on different occasions in ⅝ ♪♪ ♪ ♩ or in ⅝ ♪♩ ♪♩ .[39]

In the Hellenistic period no such uncertainty prevails: paeonic compositions keep strictly to quintuple time. In addition to the Classical patterns | ♩ ♪♩ |, | ♩ ♫ |, | ♫ ♩ |, we now also encounter | ♫♫ |. The two Delphic paeans of the late second century BC which are the most extensive musically notated texts that we have are almost entirely in paeonic rhythm. Here a long syllable is not infrequently divided between two notes, so that what appears as – ◡ – or – ◡ ◡ ◡

---

[33] My *Greek Metre*, 106.

[34] Cf. Arist. *Rh.* 1409ᵃ17, who advises that the ◡ ◡ ◡ – paeon is suitable as a closing rhythm in oratory, but not – ◡ ◡ ◡ because a long syllable is needed to make a clear and full-sounding ending.

[35] *Greek Metre*, 106–8.

[36] Cratinus fr. 237, Ar. *Eccl.* 1165, cf. *Ran.* 1356, Anon. *PMG* 967; 'very energetic' according to Ephorus, *FGrH* 70 F 149 p. 86. 20 J.; cf. Ar. *Ach.* 665f.

[37] Heph. pp. 11. 13 (specifying quintuple time), 40. 3 ff., Anon. Ambros. p. 225. 27, 228. 5, 11, etc.

[38] Aristox. ap. Anon. Ambros. p. 229. 13; *POxy.* 2687 ii 7, iii 32, v 12; Aristid. Quint. p. 38. 3.

[39] S. Baud-Bovy, *Revue de musicologie* 54 (1968), 3–8; cf. Reinach, *La Musique grecque*, 82; Georgiades, 84–6.

in the poetic text may be ♩♪♪♪♩ melodically. The frequency of the different bar-forms is shown in Example 5.3. Any can follow any other. Quite often two or three consecutive bars have the same form, but a pleasant unpredictability and variety are maintained.

Ex. 5.3

	Athenaeus	Limenius
♩ ♪♩	22	33
♫♩ ♩	28	35
♩ ♫♩	17	24
♫♫♩	13	5

The latest surviving text in paeonic rhythm is a poem by Meso-medes from the age of Hadrian. Here we have not got the music (as we have for some of Mesomedes' compositions), but the verbal metre shows three new ways of disposing the longs and shorts in addition to all the old ways: $- - \cup$, $\cup \cup - \cup$, and $\cup - \cup \cup$. We cannot be certain that they reflect musical bars with long and short notes in these patterns, because the long syllables may have been set to two short notes. But there would be little point in introducing these novelties at the verbal level only.[40]

In the case of this rhythm, then, we can trace a gradual develop-ment across the centuries from a simple prototype to a set of seven interchangeable and equivalent variants. We have sights of it at four epochs. Table 5.1 shows the increasing variety of forms in use at each.

Dochmiac

This rather complex rhythm is as characteristic of tragedy as paeonic is of comedy. But it does not enjoy so long a history. We cannot trace it before the fifth century, and after the fourth we find it only in one Hellenistic text, a concert aria which in this respect reflects the influ-ence of Euripidean melodrama.

The measure contains the equivalent of eight short notes, divided unequally in groups of three and five. The paradigm form is $\begin{smallmatrix}3+5\\8\end{smallmatrix}$ ♪♩ ♩ ♪♩ . In each group the first note was the arsis and the

[40] Mesomedes 5 Heitsch, cf. Heph. p. 40. 4; *Greek Metre*, 170.

TABLE 5.1. *The increasing variety of paeonic rhythmic forms (7th c. BC–2nd c. AD).*

	7th c. (Alcman)	5th c. (comedy, etc.)	3rd–2nd c. (Simias, Delphic Paeans)	2nd c. AD (Mesomedes)
♩ ♪♩	+	+	+	+
♩ ♩.‖	+	(?)		
♩ ♫♫		+	+	+
♫♫ ♩		+	+	+
♫♫♫♫			+	+
♩ ♩ ♪				+
♫♫ ♩ ♪				+
♪♩ ♫				+

remainder the thesis:[41] ♩ ♩ ♩ ♩♩. Any of the long notes (but most frequently the first) could be divided into two short ones, except, of course, for the final note of the final bar before a pause. In Euripides this can result in long strings of short notes. In one passage there are no fewer than thirty-two consecutively, making up four bars, with each bar-line coinciding with the end of a word.

The first of the two short notes in the paradigm form, rather as in the iambic rhythm, could be replaced by an 'irrational' long: |♩ ♩ ♩ ♪♩ | or (much more often) |♩ ♫ ♩ ♪♩ |. The second short note could also be replaced by a long, but normally only if the two long notes on either side of it remained undivided:|♪♩ ♩♩♩|. The two irrational longs could occur in the same bar:|♩♩♩♩♩|or|♩ ♫♩♩♩|. It was not until Euripides that the second irrational became at all frequent.

The contexts in which dochmiac rhythm is used are always urgent or emotional. It is in keeping with this that we find some fluctuation between dochmiac and other measures, with changes of bar-length. Dochmiac and iambic rhythms often alternate, and the one may run

[41] So marked in the papyrus fragment of Euripides' *Orestes* (3).

straight into the other, as for example in Aeschylus, *Agamemnon*
1156–9 = 1167–70 (Ex. 5.4).

Ex. 5.4

The dochmiac measure itself may fragment: the groups of three
and five occasionally appear in reverse order to make the so-called
hypodochmius, | ♩ ♪♩ ⫶ ♪♩ |, and the five-group (a paeon, when con-
sidered by itself) may be repeated a few times on its own, as at *Agamemnon* 1136–7 = 1146–7 (Ex. 5.5).

Ex. 5.5

Here and there we encounter an isolated measure of the apparent
form | ♪♩ ♪♩ ♪♩ |, which could be seen as the three-group of the
dochmius prefixed to an iambic instead of a paeonic unit.

Various other irregular forms occur in places, and it is not always
clear what rhythmic interpretation is to be put on the metrical data.
There may be two short notes where the normal dochmius in the
responding strophe has one: | ♫♩ ♩ ♪♩ | or | ♪♩ ♩♫ |. Or the second
short may be absent, ◡ – – –; this rarity sometimes stands at a pause,
and should perhaps be interpreted on the analogy of iambic | ◡ – – |
as | ♪♩ ♩ ♩. |.

The asymmetrical groupings which are the essence of dochmiac
rhythm are paralleled in the folk music of various countries, but particularly in that of the Balkans.[42] Bartók's specimens of Hungarian
folk music include a song from Transylvania which is in perfect
dochmiac rhythm (Ex. 5.6).[43]

[42] Sachs, *RT* 93f.; *WM* 116–18; Nettl, *FTM* 87–91.
[43] *Hungarian Folk Music*, ex. 36, cf. p. 57.

Ex. 5.6

♩ ♫♩ ♪♩ | ♪♩ ♫♩♩ ‖ ♫♩♩ ♪♩ | ♪♩ ♫♩♩ |

Georgiades cites from Greek folk music the measure ♩. ♩ ♪♩ alternating with ♪♩ ♩. ♩.[44] S. Baud-Bovy has drawn attention to Albanian melodies in $\frac{3+5}{16}$ time.[45] Sachs refers to 'the $3 + 3 + 2$ articulation of eight beats' as one 'which we find in practically all civilizations', and elsewhere to the currency in the Sudan and in Bantu Africa of the metre $3 + 3 + 2$, in which the members can be exchanged, $3 + 2 + 3$ or $2 + 3 + 3$.[46] The ancient Greek dochmiac's behaviour presents an interesting analogy with this formula.

Ionic

The so-called ionic rhythm, first attested in Sappho and Alcaeus, remained popular throughout Antiquity. Its basic form is ♩♩♫. The two short notes constituted the arsis and the two long ones the thesis.[47] The oldest and commonest variation consisted of linking two measures together by syncopation across the bar-line, ♩ | ♪ being inverted to become ♪♩ as in Example 5.7.

Ex. 5.7

♫♩ ♪♪♪ | ♪♪♪ ♩ | = ♩♫♩ ♪♩ ♪♩ ♩ ‖

This is the 'anacreontic' verse. Sometimes an irrational long was admitted in place of the short note in fourth place:[48]

♩♩ ♪♪ ♩♩ ♩ .

Further variety was achieved by shortening or lengthening the measure. Anacreon used the verse | ♫♩ ♩ | ♫♩ ♪♩ ♪♩ ♪♩ ♩ ‖, in the latter part of which bar-lines are of no use;[49] while in drama an ionic

[44] Georgiades, 82 f.
[45] *Revue de musicologie* 54 (1968), 14 f.
[46] *RT* 41, cf. 40, 65, 91, 102, 136, 191, 247–50, 357, 359, 367, 369, 371.
[47] 'Mar. Vict.' (Aphth.) *Gramm. Lat.* vi. 42. 16 ff., cf. 89. 21.
[48] A modern Thracian parallel: Georgiades 89, cf. 97.
[49] *PMG* 413, 414.

series can end with the extended figure |♫♩ ♪♩ ♩ ‖ as well as in various other ways. Interspersed among the triple-time measures there may be some in duple time, as in Aeschylus, *Persians* 68–72 = 76–80 (Ex. 5.8).

Ex. 5.8

It is sometimes supposed that these apparent duple bars were in fact triple, the long note being extended to twice its length, |♫♩ |, but this is an arbitrary hypothesis. The assumption of variable bar-length fits better with what we know of Classical Greek music than the assumption of doubled note-length. Other forms of lengthening and shortening occur at the beginning of a series: ♩ |♫♩ ♩ | or |♪♩ ♪♩ ♩ | or |𝄾♪♩ ♩ |.

In the course of time many alternative forms of ionic measure were evolved by the division of a long note into two short ones or the amalgamation of two shorts into a long: |♩ ♩ ♩ |, |♩ ♫♩ |, |♫♫♩ |, |♫♩ ♫|, and by the Hellenistic period |♩ ♫♫|, |♩ ♩ ♫|, and |♫♫♫|.

That might seem to exhaust the possibilities. But in Aristophanes a rather freer style of ionic makes it appearance, in which such measures as |♫♩ ♪| or |♩ ♪♩ ♩ |, where the note-values do not quite add up to the notional figure, are allowed to stand in responsion with the normal |♫♩ ♩ |. These free forms recur in later texts, together with others such as |♩ ♪♩ ♫|, |♩ ♪♫♩ |, |♩ ♩ ♪|, |♩ ♪♩ ♪|, |♩ ♩ ♩ ♪|, |♩ ♩ ♪♩ |, etc.[50] The texts in question are popular compositions, ranging from religious hymns to erotic songs. Sophisticated poets who used ionics maintained stricter standards. It is interesting to see this difference opening up, from the late fifth century onward,

[50] See my *Greek Metre*, 127, 142–7, 167–8.

between the metrical precision of educated composers and the greater flexibility and tolerance of popular music, at least in this rhythmical genus.

Aeolic

In all the rhythms considered so far, the short notes—apart from those obtained by dividing long notes in two—occur either singly (iambic, trochaic, paeonic, dochmiac) or in pairs (dactylic, anapaestic, ionic). Where both singles and doubles appear, it is as a result of some inversion with respect to the prototype, such as gives us the choriamb in iambic rhythm and the anacreontic in ionic. The aeolic category, on the other hand, is characterized from the start, one may almost say defined, by the coexistence of single and paired short notes.[51]

These appear most frequently in certain stereotyped patterns that recur through the centuries, usually clearly marked off as self-contained verses in a stanza or larger melodic structure. The most familiar is the 'glyconic', which presents the metrical scheme × × – ◡ ◡ – ◡ – or sometimes × × – × – ◡ ◡ – or – ◡ ◡ – ◡ – ◡ –. Associated with it, often closing a series, is the pherecratean, × × – ◡ ◡ – –. Other types commonly found have one syllable less at the beginning, and/or one more at the end (. . . ◡ – –).

How are we to interpret such sequences in terms of musical rhythm? First we must take note of the curious fact that several of these aeolic verses, as they appear in Sappho and Alcaeus, begin with two metrical positions of indifferent quantity: they may be both long, or both short, or one of each. This is a degree of freedom unknown in any other Greek metre. Normally any positions in a verse that do not have a fixed and definite length are separated by at least three that do. However, comparison with the metres of the *Rgveda* and of other Indo-European traditions indicates that the freedom at the beginning of the aeolic verses is a relic from a very ancient type of song in which, while the number of syllables (notes) in each line was fixed, it was only towards the end of the line that a particular pattern of long and short notes was imposed on them.[52]

[51] The use of the term 'aeolic' with this denotation is modern; such rhythms are frequent in the Aeolian poets Sappho and Alcaeus, but they were in common use throughout the Classical and Hellenistic periods.

[52] A. Meillet, *Les Origines indo-européennes des mètres grecs* (Paris, 1923); M. L. West, *Glotta* 51 (1973), 161–87; *Greek Metre*, 2–4.

Each line was clearly marked off from the next, but its internal structure did not lend itself to bar-divisions. One could not usefully beat time to it.

By Sappho's time this type of verse had acquired a more definite form. Her glyconic can be described as two unregulated notes which stand outside the rhythm, leading in to a rhythmized set of six notes: ● ● [♪ musical notation] ‖. The initial indeterminate notes are such an integral feature of the structure that they remain even when she extends the verse by prefixing the figure − ∪ − (fr. 98): − ∪ − : × × − ∪ ∪ − ∪ −.

But after Sappho and Alcaeus the freedom of these two notes was curbed. It became established that at least one of them should be long, and presently that such a long might be divided into two shorts. The quantitative principle, the counting of time, took them into its control. There was still freedom as between − ∪ and − −, but this is no greater freedom than we find in several other types of rhythm, where it represents the pressing of two long notes into the space appropriate for a long and a short.

The whole verse should now be amenable to rhythmic analysis. The ancients divided it into two measures, one 'antispastic' ('retroflex'), i.e. ∪ ⏑ − ∪, the other iambic, ∪ − ∪ −, each containing a thesis and arsis of equal duration.[53] In modern notation: [musical notation].

We should certainly accept this analysis in preference to nineteenth-century attempts on the lines of [musical notation] which are based on the premise, laid down by August Boeckh, that the verse is made up of trochaic and (irrational) dactylic feet, each bar beginning with a long note.[54] This reflects the way in which German- and English-speakers instinctively read such metre, aligning long syllables with stressed beats which we make equidistant, and taking the intervening short syllables faster or slower according to whether there are more or fewer of them.[55] The ancient analysis gives an altogether more interesting rhythm, hinging on the juxtaposition of ♩ ♪ with ♪♩, something that we have already met in the choriambic inversion of iambic. The glyconic variants in which the sequence ♩ ♪♪♩ occupies the first or the second half of the verse instead of the centre appear

---

[53] Heph. *Ench.* 10, Aristid. Quint. p. 49. 20 ff.; 'Mar. Vict.' (Aphth.) *Gramm. Lat.* vi. 42. 13, 88. 6 ff.   [54] Cf. R. Westphal, *Griechische Rhythmik*, 134.
[55] Cf. Georgiades 64–71; my *Greek Metre*, 23.

quite natural from this point of view. So do the extended verses which
we often find in the Lesbian poets and later, in which the glyconic, or
one of the other aeolic prototypes, undergoes 'choriambic expansion', as in Example 5.9,

Ex. 5.9

or, with the two initial notes brought into the rhythm, as in Example
5.10.

Ex. 5.10

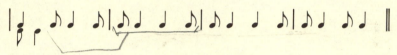

In other poems we find 'dactylic expansion', in which only the
segment − ∪ ∪ (or ∪ ∪ −) is repeated: × × − ∪ ∪ − ∪ ∪ − ∪ ∪ − ∪ −.
One might say that here successive 'bars' of the form ♩ ♪♪♩ are
being overlapped or impacted, as if different voices were chiming in,
each taking the last note of the previous voice's bar as the first of its
own. But only once voice is involved.

The notion of impacted bars may seem artificial. But it makes
sense of certain odd sequences that we find elsewhere in aeolic verse,
where the rhythm apparently goes awry. In the so-called Sapphic
stanza we find two readily analysable lines of the form shown in
Example 5.11,

Ex. 5.11

and then one of the form illustrated by Example 5.12.

Ex. 5.12

What is here represented as a 10/8 bar arises from the impaction of two of the 6/8 bar-types used in the preceding lines: ♩ ♪♪♩ ♪♪ · . It is similar with the Alcaic stanza, which is also built from two matching lines followed by a third which is longer and develops their rhythms further. The pattern of the first two lines is

Ex. 5.13

$$\mathbf{^6_8} \; \bullet \; | \; \text{♩} \; \text{♪♩} \; \bullet \; | \; \text{♩} \; \text{♪♪♩} \; | \; \text{♪♩} \; \text{⸗}$$

And of the third:

Ex. 5.14

$$\mathbf{^6_8} \; \bullet \; | \; \text{♩} \; \text{♪♩} \; \bullet \; | \; \text{♩} \; \text{♪♩} \; \bullet \; | \mathbf{^{10}_{8}} \text{♩} \; \text{♪♪♩} \; \text{♪♪♩} \; | \mathbf{^6_8} \text{♪♩} \; \text{♩} \; \text{⸗} \; \|$$

Again the 10/8 bar represents two of the 6/8 bars overlapped, this time both of the same form, as in the dactylic expansion discussed above.

To some people it will perhaps seem more natural to measure the line according to the pattern of Example 5.15;

Ex. 5.15

$$\mathbf{^6_8} \; \bullet \; | \; \text{♩} \; \text{♪♩} \; \bullet \; | \; \text{♩} \; \text{♪♩} \; \bullet \; | \; \text{♩} \; \overline{\text{♪♪♩}}^4 \; \overline{\text{♪♫}}^4 | \; \text{♩} \; \text{♪♩} \; \bullet \; \|$$

but we should not allow our own culturally determined sense of what is natural in these matters to induce us to reject an odd-looking but vital rhythm in favour of a relatively bland one. All aeolic verses can be made to sound like gently babbling brooks if one adopts the Boeckhian method of assuming that $-\cup\cup$ and $-\cup$ occupy equal time. If, on the other hand, one takes these metrical asymmetries to betoken rhythmic asymmetries, one is rewarded by the discovery of many snappy syncopations and lively, wrong-footing changes of bar-length, disconcerting to people brought up on English nursery rhymes and the Viennese or Liverpudlian classics, but in keeping with what we have found in several other of the ancient Greek rhythmical genres, and with the character of Balkan music as it exists today.

Juxtaposition of different rhythms

Each of the six types of rhythm described above may be found maintained from beginning to end of a song. But it is also common for
more than one of them to appear. Among the very simple strophic
forms used by Archilochus, for example, we find one that consists of
a dactylic hexameter followed by an iambic dimeter, and another
(Ex. 5.16) that changes from dactylic to trochaic within the first line
(with word-end at the point of transition).

Ex. 5.16

[musical notation]

Another has three verses: an iambic trimeter and dimeter (6/8 time)
separated by *[musical notation]*.[56]

From the sixth century to the third much use was made of the
metrical type called dactylo-epitrite, in which the configuration
[musical notation], or occasionally some other with paired short
notes, combined freely with the trochaic *[musical notation]*. In this
type of metre the trochaic measure had the form *[musical notation]* much more
regularly than *[musical notation]*, so that rather than treating the fourth note as
an irrational long admitted on sufferance, we may as well say that the
standard form is *[musical notation]*, with *[musical notation]* occasionally allowed
instead.[57] The rhythmical scheme of the strophe of Pindar's First
Pythian Ode may tentatively be analysed as in Example 5.17. A
comma marks the ends of periods, in other words, places at which
there was a pause and metrical continuity was interrupted. The two
5/4 bars could be made up to 3/2 by assuming the last long note to
be prolonged to twice its length. Some support for this procedure

---

[56] This 5/4 bar is a form of the so-called *paiōn epibatos*, for which see below,
p. 156. It seems to be this strophe-form that is meant when Archilochus is credited
with being the first to combine iambic lines with the *paiōn epibatos* (ps.-Plut. *De mus.*
1141a).

[57] Similar 7/8 rhythms are found in modern Greece, Bulgaria, Hungary, etc. See
S. Baud-Bovy, *Hellenika* 34 (1982/3), 191–201.

Ex. 5.17

may be found in a papyrus fragment in dactylo-epitrite metre (**42** *PBerol.* 6870. 16–19), where the rhythmical notation clearly indicates ♩ ♫♩ ♫♩ |♩ ♫… However, while this text may possibly be from a drama of Classical date, the musical setting is probably of the Roman period, and it may not be a reliable guide to Pindaric practice.

A similar doubt arises with the commonest of all Archaic song forms, the elegiac couplet, which is a little strophe composed of a dactylic hexameter followed by $- \overline{\cup\cup} - \overline{\cup\cup} - | - \cup\cup - \cup\cup - \|$. People generally assume a lengthening of the syllable before the central join, or a pause after it, to make the rhythm run evenly according to our notions. But from a Greek standpoint there is no reason why 5/4 bars, |♩ ♫♩ ♫♩ |, should not succeed each other directly, as do 5/8 paeonic bars, |♩ ♪♩ |♩ ♪♩ |.

Much fifth-century choral and dramatic lyric is characterized by the use of rhythms of more than one category. Sometimes it is a matter of introducing a brief element of contrast with a prevailing rhythm, as when a dactylic line appears near the end of an iambic strophe, the last line being again iambic.[58] Sometimes there is a definite change of horses, as in the third Epinician Ode of Bacchylides and the Thirteenth Olympian of Pindar, where aeolic passes into dactylo-epitrite. Often the situation is more complex. The

---

[58] Aesch. *Ag.* 165, *al.*; *Greek Metre*, 100, 104.

greatest diversity of rhythms is found towards the end of the fifth century and in the early fourth, in the elaborate compositions of citharodes such as Timotheus and in some of the long solo arias and lyric dialogues of late Euripides and Sophocles. An analysis of Philoctetes' dialogue with the sailor chorus in Sophocles' *Philoctetes*, 1169–217, will serve to illustrate the point: 1169–74 iambic, 1175–85 ionic, 1186–7 anapaestic, 1188–95 aeolic, twice diversified with dactylic lines, 1196–208 dactylic, 1209 aeolic, 1210–12 iambic, 1213 aeolic, 1214–15 dactylo-epitrite, 1216–17 aeolic.

It should be emphasized that this heterogeneity was a feature of a particular style of music fashionable at that period, and not of Greek music overall. By Aristoxenus' time the fashion had faded. He observes:

Complexity of rhythmic composition was taken further by the older musicians. They certainly valued rhythmic intricacy, and the business of the instrumental discourses was more complex then. For whereas the moderns are lovers of melody, the men of that time were lovers of rhythm.[59]

Most later Classical, Hellenistic, and post-Hellenistic texts, including the fragments that we possess with musical notation, are characterized by homogeneous rhythms.

TEMPO

Some kinds of dance were faster than others, and some kinds of song. A dramatic chorus or aria expressing urgency or excitement, for example, would have gone quicker than a solemn hymn sung round an altar. Greek writers recognize tempo (*agōgē*) as one of the variable factors in music that make a difference to its effect. To some extent it was bound up with rhythm, certain rhythms being perceived as intrinsically faster or slower than others.[60] We saw that the trochaic rhythm was felt to have a running or tripping effect, that paeonic was associated with lively dancing, and that dochmiac was used only when the tone was urgent or impassioned. A predominance of short notes went with rapidity, and a predominance of long ones with the opposite.[61] On the other hand, a measure in a given rhythm might be taken at perceptibly different tempi.[62]

---

[59] Aristox. ap. ps.-Plut. *De mus.* 1138bc.
[60] Cf. Damon ap. Pl. *Resp.* 400c, Aristid. Quint. pp. 82. 15, 83. 3, 84. 3.
[61] Aristid. Quint. p. 82. 15.
[62] Aristox. *Harm.* 2. 34 and fr. ap. Porph. in Ptol. *Harm.* pp. 78 f. (pp. 32–4 Pearson); Aristid. Quint. p. 39. 26 ff.

The ancients have, of course, left us no metronome markings. But we are not completely without means of forming some ideas about absolute tempo. Nearly all of the music with which we are concerned was vocal music in which the short and long notes corresponded to short and long syllables. So there was a natural limit to the speed at which it could go, in the speed at which the words could be articulated; and we have no reason to suspect that there was any form of song in which the words were gabbled as fast as possible. Nor is it likely that they were sung much more slowly than they would be uttered in ordinary speech, because short syllables cannot support undue lengthening in delivery. That is a fundamental feature of the opposition between short syllables and long ones: long syllables can be prolonged ad lib., short ones cannot. When the Greeks wanted texts for very slow singing, they composed them without short syllables (see below). For normal texts, then, we should assume a tempo-range related to that of ordinary speech, though perhaps in general a little more deliberate, as in the musical rhythm (*tempo giusto* as opposed to *parlando-rubato*) the long syllables had to be slightly longer in relation to the shorts than in speech. The tempo would also be more uniform (within a given song); there may have been some expressive variation, but it would hardly be as great as the variations of tempo inherent in natural speech.[63]

Further indications can be drawn from the relation of music to movement. We do not know how to match notes to dance-steps. But when a tragic chorus (of old men, it may be) makes an unhurried entrance marching in anapaestic rhythm—chanting, not singing, but the aulos accompaniment was melodic—we can match their syllables to their steps easily enough. One measure, | ♩♩♩♩ ♩♩♩ |, must correspond to a double pace; no alternative has any plausibility. That gives us a fair idea of the tempo. Similarly, when a comic chorus arrives in hot pursuit of someone while chanting or singing in trochaic rhythm—again perhaps old men, not able to run as fast as they used to, but still jogging along—we can equate the trochaic measure | ♩♪♩ ♪ | with their double pace.[64] When they are not

---

[63] Aristid. Quint. p. 40. 1 speaks of change of tempo as one type of rhythmic modulation.

[64] Ar. *Nub.* 204 ff., cf. *Eq.* 247 ff., *Pax* 301 ff. Trochaic rhythm is also found in tragedy in association with running or hasty entries, but perhaps not such direct (performative) association: Eur. *Ion* 1250, *Or.* 729, 1506, 1549; Soph. *OC* 887.

running but walking at a good speed, Aristophanes makes the rhythm iambic.[65]

Spondaic tempo

From the Archaic period to the Imperial age we find occasional texts composed entirely of long syllables.[66] With one exception (a children's game-song) they are invocations of gods, especially in the context of libations, or otherwise expressive of religious solemnity. They bear witness to an enduring tradition of liturgical song in which the tempo was too slow to tolerate short syllables.

Because of the association with libations (*spondē*) the ancients gave the name 'spondee' (*spondeios*) to the foot consisting of two long syllables,[67] and the metre of the texts in question is usually described as spondaic. In fact several different metres are represented, and it would be better to say that it is the tempo that is spondaic.

From the texts themselves we can see that the long syllables (notes) are organized in groups of ten, or in other cases three, five, or seven. From the Berlin Paean (**40**), which is furnished with melodic and rhythmical notation, we know that some of the long notes had twice the duration of others. In other words the contrast of short and long notes did not disappear in this slow music, but instead of being a contrast of monoseme and diseme ($\cup$: −) it became a contrast of diseme and tetraseme (− : $\sqcup$). Where we only have the words of the text, the pattern of contrast is concealed. The rhythm of the Paean is in fact slowed-down anapaestic (Ex. 5.18).

Ex. 5.18

---

[65] *Vesp.* 230 ff., *Lys.* 254 ff., *Eccl.* 285 ff., *Plut.* 257 ff.

[66] 'Terpander', *PMG* 698, Anon. *PMG* 876 (*a*), 941, 1027 (*c*), cf. Eur. *Ion* 125–7, Ar. *Av.* 1058–64, 1067–8; **40** Berlin Paean; Mesomedes 2. 1–5 and 4 Heitsch; hymn to Attis ap. Hippol. *Haer.* 5. 9. 9 (Heitsch, *Die griechischen Dichterfragmente der römischen Kaiserzeit*, no. 44. 3); Synesius *Hymn* 3.

[67] 'From the rhythm that is played on the auloi and sung to at libations', Anon. Ambros. p. 224. 10 Stud. It was this music that calmed the disorderly young man in the anecdote about Pythagoras (above, p. 31), and Cicero in telling the story refers specifically to the slow tempo of the tune.

The notes are often subdivided melodically (♩ into ♫, ♩ into ♪ ♫), but not divided between more than one syllable. The poetic text accordingly shows, or would show if we had it complete, a regular alternation of five and seven long syllables.

The same rhythm appears in the first of two short instrumental pieces in the same papyrus (**41**), while the other piece (**43**)—also in slow time, as the number of arsis-signs shows—is in paeonic 5/4. The up- and down-beats, as indicated by the points above the notes, fluctuate interestingly between 𝆑 𝆑 𝆑 𝆑 𝆑 (2 + 3) and 𝆑 𝆑 𝆑 𝆑 𝆑 (3 + 2). We recognize here a measure described by Aristides Quintilianus: the *paiōn epibatos* (perhaps 'paeon for walking to'), ⌣ — ⌣ — —. He also attests the Greater or Double Spondee, ⌣ ⌣.[68]

In the spondaic texts without musical notation we are reduced to guessing which were the double-length notes and what the rhythmical scheme was. Possible equivalences for the different phraselengths are

Three-syllable: ⌣ — ⌣ (paeon) or — — ⌣ (anapaest).
Five- or ten-syllable: — — — — — (paeon).
Seven-syllable: — — — — ⋮ — — ⌣ (anapaest).[69]

Expanded beats

The ancient rhythmicians also knew of measures called *orthios* and *trochaios sēmantos* ('marked trochee'). The first consisted of a tetraseme arsis and a thesis of twice that length (⌣ ⌣ ⌣), the second consisted of the same elements reversed (⌣ ⌣ ⌣).[70] These may look like further forms of slow tempo, even slower than those we have just considered. But the tetraseme and octaseme durations do not necessarily correspond to single syllables. It is true that Aristides Quintilianus states that these rhythms conduce to dignity because of the number of notes of the longest values. But no single note had octaseme length.[71] From the unidentified writer on rhythm in *POxy.*

---

[68] Aristid. Quint. pp. 35. 12, 37. 7; cf. ps.-Plut. *De mus.* 1141a, 1143b. In the instrumental piece a crotchet on an up-beat is sometimes replaced by a rest.

[69] Cf. my *Greek Metre*, 55f., 172.

[70] Aristid. Quint. p. 36. 3, cf. 36. 29, 83. 4; ps.-Plut. *De mus.* 1140f.

[71] Aristid. Quint. p. 32. 27 makes tetraseme the maximum; in Anon. Bellerm. 1 (= 83) and 3 the series goes up to pentaseme, five shorts (cf. Al-Fārābī pp. 150f. D'Erlanger).

2687 we hear that the *orthios* or the marked trochee might be realized as $(6/8 + 12/8)$ $|-\cup-\cup\,\vdots-\cup-\cup-\cup-\cup|$ or as $(9/8)$ $|-\cup-\cup-\cup|$.[72] The exact interpretation of the passage is somewhat uncertain, but the point is evidently that the terms *orthios* and marked trochee were applicable where rhythmic cells were organized in threes to make a higher unity with a single down-beat. In modern terms they would correspond to the longer bars in triple time. The dactylo-epitrite segments described above as bars in 3/2 rhythm, $|\,\flat\,\,\flat\flat\,\flat\,\,\flat\flat\,\flat\,\,\flat\,|$, might presumably qualify as a 'marked trochee'.

The writer goes on to say that a paeon might be made up analogously from five-syllable groups. This connects with a statement by Michael Psellus, who was drawing on a lost section of Aristoxenus' work, that the paeonic type of foot could be expanded up to the total duration of twenty-five shorts.[73] In other words, an assembly of notes as large as $|\,\flat\,\,\flat\flat\flat\,\flat\,\,\flat\flat\flat\,\flat\,\,\flat\flat\flat\,\flat\,\,\flat\flat\flat\,\flat\,\,\flat\flat\,|$

could be encompassed in the five-beat scheme ⌐⊓⊓⊓⊓⌐.[74]

What is involved in all these cases is a relatively slow beat, but not at all a slow musical tempo. On the contrary, it was with a reasonably brisk tempo that the shorter note-groups were most likely to be felt as constituents of larger groupings.

The ethos of different rhythms

The Greek composer's choice of rhythms was to some extent limited, if not determined, by the current conventions of the particular tradition or genre in which he was working. To the extent that he had freedom of choice, he might have exercised it on more than one principle. He might have been influenced by some other music that happened to be running in his head, or by the shape of the words that presented themselves most readily to his mind, or by his own established habits. But sometimes, certainly, he must have chosen a rhythm for the particular mood or effect that it was suited to convey.

From the time of the sophists there existed a body of doctrine on

---

[72] Col. iii 30–iv 1, cf. Pearson 41, 82f.

[73] *Preliminaries to the Science of Rhythm* 12 (Pearson 24), cf. Excerpta Neapol. 14 (Pearson 30), Aristid. Quint. p. 34. 10.

[74] The comic poet Theopompus used such paeonic pentameters, as the metricians called them, in his *Boys* (fr. 39), and Hephaestion says they bore the name *Theopompeion* because of it.

the ethos of different rhythms. It served for the criticism both of music and of prose writing, especially oratory.[75] Aesthetic and moral qualities were attributed to various rhythms, partly on the basis of their actual associations with dances or songs of a particular character, partly subjectively, and partly from theoretical considerations such as whether the thesis and arsis were equal in duration or, if they were unequal, what sort of mathematical relationship obtained between them. Rhythms were evaluated especially in terms of the oppositions

> calm, steady : quick, fervid
> dignified, grand : undignified, lowly
> manly, stirring : effeminate, sensuous.

Dactylic rhythm, especially as manifested in the heroic hexameter, was considered grand, noble, and steady.[76] Iambic and trochaic were more mobile; of the two, iambic was close to the rhythm of ordinary speech, businesslike, not deficient in dignity, while trochaic was less dignified, more tripping, more dancing, and indeed more *kordākikos*, that is, with the character of the lively and vulgar dance called the *kordāx*.[77]

The higher the proportion of long to short syllables/notes, the grander and more dignified the rhythm was perceived as being.[78] So feet containing only shorts were fast, fervid, lacking in dignity, but suitable to the quick dance in armour called the *pyrrhichē*.[79] Feet containing only longs, on the other hand, were solemn and stately, above all when extra-long time values were involved.[80] This was

---

[75] For music see especially Aristid. Quint. 2. 15 p. 82. 4–84. 10; for oratory, Arist. *Rh.* 1408[b]32 ff.; Dion. Hal. *Comp.* 104 ff. The whole subject is treated by G. Amsel, *De vi atque indole rhythmorum quid veteres iudicaverint* (Breslau, 1887). See also below, pp. 246 ff.

[76] Arist. *Poet.* 1459[b]32, cf. *Pol.* 1340[b]8, *Rh.* 1408[b]32, Dion. Hal. *Comp.* 108 (who finds anapaests also grand), 'Longinus', *Subl.* 39. 4, Aristid. Quint. p. 47. 4.

[77] Arist. *Rh.* 1408[b]33–7, cf. *Poet.* 1449[a]24, 1459[a]12, 1460[a]1, *Pol.* 1340[b]9, Dion. Hal. *Comp.* 106, 'Longinus', *Subl.* 41. 1. Aristid. Quint. p. 83. 2 calls both rhythms rapid, hot, and dancelike. On p. 82. 4 he makes the surprising statement that rhythms which begin on the down-beat (this would include trochaic) are calmer than those starting on the up-beat. Cf. also above, p. 140 n. 30.

[78] Cf. Aristid. Quint. p. 76. 21 ff. Long rests too were grander than brief ones (p. 82. 8).

[79] Dion. Hal. *Comp.* 105, 107, cf. 'Longinus' *Subl.* 41. 1, Aristid. Quint. pp. 82. 15 ff., 83. 30. The name pyrrhich was given to the measure ‿ ‿ or ‿ ‿ ‿ ‿.

[80] Dion. Hal. *Comp.* 105, 107, Aristid. Quint. pp. 82. 16 ff., 83. 5.

held to conduce to a calm and serious (but not quiescent) state of mind.[81]

Rhythms with equal thesis and arsis, or as we should say, those in duple time, were judged more even, orderly, and grateful. Those in 2 : 1 ratio (triple time) were less so, though the purity of the arithmetic left them with an element of evenness. Those in 3 : 2 or 4 : 3 ratio (quintuple or septuple time) were more disturbed, more carried away.[82] Aristides Quintilianus adds an interesting remark on the *paiōn epibatos* with its combination of quintuple time and long notes. It disturbs the soul with its double thesis (cf. above, p. 156), while at the same time arousing the mind to exaltation with the length of its arsis. As a response to religious music this seems altogether suitable.

Regularity of rhythm goes with equanimity, so it is natural that Aristides finds an emotional character in what he calls compound rhythms, that is, those in which (according to ancient analysis) feet of different kinds were put together. They include our dochmiac, ionic, and aeolic categories.[83] Dochmiac, as we saw, was certainly a passionate metre. We cannot say the same generally of ionic and aeolic, which are rather versatile, but it is true as regards some of the uses to which they are put.

We should beware of assuming that all these theorists' statements represent an ancient consensus, and of using them mechanically to account for the choice of particular rhythms in particular compositions. I have suggested some of the other factors that may be involved. But some of the ancients' observations make good sense to us. We can readily appreciate the 'running' character of trochaics, the solemnity of long and slow notes, the lack of solemnity in short and rapid ones, and the unsettling quality of asymmetrical rhythms. We should have been inclined to find these characteristics for ourselves, and we are fortunate in having the evidence that they appeared to ancient critics in a similar light.

---

[81] Dion. Hal. *Dem.* 22, Aristid. Quint. p. 82. 18 ff., cf. 83. 26 f.; above, p. 155 n. 67. Galen, *De placitis Hippocratis et Platonis* p. 452 Müller, says that *orthios* rhythms are suitable for pulling the sluggish and despondent together.

[82] Aristid. Quint. p. 82. 10–29, with a reference to the rhythms of the human pulse.

[83] Aristid. Quint. p. 83. 7 ff. *A fortiori*, music in which the rhythms keep changing, perhaps with corresponding changes in dance-steps, plunge the mind into turmoil, p. 83. 14 ff.

6

Scales and Modes

Before we come to melody itself we must investigate the rails on which it ran: the scales that provided a framework of discipline by limiting the infinity of possible notes and intervals to an ordered set, and the varieties of their structures and associations that make it appropriate and conventional to speak of modes.

Our information is, of course, far from complete. But Aristoxenus and other theoreticians formulate general principles which are supposed to govern the structure of scales, and they specify the sizes of intervals between successive degrees of the scale in various different tuning systems. There are some records of actual scales used in the Classical period, and numerous references to the names and characters of different modes. The surviving fragments of musical texts give us glimpses of scale systems in use.

The anatomy of the octave

The ancient writers attach great importance to the distinction between 'concordant' and 'discordant' intervals (*symphōna, diaphōna*). By concordant intervals they mean those at which two notes, sounded either simultaneously or successively, go well together or seem to blend harmoniously. The intervals which they regard as concordant are the fourth, the fifth, and the octave (or larger intervals compounded from these, octave + fourth, etc.). All other intervals were classed as discordant, though considered perfectly acceptable in melody provided that they arose between notes of a properly constituted scale.

The higher status of the recognized concords was reflected in the structure of scales. All scales (according to Greek theory) are built up from 'tetrachords', that is, from systems of four notes spanning the interval of a fourth. Successive tetrachords were either 'conjunct', that is, with a shared note (for example, *d–g–c'*), or 'disjunct', separated by a tone (for example, *d–g: a–d'*). Since a fourth plus a tone equals a fifth, a pair of disjunct tetrachords is in effect a fourth (subdivided into three smaller steps) and a fifth (subdivided into four), making up an octave (for example, *d–g: g–a–d'*, or *d–g–a: a–d'*). A pair of conjunct tetrachords, with the addition of a tone at the top or bottom, likewise make up an octave resolvable into a fourth + fifth, or fifth + fourth. These are in fact the ways in which the octave, where it appears in Greek music as a significant entity, is constructed. The three alternatives are shown in Fig. 6.1. The tone not included in the tetrachords is called the disjunction (*diazeuxis*).

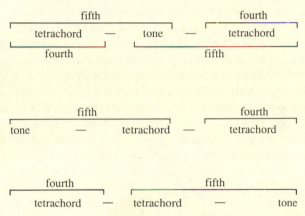

Fig. 6.1. The construction of the octave in Greek music

Not all music had a compass as wide as an octave. As we shall see, some music did not extend over even two conjunct tetrachords (a seventh). Yet always, so far as we can see, the intervals of the fifth and especially the fourth had a cardinal place in any scale. These lesser spans are of more fundamental and primordial importance in Greek music than the octave compounded from them.

The anatomy of the fourth

The scales familiar to us in Western music are diatonic, that is, they are made up of steps that are never larger than a tone nor smaller than a semitone. Two tones and a semitone make up a fourth, three tones and a semitone make up a fifth, so that a typical octave scale has a form such as

	fifth			fourth		
T	T	S	T	T	T	S

The Greeks knew this diatonic principle of dividing up fourths and fifths, so that a tetrachord spanning the interval *e* to *a* might consist straightforwardly of the four notes *e f g a* (S T T). But they also knew alternative, non-diatonic systems, and in the Classical period these predominated. In such systems the octave contained only *one* step of a tone, namely the disjunction. The steps within the tetrachords were all either larger or smaller than a tone. This is one reason why it was natural for Greek theorists to see the tetrachord as a unit of analysis. It stood out more clearly than it does in a diatonic scale.

The ancients distinguished three 'types' of scale, or 'genera' as it is customary to say, rendering the Greek *genos* by the Latin *genus*. The diatonic was one. The other two were called enharmonic and chromatic.[1] In the enharmonic, the two inner notes of the tetrachord were crowded down close to the bottom, at intervals of only about a quarter-tone, leaving a wide gap of two tones above them. In the chromatic genus they were again bunched low down, but at intervals of more like a semitone. The wider interval above them was in this case something like a minor third ($1\frac{1}{2}$ tones). The pattern of the tetrachord in the three genera was:[2]

enharmonic *e e↑ f a*
chromatic *e f f♯ a*
diatonic *e f g a*

These are the standard definitions, but the pitching of the inner notes could fluctuate within certain limits. More on this below.

Two further points of ancient terminology may conveniently be mentioned here. The outer notes of the tetrachord, which remained fixed in their mutual relationship a fourth apart in all genera and marked out the skeleton of the octave, were called the standing notes, while the inner ones, whose position varied from genus to genus, were called the moving notes. The bunch of three notes close together at the bottom of the enharmonic and chromatic tetrachords was known as the *pyknon* ('close-packed').

Before we go further, let us see if we can discover what lies behind this odd diversity in the arrangement of degrees of the scale. Ethnomusicology has light to shed on the matter.

[1] Those familiar with these terms in connection with Western music will note that their meanings have changed since Antiquity.

[2] The reader is reminded that a small arrow pointing up or down indicates a note raised or lowered by a microtone, that is, an interval less than a semitone. Where no further precision is given it may be taken as more or less a quarter-tone.

The interval of the fourth has an important structural role in the music of many peoples, particularly in certain geographical zones: Scotland and Ireland, eastern and south-eastern Europe, northern Africa, southern Asia as far east as Indonesia, and Indian North America.[3] Here and there melodies can be found based wholly on two notes a fourth apart with no (or only occasional) intermediate notes to bridge the gap.[4] More usually there is at least one 'infix', an additional note dividing the fourth into smaller steps. The steps are always unequal, the larger one being anything between a minor and a major third, and the smaller one accordingly something between a tone and a semitone.

In this case, where there is just one infix in the fourth, we have a scale of the type called pentatonic, because in an octave constructed in this way there will be just five steps, for example, *A c d e g a*, or *e f a b c' e'*. Pentatonic systems are found in the folk music of many parts of the world, including these islands; many Scottish melodies in particular are pentatonic.

Now, Aristoxenus (and other, unspecified experts before him) believed that the Greek enharmonic tetrachord (*e e↑ f a*) had evolved from a simpler, pentatonic trichord, *e f a*, by division of the semitone *e–f* into two quarter-tones. The evidence adduced was a traditional aulos tune played at libations and attributed to the semi-legendary piper Olympus. In Aristoxenus' time it was generally played with the divided semitone, but, he said, if you listen to someone playing it in the old-fashioned way, you can see that the semitone is meant to be undivided. In other compositions—deemed to be later ones—Olympus did divide the semitone and so invented the enharmonic genus.[5] Whether Olympus was really the author of the various traditional airs ascribed to him, we cannot tell. But the important fact is that there was an 'old-fashioned' way of playing at least one of them without dividing the semitone. Aristoxenus drew the right inference: that the enharmonic type of scale evolved from one in which the fourth was divided by a single infix into semitone and major third.

---

[3] Sachs, *WM* 63, 163; cf. *The Musical Quarterly* 29 (1943), 381–404. By contrast, according to the same authority, the third is the important interval in black Africa, most of Europe, and northern Asia.

[4] Sachs, *WM* 62. One passing reference in Aristoxenus implies the existence of melodies composed entirely from 'standing' notes, i.e. using empty fourths (*Harm.* 2. 44, amplified in Cleon. *Harm.* p. 189. 9–15).

[5] Aristox. fr. 83 ap. ps.-Plut. *De mus.* 1134f–1135b; cf. Thrasyllus ap. Theon. Smyrn. p. 93. 1 (Barker, *GMW* ii. 229 with n. 91).

Echoes of this old pentatonic style can still be found in certain musical texts from the third and second centuries BC.

Aristoxenus went wrong, however, in supposing that Olympus arrived at his *e f a* trichord by starting from the diatonic *e f g a* and leaving out a note.[6] On the contrary, the diatonic system represents the filling in of the wide interval in the trichord by means of a second infix.[7] The enharmonic and diatonic genera are to be seen as alternative developments from the same pentatonic matrix:

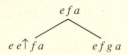

As for the chromatic (*e f f♯ a*), it seems to be analogous to the enharmonic, only based on a primary division of the fourth into tone + minor third rather than semitone + major third. As in the enharmonic, it is the smaller of the two intervals that is filled in by a secondary infix, creating a cluster of notes, the *pyknon*, while the larger interval remains inviolate.

The advance of diatonicism

In the fifth century BC, music of a serious character appears to have been normally of the enharmonic type. This genus is reported to have been typical of Simonides, Pindar, tragedy, and the old style generally.[8] Old tunes attributed to Olympus and Polymnestus were enharmonic or came to be played enharmonically.[9] A set of six 'very ancient' (no doubt fifth-century) scales described by Aristides Quintilianus are all enharmonic.[10] Aristoxenus says that theoreticians before him had concerned themselves exclusively with this genus.[11] The name 'enharmonic' itself implies its prime status, as it means 'in tune'; the enharmonic genus is quite often referred to simply as

[6] Loc. cit. Aristoxenus held the diatonic genus to be the most natural and the first to have been discovered (*Harm.* 1. 19).

[7] Cf. Sachs, *WM* 64f.; Kunst, 43.

[8] Alcidamas(?) in *PHib.* 13. 20, Plut. *De audiendo* 46b(?), ps.-Plut. *De mus.* 1137d–f, 1145a, Psell. *De trag.* 5.

[9] Polymnestus, a 7th-c. piper from Colophon, is said to have widened (or created by widening) certain intervals of ¾ tone falling and 1¼ tone rising, called respectively *eklysis* (release) and *ekbolē* (discharge); they were uncommon, and occurred only in the enharmonic genus (ps.-Plut. *De mus.* 1141b, Aristid. Quint. p. 28. 1, Bacchius, *Harm.* 36–7, 41–2).

[10] Aristid. Quint. p. 18. 5ff. See below, p. 174.

[11] Aristox. *Harm.* 1. 2, 2. 35, ps.-Plut. *De mus.* 1143e.

harmoniā, 'the (standard) tuning', whereas the chromatic genus, *chrōma* for short, is marked by its name as a kind of deviation, a 'colouring'. Chromatic was associated with professional citharodes, probably since about the mid-fifth century.[12] Modernists such as Euripides and Agathon made some use of it in tragedy, but it remained abnormal there.[13] Some maintained that it made men soft and effeminate, whereas enharmonic music made them manly.[14]

As for diatonic, we hear that some tragic enharmonic had an admixture of diatonic,[15] and that dithyrambic poets like Timotheus, Philoxenus, and Telestes were liable to modulate between all three genera.[16] Pure diatonic music, however, may have been typical only of certain regions of the Greek world at this period. A sophist, perhaps Alcidamas, claims that everyone knows that diatonic music is to be found among the Aetolians, the Dolopes, and all the tribes that sacrifice at Thermopylae.[17] In the South Italian Pythagorean school it seems to have been the diatonic genus, not the enharmonic, that enjoyed the primary status in musical theory.[18]

By the late fourth century enharmonic had lost a good deal of ground. Aristoxenus upheld it as being the most sophisticated and beautiful of the genera, but lamented the fact that it was now largely neglected in favour of the chromatic, which people found easier to appreciate and more ingratiating.[19] The musical fragments from the third and second centuries BC show a mixture of chromatic and diatonic.[20] Those from the Roman period are almost wholly diatonic.[21] There is some evidence for a marginal survival of enharmonic. Dionysius of Halicarnassus writes that when he reads Isocrates' speeches he becomes calm and solemn in mood, 'like

---

[12] Praxidamas ap. Phot./Sud. s.v. *chīazein* (Ar. fr. 930); fake Laconian decree about Timotheus in Boethius, *Inst. Mus.* 1. 1 p. 182. 12 Friedl.; Dion. Hal. *Comp.* 132; ps.-Plut. *De mus.* 1137ef.

[13] Plut. *Quaest. conv.* 645de, Psell. *De trag.* 5; ps.-Plut. loc. cit.

[14] See pp. 247f.

[15] Psell. loc. cit.

[16] Dion. Hal. *Comp.* 132.

[17] *PHib.* 13. 17ff. The statement may mean that diatonic songs were sung at the meetings of the Amphictionic League.

[18] Philolaus fr. 6, cf. Pl. *Tim.* 35b–36b. Philolaus in fact considered all three genera, and so did Archytas and his fellow-Tarentine Aristoxenus; but thereby they certainly gave the diatonic more attention than it had had.

[19] *Harm.* 1. 23 and ap. ps.-Plut. *De mus.* 1145a; echoed by Theon Smyrn. p. 55. 15–56. 3.

[20] Ch. 10, nos. **7–13**.

[21] Ch. 10, nos. **15–51**.

people listening to libation-airs on the pipes, or to enharmonic Dorian songs'; 'classical' music is evidently in question.[22] Philo says that the seven-stringed lyre is the best of instruments because it best displays the most dignified of the genera used in song, the enharmonic. He may, however, simply be echoing older theory.[23] Ptolemy, after specifying harmonic ratios for the intervals in the various genera and their sub-types, says:

> Now of the genera that have been set out, we would find all the diatonic ones familiar to our ears, but not to the same extent the enharmonic, nor the soft one of the chromatics, because people do not altogether enjoy those of the characters (*ēthē*) that are exceedingly slackened.[24]

A couple of pages later, however, he makes it clear that there still were people who sang in the enharmonic genus.[25] Aristides Quintilianus writes that the diatonic is the most natural genus,

> since it can be performed by everyone, even the wholly untutored: the chromatic is more technically sophisticated, being performed only by those who have been trained: and the enharmonic demands stricter precision, being accepted only by the most outstanding musicians, while for most people it is impossible.[26]

Macrobius states that the enharmonic has gone out of currency because of its difficulty, while Gaudentius says roundly that only the diatonic is still in general use in his time, the other two being 'perhaps obsolete'.[27]

Fine tuning

So far we have defined the genera in terms of a single set of intervals for each, and described the intervals by means of the familiar and convenient measures 'semitone', 'tone', 'minor third', etc. But lyre-strings could be tuned to give many shades of intonation that do not precisely correspond to those of our tempered scale, and certain of

---

[22] *Dem.* 22. On the other hand in *Comp.* 62–3 he treats it as a controversial matter whether quarter-tones are perceptible.
[23] *Sacrarum Legum Allegoriae* 1. 5 (i. 64. 13 Cohn).
[24] *Harm.* 1. 16 p. 38. 2, translated by Barker, *GMW* ii. 311. By 'slackened' Ptolemy refers to the lowering of the inner notes of the tetrachord.
[25] *Harm.* 1. 16 p. 40. 6.
[26] *De mus.* p. 16. 10ff., trans. Barker, *GMW* ii. 418.
[27] Macrob. *in Somn. Scip.* 2. 4. 13, Gaud. *Harm.* p. 332. 1. Cf. also Winnington-Ingram, *Mode*, 78.

the Greek specialist writers distinguish several different tunings within each of the named genera.

Apart from that, there is a problem about what exactly is meant by a 'tone'. The Greek writers define it as the interval by which a fifth is greater than a fourth. Strictly speaking, that is the interval given by the ratio 9 : 8, or 204 cents. But Aristoxenus regards it as being at the same time a unit of which a fourth (properly 498 cents) contains exactly two and a half. In effect he is operating with a tempered tone of 200 cents and a tempered fourth of 500 cents. He does not understand that that is what he is doing; he is simply working by ear. He dismisses as contrary to the evidence of the senses the mathematicians' proofs that a fourth less two tones leaves a remainder of something smaller than half a tone ($4/3$ divided twice by $9/8 = 256/243$; in cents, 498 minus twice $204 = 90$). Sometimes he speaks of intervals such as a third of a tone or three eighths of a tone. We must take these with a little pinch of salt, not as mathematically precise measurements but as approximations gauged by the ear. Writers of the Pythagorean tradition, on the other hand, insist on defining intervals as mathematical ratios, and are obliged to impose mathematical interpretations on whatever intervals were established in musical practice. They are, moreover, concerned to achieve a certain degree of mathematical elegance, and prepared to revise their formulae to this end. These authors, therefore, give us absolutely precise specifications for the genera and their varieties, but again we must take them with salt. The precision is specious. All the same, these data are valuable as providing some indication of the intervals in actual use.

The earliest of them, Philolaus (latter part of the fifth century BC), is in fact the least sophisticated mathematically, and his analyses, which in part have to be inferred from reports of the terms he used for various subdivisions of intervals,[28] probably do reflect contemporary tuning practice in quite a direct way. In the diatonic tetrachord he found two 9 : 8 tones and a remainder which he called by the name of *diesis*. In the chromatic the lowest interval was again the *diesis*, while the two lowest together added up to exactly a tone. In the enharmonic the two small intervals were obtained by bisecting one or other of those in the chromatic; Philolaus may have offered both alternatives. All these tunings could be arrived at in practice, and very likely were, by constructing steps of a tone from strings already tuned, by going up a fourth and down a fifth, or up a fifth and

[28] See Ch. 8.

down a fourth. Converted into cents, Philolaus' scheme of intervals
would appear thus:

enharmonic	45	45	408
or	57	57	384
chromatic	90	114	294
diatonic	90	204	204

— Close to "just" (handwritten note beside the 57 57 384 row)

Archytas in the first half of the fourth century achieved greater
mathematical rigour.[29] He expressed all his intervals as ratios, but I
shall again convert them into cents so that their magnitudes can be
appreciated; we are not concerned in this context with the beauty of
Archytas' arithmetic.

enharmonic	63	48	387
chromatic	63	141	294
diatonic	63	231	204

There is one interesting peculiarity which sets Archytas' system
apart from everyone else's. According to him the lower 'movable'
note is not movable at all: the lowest interval in the tetrachord
remains constant in all three genera at approximately a third of a
tone.[30] The Greek system of musical notation, which will be
described in another chapter, agrees with Archytas inasmuch as it
uses the same symbol for the lower movable note in every genus.[31] In
the chromatic, Archytas agrees with Philolaus in making the two
smaller intervals together exactly equal to a tone.[32] His scheme for
the enharmonic is also strikingly close to one of the two postulated
for Philolaus.

Aristoxenus' approach is very different. According to him the two
inner notes of the tetrachord can be pitched anywhere within a
continuous band, and it is necessary to lay down boundaries to
demarcate one genus from another. The lower movable note may be
anything from a quarter to a third of a tone above the bottom note of
the tetrachord in the enharmonic genus, and anything from a third to
half a tone in the chromatic and diatonic. The upper one may be any-

[29] His results are reported by Ptolemy, *Harm.* 1. 13 p. 30. 9 ff.; see Barker, *GMW*
ii. 43–52.

[30] In the enharmonic it is a shade wider than the next interval above it, something
that Aristoxenus (*Harm.* 1. 27, 2. 52) says never happens.

[31] For the upper one, to be sure, it uses the same symbol in chromatic as in enharmonic, but a different one in diatonic.

[32] This feature of chromatic tuning also appears in Thrasyllus ap. Theon. Smyrn.
p. 91. 19 f., Gaud. *Harm.* p. 343. 15, and *Anecdota Varia*, pp. 5–7 Studemund.

thing from a half to two thirds of a tone from the bottom in enharmonic, anything from two thirds to $1\frac{1}{4}$ tones in chromatic, and anything from $1\frac{1}{4}$ to $1\frac{1}{2}$ in diatonic. Converted into cents, the tolerance-bands appear as follows:

enharmonic	50–66	50–66	367–400
chromatic	67–100	67–183	250–366
diatonic	67–100	150–233	200–250

Within these catch-all bands Aristoxenus recognizes the following specific 'shades' or 'hues' as being familiar (the figures representing the intervals in tone-units):

enharmonic	$\frac{1}{4}$	$\frac{1}{4}$	2
soft chromatic	$\frac{1}{3}$	$\frac{1}{3}$	$1\frac{5}{6}$
hemiolic chromatic	$\frac{3}{8}$	$\frac{3}{8}$	$1\frac{3}{4}$
tonic chromatic	$\frac{1}{2}$	$\frac{1}{2}$	$1\frac{1}{2}$
soft diatonic	$\frac{1}{2}$	$\frac{3}{4}$	$1\frac{1}{4}$
tense diatonic	$\frac{1}{2}$	1	1

He also mentions as being melodically proper an unlabelled form of chromatic with the intervals $\frac{1}{3} + \frac{2}{3} + 1\frac{1}{2}$, and an unlabelled form of diatonic with the intervals $\frac{1}{3} + 1\frac{1}{6} + 1$.[33]

In the Euclidean *Sectio Canonis* we find the diatonic constructed on the same pattern as in Philolaus, with two 9 : 8 tones; this is also presupposed in Plato's *Timaeus*. The *Sectio* refers likewise to an enharmonic scale featuring the full ditone interval of 408 cents obtained by tuning from the higher note by ascending fourths and descending fifths. It is demonstrated that the small intervals below the ditone cannot be equal; but the implication is that people thought of them as being equal.[34]

Ptolemy cites the ratios arrived at by two other mathematicians of before his own time besides Archytas: Eratosthenes (third century BC) and Didymus (first century AD). Converted into cents, they appear thus:

	Eratosthenes			Didymus		
enharmonic	44	45	409	54	57	387
chromatic	89	94	315	112	71	315
diatonic	90	204	204	112	182	204

[33] *Harm.* 1. 22–7, 2. 49–52.
[34] *Sectio Canonis* 17–20 (Barker, *GMW* ii. 203–8); Pl. *Tim.* 35b–36b.

Eratosthenes' diatonic is the same as Philolaus', Plato's, and Euclid's, and his enharmonic is also based on the practice of constructing two tones down from the top of the tetrachord. Didymus', on the other hand, like Archytas', is a mathematical refinement of the other Philolaic form of enharmonic in which the ditone was slightly reduced. Didymus' chromatic is somewhat anomalous. Like Archytas' enharmonic, it breaks Aristoxenus' rule that the lowest interval is never bigger than the middle one. Ptolemy criticizes this feature of Didymus' scheme as unmelodic in principle and out of accord with the evidence of our ears.[35]

Ptolemy's own analyses are more clearly related to the actual musical practice of his time. Only two varieties of chromatic are to be distinguished, he maintains, as against Aristoxenus' three; on the other hand, two species of diatonic are not enough, as 'it is obvious that those that are sung are more'. He also disagrees with Aristoxenus' treatment of the two small intervals in the enharmonic and chromatic *pyknon* as equal, stating that the upper one is always perceived as being greater than the lower.[36] In his own tables it is about twice as large. This evidently represents a historical change since Aristoxenus' time. Aristoxenus' two forms of diatonic both have counterparts in Ptolemy's system, though his 'soft diatonic' corresponds to what Ptolemy calls 'tense chromatic'. The unnamed forms of chromatic and diatonic that Aristoxenus mentions, with respectively $\frac{1}{3} + \frac{2}{3} + 1\frac{1}{3}$ and $\frac{1}{3} + 1\frac{1}{6} + 1$ tones, correspond to what Ptolemy calls 'soft chromatic' and 'tonic diatonic'.

Ptolemy's categories are as follows.[37] Besides giving the intervals in cents I show what each tetrachord looks like when expressed in modern notes with appropriate modifiers.

enharmonic	38	73	387	$e\,e{\uparrow}^{40}\,f{\uparrow}^{10}\,a$
soft chromatic	63	120	315	$e\,f{\downarrow}^{40}\,f{\sharp}{\downarrow}^{15}\,a$
tense chromatic	81	150	267	$e\,f{\downarrow}^{20}\,f{\sharp}{\uparrow}^{30}\,a$
soft diatonic	84	183	231	$e\,f{\downarrow}^{15}\,g{\downarrow}^{30}\,a$
tonic diatonic	63	231	204	$e\,f{\downarrow}^{40}\,g\,a$
tense diatonic	111	204	183	$e\,f{\uparrow}^{15}\,g{\uparrow}^{15}\,a$
even diatonic	150	165	183	$e\,f{\uparrow}^{50}\,g{\uparrow}^{15}\,a$

---

[35] *Harm.* 2. 13 p. 68. 24ff. Eratosthenes' and Didymus' ratios are set out in 2. 14 pp. 71–3; see Barker, *GMW* ii. 346–9.

[36] *Harm.* 1. 14 p. 32. 15ff., cf. 1. 15 p. 33. 22; Barker, *GMW* ii. 305–7.

[37] *Harm.* 1. 15–16, 2. 14.

The first two of these, we recall (p. 166), Ptolemy describes as being not widely current. The last, the 'even' diatonic, is his own invention. He has tried it out, and reports that the effect is 'rather foreign and rustic, but exceptionally gentle'. The rest must be taken as mathematical idealizations of tunings actually to be heard.

In two cases Ptolemy observes that citharodes do not tune exactly as they should. In the tense diatonic, while they sing with the correct intonation, they tune their instruments with two full tones as the upper intervals of the tetrachord (90 + 204 + 204 cents); and similarly in the enharmonic they use a full ditone (408 cents) as the major interval. These 204-cent tones were easily obtained by tuning down a fifth and up a fourth, and this was no doubt the citharodes' procedure. But Ptolemy allows that the discrepancies are too small to be noticeable.[38] He proceeds to admit the 'ditonic' as another variety of diatonic.

Aristoxenus lays down rules about concord between corresponding notes in neighbouring tetrachords which appear to exclude the combination in one scale of tetrachords tuned with different series of intervals.[39] Ptolemy, on the other hand, treats the tonic diatonic as the *only* form of tuning, of those in common use, that is employed in successive tetrachords; the rest are coupled with tonic diatonic tetrachords, with the tenser form of tetrachord above the disjunctive tone and the less tense below, or vice versa in the case of conjunct tetrachords. He provides details of six specific kithara attunements embodying these arrangements, with their technical names, and two generic lyra ones.[40] Rendered in modern notation on the octave *e–e'*, which is probably about a tone too high, the kithara tunings appear as follows:

Tritai (tonic diatonic)	e f♯	g↓³⁰	a b c'↓³⁰	d'		e'
Hypertropa (tonic diat.)	e f♯	g↓³⁰	a b c♯'	d'↓³⁰		e'
Parhypatai (soft + tonic diat.)	e f↓¹⁵	g↓³⁰	a b c'↓³⁰	d'		e'
Tropoi (tonic diat. + tense chr.)	e f♯	g↓³⁰	a b c'↓²⁰	c♯'↑³⁰		e'
Iastiaiolia (ditonic + tonic diat.)	e f♯	g♯	a b c♯'	d'↓³⁰		e'
Lȳdia (tonic + ditonic diat.)	e f↓⁴⁰	g	a b c'	d'		e'

---

[38] *Harm.* 1. 16 p. 39. 14–40. 8, cf. 2. 1 p. 44. 1–5; Barker, *GMW* ii. 312 f., 317 f. The 90 : 204 : 204 division had long been established (Philolaus, Plato, Euclid).

[39] *Harm.* 1. 29, 2. 54. At 1. 7, however, he recognizes some kind of mixture of genera, and at 2. 44 (cf. Cleon. *Harm.* p. 189. 11–18) their combination (by modulation) in the course of a melody.

[40] *Harm.* 2. 15–16, cf. 1. 16, 2. 1; Barker, *GMW* ii. 312 f., 350 f., 356–61. The names are somewhat obscure; see Barker's discussion, p. 360.

The lyra tunings are classified simply as 'hard' and 'soft', 'hard' being pure tonic diatonic and 'soft' being its conjunction with tense chromatic.

We observe in the kithara tunings that the notes $e-a-b-e'$ remain constant, giving a framework of fourths and fifths; and in each scale either the a or the b has notes making a fourth both above and below it, in other words either $e-f\sharp-b-e'$ or $e-a-d'-e'$. No more than four out of eight strings had to be adjusted in substituting one of these scales for another.

From one point of view, $e-a$ and $b-e'$ can be regarded as disjunct tetrachords with movable inner notes. However, they do not necessarily correspond to the tetrachords of Greek theoretical analysis. The latter exist on an abstract scale which can be variously calibrated against the scale of an actual piece of music. In the above scales the tetrachords of theory, which have the smallest interval at the bottom, may begin on the first and fifth degrees (*Parhypatai, Lȳdia*), on the second and fifth (*Tritai, Tropoi*), on the second and sixth (*Hypertropa*), or on the third and sixth (*Iastiaiolia*), and they may run off the end of the scale. I explain this here only so that the reader may be able to work out how it is that Ptolemy's analysis into soft diatonic, tonic diatonic, etc., fits the actual note-series. Fuller explanation of this aspect of Greek theory must await Chapter 8.

Ambitus

So far we have been investigating scale structures without considering their extension. In dealing with Western music the question hardly arises. It is taken for granted that a scale once defined for an octave repeats itself indefinitely in higher or lower octaves—which we see plentifully laid out on our piano keyboard—and that the music may roam freely up and down as far as the compass of voices or instruments may allow. Our names for notes repeat at the octave, and we tend to think of a high C and a low C as being essentially *the same note*, much as the dustmen come on *the same day* one week after another. We call it the same because it stands in the same position in a structured series.

We should beware of projecting this way of thinking upon the ancient or ethnic musician. Primitive melody, on the whole, does not extend much, if at all, beyond the range of a single octave, and it often restricts itself to a narrower compass than that. It may use just five or

six different notes, or in some cases only two or three.[41] These notes
form a closed system, characterized by a particular structure and
hierarchy and suspended in a tonal void. So far as that melody is concerned, other notes—including 'the same' notes in another octave—
do not exist. To define the melody's tonality or modality it will not be
sufficient to say that it is in E flat major (or whatever modern scale
the notes may fit). It is necessary to specify its ambitus, what segment
of the theoretical scale is actually employed, how many notes above
and below the predominant or tonic note, and their relative importance in the melody.

Ancient Greek music requires this kind of analysis if its modal
variety is to be understood and the character of individual specimens
appreciated. Particularly in the earlier period there is evidence for
melodies of limited compass. The airs of Olympus and Terpander
are reported to have used only a small number of notes as compared
with those of later composers, and more specifically to have been
'simple and three-note'.[42] 'Three-note', *trichorda*, could be interpreted as meaning that there were only three notes in what later were
tetrachords, in other words that the fourths were divided by only one
infix and the scale was pentatonic.[43] But it may mean literally that
some of these old ritual tunes used only three notes. After all,
according to Bruno Nettl,

Cultures with more complex scale systems nevertheless tend to have some
songs with only two or three tones, and this is also true of European folk
cultures. In most cases (in Europe and elsewhere) these are children's songs,
game songs, lullabies, and old ritual melodies.[44]

If the first interpretation is correct, the reference may still be to
melodies with as few as five distinct notes and an ambitus of less than
an octave. One of the ceremonial tunes attributed to Olympus, the
Spondeion or *Libatory*, was apparently based on the five notes
e f a b c'.[45] In *e f a* we recognize the fourth with infix, and it seems

---

[41] C. Engel, *An Introduction to the Study of National Music* (London, 1866), 120–
3; Nettl, *FTM* 45 f.; C. Sachs, *The Rise of Music in the Ancient World* (New York,
1943), 31–9 and *WM* 59–72.   [42] Ps.-Plut. *De mus.* 1137ab.
[43] See above, p. 163. According to Clement, *Strom.* 1. 76. 5, Agnis (Hyagnis) the
Phrygian—a legendary prehistoric figure—invented 'the trichord and the diatonic
scale'; but it is not entirely clear whether 'trichord' here is adjectival, referring to a type
of scale, or a noun, the instrument that bore this name (above, p. 80).
[44] Op. cit. 45.
[45] Ps.-Plut. *De mus.* 1135ab, 1137b–d; Barker, *GMW* i. 255f. The note-values
given here serve merely to characterize the intervals of the scale: we do not know the
proper pitch.

likely that the *a* was the 'tonic', the centre of reference, the cardinal note in the melody. The *b* made a fifth with the lowest note *e*, while the *c*↑', three-quarters of a tone higher, perhaps served as a leading note or affix to the *b*.[46]

The Damonian scales

Six other early scales are recorded. Aristides Quintilianus preserves them, saying that they were used by 'the most ancient' musicians. It is probable that they were originally described by Damon, the teacher of Pericles, since Aristides mentions Damon elsewhere as having recorded some irregular scales; I shall refer to them as the Damonian scales. Certainly they seem to date from the latter part of the fifth century.[47] They are all closed systems containing enharmonic tetrachords. Two of them, identified as 'tense Lydian' and 'Ionian', resemble the *Spondeion* scale in spanning less than an octave and in being constructed from one infixed fourth plus one or two higher notes:

Tense Lydian   *e e*↑ *f a c*′
Ionian   *e e*↑ *f a c*′ *d*′[48]

The *c*′ makes the concord of a fifth with the *f*, and the *d*′ in the Ionian makes a fourth with the *a*.

The other four scales span an octave or, in the case of the Dorian, a ninth:

Dorian   *d e e*↑ *f a b b*↑ *c*′ *e*′
Phrygian   *d e e*↑ *f a b b*↑ *c*′ *d*′
Lydian   *e*↑ *f a b b*↑ *c*′ *e*′ *e*↑′
Mixolydian   *e e*↑ *f g a a*↑ *b*♭ *e*′

It is to be noted that the Dorian's extension beyond the octave does not involve recurrence of the interval-series at the octave: the low *d*

---

[46] If Winnington-Ingram, *CQ* 22 (1928), 89 f., is right in restoring *f*↑ in place of *f*, the relationship of this note to the *e* would be replicated a fifth higher by that of *c*↑′ to *b*.

[47] Aristid. Quint. p. 18. 5–19. 10, cf. 80. 29; J. F. Mountford, *CQ* 17 (1923), 126–9; Winnington-Ingram, *Mode*, 22–30, 59; M. L. West, *JHS* 101 (1981), 117–19; below, p. 247.

[48] Again the notes should not be taken as indicating absolute pitch. Aristides appends to his descriptions note-tables which would place them about a minor third lower, but it is unlikely that the original fifth-century source had the means to specify pitches. For the other four scales the pitch-ranges indicated by the tables are: Dorian *e*–*f*♯′, Phrygian *e*–*e*′, Lydian *d*↓–*d*↓′, Mixolydian *c*♯–*c*♯′.

and the tone-interval that it makes with the *e* are not matched at the top end. This *d*, which also appears in the Phrygian scale, can be characterized as an 'infrafix' attached to the tetrachord *e–a*, providing the concord of a fifth with *a* and also a note useful for circling about the *e* at the bottom of the tetrachord. The arrangement is replicated a fifth higher, in the Dorian, by the disjunctive tone *a–b* and the upper tetrachord *b–e'*. In the Phrygian, on the other hand, the top note is *d'*, making a fourth with the presumptive 'tonic' *a* and giving the upper part of the scale a more diatonic character.[49]

The Mixolydian scale presents a diatonic aspect in its lower section, with the *g* intruding into the enharmonic tetrachord *e e↑ f a*; but it has an exceptionally wide gap at the top, between *b♭* and *e'*. Probably it represents a combination of two mini-scales between which the melody alternated: the usual tetrachord *e e↑ f a*, and an open fifth erected on the *a* with infixes of the enharmonic type and an infrafix a tone below:

> *e e↑ f a*
>   *g a a↑ b♭   e'*

The name 'Mixolydian' ought to denote something that is a cross between Lydian and some other type, but it is hard to see what the Mixolydian and Lydian of this Damonian set have in common. The Lydian contains one regular tetrachord, *b–e'*; we can also find in it two overlapping fifths, *f–c'* and *a–e'*, or from another viewpoint a chain of thirds, *f–a–c'–e'*, but whether they were used as such in melody we cannot tell.[50] The two extreme degrees, *e↑* (or *f↓*) and *e↑'*, look like ornamental affixes serving as leading notes to their immediate neighbours.

Heptachord tunings

Taken together, these six Damonian scales and the *Spondeion* scale reflect a corresponding number of melodic types with an ambitus

[49] This may have something to do with a remark by Aristoxenus (fr. 84) that 'the enharmonic genus is very well suited to the Dorian tuning, and the diatonic to the Phrygian'. Elsewhere (ap. ps.-Plut. *De mus.* 1137 d) he referred to Olympus and his followers using a scale containing the notes *a b c' d'* in some of their Phrygian melodies. Cf. Winnington-Ingram, *Mode*, 27. The nine-note Dorian scale reappears in a chromatic form (*d e f f♯ a b c' c♯' e'*) in Pliny, *HN* 2. 84 from a Hellenistic Pythagorean source. See W. Burkert, *Philol.* 105 (1961), 28–43.

[50] Possibly the connection between this Lydian and the Tense Lydian is that both emphasized a note making a fifth with the note at the top of the *pyknon*, below it in the Lydian (*f(–b b↑) c'*), above it in the Tense Lydian ((*e e↑*) *f–c'*).

varying from a sixth to a ninth. Inferences may also be drawn from
the limitations of early instruments. The aulos, before Pronomus'
invention of collars, offered only six fundamental notes. They could
be augmented by microtones or semitones through half-stopping,
and also varied by other techniques. But unless overblowing was
used, the total range does not seem to have exceeded an octave or
so.[51] In Chapter 3 we saw that there was evidence for early lyres with
only three, four, five, or six strings, and no easy way of getting more
than one note from each. The commonest number in the Archaic
and Classical periods, seven, was still not enough for a full diatonic
octave. Pindar describes his lyre as having seven 'percussions' or
'tongues'—that is, one note per string.[52]

It may seem awkward, in the face of this, that several of the
Damonian scales have eight or nine degrees. But if we recall what
was said previously about the development of the enharmonic tetrachord from an older trichord, and if we assume that the divided
semitones in the Damonian scales had a little earlier, say *c.*450 BC,
been undivided, then they reduce to six or seven notes.

There are several references to seven-string tunings, spanning
either an octave or a seventh. In the earliest extant account of the
structure of the octave it is divided into a fourth below and a fifth
above; within the fifth there is a note a tone from the bottom, but
apparently only one note within the upper fourth demarcated by it.[53]
According to Nicomachus, who quotes the fragment, this note was a
tone from the top. The scale would then have the form *e f* (?) *g* (?) *a b*
d' e', with *a* as the pivotal note. In the pseudo-Aristotelian *Problems*
there is discussion of ancient heptachord tunings in which the lower
tetrachord was complete but the upper one was either conjunct or, if
disjunct, lacking its second or fourth degree. The alternatives are:

1. Conjunct tetrachords. In the diatonic genus this would mean
e f g a b♭ c' d', and Nicomachus alludes to this as a scale that was
current until Pythagoras disjoined the tetrachords to fill the octave.
The author of the *Problems*, however, refers to a *pyknon*, implying
an enharmonic or chromatic scale.[54]

---

[51] See above, pp. 87, 94–102.
[52] *Pyth.* 2. 70, *Nem.* 5. 24.
[53] Philolaus fr. 6; see Burkert, *LS* 391–4; Barker, *GMW* ii. 37 n. 34. Aristotle,
Metaph. 1093ᵃ14, argues against Pythagoreans who find sevens everywhere and one
of whose examples is that the scale consists of seven notes.
[54] *Pr.* 19. 47; Nicom. *Ench.* 5 pp. 244f.

2. Disjunct without the highest note. In diatonic this is *e f g a b c′ d′*; compare the Phrygian scale attributed to Olympus.[55]

3. Disjunct without the third note from the top: diatonic *e f g a b d′ e′*, as in Philolaus' scale. Terpander is credited with substituting this, or an enharmonic version of it, for (2).[56]

Among the surviving musical fragments the greatest number have the compass of an octave or a ninth. A few have a wider range, up to an eleventh or in three cases a twelfth. One complete little song of late date, the anonymous invocation of the Muse (16), has an ambitus of only a minor seventh, and there are several papyrus fragments in which, so far as they go, the melody is confined within an even smaller range, though if we had longer excerpts it might well become apparent that the limitation was only temporary.

Mode

The old scales set forth by Aristides Quintilianus and identified as Dorian, Phrygian, and so on, are described as *harmoniai*. The word means literally 'tunings, attunements'. It is often translated as 'mode', a term which in music implies above all a distinctive series of intervals in the scale, though it usually has other connotations in addition, as in Western music the major mode is generally felt to be sunnier and more extrovert than the minor.

In fifth- and fourth-century literature we encounter numerous references to musical *harmoniai*. The differences between one and another in respect of their aesthetic and emotional qualities, and their effect upon the disposition of the listener, were considered a subject of great interest and importance. The ones most often mentioned are the Dorian, Phrygian, and Lydian, but we also hear of Ionian, Aeolian, Locrian, Mixolydian, and others. Some of the names were established early in the Archaic period. Alcman and Stesichorus already refer to a 'Phrygian melody'.[57]

What did the names stand for? The solidest information comes from that passage of Aristides with the details of six fifth-century

---

[55] *Pr.* 19. 7; above, n. 49.

[56] *Pr.* 19. 32, cf. 7; ps.-Plut. *De mus.* 1140f, cf. 1137bc. According to *Suda* iv. 361. 8 the missing *c′* was supplied by Simonides.

[57] *PMG* 126, 212. The use of the word 'melody' (*melos*) with reference to a particular mode is paralleled in Pratinas, *PMG* 712 (*a*). 4, Pind. fr. 67, Aristox. *Harm.* 2. 39. A composition ascribed to Sakadas or Klonas with sections in three different modes was called the *trimelēs nomos* (ps.-Plut. *De mus.* 1134ab, cf. 1132d).

scales. We cannot, of course, take Aristides' account as a comprehensive record of Classical modes; but we can take it as a record of
the forms that some of the main ones had at a particular epoch. It
tells us that the Dorian, the Phrygian, and the other *harmoniai*, while
having some elements in common, such as the enharmonic tetrachord, differed from one another in the selection of notes used, and
to some extent in ambitus. Each one contained its own particular set
of intervallic relationships, which we are not in a position to define.
From the lists of notes we can read off all the intervals that *might*
have been used in melody, but the individuality of the mode would
depend to a considerable extent on which ones actually were, and
with what emphasis, and also on the relative frequency of the several
notes.[58]

No doubt there were other differential characteristics that do not
appear from the bare scales. Some types of rhythm were probably
felt to go with one mode rather than another.[59] There may have been
particular melodic formulae associated with particular modes. The
connection between mode and melodic style is implicit in the overlapping usage of *melos* and *harmoniā* (above), and explicit in
Heraclides Ponticus' hypothetical history of music in which he
stated that 'the sequence of melody that the Dorians used to perform
they called the Dorian *harmoniā*'.[60]

Certainly the modes appear to have been marked in some cases by
differences of tessitura—differences in the degree to which high or
low singing was required. Lasus of Hermione, in a hymn to Demeter
and Kore, says he is singing 'in the deep-resounding Aeolian
harmoniā'. Pratinas recommends this mode with the words

> Do not pursue either the tense
> or the relaxed Ionian Muse,
> but plough the intermediate field
> and be Aeolian in your song.
>
> ... Befitting
> all song-roisterers
> is the Aeolian *harmoniā*.[61]

---

[58] Cf. Aristid. Quint. p. 29. 18–21 (Barker, *GMW* ii. 431); Winnington-Ingram, *Mode*, 57–9.

[59] Cf. below, p. 181.

[60] Fr. 163 W. ap. Ath. 624d.

[61] Lasus, *PMG* 702; Pratinas, *PMG* 712. The word 'Ionian' is thought by D. L. Page to be interpolated.

Among the Damonian scales there is a 'tense Lydian'. Plato mentions it together with Mixolydian as lamentatory and suitable for women, and he distinguishes these from 'slack' modes, Ionian and Lydian, which are soft and suited to the symposium.[62] The meaning of 'tense' and 'slack' in this context is made plainer by Aristotle's remark that the tense *harmoniai* are not easy for old men to sing; nature offers them the slack ones instead.[63] Clearly a 'tense' mode involved more high notes and was taxing for that reason. It was not necessarily higher in pitch overall than a slack mode. It might be that both occupied the range *d–d'*, for example, but that in the tense mode the melody moved more in the upper part of that octave, in the slack one more in the lower. In any case, 'tenseness' must have affected the character of the mode by putting greater strain on the voice and altering its quality. It is significant that Plato uses tenseness and slackness as a principle of classification connected with ethos.

Let us now survey the references made to the various modes in Greek writers, especially those before 300 BC. Later authors are sometimes worth citing, but their testimony has to be treated cautiously, because, as will be explained in the chapter on theory, the concept of mode came to be mixed up with that of key.

The Dorian mode was one of the most widely used in the fifth century and probably earlier, and it was always well regarded. A traditional spondaic invocation attributed to Terpander was deemed to be in this mode, and so were some of Alcman's *Partheneia* and various poems of Anacreon, Simonides, Bacchylides, and Pindar. It was used for processionals, paeans, songs of love, and in tragedy, especially for laments.[64] Clearly it was a versatile mode, often employed for choral song but not confined to it, and compatible with more than one mood. Generally, however, it was perceived as dignified and manly. Pratinas perhaps alludes to the musical mode when he contrasts his 'Dorian' dance-song with a wilder performance in which the aulos provided a more prominent and elaborate accompaniment. Pindar certainly, in a Paean, acclaimed the 'Dorian melody' as being the most dignified or

---

[62] *Resp.* 398 e, cf. Arist. *Pol.* 1340^{a}40 ff., Poll. 4. 78.
[63] *Pol.* 1342^{b}20; cf. Plut. *An seni* 793 a. On the difficulty of singing high notes and the sort of composition involving them cf. ps.-Arist. *Pr.* 19. 37.
[64] Aristox. frs. 81, 84, Posidonius fr. 471 Th., ps.-Plut. *De mus.* 1136 f, Psell. *De trag.* 5.

solemn.[65] Plato approves it as the finest of modes, one that mirrors the character of the man who is brave in battle and drastic action, self-controlled and enduring in the face of death or disaster—a model for life.[66] According to Aristotle, 'everyone agrees that it is the steadiest and the one that most has a manly character'.[67] Heraclides Ponticus considers that it displays manliness and grandeur; it is not merry or relaxed but stern and forceful, without complexities and frills.[68] In view of its general prestige it is not surprising that the Dorian was the first tuning taught to boys when they were learning to play the lyre.[69]

The Phrygian mode was more associated with the aulos, though not exclusively so. Stesichorus referred to his *Oresteia* as a Phrygian song, and no one doubts that it was sung to the kithara.[70] Phrygian seems to have been appropriate to a range of moods, from cheerful bonhomie or piety to wild excitement or religious frenzy. Plato surprisingly ignores the latter aspect, which we might have expected him to deprecate, and welcomes this mode to his ideal state—the only one he does admit besides the Dorian—as expressing the character of the man who, when there is no war or crisis, conducts his affairs sensibly in an unforced way, approaching God with prayers, and with his fellow men making and responding to reasonable requirements.[71] Aristotle, on the other hand, writes:

The Socrates of the *Republic* is wrong to leave only the Phrygian mode beside the Dorian, especially as in the matter of instruments he disapproves of the aulos. For of the modes, the Phrygian has the same potential as the aulos among instruments: both of them are exciting (*orgiastika*) and emotional. This is evident in practice, for all Bacchic celebration and that sort of dancing is predominantly accompanied by auloi, and goes most appropriately with melodies in the Phrygian mode. The dithyramb, for instance, is by general consent held to be a Phrygian thing. The experts give many illustrations of this, notably that Philoxenus attempted to compose a

[65] Pratinas, *PMG* 708; Pind. fr. 67. There are several other apparent or possible references to the Dorian mode in Pindar: *Ol.* 1. 17, 3. 5, *Pyth.* 8. 20, fr. 191.
[66] *Lach.* 188 d, 193 d, *Resp.* 398 e–9 c, *Epistle* 7. 336 c.
[67] *Pol.* 1342ᵇ12, cf. 1340ᵇ4.
[68] Fr. 163 ap. Ath. 624 d. Cf. also ps.-Plut. *De mus.* 1136 d–f (Aristox. fr. 81), Dion. Hal. *Dem.* 22, Lucian, *Harmonides* 1, Apul. *Flor.* 4, Ptol. *Harm.* 3. 7, Psell. *De trag.* 5.　　　　　　　　　　[69] This seems to be implied by Ar. *Eq.* 985–96.
[70] *PMG* 212; cf. *CQ* 21 (1971) 310. Plato, *Lach.* 188 d, also suggests that a lyre might be tuned to the Phrygian scale (Winnington-Ingram, *CQ* 6 (1956), 172, 181 n. 2).
[71] *Resp.* 399 a–c. Cf. W. D. Anderson, *Ethos and Education in Greek Music* (Cambridge, Mass., 1966), 107–9.

dithyramb, the *Mysians*, in the Dorian mode but was unable to carry it through; the nature of the genre forced him back into the proper mode, the Phrygian.[72]

The dithyramb had not always been such as to exclude the Dorian mode; an epigram recording a dithyrambic victory at the Athenian Dionysia, probably from the first half of the fifth century, refers to the piper as having 'nursed' the song 'in Dorian auloi'.[73] It may be that the Phrygian mode did not become well established in Attica until a little later. We hear that it was first introduced to tragedy by Sophocles, who used it in a 'dithyrambic' manner.[74] Euripides alludes to it, seemingly, in connection with Asiatics and with their ecstatic Bacchic worship.[75] There was ritual aulos music in the Phrygian mode attributed to Olympus, including some used in the cult of the Mother of the Gods.[76] Two of its characteristic rhythms are mentioned, the *paiōn epibatos* and the trochaic.[77] These were perhaps the pieces of Olympus that Plato and Aristotle admired as having the power to arouse and inspire, and as revealing those who stand in need of the gods.[78] If so, it goes some way towards explaining Plato's hospitality towards Phrygian. The more negative view of the mode as dangerously inflammatory finds its classic expression in the often-retold story of Pythagoras and the over-excited young man.[79]

The Lydian mode was also represented among the aulos airs ascribed to Olympus.[80] Plato, as we have seen, groups it with Ionian as a 'slack' mode, soft and sympotic. This certainly goes well with its use by Anacreon.[81] Pindar imagined its being used in song at Niobe's

---

[72] *Pol.* 1342ª32–ᵇ12, cf. 1340ᵇ4, Procl. *Chrestomathy* ap. Phot. *Bibl.* 320b. On the basis for the story about Philoxenus see pp. 364 f.

[73] Antigenes, *Anth. Pal.* 13. 28 (*FGE* p. 12). Parallel expressions, 'in Lydian auloi', 'in Aeolian blowings of auloi', occur at Pind. *Ol.* [5]. 19, *Nem.* 3. 79. It will be recalled that early auletes needed different auloi for different modes.

[74] Aristox. fr. 79; Psell. *De trag.* 5.

[75] *Bacch.* 159 ff., cf. *Tro.* 545, *IA* 576–8 (Trojans); Ar. *Thesm.* 121 (Agathon in religious vein, cf. schol. ad loc.); cf. ps.-Arist. *Pr.* 19. 48.

[76] Telestes, *PMG* 810, Poll. 4. 78, ps.-Plut. *De mus.* 1135b, 1137d, 1141b, 1143b.   [77] Ps.-Plut. *De mus.* 1141b, 1143b; cf. Plut. *Amat.* 759ab.

[78] Pl. *Symp.* 215c (~ ps.-Pl. *Minos* 318b), Arist. *Pol.* 1340ª9. For the inspired or religious character of the Phrygian mode cf. Lucian, *Harmonides* 1, Apul. *Flor.* 4.

[79] See above, p. 31. Cf. also Lucr. 2. 620, Quint. *Inst.* 1. 10. 32 f., Cassiod. *Var.* 2. 40. 4.

[80] Telestes, *PMG* 806(?), Aristox. frs. 80, 83, Clem. *Strom.* 1. 76. 4.

[81] Pl. *Resp.* 398e; Posidonius fr. 471 Th. The statement that the Slack Lydian was invented by Damon (ps.-Plut. *De mus.* 1136e) may mean that he was the first to

wedding, and he himself used it in several celebratory odes for young athletes.[82] Sophocles introduced it to tragedy; but it was more characteristic of citharodes' solos.[83] Despite its 'slackness', there are indications that it had a high tessitura.[84] Aristotle considers it suitable for boys to learn because it is manageable for them and decorous as well as fun.[85]

The other of Plato's slack modes, the Ionian, presents several faces. For Plato it is soft and sympotic, and there were indeed sympotic songs of the sixth-century poet Pythermus of Teos in this mode. But Heraclides Ponticus described it as 'not pretty or merry, but severe and tough, with a certain dignity and weight, which is why this mode is welcomed by tragedy'.[86] It was at home in an Asiatic type of lament sung to the pipes, known as Mariandynian after a people on the south shore of the Black Sea.[87] The famous citharode Phrynis is called by his younger rival Timotheus an *iōnokamptās*, which seems to combine the notions of Ionian mode and persistent modulation. For Aristophanes saucy songs sung by prostitutes are Ionic.[88]

The Mixolydian was, beside the Dorian, the principal mode used in tragedy, at any rate before Sophocles and others introduced a wider variety. Aristoxenus also found it in Sappho, and supposed that the tragedians had got it from her. It is described as emotional, appropriate to laments and the arousal of pity.[89]

differentiate the Tense Lydian from Lydian unqualified, as in Aristides Quintilianus' list of ancient modes and in Plato loc. cit.

[82] Pind. fr. 64 = 52n adn. (cf. Paus. 9. 5. 7), *Ol.* 14. 17 (a dancing procession), *Nem.* 4. 45, 8. 15; ps.-Pind. *Ol.* 5. 19.

[83] Aristox. fr. 79, cf. ps.-Plut. *De mus.* 1137 a, Procl. ap. Phot. *Bibl.* 320 b, Psell. *De trag.* 5.

[84] Telestes, *PMG* 810. 4, Aristid. Quint. p. 23. 3 with 30. 2. Perhaps the Tense Lydian is meant. Apuleius, *Flor.* 4, characterizes the Lydian as plaintive.

[85] *Pol.* 1342ᵇ30, reading *paidián* for *paideían*. Cassiodorus, *Var.* 2. 40. 4, describes the Lydian as relaxing and restorative; schol. Pind. *Ol.* 5. 44 g calls it sweet.

[86] *PMG* 910; Heraclid. Pont. fr. 163 (both in Ath. 625 bc). For the Ionian mode in tragedy cf. also Aesch. *Supp.* 69 (a lament, compared to that of a nightingale), Aristox. fr. 82, Psell. *De trag.* 5. In the Psellus passage it is again called slack; for this cf. Pratinas quoted above, p. 178.

[87] *PMG* 878, cf. Aesch. *Pers.* 938. For Plato the modes associated with laments are the Mixolydian and Tense Lydian.

[88] Timoth. *PMG* 802. 3; Ar. *Eccl.* 883, cf. 918. Late sources (no doubt echoing earlier ones) characterize Ionian as variegated (Apul. *Flor.* 4), elegant (Lucian, *Harmonides* 1), or intellect-sharpening and spiritually uplifting (Cassiod. *Var.* 2. 40. 4).

[89] Aristox. fr. 81, ps.-Arist. *Pr.* 19. 48 (restored from Theodorus of Gaza's version), Plut. *De audiendo* 46 b (Euripides), Psell. *De trag.* 5; Pl. *Resp.* 398 de, Arist. *Pol.* 1340ᵇ1, ps.-Plut. *De mus.* 1140 f.

We have now covered the six modes for which we have Damonian scales. Plato seems to treat them as a closed set. After excluding from his state the Mixolydian, Tense Lydian, Lydian, and Ionian, the only ones that remain available are the Dorian and the Phrygian. Outside Plato, however, we find sporadic mention of others.

We have already cited Lasus' and Pratinas' references to an Aeolian mode. Pindar too seems to register his use of it.[90] Thereafter it either went out of use or came to be called by another name. Heraclides Ponticus, however, needed it for his reconstruction of the history of Greek music, so that the commonly recognized broad division of the nation into Dorians, Aeolians, and Ionians should be matched by a trio of three primary modes with the same names. Finding the allusions to an Aeolian mode in Lasus and Pratinas, and observing that the Lasus hymn was actually sung in what was currently called the Hypodorian mode, he concluded that Aeolian was the old name for Hypodorian, in which he found qualities similar to those of the oldest Aeolic people, the Thessalians: open-hearted, honest, generous, swaggering.[91]

There were two 'Hypo-' modes, Hypodorian and Hypophrygian, and they were indeed, so far as our evidence goes, not identified under these names before the late fifth or early fourth century.[92] They were mutations of Dorian and Phrygian—probably occurring in association with them, through modulation—in which disjunct tetrachords became conjunct ones. Someone performing in the Dorian scale, $d\,e\,e\uparrow f\,a\,b\,b\uparrow\,c'\,e'$, would go into Hypodorian if from the a he went up $a\,a\uparrow\,bb\,d'$, making d' his highest note. In the Phrygian, $d\,e\,e\uparrow f\,a\,b\,b\uparrow\,c'\,d'$, the change to Hypophrygian came about in the opposite way, by going down from the b through the descending tetrachord $b\,g\,g\downarrow\,f\sharp$ and (probably) making e the bottom note.[93]

[90] Above, p. 178; Pind. *Ol.* 1. 102(?), *Pyth.* 2. 69(?), *Nem.* 3. 79 with schol. (cf. above, n. 73). The interpretation of the Pindaric passages is controversial. I. Henderson in E. Wellesz (ed.), *Ancient and Oriental Music* (*New Oxford History of Music*, i, Oxford, 1957), 383, suspects that the terms Dorian and Aeolian could be applied to the same music.

[91] Heraclid. Pont. fr. 163 ap. Ath. 624c–625e; cf. Poll. 4. 65. Late sources characterize the Aeolian mode as 'straightforward' (Apul. *Flor.* 4) or 'calming and soporific' (Cassiod. *Var.* 2. 40. 4).

[92] 'Hypolydian' does not have the same modal status. It is a name created for a theoretical systematization of keys. See pp. 227f.

[93] This account is based on inference from the later systematized scheme and the known use of modulation between disjunct and conjunct tetrachords from the late 5th c. onwards.

A Peripatetic writer discusses the question why choruses in tragedy do not sing in either Hypodorian or Hypophrygian. His answer is that these modes are more suited to the heroic figures on the stage; Hypodorian is grand and steady (we have seen Dorian described in similar terms), and accordingly the most 'citharodic' of modes, while Hypophrygian is appropriate to action.[94] It may have been from citharodes that Heraclides heard Lasus' 'Aeolian' hymn sung in Hypodorian. Provided that the melody was the original one, his inference seems sound: that the old Aeolian mode was, if not identical with the later Hypodorian in its principles and ambitus, at any rate similar enough to be so interpreted.

Another mode mentioned in early poetry, but unfamiliar later, was the Locrian. It is said to have been invented by Xenocritus, a composer of narrative songs from Locri on the toe of Italy, and to have been still in use in the time of Simonides and Pindar.[95] In the harmonic handbooks of the Aristoxenian tradition it is equated with Hypodorian, just as the Aeolian mode was by Heraclides, and presumably for a similar reason: some piece by Simonides or Pindar, in which the mode appeared to be specified as Locrian, was heard sung in a mode identified as Hypodorian.[96]

Such is the evidence for the modes as regards the Classical period.[97] It suffices to confirm what we should have expected in any case, that modes were not fixed and unchanging for all time. There was evolution and modification. Old ones were discarded, new ones grew.

Mode in the post-Classical era

So what happened after Plato and Heraclides? The development of theoretical analysis, which ought to illuminate the picture, in fact

[94] Ps.-Arist. *Pr.* 19. 48. The author is able to cite the use of Hypophrygian in a scene of action in a recent play (cf. *TrGF* 127 F 3). Proclus couples it with Phrygian as proper to the dithyramb (ap. Phot. *Bibl.* 320b). Psellus, *De trag.* 5, says that both Hypodorian and Hypophrygian were dithyrambic, and that Agathon first made use of them in tragedy. The inflammatory Phrygian piping in the story about Pythagoras becomes Hypophrygian in Boethius' version, *Inst. Mus.* 1. 1 pp. 184f. Friedl.

[95] Pind. fr. 104b, Callim. fr. 669, schol. Pind. *Ol.* 10. 18b, Ath. 625e, Poll. 4. 65 (where 'Philoxenus' must be an error for Xenocritus).

[96] Cleon. p. 198. 13, Bacchius p. 309. 9, Gaud. p. 347. 10.

[97] The Boeotian *harmoniā* mentioned in schol. Ar. *Eq.* 989 (cf. schol. *Ach.* 14) is probably a mis-categorization of the 'Boeotian *nomos*' (Soph. fr. 966, Poll. 4. 65, intended by Ar. *Ach.* loc. cit.). Clement's mention of a Mixophrygian mode (*Strom.* 1. 76. 6) is isolated and probably a mistake. The Pamphylian mode or key referred to in Philostr. *VA* 1. 30 is as fictitious as the poetess, a rival of Sappho's, who is supposed to have used it.

obscures it. After various efforts to accommodate the modal scales within the framework of one master scale, a system for doing so was worked out that gave general satisfaction. A fuller account of it will be given in Chapter 8. Here it must suffice to say that in place of an untidy collection of autonomous scales with individual features the student was invited to see a neat series of overlapping segments from the great scale. As this scale was transposed to a higher or lower pitch, different sections of it appeared within the compass of the voice or instrument. So according to this model it was key-changes that lay behind the variety of heard scales. A set of names for all the keys (*tonoi*) was devised, derived from names of the modes, and these key-names largely displaced the mode-names. It became difficult to speak of mode except in terms of key. But in being interpreted as a function of key, the modes were de-natured. They lost all idiosyncrasy. Only their scale-forms were considered; particularities such as differences of ambitus, emphasis on high or low notes, frequency of use, favoured intervals and melodic figures, and so forth, were ignored.

In musical practice, of course, the differences remained. In the musical texts and fragments from the Hellenistic and Roman periods we observe a variety of scales, predominantly diatonic, occasionally (in the earlier centuries) pentatonic or chromatic. These differences of genus are one form of modal difference, despite the ancient separation of the concepts. Apart from that, how are we to classify these scales, in particular the diatonic majority?

One might think that a clue would be given by the notation of different pieces in different keys. (The keys were each represented by a different selection from the repertory of note-symbols.) However, there is no necessary correlation between the actual modality of a piece of music, as it appears to us, and the key chosen for notating it. The choice of key depended much more on the pitch at which it would be convenient to perform the piece, and on the instrument to be used.[98]

Another criterion that looks promising but turns out to be problematic is that of octave-species. The octave-species[99] are the seven different series of tone and semitone intervals obtained by

---

[98] According to Anon. Bellerm. 28 there were four particular keys used by citharodes, while auletes used seven and organists six.

[99] 'Species' is the conventional rendering of the Greek *eidos*, but 'aspect' would be better (Chailley, 99 n. 1).

taking each note of the octave scale in turn as the starting-point. The effect of the theory of keys was to reduce the old *harmoniai* to scales differentiated by species. Already before Aristoxenus the seven species of the enharmonic octave had been enumerated and labelled with names borrowed or adapted from traditional modal names: Mixolydian, Lydian, Phrygian, Dorian, Hypolydian, Hypophrygian, Locrian (or Hypodorian). The names were subsequently applied to the species of the diatonic octave too.[100] Whether this nomenclature was used by practising musicians or only by theorists is uncertain. In any case, it applied to the note-series on view in a given piece of music, the octave that best corresponded to its ambitus. So if we find a piece of music that has a compass of just an octave, with the tone/ semitone sequence T S T T T S T—as is actually the case with the Seikilos epitaph (**15**)—we could say that its scale is the Phrygian octave. The key in which the piece is notated is not Phrygian but Ionian. But the shape of the scale must be more significant than the notation.

Yet its significance remains slight until we identify the tonic note. Only when we determine how the pattern of tones and semitones relates to the tonic will we know something about the modality of the piece. In the case of the Seikilos epitaph it is easy to establish that the fourth degree of the scale is the tonic. So its scale pattern may be represented as *d e f g a b c′ d′*, with tonic *g*. We can say that it displays the D or Phrygian octave-species, but as regards mode, we must say that it is in the G mode, and be resigned to knowing no Greek label that will express this. By the G mode we mean the mode in which the successive scale degrees from the tonic upwards are T T S T . . . and downwards T S T T . . .

There is no fixed relationship between the octave-species shown by a scale and the mode as defined by the position of the tonic. For example, Mesomedes' two hymns to the Sun and to Nemesis (**18,** **19**) have the compass of an octave and a ninth respectively, both in the C or Lydian species (if we take the lowest note as determinative), and both in fact notated in the Lydian key. But the Sun hymn has its

---

[100] Cleon. *Harm.* pp. 197. 7 ff., 199. 3, records both uses; the diatonic alone appears in Aristid. Quint. p. 15. 10 ff., Gaud. *Harm.* p. 346. 6 ff. It was not until the 9th c. that the eight church modes received Greek names, and then on a false principle; see Chailley, op. cit. 115–19, *NG* xii. 381 f. The use of terms such as 'Dorian', 'Lydian', etc., in relation to Western music, as when the third movement of Beethoven's Quartet op. 132 is said to be in the Lydian mode, is based on the nomenclature of the church modes and in no way reflects the ancient usage.

tonic on the third degree (E mode), the Nemesis hymn has it on the fifth (G mode).

Actually the lowest note in the Nemesis hymn is the least used, and it might be maintained that it is the other eight notes that should be taken as defining the octave species, which will then be D. There will always be this kind of ambiguity with pieces which have an ambitus of more or less than an octave, and this further diminishes the usefulness of the species-names as a basis for classification.

A tonic, on the other hand, is regularly identifiable. This is not to say that the music always stays in thrall to one and the same tonal focus. The notes a fourth below the tonic and a fourth or a fifth above it—if the ambitus of the pieces reaches so far—function as secondary foci (analogous to the 'dominant' in the Western tonal system), and they take over whenever the melody is in their region, like planets capturing a roving satellite in their gravitational fields. There are also cases of true modulation within a piece, where either the focus shifts to a different note (normally a tone higher or lower) or it remains on the same note but the interval-pattern made by other notes changes. This will be discussed further in the next chapter.

The Hellenistic material (insofar as it is diatonic) is predominantly in the E or A mode. Sometimes there was a secondary focus a fourth below the tonic, and this might become the melody's final resting-place. Limenius' Paean (**13**) is well enough preserved for us to see that overall it was in the A mode; after a shift of focus from *a* to *b*, and several alternations between *b* and the *e* below, there was a return to *a*, but at the end the melody subsided to the *e*.

The later texts are nearly all in the E, G, or C modes. Two pieces descend a fourth from the tonic to reach their finals, like the Limenius;[101] others end on the tonic. We find modulation between E and C modes, and between C and G. One piece, the Berlin Paean (**40**), may be assigned to the D mode, though it has a secondary focus a fifth higher (A mode) which bears much of the work.

Within these groupings we might attempt further distinctions according to ambitus. The interval-structure of the tonal nucleus by itself may not be enough to define a mode. For example, in the parts of **30** *POsl.* 1413. 1–15 which are in the C mode the melody ranges freely over an octave, from the fourth below the tonic to the fifth above it. This hardly seems to belong in the same category as the

---

[101] The Seikilos epitaph; **30** *POsl.* 1413. 15; cf. **51** *POxy.* 1786.

Berlin Ajax fragment (**42**), also a tragic song in the C mode, where the compass is only a fifth (a third on each side of the tonic), and moreover the major third is divided unusually into $1\frac{1}{4} + \frac{3}{4}$ tones, the whole scale being *a′ b′ c″ d↑″ e″*.[102]

We can neatly indicate structure and ambitus together by writing for the Oslo fragment '3C4' (i.e. the three degrees below the tonic C and the four above), and for the Berlin one '2C2'. If we had many more texts than we have, and in a more complete state, it might be instructive to sort them on this principle, to see how many distinct groups emerged. As it is, many of our fragments are too small for us to be sure that all the notes of the scale are represented, and the rest are too few for clear groupings to be established. We can see that this piece is quite unlike that one, but not how many different modalities were current. It might turn out, if we had an abundance of evidence, that there was no definite number, and that to a certain extent any song might create its own modality. There might be endless dispute over criteria for classification, and over whether four or four dozen modes were to be distinguished.

It is a separate question to what extent modal categorization continued to be significant to practising musicians. Did they retain a concept of a Dorian or Phrygian mode as something distinct from the keys or octave-species of those names? Authors who refer to the ethical effects of these modes may simply be parroting old dogmas and supposing them to apply to the keys. We certainly find the view argued that the keys differ from one another in ethos, or represent distinct *harmoniai*, only to the extent that they yield different octave-species.[103] But did someone like Mesomedes, who composed one song in the E mode and another in the G, but notated them both in the Lydian key, consciously think of them as belonging to different modal categories?

It might depend whether he needed to change the tuning of his kithara. We know from Ptolemy (above, p. 171) that various accordaturas had agreed names. Each of them is linked to a particular key and presents a particular octave-species—sometimes the

---

[102] In general we must remember that diatonic scales in different texts, though identically notated, may have differed perceptibly in their schemes of attunement—'soft' or 'tonic' diatonic, etc. We can, however, identify a soft diatonic tuning in certain of the Hellenistic fragments (**7, 10**).

[103] Ptol. *Harm.* 2. 8–11; Ath. 625 d; cf. Aristid. Quint. p. 15. 15–19, 80. 6–81. 31. Plutarch believes *harmoniā* to be simply a musicians' equivalent of *tonos* or *tropos* (*An seni* 793 a, cf. *De E apud Delphos* 389 e).

same one with one or two notes slightly sharpened or flattened. Yet they do not seem to be mode-specific. The tuning called *Hypertropa* is compatible with three extant pieces of music, two of which are in the E mode (tonic on the second string) and one in the G mode (tonic on the fourth string). And Ptolemy calls the tunings not *harmoniai*, which would potentially have had modal overtones, but *harmogai*, which lacks them and simply refers to the physical process of tuning.

It seems that the absorption of the old modal names in a unified system of keys that was supposed to account for the modes, but did so only partially, left a conceptual and onomastic void. The modes must have continued in practice to exist, to evolve, and to give way to newcomers. But musicians' awareness of them no longer had the means of articulation.

7
Melody and Form

MELODY

MELODY

Despite our poverty in actual music from Antiquity, it is possible to say a certain amount about the character of Greek melody. Ancient sources make occasional reference to melodic features of the music of certain composers or styles. The extant musical documents, few and fragmentary though they are, add appreciably to our understanding. Even from pieces of which only a dozen bars or notes survive, we may get some sense of whether the music has a tonal centre, whether it tends to dwell on particular notes or is constantly moving up and down, whether this movement is predominantly between adjacent degrees of the scale or across larger intervals, to what extent syllables of the song are divided between two or more notes.

Of course we must be cautious about generalizing from what is, after all, a very limited body of evidence. We must take account of the age and character of each text, and consider whether any of its melodic features may mark a particular style or epoch. There must have been changes over the centuries, and even if we cannot get very far in establishing what they were, the material does suggest some directions in which historical development can be traced.

General features of melody

Aristoxenus' discussion of the principles of melodic composition unfortunately does not survive, but later writers preserve notice of some of the basic distinctions that he made. As Aristides Quintilianus represents the matter,[1] the musician begins by deciding whether he is going to place the starting-point of his scale (this probably means the tonic, not the highest or lowest note) in the upper, middle, or lower register of the voice. Next he fixes the structure of

---

[1] Aristid. Quint. p. 29. 2–21, cf. 16. 18–17. 2, 81. 4–6, 130. 2, Ptol. *Harm.* 2. 12 p. 67. 6–8 (Barker, *GMW* ii. 341 n. 96, 418, 430f., 483, 531).

his scale, that is, the intervallic relationships of the notes. In other words, he selects his genus and key. Then comes the delineation of the melody. This has three components: 'duction' (*agōgē*), that is, moving through successive degrees of the scale; 'plaiting' (*plokē*), or jumping to non-adjacent notes; and 'deployment' (*petteiā*), choosing which notes to use and with what frequency, and where to begin and end.[2] 'Duction' is itself divided into three types: 'direct', i.e. ascending; 'returning', i.e. descending; and 'circling', which means travelling to an adjacent note by ascending through a conjunct tetrachord, modulating to a disjunct one, and descending through that (or vice versa). Examples of this would be *a b♭ c′ d′* : *c′ b♭ a♭ g*, or *d′ c′ b♭ a* : *b♮ c′ d′ e′*. 'Plaiting' is represented in Ptolemy by the two terms *anaplokē* and *kataplokē*, meaning presumably ascending and descending *plokē*, and perhaps also by *syrma* 'trailing', which may possibly refer to some kind of smooth arpeggio or chain of intervals.

Not all of this is informative, but it does include some interesting points. First there is the choice of higher or lower pitch for the tonic, the focus of the melody. If it was low in the vocal register, presumably there were more notes above it than below it in the scale used for the melody, and if it was high, there were more notes below. This is a matter in which we observe some variety in the fragments. For instance, in the Berlin Paean (**40**) the scale extends for an octave up from the tonic, but there is only one note below it, whereas in some other pieces there seem to be only one or two notes above the tonic.

Secondly there is the distinction made between movement to adjacent and to non-adjacent notes—what modern musicians call conjunct or disjunct motion. They are, of course, the only logical possibilities if the note is to change at all. But it is interesting that the distinction was thought significant. Or we may put it this way: it is interesting that disjunct motion was felt to be something meriting separate classification. The fact is that conjunct or stepwise motion is what predominates in Greek music. Out of some 2200 note-successions in the published texts, a little over a thousand, or 47 per cent, show a move to an adjacent degree of the scale, and this

---

[2] Cleonides p. 207. 4 gives a conflicting definition of *petteiā* as the multiple repetition of one note. This seems a logical complement to duction and plaiting, and it is something that occasionally occurs in the fragments; but it is less appropriate to the primary sense of *petteiā*, which is playing a strategic board game. Cf. Winnington-Ingram, *Mode*, 56 n. 3. Cleonides adds a fourth term, *tonē*, explained as the prolongation of a note.

preponderance appears consistently in every fragment of more than a few bars' length. In 19 per cent the move is to the second nearest degree, and in 12 per cent to a more distant one. In the other 22 per cent the note remains the same.

If the fragments are consistent in using conjunct motion as the prevalent procedure, they are less so in their use of the wider intervals. This provides a significant criterion for distinguishing different styles. In most pieces the third enjoys a comfortable preponderance over all larger intervals, but there are some where this is not so. Statistics apart, we cannot help noticing that in some music leaps of a sixth, a seventh, an octave, or even a ninth, either upward or downward, are used from time to time for effect. We can identify certain recurrent patterns: an upward leap on the first or second note of a new line or section, following a pause; a downward plunge at the end of a section; a leap within a section, followed at once by a return to the previous pitch region. In this last type it is usually a downward dive, but the converse is also found, apparently already in the fragment from Euripides' *Iphigeneia in Aulis* (**4**). Later texts notable for these leaps are the two Delphic Paeans (**12–13**), the Oslo papyrus (**30–1**), and the Oxyrhynchus papyri 3161 and 3704 (**45–6, 34**). ˑ

The third point of interest in Aristides' discussion is his (and probably originally Aristoxenus') use of the terms 'direct' and 'returning' for ascending and descending motion. The implication is that a melody, by and large, goes up before it goes down. This is the more noteworthy in view of the fact that the Greeks were accustomed to think of scales as descending, and their notation system was based on a downward alphabetic series. In one of the pseudo-Aristotelian *Problems* the question is raised why a descending motion through the tetrachord is more harmonious than an ascending one. One answer suggested is that it means beginning at the beginning, because a tetrachord begins at its top note and ends at the bottom; another answer is that low notes after higher ones are nobler and more euphonious than the opposite.[3] However, melodies could not descend all the time, and the evidence of the fragments is that from late Hellenistic times, at least, melodies and sections of melodies mostly began with a rise.

---

[3] *Pr.* 19. 33, cf. 47; D. B. Monro, *The Modes of Ancient Greek Music* (Oxford, 1894), 44–6; Winnington-Ingram, *Mode*, 4 f.

12 Athenaeus, line 16: octave leap up.

13 Limenius, 13: falling third. 15: rising fourth. 23: rising fourth. 26: octave leap up.

15 Seikilos epitaph: rising fifth from tonic.

16 Hymn to Muse: rising fifth from tonic.[4]

17 Mesomedes, Hymn to Muse: rising phrase from tonic.

18 Mesomedes, Hymn to Sun: level on tonic.

19 Mesomedes, Hymn to Nemesis: first note raised slightly, but basically level on tonic.

23–8 Instrumental pieces: all rising.

29 *POxy.* 2436, 6: first note raised slightly, but basically level.

30 *POsl.* 1413, 8: three notes on level, then rising fourth to tonic. 9: rising third from note above tonic. 10: three notes on level, then rising third to semitone below tonic.

31 *POsl.* 1413, 15: rocking phrase down to tonic from fourth above. 16: rising second. 17: climbing stepwise through a fifth. 18: octave leap up.

40 Berlin Paean: rising phrase starting on note below tonic.

41 Berlin instrumental piece A: falling phrase from fifth to third above tonic.

42 Berlin Ajax: falling third from tonic.

43 Berlin instrumental piece B: rising phrase from third to fifth above tonic.

At the close of a section or of a piece the melodic line tends to be descending, with the final note either the tonic or a fourth below it:

12 Athenaeus, 8: falling fourth from tonic.

13 Limenius, 7: probably falling fourth from tonic. 21: octave drop from tone above tonic. In the last two lines of the composition the melody confines itself to the fifth from the tonic down, and it probably ended with the third and fourth below the tonic.

15 Seikilos epitaph: a similar clausula, falling from the tonic to the third and fourth below, notes not otherwise used in the piece.

16 Hymn to Muse: ends on tonic after circling round it. Most of the melody has been above it.

17 Mesomedes, Hymn to Muse: tonic approached from above, with the note below sounded just before the goal is reached.

18 Mesomedes, Hymn to Sun: similar, but with a little decorative figure when the tonic is reached.

19 Mesomedes, Hymn to Nemesis, 15: tonic reached from fourth above in a gently undulating line.

---

[4] These two cases are especially significant because the melodic rise contradicts the proper pitch-accents of the words set to it; otherwise in these two little songs melodic and verbal accent are in accord. See the section below on words and music.

24 Anon. Bellerm. 98: falling thirds to tonic.
27 Ibid. 101: falling to tonic from fourth and third above.
28 Ibid. 104: fall from fifth to third above tonic.
30 *POsl.* 1413, 15: falling fourth from tonic.
32 *PMichigan* 2958, 5: octave drop. 6: falling thirds. 16: falling fifth.
40 Berlin Paean: descending to tonic.
51 *POxy.* 1786: rocking descent from tonic to fourth below.

The type of close where there is a fall from the tonic to the fourth below (*a e*, *a f e*, etc.) has an exotic sound to our ears, but parallels can be cited from modern folk music of the Balkans.[5] In origin it is perhaps the formalization of a natural drop of the voice as the pressure is taken off.

Greek melody in general has a sinuous, writhing character. From the figures cited earlier it will be seen that if you take any two consecutive notes, four times out of five they will be different. Just occasionally the music seems to become stuck on one note for two or three bars,[6] but for the most part it is in constant, restless motion. There is little repetition of phrases; the composers seem to be always finding new paths through their scales, though I suspect that if we had more extended fragments from the Classical period we should see less of this variety and more that looked formulaic. There are signs of it in the two scraps that we have from Euripides (**3–4**), where we observe repeated playing on the notes of the enharmonic *pyknon*. In the *Orestes* fragment the sequence *f f↓ e* appears twice, besides *e f↓ f e f↓ d e* and *f f↓ f*; in the *Iphigeneia* fragment *f↓ e* three times, besides *f e f↓* and *f e*. We may suppose that this was typical of music in the enharmonic genus with the divided semitone. In the later diatonic texts we notice here and there what seem to be melodic clichés. Attention will be drawn to them as appropriate when we come to study the texts.

Tonal stability and modulation

The citharody of Terpander's time and up to the age of Phrynis remained quite simple in style. For anciently it was not considered legitimate to do as

---

[5] Cf. Manuel Bryennius, *Harm.* 3. 5 p. 324 Jonker (classification of melodies into those that end on the initial/tonic note and those that end a fourth below); C. Sachs, *Musik des Altertums* (Breslau, 1924), 63; B. Bartók, *Volksmusik der Rumänen von Maramures, Sammelbände für vergleichende Musikwissenschaft* 4 (1923), xvi and nos. 53*c*, 69, 70*a*; S. Baud-Bovy, *Essai sur la chanson populaire grecque*, 9 (a klephtic song from Parnassus).

[6] Cf. above, n. 2.

they do nowadays, modulating between scales and rhythms: in each set-piece (*nomos*) they used to preserve the appropriate tuning throughout.[7]

There are other references to modulation of mode and genus as a feature of citharodes' style in the late fifth and early fourth centuries,[8] and it is a subject discussed by the theoreticians.[9] They distinguish four categories of melodic modulation:

1. modulation of genus, e.g. from diatonic to chromatic or enharmonic;
2. of scale-constitution (*systēma*), i.e. from a conjunct to a disjunct sequence of tetrachords, or vice versa;
3. of key;
4. of ethos, e.g. from grand to sensuous, or from calm to vigorous.

Ptolemy interprets the second type as being essentially a change of key; but he draws a crucial distinction between this sort of modulation, which (like modulation of genus) palpably alters the contours of the melody, from the sort of key-change by which the melody is transposed to another pitch without its internal structure being affected.

In the musical fragments we fail to recognize any instance of the latter type of key-change.[10] We do find examples of (*a*) alternation of diatonic with chromatic, in Hellenistic texts (Vienna fragments, Delphic Paeans). (*b*) Modulation between conjunct and disjunct systems, both in Hellenistic and in later pieces (Vienna fragments, Delphic Paeans; **47** *POxy.* 3162). The tonic may remain the same, or be shifted by a tone; thus a scale *e f g a b c′ d′ e′* (disjunct tetrachords with tonic *a*) might change either to *e f g a b♭ c′ d′* (tonic still *a*) or to *f♯ g a b c′ d′ e′* (tonic *b*). Cf. p. 191. (*c*) Shift of melodic focus to a different degree of the scale without change of the scale itself. This seems to occur at all periods, and it is probably not always to be

---

[7] Ps.-Plut. *De mus.* 1133b. Phrynis belongs to the third quarter of the 5th c. For *nomos* see below, p. 215.

[8] See Ch. 12.

[9] Aristoxenus' discussion, programmed at *Harm.* 2. 38, is lost, but reflected in those of later writers: Cleon. p. 204. 19–206. 5, Aristid. Quint. pp. 16. 24, 22. 11–26, 29. 12–14, Bacchius pp. 304. 6–22, 312. 7–11, Anon. Bellerm. 65; a more independent account in Ptol. *Harm.* 2. 6. Cf. E. Pöhlmann, *Griechische Musikfragmente* (Nürnberg, 1960), 51–3; Barker, *GMW* ii. 424 n. 126; also Phrynichus, *Praeparatio Sophistica* p. 24. 16 Borries.

[10] In one of the Vienna papyri (**8** *PVindob.* 29825 fr. a/b recto 6 and verso 11) there are signatures 'Phrygian' and perhaps 'Lydian' marking changes of notation-key, but the fragments are too exiguous for us to judge the melodic significance.

understood as a change of tonic (and thus of modality). But in some cases, as in the hymns of Mesomedes, one has a definite sense of reorientation. (*d*) Change of scale combined with change of tonic. The first recitative in the Oslo papyrus (**30**) alternates between the scale *d e f g a b♭ c′ d′*, with *f* as tonic, and *d e f♯ g a b* (*c′*) *d′* with *g* as tonic.

Chromaticism

The word chromaticism is here used not with reference to the chromatic genus but in its modern sense, of the use of semitone or other intervals that are extraneous to the key or scale in which a piece is written, for ornamental or expressive effect. If we want a term that avoids the possible ambiguity of 'chromatic' in ancient contexts, 'exharmonic' would be appropriate.

While not a regular feature of Greek music, at any rate in the Roman period, chromaticism does occur in some texts. The earliest of them is the Zeno Archive papyrus (**7**) of about 250 BC, apparently a passage from an impassioned tragic supplication. In the fragment as preserved, the basic scale notes are *f g a b♭ c↓′*, with the focus on *a*. But in the second line the descending steps *g f* and *c↓′ b♭* are embellished with inserted semitones, one of them emphasized by being set to a long note (Ex. 7.1).

Ex. 7.1.

In some unpublished Hellenistic fragments that have a similar basic scale, *f g a b♭ c↓′*, the additional note *a♭* appears a number of times, especially in association with *f* or *b♭*. This note a semitone below the tonic is paralleled in Athenaeus' Paean (**12**), where, particularly in one clearly demarcated section (lines 9–16), irregular semitones are used with confident discipline to gorgeous effect. Moving in the basic framework of the fifth *a* (tonic) *b c′ d′ e′*, the composer suddenly slides us down a little scree of semitones, *e′ d′ b b♭ a g♯*, to land on the unconventional note just below the tonic, and it becomes temporarily an extra degree of the scale. Meanwhile the notes *a b♭ b d′* are used as a chromatic (in the ancient sense) tetrachord, and beside the *d′* appears

an ornamental *eb′*. The adventitious semitones are used in particular
in undulating figures, 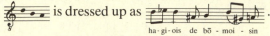 , or to embellish the outer
edges of scalar intervals, as when the underlying melodic progression

 is dressed up as

ha - gi - ois   de   bō - moi - sin

The same mannerism appears in the little anonymous hymn to the
Muse (**16**). The basic scale consists of the six notes *d e f g a b* (tonic
e), but a couple of semitonal ornaments enable the progression

to become

au - rē de sōn   ap' al - se - ōn   e - mās phre - nas   do - nei - tō [11]

The Oslo papyrus (**30**) also shows touches of chromaticism. I have
mentioned that it modulates between a scale with *f* and *bb* and one
with *f♯* and *b♮*. But in places *f* and *f♯* are deployed alternately for the
space of a bar or two, as if to keep surprising the hearer. And in the
sections that have *b♮*, we also encounter an exharmonic *bb*. It is
juxtaposed with the 'correct' *b♮* in the figures *b a bb* and *b bb b♮*, each
set to a single word.

The Berlin Ajax fragment (**42**) perhaps deserves a mention here
because, although it has no notes outside those of its own scale, the
scale itself has an irregularity of which the effect is similar to that of
occasional chromaticism. The compass, at any rate in the surviving
bars, is limited to a fifth, with the tonic (*c″*) in the middle and two
degrees below and above it. But instead of the expected *a′ b′ c″ d″
e″*, we find *a′ b′ c″ d♯″ e″*, with the fourth degree slightly sharpened.
This gives the melody an interesting tang.

Words and music

The surviving texts are predominantly vocal, as was Greek music
overall. We must next consider the relationship of the music to the
words.

The rhythm, as explained in Chapter 5, reflected in a formalized

---

[11] Following the MS text. See the notes on the piece in Ch. 10.

way the natural rhythm of the words, with their built-in opposition of longer and shorter durations. To a certain extent melody too had a basis in an intrinsic feature of the language. From the earliest times Greek had a tonal accent. In every word (except for certain particles, prepositions, conjunctions, and a handful of others) there was one syllable which was given prominence over the others, not by stress as in English (and modern Greek) but by raised pitch. The Greeks interpreted the phenomenon in musical terms. They called it 'singing along', *prosōidiā*, which the Romans translated as *ad-cantus*, *accentus*. They applied to it the same vocabulary of high/low, tension/relaxation, as they did to melodic pitch, and they could even speak of its 'attunement', *harmoniā*.[12] Aristoxenus lays it down that it is movement by definite intervals that distinguishes musical melody from that of speech, 'for there is said to be a kind of melody of speech too, the one constituted by the word-accents'.[13] The differences of pitch in this speech-melody were conspicuous. According to Dionysius of Halicarnassus, writing in the time of Augustus, they amounted to approximately a fifth.[14]

When such a language was set to music and sung, one might expect that the verbal accent, as an essential and inalienable feature of words, serving in some cases to distinguish one meaning or grammatical form from another, would be respected by the melodic line, just as each word's metrical shape was respected in the metre of the song. This relationship often exists in the music of other countries where tonal languages are spoken, for example in China, where the melody of many songs 'is but an exaggeration of the tonal accents', and in Uganda.[15]

The evidence of the Greek musical documents is that the accent was indeed respected to a large extent in non-strophic compositions, where the melody did not have to repeat with different sets of words but was 'through-composed', designed for a unique text. But in strophic compositions, such as the majority of choral odes in tragedy, correspondence of accents and melody could only have been achieved if each strophe sung to a given melody had been so composed as to have the same pattern of word accents. So far as we

[12] Anon. *Dissoi logoi* 5. 11, Arist. *Rh.* 1403^{b}31. Cf. W. S. Allen, *Vox Graeca*, 3rd edn. (Cambridge, 1987), 116.
[13] *Harm.* 1. 18; cf. Dion. Hal. *Comp.* 57f., 64f., Cic. *Orat.* 57.
[14] *Comp.* 58–62; cf. Allen, op. cit., 120f.
[15] L. Picken in E. Wellesz (ed.), *Ancient and Oriental Music*, 113; Sachs, *WM* 35–8; Nettl, *FTM* 138f.

can see, this was never attempted. Dionysius of Halicarnassus remarks on the disagreements of accent and melody in the first words of the first song in Euripides' most popular drama, *Orestes*.[16] In the papyrus fragment that gives us a little of the music to a later ode in the same play, we find that it matches the accentual pattern neither of the strophe nor of the antistrophe. There is partial agreement, sometimes with the one, sometimes with the other, but accord is not a principle of the composition.[17] It is reasonable to suppose that other dramatic fragments in which the melody shows no particular regard for the word accents were originally strophic.[18]

Where the accent is respected, the respect is expressed in the following principles:

1. The accented syllable is given a note *at least as high* as any other in the same word.[19] Often, especially in polysyllabic words, it is set at the summit of a rising and falling figure.

2. A syllable bearing a circumflex accent (which represents a high pitch followed by a fall, and can only occur on a long vowel or diphthong) is often set on two notes of which the first is the higher.

3. When the accent falls on the final syllable of a word, and is not circumflex, and not succeeded by a grammatical pause, then the melody does not fall again until after the next accent.

It is in the Delphic Paeans that these rules are observed most consistently, though even there one or two breaches occur. In other texts practice is a little freer, particularly, perhaps, as regards the third rule.[20] There is some reason to suspect that it becomes freer the later the composition, though with several of the papyri we cannot be sure whether the composition was of the same age as the papyrus or

---

[16] *Comp.* 63 f. He omits to mention that the song is strophic.

[17] See, however, D. D. Feaver, *AJPhil.* 81 (1960), 7–15, who argues that there is a more than casual degree of correspondence, especially in the strophe.

[18] This applies to the Zeno Archive fragment, parts of the Vienna fragments, and the Berlin Ajax (**7**, **8**, **42**; *Trag. Adesp.* (*TrGF*) 678, 679, 683).

[19] Similarly a sample of songs of the Ibo in Nigeria suggests 'that the musical pitch sometimes moves up and down in the same direction as the pitch in speech, and that it sometimes remains the same while the speech tones change, but that pitch movement in the music is hardly ever contrary to that of the language' (Nettl, *FTM* 139; cf. his *Theory and Method in Ethnomusicology* (New York, 1964), 290 f.).

[20] Winnington-Ingram, *Symb. Osl.* 31 (1955), 64–73, gives a careful and detailed account of the evidence known up to that date; one additional fragment was known to Pöhlmann, *Griechische Musikfragmente*, 26–9. It is to be noted that a number of the violations cited from Mesomedes disappear in the improved edition by Pöhlmann in his 1970 corpus.

older. The suspected increase in licentiousness has been connected with the fact that in the early centuries of our era the Greek verbal accent was gradually changing its nature and becoming a stress accent.[21] However, it continued to have a tonal element for a long time: the old relationship between accent and melody still generally holds in the imperial acclamations of the fifteenth-century Byzantine empire.[22]

An interesting departure from the usual rules is common to two of our texts which in other respects too show a certain likeness, the Seikilos epitaph and the anonymous invocation of the Muse (**15, 16**). They both begin with a bold rising fifth, starting from the tonic, and quite contrary to the accent, which is on the first syllable. Evidently the rising fifth was a conventional opening gesture which overrode accentual considerations. Cf. above, p. 193.

Another aspect of the interrelationship of words and music is the use of melodic means to underline or enhance the sense of particular words or phrases. In Pindar, Bacchylides, and tragedy it is sometimes observable that a word or phrase in one strophe is echoed by the same or similar-sounding words at the corresponding place in another. In such cases there must have been some association with a particular musical phrase, but we can only guess how far it had an expressive function.

The intention is clearer, perhaps, in Simonides' and Pindar's occasional placing of a significant word in a rhythmically prominent position where the length of its syllables is exaggerated. If I may attempt to render the effect in translation:

> (On the impermanence of fortune)
> > Not even the delicate-winged *house-fly*
> > changes perch so fast.

> (On the foolish boasting of Cleobulus)
> > against the perennial flow of the rivers, flowers of spring,
> > the flame of the sun, the gold of the moon
> > and swirl of the sea
> > pitting the strength of a mere *tombstone*.

---

[21] T. Reinach, *La Musique grecque*, 69; Pöhlmann, *Griechische Musikfragmente*, 28 f. For the metrical evidence of the change see my *Greek Metre*, 162–4.

[22] See E. Wellesz, *A History of Byzantine Music and Hymnography*, 2nd edn., 114–22.

(Music lulls the fierce eagle of Zeus)
> Your dark cloud settles over his hook-nosed head
> gently to shutter his eyelids, and he, *snoring*,
> rhythms his rippling back.[23]

The same onomatopoeic word for 'snore, slumber', *knōssō*, is likewise stretched out by Simonides in a fragment where it is actually written *knooss*- (♪♩). He is also cited for doing something similar with the word for fire, *pȳr*, making it disyllabic, *pyȳr*. We may guess that the music at this point was shaped to suggest the flickering flames.[24]

A related device is reflected in Aristophanes' delicious parody of Euripidean lyrics, where he twice writes the verb *heilissō* 'twirl' as *heieieieieilissō* (the manuscripts are at variance on the exact number of *ei*s).[25] In the Hellenistic papyri and inscriptions with musical notation a long vowel or diphthong is written double when it is divided between two notes; no increase in duration (as in the two Simonides instances) is implied or indeed admissible in these cases. So the Aristophanes passage suggests a multiple—probably in fact no more than a triple—division as a novelty of modern lyrics: not as a general-purpose ornament, but in association with a particular word and as a melodic comment on the word's meaning. Imitative expressionism was a feature of the new music of the period.[26]

In the Delphic Paeans, nearly three centuries later, we still find clear examples. In both compositions, at mention of the twin peaks of Parnassus, the melody duly makes two peaks in the upper part of the scale (in one case against the word accent). The words 'shimmering tunes' are set to a shimmering musical phrase: ♫♫♫. The

flickering of the altar flames is likewise evoked (cf. above on Simonides) in Example 7.2.

Ex. 7.2

Hā - phais - tos aí - thei né -ōn   mê - ra taú - rōn

---

[23] Simon. *PMG* 521, 581, Pind. *Pyth.* 1. 7 f.
[24] *PMG* 543. 9, 587; cf. *ZPE* 37 (1980) 153–5.
[25] *Ran.* 1314, 1348.   [26] See Ch. 12.

It is difficult to find parallels for this sort of thing in the post-Hellenistic fragments.

What we do find there is a growing tendency to ornamental division of notes, so that an increasing number of long syllables are sung on two or three notes (never more), and even some short syllables are sung on two. To borrow from the terminology applied to plainchant, there is a shift from syllabic to neumatic style, with premonitions of the melismatic.[27]

In traditional Greek vocal music the binary opposition of long and short syllables was matched by a binary opposition of long and short notes. Within certain limits a long syllable might take the place of two short ones, or vice versa. It is reasonable to imagine that, corresponding to this equivalence, it was sometimes acceptable to set a long syllable to two short notes. (The alternative would be to suppose that all pairs of short syllables that were capable of being replaced by one long were sung on the same note.) Certainly in the late fifth century melodic bisection of long syllables was commonplace. In the fragment from Euripides' *Orestes* one instance is directly visible, and if we calculate the number of letters written in the broken-off portions of the lines, we discover that at least three other double-vowel spellings are probable. In this short sample it seems that about one long syllable in six was divided between two notes.

In the Delphic Paeans the proportion is one in three or four, but the principle is the same. We cannot necessarily take these pieces as representative of Hellenistic technique generally. There must have been much variation between different composers and genres. In Mesomedes the frequency of division is much lower.

In Mesomedes, the anonymous invocation of the Muse, and the Seikilos epitaph we get our first evidence concerning the melodization of triseme syllables. Logically they should be allocable to three short notes just as readily as ordinary disemes are to two. And indeed we find this, ♫♩ besides ♩. and ♪♩; not, however, ♩ ♪, even where that is the underlying metre.[28] There is no reason why this should not correspond to classical practice.

In the papyri from the second and third centuries AD we encounter a more florid technique. Apart from a generally higher frequency of divided longs, there are three distinctive features:

---

[27] Neumatic, in this usage, means from two to four notes to a syllable; melismatic means five or more.   [28] See the section on Mesomedes in Ch. 10.

1. Diseme syllables may be sung on three notes, normally of the rhythmic pattern ♪♫, with the second short note of the usual binary division ♫ itself divided into two. In one instance it seems to be ♫♪, and in a couple of others the notation (so far as legible) is not exact enough for the rhythm to be determined. An earlier example than those of the papyri can be recognized in the late Hellenistic inscription from the neighbourhood of Mylasa (**14**).[29]

2. Short syllables may be sung on two notes, the standard short note ♪ being bisected, ♫. In two places a short final vowel, which would normally be treated as elided before another short vowel, is written unelided, both vowels being assigned notes which, to fit the rhythm, must be interpreted as ♪♪. In these and some other cases of bisected short, the second note is the same as that on the following syllable, and it could be classified as the ornament known as the note of anticipation or 'cadent'.[30]

3. In the Oslo papyrus (**30**) three times, in the Berlin Ajax excerpt (**42**), and in *POxy.* 3161 (**45**) we find mythological names—Ajax, Ixion, Tantalus, Deidameia, Nereus—treated in an especially elaborate fashion (Ex. 7.3), with one of their syllables, usually the first, prolonged to twice its proper length.

Ex. 7.3

(The rhythmical interpretation of Nereus is uncertain. Tantalus is too battered for public exhibition.)

The Berlin Paean is a special case because of its solemn, spondaic tempo (cf. p. 155). Its diseme and tetraseme units are subject to the same patterns of melodic division as the standard shorts and longs in

---

[29] Although this triple division of disemes first appears in regular use in the later period, I suspect that it originated as an occasional ornament in Euripides' time, and that this is what Aristophanes' *heieieieilissō* is parodying.

[30] See *NG* xiii. 850.

1 and 2 above: ♩=♫, ♩=♩♩ = ♩ ♫. In addition, the last syllable of a line, in principle tetraseme, is sometimes prolonged into the vacant time before the start of the next line, finally expiring with a dying fall (Ex. 7.4).

Ex. 7.4

-lōn   phō-nãn   stép-sãs

When a syllable is sung on three notes, whether the rhythm is ♫♩, ♫♩ or ♩ ♫, it is frequently the case that the second note is higher than the first (most often by a tone), while the third is the same as the first or a little lower. We recognize here something that is recorded in a little list of melodic figures in the Anonymus Bellermanni.[31] There is one called *ekkrousmos*, explained as being 'when the same note is taken twice with a higher note in between, for example *g a g* or *a bb a*'. The others are:

prolēpsis, a rising two-note figure (♪) making an interval of up to a fifth;
eklēpsis, the same falling;
prokrousis and *ekkrousis*, the same where it is a short note divided (♫);
kompismos and *melismos*, (apparently) the figures ♫ and ♫ where the two notes are the same (but it is also called *kompismos* if the second note is an octave higher than the first);
teretismos, a combination of *kompismos* and *melismos*, ♫♫ .

The examples which the author appends to each definition are in the instrumental, not the vocal notation, and he presumably has instrumental playing primarily in view.[32] But most of the figures he describes have parallels in our vocal texts.

---

[31] Anon. Bellerm. 2–10, 84–93. Manuel Bryennius, *Harm.* 3. 3 pp. 308–12 Jonker, gives a slightly longer list, related to that of the Anonymus but conflicting with it in various details, which need not be specified here.

[32] A symbol for *kompismos* has in fact been identified in the two Berlin instrumental pieces (**41, 43**), and Pollux 4. 83 mentions *teretismoi* as part of the aulete's technique, while Agathias, *Anth. Pal.* 7. 612. 3, speaks of the *teretismata* of the lyre. *Kompismos* signs also seem to appear in two or three of the unpublished vocal frag-

Voice and instrument. Heterophony

It is convenient for singers if they can take their first note from an instrument already in play. The Homeric bard played some preliminary bars on his phorminx before embarking on his song. Pindar, addressing the lyre, speaks of its prelude serving as signal and guide to dancers and singers. Such a prelude was called *anabolē*, and the corresponding verb *anaballomai* was used from early times for playing it.[33] Pipers too played an introduction before the singer or chorus joined in. In the later fifth-century dithyramb the instrumental prelude became something quite elaborate and fantasy-like.[34]

Melanippides, one of the leading writers of these dithyrambs, is said to have composed *anabolai* instead of antistrophes.[35] This must mean that he made the dithyramb non-strophic, through-composed, and divided it into sections by means of instrumental interludes, which the term *anabolē* is here extended to cover. In later vocal scores too we occasionally meet a line or two of purely instrumental music in the middle.[36]

During the singing the accompanying instrument's main role was to duplicate the vocal melody.[37] But sometimes it played some divergent notes as well. Plato deprecates

heterophony and lyre-embroidery, when the strings give out one melody and the composer of the song another, and when people combine close with open texture, fast with slow, high with low in parallel, and likewise when they impose all sorts of rhythmic decoration on the notes of the lyre.[38]

This sounds like quite an elaborate and busy sort of accompaniment, with the lyre putting in crowds of extra notes.

---

ments. For Bryennius *kompismos* is the instrumental equivalent of *melismos*, and *teretismos* the same when voice and instrument sound together.

[33] *Od.* 1. 155, 8. 266 with schol. and Eust., 17. 261–3; Pind. *Pyth.* 1. 3 with schol., cf. schol. *Nem.* 7. 114 d, *Etym. Magn.* 80. 22; *JHS* 101 (1981), 122. Another word was *endosimon* (Hsch.).

[34] Eup. fr. 81, Ar. *Pax* 830, *Av.* 1385.

[35] Arist. *Rh.* 1409[b]25.

[36] **9** *PVindob.* G 13763/1494, **32** *PMichigan* 2958. Late sources call such insertions *mesaulika, mesaulia,* or *kōla* (Aristid. Quint. p. 23. 21, Anon. Bellerm. 68; cf. Barker, *GMW* ii. 435 n. 160; Psell. *De trag.* 9, Eust. *Il.* 862. 19). See also above, p. 67, on citharodes' strumming in the intervals of their songs.

[37] See p. 67 with n. 85.

[38] *Leg.* 812 de; see Barker's notes, *GMW* i. 163.

From other sources we get an impression of a more frugal and calculated use of heterophony. In a discussion that seems to go back to Aristoxenus[39] we read of the use of heterophony in old tunes deriving from people like Olympus; it is presupposed that it was an integral feature of the ancient tradition, not something improvised by the modern executant. We are told that in the libation style, where the melody used (it seems) only the notes *e e↑ f a b c'*,[40] the accompaniment used *b↑* and *e'* besides: *b↑* to make a concord of a fifth with *e↑*, and *e'* to make a concord with *a* and a discord with *c'*. The author goes on to say (it is not clear whether he is still referring to the same music) that the ancients used *d'* in their accompaniment—when they would have been ashamed of its effect in the melody—to clash with *f*, *b*, and *c'*. This intriguing notion of the function of heterophonic notes is echoed by the late writer Gaudentius. According to him there is, between concordant and discordant notes, an intermediate category of 'paraphones', which sound concordant in the accompaniment. He gives as examples the interval of three tones from *f* to *b* (where the tonic is *a*) and that of two tones from *g* to *b*.[41]

But we have more direct evidence. In the fragment from Euripides' *Orestes*, besides the vocal notes, there appear a small number of instrumental (aulos) notes, just one or two at a time, at significant points. With one exception they are placed between words of the text, and it is usually assumed that they were meant to sound between those words. But that would disrupt the rhythm intolerably, and I have no doubt that they were intended to sound simultaneously with the following word, possibly continuing as a drone throughout the phrase. There was nowhere else for the copyist to fit them in conveniently but before the word at which they sounded. Three different notes are represented, and two of them are not matched in the vocal

---

[39] Ps.-Plut. *De mus.* 1137 b–d.

[40] This resembles but is not identical with the scale of the *Spondeion* discussed on p. 173. See Barker, *GMW* i. 256 f.

[41] Gaud. p. 338. 3–7; cf. Bacchius p. 305. 13, and 'Longinus', *Subl.* 28. 1, who speaks of 'the so-called paraphones' being used to make 'the proper note' more pleasurable. Ps.-Arist. *Pr.* 19. 12 (corrupt text) apparently refers to the playing of *b* with *a*. The assertion sometimes made that heterophonic accompaniment in Greek music was always higher than the voice has no basis in ps.-Arist. *Pr.* 19. 39 or ps.-Plut. *De mus.* 1141 b, since *hypo tēn ōidēn* does not mean 'above' but simply 'accompanying' the song (cf. Pl. *Leg.* 670 a; Polycrates, *FGrH* 588); it has a precarious basis in Plut. *Coniugalia praecepta* 139 cd.

scale, which is *d e e↑ f a b b↑ c'* (perhaps to be supplemented with *e'*). The instrumental notes are *c*, *f*, and *d'*—this last recalling the observations of Aristoxenus. The *d'* chimes away mechanically, it seems, at the start of each dochmiac bar (or at least every second bar), coinciding on successive apparitions with vocal *e↑*, *a*, *a*, and *d*. The other two instrumental notes, *c f*, occur in tandem—twice—and it looks as if the two auloi here diverged to blow the chord of a fourth. The concurrent vocal note is lost at the first place; at the second it is *b*, which, as it happens, gives us the very combination cited by Gaudentius as an example of a tritone harmony, *f–b*.

Isolated instrumental notes appear in much the same way in two scraps from another papyrus in Vienna, discovered along with the *Orestes* piece (**8** *PVindob*. 29825 frs. c and f). In one the vocal notes visible are *e f♯ g♯ a*, the instrumental ones *B* (once with the vocal *a*, making the chord of a minor seventh) and *d'*. In the other we see again an instrumental *B*, and vocal *d e a b c'*.

The heterophony suggested by these papyri is very different from that described by Plato: no flurry of additional notes, just a few special tones repeated at intervals to create a changing series of striking chords with the vocal line. Sometimes the recognized concords of fourth, fifth, or octave were produced; sometimes other intervals such as thirds, tritones, sixths, or sevenths, which according to Greek doctrine were discords but which, it had to be acknowledged, could give quite a good effect. The author of the pseudo-Aristotelian *Problem* 19. 39 speaks of aulos accompaniments which use discords but finish in unison with the vocal line; he says that they 'give more pleasure by the ending than displeasure by the preceding divergences'.

In Chapter 3 I made sporadic reference to the lyres of East Africa. As this is the one region where the tradition of lyre-playing has survived as an inheritance from the ancient Mediterranean world, it may be of interest to note that in Ethiopia

performance on lyres includes instrumental preludes and interludes; when accompanying the voice they usually duplicate the melody, producing a certain amount of heterophony, or play an ostinato accompaniment often derived from the basic vocal pattern on which the song may be based.[42]

---

[42] *NG* vi. 272.

FORM

One can hardly speak of a minimum or maximum length for a Greek musical performance. It might be a tiny song of two lines, or at the other extreme an open-ended epic recitation going on for hours or days. But irrespective of scale, the music had to obey some principle of form if it was to give satisfaction. What kinds of principle come into question?

To a large extent form, like rhythm, is reflected in metrical structure, and useful inferences can be drawn from our whole corpus of Greek poetry (insofar as it was sung), even without knowing anything of the melodies. First we can make a basic distinction of three structural types: stichic, where a line of more or less fixed metrical form is repeated indefinitely, with no grouping into larger units; strophic, where a longer and more complex structure, usually analysable into smaller components, is the repeating unit; and free astrophic, where there is continuous development and no principle of repetition.

Stichic form

The prime example of stichic form is Homeric epic: thousands of lines of unchanging length and rhythm, differentiated only by the varying incidence of word-ends and pauses and by the haphazard alternation of feet of the form $-\cup\cup$ with feet of the form $--$. We know it was all sung to the lyre, following a brief instrumental introduction, and probably with some instrumental notes between the verses.[43] But how was it sung? Does the stereotyped hexameter metre betoken a stereotyped melodic line, repeated over and over again? This is more or less what happens in the epic singing of many countries, from Mongolia to Iceland. Sometimes, however, the bard uses more than one melody, alternating them in different types of context. And although the melodies are often characterized as 'repetitive' or 'monotonous', they are capable of accommodating many minor variations. There is reason to believe that the Homeric singer, within the framework of a repeating melodic scheme, was able to take account of the word accents, and that in this way many archaic accentuations were preserved.[44] Yugoslav epic song—as in many respects—provides an interesting parallel:

[43] See *JHS* 101 (1981), 122f.; *ZPE* 63 (1986), 42–4.
[44] *JHS* 101. 113ff.; cf. Georgiades, 123f.; G. Danek, *Wiener humanistische Blätter* 31 (1989), 5ff.

within the narrow limits of a melody that is repeated line after line many and subtle variations are introduced.... In Serbo-Croat stress, quantity and intonation are all phonemically relevant; and it might be supposed that these factors would be suppressed by the superimposition of melody. Again, those competent to judge are agreed that this is not the case: the natural rhythms of speech, while to some extent overlaid or obscured, are still perceptible.[45]

A fragment of an inscription from Epidaurus (**11**) throws a faint light on the singing of hexameters at a later period. It carried the text of a hymn, in all likelihood to Asclepius, with musical notes over the first verse only. The implication is that this line of melody was to be repeated, or adapted, to all the other verses too. It does not accord at all with the word accents. Besides the notes over the text there are apparently a few more after the end of the line, representing an instrumental flourish or cadence.[46]

Mesomedes' hymns to the Sun and Nemesis (**18–19**) show us another style of singing stichic verse. Here there is no trace of a fixed melody, though certain patterns do occur more than once. The songs are through-composed in accordance with the word accents, only a few of which are violated. Each line comes to an end with a strongly marked rhythmic clausula and pause: there is no attempt to blur or break up the stichic structure. A fair proportion of the lines, including the final one,[47] end on the tonic; but wherever they end, some sense of continuity is maintained by the way the next line begins. We see the same characteristics in the Berlin Paean (**40**) and in the settings of dramatic iambics in the Oxyrhynchus 2436, Oslo, and Michigan papyri (**29, 31, 32**).

Strophic form

Strophic forms fall rather clearly into two categories, which may be called closed and open.

The 'closed' strophe was typical of Ionian and Lesbian solo lyric and Athenian popular songs, and it remained common in post-Classical times. It was, at least in some cases, a conventional structure that served for many different songs. The elegiac couplet (p. 152) is the outstanding example of this, and the Alcaic and

---

[45] R. Auty in A. T. Hatto (ed.), *Traditions of Heroic and Epic Poetry*, i (London, 1980), 202.

[46] *SEG* 30. 390 (inscribed in the 3rd c. AD, but the hymn and melody may be some centuries older). See my discussion in *ZPE* 63 (1986), 39–46.

[47] At any rate in the Sun hymn; the notes for the last few words of the Nemesis hymn are missing, but it seems safe to make this assumption.

Sapphic stanzas used by the Lesbian poets (p. 149) also come readily to mind. The formal features of the closed strophe are that it is small in scale, between two and six lines; the lines are easily demarcated, being for the most part verses made to familiar metrical specifications (iambic or ionic dimeter, glyconic, etc.); and several of them may be metrically identical. For example, in Anacreon and elsewhere we find quatrains made up of three glyconics ($-$ × $- \cup \cup -$ $\cup -$) plus a final pherecratean one syllable shorter ($-$ × $- \cup \cup - -$). We can represent this particular arrangement as AAAB. Other common patterns include AAB, AB, ABC, AABC, AA, but not ABBA, AABB, or ABCA. Often B is a shortened or lengthened variant of A.

The tunes must have had a correspondingly clear structure, though it should not be assumed that those lines in a strophe which had the same metrical form were necessarily melodically identical. We should expect the melodic lines to form some sort of pattern of statement and answer. The strophe would have ended with a return to the tonic note, or some other form of final cadence to make it clear that it was an end. In the preceding lines this sense of finality had to be avoided; when the melody paused, it will have paused 'up in the air', or on some kind of half-cadence, leaving the hearer in no doubt that it was incomplete.

Three of the later pieces in our collection of musical documents illustrate the principle. They are not strictly speaking strophic, because there is no repetition, but each has the form of an isolated strophe of the closed type.

The Seikilos epitaph (**15**) has four lines, all metrically equivalent though with variants, and each containing a complete sentence. It starts with a rising fifth from the tonic *g* to *d'*, and the first line and sentence end on *c'*. The second and third both end hopping across the tonic from *a* to *f*. The fourth ends with a falling cadence from the tonic down to *d*.

The anonymous invocation of the Muse (**16**) also has four lines, but in the pattern ABAB. Again the opening is a rising fifth from the tonic, *e–b*. The first line returns to *e*, but as it is the first line, no one could take this for an ending. The second line ends on *g*, the third on *a*, the fourth again on *e*.

Mesomedes' invocation of the Muse (**17**) has only three lines, the pattern being AAB. The first line starts from the tonic *e* and travels to *d*. The second takes us into what feels like a different mode, going

PLATE 1. Private sacrificial procession. Corinthian painted wooden plaque. Sixth century BC. (Athens 16464)

PLATE 2. Processions of dancers and musicians. Proto-Attic hydria in Berlin. Early seventh century BC. (Berlin 31573)

PLATE 3. Merry costumed dancers with piper. Black-figure
cup in Amsterdam. Mid-sixth century BC. (Amsterdam
3356)

PLATE 4. Citharode mounting the competition podium
before wreathed judges. Attic black-figure amphora. Late
sixth century BC. (London 1926.6–28.7)

PLATE 5. Panathenaic procession. Black-figure amphora in Berlin. Third quarter of sixth century BC. (Berlin 1686)

PLATE 6. A piper accompanies a symposiast as he sings a piece of elegiac verse. The painter has shown the words coming from the singer's mouth, though they cannot be seen in the reproduction. Red-figure cup in Munich. Early fifth century BC. (Munich 2646)

PLATE 7. Women making music. Apulian pelike in Copenhagen. Fourth century BC. (Copenhagen VIII 316)

PLATE 8. Women making bread, entertained by a piper. Terracotta group from Thebes. Late sixth century BC. (Paris 804)

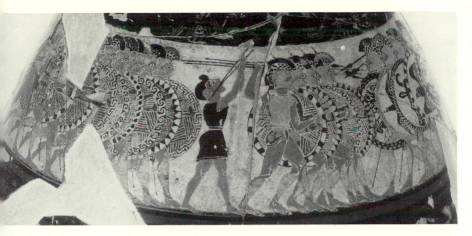

PLATE 9. Marching warriors with piper. Protocorinthian vase (the Chigi vase), *c*.630 BC. (Rome, Villa Giulia 22679)

PLATE 10. Athletes with pipers. Attic red-figure cup by Epictetus. Late sixth century BC. (Berlin F 2262)

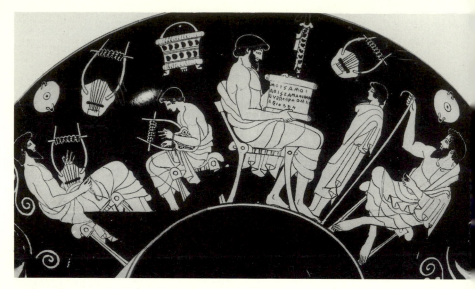

PLATE 11. Athenian school scene. Red-figure cup by
Duris. Early fifth century BC. (Berlin F 2285)

PLATE 12. Man with kithara and dancers. The Hubbard
amphora. Cypriote, about 800 BC. (*BSA* 37 pl. 8*b*)

PLATE 13. Seated minstrel. Bronze figurine from Crete. Late eighth century BC. (Heraklion 2064)

PLATE 14. Citharode. Detail from red-figure amphora in Boston. Early fifth century BC. (Boston 26.61)

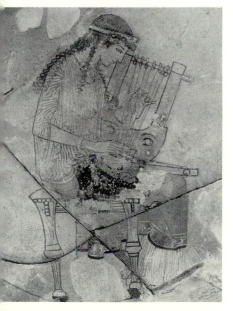

PLATE 15. Girl or Muse with round-based kithara. White-ground cup in the Louvre (Detail). Mid-fifth century BC. (Paris 482)

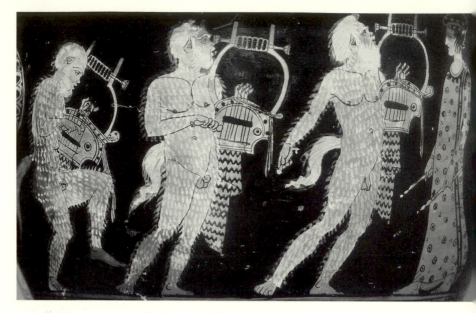

PLATE 16. Satyr chorus with 'Thracian' kitharas. Late Attic
bell crater, *c*.420 BC. (New York 25. 78. 66)

PLATE 17. Pair of auloi; crested harp (*pēlēx*); rectangular,
'Italiote' kithara. Detail from red-figure bell crater.
Second half of the fourth century BC. (Naples, Museo
Nazionale, inv. 80084)

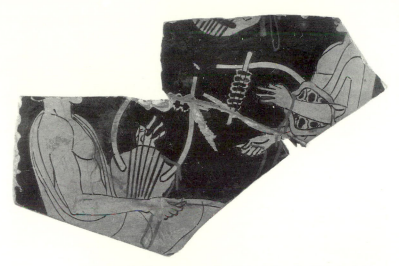

PLATE 18. Young men playing tortoise-shell lyres. Attic red-figure fragment. (Florence 128)

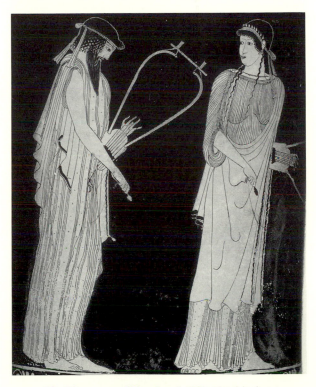

PLATE 19. Alcaeus and Sappho, holding barbitoi, as pictured by an Athenian vase-painter of the early fifth century BC. (Munich 2416)

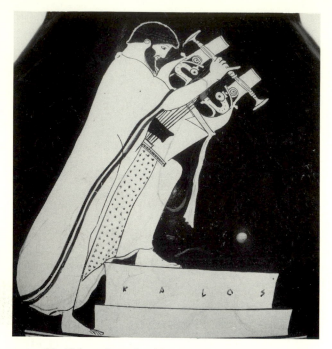

PLATE 20. Citharode tuning his lyre as he mounts the podium. Red-figure pelike, *c*.475 BC. (Münzen und Medaillen, Basle)

PLATE 21. Muse holding auloi (note the flattened reed-tips); another playing a harp (*pēktis*); Musaeus holding a lyra; (above) a round-based kithara. Attic red-figure amphora, *c*.440 BC. (London E 271)

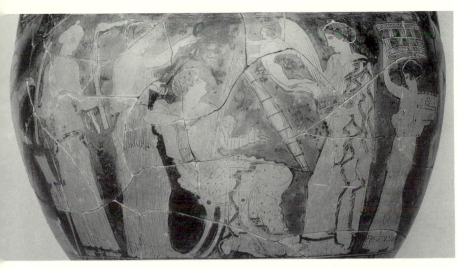

PLATE 22. Woman with triangular harp (*trigōnos*). Detail from red-figure lebes, *c*.425 BC. (New York 16. 73)

PLATE 23. Girl holding a *sambȳkē* (?). Attic white-ground lekythos (Detail). Second quarter of the fifth century BC. (Brussels A 1020)

PLATE 24. Woman playing a lute. Terracotta figurine from Cyprus. Late fourth century BC. (BM 1919.6–20.7)

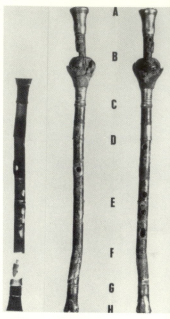

PLATE 25. Piper wearing *phorbeiā*. Attic red-figure amphora. Early fifth century BC. (London E 270)

PLATE 26. The Reading aulos. Probably from Asia Minor, and not earlier than the fourth century BC. (*BSA* 63 pl. 55)

PLATE 27. The aulete Pronomus. Detail from Attic red-figure volute crater, *c.*400 BC. (Naples H 3240)

PLATE 28. Satyr with panpipe and bagpipe. Hellenistic gem. (Boardman, Ionides Collection)

PLATE 30. Scythian archer blowing a trumpet. Black-figure dish by Psiax. Late sixth century BC. (London B591)

PLATE 29. Panpipes. Detail from Apulian situla. Mid-fourth century BC. (Bloomington 70-97 1)

PLATE 31. Young man piping; courtesan dancing with castanets. Red-figure cup by Epictetus, c.500 BC. (London E 38)

PLATE 32. Maenads with drums; piping satyr. Tarentine bell crater. Late fifth century BC. (Trendall, *Frühital. Vasen* pl. 6*b*)

PLATE 33. Woman playing *psithyrā* (?). Red-figure lekythos in Essen. Mid-fourth century BC. (Essen 74. 158 A 3)

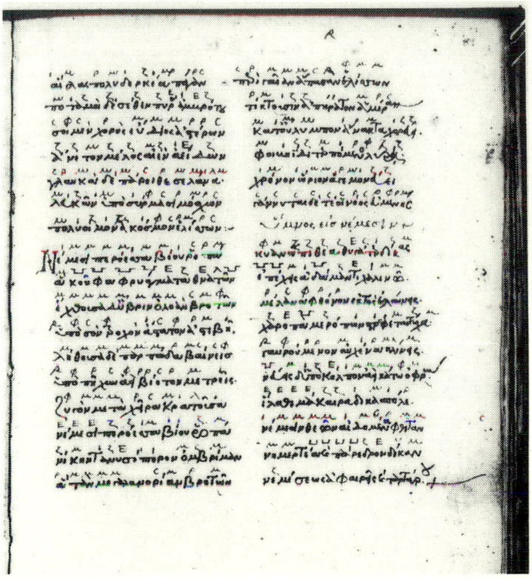

PLATE 34. Page from the Naples manuscript containing poems of Mesomedes with musical notation. Fifteenth century. (Cod. Neap. gr. III C4 fol. 83ʳ)

PLATE 35. The Berlin musical papyrus. Late second or
early third century AD. (P. Berol. 6870)

up and down the octave *c–c'* and landing on the *a*. In the short third line there is an abrupt lurch back into the original mode, duly ending on *e*.

These little songs are late in date, but it is not unreasonable to suppose that the strophes of Sappho and Anacreon obeyed similar canons of finality and non-finality, with half-cadences off the tonic and full cadences either on it or falling from it to the fourth below.

The other category of strophe, the 'open' kind, was characteristic of the Dorian tradition of choral and narrative lyric and became naturalized at Athens as a feature of dithyramb and tragedy. This kind of strophe is larger and more complex than the other. It may extend over five, ten, or fifteen lines of writing. But these lines of writing seldom correspond to distinct, metrically stereotyped verses. The strophe is built up from a number of periods (defined by the occurrence of pauses, which are themselves defined by metrical criteria), which may be of as few as four syllables or of more than forty. Sometimes they are easily analysed in terms of familiar metrical units; sometimes one can only assign the strophe to a general rhythmic category such as aeolic, but not find labels to hand for the definition of the component verses. The poets develop and embroider them as they compose, creating new mutations out of what has gone before.[48] The 'open' strophe was never, so far as we know, used for more than one composition. It was always a unique, original creation.

Such strophes represent ample musical paragraphs, too long to be called tunes. But in many cases there was an even larger structural unit. Stesichorus, Pindar, and others in their times often used the triadic system, in which two strophes sung to the same music were followed by a third, the 'epode', that had a different metrical scheme and melody; the whole sequence was then repeated as many times as required, AAB AAB AAB . . . Most (possibly all) of this triadic poetry was sung by dancers or as accompaniment to them, so that the arrangement had both a musical and a choreographic significance.

In tragedy no strophic melody was repeated more than once. A single triad might occur, but the preferred arrangement was AA BB CC . . . Aeschylus in his *Choephoroe* produces elaborate interlacings of strophes, ABA CDC EFE and the like, but this did not

---

[48] Cf. my *Greek Metre*, 63–8.

catch on. What we do find occasionally—and in comedy more often—is that a strophic melody that has been heard once recurs at a later point in the play.[49]

It may be conjectured that the musical logic of the open strophe was analogous to what has been indicated for the closed one, with a distinction of less and more final-sounding cadences at the various pauses in the structure. The only particle of direct evidence is offered by the *Orestes* papyrus. The music, so far as it is visible, circles round two tonal foci a fifth apart, and we are able to see that one period within the strophe came to rest on the upper of the two—or perhaps the lower.[50] We should guess that the strophe as a whole ended on the lower one in view of the general tendency of Greek music observed on p. 193.

Free form

Non-repetitive music, not confined by stichic or strophic organization but evolving continuously, appears to have originated not in the vocal but in the instrumental sphere. In song there are always new words when the music repeats. But when an instrumental soloist gives a performance, there is no point in his repeating the same melody several times over without change. One alternative would be variation form—repeating it with different embellishments and modifications each time—but we have no evidence for this in Antiquity. What we do hear of is a sort of programme music, extended pieces telling a story and evoking particular scenes by means of instrumental effects.

It was in the early sixth century BC, in the great pipers' competition at the Pythian Games, that the genre came into being, or at any rate into prominence. Sakadas of Argos, who won the prize at each of the first three contests, in 586, 582, and 578, was remembered as the pioneer of what became a traditional set-piece, the *Pȳthikos nomos*. This portrayed in music the central religious myth of the Pythian sanctuary, Apollo's defeat of the monstrous serpent that had beset the place before his arrival. It is not clear whether later pipers played it in anything like a fixed form or produced their own versions

---

[49] The recurrence of the melody is of course an inference from the recurrence of the metrical scheme. For the details of these various arrangements see *Greek Metre*, 79 f.

[50] A line of the text is unfortunately out of sequence at this point, and the question at issue depends on whether the associated note-series is also displaced.

according to a set programme. Our sources do state that the piece was structured in five sections, which had names. They do not altogether agree on the details, but in the version of Pollux the sections are:

1. *Peira*, 'trying out',[51] in which Apollo surveys the ground to see if it is suitable for the struggle.

2. *Katakeleusmos*, 'call of command', in which he challenges the serpent.

3. *Iambikon*, in which he fights. This part includes trumpet-like notes and 'tooth action'[52] to represent the shot serpent gnashing its teeth.

4. *Spondeion*, the stately libation music symbolizing the god's victory.

5. *Katachoreusis*, a joyful dance of celebration.

Other authorities refer to the *syringes* or *syrigmos*, in which the aulos device called the *syrinx* was used to imitate the hisses of the expiring snake.[53] The performer clearly had to be a virtuoso, able to deploy

[51] The name suggests something simple and tentative. Pollux also gives it as the name of something auletes learn at the elementary stage (4. 83). The similar *anapeira* seems to have been a technical term for the introductions of aulos 'sonatas' generally, cf. ps.-Plut. *De mus.* 1143 c. Hesychius defines it as an auletic rhythm, and we hear of auletes using 'dactylic' rhythm in prefatory sections (schol. Ar. *Nub.* 651; *Suda* iii. 43. 16).

[52] A special playing technique, also mentioned in Poll. 4. 80 and Hsch., in which 'the tongue (= reed?) is pushed against the tooth'.

[53] Poll. 4. 84, Strab. 9. 3. 10 pp. 421–2, Hypothesis in Pind. *Pyth.* p. 2. 10 ff. Dr., cf. Xen. *Symp.* 6. 5 and above, p. 102; for Sakadas, Paus. 2. 22. 8–9, 10. 7. 4, ps.-Plut. *De mus.* 1134 a, Poll. 4. 78. As an analogy in Western music one might refer to Johann Kuhnau's *Musicalische Vorstellung einiger biblischer Historien*, a set of six keyboard sonatas published in 1700, and especially to the first of them, which represents David's fight with Goliath. The various sections bear subtitles indicating the successive phases of the action: 'Le bravate di Goliath'; 'Il tremore degl' Israeliti alla comparsa del Gigante, e la loro preghiera fatta a Dio', and so on to the fall of Goliath, the flight of the Philistines, the joy of the Israelites, the women's concert in David's honour, and 'Il Giubilo comune, ed i balli d' allegrezza del Populo'. Kuhnau's preface does not suggest that he was conscious of the Greek parallel. A dramatic intermezzo on the Apollo–serpent story had been presented among the wedding festivities for the Grand Duke Ferdinando de' Medici and Christine of Lorraine in 1589, and it counts among the antecedents of Italian opera. But Kuhnau, in his use of purely instrumental means to portray a legendary battle stage by stage, is Sakadas' true counterpart.

R. Lachmann in the *Festschrift für Johannes Wolf* (Berlin, 1929), 97–106, describes what appears to be a remarkable Mediterranean relic of the *Pythikos nomos* (or possibly of an oriental antecedent): a five-sectioned flute piece, performed by a Tunisian Bedouin with a good deal of graphic gesture and mime, representing the defeat of a lion. Like the Greek *nomos*, it included a battle fanfare and ended with a dance of joy.

all the technical tricks of his profession.[54] The composition was characterized by a variety of rhythms, tempi, and timbres. It may well be that the effect of contrasted modes was exploited too, seeing that Sakadas is also credited with a *Trimelēs nomos*, 'three-melody' or 'three-mode' nome, this one a choral song in which successive 'strophes' were in the Dorian, Phrygian, and Lydian modes.[55]

Another auletic repertory item was the *Polykephalos nomos*, 'many-headed nome'. This again involved imitation of hissing serpents, the ones that grew from the scalp of the Gorgon Euryale; the hissing was a lament over the killing of her sister Medusa by Perseus. Midas of Acragas played this piece when he won the Pythian contest in 490.[56]

In 558 BC unaccompanied kithara-playing was added to the events at the Pythian contest. We might expect the citharists to attempt the same sort of thing as the auletes had been doing with éclat since 586, and in fact Strabo represents the *Pȳthikos nomos* as being the prescribed piece for both.[57] The kithara may seem a less suitable instrument than the auloi for mimicking chagrined ophidians. *Sȳrigmos*, however, is among the effects said to have been developed by the early Classical citharist Lysander of Sicyon.[58]

We do not know how early the free form of this instrumental music was extended to compositions for the voice. The *Trimelēs nomos* of Sakadas or Klonas sounds as if it might have been an example, though the source refers to 'strophes' and to a chorus. In later times astrophic song is much more associated with solo performers. From the mid-fifth century it was characteristic of citharodes' competition and recital pieces (called *nomoi*, like those of the instrumentalists). Melanippides introduced it to the dithyramb (p. 205); and gradually it won its way into tragedy, but usually for actors' arias, not choruses. As in the instrumental compositions, the emphasis was on virtuosity, variety of rhythm and mood,

[54] Cf. p. 93 for the specialized 'Pythian aulos' and 'Pythian aulete' of later times.
[55] Ps.-Plut. *De mus.* 1134b, cf. 1132d. Others attributed the composition to Klonas of Tegea or Thebes.
[56] Pind. *Pyth.* 12 with schol.; cf. U. von Wilamowitz-Moellendorff, *Pindaros* (Berlin, 1922), 144. Some attributed the composition to one Crates, others to Olympus, or to someone else of the same name (Pratinas, *PMG* 713, ps.-Plut. *De mus.* 1133de). According to Aristox. fr. 80, Olympus was also the first to perform on the auloi a lament for the Pythian serpent in the Lydian mode; others said Melanippides (ps.-Plut. 1136c). This sounds like a variation on the *Pȳthikos nomos*.
[57] Paus. 10. 7. 7, Strab. 9. 3. 10 p. 421.
[58] See p. 69.

mimetic effects, things difficult for a non-professional chorus to put across.[59] As the melody was not bound to a recurring strophic scheme, it could be shaped throughout to express every pictorial aspect or emotional nuance of the words.

Like the *Pȳthikos nomos*, the citharodic *nomos* fell into conventionally recognized sections. Pollux enumerates seven, supposedly established by Terpander: beginning, after-the-beginning, down-turn(?), after-the-down-turn, navel, seal, and epilogue.[60] The names are not very informative, and we do not know how strictly the scheme was observed by those who understood it. In the only specimen of the genre of which we have a substantial portion, Timotheus' *Persians*, we can certainly see a well-marked transition from the main narrative to a closing section that might suitably be described as a 'seal' (in that Timotheus establishes his ownership of the composition by speaking of himself) and/or an epilogue. The work began with a hexameter or hexameters, the main part is in a mixture of iambic and various other rhythms, and the concluding section is pure aeolic.

The two Delphic Paeans owe something to the style of the citharodic nome. They are free astrophic compositions, each falling into several clearly distinct musical paragraphs. Most of these end on the tonic or a fifth above it or a fourth below. There are various shifts of tonal focus in the course of each work. Both refer to Apollo's killing of the serpent and to the dying creature's hisses, with a presumably mimetic melodic inflection on the word *sȳrigma*. Limenius' paean has a change of rhythm to aeolic in its concluding prayer, much like what we have just noted in Timotheus, but apart from that both paeans are in uniform paeonic rhythm.

Nomos

The term *nomos* has been appearing in the last couple of pages. It calls for some further commentary. Poets use the word in a non-technical way, of any melody with a definite identity or character: the songs of different birds, a mourner's song, the various songs in a

---

[59] See ps.-Arist. *Pr.* 19. 15, discussing the question why *nomoi* are not strophic like choral songs.

[60] Poll. 4. 66: *archā, metarchā, katatropā, metakatatropā, omphalos, sphrāgis, epilogos.* Aelius Dionysius a 76 refers to a 'going-out' section at the end (*exodion*, like the exodos of a tragedy), introduced by a farewell salutation to the god. Cf. U. von Wilamowitz-Moellendorff, *Timotheos. Die Perser* (Leipzig, 1903), 96–100.

particular musician's repertory, and so forth.[61] In ordinary usage it had a narrower application. It referred to a specific, nameable melody, or a composition in its melodic aspect, sung or played in a formal setting in which it was conventionally appropriate: a sacrifice, a funeral, a festival competition, or a professional display. It was not, initially, genre-specific: the word could be applied to melodies accompanying hexameter poetry, elegy, iambic verse, lyric narrative, epinicians, dithyrambs.[62] There were citharodic, citharistic, aulodic, and auletic *nomoi*, and we know a number of their names in each category.[63] Some were named after the god in whose honour they were performed: the *nomos* of Athena, of Zeus, of Apollo, of Ares, of Pan, of Dionysus, of the Mother of the Gods. Some had ethnic names: Boeotian, Aeolian. Some were identified by their supposed composers: Polymnestean, Terpandrean, *nomos* of Olympus, of Hierax; by the purpose or occasion with which they were associated: *Kradiās* (fig-branch),[64] *Epitymbidios* (funeral), *Elegoi, Iamboi, Kyklios* (dithyrambic), *Kōmarchios* (starting the revel), *Exodios* (exit of a chorus), *Pȳthikos*; by the rhythm: Trochaic, Enoplian; or by some other intrinsic feature: *Oxys* (high-pitched), *Orthios* (steep), *Kolobos* (truncated), *Polykephalos* (many-headed), *Schoiniōn* (drawn out like a rope), *Trimelēs* (three-mode), *Tetraoidios* (four-note). This is not a complete catalogue.

It is unclear what degree of fixity and detail was implicit in a *nomos*' identity. Take, for example, the *nomos of Athena*, which was probably a standard item at the Panathenaic musical contests. We are told that it was a creation of Olympus', and that it was in the enharmonic genus and the Phrygian mode (or key). The introduction was in the *paiōn epibatos* rhythm, and then came a part called 'the *harmoniā*' in trochaic rhythm, which considerably changed the

---

[61] Alcm. *PMG* 40, Pind. *Nem.* 5. 35, fr. 35c, Aesch. *Supp.* 69, *Ag.* 1142, 1153, *Cho.* 424, 822, ps.-Aesch. *PV* 575, Soph. frs. 245, 463, 861, Eur. *Hec.* 685, *Hel.* 188, Telestes, *PMG* 810. 3.

[62] See *CQ* 21 (1971), 310.

[63] Mostly from the Parian Marble *FGrH* 239 A 10, ps.-Plut. *De mus.* 1132 d, 1133 a, 1133 d–1134 b, 1141 b, 1143 bc, Poll. 4. 65–6, 78–9, 83, Hsch., *Suda*; various Classical references, as Hipponax fr. 153, Pratinas, *PMG* 713 (*i*), Pind. *Ol.* 1. 102, *Pyth.* 12. 23, Hdt. 1. 24. 5, Soph. fr. 966, Ar. *Ach.* 14, 16, *Eq.* 9, 1279, Cratinus fr. 308, Glaucus of Rhegium fr. 2, Epicrates fr. 2, Pl. *Cra.* 417 e. One or two names are common to more than one category.

[64] Referring to an Ionian ritual in which a scapegoat figure was flagellated with fig-branches.

ethos.[65] Now, was this a fully worked out composition that did not change from one performance to another, or rather a melodic programme within which each performer had a certain freedom to create something individual? We certainly get the impression that 'he played the nome of Athena' would have conveyed more precise information than 'he played a mazurka'. On the other hand it seems likely that it was rather less precise than 'he played Chopin's opus 30 no. 1'. When the competing auletes at Delphi played the *Pȳthikos nomos*, they surely had some freedom to vary it and to interpret the story using musical phrases and gestures of their own, at shorter or greater length.[66]

At Athens it was the citharodes who were the great display musicians, and *nomos* came to be used especially of their compositions. In this way it came to denote a literary genre.[67] It is this kind of *nomos*, in its fourth-century form, that we must understand when a Peripatetic writer says that *nomoi* are astrophic; and when Aristides Quintilianus declares that the nomic style of melody tends to high notes, the dithyrambic to middle ones, the tragic to low ones; and when Proclus speaks of the orderly grandeur of the *nomos* and its penchant for the Lydian mode.[68] Failure to distinguish between contexts where *nomos* does and does not have this generic status has been the source of much confusion.[69]

---

[65] Ps.-Plut. *De mus.* 1143bc. Cf. Pl. *Cra.* 417e. The account of the rhythms suggests something like dactylo-epitrite. Schol. Eur. *Or.* 1384 identifies the *nomos of Athena* with the *harmateios* ('chariot') *nomos*; and the *harmateios nomos* is associated with dactylic rhythm and said to have served as a model to Stesichorus (Glaucus fr. 2 ap. ps.-Plut. *De. mus.* 1133f).

[66] Prescriptive modal-melodic structures in other cultures, especially the *rāgas* of Indian music, provide suggestive analogies, but cannot be gone into here. See *NG* xii. 422ff.

[67] Ar. *Ran.* 1282, Pl. *Leg.* 700b, 799e.

[68] Ps.-Arist. *Pr.* 19. 15 (cf. above, n. 59), Aristid. Quint. p. 30. 2 (cf. 23. 3), Procl. ap. Phot. *Bibl.* 320b.

[69] On *nomos* as a musical term see W. Vetter, *RE* xvii. 840–3; H. Grieser, *Nomos: ein Beitrag zur griechischen Musikgeschichte* (Diss. Heidelberg, 1937); E. Laroche, *Histoire de la racine NEM- en grec ancien* (Paris, 1949), 166–71; T. J. Fleming, *CJ* 72 (1977), 222–33.

8

Theory

From the earliest times, we may suppose, practitioners and teachers of instrumental playing possessed a certain amount of technical terminology and lore connected with their instrument: a system of nomenclature for strings, notes, and tunings, formulae for changing from one lyre-tuning to another, traditions and legends concerning past players, their inventions and innovations. But from the late sixth century BC, and possibly earlier, we can see the beginnings of more developed forms of theoretical inquiry into the foundations of music.

At Athens in the time of the sophists there were a number of self-appointed experts on music theory giving lectures and demonstrations. They were called *harmonikoi*, a term which for Aristotle, at least, covered both those who calculated interval ratios mathematically and those who judged them by ear.[1] Stratonicus, a virtuoso citharist and a renowned wit, is named as the first to teach *ta harmonika* and to construct a 'diagram'.[2] Others used instruments for demonstration purposes without being able to play them skilfully.[3] Theophrastus, in his thumbnail sketch of the obsequious man, represents him as owning a little sports-court that he lends out to philosophers, sophists, arms-instructors, and *harmonikoi* for their lectures.[4] After the fourth century we hear little of these oral expositors, but written treatises continued to multiply. In the end, Antiquity was destined to leave us far more musical theory than music.

That is why the theory bulks so large in most expositions of the

---

[1] *An. Post.* 79ª1, cf. 87ª34, *Top.* 107ª15, *Ph.* 194ª8, *Metaph.* 997ᵇ21, 1077ª5, 1078ª14. But Theophrastus fr. 89 contrasts those who give a mathematical account of intervals with 'the *harmonikoi* and those who judge by sense-perception'. Cf. Pl. *Resp.* 531 ab, *Phdr.* 268 de, *Chrm.* 170 c.

[2] Phaenias fr. 32 Wehrli. The diagram will have illustrated a combination of modal scales in one system. Aristoxenus, *Harm.* 1. 2, 7, 28, refers critically to his predecessors' use of diagrams.

[3] Alcidamas(?) in *PHib.* 13; Arist. fr. 52.

[4] Theophr. *Char.* 5. 10.

music of ancient Greece. In the present work the attempt has been made to focus on the music first, mentioning ancient theory only insofar as it was part of the evidence. But the time has come to attend to the theory. It will not be possible in the space of a chapter to give an exhaustive account. The aim will be to trace the main outlines of development, and to understand the ancient theorists' objectives and methods.

The naming of notes

The seven strings of the early Classical lyre had names which became transferred to degrees of the scale. In descending order of pitch:

Nētē (or *neatē*)	'bottom'	*high pitch*
Paranētē	'alongside-bottom'	
Tritē	'third'	
Mesē	'middle'	
Lichanos	'forefinger'	
Parhypatē	'alongside-topmost'	
Hypatē	'topmost'.[5]	*low pitch*

The scale in question might cover an octave, or only a seventh (see p. 176). In either case the notes from Hypatē to Mesē formed a tetrachord. There is reason to think that Mesē commonly served as a tonal centre. It seems generally to enjoy this status in the pre-Hellenistic and Hellenistic fragments. A Peripatetic writer remarks that all good melodies and melodists constantly return to Mesē as they do to no other note; and that it is the one note which, if put out of tune, will throw the whole melody out of joint.[6]

When the scale covered a seventh, Nētē was a fourth above Mesē. When it covered an octave, Tritē was a tone above Mesē, and Nētē a fourth above Tritē. This at any rate is the arrangement in our oldest source, Philolaus (second half of the fifth century).[7] But in all later

---

[5] The reason why the highest note is called 'bottom' and the lowest 'topmost' has been explained on p. 64.

[6] Ps.-Arist. *Pr.* 19. 20. Cf. 19. 36: all other notes are ordered in relation to Mesē. Similarly Dio Chrys. *Or.* 51. 7 (ii. 174. 3 Arnim). Callicratidas (Thesleff, *Pythagorean Texts*, p. 106. 21) says that the singer, knowing the range of his voice, tries to pitch his Mesē accordingly, so that he can manage both the high and the low notes well. Varro fr. 282 p. 302. 32 Funaioli describes Mesē as the beginning of the song. See further Winnington-Ingram, *Mode*, 4–9.

[7] Philolaus fr. 6; above, p. 176. The fragment preserves the terms *syllabā* 'span' for the lower section of the octave, Hypatē to Mesē, and *di' oxeiān* 'across the high strings' for the fifth from Mesē to Nētē. They evidently belong to the language of

sources, when the octave is to be covered, an eighth note, Paramesē 'alongside-Mesē', appears between Mesē and Tritē, and it is this that stands a tone above Mesē. The notes then form two similar, disjunct tetrachords (Table 8.1.).

TABLE 8.1. *Names and relationships of notes*

7-note scale covering		8-note scale
seventh	octave (Philolaus)	(later writers)
	e' Nētē	e' Nētē
d' Nētē		×
×	×	× Tritē
×	b Tritē	b Paramesē
a Mesē	a Mesē	a Mesē
×	×	×
×	×	×
e Hypatē	e Hypatē	e Hypatē

In its seven-note form, at least, the nomenclature no doubt goes back long before Philolaus; some of it may be inherited from the times when lyres generally had only three or four strings. *Hypatos* and *neatos* are archaic words, scarcely found otherwise in Classical Greek except in poetry and in fossilized cult titles.[8] And 'forefinger string' may seem a more natural term to choose for a four-stringed lyre than for a seven-stringed one, where fingers had to move about, and the forefinger was surely one of the most mobile.

We saw in Chapter 6 that most of the fifth-century scales of which we have any knowledge did not exceed the octave. One of them, however, the Dorian of the Damonian set, extended over a ninth. It incorporated two disjunct tetrachords (corresponding to Hypatē–Mesē–Paramesē–Nētē) plus a further note a tone below Hypatē. The

professional performers. Cf. 'Hippoc.' *De Victu* 1. 8. 2, ps.-Arist. *Pr.* 19. 34, 41, *PTeb.* 694, Aristid. Quint. p. 15. 8, Porph. in Ptol. *Harm.* p. 96. 21 ff.; Burkert, *LS* 390.

[8] *Neatos* survived in Hippocratic writing and in the slow-moving Arcadian dialect.

lower part of the Phrygian scale had a similar structure. For the supernumerary low note, or infrafix, the name Hyperhypatē ('beyond Hypatē') is occasionally found.[9] It is obviously an addition to the original set of names, since Hypatē's name marks it as the end point. The addition implies that Hypatē is no longer the name of the first and lowest-tuned string, but of a scalar degree defined by its intervallic relationships with other degrees. Besides its original 'thetic' sense referring to physical position, the term has acquired a 'dynamic' sense relating to its scalar function.[10]

By Aristoxenus' time the integrity of the scheme had been compromised more severely. The original octave was extended to nearly two by adding a whole conjunct tetrachord at each end. The note-names below Mesē and above Paramesē were repeated in the new annexes to the scale, and therefore it now became necessary to specify which tetrachord one was talking about. The notes added below Hypatē were unimaginatively called the Hypatai, so that the bottom note became Hypatē of the Hypatai (*hypatē hypatōn*), while the original Hypatē became Hypatē of the Middle Notes (*hypatē mesōn*). At the other end of the scale it was slightly more complicated. There still remained the alternative patterns with and without Paramesē, in other words, with either a conjunct or a disjunct tetrachord above Mesē. The scale was treated as bifurcating at Mesē. The conjunct tetrachord (*synēmmenai*) was a cul-de-sac, while the disjunct one (*diezeugmenai*) led on to the additional tetrachord, which was called that of the Overshoot Notes (*hyperbolaiai*). Thus the name Tritē or Nētē could now signify three different notes, according to whether it was qualified by *synēmmenōn*, *diezeugmenōn*, or *hyperbolaiōn*.

By now, of course, we are no longer dealing with the scale of a particular instrument or a particular piece of music, but with an abstract scheme intended to be comprehensive. The final step was to tack on another note at the bottom, a tone below Hypatē hypatōn.

[9] Thrasyllus ap. Theon. Smyrn. p. 88. 18 ff., Boeth. *Inst. Mus.* 1. 20, cf. Aristid. Quint. p. 8. 12. In the curious document called the *Common Hormasia* (Pöhlmann, *DAM* 32 f.) it is called *diapemptos*, 'at the fifth' (from Mesē downwards). Cf. Winnington-Ingram, *Mode* 25.

[10] This distinction between the thetic and dynamic was articulated by Ptolemy, *Harm.* 2. 5, perhaps, as Barker says (*GMW* ii. 325 n. 37), 'in an attempt to reduce the ambiguities of ordinary musical talk to clarity and order'. In the theorists' writings Hypatē and the other names are almost always used in the dynamic sense, while lyre-players may have continued to use them in the thetic sense, i.e. Hypatē = 'my bottom note', irrespective of the sequence of intervals separating it from my top note.

This completed a system consisting of two octaves with Mesē at the centre. The latest addition received the name Proslambanomenos, 'the note we take as an extra'. Its masculine form shows that its inventor had forgotten all idea of a string (*chordē*); he was thinking of it simply as a note (*phthongos*).

The whole scheme, which was to remain canonical, is set out in Fig. 8.1. Of the 'movable' notes whose positions varied in different genera, Lichanos was treated as especially diagnostic of genus, and as a note-name it is sometimes augmented or replaced by *enharmonios*, *chrōmatikē*, or *diatonos*, depending on its actual station. The same happens more rarely with Paranētē. Now, none of these notes had a fixed pitch in absolute terms. What a note's name defined was its position in an intervallic series; we can compare the *do–re–mi* of the sol-fa system. Paramesē, for example, was not '*b*' but 'that note above which the scale (in the diatonic genus) goes S T T and below which it descends T T T S'. A singer pitched his

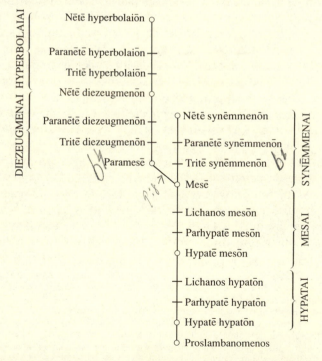

Fig. 8.1. The comprehensive notation scheme (the Unmodulating System)

Mesē to suit his voice's compass.[11] Theorists pitched it, as we shall see, according to a formula, to bring different segments of the whole system within a particular pitch-range. By doing this they could extract from the system any regularly-formed scale in actual use. And that was what the system in its extended form was designed for, not to cater for two-octave melodies, which probably did not exist.

'System', *systēma*, literally 'constitution', is in fact the Greek theorists' word for any articulated scale or scale-section (tetrachord, pentachord, etc.). A grand scale that comprehended others they called a 'complete' (*teleion*) system, or as it is conventionally rendered, a 'perfect' system. The two scales running from Proslambanomenos, one to Nētē hyperbolaiōn and the other to Nētē synēmmenōn, were known respectively as the Greater and the Lesser Perfect System. The combination of the two, as in the diagram above, was called the Unmodulating (*ametabolon*) System, because with it one could pretend that music which oscillated between the two alternative paths above Mesē was not really modulating but simply using different parts of a single system.[12]

Systematization of the modes

This universal scale with its unwieldy set of names was the outcome of long efforts to accommodate the various modal scales in a unified system and to define their mutual relationships. To some extent this was bound up with musicians' practical needs; many of the early theorists were practising performers. A player who had to retune his lyre in order to play a piece in a different mode would be interested in finding common ground between the scales concerned and in identifying, where possible, certain notes in one with notes in the other, so that fewer rather than more strings had to be retuned. The poet-musician Lamprocles (mid-fifth century) is said to have 'realized' that the Mixolydian scale did not have its disjunctive tone where it was generally thought to, but high up, and to have established its form as extending from Paramesē down to Hypatē

[11] Above, n. 6.
[12] Euclid, *Sect. Can.* 19–20, Thrasyllus ap. Theon. Smyrn. p. 92. 26, Cleon. p. 200. 10 ff., Bacchius p. 299. 1 ff. (also 308. 3 ff., where the tetrachord Hyperbolaiōn is ignored), Gaud. p. 333. 19 ff. Nicomachus pp. 256. 5–260. 4 describes the usual system but gives an unconventional, probably speculative account of its development. Cf. Barker, *GMW* ii. 264 n. 80. Ptolemy, *Harm.* 2. 5–6, differs in his terminology: he applies the title Unmodulating to the Greater Perfect System in contradistinction to the 'modulating' Lesser Perfect System.

<u>hypatōn</u>. The terminology is very probably anachronistic, but the sense is that Lamprocles found a neater way of relating the Mixolydian to other modal scales.[13] Later the development of larger kitharas and adjustable auloi made modal modulation during performance a more practical possibility, but this again involved fixing scales in definite positions relative to one another. However, practical requirements provided only part of the impetus. For the rest, it was a matter of delineating an intellectually satisfying system, in other words a neat and symmetrical one.

We get only glimpses of the course of these struggles. The earliest fragment of evidence is, I believe, to be gleaned from Alcman. In one of his *Partheneia* he invoked the Muse and then, finding in his own music the proof of her response, made his choir-girls exclaim 'the Muse cries forth, the clear-voiced Siren!' This Muse-Siren must represent the true, perfect sound that Alcman desired. Now, in another song his chorus more modestly says

> the Sirens' voice
> is indeed more musical than ours,
> for they are divine, and instead of (their) eleven
> it is only ten girls that sing here.

Why should there be *eleven* Sirens? Presumably because there are just eleven true and perfect notes. According to an old Pythagorean saying, the octave which embodies the fundamental harmonic ratios (1 : 2, 2 : 3, 3 : 4) 'has the Sirens in it'; and in the cosmology of Plato's *Republic* the music of the spheres is made by eight Sirens, each responsible for a different note of the diatonic scale.[14] Alcman, then, recognizes a divine system of eleven notes. If his music was pentatonic, the number might represent two whole octaves, for example *A B c e f a b c′ e′ f′ a′*. If it was heptatonic, it might represent a combination of two disjunct tetrachords (= an octave) with one conjunct, or perhaps some other composite structure from which alternative scales could be abstracted.

---

[13] Aristox.(?) ap. ps.-Plut. *De mus.* 1136d. See *JHS* 101 (1981), 127.

[14] Alcm. *PMG* 30; 1. 96–9; Iambl. *De vita Pythagorica* 82; M. L. West, *CQ* 15 (1965), 200, 17 (1967), 11–14, *JHS* 101 (1981), 127. Nētē, Mesē, and Hypatē are said to have been recognized as Muses at Delphi (Plut. *Quaest. conv.* 744c, cf. Censorinus fr. p. 90. 6 Jahn); and on an Argive dedication of about 300 BC (*SEG* 30. 382) they appear together with a fourth, Prātā (dialect for Prōtā 'first'), who presumably corresponds to a local name for some other important note, e.g. Hyperhypatē.

Aristoxenus makes many disparaging references to his predecessors in the extant part of his *Harmonics*; unfortunately a more systematic review of their doctrines which he says he has made previously has not survived. The earliest theorist he mentions is Lasus of Hermione, an enterprising and innovative musician who was active in Athens in the last quarter of the sixth century and who is credited with writing the first book about music.[15] It is possible that he actually coined the word 'music' (*mousikē*, the craft connected with the Muses), which is first attested shortly afterwards in Pindar and Epicharmus.[16] All that Aristoxenus tells us is that Lasus held notes to have breadth in the scale, that is, they occupied a certain finite portion of the line on which pitches were plotted, they were not mere points on it. This view was shared by 'some of the followers of Epigonus'. Epigonus was another progressive musician, active in Sicyon, perhaps a contemporary of Lasus, though the evidence for his date is very shaky.[17] He appears not to have written anything, but to have been remembered as an artist and teacher by one or two disciples who did write. Possibly Lasus referred to him.

In Chapter 3 we had occasion to consider the forty-stringed instrument named after Epigonus. It was suggested that it was a board zither designed not for musical performances but for the dissection of the gamut into the smallest possible intervals, with a view to mapping out the various modal scales against this grid. A similar instrument seems to have been named after the fifth-century theorist Simos.[18] The division of the octave into quarter-tones is an approach that Aristoxenus repeatedly criticizes, without naming its adherents. Some of them were evidently still at it in Plato's time. Plato describes students of harmonics who toil vainly to measure intervals by minimal units, which they try to determine by torturing strings as if on the rack, listening closely as if eavesdropping on their neighbours, and arguing about whether they have found the smallest interval to use as a unit or whether another yet smaller can be detected.[19]

---

[15] Aristox. *Harm.* 1. 3; Mart. Cap. 9. 936, *Suda*.

[16] Pind. *Ol.* 1. 15, fr. 32, Epicharmus fr. 91. Craft-names in *-ikē* proliferate in the 5th c.; *mousikē* is, I think, the earliest attested.

[17] See Jacoby on Philochorus, *FGrH* 328 F 23.   [18] Above, p. 79.

[19] *Resp.* 531 ab; Aristox. *Harm.* 1. 7, 28, 2. 38, 53. Alcidamas(?) in *PHib.* 13 derides lecturers on harmony who use a *psaltērion* (this is the earliest occurrence of the word) for demonstration purposes, though he says nothing of measurement by micro-intervals.

The doctrine about notes having breadth is intelligible in this context. The people of whom Plato speaks were looking for notes so close together that it was impossible to fit another in between them. But this implies that the notes take up space on the scale. If they are mere points on a line (as Aristoxenus holds), there can never be two so close together that a third cannot be put between them, even if our ears can no longer distinguish them. On the latter view there can be no minimum interval in nature qualified to serve as a measuring unit. But if notes have a finite size, there is a real minimum. It is tempting to infer that Epigonus and Lasus favoured micro-measurement, whether or not they experimented with zithers.[20]

Two other names bracketed together by Aristoxenus are those of Pythagoras of Zacynthus and Agenor of Mytilene. He praises them, very faintly, for having made attempts to articulate differences between different forms of tetrachord, pentachord, etc., though they did not catalogue them fully or grasp any general melodic law governing them.[21] This Pythagoras, not to be confused with the famous pundit, perhaps belongs to the mid-fifth century. We also hear of him as the inventor and virtuoso of an instrument called a tripod, on which he could modulate freely between the Dorian, Phrygian, and Lydian scales. It had the general form of the holy tripod at Delphi. The legs served as the frames for three differently tuned kitharas, the bowl made a big common soundbox, and the whole contraption was mounted on a revolving base so that Pythagoras could flip it round with his foot and bring one set of strings or another to his hands with no audible interruption.[22] Once again we see the combination of practising musician and theoretician. He wants to combine modal scales in music, but he has not got as far as amalgamating them in one scale or eliciting them from a single enlarged kithara. Agenor of Mytilene lived some generations later. He was a musician of high repute about 350 BC, and teacher to Isocrates' grandsons.[23]

Aristoxenus also allows some limited achievements to one Erato-

---

[20] There is an interesting parallel in ancient Indian theory, which divided the octave, for measuring purposes only, into twenty-two *śruti* (practically equivalent to quarter-tones) and defined the degree intervals in different scales as two, three, or four of these. See *NG* ix. 91 ff.

[21] *Harm.* 2. 36.

[22] Artemon of Cassandrea ap. Ath. 637 c–f. Diog. Laert. 8. 46 gives a vague dating, 'not far removed in time' from the philosopher Pythagoras.

[23] Isoc. *Epistle* 8.

cles and his school. Eratocles enumerated the seven species of the octave in one genus, which must have been the enharmonic, and showed that they arose by cyclical transfer of intervals from one end to the other. But (according to Aristoxenus) he had no awareness of the rules controlling the sequence of intervals and the forms of tetrachords and pentachords. He observed only that from the tetrachord the melodic scale divides in two in both directions, in other words, the next tetrachord may be conjunct or disjunct. He failed to say why, or whether it is true for all tetrachords.[24] Eratocles' date is uncertain, but the notion of the scale 'dividing in two' seems to be reflected in Ion of Chios' epigram on the eleven-stringed lyre, not later than 422 BC, where he speaks of the instrument's 'ten-step arrangement and (?) concordant road-junction(s) of *harmoniā*'. The point is perhaps that this lyre could modulate between the *synēmmenai* and *diezeugmenai* tetrachords.[25]

The purpose of enumerating the octave species was to show how modally different scales were generated from a single source. Eratocles must have interpreted existing *harmoniai* as approximations to octave species, disregarding other individual features that they might have. He was presumably responsible for the labelling of the species with modal names:[26]

B B↑ c e e↑ f a b	Mixolydian
B↑ c e e↑ f a b b↑	Lydian
c e e↑ f a b b↑ c'	Phrygian
e e↑ f a b b↑ c' e'	Dorian
e↑ f a b b↑ c' e' e↑'	Hypolydian
f a b b↑ c' e' e↑' f'	Hypophrygian
a b b↑ c' e' e↑' f' a'	Locrian or Hypodorian

If we compare the Damonian scales set out on p. 174, we see that the four whose names match those in the above table require only a little adjustment to make them fit the homonymous species-pattern, so far as their scheme of intervals goes, except that the Damonian Lydian corresponds to Eratocles' Hypolydian. Transposed to the pitches used above, they appear as

[24] *Harm.* 1. 5–6, cf. 1. 2, 2. 35, 36.
[25] Fr. 32 West. For the road-junction image cf. Aristox. *Harm.* 3. 66f., Aristid. Quint. pp. 116. 18–117. 17.
[26] See p. 186. The sources are post-Aristoxenian, but their language implies that the system and nomenclature were pre-Aristoxenian; see Winnington-Ingram, *Mode*, 52. I give the table in its original enharmonic form. The diatonic version came later.

B B↑ c d e e↑ f b	Mixolydian
d e↑ f a b b↑ c′ d′	Phrygian
d e↑ f a b b↑ c′ e′	Dorian
e↑ f a b b↑ c′ e′ e↑′	(Hypo)lydian

To assimilate these to Eratocles' regular species, we have to ignore the anomalous *d* in the Mixolydian and supply a missing *a*; delete the Dorian *d*, which exceeds the octave; and make an only slightly greater modification of the Phrygian, purging it of its top *d′* and changing the lower *d* down to *c*.

Eratocles also digested into his scheme a current Hypophrygian and a Locrian/Hypodorian mode. 'Hypolydian' is not attested as a Classical mode, and he may have devised this name for the sake of parallelism, so that Lydian, Phrygian, and Dorian each had a corresponding Hypo- species starting on the note a fourth higher in the abstract revolving scale. As Eratocles' Hypolydian is the Damonian Lydian, his Lydian *B↑–b↑* must be based on some alternative form of Lydian, unless it is his own creation for the sake of the scheme.

Keys

Other expositors constructed Perfect Systems extending over a twelfth or more, by staggering the modal scales in such a way that similar interval-sequences could be aligned and they could all be fitted into one sequence. But then, to counteract the displacement of one mode relative to another, a system of notional keys (*tonoi*, 'pitches') was invented. These were different pitches at which the Perfect System as a whole could be set. The higher up the composite scale a particular modal scale lay, the lower the key it was declared to be played in, so that in actuality they all stayed in more or less the same register, as for practical purposes they had to. The keys were named after the modes they went with.

We do not know many details of the pre-Aristoxenian systems of this type, but we gather that there were several rival ones. Aristoxenus likens the situation to the chaos that characterized Greek local calendars, 'as when it is the tenth of the month in Corinth but the fifth in Athens and the eighth somewhere else'. He refers to one scheme in which the Hypodorian key, as the lowest, was followed by the Mixolydian, Dorian, Phrygian, and Lydian, at intervals of semitone, semitone, tone, tone; another in which there was a Hypophrygian below the Hypodorian; another in which the order was Hypophrygian, Hypodorian, Dorian, Phrygian, Lydian, Mixolydian, and the intervals separating them, based on those of aulos-holes, were $\frac{3}{4}$ tone, $\frac{3}{4}$ tone, tone, $\frac{3}{4}$ tone, $\frac{3}{4}$ tone.[27] There seems to have been general agreement on the sequence Dorian, Phrygian, Lydian, but only partial agreement about others. Several systems apparently lacked a Hypolydian, which, I have suggested, may have been Eratocles' invention. With Hypodorian and Hypophrygian, the principle was that they had conjunct tetrachords where Dorian and Phrygian had disjunct ones.[28]

Aristoxenus criticizes all these schemes as lacking an overall rationale. What governs the number of the keys and the intervals at which they are arranged? His own system is founded on a set of axioms concerning the structure of scales, axioms held to reflect natural laws of melody. The main ones are:

1. All melodic scales are constructed of tetrachords, which are either conjunct or disjunct, and if disjunct separated by a tone.

2. The sequence of intervals within tetrachords follows the rules for the genus in question.

3. As a general corollary of (1) and (2), every note must either make the concord of a fourth with the fourth note along from it, or the concord of a fifth with the fifth note, or both. There are many particular corollaries, for example that a scale cannot contain more than two successive quarter-tones or semitones; it can have three successive tones only in the diatonic genus; and so on.

In working out his system of keys Aristoxenus was not primarily concerned with the placement of modal scales interpreted as octave species: there are only seven species, but he made thirteen keys. He appears not to have spoken of the species under their Eratoclean modal names at all, but allowed the concept of mode to be submerged in that of key. What he was more concerned about was to provide for and account for every kind of modulation.

Modulation, he determined, presupposed a note, interval, or tetrachord common to two keys. The most harmonious modulations (and actually the most usual) were those which exploited the one

<hr />

[27] *Harm.* 2. 37; see Barker, *GMW* ii. 154 n. 33. This last system (apparently alluded to also by Heraclid. Pont. fr. 163 ap. Ath. 625 a) implies aulos scales in which the diatonic tetrachord had the form $\frac{3}{4} + \frac{3}{4} + 1$ tone; cf. pp. 97–100. The Mixolydian species is here $B\,c\uparrow\,d\,e\,f\uparrow\,g\,a\,b$, the Lydian $c\uparrow\!-c\uparrow'$, the Phrygian $d\!-\!d'$, and so on, with $c\uparrow$ and $f\uparrow$ throughout for c and f.

[28] Cf. p. 183.

freedom enshrined in the laws of melody, namely that tetrachords could be conjunct or disjunct. For example, suppose you were in chromatic Phrygian and you went up from Hypatē to Mesē, *e f g♭ a*. You might continue up to Paramesē, *b*, the start of the disjunct tetrachord, but then proceed as if that note were the meeting-point of two conjunct tetrachords, and descend *b a♭ g f♯*. Aristoxenus would say that you had turned Paramesē into Nētē (diezeugmenōn), and modulated to a key in which that degree stood at the same pitch as Phrygian Paramesē; a key, in other words, a fourth lower than Phrygian. All such conjunct–disjunct modulations, interpreted on the same principle, implied keys a tone, a fourth, or a fifth removed from the original one, reflecting the intervals involved in the collocation of tetrachords.

These, said Aristoxenus, were the harmonious types of modulation; but there were many other sorts, more or less harmonious according to how much the keys concerned had in common. They could be anything from a semitone to a whole octave apart.[29] We do not know the details of his workings.[30] But he found it necessary to have keys at regular semitone intervals over a whole octave.

In naming them he adapted existing nomenclature. He used the seven names which Eratocles had applied to his enharmonic octave species, and which others had perhaps translated into diatonic terms: Mixolydian for the B species, Lydian for the C, Phrygian for the D, Dorian for the E, Hypolydian for the F, Hypophrygian for the G, and Hypodorian for the A. In the table of keys, to cancel out the pitch differentials, the sequence of names and intervals had to be inverted, with Hypodorian the lowest and Mixolydian the highest. The series of intervals separating these seven keys was thus the inversion of that in the note-series B C D E F G A; it was T T S T T S, which we can most simply represent by the note-series G A B C D E F, though it must be stressed that these notes have no significance for the keys in themselves but serve simply as a code indicating their relative positions:

    f′ Mixolydian
    e′ Lydian
    d′ Phrygian
    c′ Dorian

[29] Cleon. pp. 205. 6–206. 2; cf. Aristid. Quint. p. 22. 15 ff.
[30] For a recent attempt to reconstruct them see Barker, *GMW* ii. 23–5.

b Hypolydian
a Hypophrygian
g Hypodorian

Aristoxenus added an eighth at the top to complete the octave, (*g'*) Hypermixolydian. Then he filled in the semitone gaps by declaring that each of the names except Hypodorian, Dorian, and Hypermixolydian stood for two keys, a higher and a lower one a semitone apart. If this sounds odd, let us reflect that it is not so very different from what we do when we speak of A flat and A natural, or F natural and F sharp. Aristoxenus' reason for doubling names in this way was not that he could not think of any extra ones. It was that the 'flat' or 'sharp' keys did not correspond to any new octave species. The Dorian ('C') key brought the Dorian E species onto the screen, as it were. The Phrygian ('D') key brought the Phrygian D species. But an intermediate 'C♯' key could only produce the E species a semitone higher or the D species a semitone lower; there is no D♯ species between them.

Aristoxenus' system was close to the one generally accepted in later Antiquity. The final step was taken sometime before Varro, we do not know by whom. It was a reform of the nomenclature, with the addition of two further keys for the sake of symmetry. In Aristoxenus' scheme the Hypo- names, Hypodorian, Hypophrygian, Hypolydian, had come to stand for the keys a fourth below Dorian, Phrygian, and Lydian respectively.[31] In the new system the old names Ionian and Aeolian were brought in and arbitrarily attached to the 'flat' keys between Dorian and Phrygian (D♭) and Phrygian and Lydian (E♭); the prefix Hypo- was generalized so that it applied to all five in the same way; and the prefix Hyper-, which Aristoxenus had casually introduced in baptizing his Hypermixolydian, was likewise compounded with the names of the five central keys to denote the keys a fourth higher, Hypermixolydian being accordingly renamed Hyperphrygian. The two new keys, Hyperlydian and Hyperaeolian, were invented to fill out this scheme. They were really superfluous, because they duplicated existing keys an octave lower. Table 8.2 sets out Aristoxenus' thirteen-key and the reformed fifteen-key system.[32]

---

[31] It had not always been so, cf. pp. 228f. above.

[32] The main sources are Cleon. p. 203. 5ff. and Aristid. Quint. p. 20. 5ff., where Aristoxenus' keys are listed and glossed with their current equivalents. Cf. also Varro fr. 282 p. 304 Funaioli; Heliodorus ap. schol. Dion. Thrax (*Grammatici Graeci*, i. 3)

TABLE 8.2. *The 13-key system of Aristoxenus*
and the reformed 15-key system

	Aristoxenus		Reformed system
a'	—		Hyperlydian
ab'	—		Hyperaeolian
g'	Hypermixolydian		Hyperphrygian
$f\sharp'$	high ⎫		Hyperionian
f'	low ⎭ Mixolydian		Hyperdorian
e'	high ⎫		Lydian
eb'	low ⎭ Lydian		Aeolian
d'	high ⎫		Phrygian
db'	low ⎭ Phrygian		Ionian
c'	Dorian		Dorian
b	high ⎫		Hypolydian
bb	low ⎭ Hypolydian		Hypoaeolian
a	high ⎫		Hypophrygian
ab	low ⎭ Hypophrygian		Hypoionian
g	Hypodorian		Hypodorian

[handwritten margin note: "intense / dark" with arrow pointing to f♯′, f′ rows; arrow pointing to c′ row]

The fifteen-key system left no practical need unprovided for, and on a superficial appraisal it seemed admirably neat and coherent. It won general acceptance, though the prestige of Aristoxenus' name ensured that his system too was remembered. One later theorist, however, produced a powerful critique of both: Ptolemy. He reasserts the principle that the purpose of keys is to bring different segments of the Greater Perfect System,[33] i.e. different octave species, each with its own particular ethos, into the most comfortable vocal register. Since there are just seven species, the requisite

p. 476. 33; Censorinus fr. 12 pp. 89. 10–90. 4 Jahn; Phrynichus, *Praeparatio sophistica* p. 24. 16 ff. Borries.

[33] Ptolemy points out that the System must span the two octaves from Proslambanomenos to Nētē hyperbolaiōn, but that the tetrachord Synēmmenōn is superfluous, as diversions into it can always be explained as key-changes. Thus he uses what the Aristoxenians call the Greater Perfect System, though he himself calls it the Unmodulating System.

number of keys is precisely seven and no more. These are sufficient to account for modulation, so long as each key has a counterpart at the distance of a fourth. So let the series be constructed from a cycle of descending fourths, $f''-c''-g'-d'-a-e-B$. Arrange these in order in one octave, keeping F at the top, and it emerges as the old series $g\,a\,b\,c'\,d'\,e'\,f'$. $g-c'$ make a fourth, and so do $a-d'$, $b-e'$, $c'-f'$. Ptolemy keeps to the old names, Hypodorian, Hypophrygian, Hypolydian, Dorian, Phrygian, Lydian, Mixolydian. To complete the octave with Hypermixolydian, as Aristoxenus did, is condemned as mere duplication; going beyond the octave, as his successors did, compounded the error. Filling in the semitone steps is redundant, because these sharp or flat keys (Ionian and Aeolian with their Hypos and Hypers) cannot bring new species into view but merely reproduce, a semitone higher or lower, the species associated with an adjacent key.[34]

Ptolemy's penetrating intellect went to the heart of the matter. But he came too late. The fifteen-key system had become firmly established in the theoretical tradition and, as we shall see in the next chapter, enshrined in notational practice.

Calculation of harmonic ratios

A separate branch of theory concerned itself with the mathematical values of the intervals making up an octave. In the Classical period this approach was particularly associated with the Pythagorean tradition. Aristoxenus and his later followers disregarded it, sticking to the simple empirical equation, a fourth $= 2\frac{1}{2}$ tones, and to the belief that all musical intervals are to be measured in tones and fractions of a tone.

The Pythagoreans were fascinated by number and inclined to see it as the key to the universe. One of their old sayings went: 'What is cleverest?–Number; and in second place whoever gave things their names.'[35] Philolaus wrote that everything has a number which gives it definition; without this we would have no perception or conception of things.[36] The realization that numbers underlie the basic concords of fourth, fifth, and octave must have been, if not the source, at any rate a powerful reinforcement of this exaltation of number. These musical phenomena provided concepts and formulae that could be

[34] Ptol. *Harm.* 2. 7–11. His criticism finds an echo at Ath. 625 d.
[35] Iambl. *De vita Pythagorica* 82, Ael. *VH* 4. 17.
[36] Diels, *Vorsokr.* 44 B 4; Burkert, *LS* 261–6.

extended beyond music to general cosmology. The health of the
body or of the soul could be explained as dependent on proper
'attunement', on harmonic relationships ultimately reducible to
numbers. The whole cosmos, the planetary and stellar spheres with
their orderly revolutions, could be seen as a vast musical instrument
with each component attuned according to the same scheme of
ratios as obtains in our mortal music. Plato's harmony of the spheres
is not some unimaginable, transcendental passacaglia or fugue, but
the naked glory of the diatonic octave.

Pythagorean theory was regularly projected back onto Pythagoras
himself, and from the fourth century BC he is credited with having
personally discovered the numerical basis of the concords. He is
alleged to have heard them in hammer-blows coming from a smithy,
and on investigation to have found that the weights of the hammers
stood in the ratios 4 : 3, 3 : 2, and 2 : 1. He is then supposed to have
reproduced the concords by putting equal strings under tension
from a similarly graded set of weights. It has been pointed out ever
since the seventeenth century that neither part of the story is in
accord with the laws of physics.[37]

A more plausible account has the early Pythagorean Hippasus of
Metapontum discovering or demonstrating the concords with
bronze discs of equal diameter but different thicknesses: these really
would give the required results. We may guess that Hippasus experimented with them not as a result of a brainwave coming out of the
blue, but on the basis of knowledge built up by South Italian jingle-
makers; for in that part of the world there was a tradition, going back
to the eighth century, of metal tube and disc chimes.[38] Hippasus'
contemporary Lasus of Hermione, whom we have met earlier as a
musicologist, is also mentioned as having studied the concord ratios,
this time by striking vessels partly filled with liquid. This is again a
scientifically dubious procedure, but there must have been some
ground for naming Lasus in such a context. He is never called a
Pythagorean. Perhaps he said something about harmonic ratios in
his book.[39]

[37] Burkert, *LS* 375–7.
[38] See p. 126. One of the early Pythagorean dicta was that the sound made by
striking bronze is the voice of a *daimōn* residing in the metal (Arist. fr. 196; we are
reminded of the Sirens' connection with musical notes, above, p. 224). Glaucus of
Rhegium, *c.* 400 BC, cultivated the playing of tuned discs as an art, which seems to have
been personal to him: Aristox. fr. 90; Burkert, *LS* 377.
[39] Theon Smyrn. p. 59. 7 ff. (corrupt text); see Burkert, *LS* 377 f.

The earliest Pythagoreans appear to have been entranced by the simple ratios of the octave, fifth, and fourth, and to have treated them as an exclusive set with a mystical significance. One of their catechistical propositions ran: 'What is the oracle at Delphi?—*Tetraktỹs*, which is the octave (*harmoniā*), which has the Sirens in it.'[40] *Tetraktỹs* (*tēs dekados*), 'tetradizing (of ten)', was the name they gave to an arrangement of the numbers 1, 2, 3, and 4 in a triangular figure:

Among other properties, it embodied the concord ratios 4 : 3, 3 : 2, 2 : 1; that is why it is identified with the octave.[41]

Philolaus, a couple of generations later than Hippasus, is the first we know of who attempted to establish mathematical values for other intervals. He states that the difference between a fifth and a fourth is *epogdoon*, i.e. 9 : 8. The interval remaining when two of these *epogdoa* are subtracted from a fourth he calls *diesis*.[42] According to Boethius, he calculated the *diesis* (correctly) to be 256 : 243, and constructed a series of further small units by subtractions and subdivisions:

tone minus *diesis* = *apotomē* 'offcut'.
apotomē minus *diesis* = *komma* 'chip'.
half of *diesis* = *diaschisma* 'splinter'.
half of *komma* = *schisma* 'crack'.[43]

The purpose of bisecting the *diesis* and the minute *komma* must have been to produce values for the two equal small intervals of the

[40] Iambl. *De vita Pythagorica* 82. For the Sirens cf. p. 224.

[41] See Burkert, *LS* 72, 186 f.; 'The tetractys has within it the secret of the world; and in this manner we can also understand the connection with Delphi, the seat of the highest and most secret wisdom. Perhaps Pythagorean speculation touched upon that focal point, or embodiment, of Delphic wisdom, the bronze tripod of Apollo' (187). We recall that Pythagoras of Zacynthus' triple kithara, upon which the Dorian, Phrygian, and Lydian modes could all be played, was built in the likeness of the Delphic tripod.

[42] Philolaus fr. 6. *Diesis* means literally 'a letting-through', probably from the way in which an aulete raised a note slightly by half-stopping. Aristoxenus and his followers use the word to mean a quarter-tone or other microtone as used in the enharmonic and chromatic genera.

[43] Boeth. *Inst. Mus.* 3. 8 p. 278. 11 Friedl.

enharmonic *pyknon*, which together made up a *diesis* or an *apotomē* (= *diesis* plus *komma*). The purpose of the *apotomē* was to make the chromatic *pyknon* up to a tone, its lower interval being a *diesis*. The pattern of the tetrachords for Philolaus is shown in Fig. 8.2. (For cent values see p. 168.) Philolaus' mathematics went completely off the rails when he tried to assign numbers to these new units. He did not understand that only ratios between numbers were musically significant, and that absolute quantities were not to be sought in them. He could only visualize a set of ratios in terms of a set of whole numbers in which they were embodied. For the intervals of the diatonic tetrachord the required numbers were 192 : 216 : 243 : 256. From this Philolaus mistakenly concluded that the last interval, the *diesis*, could meaningfully be equated with the number 13 (256 minus 243).

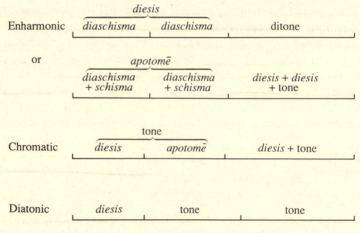

Fɪɢ. 8.2. Philolaus' pattern of tetrachords

On the same principle he subtracted 216 from 243 to get 27 for a tone (243 : 216 = 9 : 8), and then he subtracted his 13 from his 27 to get a figure for the *apotomē*. He thought it significant that 13 = 1 + 3 + 3^2 (three being the first odd number by Greek reckoning), while 27 = 3^3, and also 27 : 24 = a tone. This is as much number-mysticism as mathematics.[44]

Archytas of Tarentum moved on an altogether more sophisticated plane. He worked out a coherent system of ratios for all the intervals

[44] Boeth. *Inst. Mus.* 3. 5 p. 276. 15 ff. Friedl. See Burkert, *LS* 394–9.

of the tetrachord in each genus.[45] As ratios of 3 : 2, 4 : 3, and 9 : 8 were already established as being of harmonic importance, Archytas thought it logical to look for 5 : 4, 6 : 5, 7 : 6, and 8 : 7. He probably constructed these intervals experimentally on some instrument and then decided where they belonged in the scale. Two of them, 6 : 5 and 7 : 6, he found only between non-adjacent notes. 6 : 5 suited the interval from the enharmonic Paranētē diezeugmenōn to Mesē (or Lichanos to Hyperhypatē); 7 : 6 suited that from Tritē diezeugmenōn (in any genus) to Mesē, or Parhypatē to Hyperhypatē. More recherché figures had to be found for the various intervals of less than a tone, but he was able to deduce them from those which he had already put in place (Table 8.3). Nearly all these ratios are 'superparticular', that is, of the type $n + 1 : n$. Ptolemy speaks as if Archytas sought this on principle. Archytas was certainly interested in superparticulars, and worked out a proof that they could not be divided into two equal parts; the 9 : 8 tone, for example, cannot be divided into precisely equal semitones.[46]

This and a number of other general propositions about superparticular and multiple ratios ($n : 1$) are demonstrated in the Euclidean *Sectio Canonis*. The work also contains proofs of various basic facts about the relationships of the concordant intervals and the tone, for example that the octave is less than six tones, and the fourth less than two and a half. Archytas' elegantly proportioned scales are ignored: the diatonic tetrachord is assumed to contain two 9 : 8 tonal steps, as in Philolaus, and the enharmonic tetrachord a ditone step.[47]

This form of diatonic is also presupposed in Plato[48] and in several later writers. Among them is Eratosthenes of Cyrene, the versatile scholar and scientist who presided over the Alexandrian Library for most of the second half of the third century BC. Ptolemy cites Eratosthenes' sets of ratios for all three genera. From Hypate to Parhypatē to Lichanos to Mesē they are:

Enharmonic	40 : 39	39 : 38	19 : 15
Chromatic	20 : 19	19 : 18	6 : 5
Diatonic	256 : 243	9 : 8	9 : 8

---

[45] Cf. above, p. 168. The following analysis owes much to Barker, *GMW* ii. 46–52. Plato, *Resp.* 531 a/c, apparently contrasts Philolaus' with Archytas' approach.

[46] Ptol. *Harm.* 1. 13 p. 30. 9; Boeth. *Inst. Mus.* 3. 11 (Diels, *Vorsokr.* 47 A 19); cf. Barker, *GMW* ii. 43 n. 63, 46 f., 195 n. 12.

[47] Cf. p. 169.   [48] *Tim.* 35 b–36 b; see Barker, *GMW* ii. 59 f.

TABLE 8.3. *Interval-ratios according to Archytas*

	Hyperhypatē to Hypatē	to Parhypatē	to Lichanos	to Mesē
Enharmonic	9:8	28:27	36:35	5:4
	7:6			
		6:5		
Chromatic	9:8	28:27	243:224	32:27
	7:6	9:8		
Diatonic	9:8	28:27	8:7	9:8
	7:6			

Handwritten annotation beside 5:4: just M3 — (Pyth M3 = 81:64)

He obviously followed a quite different procedure from Archytas. It seems that his object was to find ratios that would correspond as closely as possible to the standard definitions of Aristoxenus. The 19 : 15 interval in the enharmonic is almost exactly a ditone, and the 6 : 5 interval in the chromatic is only 9 cents over $1\frac{1}{2}$ tones (Aristoxenus' tonic chromatic). Eratosthenes divides the remainder in each case, the *pyknon*, into two parts as nearly equal as possible.

It would be interesting to know the relationship between Eratosthenes and Ptolemais, a female musicologist of uncertain date who also came from Cyrene. She wrote a work entitled *Pythagorean Elements of Music*, in the course of which she contrasted the Pythagoreans' mathematical approach with the Aristoxenians' empiricism, and argued that something of both was required. Reason and perception should go hand in hand.[49]

A theorist of the time of Nero called Didymus took a similar line in a work *On the Difference between the Aristoxenians and the Pythagoreans*. It was probably from him that Porphyry took the quotations from Ptolemais. Didymus offered another set of formulae for the intervals of the tetrachord:

Enharmonic	32 : 31	31 : 30	5 : 4
Chromatic	16 : 15	25 : 24	6 : 5
Diatonic	16 : 15	10 : 9	9 : 8

I have commented on these values in Chapter 6.[50]

It remains to give Ptolemy's ratios, from which the table on p. 170 is derived. As was noted there, Ptolemy differs systematically from his predecessors in making the middle interval in the enharmonic and chromatic tetrachords about twice as large as the one below it.

Enharmonic	46 : 45	24 : 23	5 : 4
Soft chromatic	28 : 27	15 : 14	6 : 5
Tense chromatic	22 : 21	12 : 11	7 : 6
Soft diatonic	21 : 20	10 : 9	8 : 7
Tonic diatonic	28 : 27	8 : 7	9 : 8
Tense diatonic	16 : 15	9 : 8	10 : 9
(Ditonic diatonic	256 : 243	9 : 8	9 : 8)
Even diatonic	12 : 11	11 : 10	10 : 9

[49] Excerpts are preserved by Porph. in Ptol. *Harm.* pp. 22–6; Thesleff, *Pythagorean Texts*, 242 f. (abridged); Barker, *GMW* ii. 239–42.

[50] See p. 169 for both Eratosthenes and Didymus.

Except for the ditonic diatonic, which Ptolemy includes as a concession to common musical practice, he contrives throughout to make each ratio superparticular. He regards this as an essential requisite of melodic intervals for reasons explained in an earlier chapter of his work.[51] The smooth progression in the right-hand column (the interval between Lichanos and Mesē) from 5 : 4 to 10 : 9 will be noted.

A few words should be added about devices for measuring, testing, and demonstrating intervals with various ratios. The zithers used by some early lecturers on harmonics could have served this purpose only if the strings were equally tuned and the soundboard under them so calibrated that a string could be stopped at precisely measurable fractions of its length. More probably these instruments were used with open strings, each differently tuned. The string-torturers described by Plato (above, p. 225) are not measuring intervals but trying to settle on an interval to measure by. If they had been measuring by ratios they would not have been looking for a minimal unit.

However, the harmonicist who apparently gave his name to one of these zithers, Simos, is also associated with the invention of the monochord, the instrument commonly used for ratio measurement. It had a single string stretched over a graduated rule (*kanōn*), with a movable bridge by which the vibrating length of the string could be shortened or divided in measured proportions. Pythagoreans later claimed that Simos had appropriated knowledge of the *kanōn* from an exposition of Pythagoras' wisdom set up on an inscription at Samos by a son of Pythagoras, and promulgated it as his own. The story implies that Simos was widely credited with the invention.[52] Perhaps it was on the monochord that Archytas tried out the ratios of 5 : 4, 6 : 5, etc., that he incorporated in his system. It was certainly in use by the time of the *Sectio Canonis*. The last two propositions of the work give directions for dividing the rule so as to construct a diatonic two-octave system.

For a long time measurements were taken only from one end of the string. Didymus in the first century AD realized that one could use the portions on both sides of the bridge and take the ratio of one part

---

[51] *Harm.* 1. 7 p. 15. 18 ff., cf. 1. 15 p. 33. 5 ff.

[52] Duris, *FGrH* 76 F 23; cf. U. von Wilamowitz-Moellendorff, *Platon* ii (Berlin, 1920), 93 f.; Burkert, *LS* 455 n. 40. For Pythagoras as inventor of the *kanōn* cf. Nicom. p. 248. 16, Gaud. p. 341. 13, Aristid. Quint. p. 97. 3, Diog. Laert. 8. 12, *Anecdota* p. 9 Studemund; other references in Burkert, *LS* 375 n. 22.

to the other as well as that of either part to the whole length.[53]
Ptolemy, however, a few generations later, found no continuing
tradition of the monochord's use; and he considers it an inadequate
instrument, though he does provide some detailed advice on how
best to construct it.[54] Elsewhere he recommends fitting out the
kanōn with eight or fifteen strings, equal in length and tuning, or (in
the case of the fifteen-stringed version) with seven strings tuned to
one pitch and the other eight an octave higher. There can be separate
bridges, or just one crossing a bank of strings diagonally.[55]

Ptolemy also describes a contrivance used by some theoreticians
and poetically called the *Helikōn*, after the mountain on which the
Muses dwell. It had four strings and one diagonal bridge. The
proportional lengths for the concords were constructed by geometrical procedures, given a square and the mid-points of its sides
(Fig. 8.3). The verticals represent the strings; the position of the third

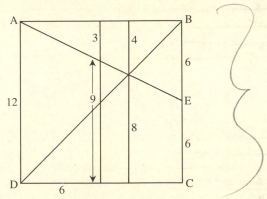

Fig. 8.3. The *Helikōn*

one on the horizontal axis is pinpointed by the intersection of the
lines BD and AE. AE represents the bridge. The various vibrating
lengths then available, 3, 4, 6, 8, 9, 12, will yield all the intervals contained in the note-series *E A e a b e'*.[56]

[53] Ptol. *Harm.* 2. 13 p. 67. 22 ff.
[54] *Harm.* 1. 8, 2. 12.
[55] *Harm.* 1. 11, 2. 1–2, 13, 16, 3. 1–2. See Barker, *GMW* ii. 300, 315, 319, 344,
356 f., 362–70.
[56] Ptol. *Harm.* 2. 2 (Barker, *GMW* ii. 319 f.), cf. Aristid. Quint. p. 99. 1 ff.

Ptolemy then proposes an ingenious combination of the *Helikōn* principle with the eight-stringed *kanōn*, enabling all the notes of the octave in any tuning to be sounded and, moreover, to be transposed wholesale to a higher pitch. It involves adjusting the distances between the strings so that they make the desired interval-ratios, as measured from a point out to the side, and stopping them by means of a long diagonal bridge pivoted at that point (Fig. 8.4). The stopped lengths, since they mark off equal triangles, stand in the same ratios to one another as the base lines, and are reduced proportionately as the bridge swings down.[57]

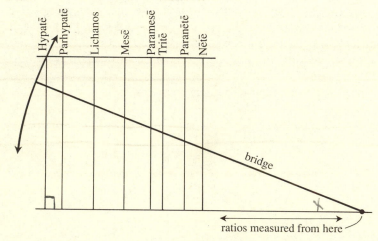

Fig. 8.4. Ptolemy's adaptation of the *Helikōn*

Rhythm

The aulete or citharist of the Archaic and Classical periods knew various *nomoi* appropriate to the accompaniment of different forms of song, dance, and recitation. Each *nomos*-name must have implied a particular rhythm or sequence of rhythms; and certain of the names either referred directly to rhythm or at a secondary stage came to serve as the names of rhythms.[58] Thus there was a rudimen-

---

[57] *Harm.* 2. 2 p. 46. 4ff.; Barker, *GMW* ii. 319–22.
[58] *Elegoi, Iamboi*, Trochaic, Enoplian; cf. p. 216. Other rhythmic terms such as dactyl, anapaest, paeon, also probably originated as types of dance, etc.

tary vocabulary by which at least some of the standard rhythms might be identified.

It is not until the second half of the fifth century that we can trace any form of systematization or theory. Herodotus, in citing verses of Archilochus, the Delphic oracle, or inscriptions, sometimes observes that they are in a 'three-measure iambos' or in 'six-measure tonos', and we have the impression that he is showing off his knowledge of a modern art of metrical analysis.[59] Metre and rhythm were distinguished as separate topics,[60] but they could not be considered entirely independent of each other; interest in them developed in parallel. Among the many writings of Democritus there was one *On Rhythms and Harmony*, and the sophist Hippias of Elis also expounded these subjects.[61] But the most important rhythmic theorist of the period seems to have been Damon, the teacher of Pericles.

From a passage in Plato's *Republic* we gather (in spite of the artistic vagueness characterizing Socrates' memory of the matter) that Damon classified rhythms according to whether the 'up' and 'down' parts of the measure were equal in duration or unequal. Socrates' interlocutor, who is Plato's brother Glaucon and a musician, says he knows from his own observation that there are three species of rhythm from which measured sequences are woven together. Socrates then introduces the name of Damon, and says

I dimly recall him specifying some 'enoplian' that was compound, and there was a 'dactyl' and a 'heroic', that's right, that he somehow analysed, making an equal up and down, and also one that divided into short and long, that he called (I think) iambus, and another one trochee, and he attached long and short durations to them.[62]

Glaucon's three categories are no doubt those with the arsis/thesis ratios 1 : 1, 1 : 2, and 2 : 3. Socrates mentions the dactyl as the representative of the first, the iambus and trochee as representative of the second; the 'compound enoplian' probably represents not the 2 : 3

---

[59] Hdt. 1. 12. 2, 47. 2, 62. 4, 174. 5; 5. 60, 61. 1; 7. 220. 3. For the terminology cf. Ar. *Nub.* 642.
[60] Ar. *Nub.* 638 ff., cf. Pl. *Phlb.* 17 d.
[61] Diog. Laert. 9. 48; Pl. *Hp. Mai.* 285 d, *Hp. Mi.* 368 d.
[62] Pl. *Resp.* 400 ab, cf. U. von Wilamowitz-Moellendorff, *Griechische Verskunst* (Berlin, 1921), 65; Barker, *GMW* i. 133 f.; and for the division of the measure into 'up' and 'down', above, p. 133.

category but a complex unit 'woven' from the simple feet.[63] Socrates goes on to say that Damon evaluated the various rhythms and the tempi associated with them, condemning some and praising others.

Plato hints at a parallelism between the series of rhythmic ratios and those governing harmony.[64] Pythagoreans would certainly have seen a deep significance in this.[65] The parallelism went further for those who recognized 4 : 3 as a valid rhythmical genus.[66] Most writers, however, acknowledge only the three categories, equal (1 : 1), double (2 : 1), and hemiolic (3 : 2). This is the position of Plato, Aristotle, Aristoxenus, and others.[67]

Aristoxenus' work on rhythm is known to us from a nine-page fragment of the second book of his *Elements of Rhythm*, a short excerpt from another work of his *On the Time-unit*, a papyrus fragment from a treatise either by Aristoxenus himself or by some follower, and echoes of his doctrines in later sources, especially Aristides Quintilianus and Michael Psellus' *Preliminaries to the Science of Rhythm.*[68] He took pains to define rhythm and to delimit musical from other forms of rhythm. As a good Aristotelian he distinguished the object shaped by rhythm—language, melody, or bodily movement—from the rhythmic form shaping it. Thus he rejected the notion of earlier rhythmicians who thought that rhythm could be measured by syllables.[69] Rhythm was an organization of

---

[63] 'Compound' means resolvable into smaller constituents, cf. Aristox. *Rhythm.* 2. 26, Aristid. Quint. p. 33. 16. Enoplian and dactyl also appear as key terms of rhythmic theory in Ar. *Nub.* 651. One scholiast on that line identifies enoplian with the cretic – ◡ –, a rhythm certainly sometimes associated with the dances in armour from which 'enoplian' took its name. But usually enoplian as a metrical term stands for × – ◡ ◡ – ◡ ◡ – (×) or something similar. See my *Greek Metre*, 195.

[64] *Resp.* 400 a, 'there are three forms [i.e. ratios] from which step-sequences are woven, just as among notes there are four (forms) from which all *harmoniai* come'. He probably means the ratios 2 : 1, 3 : 2, 4 : 3, and 9 : 8. Cf. Barker, *GMW* i. 133 n. 35.

[65] Cf. Dionysius Musicus ap. Porph. in Ptol. *Harm.* p. 37. 17, Aristid. Quint. p. 66. 1, Psell. *Rhythm.* 11.

[66] 'Some' ap. Aristid. Quint. pp. 33. 30, 38. 20; Dionysius loc. cit.; Psell. *Rhythm.* 9.

[67] Pl. loc. cit., Arist. *Rh.* 1409ª2–4, Aristox. *Rhythm.* 2. 30 ff., Aristid. Quint. p. 33. 29; other references above, p. 131 n. 7.

[68] The relevant section of Aristides Quintilianus is 1. 13–19 pp. 31. 3–40. 25; cf. Barker, *GMW* ii. 433–45. The other texts are collected with translations and notes by L. Pearson, *Aristoxenus, Elementa Rhythmica* (Oxford, 1990). The papyrus is *POxy.* 2687.

[69] The criticism, recorded by Psellus 1, may have been directed against Phaedrus, an otherwise unknown writer whose definition of rhythm as 'the measured placing of syllables in a certain mutual relationship' is listed before Aristoxenus' by Bacchius p. 313. 2.

time, and to be measured by time-units. The minimal unit, the 'primary duration' (*prōtos chronos*), was not a physical constant: it was whatever served as the smallest indivisible unit in a given piece of music. In the case of vocal music it normally corresponded to the time occupied by a short syllable, since at Aristoxenus' period short syllables were never divided between more than one note. But in a piece in spondaic tempo the primary duration would be significantly longer. Besides the primary duration there are other durations that are multiples of it (diseme, triseme, etc.) or else irrational. The durations must be arranged according to certain rules if the sequence is to be rhythmical, just as notes and intervals must be if their sequence is to be melodic. Hence we get feet of various shapes and sizes.[70] But the abstract scheme is only realized when time is actually divided up by the rhythmicization of a text. The syllables of the text do not necessarily match on a one-to-one basis the durations that constitute the feet. A syllable is flexible, and a particular sequence of syllables may fit more than one rhythmic scheme. In the papyrus fragment the principle is illustrated with the syllabic sequence – ᴗ –. The author explains how, by treating one of the long syllables as triseme, we can use such a sequence to fill feet of the form – ᴗ – ᴗ or ᴗ – ᴗ – or – ᴗ ᴗ –.

Post-Aristoxenian writers do not seem to have added much of significance to the theory of rhythm. Definitions of rhythm by one Leophantus and by Didymus and Nicomachus, cited by Bacchius, are mere variations on Aristoxenus'.[71] Aristides Quintilianus, after expounding rhythm on Aristoxenian lines, describes the approach of others who made a clearer separation between rhythm and metre. They analysed rhythmic structures purely in terms of numerical ratios without, apparently, using terms such as 'dactylic' and 'iambic', which were shared with metrics.[72] For the rest, while they differed from Aristoxenus over some details, their concepts seem generally to have been in accord with his.[73]

---

[70] It is not necessary to go into the details of them. Reference has been made as appropriate in Ch. 5.

[71] Bacchius p. 313. 6–10.

[72] Metricians' usage of these terms, however, did not coincide with that of rhythmicians; cf. pp. 136, 137 with n. 22. Metricians were those who analysed the metres of verse texts without reference to performance.

[73] Aristid. Quint. pp. 38. 17–39. 25.

Ethos

Mode, genus, rhythm, and tempo naturally had a considerable role to play in determining the character and emotional effect of a musical composition. Defining and accounting for this variety of effect became a recognized, if controversial, objective among theorists. Already in the first half of the fifth century we find some lyric poets making programmatic assertions that a certain mode is the best for a particular purpose.[74] The Pythagoreans are reported to have classified (and made systematic practical use of) types of music producing different effects, rousing or calming. They probably took both harmonic intervals and rhythms into account in their classification and regarded number ratios as the crucial factor in each case.[75]

It is possible that Lasus had said something on these matters in his pioneering treatise on music. However, the first writer we know of who expounded them in detail is Damon. This man, considered the greatest Athenian intellect of his time, an associate of Pericles, Prodicus, and Socrates, was probably a well-known figure by the 440s—it may have been then that he was ostracized—and still about in the 420s.[76] He published an essay in the form of an address to the Areopagus Council, which was a sort of Athenian House of Lords, filled with retired state officials, enjoying little real power but vested with some high judicial functions and nominally with the responsibility of supervising public morality in general.[77] This last was the relevant point for Damon, who wished to argue that musical modes and rhythms were intimately connected with ethical qualities, and that accordingly it was important for the state to concern itself with the regulation of music and musical education. 'A musical revolution always means a social revolution':[78] it sounds as if Damon wanted

---

[74] Pratinas, *PMG* 712, quoted above, p. 178; id. *PMG* 708 and Pind. fr. 67, cited p. 179.

[75] See pp. 31 f. The earliest source is Aristoxenus. We cannot trust the attribution of this science to Pythagoras himself, but it almost certainly goes back to the 5th c.

[76] Cf. Plato Com. fr. 207, Pl. *Alc.* i. 118 c with schol., *La.* 180 d, 197 d, Isoc. 15. 235, Arist. *Ath. Pol.* 27. 4, Plut. *Per.* 4. 1–4, *Nicias* 6. 1, *Aristides* 1. 7; U. von Wilamowitz-Moellendorff, *Aristoteles und Athen* (Berlin, 1893), i. 134 f., *Griechische Verskunst*, 59 f.; K. von Jan, *RE* iv. 2072; W. Kroll, *RE* Supp. iii. 324; H. Ryffel, *Museum Helveticum* 4 (1947), 23–38; F. Lasserre, *Plutarque: De la musique* (Olten and Lausanne, 1954), 53–79.

[77] Isoc. 7. 37. Cf. U. von Wilamowitz-Moellendorff, *Einleitung in die attische Tragödie* (Berlin, 1889), 21 n. 35.

[78] Pl. *Resp.* 424 c = Diels, *Vorsokr.* 37 B 10.

official action taken to curb the originality of contemporary music. Song and dance, he maintained, entailed particular commotions of the soul and thus set up particular patterns in it, mirroring their own qualities, shaping a boy's unformed character or bringing out latent traits in those of maturer years.[79] Boys should be taught to sing and play melodies characterized by manliness, self-control, and even-handedness.[80] Damon set out a series of modal scales, not merely listing them by name but enumerating their notes and intervals and commenting on their qualities.[81] He did likewise with rhythms and tempi, commending some, condemning others as expressive of undignified aggression, frenzy, or other vices.[82] Here numerical ratios played a part in his theory, so that a Pythagorean influence may perhaps be suspected.[83]

The author of a diatribe composed perhaps around 390 BC, the beginning of which is preserved on papyrus, attacks certain *harmonikoi* who claim that different melodies can make men self-controlled, sensible, righteous, manly, or the opposite of all these.[84] The list of qualities corresponds closely to those of which Damon spoke; but he must have been dead many years by this time.

[79] Ath. 628 c, Aristid. Quint. p. 80. 25 ff. = Diels, *Vorsokr.* 37 B 6–7. Similarly in 1926 the Salvation Army in Cincinnati raised its voice in protest at the prospect 'that babies born in the maternity hospital are to be legally subjected to the implanting of jazz emotions by such enforced propinquity to a theatre and jazz palace' (*New York Times*, 4 Feb. 1926, quoted by Merriam 242). That jazz was evil and corrupting was a widely held conviction in the 1920s and 1930s, and it was actually banned in some places; see Merriam 241–4. 'After the dissemination of jazz,' wrote Cyril Scott, '. . . a very marked decline in sexual morals became noticeable' (quoted by N. Slonimsky, *Lexicon of Musical Invective* (Seattle, 2nd edn. 1969), 25).

[80] Philod. *Mus.* pp. 54 f. Kemke = 116 van Krevelen, cf. p. 7 K. = 14 Kr. = 115 Rispoli; Diels, *Vorsokr.* 37 B 4; Wilamowitz, *Griechische Verskunst*, 63 f.

[81] Aristid. Quint. loc. cit., 'in the *harmoniai* handed down by him one finds that, of the movable notes, it is sometimes the female ones and sometimes the male that predominate or are included to a lesser extent or not at all'. Female and male = lower and higher, cf. p. 77. 19. It is not clear whether these are Damon's terms or only Aristides', but they would suit Damon's concern with manliness. We can hardly doubt that these heterogeneous scales of Damon's are identical with the six that Aristides elsewhere adduces from 'the most ancient' sources (above, p. 174), especially as he adds that those are the ones Plato refers to in *Resp.* 398 e–399 c. See below.

[82] Pl. *Resp.* 400 a–c; Diels, *Vorsokr.* 37 B 9; see above, p. 243.

[83] Schol. Pl. *Alc.* i 118 c (p. 95 Greene) connects Damon through a succession of teacher-pupil relationships with Pythoclides, an aulete of the earlier 5th c., here said to be a Pythagorean.

[84] *PHib.* 13, translated with notes in Barker, *GMW* i. 183–5; improved text in *ZPE* 92 (1992), 16 f. A plausible case has recently been made for identifying the author as Alcidamas: A. Brancacci in A. Brancacci *et al.*, *Aristoxenica, Menandrea, Fragmenta Philosophica* (Accad. Toscana, *Studi* xci, 1988), 61–84.

Evidently his ideas had been taken up by younger men. They referred specifically to the ethos of the genera, praising the enharmonic as conducive to manliness and condemning the chromatic as making them wimpish. The writer of the oration briskly denies these effects, on the ground that diatonic music (which he oddly treats as a variety of chromatic) is regularly used by central Greek tribes much manlier than the vocalists of the tragic stage who use enharmonic.

Plato too took up Damon's ideas; he is said to have been taught music by a pupil of Damon's, Dracon, and he mentions Damon in the most commendatory terms.[85] He says nothing of the genera, but refers repeatedly to mode and rhythm as agents of ethical influence.

And the music-teachers . . . teach boys the compositions of other good melic poets, matching them to the lyre music, and they make the rhythms and *harmoniai* settle in the boys' souls so that they may be less wild and, through being better rhythmed and attuned, good at speaking and in action; for a man's whole life calls for good rhythm and good attunement.[86]

So is this the reason, Glaucon, why musical education is the most important, that rhythm and attunement are what most penetrate the inner soul and grasp it most powerfully, bringing good order, and make a person well-regulated if he is educated correctly and the opposite if he is not?[87]

Attunement possesses motions akin to the soul-circuits in us, and it is a gift of the Muses to the man who employs music intelligently, not for irrational pleasure, as is now supposed to be its utility, but as an ally against the unattuned soul-circuit that exists in us, to bring it into order and concord (*symphōniā*) with itself. And rhythm likewise, on account of the unmeasured and graceless condition in most of us, was given by them to assist us in the same fight.[88]

Modes and rhythms (rhythms of dance as well as song) are charged with ethos because they are themselves imitations of the voices and movements of people characterized by particular qualities or emotional conditions.[89] Music and dance therefore encode ethical qualities already manifested in human conduct and feed them back into the souls of performers and audiences. Consequently it is important—especially in education—to choose music that conveys

[85] *La.* 180d, cf. 197d. Dracon: ps.-Plut. *De mus.* 1136f, Olympiodorus, *Vita Platonis* 1. 38 Westerm., Anon. *Vita Platonis* p. 6. 43 W. = *Proleg. philos. Plat.* 2 Herm.   [86] *Prt.* 326ab.
[87] *Resp.* 401d.   [88] *Tim.* 47de.
[89] *Resp.* 399a–c, 399e–400a, *Leg.* 654e–655d, 660a, 668a–670c, 798d, 812c.

good qualities. In song it is the words and subject matter that play the primary role, but they must be combined with the appropriate modes and rhythms, used in a consistent and straightforward way, or the ethical effect will be confused and obscured. Out of six *harmoniai*—apparently the six discussed by Damon—only the Dorian and Phrygian are approved.[90] In the case of rhythms Damon is explicitly named as the authority.[91] Later his warning against changes in musical style is cited with approval.[92] Plato may not have followed Damon in all particulars, but he shared his general theory of music's ethical power, his anti-modernism, and his totalitarian tendencies. Both in the *Republic* and in the *Laws* Plato manipulates theory to legislate for the Classical forms of music and dance that he liked, and to exclude other kinds as useless or pernicious.

Aristotle takes it as an evident fact that music can alter us; he refers to Olympus' melodies, which are acknowledged to make us feel exalted. His explanation is essentially identical with Plato's. Melodies and rhythms contain likenesses of ethical qualities and states—anger, mildness, manliness, self-control, and so on—and our souls respond to these likenesses when we hear them. Differences of ethos and effect are especially manifested in the *harmoniai*. Aristotle specifies some of these and the ways in which they affect people.

It is the same with rhythms: some of them have a more stationary, some a more mobile character, and of the latter some have more vulgar movements, others more respectable. From all this it is clear that music is capable of conferring a particular quality on the soul's character . . . And there seems to be (in the soul) some sort of kinship with the *harmoniai* and the rhythms, so that many of the sages say, some of them that the soul is an attunement (*harmoniā*), others that it possesses attunement.[93]

When he goes on to deal with the use of the *harmoniai* in education, Aristotle refers explicitly to Plato's discussion in the *Republic*, and it is clear that his ideas of the whole matter are strongly influenced by Plato's.

[90] *Resp.* 376 eff., 395 c–e, 398 b–399 c (cf. above, pp. 180–3); *Leg.* 802 c–e, 812 c–e. Cf. *La.* 188 d, where, if 'Lydian' is taken to include Tense Lydian and Mixolydian, the same modes are mentioned and Dorian, 'the only true Greek mode' (Ionian is not counted), is picked out as the mode to which the manly man's life is attuned.
[91] *Resp.* 399 e–400 c.   [92] *Resp.* 424 c.
[93] Arist. *Pol.* 1340ª6–ᵇ19 (Barker, *GMW* i. 174–6). For Aristotle's comments on individual rhythms and modes see above, pp. 158 and 180–2. The idea that the soul itself is an attunement may go back to Philolaus; see Burkert, *LS* 272.

Many of Aristotle's pupils and associates subscribed to similar theories.[94] They were developed further by the Stoic Diogenes of Seleucia (*c.* 240–152 BC) in a substantial work in which he praised music and its manifold potencies and uses; what we know of the book derives entirely from Philodemus' extended critique in his *On Music*, itself fragmentary.[95] Diogenes again spoke of music containing 'likenesses' of ethical qualities, every possible one, though he held that they did not arise from imitation, and would not affect every hearer in an identical way. He referred to specific songs and hymns that would be much less impressive as bare texts without their melodies. We do not know whether he went into individual modes and rhythms, but he does seem to have endorsed the evaluation of the genera according to which the enharmonic was noble, dignified, simple, and pure, while the chromatic was unmanly and vulgar.[96] We have seen this view already being attacked in the early fourth century, and Diogenes must be echoing earlier authorities, since the enharmonic genus was largely obsolete in his time. Philodemus mentions an alternative view upheld by advocates of chromatic: they dismissed enharmonic as austere and uncompromising, whereas chromatic was gentle and yielding.[97]

[94] Cf. Heraclid. Pont. frs. 162–3 W., Aristox. frs. 80–3, 122–3, Theophr. fr. 91 W. and ap. Philod. *Mus.* 3 p. 37 K. = 84 Kr., ps.-Arist. *Pr.* 19. 27, 29, 30, 48; Neubecker 135–7.

[95] The passages relevant to Diogenes are collected in J. von Arnim, *Stoicorum Veterum Fragmenta* iii (Leipzig, 1903), 221–35; improved texts in the more recent editions of Philodemus by D. A. van Krevelen (1939), G. M. Rispoli (bk. 1, *c.* 1969), and A. J. Neubecker (bk. 4, 1986). See also A. J. Neubecker, *Die Bewertung der Musik bei Stoikern und Epikureern* (Berlin, 1956); W. D. Anderson, *Ethos and Education in Greek Music*, 153–76; G. M. Rispoli, *Cronache Ercolanesi* 4 (1974), 57–87, esp. 77 ff.

[96] Philod. *Mus.* 4 pp. 40, 49 f., 39 Neub.

[97] Plut. *Non posse suaviter vivi sec. Epicurum* 1096 b cites as a typical problem of Aristotle's school 'why is it that the chromatic genus relaxes us, while the enharmonic pulls us together?' In later authors' assessments the diatonic genus is included, and each genus on the whole is assigned positive qualities. With the decline of enharmonic and the increased importance of diatonic, the qualities originally assigned to the former in antithesis to chromatic tend to be transferred to diatonic. (i) Theon Smyrn. pp. 54. 12–56. 5 (from Adrastus?): diatonic is strong, dignified, muscular, noble; chromatic is more plaintive and emotional; enharmonic is difficult and not often used. (ii) Sext. Emp. *Math.* 6. 50: diatonic is rugged, a little lacking in elegance; chromatic is clear-toned (*ligyron*) and lamentatory; enharmonic is austere and dignified. (iii) Interpolation in Aristid. Quint. p. 92. 19 ff.: diatonic is masculine and rather austere, chromatic is plaintive and most pleasant, enharmonic is rousing and gentle (? text probably corrupt). Cf. Anon. Bellerm. 26: diatonic is rather manly and austere, chromatic is plaintive and most pleasant. (iv) Procl. *In Ti.* ii. 169. 1 ff. D.: diatonic is full-bodied, simple, noble, chromatic is slack and ignoble, enharmonic is educational.

Others again, says Philodemus, those more devoted to physical science, deny that the genera have any such intrinsic properties, and advise us to go for whichever one happens to please our ears; and likewise with rhythms and melodic types. The reference is to the Epicureans, perhaps to Epicurus himself, who had written a book on music.[98] Philodemus was an Epicurean and shared the point of view that the means of musical expression are ethically neutral. His *On Music* was devoted to reviewing and rebutting earlier philosophers' arguments about music's potency and educational value. He argued that music in itself, as distinct from the words with which it may be associated, is incapable of exercising any moral effect upon the hearer, and that its only usefulness is as the source of an inessential kind of pleasure.

This denial of the ethos theory was not exclusively Epicurean. We have already seen the theory attacked by a sophist of the early fourth century BC. About the end of the second century AD the Sceptic Sextus Empiricus devotes the sixth book of his work *Against the Scientists* to argument against musical theorists, on similar lines to Philodemus.

In general, however, belief in the ethical power of music continued to prevail. With the increasing influence of Platonist philosophy from the first century AD onwards, it came to be yet more firmly integrated in cosmological theory. For Ptolemy the whole order of nature, and especially the revolution of the heavenly bodies, is characterized by proportional arrangements akin to those of musical attunement. The soul is analysed into three components which correspond to the principal concords (octave, fifth, fourth), and they have respectively seven, four, and three faculties or virtues, corresponding to the species of the octave, fifth, and fourth. The condition of the soul depends on how all these parts are attuned. Changes in its attunement in response to changed circumstances of life are analogous to musical modulations: greater intensity and activity correspond to tuning to a higher key, greater relaxation and torpor to a lower one, while moderation and stability correspond to median keys such as the Dorian.

---

[98] Diog. Laert. 10. 28. Plutarch, *Non posse vivi* 1095 c, cites from other works of Epicurus his view that one should enjoy music but not waste time in boring scholarly debate about it.

Indeed, our souls are quite plainly affected in sympathy with the actual activities of a melody, recognizing the kinship, as it were, of the ratios belonging to its particular kind of constitution, and being moulded by the movements specific to the idiosyncrasies of the melodies, so that they are led sometimes into pleasures and relaxations, sometimes into grief and contractions; they are sometimes stupefied and lulled to sleep, sometimes invigorated and aroused; and they are sometimes turned towards peacefulness and restraint, sometimes towards frenzy and ecstasy, as the melody itself modulates in different ways at different times, and draws our souls towards the conditions constituted from the likenesses of the ratios.[99]

These likenesses do not seem to arise, as in Plato, from imitation of psychic states by music, but to be inherent in the various combinations of higher and lower tensions.

Aristides Quintilianus presents a more elaborate system of cosmic harmony. Everything is based on number and proportion. Our earthly music is an imperfect imitation of the heavenly attunement manifested in the working of the universe.[100] The soul itself is an attunement, having the same set of ratios as a musical scale and therefore moved by music which uses these ratios. Alternatively, it is moved because, descending from purer regions, it has become enmeshed in a structure founded on sinews and breath; these vibrate in sympathy when stringed or wind instruments are sounded.[101] The soul chooses a body with male or female attributes or some combination, according to its inclination, and develops emotions reflecting its male, female, or mixed affinities. Musical scales and keys, too, are more or less male or female in character, and will appeal to the individual hearer according to his or her own sexual mix. Lower keys are male, higher ones female. In the case of different modal scales the sex quotient depends on the prominence of male or female notes.[102] Instruments too are graded on a sexual scale according to register or timbre, and this makes them suited to different *harmoniai* and rhythms.[103]

[99] *Harm.* 3. 4–7 (Barker, *GMW* ii. 374–9). The passage quoted is as translated by Barker.

[100] Aristid. Quint. 3. 7, 9 ff.   [101] Id. 2. 17–18.

[102] Id. 2. 8, 14. The lower movable note of each tetrachord is represented as being the most female and emotional, the upper one the most male and vigorous, the standing notes more male than female, except for Mesē, which is more female, as also is Proslambanomenos. The sexing is bound up with an aesthetic classification of the vowels used in a sol-fa system, for which see below, p. 265.

[103] Id. 2. 16. In the chapters where the sex theory is expounded it is implied that the number of different possible emotions and mixtures of them, all potentially expres-

Aristides is convinced of the value of music for educational and therapeutic purposes. Orderly, manly melodies are required in education; others may be useful in treating people in different emotional states. Not everyone responds as quickly or in the same way as everyone else to a given type of music. Sex, age, and other factors may make a difference, and some experimentation may be necessary.[104]

sible in music, is very large; see especially 2. 8 p. 67. 5–14. But elsewhere Aristides reckons with a simple trinity of musical characters: depressant, stimulant, and calming (pp. 30. 12–17, 40. 14–15). Cf. Cleon. p. 206. 6–18, 'the stimulant kind of composition is that which conveys grandeur, manly exaltation, heroic deeds, and related emotions, as used especially by tragedy . . . The depressant is that which reduces the soul to an abject, unmanly state; it will be appropriate to unhappy love, death, disaster, and the like. The calming type is that associated with equanimity and a situation of freedom and peace. Suited to it will be hymns, paeans, encomia, precepts, etc.'

[104] Aristid. Quint. 2. 3–6, 14.

9
Notation and Pitch

NOTATION

By the middle of the third century BC, at latest, an agreed system of musical notation was in use among professionals. It is employed consistently in the surviving papyri and inscriptions, which extend from that time down to the late third century AD, and also in tables and examples in several of the later writers.[1] It is still to be seen in the medieval tradition of Mesomedes' songs, though its use by practising musicians probably ceased around the fourth or fifth century. Our understanding of the system is derived principally from Alypius' extensive tables of the notes available in each of the fifteen keys and in each genus.

The pitches of notes are indicated by letter symbols, which in the case of vocal music are written above the syllables of the text. In documents of Hellenistic date, when successive syllables are to be sung on the same note, the symbol stands only over the first, but in later texts it is repeated over each syllable.[2] There are two separate series of symbols, one normally used for vocal, the other for instrumental music.[3] Rhythmical values are defined where necessary by certain supplementary signs; but in vocal texts the rhythms are for the most part left to be inferred from the metre of the verse. There

---

[1] Alypius pp. 368–406 J., Aristid. Quint. pp. 19–20, 24–7, Gaud. pp. 347–55, Bacchius pp. 293–302, Anon. Bellerm. 1–11, 67–8, 77–104, Mart. Cap. 9. 943, Boeth. *Inst. Mus.* 4. 3 f., 15 f.

[2] In a few papyri we find a horizontal bar appearing here and there among the notes. It may perhaps represent an alternative way of marking a repeat of the preceding note.

[3] This is stated by Aristid. Quint. p. 23. 20–2, cf. Alyp. p. 367. 22, Gaud. p. 350. 10, Anon. Bellerm. 67, 68; and the distinction is nearly always maintained in the musical documents. The only exceptions are **13** Limenius' Paean, where the instrumental notation is used (we know that the composer was a professional citharist); **32** *PMichigan* 2958, where a sung text has vocal notation, but there is one line of notation without accompanying text, perhaps an instrumental insert; and **11** *SEG* 30. 390, where again vocal notation seems to be used for a short instrumental interpolation in a sung text.

are also a few symbols that are used in later texts to clarify the articulation of notes where more than one is allocated to the same syllable.

Pitch notation

The pitch symbols are set out in Fig. 9.1 on p. 256, starting from the highest. The vocal and instrumental symbols are shown in parallel columns, and each pair is assigned a number for convenience of reference.[4] The whole scheme covers a little over three octaves. The symbols form groups of three, as is visually apparent in the instrumental series. The bottom symbol in each triad represents a 'natural' note on a diatonic scale. The modern notes shown in the boxes are the conventional equivalents used in most scholarly literature, chosen to avoid sharps and flats, but the true pitch will have been about a minor third lower.[5] The two other symbols in each triad represent successive sharpenings of the 'natural' note; I shall call them the first sharp and the second sharp. The degree of sharpening is not fixed but varies between a quarter-tone and a semitone, depending on the genus of the composition or the conventions of the key. For example, in the enharmonic genus the notes 22, 23, 24 would be interpreted as *e, e↑, f*, whereas in chromatic they would stand for *e, f, f♯*. (In this latter case 24 is a higher note than 25, just as in modern notation E double sharp is higher than F.) The notation does not in fact distinguish between enharmonic and chromatic scales.[6]

The first sharps are normally used only for the lower movable note of a tetrachord (Parhypatē hypatōn or mesōn, Tritē synēmmenōn, diezeugmenōn, or hyperbolaiōn); and when the standing note at the base of the tetrachord is represented by a natural, the lower movable note is always represented by the first sharp, whatever the genus.[7] The upper movable note is then represented in the enharmonic and chromatic genera by the second sharp, and in the diatonic either by

---

[4] The numbers are those used by J. M. Barbour, *Jour. Am. Musicol. Soc.* 13 (1960), 3, and Barker, *GMW* ii. 426 ff. Pöhlmann, *DAM* 144, following J. Chailley, has a slightly different numbering.

[5] The basis of this estimate is explained at the end of the chapter. The conventional equivalences were established by F. Bellermann, *Die Tonleitern und Musiknoten der Griechen* (Berlin, 1847), 54–6.

[6] In Alypius' tables of chromatic scales, but in the Lydian key only (p. 384 J.), the second sharps are marked as chromatic by having a small transverse stroke through them; so also in Boeth. *Inst. Mus.* 4. 3–4. But this diacritic is nowhere attested in the musical documents.

[7] One might have expected a diatonic sequence of naturals such as 43, 46, 49, 52 to be used in notating the corresponding diatonic tetrachord (*e' f' g' a'*), but it never is: the notation is 43, 44, 49, 52.

		Vocal	Instr.			Vocal	Instr.			Vocal	Instr.			Vocal	Instr.
					54	⊥	⅄		33	Π	Ɔ		12	И	Я
					53	⅄	⸌		32	P	U		11	M	Н
				a'	52	Θ	ꓨ	*a*	31	C	C	*A*	10	٩	H
					51	✳	ⵔ		30	T	Ⅎ		9	Ц	3
					50	ꜩ	⼂		29	Y	Ⴠ		8	Ь	ɯ
g"	70	Ʊ'	⅂'	*g'*	49	Ʊ	⅂	*g*	28	Φ	F	*G*	7	3	Є
	69	A'	\'		48	A	\		27	X	Ч		6	ꓤ	T
	68	B'	/'		47	B	/		26	Ψ	⅃		5	≺	⅄
f"	67	Γ'	N'	*f'*	46	Γ	N	*f*	25	Ω	Ρ	*F*	4	ᗡ	ᐱ
	66	Δ'	⅃'		45	Δ	⅃		24	Ɐ	˥		3	✳	✳
	65	E'	U'		44	E	U		23	R	L		2	Ә	Ɛ
e"	64	Z'	Ⴀ'	*e'*	43	Z	Ⴀ	*e*	22	˥	Γ	*E*	1	Ϙ	Ϛ
	63	H'	>'		42	H	>		21	▽	⊣				
	62	Θ'	V'		41	Θ	V		20	F	⊥				
d"	61	I'	<'	*d'*	40	I	<	*d*	19	7	⊢				
	60	K'	Λ'		39	K	Λ		18	ꓩ	Ǝ				
	59	Λ'	⊴'		38	Λ	⊴		17	ᴧ	Ш				
c"	58	M'	⅂'	*c'*	37	M	⅂	*c*	16	\	E				
	57	N'	⋋'		36	N	⋋		15	Ⅎ	ꓩ				
	56	Ƹ'	Ⴑ'		35	Ƹ	Ⴑ		14	V	⊏				
b'	55	O'	K'	*b*	34	O	K	*B*	13	W	h				

FIG. 9.1. Repertory of symbols

Notes: Many divergent and corrupted forms of the symbols occur in manuscripts. The most significant variants and uncertainties relate to the following:

54–53 and 51– instr., see Winnington-Ingram, *Philol.* 122 (1978) 241–8.

24 instr.: Gaudentius and Boethius give ⵎ and ꓔ (chromatic ꓞ) respectively, Alypius Ⱶ

16 vocal: or perhaps —. See Winnington-Ingram, *Philol.* 117 (1973) 247 n.9.

6–4, Aristides Quintilianus gives ⊣Ⱶ ,⅄≺ ,-oo-

For 6 Gaudentius gives ⱴⱱ (and at 8 vocal he gives d).

The design of the above table is modelled on Pöhlmann, *DAM* 144, but there are modifications of detail.

the second sharp of the next triad up or by the natural above that, depending on whether this natural is a major or a minor third higher than the one we started from.[8] The second sharps also serve in other

---

[8] In a few of the unpublished Hellenistic fragments (**10**)—possibly belonging to a single text—the upper movable is notated by the first sharp instead of the second

	Dorian		Ionian		Phrygian		Aeolian		Lydian	
	63		64		67		69		70	
	60/57		61/57		63/60		64/63		67/63	
	55		56		59		61		62	
	54		55		58		60		61	
	51/48	51	52/51	52	54/51	54	55/54	55	58/54	58
	47	48/45	49	49/45	50	51/48	52	52/51	53	54/51
	46	43	48	44	49	47	51	49	52	50
	42/39	42	43/42	43	46/42	46	48/45	48	49/45	49
	38	39/36	40	40/36	41	42/39	43	43/42	44	46/42
	37	34	39	35	40	38	42	40	43	41
	33/30	33	34/33	34	37/33	37	39/36	39	40/36	40
	29	30/27	31	31/30	32	33/30	34	34/33	35	37/33
	28	26	30	28	31	29	33	31	34	32
		25		27		28		30		31
	21/18		22/21		25/21		27/24		28/24	
	17		19		20		22		23	
	16		18		19		21		22	
	12/9		13/12		16/12		18/15		19/15	
	8		10		11		13		14	
	7		9		10		12		13	
	4		6		7		9		10	

Fɪɢ. 9.2. Key to the keys

Note: A tip for finding these charts quickly in future: trim 2 mm. off the margin of the left-hand page.

circumstances when an intermediate step between the naturals is required. In the Ionian and Aeolian keys (cf. p. 231) and in Hypo-dorian, many of the standing notes are represented by second sharps. The next note up, if it is a lower movable, is then represented by the adjacent natural. The upper movable will be the second sharp of this natural in the enharmonic and chromatic genera, and in the diatonic either the next natural up or, if this is only a semitone up from the preceding natural, its second sharp.

(Phrygian 37, 38, 41, 46 instead of 37, 38, 42, 46). This may represent Aristoxenus' 'soft diatonic' tuning (see p. 169), i.e. *c′ c♯′ d♭′ f′*. So too, apparently, in **7**.

These principles, which are applied with remarkable consistency, may be easier to grasp from Table 9.1. It shows the formulae according to which notation symbols are chosen for the notes of any tetrachord. Find in the left-hand column the scale degree corresponding to the lowest note of the tetrachord. In the right-hand columns the figures 1, 2, 3, 4 refer to successive triads of symbols, reading up the repertory on p. 256. The bare figure denotes the base note of the triad, the 'natural', and a/b denote the first and second sharps.

TABLE 9.1. *Formulae for choosing notation*
symbols of tetrachords

	Enharmonic/ chromatic				Diatonic			
A, B, D, or E	1	1a	1b	4	1	1a	3	4
C or G	1	1a	1b	4	1	1a	2b	4
F	1	1a	1b	3b	1	1a	2b	3b
A♯ or D♯	1b	2	2b	4b	1b	2	3b	4b
C♯ or G♯	1b	2	2b	4b	1b	2	3	4b
F♯	1b	2	2b	4	1b	2	3	4

For each of the fifteen keys of post-Aristoxenian theory a selection of note-symbols was drawn up according to these formulae, one for each degree of the Unmodulating System. They are all set out in Fig. 9.2, using the identification numbers of the chart facing it (Fig. 9.1). The 'railway map' shows the forked structure of the Unmodulating System (cf. p. 222), triplicated at intervals of a fourth. The central line in heavy black represents the basic Dorian, Ionian, Phrygian, Aeolian, or Lydian, while the higher and lower ones represent respectively the associated Hyper- and Hypo- keys, which serve to provide a choice between conjunct and disjunct tetrachords throughout the middle register. Mesē in each key is to be found at the point where the line forks, and the other standing notes of the system are shown as 'principal stations'. The note-series for the various keys are listed in five columns, each of which includes the Hyper- and Hypo- key together with the central one. The layout matches that of the diagram, with a double set of numbers where there is a divergence between disjunct tetrachords (on the left) and conjunct (on the right). For the upper movable note in each tetrachord two numbers are given, divided by an oblique stroke: the higher one applies to the diatonic genus, the lower one to chromatic or enharmonic.

This elaborate system is employed with great consistency in the Hellenistic and post-Hellenistic documents. The transcriber of a melody matched its scale with a segment of the Unmodulated System, chose the key in which the said segment appeared at the desired pitch,[9] and then used the note-symbols proper to that key until forced, by modulation or chromaticism on the composer's part, to use others. Whenever a new fragment of Greek music is published, therefore, the editor analyses the selection of notes that appear in it with a view to identifying the key. Any note that does not fit the apparent key will merit special comment.

There are a few notes near the top and bottom ends of the repertory—numbers 1–3, 5, 65, 66, 68—that have no home in any key. However, 65 is employed in the exotic modal scale of **42** *PBerol.* 6870, 16–19, and there is no reason why the others should not have been used occasionally, even if they owe their existence primarily to the logic of the notational system itself.

Origins of the pitch notation

Opinions as to the age of this system have varied widely, between the eighth and the third centuries BC. What is fairly clear, and agreed by most investigators, is that it did not come into being all at once but was built up in successive stages. It is also commonly acknowledged that the two parallel series of vocal and instrumental symbols were not invented simultaneously. The instrumental system, or rather its basic core, is generally, and I believe rightly, regarded as the older.

The vocal symbols are perspicuous. The twenty-four letters of the standard Ionic alphabet are assigned to the eight triads of the central octave ($f'-f$ with first and second sharps, notes 48–25), corresponding to the average register of the male voice.[10] The series is extended

[9] In practice some keys are favoured more than others. Lydian/Hypolydian accounts for over half of the extant fragments, and Ionian/Hyperionian for over half the rest, whereas we have no certain example of the Dorian set. Of those notated in Phrygian, none seems to be a post-Hellenistic composition.

[10] The reader is reminded that '$f'-f$' is merely a conventional description of this octave reflecting its interval structure, not its actual pitch, which would have been more like $d'-d$.

in both directions by using the letters again but turning them upside down, sideways, or back to front, or by amputating them or adding a diacritic stroke. Closer inspection reveals that this extension was made in at least two stages.

In the first stage, letters were on the whole inverted (without exchange of left and right), other expedients being resorted to if inversion did not produce a clearly differentiated symbol. The downward extension at this stage used the letters alpha to sigma (24 to 7); the remaining letters, tau to omega, were used at the upper end (54 to 49). The scheme now covered just over two octaves (*a'–G* with sharps).

In a further expansion or expansions the incomplete alphabet at the lower end of the scale was filled out with another tau-to-omega group (6 to 1), with the letters turned sideways instead of upside down.[11] At the upper end the scale was extended to *g″* by repeating the notes of the octave below and distinguishing them with a diagonal stroke (70 to 55).

If we now look at the instrumental signs, it is obvious that 70–55 and 6–1 represent expansions made in parallel with the expansions of the vocal system. 70–55 show the same principle of octave strokes applied to the signs 49–34, while 6–1 are derived directly from the corresponding vocal symbols, abandoning the principle, prevailing otherwise in the instrumental series, that the symbols within each triad are variations on a single form.

Concentrating our attention on the series 54 to 7, and in particular on the primary note of each triad, we find a strange set of symbols that have on the whole the appearance of letters, but letters of often abnormal or unrecognizable form, arranged in no intelligible order:

Ч Ɪ Ν Ⴀ < ⟨ Κ ⊂ Ϝ Ϻ Γ Ⱶ Ε ᚺ Η Ε

There are features at both ends of the series that may require special consideration. The last sign, number 7, may be derived from the corresponding vocal note, as are 6–1, though its sharps are formed from it in the usual way. The top three, 52, 49, and 46, seem to be related like the notes of a triad; the six symbols for their sharps seem to be related amongst themselves, but not derived from the primaries.

There are three principal theories about the origin of these

---

[11] Symbol 3 (chi with a stroke through it) is 51 turned sideways. A sideways phi had already had to be used at 52; it was amputated to make 4.

eccentric characters: that they are borrowed from a Semitic alphabet; that they come from an early Greek local script, perhaps that of Argos; and that they are late and artificial symbols adapted from ordinary letters.

There is nothing to be said in favour of the first hypothesis.[12] None of the symbols appears to be closer in form to a Semitic letter than to an Archaic Greek one. The third hypothesis, which presupposes the priority of the vocal notation,[13] is hardly more plausible. Why should a straightforward alphabetic system, once established, be fragmented and tortured into something so much more obscure?

The second hypothesis, advocated by Westphal in 1867, still remains in principle the most persuasive, although Westphal's detailed identifications of letter-forms are open to criticism at several points. The instrumental symbols in their basic forms can on the whole be matched with letters in sixth- and fifth-century local Greek scripts, or easily derived from them. The hardest to account for is 13, but the difficulty is not so great as to constitute an insuperable obstacle to this approach. In most cases one can find analogues in many parts of Greece—sometimes with several different letter values in different regions.

Of course, we want to identify one particular local script to which all the symbols can be related. The inventor of the system cannot be supposed to have taken some of them from one script and others from another.[14] It is indeed the Argive script, as Westphal said, that offers the most satisfactory set of correspondences.[15]

This points to the conclusion that the instrumental notation, or at any rate its original core, was invented by a musician from the Argolid, not much later than the mid-fifth century and perhaps somewhat earlier. One cannot help being struck by the coincidence that two of the earliest identifiable musical theorists came from this region or close to it: Lasus of Hermione and Epigonus of Sicyon. The latter, we recall (p. 225), left followers who carried on a tradition. However, Lasus and Epigonus, if our inferences were correct, followed the approach of dividing the octave into the

---

[12] For the Semitic hypothesis see H. Husmann, *Gött. Anz.* 211 (1957), 57 f. and his *Grundlagen der antiken und orientalischen Musikkultur* (Berlin, 1961), 79 f.

[13] A. Bataille, *Recherches de Papyrologie* 1 (1961), 5–20; J. Chailley, ibid. 4 (1967), 201–16.

[14] As D. B. Monro thinks, *The Modes of Ancient Greek Music*, 74 f.

[15] This requires more detailed argument than can be accommodated here. See *ZPE* 92 (1992), 38–41.

smallest possible intervals. So a notation invented by them might be expected to reflect this approach, for example by dividing each semitone into two steps and each tone into four. The principle of the notation we are examining is fundamentally different.

Its inventor took the notes of the diatonic scale across the span of two octaves or just over ($a'-A$, or G?) and designated them by letters, whose apparently chaotic order[16] must reflect a sequence of technical names or mnemonic syllables that lies beyond our ken.[17] The system of triads, in which the symbol rotated through ninety degrees to the left denoted the first sharp and the symbol reversed the second sharp,[18] was surely designed to deal with the enharmonic/chromatic *pyknon*, with which it is intimately bound up in the fully developed notation. It characterizes the movable notes as modifications of the standing note below them. Sachs and Gombosi argued that this reflected techniques of obtaining all three notes of the *pyknon* from the same lyre-string; but their position has been subjected to damaging attack. It is much more likely that what lies behind the triadic notation is the production of the three notes by closing or partly opening the same hole of the aulos.[19] In the diatonic genus the lower movable note would still be produced in this way, by half-stopping, but not the upper one; and in the notation the first sharp is used for the lower note in diatonic, just as in enharmonic and chromatic.[20]

There was no need for sharps on any note above e', since $e'-a'$ was the highest tetrachord in the two-octave scale. This must be connected with the fact that the three positions of 46 **N** are used not to provide f' with sharps but to notate the top three notes f' g' a'. We

---

[16] We cannot be sure of all their identities, but in the article cited I suggest that they were, from 46 downwards, nu, beta, gamma, pi, kappa, omikron, vau, upsilon, tau, lambda, epsilon, heta, rho, sigma. Westphal's interpretation, according to which notes an octave apart are regularly designated by adjacent letters (cf. Monro, op. cit. 71), depends on some untenable identifications.

[17] Cf. *NG* xiii. 336, s.v. Notation: 'There further exist non-alphabetical letter notations: that is, notations in which an item in the musical order is specified by reference to the position of the letter not in an alphabet but in some other order. Such letters are abbreviations of syllables or words ...'. An Indian example is quoted, in which notes are designated by Sanskrit letters that stand for names of the degrees of the scale.

[18] The triad 10–12 H ⊔ Ꞙ does not, as transmitted, fit this formula, but perhaps originally it was R ɑ Ꝗ. Some distortion has occurred in the triad 37–39.

[19] See pp. 66, 95, 235 n. 42; H. Husmann (as above, n. 12).

[20] This use of the same symbol for the lower movable in all genera is often connected with Archytas' scheme of harmonic ratios, where, contrary to all later reckonings, the lowest interval of the tetrachord is of equal size in each genus (p. 168).

cannot take it for granted that the system in its original conception supplied sharps for all the lower notes from *e'* down to *A* or *G*. But presumably it supplied enough to cater for the current modal scales, and perhaps for some of them to be taken at more than one pitch (on larger or smaller auloi) to suit different voices.

We must suppose that the Argive notation was handed down among professional musicians, perhaps especially auletes, not immune from accretions, yet preserved in its basic substance with great fidelity. Originally it was meant as a means of writing down music generally, not specifically instrumental music. At some later time a need was felt for a less esoteric set of symbols, particularly, perhaps, for the use of vocalists. The triadic structure of the Argive system was taken as given but was concealed by lettering continuously without regard for the distinction between primary and modified notes. Initially, it seems, the new notation was provided just for the common singing octave *f'*–*f*.[21] In a subsequent systematization it was made coextensive with the older notation, although this meant providing 'vocal' symbols for notes deeper than any normally sung. After that both notations were extended in parallel.

The vocal notation probably dates from the late fifth or the fourth century BC. The Ionic alphabet on which it is based was officially adopted at Athens in 403/2, and had been in widespread unofficial use there for a generation before that. It was also establishing itself in other Greek cities at this period. The actual letter forms used in the notation point to a date before rather than after 300: the square **E**, and the Classical **Σ** and **Ω**.[22]

Rival systems

The first definite reference to the existence of musical notation comes in Aristoxenus.[23] He criticizes people who treat the notation

---

[21] Or perhaps the tenth *a'*–*f*, if the letters A B Γ at first corresponded to the instrumental triad Ͱ Ⅎ N and represented the notes *a' g' f'*, as suggested by J. M. Barbour, *Jour. Am. Musicol. Soc.* 13 (1960), 5f.

[22] The original **Σ** at 31 has given way to the later form **C**, but the reversed form **3** at 7 reveals what it had been (Winnington-Ingram, *Philol.* 122 (1978), 240f.). More problematic is 43 **Z** with its modified form 197, as in the 4th cent. zeta had the shape **Ⅰ**. It is easy to suppose that 43 was modernized in the course of transmission, as 31 was, but it is also necessary to postulate a corresponding alteration of 19, perhaps from Ⅎ; see Winnington-Ingram, loc. cit.

[23] *Harm.* 2. 39–41. It has sometimes been claimed that book-rolls shown being read in musical performances in certain 5th-cent. vase-paintings must be scores: see especially Pöhlmann, *Griechische Musikfragmente*, 10f., 83f. and *Beiträge*, 61–9. But

of melodies as the only aim of harmonic analysis. So far from being
its goal, he protests, it is not even a part of the science. He speaks as if
there was just one notational system. He complains that it merely
indicates intervals without defining functions. For instance, it tells
you that two notes are a fourth apart, but the notation is the same
whether they are the outer notes of a tetrachord (of whatever genus)
or not, and, if they are the outer notes, it is the same whether the
tetrachord is Hyperbolaiōn or Mesōn. There is no agreement among
scholars as to whether Aristoxenus is referring to the system of notation that we know or to some other. In view of our conclusions about
the age of the common system and its general currency from the
third century BC onwards, it would be surprising if Aristoxenus was
unacquainted with it and regarded some other system as the only one
available. Although his criticisms seem somewhat tendentious, I
agree with Macran and Pöhlmann that they can be understood in
relation to the standard system.[24]

We do, nevertheless, know of another system. Aristides Quintilianus, after stating that the ancients (i.e. pre-Aristoxenian theorists) divided the octave into twenty-four quarter-tone steps, appends
a table of note-symbols associated with this division. It covers two
octaves, and appears to be based on the letters of the Ionic alphabet
in their normal order, though some of them have become displaced
in the course of transmission. Each letter provided two symbols, one
of which was the other reversed or inverted. The primary forms
(some of them amputated or otherwise altered in the interests of
reversibility) were assigned to the twenty-four semitone steps contained in the double octave, and the reversed forms to the intervening quarter-tones.[25] The twenty-four quarter-tone steps into which
each octave was divided, therefore, were not treated as all of equal
status, but the twelve semitone steps were. The system differs significantly in this respect from the usual one based on diatonic steps. It

there is no sure ground for supposing them to be more than libretti; see Winnington-
Ingram, *Gnomon* 33 (1961), 693.

[24] H. S. Macran, *The Harmonics of Aristoxenus* (Oxford, 1902), 270–2; Pöhlmann, *Beiträge*, 74–6. For example, the notes Γ Μ (46, 37) represent the outer notes
of the tetrachord Hyperbolaiōn in Hypodorian, and of the tetrachord Mesōn in
Hyperphrygian (or Hypermixolydian, as it was called in Aristoxenus' key-system); or
Paranētē synēmmenōn and Lichanos in diatonic Lydian. See also Barker, *GMW*
ii. 156 n. 46, who takes a different view.

[25] For detailed interpretation see Winnington-Ingram, *Philol.* 117 (1973), 243–9;
M. L. West, *ZPE* 92 (1992), 42–6.

cannot be of great antiquity, but there is no reason to doubt that it is, as Aristides implies, pre-Aristoxenian. It is only in the pre-Aristoxenian period that we hear of harmonic theorists mapping out the octave in quarter-tones.[26] From Aristoxenus onwards, so far as we know, everyone operated with some form of heptatonic Perfect System, and the standard notation had by then probably established itself to the exclusion of all rivals.

Solmization

Although it does not properly belong under the heading of notation, a rudimentary scheme of solmization attested in late sources may best be mentioned here. By solmization is meant the association of degrees of the scale with different syllables for mnemonic or didactic purposes.[27] In the Greek system the syllables repeat in each tetrachord; they do not therefore identify specific degrees of an octave or double octave scale, but only the position of a note in its local interval-sequence. The notes of the disjunctive tone (Proslambanomenos to Hypatē hypatōn, or Mesē to Paramesē) are designated tĕ ta; other standing notes are ta; and the movable notes in any tetrachord are (rising) tē tō. The Unmodulating System is thus solmized as illustrated in Fig. 9.3. Aristides Quintilianus, who is our main source for the scheme, explains it in terms of a sexual classification of vowel sounds, according to which o is masculine, ĕ/ē feminine, and a intermediate. He finds these qualities in the corresponding notes of the tetrachord. It is uncertain how old this idea is, and whether the solmization scheme originally had any such associations.[28]

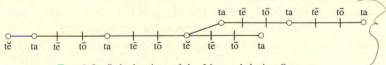

FIG. 9.3. Solmization of the Unmodulating System

---

[26] Cf. p. 225.

[27] See *NG* xvii. 458 ff. for a survey of such systems in European and oriental musics; the ancient Greek system is recorded on p. 466.

[28] Aristid. Quint. pp. 77. 30–81. 6, cf. above, p. 247 n. 81, and Barker, *GMW* ii. 479 ff. with notes; Anon. Bellerm. 9–10, 77, 86, 91, who gives *tō* for Proslambanomenos, and represents the diatonic intervals from Proslambanomenos to Mesē as *tō–a, ta–e, tē–ō, tō–a, ta–e, tē–ō, tō–ĕ*. For A. Bélis's proposal to recognize the solmization syllables in the representation of a trumpet signal on an early Classical painting see p. 120 n. 184.

Rhythmic and articulatory notation

We saw in Chapter 5 that Greek music for the most part used only two different note values, monoseme and diseme, while certain rhythms also made use of trisemes. Not until the second century AD (p. 202) do we find a wider range of possibilities in common use. The need for a multiplicity of rhythmic symbols was accordingly limited. The Anonymus Bellermanni (1, 3, 83) lists the following:

- _ 'two-time long' (diseme)
- ∟ 'three-time long' (triseme)
- ⊔ 'four-time long' (tetraseme)
- ⊔⊔ 'five-time long' (pentaseme).

In the musical documents the diseme symbol occurs frequently, written above (or occasionally just to the right of) vocal or instrumental notes. In vocal texts, however, diseme notes are often unmarked as such, their rhythmic value being left to be inferred from the metre of the words. The triseme symbol is found in one or two papyri and one inscription, but generally in the form ─╱.[29] The tetraseme and pentaseme signs are not attested outside the Anonymus; in the Berlin Paean (**40**), where the tempo is slow and long syllables are set to the shorter note-values and double-length longs to the longer ones, diseme signs are used for the latter. No sign for monosemes is attested, though in non-musical verse texts the metrical long-sign ─ had a short counterpart ∪, and presumably this might have been used if need arose.

The duration of a long note could be made up from a shorter note plus a rest. A monoseme rest, called a *leimma*,[30] was denoted by the initial letter of that word, Λ, sometimes given a peculiar rounded shape, ⌒. A diseme rest was denoted by the same sign surmounted by the diseme symbol, Λ̄ or ⌒̄.[31] Besides being used to mark actual pauses, rests are sometimes written to show that the following note is delayed, in other words that the preceding note is prolonged. For

---

[29] **8** *PVindob.* G 29825(c) 2; **15** Seikilos epitaph. For other papyri see Pöhlmann, *DAM* 125, 138; M. W. Haslam in *The Oxyrhynchus Papyri* xliv (1976), 60, n. on fr. 4.3. One of the unpublished Hellenistic fragments appears to have the form ∟.

[30] Aristid. Quint. p. 38. 29, defined as 'minimum empty time'. Anon. Bellerm. 102 calls it a 'short empty (time)' (*kenos brachys*).

[31] Aristides loc. cit. calls this *prosthesis*; Anon. Bellerm. calls it a 'long empty', and adds a 'triple long empty' (Λ̠) and 'quadruple long empty' (Λ̈). Cf. Quint. *Inst.* 9. 4. 51.

example, in Mesomedes, *Hymn to Nemesis* 3, the word *thnātōn* has over it the notes **ΕΛⴜ**. The pitch-symbols **Ε ⴜ** are understood as having diseme value, because the word consists of two long syllables; the addition of the *leimma* makes the first one into a triseme. Similarly in **29** *POxy.* 2436 ii 6,

Ī Λ ⴜ Ζ Ι

pyrsos eti = ♩. ♪♪♪.

   In the Hellenistic documents, when a long syllable is divided between two notes, the note symbols are simply written above it, and the vowel of the syllable is written double to indicate its resolution into two parts.[32] In post-Hellenistic texts this doubling disappears except in a few special cases.[33] Instead we normally find some graphical indication that the notes above the syllable belong closely together. This most often takes the form of a slur[34] under the notes, e.g. **ΑⅠ**. There may be a diseme sign over them too. Alternatively, or in addition, they are preceded by a double point, **:ΑⅠ**.[35] Where a syllable is sung to three notes, the double point and diseme show that the notes form a group with diseme value, and the slur usually links the second and third notes, showing that they are more closely connected; so in the Berlin Paean, **:ⴜϴⴜ**, **:ΑⴜΖ**, etc. This pattern is interpreted as the rhythm ♪♪♪ or ♩ ♫. Other rhythmic configurations can be expressed by including a *leimma*. This, bracketed to the following note-symbol, indicates the division of the time-unit between a prolongation of the preceding note and the succeeding

---

[32] The diphthongs *ai*, *au*, *eu* are in this case written *aei* or *aiei*, *aou*, *eou*; but *ei*, *oi*, *ou* become *eiei*, *oioi* (once *oei* or *oiei*), *ouou*. When the vowel is a short one, the syllable is almost always closed by a liquid or nasal consonant, which must have been sung on the second note. For example, **ᐸᅟ ⊔ᅟ** (**13** Limenius 18) would have been *aambrotan* sung ♪♪♪ ♩.
a - m - bro · tān

[33] The exceptions occur among the instances noted on p. 203 where one syllable of a name is prolonged to twice its natural length: *Aiian* in the Berlin papyrus, *Taantalos* and *Dēēidameia* in the Oslo papyrus.

[34] In Greek: *hyphen*. Cf. Anon. Bellerm. 4, 86 f. The same sign was sometimes used in literary texts at the junctures of compound words, to confirm to the reader that the two elements of the compound were not separate words but formed a unity.

[35] The double point too occurs as a lectional sign in literary texts. It is a mark of separation, used in particular to signal a change of speaker in dialogue. In early inscriptions it serves as a simple word-divider.

one. Thus : $\overline{A}U\cap Z$ = ♩ ♩. ♪ (spondaic tempo), $\overline{\Xi}\cap\Phi$ = ♩ ♫ (spondaic tempo), : I′K′∩I′ = ♪♩ ♪.

In instrumental music a time-unit might occasionally be divided between two notes of equal pitch (♬ for ♪). This was called *kompismós*, and indicated by writing the note symbols with the sign ⊥ between them. There are three instances in the Berlin instrumental pieces, and the device is recorded in the Anonymus Bellermanni together with similar ones called *melismos* and *teretismos*, which apparently represented the division of ♩ into ♫ and ♬ respectively.[36] In the manuscripts of the Anonymus the *kompismos* symbol appears as ⊥, the *melismos* symbol as X or ϗ or ✕ or ⵔ or ϛ. *Teretismos* is notated with a combination of the two, e.g. F+F✕F. In two of the three examples in the Berlin papyrus the group of symbols is followed by the double point, < ⊥ <:. This evidently serves, as in the usage described above, to draw attention to the connectedness of the group by marking it off from its surroundings; but it is surprising that the double point is placed after and not before the group. A double point appears twice elsewhere in the second Berlin piece, once preceding a compound rhythmic figure (:Ⴀ∖∩ϗ = ♩. ♩), and once for no reason that we can discern, but presumably indicating something about the phrasing.

Another symbol of frequent occurrence is the single point (*stigmē*) added above or just to the right of note-signs (and above any diseme or triseme symbol). This marks the arsis or up-beat, as the Anonymus states: 'The thesis is indicated when there is simply the note-symbol without the point, and the arsis when it has the point.'[37] Where the arsis embraces two or three notes, each of them commonly has the *stigmē*, but sometimes only one of them has it. Some texts, such as the Delphic Paeans, have no pointing, and in others it is sporadic. Sometimes it is difficult to make sense of, and seems to have become confused. A mere point was especially vulnerable to faults of transmission: it was easily overlooked, and on the other hand it was possible for a stray spot of ink, or of some alien substance, to be mistaken for a *stigmē*.[38]

[36] Cf. p. 204. The Anonymus renders the effects in solmization code as follows: (*kompismos*) *tōntō*, *tanta*; (*melismos*) *tōnnō*, *tanna*; (*teretismos*) *tōntōnnō*.

[37] Anon. Bellerm. 3 = 85.

[38] For detailed remarks on the pointing and other rhythmical notation in texts known up to 1955 see Winnington-Ingram, *Symb. Osl.* 31 (1955), 35–42, 73–87;

The Anonymus refers also to the *diastolē*, used both in vocal and in instrumental music as a mark of punctuation, separating what precedes from what follows.[39] The manuscripts of the treatise give its shape as /: · or : · or :. The use of the double point has already been described. But in the papyri we find symbols of other forms being used in a more definitely separative function, and the name *diastolē* would be properly applied to them. The *Orestes* papyrus and other Hellenistic fragments in the Vienna collection (**3**, **8**) have the sign ⌐ in the poetic text,[40] in some cases followed by instrumental notes which are thus marked off as something separate from the text— though in the *Orestes* fragment there are also single instrumental notes in the text which are not so introduced. In one of the Vienna fragments a new section at which the music modulates is marked off by a large χ in the text, with the direction *phrygisti* ('Phrygian mode/key') written above it. In several of the later papyri a simple oblique stroke occurs here and there in the row of vocal notes.[41] Its purpose appears to be to mark breaks of continuity due to major sense-pause, change of voice (in dialogue), end of a section, etc. In one of these fragments the end of a section or of a piece is celebrated by an ornamental)⌐ both in the notation line and in the text.[42]

Development and diffusion of notation

The first Greek musical notation of which we have any knowledge appears to have been invented sometime before 450 BC in the north-east Peloponnese, a region associated at that time with some of the most active advances in musical theory and technique. The notation was preserved among musicians, perhaps especially auletes, and in time achieved wider geographical diffusion. We may guess, for instance, that it was taken up at Thebes, a city famous for its tradition of aulos playing. In the late fifth or the fourth century a less esoteric version of the system was produced for singers' use, employing the Ionic alphabet but basically following the principles of the older

also id. in *The Oxyrhynchus Papyri* xxv (1959), 113 ff.; Pöhlmann, *Griechische Musikfragmente*, 40–8, and *DAM* on individual pieces; M. W. Haslam in *The Oxyrhynchus Papyri* xliv (1976), 63–5, 70–2, and liii (1986), 46 f.

[39] Anon. Bellerm. 11 = 93.

[40] It seems to be an enlarged version of the *diastolē* ⌐ or *hypodiastolē* ⌐ used in literary texts to clarify ambiguities of word division.

[41] **32** *PMichigan* 2958; **45–46** *POxy.* 3161; perhaps **34** *POxy.* 3704. Four of the unpublished Oxyrhynchus papyri exhibit a number of diagonal streaks, starting below the line of notes. Their significance is so far obscure.

[42] **46** *POxy.* 3161 fr. 3 verso 4.

scheme, which now became specialized in function as the notation used for instrumental music. The two notations circulated in conjunction, and extensions to cover a wider compass were applied to both together. Some refinements of the rhythmic and articulatory notation seem on present evidence to have been devised later than 100 BC: the *hyphen* and double point, the *kompismos* and *melismos* signs, and possibly the *leimma*. There was also a change, after 100 BC, in the convention regarding successive syllables sung to the same note; again it was a change in the direction of greater explicitness. But in all their basic essentials the notations were well established by the mid-third century BC at the latest. They were in use by that date in Egypt and, by implication, over most of the Greek world.

It is doubtful, however, whether they were understood by many non-professionals. They were by no means necessary for the propagation of music. From time immemorial people learned songs simply by hearing them. Poet-composers taught choruses by singing to them. By the fifth century it may be that copies of the words were provided to assist the learning process, but as for the melodies, much the easiest way to pick them up was aurally, and few would have been helped by note-symbols. Plutarch relates an anecdote about Euripides singing an ode in front of his chorus to teach it to them, and reproving one of them for laughing at his enharmonic Mixolydian.[43]

Having learned it, they would very likely remember it all their lives, and if a tragedy was revived within a generation or so, there would be people available—not only the original choreuts—who could recall the music. So it was perfectly possible for the music of popular plays to be preserved orally for half a century or more before being committed to writing. The fragments of music to Euripidean plays that have survived are from two of his popular melodramas, *Orestes* and *Iphigeneia at Aulis*.[44] There is no reason to doubt that it is the original music, but it is not necessary to assume that it was transmitted *in writing* from before 400 BC. It is important to remember that lyric and dramatic texts were normally copied without music. The fragments with notes are exceptional, and re-

---

[43] Plut. *De audiendo* 46 b. Cf. C. J. Herington, *Poetry into Drama* (Berkeley and LA, 1985), 43–5.

[44] *Orestes* was his most popular play. We know that there was a performance of it in 340 BC, and of one of his *Iphigeneia*s (we do not know which) in the previous year.

present excerpts made by or for musicians, not complete texts of the plays in question.

Again, when writers such as Glaucus of Rhegium or Aristoxenus make observations about the music of Olympus, Terpander, Sappho, Stesichorus, etc., we should not imagine that there was a written tradition of this music. There was a tradition, but it was oral. In the fourth century there were still many opportunities of hearing older songs and instrumental tunes, just as today most Englishmen, whether or not they can read music, and irrespective of interest in 'classical' music, are familiar with *Greensleeves, God Save the King/ Queen, Rule Britannia, Clementine,* and dozens of other songs that are at least a century old.

Aristoxenus, as we have seen, regards the notation of music as unimportant, something practised by 'the so-called *harmonikoi*' either from simple incomprehension of the true aims of harmonic science or as a concession to laymen, to give them something visible to grasp.[45] He might have made some use of notation in giving examples of intervals, as is done in some of the late treatises, but he nowhere does so. He also mentions the existence of metrical notation, and takes a similarly scornful view of its significance for theoretical inquiry.

Given that the man who can notate the iambic metre does not necessarily know what the iambic is, and likewise with melody, the man who writes out the notes of the Phrygian melody does not necessarily know what the Phrygian melody is, obviously notation cannot be the goal of the science in question.[46]

At a later period there is some evidence for rhythmic and melodic notation as (separate) subjects studied in Ionian high schools. An inscription from Teos honouring prizewinners lists *rhythmographiā* and *melographiā* among other musical and literary accomplishments, and *melographiā* also appears on a similar list from Magnesia on the Maeander.[47] Whether these were compulsory subjects we cannot tell. But these inscriptions do show that in the high Hellenistic age, at least in Ionia, a knowledge of musical notation could be

[45] *Harm.* 2. 39–40.   [46] *Harm.* 2. 39.
[47] C. Michel, *Recueil d'inscriptions grecques* (Brussels, 1900), no. 913 = *CIG* 3088 (*c.*200 BC); *SIG* 960 (2nd c. BC); differently interpreted by H. I. Marrou, *Ant. Class.* 15 (1946), 289–96. The word for instrumental notation is *kroumatographiā* (Anon. Bellerm. 11 = 93).

considered to have a place in general education, as the practice of music had always had. The occasional publication of song texts on stone, notes and all, might suggest that some passers-by, at least, could be expected to be able to read the melody. And the number of papyri with musical notes, though very small in comparison with the number of lyric and dramatic papyri without notes, is now more than a handful, and it continues to grow.

It remains nevertheless unlikely that reading music was an attainment of more than a small minority. When Dionysius of Halicarnassus decides to illustrate from Euripides the absence of correspondence between musical and speech melody, he cites the first bit of song in the most often performed of tragedies, *Orestes*: it was surely from hearing it in the theatre that he was able to refer to it, not from consulting a score. He describes the relationship of the melody to the word accents laboriously in terms of higher, lower, or equal pitches. It would have been shorter and more precise to use musical notation if he had understood it and been able to count on his readers' understanding it.[48] Quintilian advises that the budding orator should study music, but that he will not have time to go into it so thoroughly as to learn to sing from a score.[49] The humorous epigrammatist Lucillius compares a boxer's manifold scars to the 'oblique and upright Lydian and Phrygian letters of the lyricists'; musical notation is here conceived as a peculiar form of writing, familiar in general appearance but to most people indecipherable.[50]

Of the later writers on music, Cleonides, Theon of Smyrna, Ptolemy, Porphyry, and Nicomachus make no use of notation, whereas Aristides Quintilianus, Gaudentius, Alypius, Bacchius, and the Anonymus Bellermanni all do; most of them set out tables of the notes belonging to each key, though these have largely fallen away in the manuscript tradition. This latter group of writers are perhaps all later in date than the former group, and it looks as if a new fashion set in, in the third century, for including in harmonic and other musical treatises the notation tables which had previously enjoyed a more limited, independent circulation.[51]

Gaudentius speaks of the notation as something used by the

---

[48] *Comp.* 63f.   [49] *Inst.* 1. 10. 1–33; 1. 12. 14.

[50] *Anth. Pal.* 11. 78 (generally mispunctuated).

[51] They were apparently known as *Tropika* i.e. tables of *tropoi* (= *tonoi*, keys): 'Marius Victorinus' (Aphthonius) *Gramm. Lat.* vi. 183. 23. The earliest reference to them is in Varro, fr. 282 p. 304 Funaioli. He mentions that the Hyperlydian key was shown at the top and the Hypodorian at the bottom.

ancients, convenient as a means of indicating particular notes, but—
so his language seems to imply—no longer in general currency.[52] We
cannot date Gaudentius closely, but he probably belongs to the
fourth or fifth century. The latest papyri with notation so far known,
POxy. 1786 and 3161, are assigned to the latter part of the third
century. Synesius, who knew how to sing Mesomedes' compositions
to the lyre about 400, was presumably taught them (in Alexandria?)
on the basis of the book tradition.[53] Martianus Capella still equips
his Muses with scores,[54] and academic knowledge of notation was
perpetuated by the technical literature. It was this tradition that
preserved some of Mesomedes' music into the Middle Ages.[55] But
among practising musicians it looks as if the notations virtually
ceased to be used by about the fourth century.

ABSOLUTE PITCH

This seems the most convenient place to deal with the problem of
correlating the ancient notation with absolute pitch-levels.

One's first instinct is to question whether there can have been any
fixed correlation. The ancients, after all, were not blessed with tuning
forks, and their lyre strings would not have stayed in tune for long
even if they had left them taut between performances. On the other
hand they did have pitch pipes, and countless other pipes whose
register was more or less constant and which could serve to maintain
a pitch standard. Xenophon describes a young singer at a symposium tuning his lyre to the girl piper's aulos before beginning.[56]
The decisive fact is that the notation system, with its elaborate array
of keys, itself presupposes a fixed standard of pitch. Otherwise there
would be no reason to choose one key rather than another for a given
piece of music, and far fewer symbols would be needed. This complicated system with its postulate of fixed pitch was not only
invented, it was adopted and operated, to the exclusion of other
systems, for several hundred years. It was operated, so far as we can
see, with impressive consistency, so that again and again we find
different pieces of music settled in the same pitch range or close to it.

---

[52] Gaud. pp. 347. 11, 349. 8, 15, 23, 350. 9, 11, followed by Boeth. *Inst. Mus.* 4. 3.
[53] Synes. *Epist.* 95.
[54] Mart. Cap. 2. 138. He shows some knowledge of notation also at 9. 943.
[55] Besides the writings already mentioned we should advert to the enigmatic note-
table entitled 'the *Common Hormasia*, transferred from the *Art of Music*' (Pöhlmann,
DAM 32–5). [56] *Symp.* 3. 1.

Of course it is unlikely that a specific standard was maintained everywhere at all times without error; but any fluctuation seems to have been small.

We have some thirty-four vocal pieces for which we can make an assessment of the range on the notation-scale within which the melody disported itself. In six the compass is less than a seventh, so far as can be seen from the notes preserved; it may of course really have been wider in some cases. In twenty-two pieces it is between a seventh and a ninth. In one it is a tenth, and in the remaining five it is an eleventh or a twelfth. There seems a clear division between the second and last groups, the latter being presumably compositions for professional vocalists (as is clearly the case with two of them, the Delphic paeans **12–13**).

We will leave aside the first group, which afford little basis for inference, and consider the second, the twenty-two pieces with a compass of between a seventh and a ninth. Figure 9.4 shows how they

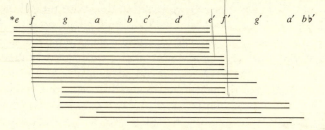

lie, if we give the notation symbols their conventional equivalents, M = *c′ etc.[57] It is apparent to the eye that the preponderant block of melodies occupies the octave *f–*f′. This is precisely the octave covered by the original alphabet in the vocal notation, and it is also the octave specified by Ptolemy as the most generally convenient for singing.[58] We must bear in mind that the ancients did not formally distinguish between tenor, baritone, and bass voices; in choral music all had to sing the same notes. This octave, then, must be identified

[57] It will be recalled that these equivalents were not chosen to represent a hypothetical absolute pitch, but merely to match the sequence of tones and semitones in the diatonic scale built into the notation system. In what follows, to avoid any confusion, I bestow an asterisk on these conventional equivalents to distinguish them from the real pitches we are now trying to establish.

[58] *Harm.* 2.11, 'to allow the voice to move about and exercise itself comfortably upon melodies of middling compass, for the most part, going out only infrequently to the extremes because of the hard work and force involved in slackening or tension that goes beyond the norm' (trans. Barker, *GMW* ii. 338).

with one particularly convenient for the baritone (the commonest male voice in nature) but also manageable by others: somewhere about *d–d'* or *e–e'*. Another group of melodies, perhaps set for a tenor soloist, avoids the lowest note of this common octave but goes a tone or two higher. The highest low note that a tenor might have difficulty with is perhaps *d*.

Let us now add the evidence of the five pieces that have a wider compass, spanning an eleventh or twelfth (Fig. 9.5). Again the main

*d	e	f	g	a	b	c'	d'	e'	f'	g'	a'	b'	c"

singing zone is located between *e and *g'. Some of the pieces go a little lower, though *d occurs (so far as present evidence goes) only in momentary dives from a higher register, and indeed the same is largely true of *e except in **30** *POsl.* 1413. 1–15. So it looks as if these notes were felt to be too deep for a melodic track, and more suitable for occasional dramatic effect. At the upper end some singers at least are quite happy to maintain a melodic line centred on *g', rising sometimes to *a' and sporadically higher. The highest certainly attested note is *c" in **34**(b) and **49**, evidently pieces for tenor.[59] If this is the top tenor note, it should be close to *a'*.

Support for these conclusions may be drawn from definitions of the regions of the voice given by the Anonymus Bellermanni:

Hypatoeidēs (low)	*c–*b♭
Mesoeidēs (middle)	*g–*f '
Nētoeidēs (high)	*d'–*c"
Hyperboloeidēs (overshoot)	Anything higher.

The fourth region must be that of boys' and women's voices, included for the sake of completeness but not deemed worthy of closer specification. The three regions of the man's voice cover the two octaves *c–*c", corresponding closely to the range attested in our fragments.[60] This is best equated with *A–a'*, the range from the

---

[59] **14**, not included in the diagrams because uncertainties of reading and the very fragmentary nature of the text preclude conclusions about its tonal range, went up at least to *b♭' and possibly to *c♯". I leave aside **42** with its exceptional register *b'–*f♯", clearly for a female voice.

[60] Anon. Bellerm. 63–4. For two octaves as the range of the voice cf. Nicom. p. 255. 25, Aristid. Quint. p. 21. 14, Gaud. p. 359. 5.

baritone's lowest note to the tenor's highest. The three overlapping registers identified by the Anonymus will then be *A–g, e–d', b–a'*. A bass could of course go a little lower. But the indications are that the Greeks esteemed high notes more than low ones. In Chapter 2 we saw evidence that a clear, full vocal tone, associated with higher rather than lower notes, was most admired, and that notes high enough to be taxing were employed.[61] For much of the Middle Ages high singing was favoured.

The evidence is as consistent as we could wish. We must conclude—as indeed scholars concluded long ago, though from a more limited body of material[62]—that the conventional note-equivalents, as given in the chart on p. 256, are too high by about a minor third. The differential might conceivably be larger by up to a tone, but it can hardly be smaller.

[61] pp. 42, 46. Cf. Isid. *Orig.* 3. 20. 14, 'the perfect voice is high, sweet, and loud: high, to be equal to the top notes; loud, to fill the ears; sweet, to soothe the listeners' spirits'.

[62] F. Bellermann, *Anonymi Scriptio de Musica* (Berlin, 1841), 3–16, and *Die Tonleitern und Musiknoten der Griechen*, 54–6; R. Westphal, *Griechische Rhythmik und Harmonik* (2nd edn., Leipzig, 1867), 367–76.

10

The Musical Documents

We come now to the musical documents themselves. First I will present a catalogue of the specimens of Greek music so far known, however fragmentary. It is arranged as far as possible chronologically. References are provided to Pöhlmann's *Denkmäler altgriechischer Musik* and to other selected secondary literature, especially to publications containing photographs of the originals. The catalogue is followed by transcriptions of most of the pieces, with Greek texts transliterated and translated and with observations on the music. The items asterisked in the catalogue are those treated more fully in the transcription section.

CATALOGUE

Classical period

1 Clay epinetron (knee-guard for sewing) with black-figure painting by the Sappho Painter showing a trumpeting Amazon and the syllables TOTĒ TOTOTE apparently representing the notes sounded. Eleusis Museum 907, early 5th c.

    A. Bélis, *BCH* 108 (1984), 99–109. Cf. above, p. 120.

2 Euripides, *Orestes* 140–207. We have scraps of information on the music of this lyric dialogue from two sources: (i) Dionysius of Halicarnassus, *Comp.* 63f., makes a number of statements on the relative pitches of syllables in lines 140–2, which must apply also to the corresponding words in the antistrophe at 153–5. (ii) The scholiast on line 176 says 'this song is sung on the top notes and is very high'. The singers were men playing female roles.

    M. L. West, *Euripides, Orestes* (Warmington, 1987), 191.

3* Euripides, *Orestes* 338–44: fragmentary score in Vienna papyrus G 2315 (Rainer inv. 8029), copied *c.* 200 BC. The same music must be assumed for the corresponding words of the strophe, 322–8.

Pöhlmann, *DAM* no. 21 with bibliography; J. F. Mountford in J. U. Powell and E. A. Barber (ed.), *New Chapters in the History of Greek Literature*, 2nd ser. (Oxford, 1929), 149–69; Winnington-Ingram, *Mode*, 31f.; D. D. Feaver, *AJPhil.* 81 (1960), 1–15; L. Richter, *Deutsches Jahrbuch der Musikwissenschaft* 16 (1971), 111–49; G. Marzi, *Scritti in onore di Luigi Ronga* (Milan, 1973), 315–29; J. Solomon, *GRBS* 18 (1977), 71–83; Chailley, 148–53; M. L. West, *Euripides, Orestes*, 203f. and *ZPE* 92 (1992), 1. Photos: *Wien. Stud.* 75 (1962), facing p. 76; *Deutsches Jahrbuch der Musikwissenschaft* 16 (1971), 123; E. G. Turner, *Greek Manuscripts of the Ancient World* (Oxford, 1971, ²1987), 71; *Scritti in onore di Luigi Ronga*, facing pp. 316, 326 (enlarged detail); *GRBS* 18 (1977), facing p. 81; *MGG* xvi (1979), facing p. 642; *NG* vi. 295; Pöhlmann, *Beiträge*, 206.

4*, 5 Euripides, *Iphigeneia in Aulis* 784–92 and 1499(?)–1509: fragmentary scores in Leiden papyrus inv. 510, copied in the 3rd c. BC (excerpts; 1499(?)–1509 precedes 784–92; only in the latter passage can any of the notes be made out). The play was first produced in 405, a year after the poet's death in Macedon, by his son, Euripides the younger, so it may be that it fell to the latter to compose the music.

D. Jourdan-Hemmerdinger, *Comptes rendus de l'Académie des Inscriptions et Belles-lettres* (1973), 292–302, and *Les Sources en musicologie* (1981), 35–65; G. Comotti, *Museum Philologicum Londiniense* 2 (1977), 69–84, and *Music in Greek and Roman Culture* (Baltimore, Md., 1989), 110f.; T. J. Mathiesen, *Acta Musicologica* 53 (1981), 23–32; A. van Akkeren, *Hermeneus* 55 (1983), 259ff.; M. K. Černý, *Listy filologické* 109 (1986), 132–40. Photos: Jourdan-Hemmerdinger, opp. citt.; *Papyrologica Lugduno-Batava* 19 (1978), pl. ɪ; Mathiesen, art. cit. 24; Černý, art. cit. after p. 192.

Late Classical or Hellenistic period

6(a–b) Two very small fragments of vocal notation, apparently from examples in a treatise: *PHib.* 231, copied in the mid-3rd c. BC.

E. G. Turner, *The Hibeh Papyri*, ii (1955), 152; Pack no. 2445; M. L. West, *ZPE* 92 (1992), 2–4.

7* Fragment from a tragedy (?): Zenon papyrus 59533, copied in the mid-3rd c. BC.

Pöhlmann, *DAM* no. 35 with bibliography; Pack no. 1916; *Trag. Adesp.* 678 Kannicht–Snell (text only); J. F. Mountford in J. U. Powell (ed.), *New Chapters in the History of Greek Literature*, 3rd series (Oxford, 1933), 260f.; Winnington-Ingram, *Mode*, 32; Chailley 144f. Photos: *JHS* 51 (1931), pl. v; C. C. Edgar, *Zenon Papyri*, iv (Cairo, 1931), pl. ɪɪ; C. Del

Grande, *La metrica greca* (*Enciclopedia classica*, v, Turin, 1960), 442; *MGG* xvi (1979), facing p. 642; Pöhlmann, *Beiträge* 206.

8(a–f) Fragments from tragic and satyric drama (?): Vienna papyrus G 29825 a–f, copied *c.* 200 BC (found with **3**). It is uncertain how many different pieces of composition are represented.

Pöhlmann, *DAM* nos. 22–7; Pack no. 2441; *Trag. Adesp.* 679 (text only); H. Hunger and E. Pöhlmann, *Wien. Stud.* 75 (1962), 51–78 with photos; Chailley, 146–8. Photos of frs. a–b also in *MGG* xvi (1979), facing p. 639; Pöhlmann, *Beiträge*, 205.

9 Fragments of vocal music with instrumental interludes: Vienna papyri G 13763 and 1494, copied *c.* 200 BC.

Pöhlmann, *Hermes* 94 (1966), 501–4, *DAM* nos. 28–29. Photo: *DAM*, Abb. 24.

10 Fragments of poetic text, parts of which are provided with vocal notation: *POxy.* inv. 89B/29–33, copied 3rd–2nd c. BC. Publication in preparation.

11* Fragment of hexameter hymn to Asclepius with notation for first line only: inscription from precinct of Asclepius at Epidaurus, *SEG* 30.390. Inscribed about the late 3rd c. AD, but the composition, like several others from this site inscribed at the same period, may be many centuries older.

M. T. Mitsos, Ἀρχ. Ἐφ. (1980), 212–16 (photo); J. Solomon, *JHS* 105 (1985), 168–71 (drawing); M. L. West, *ZPE* 63 (1986), 39–46 (drawing).

Later Hellenistic period

12* Athenaeus, Paean: substantial fragments of a choral work performed at Delphi in 127 BC by the Athenian *Technītai*, a company of professional musicians, and inscribed on an external wall of the Athenian Treasury at Delphi. Delphi Museum, inv. 517, 526, 494, 499.

Pöhlmann, *DAM* no. 19 with bibliography, and *Griechische Musikfragmente* 59–71; Winnington-Ingram, *Mode*, 33–5; Chailley, 154–8; A. Bélis in Gentili–Pretagostini, 205–18 (identifies the composer's name and fixes the date); *Nouveau corpus des inscriptions de Delphes* (forthcoming). Photos: *DAM*, Abb. 17, 18, 22; Bélis, art. cit. 208, 211.

13* Limenius, Paean and processional: substantial fragments of a work similar to **12**, performed on the same occasion and inscribed beside it. Delphi Museum, inv. 489, 1461, 1591, 209, 212, 226, 225, 224, 215, 214.

Pöhlmann, *DAM* no. 20 with bibliography, and *Griechische Musikfragmente* 59–71; Winnington-Ingram, *Mode*, 35–8; Chailley, 159–66. Photos: *DAM*, Abb. 19–22; Bélis, art. cit. 209.

14 Fragments of a vocal text or texts: inscribed blocks from a sanctuary of the Carian deity Sinuri near Mylasa, probably 1st c. BC. The text extends over many lines, but not a single complete word is preserved.

L. Robert, *Le Sanctuaire de Sinuri près de Mylasa*, i. *Les Inscriptions grecques* (*Mémoires de l'Institut Français d'Archéologie de Stamboul*, vii, Paris, 1945), 104–6 no. 81 and pl. I; M. L. West, *ZPE* 92 (1992), 8–10.

Roman period

15* Song of Seikilos: inscribed stele from Aidin near Tralles (Caria, like **14**). Copenhagen, National Museum, inv. 14897, commonly dated to the 1st c. AD.

Pöhlmann, *DAM* no. 18 with bibliography; C. Sachs, *Musik des Altertums* (Breslau, 1924), 62–6 and *WM* 58; Chailley, 166–9; J. Solomon, *AJPhil.* 107 (1986), 455–79. Photos: *MGG* v (1956), 847 f.; *DAM*, Abb. 15/16 and 23; Neubecker pl. VIII (one side only); E. Vogt (ed.), *Griechische Literatur* (*Neues Handbuch der Literaturwissenschaft* 2, Wiesbaden, 1981), 136 (one side only).

16* Invocation of the Muse, transmitted in MSS with songs of Mesomedes, but differing from them in dialect and (it may be felt) in musical style. The MSS give no indication of authorship; the dialect points to Ionian origin.

Pöhlmann, *DAM* no. 1; Winnington-Ingram, *Mode*, 41 f.; Chailley, 172 f. Photos of the MSS: *DAM*, Abb. 5, 7, 8.

17* Mesomedes, invocation of Calliope and Apollo: MS transmission. Mesomedes was a noted citharode and composer of Cretan origin, a courtier of Hadrian.

Pöhlmann, *DAM* no. 2; Winnington-Ingram, *Mode*, 42; Chailley, 173. Photos as for **16**.

18* Mesomedes, hymn to the Sun: MS transmission.

Pöhlmann, *DAM* no. 4; Sachs, *Musik des Altertums*, 60–2; Winnington-Ingram, *Mode*, 42 f.; Chailley, 174 f. Photos: *DAM*, Abb. 5, 7–9; my Pl. 34 (part).

19* Mesomedes, hymn to Nemesis: MS transmission (the music only in one MS).

Pöhlmann, *DAM* no. 5; Sachs, op. cit. 69; Winnington-Ingram, *Mode*, 43; Chailley, 176 f. Photo: *DAM*, Abb. 9; Neubecker, pl. VII; my Pl. 34.

20–22 Three further pieces by Mesomedes, though now transmitted without musical notes, are accompanied by scholia which state the key of the music. In Heitsch's edition they are poems 4 (Lydian), 5 (Hypolydian), and 7 (Lydian). But the accompanying descriptions of the metres do not altogether accord with the metres of the poems; the scholium on 7, at least, seems to have attached itself to the wrong poem, and the same may be true of that on 4. See Pöhlmann, *DAM* pp. 28 f.

23*–28* Six elementary instrumental exercises, preserved in Anon. Bellerm. 97–104.

Pöhlmann, *DAM* nos. 7–12. Photo of the MS: *DAM*, Abb. 12, partially also in Neubecker, pl. VII.

29* Fragment of a satyric drama (?): *POxy.* 2436, copied in the 1st or 2nd c. The poetic text might be old (though satyr-plays were still written in the 2nd cent. AD), but the music is in the later style.

Pöhlmann, *DAM* no. 38; *PMG* 1024 (text only); Pack no. 2440; *Trag. Adesp.* 681 (text only); R. P. Winnington-Ingram (with E. G. Turner), *The Oxyrhynchus Papyri*, xxv (1959), 113–22; Chailley, 178. Photo: E. G. Turner, *Greek Manuscripts of the Ancient World*, 70.

30* Dramatic recitative: Oslo papyrus inv. 1413 fr. *a*, ll. 1–15, and frs. *b–e*, copied in the late 1st or 2nd c. AD.

Pöhlmann, *DAM* no. 36; Pack no. 1706; *Trag. Adesp.* 680a, c (text only); S. Eitrem, L. Amundsen, R. P. Winnington-Ingram, *Symb. Osl.* 31 (1955), 1–87; Chailley, 170 f. Photos: *Symb. Osl.* 31, facing pp. 2–3; Del Grande (as under **7**), 448.

31* Speech from a drama about Philoctetes: same papyrus, fr. *a* 15–19 and frs. *f–m*.

Pöhlmann, *DAM* no. 37; *Trag. Adesp.* 680b, c; other literature as above.

32* Dramatic dialogue on the return of Orestes: Michigan papyrus inv. 2958, ll. 1–18, copied in the 2nd c. AD.

Pöhlmann, *DAM* no. 39; Pack no. 2442; *Trag. Adesp.* 682a (text only, improved); O. M. Pearl, R. P. Winnington-Ingram, *JEg. Arch.* 51 (1965), 179–95 and pl. XIX; Chailley, 179 f.

33 Fragment of obscure content: same papyrus, ll. 20–7.

Pöhlmann, *DAM* no. 40; *Trag. Adesp.* 682b.

34*(a–e) Fragments of obscure content: *POxy.* 3704, copied in the 2nd c. It is not clear whether more than one composition is represented.

M. W. Haslam in *The Oxyrhynchus Papyri*, liii (1986), 41–7 and pl. IV, VI.

35, 36 Fragments of uncertain content: *POxy.* inv. 102/58(c)↓ and 105/31(c), copied in the 2nd c. AD. Publication in preparation.

37–39 Others: *POxy.* inv. 63 6B 63/K(1–3)(b)→, 72.13(g)→, and 100/122(c), copied in the late 2nd or early 3rd c. Publication in preparation.

40* Fragmentary paean: Berlin papyrus inv. 6870, ll. 1–12, copied in the later 2nd or early 3rd c. (on the verso of a document dated to 156 AD).

Pöhlmann, *DAM* no. 30; Pack no. 2439; R. Wagner, *Philol.* 77 (1921), 256–310; J. F. Mountford (as under **3**), 172–4; Winnington-Ingram, *Mode*, 39 f.; G. B. Pighi, *Aegyptus* 23 (1943), 169–243; E. Heitsch, *Die griechischen Dichterfragmente der römischen Kaiserzeit*, i. 168–70 (text only); M. L. West, *ZPE* 92 (1992), 12–14. Photos: *Sitz. Berl.* 1918 pl. IV facing p. 768; *MGG*, V, facing p. 831; my Pl. 35.

41* Fragmentary instrumental piece: same papyrus, ll. 13–15.

Pöhlmann, *DAM* no. 31; Mountford, op. cit. 174 f.; other literature as above.

42* Fragment of a dramatic lament on the death of Ajax: same papyrus, ll. 16–19.

Pöhlmann, *DAM* no. 32; *Trag. Adesp.* 683 a (text only); Mountford, op. cit. 175 f.; Winnington-Ingram, *Mode*, 40 f.; other literature as above.

43* Fragmentary instrumental piece: same papyrus, ll. 20–2.

Pöhlmann, *DAM* no. 33; literature as above.

44* Fragment of dramatic(?) lament: same papyrus, l. 23.

Pöhlmann, *DAM* no. 32 (with 42); *Trag. Adesp.* 683 b.

45*(a–d) Dramatic fragments concerning Thetis and Achilles: *POxy.* 3161 recto, copied in the 3rd c.

M. W. Haslam in *The Oxyrhynchus Papyri*, xliv (1976), 58–66 and pl. VI; *Trag. Adesp.* 684 (text only); T. J. Mathiesen, *Acta Musicologica* 53 (1981), 16–20 with figs. 1–3.

46*(a–c) Fragments of lament involving Persians and Lydians: same papyrus, verso.

Haslam, loc. cit. 66 f. and pl. VII; *Trag. Adesp.* 685.

47 Fragment of uncertain content: *POxy.* 3162, copied in the 3rd c.

Haslam, loc. cit. 67–72 and pl. VII; *Trag. Adesp.* 686 (text only); Mathiesen, art. cit. 20 with fig. 4.

48* Fragment of a tragic(?) verse with four alternative musical settings: *POxy.* 3705, copied in the 3rd c.

5(fragments in all

M. W. Haslam, *The Oxyrhynchus Papyri*, liii (1986), 47f.; A. Bélis, *ZPE* 72 (1988), 53–63.

49, 50 Fragments of uncertain content: *POxy.* inv. 100/81(b) and 100/125(a)↓, copied in the 3rd c. Publication in preparation.

51* Fragmentary Christian hymn: *POxy.* 1786, copied in the later 3rd c.

Pöhlmann, *DAM* no. 34 with bibliography; J. F. Mountford (as under **3**) 176–8; Winnington-Ingram, *Mode*, 44; G. B. Pighi, *Aegyptus* 21 (1941), 189–220; E. J. Wellesz, *CQ* 39 (1945), 34–45 and *A History of Byzantine Music and Hymnography*, 2nd edn. (Oxford, 1962), 152–6; E. Heitsch (as under **40**), i. 159f. (text only). Photo: *The Oxyrhynchus Papyri*, xv (1922), pl. I.

In 1968 it was announced that three marble inscriptions measuring 120 × 60 cm. and bearing vocal and instrumental notation, being part of an unknown drama 'mit monodischer Partitur der Dramenmusik', had been found in the remains of a third-century BC theatre at Dionysopolis (Balchik) in Bulgaria; but nothing further was ever heard of them, and experts on the region have no knowledge of the discovery. The report must be treated as highly suspect.[1]

TRANSCRIPTIONS

Most of the items in the catalogue are in some degree fragmentary. It does not seem worth while to transcribe here those that offer only a very few consecutive notes, unless they are of particular interest for some reason (like **4**); but we cannot afford to be too fastidious in the matter. Beggars may not be choosers.

Where there are gaps in the text or breaks between fragments, this is indicated by a wavy line crossing the stave. In places where notes are lost but the rhythm is known, it is indicated either by headless crotchet- or quaver-tails or by metrical symbols written in the bars. Where on the other hand the pitch of a note is known but not its duration, it appears as a tailless head (•).

In the transliterated Greek texts the tonal accents of the words are given for comparison with the melodic line (cf. p. 199); acute accent = high tone, circumflex = high but falling. All diphthongs and circumflexed vowels are long, and other long vowels are marked as

---

[1] A. Andrejew in R. Pečman (ed.), *Musica Antiqua* (Colloquium Brno, 1967), 153; cf. Neubecker, 153 n. 13. According to J. G. F. Hind in *Arch. Rep.* 30 (1983/4), 74, Dionysopolis 'has produced little that is pre-Roman'.

such. Translations are provided to give the Greekless reader an idea of the text's character and emotional level. Because of the flexibility of Greek word order, however, it is not practicable to match the words of the translations directly to the sequence of notes.

On the choice of pitches for transcription see the Introduction, p. 12.

3 Euripides, *Orestes* 338–44
(Original a tone higher)

ka-to-lo-phȳ-ro-mai, ka-to-lo-phȳ-ro-mai   mā - té-ros haî-ma sâs

hó s'a-na-bac-cheú-ei.   ho mé-gas ól - bos ou   mó-ni-mos en bro-toîs,

a - na de laî-phos hṓs   tis a - ká-tou tho – âs   ti - ná – xās daí-mōn

ka-té-kly-sen dei-nôn   pó-nōn hōs pón-tou lá-brois o-le-thrí-oi –

sin en   kȳ - ma-sin

(I grieve, I grieve—your mother's blood that drives you wild. Great prosperity among mortals is not lasting: upsetting it like the sail of a swift sloop some higher power swamps it in the rough doom-waves of fearful toils, as of the sea.)

There is a dislocation in the text: the words *katolophȳromai katolophȳromai* belong after *anabaccheuei*. Whether the accompanying notes are also transposed is uncertain. This is one reason why I have not inserted the corresponding words from the strophe.

The rhythm is dochmiac (suggesting a briskish tempo), with some variations between strophe and antistrophe, e.g. |◡◡◡−−−| responding with |−−−◡−|. The papyrus has pointing, marking the first and third notes of the measure (in its basic five-note form) as upbeats: ◡̇ − −̇ ◡ −. Several long syllables are divided between two notes.

The music is for male chorus (representing women) with a heterophonic aulos accompaniment. The notes in brackets are the instrumental ones. On their interpretation and the nature of the heterophony see p. 206.

The genus is enharmonic. (So far as the notation goes, it could be chromatic, but we know that enharmonic was characteristic of fifth-century tragedy and chromatic exceptional.) The notes of the *pyknon* are repeatedly played in sequence, rising or falling, sometimes combining in figures with the tone below (cf. p. 194). There are two of these tone + *pyknon* clusters, located a fifth apart. The resulting scale, *d e e↑ f a b b↑ c'*, agrees with the Damonian Dorian *harmoniā* (if completed with *e'*) or the Phrygian (if completed with *d'*).[2] But the notional upper note seems to play little or no role. The music circles in the tone + *pyknon* clusters round the two foci *e* and *a*. Transitions between the clusters seem to coincide with the arsis. As the composition is strophic, there is no correlation of melody and word accent.

---

[2] On these see p. 174. In Aristides Quintilianus' table of these scales the Lydian key-notation is used, and so it is in the Euripides fragment.

4 Euripides, *Iphigeneia in Aulis* 784–92
(Original a semitone higher)

(I pray neither I nor children of my stock may ever have those prospects that the Lydian women rich in gold and the Phrygians' wives will think on as they ply their looms: 'Which man will pull my fine hair to tears and ravish me amid the ruin of my fatherland?')

The readings of many of the notes are very uncertain, but an enharmonic *pyknon e e↑ f* is clearly identifiable. The note-sequence on *tanysās* is like that on *akatou thoas* in **3**. Notes from a higher, conjunct tetrachord (*a*) *a↑ b♭ d′* are plausibly recognized, and there is also a high *f′* which seems to play a role in wide leaps here and there. The general structure of the scale, two conjunct tetrachords with wide intervals at the top, has something in common with the Damonian Mixolydian (p. 175), *e e↑ f g a a↑ b♭ e′*, and might be a variant of it. The notation appears to be Hyperaeolian (an auletic key according to Anon. Bellerm. 28) and Aeolian.

The rhythm is aeolic. As in **3**, some long syllables appear to be divided between notes.

The passage is not strophic, and we might expect a correlation between melody and word accents. But there are several apparent contradictions. The high note on the interrogative pronoun *tis* 'which?' is paralleled in **32** and **45**.

At the end of *polychrȳsoi* there is what I read tentatively as an instrumental note, a low *Bb*. If this is right, it should perhaps sound with the first note of the following bar.

7 Zenon papyrus 59533

]koi tád' he - tá - rōn hi - ké - tin au[

]thi go - ná - tōn e - pi ka - tas - k[í - ōn

(... companions ... suppliant [*fem.*] ... at (your? gods' statues'?) knees shaded (with boughs as carried by suppliants) ...)

The rhythm is dochmiac or perhaps paeonic (in that case 5/8, | − ◡ ◡ ◡ |. There is little agreement of melody and accent, which points to a strophic composition, perhaps a tragic chorus. The lines refer to an emotional appeal by a suppliant or suppliants.

In the surviving bars *a* appears as the focal note, and the music does not go further from it than a minor third above or a major third below. It is based on the diatonic series *f g a bb c↓'* (soft diatonic in the upper tetrachord, *a bb c↓' (d')*, cf. p. 256 n. 8), but there are some chromatic glides in descending motion; see p. 196. The notation-key is Phrygian.

11 Hymn to Asclepius, *SEG* 30. 390
(Original a semitone higher)

As-klē-pi] - ón ā - eí - sō - men

(... let us sing of Asclepius, (who protects) men (from dire diseases together with the lord Paian,) Apollo of the famous bow' (etc.))

Brief as it is, this fragment is of high importance as evidence of the (or at any rate of a) manner in which hexameter texts were set to music. The same melodic scheme evidently served for every line. See p. 209.

The scale, so far as revealed, is a six-note one analysable into two conjunct chromatic tetrachords, $g(g\sharp)\ a\ c'\ c\sharp'\ d'\ f'$. The interval of a falling major third occurs three times, and that of a rising fourth twice, while the little instrumental figure that follows the vocal line presents (if we have it complete) a cadence on a falling fifth that lands on the base-note of the lower tetrachord. There is, as we should expect, no agreement of melody and word accent.

The notation-key is Hypolydian. Vocal notation is used for the instrumental as well as for the sung notes.

12 Athenaeus, Paean

The two Delphic paeans composed in 127 BC by Athenaeus and Limenius are the prize exhibits in our collection. Besides being the longest pieces of ancient music that survive, they are fine examples of a sophisticated style of composition practised by and for professional artists of the high Hellenistic age. We are fortunate to be able to compare two pieces composed at the same time and in the same milieu by different composers, and to see how much they have in common.

Both are in free astrophic form, but fall into clearly marked sections (cf. p. 215). It will be convenient to take them section by section.

[Pro-mó-leth' He-li-] kô - na ba-thý - den-dron haí   lá -[che-te, Di-ó]s

e - [rī]-bró-mou   thý-ga-tres eu - ő - l[e-noi:] mó-le-te, sy-nó-

-mai-mon hí-na Phoî - bon ōi - dâi - si mél - psē - te chrȳ -

-se - o - kó - mãn,   hós a - na di - kó - rym - ba Par – nãs – sí - dos

tâs - de pé - te – rãs   hé-dran' hám' a - ga-kly-taîs   Del – phí - sin

Kas - ta - lí - dos eu – hý -drou   nã̃ - mat' e - pi – nĩ̃ – se - tai,

Del - phón a - na   prô – na man – teî – on e - phé -põn pá- gon.

(Come forth, ye (Muses) that were allotted deep-forested Helicon, loud-booming Zeus' fair-armed daughters: come to celebrate your brother in songs, Phoebus of the golden hair, that over the twin peaks of this crag of Parnassus, accompanied by the famous maidens of Delphi, comes to the waters of the fair-flowing Castalian spring as he attends to the mountain oracle.)

The rhythm is paeonic throughout (see p. 141). At first the melody circles about the tonic *a*, with which it probably started. It rises up to *b* and *c'* (if not further), and several times dips to *f*, omitting *g* in the pentatonic manner. At *melpsēte* the compass widens with a dramatic drop from *a* to *c*. The relationship of this new note is established by the figure *c e f c*, which forms a cadence at *chrȳseokomān*: we now have a complete pentatonic scale, *c e f a b c'*. The next words repeat the *c e f* sequence an octave higher, thus extending the scale up to *e'* and *f'*. It is no accident that this high passage introduces mention of Parnassus with its twin peaks, and that it has two peaks itself. Then successive descending thirds at *Parnāssidos tāsde* bring us back to the tonic *a*. The melody proceeds in the original zone for a few bars, but at *Kastalidos* climbs again, this time diatonically through *d'* to the 'dominant' *e'* and its subordinate *f'*. Progress is mainly stepwise and undulating. At *epinīsetai* comes a plangent modulation, from the *d'* of the disjunct tetrachord *b c' d' e'* into a descending conjunct one, *d' (c') b♭ (a)*; the disturbing *b♭* is fittingly used in the half-cadence, marking a pause that demands a continuation. The last line returns to the familiar note-set $f\,a\,b\,c'$, and reaches a full cadence on e, a fourth below the tonic.

(Lo, famous Attica of the great city is here at prayer, whose home is Athena's invincible ground; and on the sacred altars Hephaestus is burning the thighs of young bulls.)

This passage is situated in the fifth from a up to e' with the semitones on each side. There is much semitonal chromaticism, especially in three-note figures such as $b\,b\flat\,b$, $d'\,e\flat'\,d'$. It contributes effectively to the picture of the flickering altar flames. See pp. 196, 201.

(At the same time Arabian incense-smoke spreads up to heaven, and the clear-braying pipe weaves shimmering tunes into the singing, while the sweet-voiced golden kithara takes its part in the song of praise.)

This has the same character as the preceding passage and forms a single section with it, but the compass now goes down to f. A characteristic five-note pattern of rising and falling semitones appears in the parallel half-cadences at *anakídnatai* and *anamélpetai*, and in the word *aiólois* 'shimmering'. The sentence about the pipe, *ligy–krekei*, is entirely in conjunct motion, gliding along as smoothly as a snake.

ho dé [te‑chnī‑] tôn   pró‑pās   hes‑mós At ‑ thí‑ da la‑chốn   [ag ‑ la ‑ í‑]

zei kly‑tón   paî ‑ da me‑gá ‑ lou [Di‑ós: soí gár é‑po]r' a ‑ kro‑ni‑phê

tón ‑ de pá‑gon, ám[‑broth' hoû]   pâ ‑ si thnā ‑ toîs   pro‑phaí ‑ nei[s ló‑ gi ‑ a,

(The whole company of Artists of Attica glorifies you, the son of mighty Zeus, who granted you this snow-capped crag, where you show forth immortal oracles for all men.)

With a clean octave leap we shake off all chromaticism and return to the pure upper reaches of the scale. This part is mostly confined to the notes $c'\ d'\ e'\ f'$, with e' as the focus. The bb at *thnātois* is a surprising diversion, especially as it contradicts the circumflex accent; a probable conjecture by Reinach replaces $\wedge$ by $\lambda = f'$.

tr]í ‑ po‑da man ‑ teî ‑ on hõs   heî ‑ [les, ech ‑ thrós hón e ‑phr]oú‑

‑rei   drá‑kōn,   hó ‑ te té[‑ kos   Gâs   a ‑ pé ‑ s]tē ‑ sas ai ‑

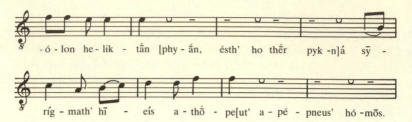

-ó - lon he - lik - tắn [phy - ắn, ésth' ho thếr pyk -n]á sȳ -

ríg - math' hī — eís a - thỗ - pe[ut' a - pé - pneus' hó -mōs.

((We sing) how you took possession of the prophetic tripod that a fearsome serpent guarded, when you removed the earth-born, shimmering, coiling creature, and with charmless hissings it expired.)

Similar to the preceding section but with more recourse to the lower notes. The melodic inflection on *sȳrigmata* 'hissings' is no doubt mimetic, in the tradition of the *Pȳthikos nomos*; cf. pp. 212ff.

Hô -]de Ga - la - tân Á - rēs [bár - ba - ros, tắnd' hós e - pi

gaî - a]n e - pé - rās' a - sép - t[ōs All' i - ỗ gén - nan[

(In this way the Gauls' war-fury, that impiously crossed into this land . . .)

The melody continues to inhabit the high register, and in the *ekkrousmos* on *Galatân* it goes up to *g♭′*. We have not seen this note before, but it occurs again among the increasingly exiguous fragments of the following lines, which are not worth transcribing here.

The total range of the paean is an octave and a half, thirteen different notes being used.[3] The singers were accompanied by aulos and kithara, as the text itself indicates. The principles of melodic respect for the word accents, as described on p. 199, are followed quite carefully. The only breach of them, apart from the doubtful case of *thnātoîs* mentioned above, is at *pheróploio* in the chromatic second section. This does not, of course, mean that the melodic line

---

[3] Or fourteen, if the *b* of the disjunct tetrachord *b c′ d′ e′* is distinguished from the *b* (or *c♭′*) of the conjunct tetrachord *a b♭ b d′*; they are represented by different symbols, as the Greek system requires in the Phrygian key, which is what is used in the notation of this piece.

is mechanically determined by word accents. Far from it. Athenaeus skilfully gives his composition form and variety by shifts of register and of tonal focus, mainly between *a* and *e'*, and by the contrast of chromatic and non-chromatic passages. At the same time he is at pains to set the words to suitably expressive melodic figures and lines.

13 Limenius, Paean and processional
(Original a tone higher)

(Come to this far-visible, twin-peaked Parnassian mountain-side and begin my hymn, Pierian Muses that dwell on the snow-covered crags of Helicon. Sing of the golden-haired Pythian god, the far-shooter with the fine lyre, Phoebus, whom blest Leto bore beside the famous lake, clasping in her labour the grey olive's vigorous stem.)

The opening is pentatonic in character, like that of **12**, mainly on the notes *f a* (tonic) *b c'*, and descending firmly to *e* at the close of the section. Twice there is modulation from disjunct (*b–e'*) to conjunct (*b♭–d'*) tetrachords, both times with the sequence *c' d' b♭ a b♭* (*a*?) *f*. *Dikóryphon* offers the only violation in the paean of the melodic-accentual principles, no doubt for the sake of expressing the idea 'twin-peaked' musically (cf. on **12**).

pâs [dé g]ā́ - thē̄ - se pó - los ou - rá - ni - os   nē̄ - né[-mous
d' és-chen ai - thḗr a-e[l - lôn ta-chy-pe - t]eîs [dr]ó-mous; lê - xe dé ba-
-rýb-ro-mon Nē̄ -[ré - ōs za-me-nés] oîdm'   ē̄ - dé mé-gas Ō̄ - ke-a-nós,
hós pé - rix g[ân hy-graîs an] - ká - lais am - pé - chei.

(The whole vault of heaven rejoiced, the air held the tempests' swift courses in windless calm, and Nereus' thunderous swell abated, and mighty Ocean that surrounds the earth with his watery embrace.)

The melody plunges to *B*, only to leap up again. The emphasis shifts in this section from *a* to *b*, which changes its function from Lydian Paramesē to Hypolydian Nētē diezeugmenōn, so that the scale down from it now runs *a g f♯ e*. There are occasional dives to *B* involving leaps of a fifth, octave, or minor ninth. Cadence on *b*.

tó-te li-pón   Kyn - thí - ān   nâ - son e - p[é - bā   the-ó]s   prō - tó - kar -

-pon kly-tắn   At - thíd' e - pi   gā - l[ó-phōi   prô - ni] Trī - tō - ní-dos.

(Then the god left the island of Mount Cynthus and went to the famed land that first grew cereals, Attica, on the jutting hill of Athena.)

Similar to the preceding section, but with one jump to *e′*. The cadence at *Trītōnídos* echoes that at *ampéchei*.

me - lí -pno -on   dé Lí-bys au - dắn ché-ō[n   lō - tós a - né -

- mel-]pen hā - deî - an ó-pa meig-ný-me-nos ai - ó- l[ois   ki -thá-ri -os

mé - le -sin, há-]ma   d'ī́ - a -chen   pe-tro - ka -toí - kē - tos ā - ch[ṓ

(Pouring forth its honey-breathed voice, the Libyan pipe sang sweetly, blending with the shimmering tunes of the kithara, while Echo who lives among the rocks joined in the holy song.)

The focus shifts to *e*, the bottom note of a conjunct pair of chromatic tetrachords: *e f g♭ a b♭ d′*. The expressive figure on *aiólois* 'shimmering' may well have been identical to that used in the same phrase in **12**.

[hó] dé gé-gāth' hó - ti nó - ōi de - xá - me-nos am - bró-tān

Di - [ós e - pég - nō phré]n'; anth' hôn e - keí - nās ap' ar -

-châs Pai - ḗ - o - na ki-klḗi - sk[o-men há-pās l]ā - ós au - toch-thó-nōn

ḗ - dé Bác - chou mé - gas thyr - so - plḗ[x hes - mós hi] - e -

-rós te-chnī - tôn é - noi - kos pó - lei Ke-kro-pí - āi.

(And he was glad, because his mind took in the immortal thinking of Zeus. Therefore, since that beginning, we call him Paieon, the aboriginal Attic people and Bacchus' great inspired company of Artists that dwells in the city of Cecrops.)

We return to a diatonic scale, $B\,c\,e\,f\sharp\,g\,a\,b\,c'$, with a as the focus. As before, the lowest notes (B, c) appear only transitorily and well separated from their nearest neighbours. Cadence on b with a dramatic octave plunge to B on the final note.

al[- la chrēs -m]ōi -dón hós é - cheis   trí - po - da, baîn' e - pi the -

-os - ti -b[é - a   tấn - de P]ar- nā - sí - ān   dei - rá-da phi- lén- the-on.

(So, thou that possessest the oracular tripod, come to this Parnassian ridge where gods walk, where the inspired are favoured.)

Mostly on *a b c'*, with the low notes used as in the preceding section and a similar cadence.

am - phi plók[a - mon sý d' oi-]   nô - [pa] dáph - nās   klá-don

ple - xá - me - nos ap[am - bró - tāi   chei - rí sý̄ -

-rōn,   á - nax,   G[âs pe - ló - rōi   sy - nan - tâis] kó - rāi.

(Plaiting a bay-stem about thy hair and trailing thy bow(?) in thy immortal hand, lord, . . .)

The focus reverts to *e* and the genus to chromatic, scale *d e f g♭ a b♭ b*. The treatment of the *pykna*, with the flutterings round *e* and *a*, is not far removed from the Classical style seen in **3** and **4**, particularly now that the tone below the lower *pyknon*, *d*, is involved. The section ends on this *d*.

al - la Lā - toûs e - ra - to - g[lé-pha-ron ér - nos a - grí - ā]n   paî - da Gâs

t' é-pe-phnes ī - oîs, ho[-moí - ōs   te Ti-ty - ón hó-ti] pó-thon és - che mā -

- trós [te-âs]   thēr   hā̃ ka-ték - tā - sos[s] ȳ̃ - rigm' ap' e[u - n]ôn[

(But, lovely-eyed son of Leto, thou didst slay the child of Earth with thy
arrows, and likewise Tityos who conceived a desire for thy mother . . . Thou
didst kill the creature . . . hissing from its lair . . .)

The octave leap from *B* to *b* that begins the section is the converse of
the previous closing descents at *Kekropiāi* and *philentheon*. The
emphasis now is on *b*, framed by the adjacent notes *a* and *c'*, with
some use of lower ones, *g*, *e*, and *B* (which is again jumped on from a
great height). On *sȳrigma* cf. the note on **12**.

[eît'] e-phroú - reis   dé Gâ[s   ho bár-] ba - ros Á-rēs   hó - te [te-]ón

man - tó-sy[-non   lē - zó-me-nos ṍ - leth' hyg - râi chi[- ó-nos en   zá-lāi.

(Again thou didst guard the shrine at the earth's navel when the barbarian
war-fury, making to plunder thy oracular seat, perished in wintry storm.)

The melody now goes up into the highest register, soaring in two
notes from the deep *B* to the top *e'*, which becomes the focus. As in
12, the highest note used in the piece, in this case *f'*, makes its
appearance in a passage referring to the Gaulish invasion of Delphi
in 279 BC.

Up to here the rhythm has been uniformly paeonic. For the final section it changes to aeolic (glyconics, with a pherecratean to close). The heading of the piece describes it as a 'paean and processional'. The aeolic portion presumably corresponds to the processional.

(O Phoebus, preserve Pallas' divinely-founded city and glorious people, and thou too, goddess, mistress of Cretan archery and hunting hounds, Artemis, and august Leto. And keep the Delphians secure in house, family, and livelihood. And come in favouring mood for Bacchus' servant musicians; and increase the Romans' spear-crowned rule with age-long power, so that it thrives victorious.)

The music returns to the register and harmonic frame of the opening section: tonic *a* with *b c'* (and intermittently *b♭/d'*) above, *f* and *e* below. In the last two lines *a* is the highest note, and the melody settles down towards *e*; the *d* below makes an appearance to encircle the *e* at *auxet' agēratōi* (*f d d f f e*). The final cadence was probably on *f e*. The sequence of tonal foci in the work as a whole is

$$a; b, e, b; e; b, e'; a, e.$$

The general remarks made above on Athenaeus' paean are on the whole applicable also to Limenius'. In this case fourteen notes are used,[4] extending from what we have called *B* to what we have called *f'*; adjusted to the hypothetical real pitch this becomes *c♯–g'*, which is close to Athenaeus' ambitus *c–g♭'*. The two composers are virtually agreed on the vocal range to be used. But Limenius sets his tonic Mesē a semitone higher within that range than Athenaeus. Consequently, whereas Athenaeus goes down the Perfect System as far as Parhypatē hypatōn and up as far as chromatic Paranētē hyperbolaiōn, Limenius goes down a step further, to Hypatē hypatōn, and stops at Tritē hyperbolaiōn at the upper end. The different pitches at which they set their Systems determine that they choose different key-notations, Athenaeus using Phrygian/Hyperphrygian and Limenius Lydian/Hypolydian.[5] It is noteworthy that Limenius uses instrumental notation: being a professional citharist,[6] he was accustomed to using it.

The diagrams in Fig. 10.1 illustrate the scales and modulation-paths employed in the two works.

---

[4] Or fifteen, if Hypolydian *f♯* is distinguished from Lydian *g♭*.

[5] Phrygian and Lydian differ by a tone. As the difference between the corresponding degrees of Athenaeus' and Limenius' scales is only a semitone, it would not have been surprising if one or other of them had used the intermediate key-group, the Aeolian.

[6] *SIG* 698 A 21.

Athenaeus

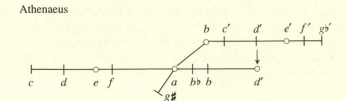

Limenius

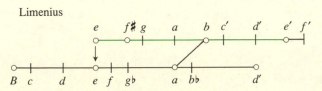

Fig. 10.1. The paeans of Athenaeus and Limenius: scales and modulations

15 Song of Seikilos
(Original a semitone lower)

(1) Hó-son zês,   phaí - nou; (2) mē - dén hó-lōs   sý lȳ - poû.

(3) pros o - lí-gon és - ti to - zzên: (4) to té-los ho chró-nos a - pai - teî.

(While you're alive, shine, man, | don't be the least bit blue. | Life's for a little span; | Time demands its due.)

A simple ditty in four clearly distinct lines, each of two iambic measures (variously realized, cf. p. 138). The melody is diatonic, in the G mode (cf. p. 186). It moves wholly within the limits of the fifth above the tonic and the tone below, until on the final syllable it descends in a traditional-sounding pentatonic cadence to the fourth below the tonic (cf. p. 194). It accords with the word-accents except at the beginning, where the rising fifth from the tonic *g* was evidently a conventional incipit (p. 193).

The structure of the scale does not fit well with the tetrachords of theory. The fifth *g–d′* is not the sum of a tetrachord and a disjunctive tone; it is clearly felt to divide into a major and a minor third, with *b* as the principal stepping-stone. These cardinal degrees *g–b–d′* are avoided in the half-cadences at the ends of the first three lines, *c′* and *f* being used instead so that no premature impression of finality is given (cf. p. 210).

In the first line the melody rises from the tonic *g* to the 'dominant' *d′*, in the second it descends again, and in both the third and the fourth it starts from the tonic, rises to the *d′*, and returns past *g*. The only consecutively repeated notes in the piece are the first *d′* and the last *g*.

For notational purposes the tonic *g* had to be identified with the diatonic Lichanos of the Perfect System to achieve the desired interval sequences. So in this case the standing notes of the System such as Mesē and Hypatē do not correspond at all with the notes that are structurally important in the music. The notation-key is Ionian.

16 Invocation of the Muse
(Original a tone higher)

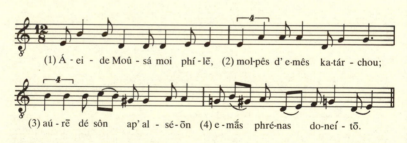

(1) Á - ei - de Moû - sá moi phí - lē, (2) mol-pês d' e-mês ka-tár - chou;

(3) aú - rē dé sôn   ap' al - sé - ōn (4) e - mãs phré-nas   do-neí - tō.

(Sing for me, dear Muse, | begin my tuneful strain; | a breeze blow from your groves | to stir my listless brain.)

The first, second, and fourth notes of line 2 are missing in the manuscripts and supplied by conjecture. The note transcribed as *g♯* in lines 3–4 is an 'accidental' alien to the notation-key in use (Lydian), and its interpretation is not wholly certain in the circumstances: it might be *g♭*. I have followed the usual view.[7]

___

[7] See Winnington-Ingram, *Mode*, 41; S. Baud-Bovy, *Revue de musicologie* 70 (1984), 259f.

This little diatonic piece is in the E mode. It has some similarities
with **15**. Again four iambic dimeter lines (unless we prefer to read
them as two tetrameters), though more uniform in pattern, alternately ⌣ − ⌣ − ⌣ − ⌣ − and ⌣ − ⌣ − ⌣ − ⌣ −. Again the tune starts with a
rising fifth from the tonic, against the word accent, and this fifth
together with the tone below (and in this case also a transitory semitone above) constitutes the space within which the melody moves.
The first line simply marks out this space, returning to the tonic *e*.
The second line, by an alternation of rising fourth and falling fifth (as
in tuning a lyre), leads us to a concordant fourth, *d–g*, which cuts
across the primary fifth *e–b* and feels like a rival harmonic axis. The
third line returns to *b* and leaves us suspended on an obviously
insecure *a*. In the fourth line we slalom down into the *d–g* box again,
but at the last moment it tilts back to the tonic.

The third and fourth lines have chromatic ornament; see p. 197.
Except in the last line, there is much more repetition of notes in
successive than in **15**. For the rhythmization of *doneitō* (♪♩ ♪♩) cf.
Seikilos' *sy lȳpou*.

17 Mesomedes, invocation of Calliope and Apollo
(Original a tone higher)

(1) Kal - li - ó - pei - a so - phấ, Mou - sôn pro-ka - thā - gé - ti ter-pnôn,

(2) kai so-phé mys - to-dó - tā, Lā - toûs gó-ne, Dḗ - li - e Pai - ấn,

(3) eu - me-neîs pá - res - té moi.

(Skilful Calliope, leader of the delightsome Muses, | and skilful instructor,
son of Leto, Delian Paian, | favour and be with me.)

The melody, which is in full accord with the word accents, is characterized by smooth ascents and descents. The hexameters each fall

into two halves for melodic purposes. In the second hexameter (*kai sophe–Paiān*) the tonic shifts from the original *e* to *c*; the music marches boldly up the C major scale and most of the way down again. Only at the final words *pareste moi* does it switch back to its initial allegiance. The melodic pattern of this line (*eumeneis–moi*) resembles that of the last line of **18**, *polyeimona kosmon helissōn*.

If the manuscripts are reliable there one touch of chromatic ornament, at *Mousôn*. As in **16**, it is not quite certain whether the accidental note (**N**) should be interpreted in the Lydian context as *g♯* or as *g♭*. But Winnington-Ingram may well be right in thinking that it is a scribal error for **M** = *g*. No accidentals occur in the two longer Mesomedes pieces.

All these Mesomedes pieces are in the Lydian notation.

18 Mesomedes, Hymn to the Sun
(Original a tone higher)

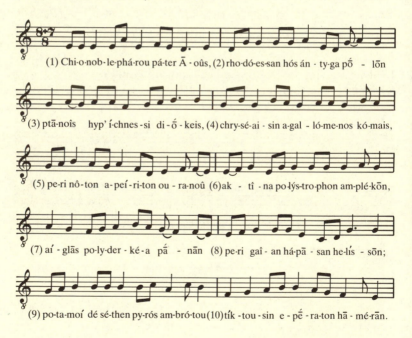

(1) Chi·o·nob·le·phá·rou pá·ter Ā · oûs, (2) rho·dó·es·san hós án · ty·ga pố - lõn

(3) ptā·noîs   hyp' í·chnes·si di·ṓ·keis, (4) chry·sé·ai · sin a·gal · ló·me·nos kó·mais,

(5) pe·ri nô·ton a·peí·ri·ton ou · ra·noû (6) ak · tî · na po·lýs·tro·phon am·plé·kōn,

(7) aí · glās po·ly·der · ké·a pā̃ - nān (8) pe·ri gaî· an há·pā · san he·lís · sōn;

(9) po·ta·moí dé sé·then py·rós am·bró·tou (10) tík·tou·sin e · pḗ · ra·ton hā · mé·rān.

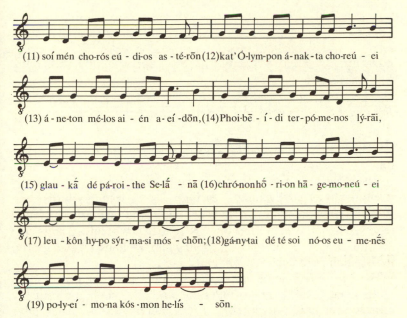

(11) soí mén cho-rós eú - di-os as - té-rōn (12) kat' Ó-lym-pon á-nak-ta cho-reú - ei

(13) á - ne-ton mé-los ai - én a - eí -dōn, (14) Phoi-bē - í - di ter-pó-me-nos lý-rāi,

(15) glau - kā̃ dé pá-roi - the Se-lā̃ - nā (16) chró-non hō̃ - ri-on hā - ge-mo-neú - ei

(17) leu - kôn hy-po sýr-ma-si mós - chōn; (18) gá-ny-tai dé té soi nó-os eu - me-nḗs

(19) po-ly-eí - mo-na kós - mon he-lís - sōn.

(Father of snow-eyed Dawn, that drivest thy rosy chariot in thy steeds' soaring steps, glorying in thy golden hair, twining thy ever-circling beam about the limitless back of the sky, winding the thread of radiance round the whole earth, while the rivers of thy immortal fire bring the lovely daylight to birth. For thee the serene chorus of the stars dances on Lord Olympus, ever singing a happy song, delighting in Phoebus' lyre, and the pale Moon in front leads time and season on with her white heifers' drawing; and thy benevolent heart is glad as it keeps the richly arrayed universe revolving.)

This and the following hymn are stichic texts, each line having the metrical form $\overline{\cup\cup} - \cup\cup - \cup\cup - \cup -$ or $\overset{\cup}{-} - \cup\cup - \cup\cup - -$.[8] The diatonic melody follows the word accents with rare exceptions, some of which may be due to miscopying of note-symbols. For further general remarks on these settings see p. 209.

The Sun hymn begins and ends on *e*, which is in general the focal note, though at times *g* and *b* take on this role. Almost every line ends on one of these three notes, and all but four begin on one of them. The diagram in Example 10.1, which shows just the first and last notes of each line, may convey some idea of the course steered by Mesomedes overall. Eleven lines end on a higher note than that

---

[8] This was a popular verse-form in the 2nd and 3rd c.; see my *Greek Metre*, 172 f.

Ex. 10.1

on which they began, and only five (including the last) on a lower one.

The scale runs from *c* to *c'*, but the two outer notes appear only occasionally as passing notes. Few intervals wider than a third occur. *Ekkrousmos* (the figure) is common, and one notices certain repeated melodic formulae: compare (i) the ends of lines 2 and 8, (ii) the ends of lines 3, 12, and 16; (iii) the ends of lines 17 and 19; (iv) the beginnings of lines 6, 8, 15, and 17.

There are uncertainties about the rhythmic interpretation of some of the line-ends. Where – – takes the place of – ⌣ –, it presumably represents either ♩. ♩ or ♩ ♩. (or ♩ ♩ 𝄽). Sometimes the first alternative is indicated by a *leimma* after the first note. A *leimma* is nowhere written after the second. It does not seem safe to assume that where no *leimma* is written, the rhythmization is other than ♩ ♩, especially as there are signs that some *leimmata* have been lost in the course of transmission.[9] Then sometimes one or both long syllables are divided between notes. In two cases the first syllable has two notes and then a *leimma*, i.e. ♪♩ (with syncopated effect in relation to the underlying rhythm – ⌣). There is never a *leimma* between the two notes, and where there is no *leimma* I tentatively assume ♪♩ again.[10]

19 Mesomedes, Hymn to Nemesis
(Original a tone higher)

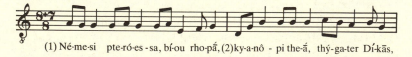

(1) Né·me·si   pte·ró·es·sa, bí·ou rho·pã̂,(2)ky·a·nõ·pi the·ã̂, thý·ga·ter Dí·kās,

---

[9] See Pöhlmann's critical apparatus in *DAM*. Note that the identical melodic figure occurs both with the *leimma* (at 3) and without it (at 12 and 16).

[10] On these problems see Winnington-Ingram, *Symb.·Osl.* 31 (1955), 82f.; Pöhlmann, *DAM* 26f.

(3) hã̂ koû-pha phry-ág - ma-ta thnā̄ - tôn (4) e-pé-cheis a-dá-man- ti cha -lī̄ - nôi,

(5) éch-thou-sa d'hý-brin o - lo-án bro-tôn (6) mé-la-na phthó-non ek - tós e -laú - neis.

(7) hy-po són tro-chón ás - ta-ton as - ti-bê (8) cha-ro-pã̂ me-ró-pōn stré-phe-tai tý-chã.

(9) lẽ̄ - thou-sa dé par pó-da baí - neis, (10) gau -roú-me-non au - ché-na klī̂ - neis;

(11) hy-po pê-chyn a - eí bí-o-ton metreîs, (12) neú-eis d'hy-po kól-pon o-phrŷn a - eí,

(13) zy-gón me-ta cheî - ra kra-toû - sa.(14) hī̂ - lẽ̄ - thi má-kai - ra di-kas - pó-le,

(15) Né-me-si pte-ró-es - sa, bí-ou rho-pã̂.(16) Né-me-sin the-ón ãĩ- do-men aph-thí-tān,

(17) Nī̂ - kēn ta-ny-síp -te-ron ob - rí-mān (18) nē̄ - mer -té- a kai pá-re-dron Dí-kās,

(19) hã̂ tān me-ga-lā̄ - no-rí-ān bro-tôn (20) ne-me-sô - sa phé-reis ka-ta Tar - tá-rou.

(Nemesis, winged one that tilts life's balance, dark-eyed goddess, daughter of Justice, that curbest the vain neighings of mortals with thy adamant bit, and in thy hatred of their pernicious insolence drivest out black resentment: under thy wheel that neither stands still nor follows a fixed track men's gleaming fortune turns about. Unobserved, thou treadest at their heel; the haughty neck thou bendest; under thy forearm thou measurest off life, and ever thou turnest thy frowning gaze into men's hearts, with the scales in thy hand. Be gracious, blest dispenser of justice, Nemesis, winged one that tilts life's balance.

Of Nemesis we sing, undying goddess, stern Victory with spreading wings, infallible, seated by the throne of Justice; of thee that resentest man's arrogance and sweepest it down to Tartarus.)

In this hymn the tonic is *g*, with *c′* and *d′* as secondary foci. It is no doubt because of the higher tonic that the scale goes a little higher than in **18**, to reach the fifth above *g*. Its lower limit is the same as in **18**. The three lowest notes occur less frequently than the rest; the bottom one occurs only in rising figures at the start of the line (*c d e* or *c d f*). Over half the lines end on *g*; those that do not, end on *d, f, a,* or *d′*. No line begins from *e*, but all other notes of the scale appear at least twice in this role (*a*, however, only as a leading note to *g*). A diagram of first and last notes looks much more widely spread out than the diagram for **18** (see Ex. 10.2).

Ex. 10.2

At least, it does so up to line 15, where the reprise of the first line gives the impression of an ending, and the following five lines look like a separate little hymn or an extension added afterwards. The diagram there flattens out noticeably. The desire for a descending final cadence on 15 overrides the accent of *rhopá*.

Multiple repetition of one note is a more conspicuous feature of this hymn than of its companion. A number of notes are missing in the only manuscript that gives notes for this poem, particularly in lines 6–8 and 19–20.

23-28 Instrumental exercises, Anon. Bellerm. 97–104
(Originals a tone higher)

25 is simply a diatonic scale (A mode). **23** and **26** are a set of permutations on four notes in two different rhythms, evidently a fingering exercise for the novice aulete. The other three pieces are

simple tunes, again, no doubt, devised specially for the learner. Like
15 Seikilos' song, they display a strong sense of the fifth dividing
into thirds, whether major above minor, *A–c–e* (**24**, **27**) or minor
above major, f–a–c′ (**28**, cf. Seikilos). We shall see this again in our
next item.

Rhythmic monotony is avoided. Lydian instrumental notation is
used throughout.

29 Satyric drama (?), *POxy.* 2436 (col. ii 2–8)
(Original a tone higher)

(... child of Ares, Hyme[ttus.] I have been luckier than [Her]mes(?) in my
offspring. Hurry to speed their deliverance from misfortune! All dance, and
do not . . . but remember . . . [*Lyrics*:] If there's still any brand alight indoors,
with fire, lads, . . . See, goatherd types . . . shepherds, cowherds, maenads . . .)

The fragmentary phrases down to *mnēmoneusate* seem to belong to an iambic or rather a trochaic speech, such as in Classical drama would have been spoken, not sung; but by the time of this papyrus dramatic recitalists commonly set them to music and sang them (cf. **31, 32, 48**). The lyrics that follow are mainly in iambic rhythm of the type that uses triseme notes. The melody is largely in accord with word accents, but there are a couple of divergences.

In spoken delivery the final vowel of *ēuteknēsa* would have been elided before *egō*—the verse would not be metrically correct otherwise—but here it is allotted a separate short note. This, and the two instances of diseme syllables sung to three notes (in *ekkrousmos*), are features of the florid style described on p. 203. In other respects, however, the music seems to have a certain crudity, with its constant emphasis on the notes of the major triad, *g* (tonic)–*b*–*d'*. There is much use of the top note (*d'*), and of the interval of the third. Was this perhaps a characteristic of the burlesque satyric drama of the time?

The scale goes down to *d*, its whole compass being an octave (which is leapt up in one bound at *boukoloi*). At *choreusate* we see the old pentatonic clausula, *g e d*. Immediately below *g* we find sometimes *f♯*, sometimes *f♮*. The modality resembles that of **15** Seikilos' song, which, however, is pitched a minor third lower.

The notation is Lydian, alternating with Hypolydian when *f♯* is used.

30 Oslo papyrus 1413, lines 1–15
(Original a semitone lower)

]phai - ō. ktý-pos agr[en - dó-my-chon né-phos elth[

]e - pe-tai phthi-mé-nōn phan-tás - mat[ ]mi-on hy - po tro-chón

I - xī - ōn d[· e-pi po-ta-món Ta - a[n-ta-] l[

]stai   phás - ga - na ka - ta gês   é - ba-lon   Phrý- gi - ai   la[

sým-ma-chos é-mo-len: thár-sei   tlḗ-mōn Dē - ē - i -dá-mei - a [

]mōn,   a - né - bē   d' e-pi phén - gos A - chil - leús.

kai gar dei - laí   Trō[phás - g]a-na gym - ná   pro-li-poû - sai.

kā - mé   gly-ke-rā́   baí - nei   phō - né   ê - chon dé sa-phôs

e - pi-gī́ -nōs-kō   kai   pâ - sa [   ] des - pó-ti ka-té-d[ȳ

]stḗ   ] i - a - k[.] n syn e -moí[P]ýr - rhou   pé-las

] ēn   a - ó - rā - ton   au-tós ty-chón a[   ]oi -dā

(A wild crash . . . dark cloud in the recesses . . . apparitions of the dead . . . on his wheel of bondage, Ixion . . . at the river, Tantalus . . . the Phrygian women dropped their swords down on the earth . . . came in support: be brave, poor Deidameia! . . . and up to the light came Achilles. For the cowardly Trojan women . . . abandoning their drawn swords. Then I heard a sweet voice . . . I recognized the sound for sure, and the whole . . . sank, mistress . . . near Pyrrhus . . . unseen . . .)

The rhythm is anapaestic, and the composition certainly of late date. The text contains more than one version of certain bars, and seems to have been written by the composer of the music, changing his mind here and there as he wrote. The music is in the florid style, with the elaborately decorative treatment of mythical names described on p. 203 and some wide leaps. The dive down on *kata gês* 'down on the ground' may be meant to fit the action described. Word accents are largely respected.

The compass is an octave, *d–d'*, pitched a little lower than average. Two modes alternate. In one, *f* appears to be the tonic. The music moves largely above it. At pauses it tends to rest on *g*, rising from *f* (*Achilleus, aorāton*) or descending from *bb* (*prolipousai*). In the other mode, *g* becomes the tonic, with the scale now descending *f♯ e d* and ascending *a b c' d'*. Besides the *b*, however, there appears a chromatic *bb* (*phasgana, tharsei, despoti katedȳ*). The composer seeks exharmonic effects by juxtaposing it with *b♮*, and elsewhere *f♯* with *f♮* (*epi potamon Tantal-*; *epi phengos Achilleus*); cf. p. 197. The piece ends with a fall from *g* to the fourth below, evidently in the second mode, in which, presumably, it also began.

The notation is Hyperionian for the first mode, Hypoionian for the second.

31 Same papyrus, lines 15–19
(Original a tone higher)

(O Lemnos and ... where Hephaestus (made Achilles' shield?) ... and mixing ... skill, and all the elements ... unseen he fashioned. Here now is Achil[les' son] ... (This has been decreed by) Zeus, of whom the gods were afraid.)

Setting of a tragic speech in iambic trimeters, mostly following the word accents, though they are spectacularly flouted in *ephobéthēsan* (if the note is rightly read). The tonal centre is here *e*. The compass is the same as in **30**, and the musical style is similar; besides general characteristics of the florid manner, and the moderate use of wide intervals, note the exharmonic *f♯* at *Achill-*. A vowel that by rights is elided is given its own short note at *de homou* (cf. on **29**), but not in other instances.

The notation is Lydian, with the sign for *f♯* borrowed from Hypolydian.

32 Michigan papyrus 2958, lines 1–18
(Original a semitone lower)

tôn eu [-] . . .   ouk ést' a - élp - tou   tér - psis [ ] pros nýn[

ál - lo d' aû m' é - ti   és - peu - de . . .   o sê - mat [   ] ouk an ei -

- deí - ēn   tá - de;   pa - rón - ta d' thám - bos em - po - eî.   ]sōn

pe - phas - mé - nōn.   ]ton Ai - gís - thou lé - geis   tō . . . ta . . . na[

]s kra - tê.   poî - on   pho - bē - theís deî - ma[

((Orestes, Old Servant) ' . . . o dearest of servants!' . . . 'Whoever are you?
Whose young . . .' 'You say this? When . . .' (*Instrumental line*) '. . . dearest
one.' '. . . you have succeeded? Tell me!' 'I will . . . salvation came about.'
'What homecoming . . . back here to me?' 'From the instruction that came
from Apollo.' 'Tell me, tell me . . . No joy is sweeter than the unexpected . . .'
'. . . And then another sign made me eager . . .' '. . . I wouldn't know; but the
present . . . fill me with wonder . . .' 'You speak of Aegisthus' . . .' 'He has . . .'
'Afraid of what . . .?')

Setting of a tragic dialogue in iambics, generally following the word
accents. Apart from one clausular fall from c' to f, the vocal part
moves almost entirely in the register bb–g', with a preference for the
higher notes. The tonal centre seems to be d'. In the line of wordless
notes—assumed to represent an instrumental insert, though the
notation is still the vocal—we find $b\natural$ as well as bb, and also the lower
notes g and (at the end, with an octave fall) d. The style is notably
florid; the trisyllabic word *aélptou*, for example, is set to seven notes.
The notation is Hyperionian.

34 *POxy.* 3704
(Original a tone higher)

(*a*)

ho sý-nai-mos em[   ]e-ke-neu-e... a-nó-mōi che-rí[

]nas E-rī-nýōn ou-ke-not[   ]ou phó-ni-on thê-ra tit[

]i-ou phei-sá-me-nos[

(My kinsman . . . with lawless hand . . . Erinyes . . . a bloody animal . . . sparing . . .)

(*b*)

]i-dí-ōi ge-né-tēi ge-ga-mē-mé-non[e]x sko-pé-lōn

ex-é-tho-ren pho[   ]Si-ke-lôn ex án-trōn

êl-the[prē]s-tér ḗ tȳ-phṓs ḗ skḗ[p-tós

(. . . married to its own sire . . . from the rocks sprang forth . . . from Sicilian caves came . . . waterspout, or whirlwind, or thunderbolt . . .)

(*a*) and (*b*) are written on the front and back of the same scrap of papyrus. It is not clear whether both are parts of the same text. They are apparently in the same rhythm (anapaestic) and the same notation-key (Hyperionian). Both show some wide leaps, and only partial regard for the word accents. In (*b*) some bars begin with rests, a feature also found in **51**; cf. p. 137.

40 Berlin papyrus 6870, lines 1–12: paean
(Original a semitone lower)

(1) Pai-ắn, ô   Pai-ắn   [cha]îr' ô - n[ax

(2) tón Dắ - lou tér-pei   tas [   ]lōn

(3) kai dî - nai Xán-thou [   ]lōn

(4) pā̄ - gaí t' Is - mē̄ - noû [   ] . . . tā:

(5) Pai-ắn,   hós Moú - sa [is   krắ - nās

(6) hým - nōn   ex - ár - [cheis   -]xās phō̄-nắn:

(7) hós pȳr   b[   ] chaí -tais stép-sās

(8) Lā-toû[s   ] mā - trós lố - bān

(9) klē - dõn [-]s

(10) tôi   Zeús   dāi - dou - cheî [   ]gān

(11) tôi   gâs   en   bố - lois   xa[n - thoí   kar-]poí.

(Paian, o Paian, hail, o Lord . . . who delights in Delos' . . . and in the eddying
waters of Xanthos . . . and Ismenos' springs . . . Paian, that leadest the Muses
in their singing by the Horse's Fountain . . . voice, thou that . . . fire . . . binding
bay on thy hair . . . (thou didst punish) the insult of Leto thy mother . . . for
whom Zeus bears the torch . . . for whom in the soil the yellow grain grows.)

This is a stichic text in anapaestic rhythm and spondaic tempo. Each
line has the metrical form ‿ − ⌣ − − ⌣ | − − − − − − − ⌣ ‖. But rhythmic
variety is maintained by dividing some syllables between two notes
(many of the tetrasemes between three), and by sometimes prolonging the last syllable of the line into the vacant time in the following
bar.[11]

The melody generally follows the word accents. Its compass is a
ninth, from *f* to *g'*. The primary tonic is *g*, with a secondary one a
fifth higher at *d'*. Of the nine preserved line-endings, all but two end
with *g* (or *g* lapsing to *f*) or with *d'*; both of the main sections end on
g (lines 4 and 11). Most lines begin rising; the exceptions are 4,
which rounds off a section of the composition, and 10 and 11 which
conclude it. And most lines end falling. It is at the beginnings and
ends of lines that most of the wider intervals (fourth or fifth) are
found.

The key is Hyperionian.

---

[11] See p. 204. Also in the first half line we find the variation ‿ − − ⌣ − ⌣ |.

41 Same papyrus, 13–15: first instrumental piece
(Original a semitone lower)

The metrical structure is the same as in **40** (which may suggest a
similarly slow tempo), and so is the key. But the melody goes a fourth
lower, encompassing altogether an octave and a fifth, and the
tonality is different. The tonic is *f*. The melody often dwells on *g*, and
fourths and fifths (*f*–*b*♭, *f*–*c′*, *c*–*g*, *g′*–*d′*, *d′*–*g*) play a conspicuous
role in it. The third bar of the first line recurs in line 5.

42 Same papyrus, 16–19: dramatic lament
(Original a semitone lower)

au - to - phó - nōi che - rí kai   phás - ga - non   Te - la -

-mō - ni - á - dā to són Aî - i - an   di' O - dys - sé -

ā ton a - lit - rón, hó   hél - ke - sin ho po - thoú - me - nos

(With suicidal hand and . . . your sword, Ajax son of Telamon . . . because of
Odysseus, the villain . . . wounds, he whom we miss . . .)

This piece is unique among our specimens of vocal music (with the
doubtful exception of **44**) in being set in the register of a female
voice. The singer presumably represents Ajax's mistress Tecmessa,
or else it is a female chorus.[12] The metre is dactylo-epitrite, and the
melody pays no attention to word accent, which implies a strophic
composition. These features suggest that the text is taken from a play
of late Classical or Hellenistic date, in which the lament was either
sung by the chorus or by Tecmessa in alternation with the chorus.[13]
The music, however, looks much later, especially in view of the
melisma on *Aian*, which distorts the original rhythm by protracting
the first syllable to twice its proper length. The absence of tetrachordal structure in the scale used is also against an early date. And
originally all female parts would have been played by male actors,
with their songs therefore in the normal register (as in **3**, **4**). It seems
therefore that in the Imperial period a new setting of an emotional

[12] The piece is preceded in the papyrus by the abbreviations 𝈀𝈦 𝈬 which mean
'another item' and perhaps 'choral'.
[13] A lament not involving the chorus would have been unlikely to be strophic.
Dactylo-epitrite began to be used in drama about 450 bc; it was very popular down to
the 3rd c. bc, but not later. We know of Ajax plays by several 4th-c. tragedians:
Astydamas the younger, Carcinus the younger, and Theodectas. Cf. *Trag. Adesp.*
110, 438b.

lament from an older tragedy was made for a woman concert singer. (A female chorus is harder to imagine.) It must have been more extensive than the few lines copied in the papyrus, covering at least a strophe and antistrophe.

The compass is no more than a fifth. The scale is unusual: *a′ b′ c″ d↑″ e″*, with the fourth degree raised by a quarter-tone or so above the diatonic standard (cf. p. 197). The tonal focus is the central note, *c″*. The two notes below it are used more than the two above.

The key is Hyperaeolian (cf. the note on **4**). For the exharmonic *d↑″* a first sharp symbol (65 **E′**) is exceptionally used.

43 Same papyrus, 20–2: second instrumental piece
(Original a semitone lower)

This piece is pitched a little higher than **41**. It seems to be based on the major triad *c′ e′ g′*. It is notable for its rhythmic variety; it is not, like **41**, the instrumental realization of a verse rhythm, but something conceived specifically for the instrument. The distinction made between short note + *leimma* and long note (♪ ‖ and ♩) may suggest the aulos rather than the lyre. The placing of arsis-points over the notes indicates that the tempo was slow enough for two down-beats per bar, i.e. 5/4 rather than 5/8; and it implies a variable beat that sometimes divides the bar into 2 + 3, sometimes into 3 + 2 (cf. p. 156). I have indicated this in the transcription by accent marks. In the fifth bar a colon after the first note seems most likely to be a mark of phrasing.

The notation is Hyperionian (instrumental).

44 Same papyrus, 23
(Original a semitone higher)

          hâi – ma ka - ta   chtho-nós a - po[

(Blood on the ground . . .)

This was the last line on the papyrus sheet: evidently a very short
snatch of song. The metre is obscure, and anyway distorted by the
melisma on *haima*, which resembles that on *Aian* in **42**. The reading
of the second note is uncertain; **X** (= *d*) would suit the key (Hyperaeolian), but the trace looks more like **Y**, which would be an
exharmonic semitone or microtone down from *e*.

The note for *a*(*po*-) has a bold and clear octave stroke attached to
it, putting it an octave higher than transcribed. But this is out of the
question, unless the whole line was meant to be in that register. Perhaps the scribe, after writing strokes throughout **42**, put one here in a
momentary lapse.

45 *POxy*. 3161 recto
(Original a semitone lower)

(a)]i - dí - oi - sin en   nó-m[ois   -]rē   té-knon el - thé[

]tí - ni taû - ta la - leî[s?   ]ri syn e - moí   to tha-neî[n

t]é-knon e-món ai[   ]lle bo- ē̄ - ḗ phthenx[-]tōn phō - nén

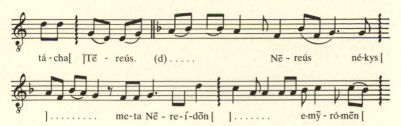

tá-cha[ ]Tē - reús. (d) . . . . . Nē - reús né-kys [

] . . . . me-ta Nē - re-í-dōn [ ] . . . . e-mȳ - ró-mēn [

((*a*) '. . . Come, child . . .' 'Who are you saying this to? . . . with me; death . . . my child . . . a cry . . . voice . . . Tereus . . .' (*d*) '. . . Nereus; and his corpse . . . I beheld stupefied with the Nereids . . . I lamented . . .')

These fragments are so broken that nothing can be clearly established about their metre(s). The melody on the whole respects the word accents. The compass exceeds an octave, extending down to *d* and *c* if the readings are correct. In (*a*) there are several leaps of a sixth or a seventh; the composer seems to favour the latter interval particularly. The focal notes here seem to be *g* and *d′*, while *e* and *b* rarely appear and *e′* not at all; there are no semitone intervals. In (*d*) it is otherwise. Here the scale has *b*♭ instead of *b*♮, and the note appears frequently. For the melisma on the name Nereus see p. 203; its exact rhythmic form is uncertain.

The notation-keys are Ionian (*b*♮) and Hyperionian (*b*♭).

46(c) Same papyrus, fr. 3 verso
(Original a semitone lower)

]s.ō - sō gé-nos ô Per-sôn[pa-trós āth - lí- ou pe[

ba - si - lé -ā. . mōn]n ka-ta-thrē - né-s . .

(O nation, o Persian . . . my wretched father's . . . king . . . lament . . .)

There seems to be more division of syllables between notes in **46c** than in **45**. The key is Ionian.

48 *POxy.* 3705
(Originals a tone higher)

toû   dḗ   tó - pou?   tí   mnē̄[

(Of what region? What memor- . . .?)

Part of an iambic trimeter, with four alternative musical settings, perhaps to illustrate different styles. Each has either one note per syllable or two. All except the first start on *g*. All but the third share a similar melodic contour, which seems related to the word accents.

The notation is Lydian (modulating to Hypolydian in 2 and 4). The sign I have interpreted as **K** = *ab* is oddly written and (if rightly identified) alien to the key.

51 *POxy.* 1786: Christian hymn
(Original a tone higher)

]ȳ - tā - nē - ō   sī - gā́ - tō,   mēd' ás - tra pha - es -

- phó - ra lam - pés - thōn   po - ta - môn   rho - thí - ōn   pâ - sai;

hym-noún - tōn   d' hē - môn pa-té-ra   k'hyi-ón   k'há-gi-on

pneû - ma   pâ - sai   dy - ná-meis   e - pi -phō-noún - tōn

Ā - mēn,   Ā - mēn,   krá-tos, aî - nos a -eí   kai dó - xa the-ôi

dō - tê - ri mó-nōi   pán - tōn   a -ga-thôn.   Ā - mēn, Ā - mēn.

(. . . Let it be silent, let the luminous stars not shine, let the winds (?) and all the noisy rivers die down; and as we hymn the Father, the Son, and the Holy Spirit, let all the powers add 'Amen, amen'. Empire, praise always, and glory to God, the sole giver of all good things. Amen, amen.)

This hymn is perhaps the latest in date of the known pieces recorded in the ancient Greek notation; at the same time it is the earliest example of Christian hymnody. Egon Wellesz maintained that it was modelled on melodic patterns deriving from oriental sources, perhaps adapted from a Syriac hymn, and had nothing to do with the native Greek musical tradition. However, I can see no feature of the music that cannot be illustrated from the foregoing documents of the art as it existed in the second- and third-century Empire. It is only a little further along the path towards ever greater ornament, as might be expected from its date.

The metre is anapaestic, a favourite form in those centuries.[14] The practice of beginning some bars with a rest, as before *sīgātō* and *hymnountōn*, is unusual but paralleled in **34**. The melody, purely diatonic, has the compass of an octave. The tonal foci are *d* and *g*; the final Amen descends from *g* to *d*. The two notes next above *g* are much used, but the outer notes of the octave, *c* and *c'*, only transitorily. Accord of melody and accent is only partial. We see the standard manifestations of the florid style: occasional division of

[14] Cf. **30**, **34**, **40**, **41**; *Greek Metre*, 170–2.

monosemes into ♫, more frequent division of disemes into ♫ or ♫♫. Such ornament is used liberally, but individual instances are no more extravagant than those seen in **32**.

The key is Hypolydian.

11

Historical Synthesis
1. Sunrise and Forenoon

In the preceding chapters we have studied the various elements that
go to make up ancient Greek music as a performing art, as an object
of theoretical inquiry, and as a cultural phenomenon. It remains to
attempt a synthesis in which we bring the chronological aspect to the
fore and outline the historical development of Greek music from
century to century.

THE BRONZE AGE AND THE EARLY IRON AGE

We begin with the Mycenaeans. The Cycladic civilization of the third
millennium, with its figurines of men playing harps, paired pipes, and
panpipes, is earlier in date, but although it falls geographically within
the limits of what were later Greek lands, it is a non-Hellenic culture
with Anatolian affinities. The Minoan civilization centred on Crete
is also non-Hellenic, though important as a major source of cultural
influence on the Mycenaean Greeks. It was from the Minoans that
the Mycenaeans acquired the lyre, an instrument that had been
slowly evolving in the Near East for over a millennium. The lyre is
the only musical instrument so far attested for the Mycenaeans, and
it appears to have enjoyed the highest prestige. It was played in the
palaces, to judge from the representation of a lyre-player in a fresco
from Pylos, and fragments of two ivory-faced lyres were found in the
royal 'beehive' tomb at Menidi in Attica. It is, of course, a reasonable
assumption that some other instruments were also in use. The
Minoans, at any rate, knew the 'Phrygian' double pipes, cymbals,
conchs, sistra, and perhaps harps. The Mycenaeans, besides whatever they took over from the Minoans, are likely to have had their
own native instruments, probably simple traditional things such as
panpipe and horn.

They must have had their own musical tradition too. It is possible that they took over something of Minoan musical style together with Minoan instruments; they may have employed Minoan musicians at their festivities. However, according to the author of a wide-ranging survey of primitive music,

Even when two races of different culture are in constant economic or military contact there is little evidence that they adopt each other's musical forms ... Even when foreign musical instruments are adopted, the relevant literature seems to be taken over only to a small extent or in mutilated form.[1]

The Mycenaeans continued to sing in certain traditional rhythms and verse-forms inherited from their Indo-European past, as we can infer from the survival of these rhythms and forms, only somewhat modified, in Classical times.[2]

The Minoan–Mycenaean lyre normally had seven or eight strings. As the strings were of equal length, it is unlikely that they would be tuned to cover a wider compass than an octave or so. Their number then implies a hexatonic or heptatonic scale or set of scales.

After the Mycenaean period, however, between about 1100 and 700 BC, lyres are regularly represented with only three or four strings. If we accept that this is what they had, it suggests a more restrained style of singing that used a smaller compass, perhaps not more than a fifth.

One type of singing that continued throughout these centuries (though perhaps not in all parts of Greece) was the performance of epic poetry. In the eighth century, at any rate, it was accompanied by the lyre. Study of the most archaic elements in the Homeric language leads to the conclusion that there was an unbroken tradition of heroic epic in dactylic hexameters from the fourteenth century or before. The technique of its performance, like that of its composition, is likely to have been highly conservative. I have said something about it on p. 208. I believe that the epic singer used a limited scale of three or four notes (at a guess, perhaps *a b c′ e′*, tone + fourth, with *b* as the focus), and disposed his syllables over them with regard both to the word accents and to a repeating melodic scheme.

There were, naturally, many other types of song. Homer mentions paeans, laments for the dead, wedding songs, a song of the vintage, singing at the loom, singing drinkers, girls' choruses that sing and dance, a healing incantation. In one passage a singer performs an

---

[1]   M. Schneider in E. Wellesz (ed.), *Ancient and Oriental Music*, 29.
[2]   Above, p. 147 with the literature cited in n. 52.

entertaining narrative song to the lyre while a chorus of young men dances round him, presumably illustrating the story in a sort of ballet. There must have been much else that Homer has no occasion to mention: cult songs, songs of work and play, lullabies, and so on.

There are one or two passing allusions in Homer to auloi and panpipes as instruments of popular music-making. But the lyre is far more prominent. It has been pointed out (p. 82) that the aulos goes unmentioned in various contexts where it might have been expected on the basis of later usage. Choral dancing, for example, is accompanied by the lyre.[3] In the dances represented in the vase-painting of the eighth and early seventh century, the lyre is the usual accompanying instrument. The rhythm might be accentuated by hand-clapping, stamping, or wooden clappers.[4]

THE EARLY ARCHAIC PERIOD

From the beginning of the Archaic period, which for this purpose we will consider as starting somewhat before 700, the evidence of archaeology, literature, and legend becomes much more abundant. We get the impression that music at this time underwent important developments and diversification. It may be an impression exaggerated by the relative dearth of earlier evidence; yet it does not seem to be altogether false.

There are developments in lyre design. The seven-stringed instrument, last seen in the Mycenaean period, makes isolated appearances in the eighth century and is depicted more regularly from the seventh. Beside the round-based kithara a new type appears, with a flat base and a different construction of the arms.[5] The evidence of art links up with the literary tradition of innovations by Terpander and his pupil Kepion.

Terpander was remembered as an outstanding citharode from Lesbos or Aeolian Cyme. Hellanicus put him in the time of Midas, who died *c.* 696, and also listed him as the first victor in the Spartan Karneia, which are said to have been founded in 676/3. Glaucus of Rhegium agreed in dating him before Archilochus, whereas other sources bring him down to the 640s. He won four successive victories at the Pythian festival, which at that time was octennial, so that

---

[3] *Od.* 8. 250–369, 23. 133–47; so too the processional paean in *Hymn. Hom. Ap.* 514 ff.   [4] See p. 123.
[5] See pp. 52 n. 12, 53.

a career peak of at least twenty-five years is indicated. Many accomplishments were set to his credit: increasing the number of the lyre's strings from four to seven; inventing the barbitos; organizing musical institutions at Sparta for the first time; composing the first citharodic *nomoi* and establishing their formal structural divisions; inventing drinking songs; extending the scale from a seventh to an octave by using the 'Dorian' Nētē, a fifth above Mesē; introducing the Mixolydian mode, and the slow measures called *orthios* and 'marked trochee'; composing a set of citharodic prooimia with which to preface melodic arrangements of Homeric and other verse.[6]

Much of this was no doubt constructed by projecting Classical citharodes' practices and repertory back upon the first famous citharode to be remembered. But Terpander must have been an exceptionally gifted musician, and it is likely enough that he made some technical and artistic innovations. It cannot be literally true that he was personally responsible for increasing the kithara's strings to seven. But he may well have been the first to win wide acclaim with the seven-stringed instrument and with a new, less monotonous style of epic singing, in which a wider melodic compass and more different notes were used.[7]

Kepion is a much less famous figure. But besides giving his name to a citharodic *nomos*, he is associated with the establishment of the kithara's (classical) form, which is put in his time.[8] He is called a pupil of Terpander's. This, however, is a standard ancient way of linking up persons who were successively important in a given field of endeavour, and the information should be treated guardedly.

The aulos is first attested at the end of the eighth century. From at least the fifth century the Greeks believed that they owed the introduction of aulos music to a Phrygian or Mysian piper called Olympus, a semi-legendary figure who had learned his art from the satyr Marsyas. Another Phrygian, Hyagnis or Agnis, was held to

---

[6] The sources for all this are conveniently collected by D. A. Campbell in the Loeb *Greek Lyric* ii (Cambridge, Mass., 1988), 294 ff.

[7] Cf. *CQ* 21 (1971), 307–9; *JHS* 101 (1981), 113 f., 116; *ZPE* 73 (1986), 44–6.

[8] Ps.-Plut. *De mus.* 1132 d, 1133 c. See p. 53. The second passage continues: 'And it (the kithara) was called Asiatic, because the Lesbian citharodes, living close to Asia, used it. And lastly they say that the citharode Perikleitos, a native of Lesbos, won the Karneia at Sparta. With his death the unbroken succession of Lesbian citharodes came to an end.' This must surely come from Hellanicus' work on Karneian victors, in which he celebrated the successes of his native Lesbos (see *FGrH* 4 F 85). Kepion perhaps belongs in the Lesbian series.

have been the first aulete of all, and Marsyas was subordinated to him by being made his son. Some Greeks thought of these people as having lived long before the Trojan War, but others put Olympus in the reign of Midas (*c.*738–696). The discrepancy was dealt with by the typical device of assuming two men of the same name, an older and a younger Olympus.[9]

It was precisely in the time of Midas that Greeks had cultural dealings with Phrygians at the highest level. Midas sent a splendid throne to Delphi as a gift. He married the daughter of a king of Cyme. And his tomb was said by the Cymaeans to bear an epigram composed by Homer when the poet was at Cyme. Perhaps it was from Cyme that Olympus' reputation went forth. One cannot feel much confidence in his historicity. But certainly the Greeks felt the aulos to be especially appropriate to the 'Phrygian' mode,[10] and Phrygian slave auletes were not unfamiliar figures in Archaic Greek society.[11]

Many of the traditional airs played on the auloi in ritual settings in the fifth and fourth centuries were attributed to Olympus, as were some of the more elaborate *nomoi* played in competitions.[12] It may be that few of them, if any, were really as old as the eighth century, but they were admired for their inimitable old-fashioned simplicity and their uplifting quality. What is said of them provides the best clues we have to the character of Archaic aulos music. Olympus' tunes, like Terpander's, used relatively few notes, without modulation; they were 'simple and three-note'. It was Olympus who invented the enharmonic genus, initially in a form without the divided semitone, that is, a scale of pentatonic character.[13] The modes he used were the Dorian, the Phrygian, and the Lydian, especially the two latter.[14]

References to 'Phrygian melody' go back as far as Alcman and

[9] Most of the sources for Olympus are set out by Campbell (as in n. 6), 272 ff., but he overlooks Pind. fr. 157, Telestes, *PMG* 806., Eur. *IA* 576, ps.-Plut. *De mus.* 1137d, Philostr. *Imag.* 1. 20, Clem. *Strom.* 1. 76. 6, Tzetz. *Chil.* 1. 373.

[10] Cf. the passage of Aristotle quoted on p. 180.

[11] Alcm. *PMG* 109, cf. 126; Hipponax fr. 118. 12; cf. Ar. *Vesp.* 1371. An aulete from Acragas called Midas, Pind. *Pyth.* 12; a Theban one called Olympichos, Aristodemus, *FGrH* 383 F 13. An aulete on an Attic amphora of *c.*560 is labelled Olympos (Athens 559; Wegner, *Bilder*, 71).

[12] Pratinas, *PMG* 713(*i*), Ar. *Eq.* 9, Pl. *Smp.* 215c, *Minos* 318b, Arist. *Pol.* 1340ᵃ9, Aristox. fr. 80, ps.-Plut. *De mus.* 1133d–f, 1141b.

[13] Aristox. fr. 83 ap. ps.-Plut. *De mus.* 1134f–1135b; 1137ab. See pp. 163, 173.

[14] Aristox. loc. cit., also ps.-Plut. *De mus.* 1137d, 1143b, Poll. 4. 78.

Stesichorus.[15] By the seventh century, then, Greek musicians seem to have recognized and defined a particular mode or melodic style as being derived from Phrygia, or at any rate similar to what could be heard in Phrygia. The Lydian mode too must have been identified at this period or not much later, as it was from the mid-seventh century to the reign of Croesus that the Aeolian and Ionian Greeks were in the closest cultural contact with Lydia. This contact is reflected especially in the poetry of Alcman, Alcaeus, and Sappho. The Lydian mode is not associated with a particular Lydian musician, as the Phrygian is with Olympus.[16]

These foreign modes are never contrasted simply with a 'Greek' one, but always with Dorian, Ionian, and other sub-national denominations. Presumably this was already the case in the seventh century, or whenever this nomenclature came into use. And presumably there was some continuity of nomenclature from then to the fifth century. At least some of the scales used in seventh- and sixth-century music were sufficiently like those known in the Classical period for compositions of Terpander and Alcman to be identified as being in the Dorian mode, airs of Olympus to be classified as Phrygian or Lydian, songs of Sappho as Mixolydian, songs of Pythermus as Ionian.[17]

For the Archaic period we should probably assume that these modes had pentatonic form, in view of Aristoxenus' remarks about Olympus' earliest enharmonic, the indivisibility of the semitone in old-style aulos-playing, and the 'trichordal' character of both Olympus' and Terpander's music. For example, if we take the Dorian and Phrygian scales as described by Damon and eliminate the divided semitones,

Dorian   *d e f a b c′ e′*
Phrygian   *d e f a b c′ d′,*

[15] Cf. p. 177.

[16] In fact Olympus is credited with inventing the Lydian mode (having learned the Phrygian from Marsyas): Telestes, *PMG* 806, Clem. *Strom.* 1. 76. 4–6. Alternatively the 7th-c. Colophonian aulete Polymnestus is said to have invented 'the *tonos* now called Hypolydian' (ps.-Plut. *De mus.* 1141 b), which probably corresponds to what was called Lydian in the 5th c. (cf. pp. 227 f.).

[17] Clem. *Strom.* 6. 88. 1; Aristox. frs. 80–3; Ath. 625 c. Himerius' flowery phrase about Alcman 'blending the Dorian lyre with Lydian songs' (*Orat.* 5. 3 p. 39. 12 Colonna) is probably based merely on the opinion that Alcman came to Sparta from Lydia, not on any musicological learning. The Dorian *harmoniā* which is attributed to Stesichorus, Ibycus, Pindar and Alcman in the epigram on the nine lyric poets in schol. Pind. i. 10 f. Dr. is nothing but their dialect.

we get seven-note scales that may well resemble what Archaic musicians knew as Dorian or Phrygian. Lydian is problematic, as Damon recorded more than one variety of Lydian. If we take the one labelled 'Lydian' as opposed to 'Tense Lydian', it is not clear whether the quarter-tone intervals at the top and bottom of the scale, which look like ornamental affixes, should be left as quarter-tones. If they are, the result will be

Lydian   (e↑) *f a b c' e'* (e↑').

The Ionian and Mixolydian scales become

Ionian   *e f a c' d'*
Mixolydian   *e f g a b♭ e'*.

But this is all somewhat speculative. There may have been variant forms of scale covered by a single name, and there may have been other changes in the course of time besides the division of semitones. It must be remembered that some old aulos tunes, like the *Spondeion* attributed to Olympus and certain pieces attributed to Polymnestus, used intervals of $\frac{3}{4}$ or $1\frac{1}{4}$ tone.[18]

Several other shadowy figures are named as having played important roles in the development of music in the early Archaic period. The creation of aulodic as opposed to auletic *nomoi* was credited to one Klonas, thought to stand chronologically between Terpander and Archilochus. Arcadians claimed he was an Arcadian, Boeotians claimed he was a Boeotian; the inference is that his name was associated with traditional aulos music in both areas. More specifically, he is linked with processionals, with hexameter and elegiac verse, and with the *nomoi* called *Apothetos* and *Schoinión*.[19]

The Troezenians claimed that aulody was established earlier by Ardalos of Troezen. Plutarch distinguishes this aulode Ardalos from a more ancient Ardalos who inaugurated the Troezenian cult of the 'Ardalid Muses'; but they may originally have been identical. According to Pausanias Ardalos was a son of Hephaestus, and invented the aulos itself. He seems to be a mythical, not a historical personage.[20]

---

[18] Cf. pp. 164 n. 9, 173 f., 229.
[19] Ps.-Plut. *De mus.* 1132 c (= Heraclid. Pont. fr. 157), 1133 a, Poll. 4. 79.
[20] Ps.-Plut. *De mus.* 1133 a, Pliny, *HN* 7. 204; Plut. *Conv. sept. sap.* 150 a; Paus. 2. 31. 3.

Polymnestus of Colophon in the later seventh century is credited with further *nomoi*, rhythmic innovations, a type of Lydian mode ('the *tonos* now called Hypolydian'), and compositions that used the unusual intervals mentioned above. Both he and Klonas apparently composed words as well as music, but Polymnestus was the more celebrated of the two, being mentioned by Alcman and Pindar.[21]

Polymnestus himself mentioned the Cretan Thales or Thaletas, who reputedly came to Sparta in accordance with the advice of the Delphic oracle and ended a plague, or civic discord, by means of his paeans and choral dance-songs. Thaletas is said to have enlarged the kind of simple strophic form used by Archilochus, and to have introduced the paeonic and 'cretic' (5/8) rhythms into vocal music. According to the fourth-century historian Ephorus, the Cretans attributed their paeans and other native songs to Thaletas, and many of their customs and rituals as well. The Spartans too used dance-songs of his at certain festivals, or ascribed to him dance-songs that they used.[22]

Thaletas seems, like Olympus and Terpander, a little larger than life. The Greeks abhorred the anonymous, and always tended to assume that the first person remembered as having done something was the first person who ever did it. When it came to assigning the credit for their cultural heritage, the few names of lawgivers, poets, and musicians remembered from early times had to do duty for all. The individual achievements of these men may therefore have been exaggerated. But they will not have been immortalized for nothing.

Regional traditions are an important aspect of early Greek musical history, as of early Greek cultural history in general. In the light of the evidence at our disposal, Lesbos and Sparta stand out as the great centres of musical excellence in the seventh century. In Sparta's case it was largely a matter of organizational encouragement. The establishment of musical contests at the Karneia festival and the provision of fine choral displays at other festivals (young men dancing in armour, girls' dances, etc.) manifested the Spartan interest in public musical entertainment and attracted musicians from other parts of Greece. The Lesbian (or Cymaean) Terpander was reputedly the first Karneian winner, followed by a series of other

---

[21] Alcm. *PMG* 145, Pind. fr. 188; other testimonia in Campbell (as n. 6), 310, 322, 330–4. Cf. Kassell–Austin on Cratinus fr. 338.

[22] For sources see Campbell, op. cit. 320–8, adding Porph. *Vita Pythagorae* 32. Cf. above, p. 33.

Lesbian citharodes including Arion and ending with Perikleitos sometime in the sixth century.[23] We hear that the Spartans always offered the platform first to descendants of Terpander, then to any other Lesbian singer who might be present. Sappho praised someone as 'supreme, like the singer from Lesbos performing abroad'.[24] Other musicians from overseas who performed at Sparta included Thaletas and Polymnestus.[25] Some say that Tyrtaeus the elegist and Alcman were also of non-Spartan origin, but this is doubtful. We hear also of one Xenodamus of Cythera, who composed songs for dancing chorus that some classified as paeans. The place of performance is not specified, but for a poet from Cythera Sparta is an obvious guess.[26]

Seventh-century song, so far as our evidence goes, was either stichic (as in epic recitation) or strophic. In the islands of the central Aegean and east of it, strophes were of the 'closed' type (p. 209), small in scale and clearly divided into single verses. In the Aeolian area there was the archaic-looking tradition represented by Sappho and Alcaeus. From Ionia we have the 'epodic' songs of Archilochus, built from simple dactylic and iambo-trochaic units, and the widely popular form that is the elegiac couplet. Elegiacs were commonly sung to aulos accompaniment in social contexts, presumably to conventional melodies that the aulete could repeat (or vary) for as long as required. Some of these melodies were probably attributed to Olympus or Klonas, both of whom are associated with elegy. The elegiac poet Mimnermus was himself an aulete, according to later sources.[27] In all this Aeolian and Ionic strophic song we may suppose that the shaping of melodic lines was subject to the general principles adumbrated in Chapter 7 (pp. 210 f.).

In mainland Greece and the west, at any rate at Sparta by the end of the century, larger strophic structures were being used in songs for dancing choruses. This is probably what is meant by Glaucus of Rhegium's statement that Thaletas 'imitated the melodic forms of Archilochus but increased their length'.[28] In Alcman we find

[23] See above, n. 8.
[24] Cratinus fr. 263, Arist. fr. 545, Aelius Dionysius λ 7, Paus. Atticista μ 14; Sappho fr. 106.
[25] Paus. 1. 14. 4.
[26] Pratinas, *PMG* 713; ps.-Plut. *De mus.* 1134bc, probably from Glaucus of Rhegium.
[27] See my *Studies in Greek Elegy and Iambus*, 12, 13 f.; K. Bartol, *Eos* 75 (1987), 261–78.   [28] Ps.-Plut. *De mus.* 1134 d.

extended strophes—fourteen lines in the case of the Louvre Partheneion—which are still, however, made up from the simplest
verse-units. The rhythms are dactylic, iambo-trochaic, and aeolic.
Occasionally Alcman used the paeonic rhythm that Thaletas is said
to have brought from Crete. It seems to be alien to the Ionian and
Aeolian traditions, where choral singing and dancing, though no
doubt known, appear not to have engaged the attentions of innovative musicians and directors as they did at Sparta.

Choral song probably continued to be accompanied predominantly by the kithara. This would be appropriate for Thaletas' paeans
(which Pythagoras is supposed to have liked singing privately to the
lyre), and he is called a composer of 'lyric' songs. Alcman represents
his chorus-girls as praising their citharist, though he also mentions
auloi and auletes more than once.[29] Alcaeus spoke of auloi in connection with choral dances or processions in the worship of
Apollo.[30] A combination of auloi and lyre is not excluded. An Attic
jar of the early seventh century shows a piper and a citharist leading a
file of women who hold hands and branches,[31] and there is plenty of
evidence for the combination of the two instruments in the Classical
period. For solo singing, whether public or domestic, no more than
one instrument would be used.

Besides the lyre and auloi, the harp makes its appearance in the
Lesbos of Sappho and Alcaeus, no doubt imported from Lydia.[32]
Two varieties of lyre first mentioned in these poets are the *barmos*
(= barbitos?) and *phoinix*. Another instrument first named in them,
though attested earlier in art, is the castanets.

THE LATER ARCHAIC PERIOD

From at least the time of Hesiod there had been opportunities, at
large gatherings, for singers to compete for prizes.[33] Terpander
carried them off not only at the Spartan Karneia but also at the

---

[29] *PMG* 38, cf. 41; 51 (Apollo as a piper), 109, 126. The verb *hypaulein* (37, 87)
properly means 'accompany on the auloi', but may have been extended to mean
'accompany' on any instrument, as apparently in Epicharmus fr. 109.

[30] Alc. fr. 307 (*b*) L.–P.

[31] Berlin, Antikenmuseum 31573; my Pl. 2. A fragment of a late Geometric cup
(Athens, National Museum 291; Wegner, *Musik und Tanz*, pl. IVc) shows a solo
dancer (?) on a podium, flanked by a citharist and an aulete.

[32] See pp. 71f.

[33] See p. 19.

Pythian festival at Delphi. But the first half of the sixth century saw a significant increase in the range and frequency of these opportunities.

In 586 BC the Pythian festival was reorganized on a grander scale, with the institution of athletic and additional musical contests. It had previously been held only every eight years: from now on it was to be every four. The new musical events were for aulodes and auletes. The victorious aulode in 586 was an Arcadian called Echembrotus. His prize was a tripod cauldron, and according to the dedicatory inscription he won it for singing 'songs and *elegoi*', probably a form of lament for the dead.[34] The aulodic contest was then apparently discontinued. Pausanias supposes the reason to have been that laments were considered too gloomy and inauspicious, but this cannot be the true explanation. There was plenty of scope for cheerful aulody.

The contest for solo auletes was vastly more successful. It continued for many centuries and was acknowledged as the most prestigious of its kind anywhere. The winner in 586, as in the two succeeding contests in 582 and 578, was Sakadas of Argos. What he played was an extended composition, the *Pȳthikos nomos*, portraying in music the story of Apollo's fight with the serpent. It became a traditional repertory piece.[35]

Sakadas may possibly have made improvements in the aulos itself, seeing that there was a type of instrument named after him.[36] In any case, his performance at Delphi is the first we hear of the aulos as a virtuoso instrument. Its development in this capacity evidently prompted kithara-players to explore the potentialities of their instrument and to see what they could achieve using it not just as an accompaniment to fine singing or dancing but as a musical voice on its own. In 558 unaccompanied kithara-playing was added to the Pythian programme.[37] The first victor is named as Agelaus of Tegea. Aristonicus of Argos, the man said to have first developed the art, may perhaps have been active about this time, though our source puts him back as far as the age of Archilochus.[38]

Meanwhile, in about 566, the Panathenaea at Athens had also

---

[34] Strab. 9. 3. 10, Paus. 10. 7. 4–6, schol. Pind. *Pyth.* argum.; on the chronology, K. Brodersen, *ZPE* 82 (1990), 25–31. See my *Studies in Greek Elegy and Iambus*, 5–7.

[35] See the fuller discussion on pp. 212–14.   [36] See p. 90 n. 42.

[37] See p. 214.   [38] Menaechmus, *FGrH* 131 F 5.

been reorganized. It became a grand city show at which, among other events, rhapsodes, citharodes, aulodes, and auletes competed for prizes.[39] For the time being, however, this festival was of only local importance. Not till the fifth century do we hear of musicians coming from elsewhere to perform at it, or, for that matter, of Athenians who attained national distinction in the musical arts.

The leading region for musical excellence in the sixth century was the Argolid. Sakadas of Argos' three Pythian victories in the auletic contest were succeeded by a run of six (574–554) by Pythocritus of Sicyon.[40] The pioneer psilocitharist Aristonicus was an Argive, though he lived in Corcyra. And we have a statement to the effect that in the time of Polycrates of Samos, about 530, 'the Argives were spoken of as occupying the first place for music among the Greeks'.[41] It is this strong regional tradition that lies behind the technical and theoretical accomplishments of Epigonus and Lysander of Sicyon and Lasus of Hermione, men to whom we shall return presently.

Among the western Greeks the 'Terpandrian' manner of singing epic to the seven-stringed kithara flourished and evolved. Xeno-critus (or Xenocrates) of Locri in south Italy made a name for himself, in the late seventh or early sixth century, with heroic narra-tive songs which some classed as paeans and others as dithyrambs.[42] One Xanthus, whose place of origin is not recorded, also seems to have composed works of this sort.[43] We may guess that he was another westerner. Later in the sixth century this line of tradition becomes more visible to us in the work of Stesichorus, who is said to have made much use of Xanthus' material. He came from the Locrian foundation of Matauros, but his activity is associated chiefly with Locri and with Himera in Sicily. There is some reason to believe that he sang at Sparta. His compositions were epic in scale and subject matter, but strophic in form. The metres were largely dactylic,[44] sometimes dactylo-epitrite (p. 151). The strophes, some-

[39] See J. A. Davison, *JHS* 78 (1958), 37, 42, and 82 (1962) 141 f. = *From Archi-lochus to Pindar*, 55 f., 64–8.

[40] Paus. 6. 14. 10. His name ('Chosen for Pytho') and his father's (Callinicus, 'Victor') suggest that he came from a family of dedicated and ambitious auletes. At Sparta in the 5th c. 'heralds, auletes, and chefs follow their fathers' crafts: aulete is born from aulete, chef from chef, and herald from herald' (Hdt. 6. 60).

[41] Hdt. 3. 131. 3 (perhaps an interpolation).

[42] Glaucus ap. ps.-Plut. *De mus.* 1134 bc, ef. For his use of the Locrian mode see p. 184.

[43] *PMG* 699.

[44] Perhaps in irrational rhythm: see p. 136.

what more voluminous and flowing than those of Alcman, were arranged on the triadic system (p. 211). In other words two broad melodies, each of up to a hundred notes, alternated, one always coming twice in succession, the other once. The alternation helped to stave off monotony, but it must be remarked that the songs were so long as to contain (in one case, at least) fifty triads or more, so that one of the melodic schemes would have been repeated over a hundred times. The performance must have lasted well over an hour. It used to be assumed that these works were sung by a chorus, but it now seems altogether likelier that Stesichorus sang them solo, accompanying himself on the kithara. Possibly there was a chorus that danced while he sang.[45]

We hear that Stesichorus used the *Harmateios* ('chariot') *nomos*, which was primarily auletic, deriving from Olympus. It was high in register, and identified with the *nomos of Athena*, which was in the Phrygian mode and the enharmonic genus. It is consistent with this that Stesichorus refers to one of his own songs as a 'Phrygian melody'.[46] If we interpret this as proposed earlier (p. 332), the implied scale is $d\,e\,f\,a\,b\,c'\,d'$.

He says that his Phrygian song is appropriate at the beginning of spring. This may be taken to mean that it is performed at a set festival. Those who considered Xenocritus' songs to be dithyrambs or paeans evidently saw nothing out of place in the performance of heroic narrative songs in a ritual setting.

The Corinthians believed that the dithyramb originated at Corinth in the time of their dictator Periander (*c.* 625–585), and that it was invented by the celebrated Lesbian citharode Arion, 'the first man we know of who composed a dithyramb, gave it this name, and taught it (to a chorus) at Corinth'.[47] This suggests that the Corinthian dithyramb may have involved a singing citharode and a chorus who sang in response to him. The formal pattern of leader (*exarchos*) and answering chorus was an ancient one, well established in cult.[48]

[45] On all this see *CQ* 21 (1971), 302–14.

[46] Glaucus ap. ps.-Plut. *De mus.* 1133f, schol. Eur. *Or.* 1384 (i. 220. 1–5 and 25 Schw.; *Etym. Magn.* 145. 25ff.), Phot. *Lex.* α 2835; Stesich. *PMG* 212. Cf. *CQ* 21 (1971) 309–11; *JHS* 101 (1981), 125; for the *nomos of Athena*, above, p. 216.

[47] Hdt. 1. 23, citing Corinthian and Lesbian sources. Hellanicus included Arion in his *Karneian Victors*, *FGrH* 4 F 86. Arion certainly did not invent the name 'dithyramb': it occurs earlier in Archilochus, and is obviously old, perhaps pre-Greek. Pindar acknowledges Corinth as the home of the dithyramb in *Ol.* 13. 18.

[48] Cf. *Il.* 18. 51, 316, 24. 720–76 (lament), Archil. fr. 120 (dithyramb), 121 (paean), Sappho fr. 140 (Adonis drama).

However, this would be something quite unlike Stesichorus' songs, and presumably unlike Xenocritus'. It is an arrangement more suited to the dramatic enactment of scenes from legend, as in the Sappho fragment where the lead singer plays the part of Aphrodite and enacts with her chorus the death of Adonis.[49] At Sicyon in the early sixth century the story of Adrastus was ritually portrayed by 'tragic' choruses, where there may well have been this kind of antiphony.[50]

The dictators who held power in various cities at various times were sometimes instrumental in reforming festivals and festival music, or, by their patronage, attracted outstanding musicians from other places and so contributed towards a cross-fertilization of local traditions. Periander's hospitality kept Arion much at Corinth, and the new form of dithyramb was instituted as a result. At Sicyon Cleisthenes, for political reasons, changed the nature of the 'tragic' performances, and put a stop to those of the rhapsodes. At Athens the organization of the Great Panathenaea as a musical festival seems slightly to pre-date Pisistratus' rise to power, but he may have influenced its further development. It was during his rule that Thespis transformed the enactment of mythical scenes by Dionysiac choruses into tragedy, by adding a speaker. At Samos Aeaces and his son Polycrates gathered notable singers to their court. Here Ibycus from Rhegium, a man trained in the same western tradition as Stesichorus, came together with Anacreon, who composed in the closed strophes of Ionian tradition. Poetically the two have certain ideas in common, but the formal difference is fascinating. In one respect it looks as if Ibycus has picked up an east Greek rhythmical device.[51]

After the fall of Polycrates Anacreon found another patron at Athens in Pisistratus' son Hipparchus. Here again different currents were running together. Hipparchus' circle also embraced Lasus of Hermione and Simonides. His elder brother Hippias was managing the city, and Hipparchus himself had power enough to influence its cultural life. It was he who developed the rhapsodes' competition at the Great Panathenaea into an organized serial performance of the whole *Iliad* and *Odyssey*.[52]

---

[49] Sappho loc. cit. Similarly in the 5th c. with Bacchylides' *Theseus*, and probably Telesilla, *PMG* 717; Eur. *Hipp*. 58–71.

[50] Hdt. 5. 67. 5.

[51] Choriambic expansion (above, p. 149). See my *Greek Metre*, 52.

[52] Ps.-Pl. *Hipparch*. 228 b, cf. 228 c (Anacreon, Simonides), Hdt. 7. 6. 3 (Lasus).

The Archaic age saw some advances in the techniques of playing solo instruments, and among the western Greeks the development of larger melodic structures. But our sources do not suggest that much change was taking place in the varieties of scale used or in general principles of matching words to music. Anacreon is said to have still used only the old modes of Olympus, the Dorian, Phrygian, and Lydian.[53] There is a vague mention of Ibycus, Anacreon, and Alcaeus (or Achaeus) having given 'flavour' to their *harmoniā*, which is somehow analogous to their wearing of elegant Ionian clothes, but we cannot tell what this amounts to.[54]

Towards the end of the sixth century, however, there are definite signs of innovation in one particular quarter, associated with an intellectual and analytical approach to music. This approach was developed by two musicians from the Argolid, Epigonus of Sicyon and Lasus of Hermione.

Epigonus, Lasus, Simonides

Epigonus was remembered as the author of certain theoretical ideas about pitch, and I have argued that he attempted to work out an integrated system of modal scales using a specially constructed zither with strings tuned at quarter-tone intervals.[55] It is further recorded that he and his school were the first to practise *enaulos kitharisis*. The meaning of this expression is debated. Many scholars take it to be kithara-playing that is either accompanied by or in some way similar to aulos-playing.[56] But *enaulos* usually means 'echoing in the ears', of something once heard that remains vividly present, with no reference to auloi. So the meaning is most likely a technique of kithara-playing with sustained notes or echo effects, perhaps using 'upper partials' by bisecting the vibrating length of strings as described on p. 66.[57] This interpretation fits very well with what is

---

[53] Posidonius fr. 471 Theiler ap. Ath. 635 cd.

[54] Ar. *Thesm.* 161–3. Ancient scholars disputed over whether Aristophanes named Alcaeus or Achaeus, and if it was the former, whether the Lesbian Alcaeus was meant or another.

[55] pp. 78 f., 225 f.

[56] Philochorus, *FGrH* 328 F 23; A. Barker, *CQ* 32 (1982) 266, 269.

[57] E. K. Borthwick ap. Winnington-Ingram in Gentili–Pretagostini, 260 n. 25.

reported of another Sicyonian performer, who perhaps belongs in the early fifth century:

Lysander the Sicyonian citharist made the first changes in solo playing, by prolonging the duration of the notes and giving body to the tone; and in *enaulos kitharisis*, which Epigonus' circle was the first to use. He ended the brevity that prevailed among psilocitharists, being the first to play fine shades of colour, and *iamboi*, and octave echoes, the so-called 'whistling' effect (*syrigmos*). He was the first to change instrument (?), and to make it a bigger affair by surrounding himself with a chorus.[58]

Lasus wrote the first book about music. He is cited as subscribing to the same notion of pitch as Epigonus' school, and as having studied the ratios underlying concords.[59] He was more widely remembered as a practising musician. There was a self-consciously intellectual element in his compositions. In two of them he excluded any word containing the letter *s*, apparently because he felt that it did not go well with the sound of the aulos.[60] One of these songs began

> Of Demeter I sing, and the Maiden, Klymenos' consort,
> raising a hymn of honey cry
> in the deep-resounding Aeolian attunement,

which is something like saying 'let us praise the Lord with one voice in G major'. Alcman and Stesichorus had mentioned the 'Phrygian melody' in passing, but to Lasus it is evidently important to draw people's attention to his use of a new or uncommon mode, or at any rate to raise their consciousness regarding the identification of modes. Similar technical references appear in Pratinas and Pindar, no doubt following Lasus' lead. Both mention the Aeolian mode, and nobody else does. To argue from Heraclides Ponticus' identification of it with Hypodorian, it may have had a scale something like *d e f a b♭ d'*.[61] Pratinas commends it as somehow a mean between tense and slack modes, and he describes its use metaphorically as 'turning over a fallow field', which implies that it had lain unexploited or under-exploited. This tends to confirm Lasus' originality in adopting it.

---

[58] Philochorus loc. cit. The significance of *iamboi* in this context is unclear. On Lysander cf. A. Barker, *CQ* 32 (1982), 266–9; Winnington-Ingram in Gentili–Pretagostini, 255.

[59] See pp. 225, 234. On Lasus generally see G. A. Privitera, *Laso di Ermione* (Rome, 1965).

[60] See pp. 39 f.   [61] See pp. 183 f.

Lasus is credited with the introduction of dithyrambic competitions; it is assumed that this means their institution at Athens, which is dated *c.* 508, a few years after the assassination of Lasus' patron Hipparchus.[62] He composed dithyrambs himself, and

> by adapting his rhythms to the tempo of the dithyramb, and using a larger number of scattered notes, in accordance with the abundance of sounds that auloi have, he changed the older music into something new.[63]

This is not as clear an account as we could wish, but it suggests a busier style of vocal music than had been customary, with more rapid and varied movement of the melodic line, perhaps in imitation of auletic solo music as it had evolved in the Argolid since Sakadas. Pindar alludes repeatedly to the multiplicity of the aulos' sounds.[64] It is possible that the division of the semitone into quarter-tones in the enharmonic genus, a development most naturally derived from auletic part-stopping, was introduced to vocal music by Lasus, particularly as his doctrine of notes having breadth in the scale suggests interest in Epigonus' investigation of minimal intervals.

The new kind of dithyramb was controversial, as innovation in music usually is. Pratinas of Phlius, a musician and dramatist active at Athens from sometime before 500, composed a dance-song—perhaps a dithyramb—in which the chorus protested at a riotous, rhythmically complex style of dancing that had arrived at Dionysus' altar; the aulos, instead of being subservient to the voice, was now calling the tune, babbling away in deep, toad-like intricacies. Pratinas sought to reassert a more conventional 'Dorian' style.[65] Pindar, on the other hand, begins a dithyramb written for performance at Thebes thus:[66]

> Formerly the dithyrambic song proceeded
> drawn out like a rope,
> and from men's mouths the false-sounding 's'.

---

[62] Schol. Pind. *Ol.* 13. 26 b, schol. Ar. *Av.* 1403, *Suda* iii. 207. 27, 236. 26; *Marm. Par. FGrH* 239 A 46 with Jacoby's comment.

[63] Ps.-Plut. *De mus.* 1141 c.

[64] See below, p. 346.

[65] *PMG* 708 = *TrGF* 4 F 3. The toad metaphor is probably the earliest attested instance of a commonplace of modern music critics, likening unfamiliar sonorities to animal noises; a number of examples are quoted by N. Slonimsky, *Lexicon of Musical Invective*, 9 f. There is no real basis for the idea that *phrȳneou* 'toad' plays derisively on the name of Phrynichus or Phrynis. Pratinas elsewhere shows interest in musical history, and in the propriety of different modes, including Lasus' Aeolian.

[66] Fr. 70 b.

> But now new gates stand open wide
> for the holy chorus-rings.

He goes on to justify the new style by a vision of a wild Dionysiac celebration among the gods, with drums and clappers, waving torches, and frenzied dancing; and by his own authority as a nationally important poet. The old-fashioned kind of dithyramb was monotonous and lacking in variety.[67] The reference to the 'false-sounding "s"' clearly serves to define 'formerly' as 'before the refinements of Lasus'. It is worth mentioning that one line of the (unreliable) biographical tradition made Pindar a pupil of Lasus.[68]

Simonides must have known Lasus as a member of Hipparchus' entourage,[69] but it is difficult to say how much he was influenced by him. All that we hear of his scale systems is that he used the Dorian mode (not necessarily always) and the enharmonic genus.[70] It may be significant that he appears in one version of the list of those who enlarged the kithara: he is named as the inventor of the eighth string, and specifically of 'the third note', i.e. Tritē, which is the note missing from the third of the heptachord scales recorded in the pseudo-Aristotelian *Problems*.[71]

Like other choral poets of the time, Simonides commonly used the triadic system of strophes. His rhythms are certainly complex and 'modern' in comparison with those of Ibycus or Anacreon. One feature of his technique that seems particularly forward-looking is his occasional stretching of a word beyond its natural measure for the sake of an expressive musical setting.[72]

Pindar

In Pindar we find a composer with a marked interest in musical and literary history. He looks back over the centuries, contemplates poets and musicians of the past, and comments on their achieve-

---

[67] 'Drawn out like a rope', *schoinoteneia*, may allude to the *schoiniōn nomos* (p. 216). It also recalls Euripides' criticism of Aeschylus' songs (in Ar. *Ran.* 1297) as like those of a rope-maker.

[68] Eustathius, *Proleg. Pind.*, iii. 296. 19 Dr.; *Vita Pindari Thomana*, i. 4. 14 Dr. Cf. G. A. Privitera, *Laso di Ermione* 60f.; I. Gallo, *Una nuova biografia di Pindaro* (Salerno, n.d.), 64.

[69] Ar. *Vesp.* 1410 represents them as rivals in a dithyrambic contest.

[70] Ps.-Plut. *De mus.* 1136f (where Bacchylides and Pindar are also mentioned for Dorian); 1137f ('the Pindaric and Simonidean manner' = enharmonic).

[71] Pliny, *HN* 7. 204, *Suda* iv. 361. 8; *Pr.* 19. 32, see p. 177.

[72] *Knoōsseis*, *pyȳr*: see p. 201.

ments and inventions.[73] He is aware that the art is not static, that it has evolved; and he regards himself as a commanding figure in his time, entitled to depart from tradition, whether in mythological matters or in musical and poetic technique. His advertisement of a modern style of dithyramb has been noticed above. In a paean he calls upon Apollo and Memory, the mother of the Muses, to sound the song, 'not following the rutted carriageway of Homer, but with different horses drawing the Muses' soaring car'.[74] Somewhere he expressed surprise at the neglect of a certain melodic mode, presumably while using it himself.[75] And in his Third Olympian ode he vaunts his discovery of a 'shining new manner' of fitting the celebration of Theron's victory at the Games into the 'Dorian shoe' represented by the noble's concurrent celebration of the Dorian Theoxenia festival.[76]

Pindar composed songs for various kinds of occasion: paeans for regular festivals or special situations; dithyrambs; processionals for male or female choirs; songs for private celebrations; dirges, hymns, etc. It is the Epinician Odes, honouring victors in sporting events, that are best represented in what survives of his work.[77] It was customary for the victor's friends to honour him with songs in a festive setting, but those who employed a poet of Pindar's rank got something special: an elaborate composition of up to a hundred lines (in one exceptional case, three hundred), in long strophes usually arranged on the triadic system. The rhythms were either of the dactylo-epitrite type or variations on iambic or aeolic sequences, often highly complex and as difficult to analyse as anything in Greek poetry. Pindar repeatedly characterizes his own music as *poikilos*, 'intricate, variegated', sometimes in association with verbs expressing craftsmanship, 'plait', 'weave', 'build (as a wall)'.[78] This intricacy

---

[73] Hesiod and Homer quoted, *Isth.* 6. 67, *Pyth.* 4. 277; literary comment on Homer, *Nem.* 7. 21, *Isth.* 3. 55, fr. 347; biographical lore, frs. 264–5 (authorship of *Cypria*); Archilochus quoted, *Ol.* 9. 1; literary-biographical comment, *Pyth.* 2. 54; Alcman, *POxy.* 2389 fr. 9 (if Pindar is the author of the quotation); Olympus, fr. 157; Terpander, frs. 125, 126a; Polymnestus, fr. 188; Sakadas, fr. 269; Xenocritus(?), fr. 140b. 4 (invention of Ionian mode); Arion(?), *Ol.* 13. 18 (Corinthian origin of dithyramb).

[74] *Paean* 7b = fr. 52h. The reference may be to a new form of the legend rather than to a novel style, but the attitude—'avoid the beaten track'—is significant. Cf. also *Ol.* 1. 36, 9. 48, *Nem.* 8. 20.   [75] Fr. 275.

[76] *Ol.* 3. 1–9. We cannot identify the novelty or the Dorian component in the combination.   [77] See p. 22.

[78] *Ol.* 3. 8, 4. 2, 6. 86f., *Nem.* 4. 14, 5. 42, 8. 15, fr. 179, 194. 2; Kaimio, 149. For a detailed survey of Pindar's musical references see ibid. 146–62.

may be rhythmical, melodic, or verbal, or all of these; but he does not mean only verbal intricacy, since in three of the passages the adjective qualifies the sound of his lyre. This lyre, however, does not produce a wider array of notes than normal: it has but seven 'percussions', seven 'tongues'.[79]

It was always assumed in Antiquity, and has mostly been accepted by modern scholars, that these songs were sung by the local choir. Recently a lively controversy has been aroused by an alternative view according to which they were sung solo by Pindar or a deputy, while the chorus that is several times mentioned performed other, less ambitious songs and dances.[80] The new hypothesis deserves serious consideration, but it seems to me to require a forced interpretation of some passages.[81]

As regards instrumentation, there are many references in the Epinicians to the *phorminx* or *lyrā* as being in action.[82] But in several odes there are auloi as well,[83] and it must be accepted that sometimes, at least, these songs were accompanied by both instruments. Perhaps the aulete supplied some notes additional to those of the kithara-strings, for while the kithara has 'seven tongues', those of the aulos are not numbered, and it is repeatedly described as *pamphōnos*, 'having every voice'.[84] Does this mean 'all the notes of the vocal melody'? We recall that Lasus had introduced to vocal music 'a larger number of scattered notes in accordance with the abundance of sounds that auloi have'. It was suggested that he developed the old pentatonic vocal scale into the (enharmonic) heptatonic. Possibly Pindar's choruses sang in this more elaborate style, with the aulete able to match their every note, but with the citharist missing out on the divided semitones.

Pindar several times refers to particular modes. In a paean he

---

[79] *Pyth.* 2. 70, *Nem.* 5. 24.

[80] Tentatively suggested for *some* odes by J. Herington, *Poetry into Drama* (Berkeley and LA, 1985), 31; argued on a broad front by M. Lefkowitz, *AJPhil.* 109 (1988), 1–11; M. Heath, ibid. 180–95; M. Davies, *CQ* 38 (1988), 52–64; Heath and Lefkowitz, *CPhil.* 86 (1991), 173–91; *contra*, A. P. Burnett, *CPhil.* 84 (1989) 283–93; C. Carey, *AJPhil.* 110 (1989) 545–65 and *CPhil.* 86 (1991), 192–200; J. M. Bremer in S. R. Slings (ed.), *The Poet's I in Archaic Greek Lyric* (Amsterdam, 1990), 50–8.   [81] For example, *Pyth.* 10. 4–6 + 51–9; *Nem.* 3. 1–12.

[82] Both words will denote a box lyre, see p. 51. Pindar and Bacchylides also know the barbitos, but only in more informal sympotic settings; see p. 58.

[83] *Ol.* 3. 8, 7. 12, 10. 84, 93 f., *Nem.* 3. 12 + 79, 9. 8. Auloi alone are mentioned in ps.-Pind. *Ol.* 5. 19, Bacchyl. 2. 12, and perhaps 9. 68, 10. 54. They also appear as the instrument accompanying the girls' chorus at the Theban Daphnephoria, Pind. fr. 94 b. 14.   [84] *Ol.* 7. 12, *Pyth.* 12. 19, *Isth.* 5. 27.

praised 'the Dorian melody' as being the most dignified; no doubt he was composing in it at that moment. At least one other reference to the Dorian mode seems fairly sure.[85] Three or four of the Epinicians are unequivocally indicated to be in the Lydian mode.[86] Others are apparently in the Aeolian.[87] The Phrygian mode is nowhere mentioned. The invention of the Ionian is discussed in a prominent position at the beginning of a fragmentary song which was presumably in that mode: it is associated with auloi, and surprisingly attributed to an unidentified Locrian from South Italy.[88]

Regional traditions: Athens

Like Simonides and Simonides' nephew Bacchylides, Pindar took commissions from patrons in many parts of the Greek world, from Thessaly in the north to Cyrene in the south, from Rhodes in the east to Italy and Sicily in the west. The geographical spread is vast, but the actual clientèle for these prestigious compositions was quite small. As in the sixth century, there were men of wealth and power here and there who were drawn to music and poetry and who, by buying it in from near and far, established at least for a time centres of a Panhellenic rather than local culture. The most outstanding of these patrons was Hieron, the lord of Syracuse, who between 478 and 467 made his city virtually the cultural capital of the Greek world.

Regional traditions subsisted nevertheless. Lesbos continued to produce outstanding citharodes. There was one Aristoclides, who claimed descent from Terpander, and who may have enjoyed Hieron's patronage.[89] There was his pupil Phrynis, whose importance is such that we will have to return to him later. 'After the Lesbian singer' was a phrase applied to those who were judged good at something but not quite the best, as if the first prize automatically

---

[85] Frs. 67; 191 'an Aeolian (sc. the Boeotian Pindar) trod the Dorian path of songs'. More debatable are *Ol.* 1. 17 'Dorian phorminx' (a later passage in the ode suggests the Aeolian mode), 3. 5 'Dorian shoe' (cf. above, p. 345), *Pyth.* 8. 20 'Dorian *kōmos*' (= the festive singers).

[86] *Ol.* 14. 17, *Nem.* 4. 45, 8. 15; ps.-Pind. *Ol.* 5. 19, where the instrument is the auloi. These odes do not all belong to the same metrical category. Pindar also spoke of this mode in a paean, where he said it was first introduced by Amphion, who married the Lydian Niobe and learned it from her family (fr. 52n adn. + Paus. 9. 5. 7).

[87] *Ol.* 1. 102; *Pyth.* 2. 69 (seems to refer to another composition; lyre); *Nem.* 3. 79 (auloi). 'Aeolian' could mean merely Boeotian, i.e. from Pindar, but close phraseological parallels with other passages favour the modal interpretation.

[88] Fr. 140b; he may have had Xenocritus in mind.

[89] Istros, *FGrH* 334 F 56, schol. Ar. *Nub.* 971.

went to a Lesbian contestant.[90] At Sparta the art of playing the auloi was handed down from father to son in certain families.[91] At Thebes too the aulos was cultivated assiduously, and towards the end of the fifth century this city established itself as the mother of the leading virtuosi, some of whom developed the capabilities of the instrument by mechanical improvements. An account of them may be postponed for the moment.

At Athens, from the beginning of the Classical period, we see a lively and varied musical culture, fed by influences both from Ionia and from mainland neighbours. At the public level there were all the dithyrambs and dramatic performances at the Dionysiac festivals; these probably owed much in their beginnings to Dorian traditions of choral song in the Megarid and the north-eastern Peloponnese. There were the paeans and hymns sung at various other festivals. At the Great Panathenaea there were also the citharodic, aulodic, and auletic displays. In the 470s Themistocles put up a special building for these contests to take place in, the 'Odeion', perhaps the world's first purpose-built concert hall. In 446, or a little before, Pericles made new ordinances for the musical events, and there were modifications to the Odeion.[92]

Meanwhile, in the houses of the leisured class, there was the eternal symposium with all its informal music-making.[93] Here, for a while at least, Ionian elegance was the vogue. Hipparchus' importation of Anacreon planted the best East Greek poet-musician of his time in Athenian society, and between about 520 and 460 various vase-paintings depict revellers attired in East Greek fashion, with turbans or bonnets, long cloaks and mantles, and sometimes earrings and parasols. One of them holds a barbitos with Anacreon's name written on it, clear evidence that this style of luxury was associated with him, whether or not he personally started the fashion. The barbitos itself first appears at Athens in his time, and we have noted the suggestion that he may have introduced it from across the Aegean.[94]

---

[90] Cratinus fr. 263. Aristotle (fr. 545) took the reference to be specifically to Terpander; others (Aelius Dionysius λ 7) took it to be to Euainetides—otherwise unknown, but evidently another notable Lesbian citharode—or Phrynis. Cf. also Paus. Atticista μ 14. [91] Hdt. 6. 60 (above, n. 40).

[92] Plut. *Per.* 13. 9–11; J. A. Davison, *JHS* 78 (1958) 33–41 = *From Archilochus to Pindar* 48–64. [93] See pp. 25 f.

[94] Above, p. 58. For the vases and their interpretation cf. M. Davies, *Mnemos.* 34 (1981), 288–99; C. Brown, *Phoenix* 37 (1983), 8–11; Maas–Snyder, 119 f., 135 figs. 13–14.

The harp is another instrument that came to Athens from East Greece. Anacreon knows it; it is only after the middle of the fifth century that it appears on Attic vases, but then in several forms. It is normally a women's instrument, but we hear of a Gnesippus and a Cleomenes who composed and sang beguiling love-songs to the *trigōnos* or *iambȳkē*.[95] A party is described at which, after a girl with auloi has played a Carian melody, another with a *trigōnos* accompanies herself in an 'Ionian' song, that is, a sexually provocative one.[96]

The symposiasts themselves might sing songs or excerpts from well-known poets from anything up to a couple of hundred years back, and from various parts of Greece (though with alien dialects modified to something nearer Attic).[97] The repertory also included popular anonymous items such as the *Harmodios*, which celebrated the memory of the two brothers who assassinated Hipparchus in 514 and hastened the fall of the Pisistratid régime.[98]

The ten civil tribes that competed against each other in the dithyrambic contests sometimes, in their zeal for the prize, engaged outstanding non-Athenian musicians to compose or to play the auloi for them. This is probably why dithyrambic music—together with citharody, which also occupied many outsiders—came to be particularly associated with novelty and avant-gardism. The music of tragedy also evolved, of course, but dithyramb and the citharodic *nomos* led the way.[99] Lasus, Simonides, Bacchylides, and Pindar all wrote dithyrambs for Athenian choruses; of their modernism we have spoken already. In the second half of the fifth century there

[95] Chionides fr. 4 (nine strings), Eup. fr. 148, cf. Cratinus fr. 104, Epicrates fr. 4. On harps see above, pp. 70 ff.

[96] Plato Com. fr. 71. 12 ff. 'Ionian songs' were known at the time as a category of erotic song; see Ar. *Eccl.* 883 (with Ussher's note), 890–9, 911–19. They may have been in the Ionian mode, though the Lydian is also associated with songs of that sort (Cratinus fr. 276). 'Ionian' may just refer to the hedonistic life-style associated with Ionia. By the late 4th c., songs of this character were called 'Locrian' (Clearchus fr. 33, *PMG* 853), probably with reference to Locri in South Italy, where the women had the reputation of being easily available; the old Locrian mode does not come into question.

[97] See p. 25; *PMG* 891 = Alc. fr. 249. 6–9; Ar. *Vesp.* 1232–5 = Alc. fr. 141.

[98] *PMG* 893–6, 911. See the whole collection of *Carmina convivalia*, *PMG* 884 ff. It can be observed from the metres that there were certain favourite tunes that were used again and again.

[99] Tragedy was sometimes written by resident aliens, such as Pratinas of Phlius and his son Aristias, Neophron of Sicyon, Ion of Chios, or Achaeus of Eretria, but they were not noted for musical originality in the same way.

were, among others, Melanippides of Melos, Timotheus of Miletus, Telestes of Selinus, and Philoxenus of Cythera, while the only native Athenian dithyrambist of note is Cinesias.[100] These, together with the Lesbian citharode Phrynis, stand out as the principal representatives of the so-called New Music that we find unfavourably contrasted with the old by comedians and philosophers.

We shall come back to the New Music in the next chapter. But first some further remarks on the general state of music in fifth-century Athens.

Many older songs, and traditional aulos melodies such as were attributed to Olympus, were still current. What we are told of the archaic style would lead us to suppose that they were essentially pentatonic and without modulation. On the other hand there were modern compositions, some of which perhaps maintained the same simplicity, while others tended to the richer enharmonic scales and the greater rhythmic complexity and variability of Lasus and his followers.

Apart from his musical innovations, Lasus had aroused new interest in the history and theory of the art. We hear of several musicians at Athens in the first half of the fifth century who seem to have been in some sense also musicologists. Plato names Pythoclides of Ceos and Agathocles of Athens as men who used music as a cover for sophistry. Pythoclides was an aulete who taught Pericles;[101] Agathocles is said to have taught Pindar and Damon.[102] Then there was Lamprocles, a composer of dithyrambs, who 'realized' that the Mixolydian scale was not related to others in the manner that had been supposed. He is said to have been a pupil of Agathocles and a teacher of Damon.[103] Then there was Damon himself, whose influential disquisition on music has been described elsewhere.[104]

Tragedy

The tragic poet, unlike the dithyrambic, had to apply to the mayor for a chorus and a performing slot. He apparently presented speci-

[100] Unless Crexus, whose place of origin is not recorded, was an Athenian.

[101] Pl. *Prt.* 316e, *Alc. I* 118c, Arist. fr. 401. Schol. Pl. *Alc.* 118c says he was a Pythagorean. His name may suggest an auletic family background. According to one opinion he invented the Mixolydian *harmoniā* (Aristox.[?] ap. ps.-Plut. *De mus.* 1136d).

[102] Pl. *Prt.* loc. cit., *La.* 180d; *Vita Pindari* i. 1. 12 Dr. and Eust. *Proleg. Pind.* iii. 301. 2 Dr., poet ap. eund. 301. 19. Schol. Pl. *Alc.* 118c makes him a pupil of Pythoclides.   [103] Above, p. 223; schol. Pl. loc. cit.

[104] Above, p. 246.

mens of his work, including musical portions.[105] One imagines that the authorities favoured proven talent, promising plots, and music that was not too alarming. As we have mentioned, where musical originality was concerned, dithyramb and the citharodic *nomos* led and tragedy followed. The tragedian had to have some musical competence, since he was his own melodist and commonly his own choreographer and chorus-trainer, besides being in the earlier period one of the principal actors.[106] But poetic, rhetorical, and dramatic skills were on the whole more important for success.

The musical elements consisted of (*a*) songs for the chorus, mostly strophic;[107] (*b*) songs, again mostly strophic, in which the chorus and an actor, or the chorus and two actors, sang in turn; (*c*) after the middle of the fifth century, and increasingly towards its end, solo arias, mostly astrophic; (*d*) certain passages recited (by chorus or actors) with instrumental accompaniment;[108] (*e*) short instrumental sections in amongst the songs.[109] Not all actors were required to sing. Many parts are written in such a way as to dispense them. The chorus numbered twelve in Aeschylus' time, but later fifteen. The instrumental accompaniment was provided by a single aulete.[110] It had elements of heterophony, at any rate by the end of the fifth century.

The music of the older tragedians, so we are told, was either of the enharmonic genus or enharmonic with an admixture of diatonic. Agathon or Euripides was the first to use the chromatic.[111] We hear also that the earlier tragedians used 'small' scale-systems, Euripides being the first to use *polychordiā*, many notes; the older style was known as *anatrētos*, 'perforated', or as we should say, 'gapped'.[112] The meaning may be that the enharmonic of early classical tragedy

---

[105] See Pickard-Cambridge, *DFA*² 84.
[106] Ibid. 84–6, 93, 130f. On the early tragedians as dance-masters see Ath. 21 e–22 a.
[107] For the form and arrangement of the strophes see pp. 211 f.
[108] See p. 40. In some cases this *parakatalogē* alternated with sung sections in symmetrical strophic structures.
[109] *Mesauli(k)on* or *diaulion*, Psell. *De trag.* 9, cf. Aristid. Quint. p. 23. 21, Hsch. δ 1417, Phot. *Lex.* δ 478–9, Eust. *Il.* 862. 19. It is not clear how early this existed.
[110] J. Beazley, *Hesp.* 24 (1955), 305–19 (vases); Pickard-Cambridge, *DFA*² 165–7. Other instruments might appear occasionally as appropriate to particular characters or situations. Thus a mythical singer such as Orpheus, Thamyras, or Amphion could carry a lyre and sing to it. Hypsipyle accompanies her song to the baby Opheltes with *krotala* (Eur. *Hyps.* p. 26 Bond), and the Bacchants are equipped with drums (*Ba.* 58 f., 124, 156).
[111] Plut. *Quaest. conv.* 645 e (*TrGF* 39 F 3 a); Psell. *De trag.* 5.
[112] Psell. loc. cit.

was still of the pentatonic type, without divided semitones, and that Euripides adopted the more modern, nuanced version described by Damon, in which the Dorian scale, for example, had nine notes instead of seven.

The principal modes employed were the dignified Dorian and the more emotional Mixolydian.[113] The Ionian and (Slack) Lydian were also used.[114] The introduction of the Lydian is attributed to Sophocles. He is also credited with introducing the Phrygian mode to tragedy and using it in a rather dithyrambic manner.[115] Agathon then brought in the Hypodorian and Hypophrygian. These too were associated with the dithyramb (the Hypodorian also with citharody), and they were not used for choral odes but only in astrophic monodies.[116]

The first tragedian on whose music any judgements are recorded is Phrynichus. Songs played a large part in his plays, and they were remembered as being highly melodious and grateful to the ear. His choreography was also noted for its inventiveness.[117]

Aeschylus' music was distinctly different in style from Phrynichus': so we gather from Aristophanes, who represents it as long-winded and repetitive, like an antiquated rope-maker's work songs. At the same time it is somehow like the citharodes' *nomoi*, requiring only lyre-strums between the lines to bring out the resemblance.[118] The point of the comparison seems to lie in Aeschylus' occasional use of rolling dactylic rhythms of an epical cast, not in any modal factor, since the modes most associated with the citharodes, Lydian and Hypodorian, were introduced to tragedy only after Aeschylus' time.[119]

---

[113] Aristox. fr. 81, cf. ps.-Arist. *Pr.* 19. 48, Plut. *De audiendo* 46b. Aristoxenus thinks the tragedians got the Mixolydian mode from Sappho; evidently it was less widespread in archaic music than Dorian. If its scale was as described in the Damonian list, *e* (*e↑*) *f g a* (*a↑*) *bb e′*, it may account for Psellus' 'enharmonic with an admixture of diatonic'.

[114] Aristox. fr. 82, Psell. *De trag.* 5, Heraclid. Pont. fr. 163 (Ath. 625b); Aesch. *Supp.* 69 'so I too lamenting in Ionian strains . . .', cf. my *Studies in Aeschylus* (Stuttgart, 1990), 130f.

[115] Aristox. fr. 79; Psell. loc. cit., who remarks that the Lydian belongs more to the citharodic style.

[116] Psell. loc. cit.; ps.-Arist. *Pr.* 19. 30, 48. See above, pp. 183f.

[117] Ar. *Vesp.* 220 and schol., 269, 1490 (with MacDowell's n.), 1524; *Av.* 748ff.; ps.-Arist. *Pr.* 19. 31; epigram in Plut. *Quaest. conv.* 732f (*TrGF* 3 T 9–10, 13).

[118] *Ran.* 1249f., 1261–300, cf. 914f.

[119] One ancient interpreter, Timachidas (ap. schol. *Ran.* 1282), explained the reference by saying (not necessarily with any evidence) that Aeschylus used the

Aeschylus' odes sometimes represent types of song that might be sung in real-life situations: ritual or incantatory hymns, formal laments accompanied by breast-beating and other gestures of mourning, and so forth. There are stylistic features such as antiphonal verbal responsion, solemn interjections, refrains, that may reflect the conventions of ritual songs. The music too may have echoed them. In the *Persians* Aeschylus may have sought to give some of the songs an Asiatic flavour. The chorus refer to their own 'barbarian cries' and to their wailing that will be like that of a Mariandynian dirger, while Xerxes calls upon them to vociferate in Mysian fashion.[120]

Sophocles gave the music of tragedy a wider range by admitting modalities more familiar in other genres. It may be that no special flash of genius was required for such developments, and that musical styles naturally tended to spread across concurrent genres and blur their individualities. Sophocles' rhythms were also more varied and complex. Here too we may see the influence of non-theatrical music. For example, the dactylo-epitrite type of metre, much used by such poets as Pindar and Bacchylides, but not, so far as we know, by Aeschylus, comes to be quite at home in Sophoclean and Euripidean tragedy.

Aristophanes lists 'songs by Sophocles' among the pleasures of the festival,[121] and he clearly preferred Sophocles' music to Euripides'. In the *Frogs* he makes Aeschylus accuse Euripides of gathering his lyrics from anywhere and everywhere: 'from tarts' songs, party songs by Meletus, Carian aulos airs, dirges, festive choral dances'.[122] There follows, to a vulgar, clacking accompaniment (see p. 123), a delightful parody of a choral ode in Euripides' late style—if only we had the music!—with the comment that it is composed on the twelve-resourceful-variations principle of Cyrene, who was a versatile *fille de joie* of the time. It looks as if this refers at least in part to metrical variations, as attention is drawn to two glyconic measures of unusual form. But there is probably also a melodic reference that we cannot appreciate. Then comes an equally brilliant parody of a Euripidean

orthios nomos (cf. Aesch. *Ag.* 1153). This was a citharodic *nomos* ascribed to Terpander (Poll. 4. 65, ps.-Plut. *De mus.* 1140f, *Suda* i. 151. 30, iii. 477. 15 = Phot. s.v. *nomos*); cf. Hdt. 1. 24. 5 (Arion).

[120] *Pers.* 635, 939, 1054. Cf. W. Kranz, *Stasimon* (Berlin, 1933), 127–42.
[121] *Pax* 531.
[122] *Ran.* 1301–3. Meletus was known for erotic songs (Epicrates fr. 4). Carian aulos pieces belong in the same sphere, cf. above, p. 349.

solo aria, a rambling lament in a kaleidoscopic medley of different rhythms.[123] Both parodies contain the word *heieieilissō*, so spelt to indicate and exaggerate the modern expressive division of the first syllable between three (?) notes.[124]

Of course, the whole criticism is exaggerated. We cannot believe that Euripides' lyrics, which are far from vulgar in their verbal style, so readily evoked the atmosphere of the night club. Yet Aristophanes is able to point a connection. Other fragments of ancient comment reflect rather the growing influence on tragedy of contemporary citharodic and dithyrambic music: Euripides uses more notes than the older tragedians, he ventures into the chromatic genus, which was too 'soft' for them, and in general he shows a greater variety of styles and colours.[125] Again we should beware of overstatement. Euripides' use of chromatic, for example, can hardly have been more than occasional, since after his death, with his plays becoming increasingly popular, we still find it asserted that the singers of tragedy 'use enharmonic throughout', and that tragedy 'has not adopted the chromatic genus even today, although the kithara, which is many generations older, has used it from the beginning'.[126] The two preserved fragments of music to Euripidean lyrics are best interpreted as enharmonic (with divided semitones), although the notation is compatible with chromatic. One is probably in the Dorian mode, the other perhaps in a form of Mixolydian.[127] They show some division of long syllables between two notes, but this was not necessarily a modernistic feature.[128] There is more reason to suppose this of the touches of heterophony in the accompaniment, but the evidence on the matter is equivocal.[129]

The much younger tragedian Agathon, who won his first victory in 416 when Euripides was in his sixties, was more closely associated with modernist tendencies. Besides being named (alternatively to Euripides) as the first to use the chromatic genus in tragedy, he is said to have introduced to it the Hypodorian and Hypophrygian modes. His melodies were full of intricate bends like ant-tracks, and had a sensuous effect. His aulos music itself had a distinctively soft and voluptuous character; presumably he used *mesaulia*, instru-

[123] *Ran.* 1331–63. For the contemporary vogue for rhythmic diversity see p. 153.
[124] See pp. 201, 203 n. 29.   [125] Psell. *De trag.* 5.
[126] Alcid.(?) in *PHib.* 13. 20f.; ps.-Plut. *De mus.* 1137e, where 'even today' must reproduce the wording of a 4th-c. source, probably Aristoxenus.
[127] pp. 285f.   [128] p. 202.   [129] pp. 206f.

mental solos. We know that he broke the conventions regarding choral odes by substituting songs that were mere interludes and had nothing to do with the play. Other dramatists took up the practice.[130]

Comedy

There is less to say about the music of fifth-century comedy. It was mainly choral or shared by the chorus with one or two actors. Solo arias are exceptional except where tragedy or other serious music is being parodied. The chorus was larger than that of tragedy, having twenty-four members. The accompanist was again an aulete.

The songs are mostly comparatively simple in rhythms and structure—again, except in tragic parody.[131] They clearly represent a more popular level of music. Sometimes they give us a distinct impression of genuine forms of popular song, for example in the wedding hymns at the end of *Peace* and *Birds* and the amorous serenades in *Ecclesiazusae* (893 ff.). On modes, genera, etc., we have no information.

Recitative in iambic, trochaic, and anapaestic metres appears to have played a more extensive role than in tragedy.[132] A recurrent and evidently traditional feature of Old Comedy is the so-called 'epirrhematic syzygy', in which a sung strophe and antistrophe are each followed by an equal number of trochaic tetrameters, either sixteen or twenty. These must have been in recitative, and the standardization in their number of lines probably reflects a stereo-typed dance sequence.

---

[130] Plut. *Quaest. conv.* 645 e, Psell. *De trag.* 5; Ar. *Thesm.* 68, 100 ff., fr. 178; Arist. *Poet.* 1456ᵃ29. (*TrGF* 39 F 3 a, T 20 c, 21, 20 ab, 18.)

[131] The rhythms are usually iambic or iambo-choriambic, trochaic, paeonic, aeolic, or anapaestic.

[132] For discussion of how extensive see Pickard-Cambridge, *DFA*² 156–65.

12

Historical Synthesis
2. High Noon and Afternoon

By the last quarter of the fifth century the progressive music of Lasus
and Simonides had become classic; but there was a more acute sense
than ever of an opposition between old and new styles. Damon's
warning against the dangers of a musical revolution (p. 246) was one
influential expression of this feeling. In a fragment of Eupolis someone asks, 'Okay, do you want to hear the present-day pattern of song,
or the old style?' One of those addressed answers, 'Give us both, and
I'll listen and take whichever I decide.' Songs ancient and modern,
with elements of exaggeration and parody, must have followed. In
Aristophanes we hear that formerly boys were brought up to sing to
the lyre such pieces as Lamprocles' hymn to Athena,

> maintaining to pitch the attunement handed down by their fathers.
> And if any of them played the fool or made any bends
> of the kind they do now, these cussed bends *à la* Phrynis,
> he got a good thrashing for doing away with the Muses.[1]

'Bends' (*kampai*) are often alluded to at this period as a characteristic of modern music. They are associated with departure from the
harmoniā, the proper attunement, and it seems likely that they are
the same as what are later called *metabolai*, i.e. modulations.[2]

Another aspect of the old/new antithesis is the increased number
of notes available and the consequent enhancement of melodic

---

[1] Eup. fr. 326; Ar. *Nub.* 966–72. 'The Muses' here stand for the true notes; cf.
p. 224.

[2] See especially Pherecr. fr. 155. 9, 15f., 26–8; also Ar. *Nub.* 333 (with schol.),
Thesm. 53, 68, fr. 753, Eup. fr. 366, Timoth. *PMG* 802, Poll. 4. 67, 73. Probably not
with this sense in Pind. fr. 107 a. 3, nor in Telestes, *PMG* 808.4. In another Aristophanic passage (fr. 930) departure from the *harmoniā* is called 'playing the Chian or
Siphnian'; according to the 4th-c. writer Praxidamas, the allusion was to Democritus
of Chios and Theoxenides of Siphnos and their use of the chromatic genus.

variety. Ion of Chios, in his poem addressed to the kithara that is now equipped with eleven strings, says

> Formerly Greeks all plucked you at seven pitches,
>   two tetrachords (?), raising a scanty Muse,

and in similar vein someone in Aristophanes, praising the modern music, says of it

> not like they sang originally, seven-note, all alike.[3]

Multiplicity of *chordai* (strings or notes), besides exharmonic 'bends', is a prominent theme in a passage quoted from Pherecrates' comedy *Chiron*, where the dishevelled figure of Music complains to Justice of the progressively more outrageous treatment she has suffered in recent times from Melanippides, Cinesias, Phrynis, and Timotheus. At two or three points she speaks of 'twelve *chordai*', though the number should probably not be taken too literally. 'A dozen' may be a better rendering.[4]

Melanippides

These ruffians were all either composers of dithyramb or citharodes; Timotheus was both. Tragedians such as Agathon and Euripides, though influenced by the new music, are never numbered among its pioneers. It is the dithyrambist Melanippides of Melos that Pherecrates' Music identifies as the first to misuse her. He came from a family of musicians; his maternal grandfather, also called Melanippides, won a dithyrambic victory at Athens in 493, and his father Criton too is described as a poet. He himself was active perhaps from about 440 to about 415.[5]

One crucial innovation attributed to him is the substitution of *anabolai* for antistrophes. As a musical term, *anabolē* usually signifies an instrumental preface to a vocal performance.[6] If it replaces an antistrophe, it becomes an intermezzo; and a dithyramb deprived of antistrophes is presumably one without responsion,

---

[3] Ion fr. 32. 3–4; Ar. fr. 467. Cf. the criticism of Aeschylus' music as 'always the same' (*Ran.* 1250).

[4] Pherecr. fr. 155. On 'twelve' as a round number see I. Düring, *Eranos* 43 (1945), 181 f.

[5] The main sources regarding Melanippides and the other musicians to be discussed in this section are most conveniently collected in J. M. Edmonds's *Lyra Graeca*, iii (Loeb, 1927). See also the relevant articles in *RE*, mostly by Paul Maas.

[6] See p. 205.

through-composed, consisting of a series of sung sections punctuated by passages for aulos alone. Strophic form had been taken for granted in Pindar's day, however original his dithyrambs may have been in other respects. Its abandonment by Melanippides in favour of the free form characteristic of auletic and citharistic programme music opened the way to a much more expressive vocal style in which the melody could be shaped to suit the words.[7]

What Pherecrates says of him is that he undid Music and slackened her with his dozen *chordai*. We can infer at least that he used extra notes besides those of the plain old scales, and probably that he favoured a mode or modes of the category called 'slack'.[8] As to the latter point, we have a vague statement, in the context of a discussion of the origins of the Lydian mode, that 'some say Melanippides originated this *melos*'.[9] As to the former, we hear from the same writer, pseudo-Plutarch, that

aulos-playing has changed from a simpler to a more intricate musical art. In the old days, up to Melanippides the dithyrambic composer, it was the case that the auletes were paid by the composers: the primary role was played by the poetry [or composition], and the auletes were subservient to the chorus-trainers [= the composers]. But later this changed for the worse.[10]

At this point the compiler turns from his source, probably Aristoxenus, to the Pherecrates passage, breaking the thread of the argument, which should have gone on to explain that after Melanippides the aulete in the dithyramb got to do more than just accompany the vocal part.

Melanippides reformed the dithyramb in an original and effective way that opened up all kinds of artistic possibilities for the future, and he may have saved the genre from declining into a routine obscurity. But we should not lay every feature of the New Music at his door. Pherecrates represents him as moderate in comparison with Cinesias, Phrynis, and Timotheus, and he does not mention modulations, *kampai*, in connection with Melanippides as he does with all the others. A gentleman of taste in the last decade of the century, whose favourite epic and tragic poets were Homer and Sophocles, might put Melanippides top for dithyramb.[11]

---

[7] Cf. pp. 198 and 212 ff.   [8] See p. 179.
[9] Ps.-Plut. *De mus.* 1136 c. Perhaps the meaning is that he was the first to use Lydian in dithyramb.   [10] Ps.-Plut. *De mus.* 1141 cd.
[11] Socrates' friend Aristodemus in Xen. *Mem.* 1. 4. 3.

Cinesias and Crexus

Cinesias is, of all these musicians, the one most commonly satirized in comedy. But that is probably because he was the only Athenian among them; the others were men from overseas who came and went. He was the son of a painfully bad citharode called Meles, who was still about in 420. He himself was a nervous, spindly, sickly creature, whose career spans roughly the period 425–390. In Aristophanes' *Birds* he is characterized by his airy-fairy, high-flown style, and there is reference to his *anabolai*. Pherecrates speaks of him as 'making exharmonic bends in his strophes', so that his dithyrambs appear the wrong way round.[12]

No specific innovation is attributed to Cinesias, and later writers do not acknowledge him as one of the important figures in the development of music. They have more to say of one Crexus, who is nowhere mentioned in the remains of Attic comedy and whose home town is not recorded. He is named in two passages of pseudo-Plutarch which are probably drawn from Aristoxenus. The first is a survey of innovative composers. The older ones, including Terpander, Polymnestus, Thaletas, Sakadas, Alcman, and Stesichorus, all adhered to noble standards of beauty,

but Crexus and Timotheus and Philoxenus and the composers of that generation have become more vulgar and devoted to novelty in their pursuit of what is now called personable and prize-quality (?); limitation to a smaller number of notes and simplicity and dignity in music has come to be old-fashioned.

In the other passage Crexus is credited with introducing into dithyramb a form of combination of singing with instrumentally accompanied spoken delivery, which Archilochus and the tragedians had previously employed; and with the invention of heterophonic accompaniment to vocal music.[13] The Stoic Diogenes of Seleucia cited a composition of Crexus as an example of poetry gaining much in impressiveness from its musical setting.[14]

[12] Ar. *Av.* 1372–409, cf. *Ran.* 1438; Pherecr. fr. 155. 8–13, cf. Düring (as above, n. 4), 182–6, and E. K. Borthwick, *Hermes* 96 (1968), 63–7. Cinesias may well be targeted among others in the unspecified references to dithyrambists at Ar. *Nub.* 333–8 (cf. schol.) and *Pax* 829–31. Here too there are *anabolai* and airy-fairy language.
[13] Ps.-Plut. *De mus.* 1135 c, 1141 a. The references to heterophony in older music (above, p. 206) apparently concern aulos pieces alone.
[14] Philod. *Mus.* 4 x pp. 49 f. Neub., *SVF* iii. 227. 32.

Phrynis

The citharode Phrynis appears after Cinesias in Pherecrates' account, but he must have been rather older, probably older than Melanippides. He followed Aristoclides in the proud line of Lesbian citharodes going back to Terpander. He won his first victory in the Panathenaic contest in (probably) 446.[15] He is said to have increased the number of kithara-strings from seven to nine, developed a style of performance characterized by harmonic modulation and rhythmic variety, and created a new kind of *nomos* that combined dactylic hexameters with passages in free form, older citharodes' *nomoi* having been simply melodic schemes for singing verse of stereotyped forms such as hexameters or elegiacs.[16] The increase to nine strings is plausible, though the literary and artistic evidence on the subject is conflicting.[17] It was suggested earlier that Lasus had introduced the form of enharmonic with divided semitones—the form that gave the Dorian and Phrygian scales nine notes (as in the Damonian list) instead of seven—and that Pindar's choruses sang in this style while the citharist could still only play seven notes. The construction of a nine-stringed kithara was an obvious next step.

Pherecrates' lines on Phrynis are not easy to understand:

> Phrynis, hurling a kind of personal whirlwind at me,
> has ravaged me completely with his bending and twisting,
> having a dozen *harmoniai* in five strings.[18]
> Even so, he too was a passable partner,
> for if he did go astray at all, he made it good again.

The first line suggests a wild flurry of notes.[19] The next two lines obviously refer to modulation between different scales. But if the

---

[15] The source, schol. Ar. *Nub.* 971, gives 'in the archonship of Callias' = 456, but as this was not a year in which the quadrennial Great Panathenaea were celebrated, 'Callias' is thought to be a mistake for 'Callimachus', whose archonship fell in 446/5.

[16] Ps.-Plut. *De mus.* 1133 bc from a 4th-c. source, perhaps Heraclides Ponticus (cf. 1132 c); Plut. *Agis* 10. 7, *De prof. virt.* 84 a, *Apophthegmata Laconica* 220 c; Procl. ap. Phot. *Bibl.* 320 b. For Phrynis' association with modulation cf. also Ar. *Nub.* 971, quoted above, p. 356.

[17] See pp. 63 f.   [18] Variant: 'in his pentachords'.

[19] For *strobīlos* 'whirlwind' in this context cf. Plato Com. fr. 285. The word may also mean 'pine-cone' and various other twisted-up things, but Düring's idea that Pherecrates is referring to some conical gadget for altering the tuning of a lyre-string is far-fetched (as in n. 4, 186 f.); cf. H. Schönewolf, *Der jungattische Dithyrambos* (Diss. Giessen, 1938) 67; E. K. Borthwick, *Hermes* 96 (1968), 67 f.; E. Pöhlmann in *Serta Indogermanica* (1982), 310 f.

number of strings is to be mentioned, one certainly expects them to be more than the standard seven, not less. The variant reading 'in his pentachords' offers no clear sense, and even if it could be understood, it would be too technical for comedy. However, with a small emendation (*eis* for *en*) the line can be made to yield the sense 'having up to five *harmoniai* in a dozen strings'. As 'a dozen strings' is a recurring formula in Pherecrates' account of the modern musicians, this is surely what is required. As for the last line of the extract, it suggests that Phrynis' exharmonic excursions were only brief and temporary. The contrast is with Timotheus, who is the subject of the succeeding lines.

Timotheus

Timotheus' name is new to Justice, and she has to ask 'What Timotheus is this?' Music replies, 'A Milesian, a red-haired fellow'. He seems to have been born about 450 or a few years earlier, and not to have become known at Athens as soon as the native Cinesias, who was of similar age. He lived to a great age—90 or 97, according to different sources—but he can hardly have continued as a virtuoso singer much after the first decade of the fourth century.

It was a great moment for him when he beat the eminent Phrynis in competition, perhaps sometime around 420. He boasted of it afterwards:

> How happy you were, Timotheus, when the herald
> announced 'Timotheus of Miletus
> defeats the son of Kamon, the Ionian-bender'.[20]

In another fragment he trumpets his originality: 'I sing not the old songs, my new ones are better . . . Away with the Muse of old.'[21] And in the epilogue of his *Persians* he says that he has found much disfavour at Sparta 'because with my young songs I dishonour the elder Muse'. But, he goes on,

> I exclude no one, young
> or old or my own age,
> from the range of these hymns:
> only those out-of-date music-spoilers,
> that's who I ban, the maulers of songs
> who strain and yell with far-ringing criers' voices.

[20] *PMG* 802. 'Ionian-bender' must refer to Phrynis' use of the Ionian mode. Timotheus himself was an Ionian, Phrynis was not.   [21] *PMG* 796.

His own singing style is evidently something more relaxed and beguiling. He proceeds modestly to identify himself as the only true successor of Orpheus and Terpander. Orpheus first brought the lyre to birth, Terpander equipped it with ten strings (?),[22]

> and now Timotheus brings forth
> his kithara with eleven-note
> measures and rhythms, opening up
> the Muses' treasure-chamber of manifold song.

The diction is somewhat obscure, but there cannot be much doubt that Timotheus is referring to the eleven-stringed instrument with which tradition connects him.[23]

The lady Music in the Pherecrates passage declares that Timotheus' maltreatment of her goes beyond all the others she has mentioned. He leads her through amazing ant-hills,[24] and if he catches her on her own—does this mean when the instrument is playing solo?—he pulls her clothes off and untunes her with his dozen strings. In three further lines which have become detached but probably still refer to Timotheus, she speaks of exharmonic and 'over-shoot' (extra-high) notes,[25] or *niglaroi*,[26] and of being filled up with wrigglies.[27]

We have a substantial portion of the text of one of Timotheus' most celebrated citharodic compositions, his *Persians*.[28] It is a vivid

---

[22] This is very surprising, but it seems to be what Timotheus means. Possibly he is combining the tradition that Terpander added three strings (sc. to the four-stringed lyre) with the legend that gave Orpheus a seven-stringed lyre. He ignores the advances of Phrynis. But in Aristotle's opinion (*Metaph.* 993ᵇ15) 'if Timotheus had not been born, there is a lot of music we would not have, yet if Phrynis had not existed, there would not have been a Timotheus'.

[23] Hellenistic forgery of Laconian decree ap. Boeth. *Inst. Mus.* 1. 1, Nicom. p. 274. 5, Paus. 3. 12. 10, etc. The poem of Ion of Chios (there is no good reason to doubt his authorship) shows that the eleven-stringed lyre was created not later than 422, the year of Ion's death.

[24] The metaphor echoes, or is echoed by, the one Aristophanes applies to Agathon's vocal lines (above, p. 354). On the intricate, twisting and back-turning paths in ant-hills cf. Plut. *De soll. an.* 968b, Ael. *NA* 6. 43.

[25] This became the technical term for the highest tetrachord of the Greater Perfect System (p. 221).

[26] Apparently some kind of instrumental effect or figure, cf. Eup. fr. 121 (with Kassel–Austin), Phrynichus Com. fr. 74. 1 cj.; D. Restani, *Rivista italiana di musicologia* 18 (1983), 186–90.

[27] There is a pun on *kampaí* 'bends' and *kámpai* 'caterpillars'.

[28] *PMG* 788–91; U. von Wilamowitz-Moellendorff, *Timotheos: Die Perser*. For an imaginative reconstruction of the first performance see J. Herington, *Poetry into Drama*, 151–60.

account of the battle of Salamis in several hundred lines, with an epilogue containing prayers to Apollo and the artistic manifesto summarized above. After a hexameter opening it was in free form, falling into clearly marked paragraphs which may have been divided by citharistic passages. The rhythms are varied but not especially complex; iambic and aeolic predominate, and in the epilogue Timotheus settles down into a steady succession of aeolic verses. The language is elaborate, exuberant, highly coloured. The narrative concentrates on pictorial details, the noise and confusion of the naval battle, the surge and the spray, the emerald sea stained red with blood, the floating and washed-up corpses; there are emotional speeches by Persians expostulating through mouthfuls of salt water, chattering with cold on a beach, or abjectly pleading with a captor for mercy in comically broken Greek. Timotheus must have used a wide range of musical resource in putting all this across, variety of mode and register, expressive variations of vocal timbre, and so forth, perhaps underlined by facial expression and body movement. It is this mimetic aspect of the citharodic *nomos* that is given as the reason for its astrophic form: once the contestants at the music festivals learned to imitate action and stretch themselves, their songs became long and varied, changing continually to suit the representation of the subject matter.[29]

Timotheus' dithyrambs showed similar characteristics. One of them contained a portrayal of a storm at sea (a critic remarked that he had seen a bigger one in a stew-pot); another dramatized the birth-pangs of Semele and her cries. It was probably in performing Timotheus' *Scylla* that auletes would make a show of grabbing at the chorus-leader, in imitation of the monster grabbing at Odysseus' sailors.[30] Homer describes Scylla as yelping like a young puppy, and Timotheus no doubt tried to achieve this effect in the aulos part. Odysseus' lament for his lost men seemed to Aristotle a prime example of unseemly and inappropriate characterization.[31] Evidently it was extravagant and unmanly. It seems that it was not related by the chorus as part of a narrative but performed by a solo singer. Similarly with Semele's birth-pangs, and perhaps others of these dithyrambs. Plato says that narrative without speeches is something particularly found in dithyramb (as opposed to epic or

---

[29] Ps.-Arist. *Pr.* 19. 15.
[30] *PMG* 785, 792–3; above, p. 106.
[31] *Poet.* 1454ª30.

tragedy and comedy), but he does not say that all dithyramb took that form, and a later fourth-century source speaks of the dithyramb as having become 'mimetic', like the citharodic nome, and for that reason astrophic. There is a suggestion of the use of soloists, and of an analogy with the actors' arias in tragedy.[32]

Philoxenus

Philoxenus of Cythera, who lived from about 435 to about 380, and is said to have been for a short time a slave of Melanippides', was another dithyrambist, often coupled with Timotheus as a representative of the same trends. Changes of mode, genus, and rhythm are particularly mentioned:

The dithyrambic composers used to change their modes too, making them Dorian, Phrygian, and Lydian in the same song; and they would exchange their melodic lines, making them sometimes enharmonic, sometimes chromatic, and sometimes diatonic, and in their rhythms they continued (sc. following Stesichorus and Pindar) to practice licences quite boldly—I mean the composers of the age of Philoxenus, Timotheus, and Telestes, because with the ancients the dithyramb was just as regulated as anything else.[33]

The Philoxenian style of dithyramb is twice contrasted with the Pindaric, as the paradigm of the new as against the older.[34]

More specific information is vouchsafed about Philoxenus' *Mysians*. According to Aristotle, he tried to compose it in the Dorian mode, but the very nature of the dithyrambic genre forced him back into the conventional Phrygian. This sounds like a rather tendentious way of saying that the work progressed from a Dorian to a Phrygian modality. Fortunately we have a more detailed analysis of it, almost certainly from Aristoxenus, which enables us to reconstruct in general outline the scheme of modulations. The first part of the work was in Hypodorian, its middle in Hypophrygian and Phrygian, and its last section in Dorian and Mixolydian.[35] The terms

---

[32] Pl. *Resp.* 394 c; ps.-Arist. *Pr.* 19. 15.

[33] Dion. Hal. *Comp.* 131 f. Telestes of Selinus is named elsewhere as one of the most important of these poets. There is record of a victory that he won at Athens in 401. His surviving fragments (*PMG* 805–12) show an interest in the legendary history of music and of instruments. It is noteworthy that he twice mentions rapid fingering: 805 c. 3 of the aulos, 808. 4 of a harp(?).

[34] Aristox. fr. 76; Diogenes of Seleucia, *SVF* iii. 222. 20 (Philod. *Mus.* i p. 133 Rispoli), who says intriguingly that despite the great difference of ethos, the underlying manner is the same.

[35] Arist. *Pol.* 1342ᵇ9–12 = *PMG* 826; ps.-Plut. *De mus.* 1142 f. The title of the work is slightly corrupted in both passages, but its restoration is virtually certain. Why

here refer to Aristoxenus' system of keys (see p. 230), 'Mixolydian' being what was later called Hyperdorian. Assuming that the modulations proceeded on the usual principle of switching between conjunct and disjunct tetrachords at the nodal points, the harmonic plan of the *Mysians* may be schematized as in Fig. 12.1.

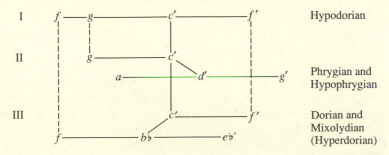

Fig. 12. 1. Harmonic plan of Philoxenus' *Mysians*.

Philoxenus' most celebrated work was his *Cyclops*, composed in singular circumstances. As a guest at the Syracusan court of Dionysius I, the ruler of much of Sicily, Philoxenus made the mistake of dallying too openly with his patron's mistress, an aulos-girl who bore the name of the sea-nymph Galatea, and he was consigned to the stone-quarries. He kept his spirits and composed an amusing work on the incarceration of the intelligent Odysseus (corresponding to himself) in the cave of the dull-witted, one-eyed ogre Polyphemus (Dionysius' eyesight was poor). Polyphemus appeared wearing a pouch full of vegetables and, accompanying himself on the lyre (Dionysius was a third-rate poet), sang in high-flown language to his sheep and goats and to his love, the distant Galatea; he called on the dolphins in the sea to tell her that he was consoling himself with music. There was also a lyrical dialogue between him and Odysseus, who perhaps persuaded him to allow him to set sail in his ship to bring Galatea back.[36] The main instrumental accompaniment to this entertainment was provided by an aulete, and it seems to have been categorized as a dithyramb. But with its two solo singers (one of whom sings to the lyre) and its entries and exits it clearly bursts the

this particular work attracted the attention of harmonic analysts it is hard to say. Perhaps its modulations were more striking than usual.

[36] *PMG* 815–24; cf. S. Medaglia, *Bollettino dei classici* (3rd ser.) 2 (1981), 200.

traditional bounds of dithyramb. It is not surprising that two late sources refer to it as a drama. We might describe it as a chamber opera or operetta.[37]

Star performers

This was an age in which, in music as in the theatre, public enthusiasm was increasingly focused on the virtuoso skills, personality, and showmanship of the individual performer. The leading auletes, for example, enjoyed a higher status than ever before. Alcibiades engaged the Pythian champion Chrysogonus, rather than any ordinary ship's piper, to set the stroke for the crew rowing him back to Athens from exile, while a well-known tragic actor in full costume proclaimed the orders.[38] The most celebrated aulete of the time was Pronomus, a Theban, like so many of the notable auletes that we hear of.[39] He captivated audiences not just by his playing but by his facial expression and the whole movement of his body.[40] He is depicted on a contemporary vase (now named after him), seated in an ornate robe, a garland on his head, playing in the centre of the rehearsal room, which is crowded with actors in satyric and stage costume.[41] But he was more than just a charismatic performer. He was a master of his instrument who significantly extended its capabilities. Just as Phrynis and Timotheus devised kitharas and citharistic techniques for playing several different modal scales with-

---

[37] Cf. Arist. *Poet.* 1448ª14; Didymus in Dem. *Phil.* xii 60 p. 46 Pearson–Stephens. Aristoxenus (frs. 135–6) referred to a composition by one Oenonas or Oenopas which parodied citharody and which portrayed the Cyclops warbling and Odysseus using ungrammatical language (?). This seems to be somehow related to Philoxenus' work. The citharode Nicocles of Tarentum in the early 3rd c. BC is recorded as having won a victory in a dithyramb (*IG* 2². 3779; see Pickard-Cambridge, *DFA*² 42 n. 2).

[38] See p. 29.

[39] From the 5th and early 4th c. we can list: Scopelinus, uncle(?) and teacher of Pindar (*Vita Pindari*, i. 1. 3, 4. 12 Dr.); Olympichus, who played for choruses of Pindar (*CEG* 509, Aristodemus, *FGrH* 383 F 13); Olympichus' son Potamon, who won at the Pythian festival (*CEG* 509); Chaeris (Cratinus fr. 126, Ar. *Ach.* 16, 866 with schol.); Pronomus' son Oeniades (*IG* 2². 3064); Olympiodorus and Orthagoras (Pl. *Prt.* 318c, Aristox. fr. 96); Cleolas, remembered for his use of bodily gesture (Theophr. fr. 92 W.); Nicopheles (Poll. 4. 77); Diodorus (ibid. 80); Ismenias (Plut. *Per.* 1. 5, Pliny *HN* 37. 6); Timotheus (Diphilus fr. 78 with Kassel–Austin, adding Lucian *Harmonides* 1); Antigeneidas (below); Lycus (*IG* 2². 3046, cf. 3071). Cf. Gevaert, ii. 568–72.

[40] Paus. 9. 12. 6.

[41] Naples, Museo Nazionale H 3240, cf. Pickard-Cambridge, *DFA*² 186 f. and pl. facing p. 188; Pl. 27.

out re-tuning, so Pronomus devised multimodal auloi, which came into general use among professionals.[42]

Scarcely less famous was the probably somewhat younger Antigeneidas, also from Thebes.[43] His activity seems to fall in the first third of the fourth century, though some anecdotes place him in settings that lie well outside this span. Apuleius describes him as 'a honey-sweet melodizer of every word and a practised player of every mode, whether you wanted the simple Aeolian or the diverse Ionian, the plaintive Lydian, the religious Phrygian, or the martial Dorian', and says that he was greatly distressed whenever he heard the noble title of piper applied to the hacks who blow hornpipes at funerals.[44] He developed and made fashionable a playing technique described as 'moulded' or 'affected', which required flexibility in the reed and led to a change in the season at which the reeds were harvested.[45] He is called the aulode—no doubt a mistake for 'aulete'—of Philoxenus; perhaps it was he who had to accompany the chorus through the modulatory labyrinth of the *Mysians*. The same source records that he was the first to wear Milesian shoes, and that in the *Reveller* (another work of Philoxenus'?) he wore a yellow cloak.[46]

These sartorial details suggest that in the dithyramb of this period the aulete had come to play a more conspicuous role than formerly. We recall the engagement of the aulete in the action of Timotheus' *Scylla*. It is significant in this connection that whereas the older inscriptions recording victories of the tribal choruses name only the *chorēgos* (the impresario) and the chorus-master (the composer, normally), in the fourth century the aulete is named too, at first mostly after the chorus-master, but later before him.[47]

The outstanding citharist of the period was Stratonicus of Athens, active from about 410 to about 360, and remembered especially for his witticisms, many of which were at the expense of other musicians.

---

[42] See p. 87, and ibid. on the related innovation attributed to another Theban aulete, Diodorus.

[43] H. L. M. Dinse, *De Antigenida Thebano musico* (Berlin, 1856); K. von Jan, *RE* i. 2400f.

[44] Apul. *Flor.* 4.

[45] Theophr. *Hist. Pl.* 4. 11. 4–5, cf. p. 84. Quint. *Inst.* 1. 11. 6–7 describes a type of 'moulded' or 'plastered' playing that involves closing the holes that give a clear tone and using the deep sound of the full pipe; it is analogous to elocution in which the voice's simple nature is coated in a fuller resonance.

[46] *Suda* i. 235. 10–12.

[47] E. Reisch, *RE* iii. 2414.

He is said to have been the first to introduce 'multiplicity of notes' (*polychordiā*) into unaccompanied kithara-playing, which probably means that he adopted one of the new instruments with up to eleven strings. He had pupils, whom he instructed in a room adorned with images of Apollo and the nine Muses. He taught not only the kithara but also harmonic theory, which he illustrated with a diagram of modal scales and their combination.[48] This was very relevant to the modulatory style of music that his polychord kithara was designed for. His music should be imagined as mimetic rather than abstract.[49]

The musician who aroused the greatest popular enthusiasm was the citharode. At the Panathenaic competitions in the late fifth and early fourth centuries it was the citharodes who got the largest prizes. In 402 the first prize (not in fact awarded) was a gold crown weighing 85 drachmas (about 370 grammes). Fuller information is provided by a slightly later inscription, where there are no less than five prizes for citharodes. The top prize is a crown worth 1000 silver drachmas, plus 500 drachmas in cash; the other prizes are worth 700, 600, 400, and 300 drachmas respectively. For aulodes there are only two prizes, worth 300 and 100 drachmas. For citharists there are three, the highest being worth 500 drachmas. For auletes the details are lost.[50] In the musical contests instituted at the Eretrian festival of Artemis about 340 BC the prizes were:[51]

	First	Second	Third
Rhapsodes	120	30	20
Citharists	110	70	55
Citharodes	200	150	100
Parodists	50	10	—

At the Macedonian court, which attracted some of Greece's leading musicians from Pindar's time on, citharodes were prominent among the entertainers after the late fifth century.[52]

[48] Phaenias fr. 32 Wehrli; Ath. 348 d; P. Maas, *RE* iva. 326 f.; above, p. 218. On hearing Timotheus' *Semele* he commented 'What cries she would utter if she were giving birth to a contractor instead of a god!' (Ath. 352 a).

[49] Arist. *Poet.* 1447ᵃ15 states this as a characteristic of solo kithara and aulos music.

[50] *IG* 2². 1388. 36; 2311 = *SIG* 1055; J. A. Davison, *JHS* 78 (1958), 37 f. = *From Archilochus to Pindar*, 56 f.

[51] *IG* 12(9). 189. 15–20. Aulodes and auletes are not provided for here.

[52] Plut. *De Alex. fort.* 334 b (Timotheus a familiar of Archelaus); Theopomp. *FGrH* 115 F 236 (Philip); Chares, *FGrH* 125 F 4 (Alexander).

Resistance to the New Music

The new trends were not to everyone's taste. There were many, both musicians and laymen, who deprecated them. We hear of one Pancrates who generally avoided the chromatic genus, declaring himself a follower of the old style of Simonides and Pindar.

The same applies to Tyrtaeus of Mantinea, Andreas of Corinth, Thrasyllus of Phlius, and many others, all of whom, we know, have as a matter of choice abstained from the chromatic genus, modulation, polychordy, and many other available resources—rhythms, tunings, diction, melodic construction and interpretation. Telephanes of Megara, for instance, was so opposed to the *syringes* that he never let his aulos-makers even put them on his auloi, and he stayed out of the Pythian competition mainly for this reason.[53]

Another conservative aulete was Dorion, who used to play for Philip of Macedon. He eschewed the fashionable style of Antigeneidas, and he was not without followers. It was he who made the scathing comment on Timotheus' storm effects cited earlier.[54]

Plato, following the lead of Damon, opposed many of the tendencies of modern music as morally harmful. In the *Republic*, discussing the cultural education of his ideal city's guardians, he rules out the imitation by men of women doing unseemly things like scolding their husbands, boasting against the gods, lamenting, dying, in love, in labour; or of slaves, or of men displaying cowardice, abusing each other, insane; or of neighing horses, bellowing bulls, noisy rivers, crashing seas, thunder and tempest, axles and pulleys, trumpets, panpipes, and other instruments. All this can only be done by using a whole range of different scales, rhythms, and changes of one to another. Once it is excluded, there will be no need of polychordy and omnimodality in the music, or of instruments such as harps or auloi that yield excessive numbers of notes and scales, or of complex rhythms.[55] In the *Laws* Plato is more explicit. Composers

---

[53] Ps.-Plut. *De mus.* 1137f–1138a, from Aristoxenus. This Telephanes, originally from Samos, was a well-known figure, cf. Dem. *Meid.* 17, *IG* 2². 3093, *CEG* 552 with Hansen's notes, Nicarchus *HE* 2747–50, Paus. 1. 44. 6, Ath. 351 e. On the mysterious *syrinx* see p. 86.

[54] Theopomp. loc. cit.; ps.-Plut. *De mus.* 1138 ab, from Aristoxenus; Ath. 337 c–338 a. Two of the authors quoted by Athenaeus, Machon (53 Gow) and Aristodemus, call him a composer of instrumental music (*kroumatopoios*).

[55] *Resp.* 395 d–400 a. Plato may have in mind, among other modern compositions, Timotheus' *Niobe* (woman boasting against gods), *Semele* (in labour), *Nauplios* (the storm), and *Ajax's Madness*.

mix up men's words with womanish 'colouring'[56] and womanish melody, or free men's melody and dance steps with slavish rhythms; they jumble into one composition the sounds of humans and animals, of musical instruments or anything else; they break up the proper union of words, melody, rhythm, and dance movement, and produce unaccompanied kithara or aulos music, in which it is very hard to understand what is supposed to be being conveyed. This is all crude and unmusical prestidigitation, this love of faultless rapidity and animal noise. The various genres used to be clearly distinct: hymns, dirges, paeans, dithyrambs, citharodic *nomoi*, and so on, each with its own kind of melody.

But as time went on, composers appeared who inaugurated unmusical rule-breaking, poetic spirits by nature but insensitive to the Muse's rights and principles, running wild and unduly possessed by pleasure, blending dirges with hymns and paeans with dithyrambs, making citharody sound like aulody, combining everything with everything, misled by their folly into denying that music has any true standard at all and saying that it is most truly judged by the pleasure it gives, be it of the better or the worse kind . . . Hence audiences became vocal instead of silent, as if they understood what is or is not fine in music, and instead of a sovereignty of the best there has come to be a loutish sovereignty of the auditorium.[57]

Aristoxenus too felt that music had become degraded by catering for the tastes of vulgar audiences. In early times, he maintained, it existed for the purpose of honouring the gods or educating the young, and there were no auditoria,

but in our own times corruption has made such inroads that there is no mention or conception of the educational, and all those who engage in music have gone over to the Muse of the concert-hall.[58]

As our auditoria have become barbarized and this vulgar music has reached an advanced state of corruption, we few in isolation recall what music used to be like.[59]

Aristoxenus' judgement on Crexus, Timotheus, and Philoxenus has been quoted earlier (p. 359). These composers of many notes and scales, he considers, are all inferior to the old inimitable Olympus.[60] They have abandoned the noble enharmonic genus, so that people

---

[56] The word, *chrōma*, is the same as that which denotes the chromatic genus; cf. p. 165.   [57] *Leg.* 669c–670a, 700a–701a.
[58] Aristox. ap. ps.-Plut. *De mus.* 1140d–f.   [59] Aristox. fr. 124.
[60] Ps.-Plut. *De mus.* 1137b.

no longer have any idea of it. The reason is that they are always
wanting to make music sweeter.[61]

'Incoherent, shrill, chaotic ... laborious trifling ... full of un-
accountable and often repulsive harmonies ... disagreeable eccen-
tricity ... morbid desire for novelty, extravagance, disdain of rule ...
odious miaowing ... does not belong to the art which I am in the
habit of considering as music ... violation of fundamental laws ...
ugly, in bad taste ... stupid and hopelessly vulgar ...'. All this was
said of Beethoven by nineteenth-century critics, some of them
writing long after his death.[62] Chopin, Liszt, Wagner, Debussy,
Mahler—these and many other great and original composers have
suffered such assaults from the unadjusted. We are in no position to
assert that Timotheus was a Beethoven. But we should beware of
adopting a disparaging attitude towards him and the other leading
composers of his time on the strength of Plato's and Aristoxenus'
complaints. It is clear that these composers extended music's technical and expressive resources and freed it from many of the con-
straints of conventional forms. It is not altogether inappropriate to
compare the transition from eighteenth-century Classicism to nineteenth-century Romanticism.

Aristoxenus records with a mixture of distaste and satisfaction the
case of a Theban musician called Telesias, who was brought up on
the best 'classical' composers, including Pindar, Dionysius of
Thebes, Lamprus, and Pratinas, and thoroughly well grounded in
aulos-playing and other aspects of musical education. In middle age
he became captivated by the elaborate theatrical music and, losing
interest in the classics, learned the most complex and untraditional
compositions of Philoxenus and Timotheus. He tried to compose in
both the Pindaric and the Philoxenian style; but his sound early
training precluded his being successful in the latter.[63]

As Plato and Aristoxenus themselves indicate, this music was
popular with the public and soon accepted as canonical.[64] A medical
philosopher of the mid-fourth century takes it as a fact that the
greatest diversity in musical notes is the most agreeable, and that the

---

[61] Ps.-Plut. *De mus.* 1145 a, cf. b–d; Aristox. *Harm.* 1. 23.

[62] Excerpted from N. Slonimsky, *Lexicon of Musical Invective*, 42–52.

[63] Aristox. fr. 76 ap. ps.-Plut. *De mus.* 1142 bc.

[64] According to Slonimsky, op. cit. 19, 'A fairly accurate time-table could be drawn
for the assimilation of unfamiliar music by the public and the critics. It takes
approximately twenty years to make an artistic curiosity out of a modernistic
monstrosity; and another twenty to elevate it to a masterpiece.'

most frequent and varied modulations give the greatest pleasure.[65] The quest for novelty continued. 'Music, like Africa, keeps producing some new kind of animal every year.'[66] Timotheus and the others were already being favourably compared with their juniors. A character in a comedy written sometime after Philoxenus' death praised him as the best of poets, with his original diction, his fine blending of melodic colourings and modulations; a god among men, he knew true music, 'whereas the men of today compose ivy-twined, spring-watery, flower-flittery songs in threadbare language, interwoven with alien melodies'.[67] This sounds like the 'patchwork' style associated with Polyidus of Selymbria, which, according to Aristoxenus, most citharodes had taken up in place of the Timothean manner. Polyidus won a dithyrambic victory at Athens sometime between 398 and 380. A pupil of his, one Philotas, managed to defeat the aging Timotheus in a contest; but when Polyidus expressed his pride at this, the citharist Stratonicus remarked that Philotas' songs were not real *nomoi* like Timotheus'.[68] The Peripatetic Phaenias wrote of two recent lyricists, Telenicus of Byzantium and Argas, who were fluent in their own manner 'but fell far short of the *nomoi* of Terpander and Phrynis': Phrynis has joined Terpander as a classic.[69]

THE LATER CENTURIES

After the time of Aristoxenus and Phaenias we find ourselves in a world seemingly devoid of acknowledged composers. The public's interest had come to be concentrated on performers, while the performers drew largely on established repertory and had their greatest successes with it. Of course new music was being composed all the time. But for the next 400 years and more, while we know the names of dozens of acclaimed poets, singers, actors, and auletes, the only composers we can name are the handful who chance to be recorded on commemorative inscriptions, such as the Athenians Athenaeus and Limenius whose paeans were sung at Delphi in 127 BC, or the few mentioned in literary sources, such as Glauce of Chios

---

[65] Ps.-Hippoc. *De Victu* 1. 18. 1.
[66] Anaxilas fr. 27 K.–A.
[67] Antiphanes fr. 207 K.–A.
[68] Aristox. in ps.-Plut. *De mus.* 1138b; *Marm. Par. FGrH* 239 A 68; Ath. 352b.
[69] Phaenias fr. 10 Wehrli. For Argas cf. Anaxandrides frs. 16. 4, 42. 17 K.–A.; Alexis fr. 19. 3 K.–A.

and Pyrrhus of Erythrae, whose songs are familiar to a rustic in Theocritus.[70] There is none otherwise until we come to Mesomedes in the time of Hadrian; and although he was remembered as 'the man who wrote the citharodic *nomoi*', it is not suggested that these were of particular significance in musical history.[71] From the literary tradition we would get the impression that musical evolution came to an end in the fourth century BC. The musical documents, however, show that it did not.

Before we summarize their evidence, it is appropriate to describe the conditions in which music flourished as a public art in the Hellenistic and early imperial periods.

There was a general increase in the number of musical festivals and competitions. The Dionysiac festivals of Athens, with their rich offerings of music and drama, inspired the institution of similar Dionysia in other cities, and dramatic performances became a feature of other festivals too. Musical contests were added to the Nemean and Isthmian Games. A monument to the early third-century citharode Nicocles of Tarentum records his victories at the Pythian and Isthmian Games, the Great Panathenaea, the Lenaea (in a dithyramb), the Hecatomboia, the Helieia, and royal festivals in Macedonia and Alexandria.[72]

The reference to royal festivals reflects the important role played by many rulers in promoting major musical events. At Alexander's five-day wedding festivities in Susa the company was entertained by a rhapsode, three psilocitharists, two citharodes, two aulodes, five auletes (who played the *Pȳthikos nomos* and then accompanied choruses), three tragic and three comic actors, and a harpist.[73] At Ecbatana he organized athletic and musical contests in which, it is said, three thousand competitors took part.[74] Demetrius Poliorcetes' nominal restoration of Athens' liberty and traditional constitution in 307 was the occasion for a competition for paeans sung in his honour.[75] Harpalus engaged Athens' leading musicians for the funeral of the courtesan Pythionice, and the cortège was attended by

---

[70] Theoc. *Id.* 4. 31 with schol., who describes Glauce as a composer of instrumental music; cf. Hedylus, *HE* 1883. She was better known as a citharode (below, p. 379).

[71] Dio Cass. 77. 13; cf. Euseb. *Chron.* Ol. 230. 4.

[72] *IG* 2². 3779, cf. Paus. 1. 37. 2. The Isthmian victory is noted as being the first there. [73] Chares, *FGrH* 125 F 4.

[74] Plut. *Alex.* 72. 1, Arr. *Anab.* 7. 14. 10.

[75] Philochorus, *FGrH* 328 F 165.

a large choir singing in unison with instruments of various kinds.[76] The grand procession of Ptolemy II at Alexandria has been mentioned elsewhere.[77] These were all single events, but rulers might also establish recurrent ones. Scores of new festivals were set up in the Hellenistic age either by or in honour of powerful persons. The Roman emperors often founded Games in their own honour, with a musical as well as a sporting programme.

Artists' guilds

An important development in the early third century BC was the formation, in more than one part of Greece, of professional associations of musicians and actors. Such entertainers had by this time come to be known by the general name of *technītai*, often translated 'artists', but connoting professional training and skill rather than artistry of the inspirational sort. Sometime about 290–280 the *technītai* of Athens formed themselves into a company or guild for the purpose of mounting shows, not only in their home city but also at other venues further afield. Very soon afterwards, if not even before, a similar body constituted itself from the artists 'who come together at the Isthmus and Nemea', that is, from those living in the north-east Peloponnese or other areas near enough for them to be regular visitors to the Isthmian and Nemean Games. Both of these guilds operated for over two centuries, sometimes in bitter rivalry, and in changing fortunes. Both of them quickly established relations with the supremely prestigious religious centre at Delphi and were granted various rights and privileges there. The Isthmian–Nemean guild, in particular, played a prominent role in the third century at the Delphic Soteria festival. In about 211 it was invited to take part in the newly reorganized festival of the Muses at Thespiae, and there is also evidence from this period for its activity at Thebes, on Delos, and around the Peloponnese. It was indeed, unlike the Athenian guild, developing into something approaching a nation-wide organization, with local branches in various places. At the same time other guilds were springing up in more distant regions. There was a major one based in Teos and covering Ionia and the Hellespont; it first appears about 235 BC, and it survived into the third century AD. There is evidence for others in Rhodes, Cyprus, Alexandria, and Sicily. From the time of Augustus there was an international associ-

---

[76] Posidonius, *FGrH* 87 F 14 = fr. 168 Th.   [77] See p. 41.

ation of *technītai* 'from the whole world', presumably embracing the older regional guilds, though at least some of them evidently maintained their identity within the larger organization.

The guilds generally called themselves Commonalty (*koinon*), or later Convention (*synodos*), of the Artists concerned with Dionysus, reflecting the traditional (Athenian) association of drama and dithyramb with the Dionysiac festivals. Much of their activity was concerned with honouring the gods with hymns, paeans, etc., at festivals, and they also took part in the sacrifices and processions there. They prided themselves on their piety, and conducted their own internal religious ceremonies at regular intervals. Their premises contained a shrine and sometimes a sacred precinct. In some cases a priest of Dionysus was the chief official of the guild.

The membership typically included rhapsodes, citharists, citharodes, auletes; tragic and comic poets, directors, and actors; choral singers and dancers for dithyrambs (boys' and men's), tragedy, and comedy; and costumiers. The dithyrambic and dramatic choruses were considerably smaller than those of fifth-century Athens, but no doubt just as effective, being composed of professionals instead of laymen (some of whom, as we know, only pretended to sing). In the inscriptions listing those who took part in the Delphic Soteria in the years from *c.*262 to *c.*252, the dithyrambic choruses do not exceed fifteen members, while the comic choruses have only seven or eight.[78]

We are well informed about three expeditions which the Athenian guild made to Delphi to celebrate the Pythaid festival in 127, 105, and 97 BC.[79] The Pythaid, nothing to do with the Pythian Games, was a pilgrimage from Athens held at irregular intervals and involving a substantial delegation of Athenians apart from the *technītai* who participated on these three occasions. In 127 some fifty-eight *technītai* took part; thirty-nine of them were singers, who formed a large choir to sing the paean to Apollo. We have most of the citharist Limenius' 'Paean and processional' and of the similar composition by Athenaeus sung at this festival (**12, 13**). There were various dramatic productions and concert performances (*akroāmata*) after the days of ceremonial. In 105 and 97 there were about a hundred

---

[78] Sifakis, 73f. The tragic choruses were apparently drawn from the same personnel as the men's dithyrambic.

[79] *SIG* 698, 728 K, 711 L + *BCH* 62 (1938) 362ff.; see Pöhlmann, *Griechische Musikfragmente*, 59–61; Sifakis, 86–94.

technītai, including a number of epic and dramatic poets, rhapsodes and actors, instrumentalists and singers. In 97, at least, besides regular citharists there were some 'accompanying citharists' (*potikitharizontes*) and a 'Pythian citharist' (see p. 60).

Varieties of public music

At festivals which included musical competitions the public could often witness performances in a whole range of genres: epic recitation, citharodic *nomoi*, instrumental solos (kithara, aulos, or harp), and dithyrambs, as well as drama in its several forms (including satyr-plays). At the Samian Heraia in the second century BC there was a competition for composers of solo kithara music.[80] Apart from the official competitions, musicians and entertainers of various kinds, acrobats, puppeteers, dancers, parodists, and so on, might put on free displays 'for the god', adding a day or more to the festival and earning themselves much favour with the authorities. We have records of such performances especially from Delos and Delphi.[81]

Many of the tragedies performed were old ones, especially plays of Euripides. Sometimes individual recitalists quarried material from these classics. The papyrus that preserves music to the *Iphigeneia in Aulis* was not a text of the whole play but contained merely lyrical excerpts (not in the proper order), and the same is probably true of the *Orestes* papyrus and other Hellenistic papyri containing tragic music. At the Pythian festival of (probably) 194 BC an eminent aulete from Samos, Satyrus by name, won the prize (no one else venturing to compete), and after the sacrifice that officially concluded the Games he gave as a bonus 'a song with chorus, *Dionysus*, and a *kitharisma* from Euripides' *Bacchae*'. Several things are unclear about this report, but there can be no doubt that it refers to some sort of arrangement made from a section of Euripides' play.[82]

[80] C. Michel, *Recueil d'inscriptions grecques*, no. 901. 5 *didaskaloi tōn kitharistōn*, where these 'instructors' are parallel to the 'poets' of new tragedies etc.

[81] Sifakis, 19f., 72f., 83, 85, 96–8, 104f. For the general phenomenon of travelling musicians in the Hellenistic age, and a collection of the civic inscriptions recording honours bestowed on them in various places, see M. Guarducci, *Atti della Reale Accademia Nazionale dei Lincei*, Classe di scienze morali, storiche e filologiche, ser. 6.2 (1927–9), 629–65.

[82] *SIG* 648 B, the inscription to an honorific statue of Satyrus. He also had a statue on Delos (*SIG* 648 A = *IG* 11. 1079), and he is known to have won victories elsewhere. The difficulties of the above notice are: how does an aulete 'give' a song with chorus, or a *kitharisma*, which should mean a kithara solo? How can a *kitharisma* be 'from' a tragedy? Were the two items separate, or was it one piece involving aulos, kithara, and voices? Cf. Sifakis, 96f. with literature.

In 118 BC the Delphians honoured two musicians from Arcadia who, apparently as trainers of boys' choruses, had presented 'items (*arithmoi*) from the old poets which were appropriate to the god and our city'.[83] Similarly the citharode Menecles of Teos, for a Cretan audience, drew from many poets and historians to make up a 'cycle' of narrative song on Cretan legend and tradition.[84] Nero sang the parts of various heroes and heroines from tragedy, wearing the appropriate masks and acting out their torments: Heracles mad, Oedipus blinded, Orestes beset by Furies, Canace in labour, and so on.[85] Philostratus in his fictional biography of Apollonius of Tyana describes a citharode of Nero's time who goes about singing a selection of lyrics from the emperor's tragedies and threatening to denounce those who fail to reward him.[86] Eunapius has a far-fetched story of another who bowled over a barbarian audience with highlights from Euripides' *Andromeda*.[87] A papyrus document of the first or second century AD lists pieces in the repertory of (or performed on a particular occasion by) an aulete Epagathus and other artists. The first and better preserved of the two columns reads:

Songs of Epagathus the *choraulēs*   40
   From dramas 6
   From *Hypsipyle* 6
   From *Deidameia*
   From *Androgynos* (?)
   From *Ransoming of Hector*
   From *Medea*
   From *Antiope*
Songs of his own   40

Epagathus was a *choraulēs*, i.e. he accompanied singers, in this case probably soloists, not a chorus. In the second column there is mention of 'songs of the tragic actor . . .', and of another *choraulēs*.[88] In the papyri of the first to third centuries AD we find excerpts from dramas in which not only the lyrics proper but also iambic speeches

---

[83] *SIG* 703. The usual interpretation of *arithmoi* as 'rhythms' is nonsensical.

[84] *Inscriptiones Creticae* i pp. 280 f., mid-2nd c. BC.

[85] Suet. *Ner.* 21, 46, Juv. 8. 220 ff., Dio Cass. 63. 9. 4, 10. 2, 22. 6, Philostr. *VA* 5. 7; Wille 342 f.   [86] *VA* 4. 39. 82.

[87] C. Boissevain, *Excerpta Historica iussu imperatoris Constantini Porphyrogeniti confecta*, iv (Berlin, 1906), 87. 21 ff.

[88] W. E. H. Cockle, *Proceedings of the XIVth International Congress of Papyrologists*, Oxford, 24–31 July 1974 (London, 1975), 59–65 with pl. xv.

have been set to music, surely going beyond the authors' intentions. In the second century the people of Miletus honoured one C. Aelius Themison, a winner of many prizes, who was 'the first and only man to set Euripides, Sophocles, and Timotheus to his own music'.[89]

Bleeding chunks of Euripides, dished up in various ways, may perhaps be classed as high- to middle-brow entertainment. Middle- to low-brow tastes were catered for by various kinds of performer to be encountered not at the great divine festivals but in more secular settings, privately organized shows, etc. There was the 'hilarode' or 'cheerful singer', who appeared in a white robe and gold crown and sang what seems to have been a straight-faced parody of tragic song, perhaps of a risqué nature, accompanied by a male or female harpist.[90] The 'simode', named after Simos of Magnesia, was regarded as similar to the hilarode. Simos, dated to the second half of the fourth century BC, 'corrupted' the melodic style of older composers, and dealt in poetic obscenity.[91] Then there were 'lysiodes', named after one Lysis, and 'magodes': both of these were more akin to comic actors. The magode is described as being equipped with drums and cymbals and dressed in feminine garments, but also as playing a variety of unseemly roles both male and female, an adulteress, a procuress, a drunk serenading his mistress, and so on.[92] The lysiode seems to have been something similar. We hear of women lysiodes, including one sexy creature who, with tipsy, melting looks at her audience, performed dances of such fluidity that she seemed to have no bones at all in her body, and left everyone extremely contented. These acts were accompanied on auloi of a particular kind.[93]

It was not only at this cabaret level that female musicians appeared before the public. There were some women citharodes, or at any rate courtesans accomplished in the art of singing to the lyre before an

[89] *SEG* 11. 52c (p. 215); O. Broneer, *Hesp.* 22 (1953), 192; cf. K. Latte, *Eranos* 52 (1954), 125–7 and 53 (1955), 75f. = *Kleine Schriften* (Munich, 1968), 590–4; J. Chailley, *Revue de musicologie* 39 (1957), 6–9 and 41 (1958), 15–26; A. Machabey, ibid. 41. 1–14; Pöhlmann, *Griechische Musikfragmente*, 15.

[90] Aristox. (fr. 110) and Aristocles (*c.* 100 BC) ap. Ath. 620d, 621bc; Festus p. 101. 10 M., *lasciui et delicati carminis cantator.*

[91] Aristocles loc. cit., Strab. 14. 1. 41 p. 648.

[92] Aristox. (frs. 110f.) and Aristocles ap. Ath. locc. citt.; Strab. loc. cit. Hesychius defines magody curtly as 'effeminate dancing'.

[93] Aristox. (fr. 111) and Aristocles ap. Ath. 620e; Strab. loc. cit. (Lysis as a poet of obscenity); Plut. *Sull.* 36. 2. Women lysiodes: Athenaeus, *FGrH* 166 F 1; Antip. Sid. *HE* 584ff. (if the mention of Lysis is correctly understood). Auloi: Posidonius, *FGrH* 87 F 4 = fr. 88 Th.; above, p. 94 n. 64. On all these kinds of entertainment (hilarody, simody, magody, lysiody) see P. Maas, *RE* iiiA. 159f.

audience, whose singing utterly captivated certain of their hearers. The most famous of them was Glauce of Chios, who sang at the court of Ptolemy Philadelphus and also composed.[94] A couple of others are immortalized by their admirers' epigrams; another was Panthea of Smyrna, a mistress of the emperor Verus.[95] The Berlin Ajax fragment (**42**) is a tragic lament set for a female singer. Evidence for female instrumentalists in outdoor events—harpists and organists— will be mentioned below.

Development of instruments

Lyre and aulos were, as always, the principal instruments. But now that music-making was so much concentrated in the hands of professionals, it was the more elaborate types of lyre and aulos that predominated. We hear much of citharodes and citharists, and presumably they often used kitharas with more than seven strings. If Limenius had a string on his kithara for each note in his Delphic paean, he needed fourteen or fifteen. We have the statement of Nicomachus that lyres were built with as many as eighteen strings, and one monument actually shows nineteen.[96] Auloi too were made increasingly versatile by the incorporation of subsidiary holes and attachments of various kinds.[97] There comes to be a clear distinction between the choral and the Pythian (solo) aulos, and we hear of a number of other specialized aulos types. There was also a specialized 'Pythian kithara' for solo playing.[98]

The harp, which in the Classical period was a domestic instrument mostly played by women, starts to appear in more public settings, in the hands of either sex. Male harpists are recorded as having performed at Alexander's wedding at Susa and at the Delian Apollo festivals of 284 and 236.[99] On the latter occasion two harpists played, each 'with accompanying (choral) song' (*meta prosōidiou*). Somewhat later there are records of female harpists who accompanied

---

[94] Theoc. *Id.* 4. 31 (above, n. 70); Pliny, *HN* 10. 51, Plut. *De Pyth. or.* 397 a, *al.*; cf. P. Maas, *RE* vii. 1396 f. and Gow on Theoc. loc. cit.

[95] Dioscorides, *HE* 1471, Antip. Sid. *HE* 496, Meleager, *HE* 4146, Anon. *Anth. Pal.* 5. 99, Crinagoras, *GP* 1777; Luc. *Imag.* 13 f.; still apparently in the 6th c., Agathias, *Anth. Pal.* 5. 222, 7. 612, Paulus Silentiarius, ibid. 16. 278.

[96] Nicom. p. 274. 6; above, p. 62 n. 69.

[97] See p. 87.

[98] See pp. 60, 93.

[99] Chares *FGrH* 125 F 4, *IG* 11. 105, 120. Anecdotes about harpists set earlier in the 4th c.: Plut. *Quomodo adul.* 67 f (entourage of Philip); Machon 104 ff. Gow. In the 5th c.: ps.-Plut. *Apophthegmata Laconica* 218 c.

choruses, *choropsaltriai.*[100] Evidently harps had been developed that had greater resonance and carrying power than the gentle-toned Classical instruments. These open-air concert harps must be distinguished from the light *sambȳkē* wielded by loosely-dressed girls at private entertainments.[101] There is evidence for the harp being taught in East Greek high schools in the second century BC.[102]

New instruments had come to Greece from the Levant at various times from the Bronze Age on. With the expansion of Hellenic culture into the East after Alexander, it was natural that further oriental instruments should find their way into Greek hands: unfamiliar types of lyre or harp (*skindapsos, klepsiambos, nablas*) and aulos (*gingros/ginglaros*); the flute, the lute, the zither, the bagpipe. None of these, however, attained more than a marginal significance.

The only new instrument that came to take a prominent role in ancient music-making was a native invention, the organ. It was apparently slow to achieve any currency; we hear nothing of it for more than a century and a half after the time of its inventor Ctesibius. But in 90 BC a Cretan organist named Antipatros went to Delphi as an official emissary from his city of Eleutherna. He so greatly impressed the Delphians with performances which he gave over a period of two days, and with his piety towards Apollo, that they loaded him with prizes at the Pythian Games and with civic honours for him and his descendants to enjoy in perpetuity.[103] Such rewards were not uncommonly bestowed on visiting musicians. But in view of the reference to Antipatros' piety towards the god, it may be conjectured that he had applied the organ to that genre of religious music that was traditional at the Pythian festival: the instrumental depiction of Apollo's arrival at Pytho and his victorious fight with the great serpent that guarded the place. If Antipatros played a version of the *Pȳthikos nomos* on the organ, the Delphians might well have felt that he had made an important contribution to their god's worship.

We find the organ in the service of religion again in Rhodes in the

---

[100] Michel (as n. 80) no. 910. 24 (Iasus, 2nd c. BC); *SIG* 689 and 738 (Pythian Games, 134 and 86 BC).

[101] See p. 77.

[102] *SIG* 578. 15 (Teos), 959. 10 (Chios); W. R. Paton and E. L. Hicks, *The Inscriptions of Cos* (Oxford, 1891), 59.

[103] *SIG* 737.

third century AD. It was employed there in the 'rousing' of Dionysus after his periodic descent to the lower world.[104] But it was more commonly to be heard in secular contexts, as in the Roman theatre and amphitheatre.[105] Gladiators fought to the death to the accompaniment of an organist, who watched them attentively and, like the cinema organist of a more recent era, improvised music to match the action; trumpeters and horn-blowers stood by to support him—or her—at dramatic moments.[106] Only loud instruments were suitable for such events, and these were the three loudest.[107] We have seen in Chapter 4 how the organ was made ever larger and louder in later Antiquity.[108]

Musical style

Timotheus remained a classic for centuries. His works were often performed, and some of the other composers of his time were also kept in circulation. At the Athenian Great Dionysia of 319 BC the boys' chorus of the Cecropid tribe won the dithyramb contest with a rendition of Timotheus' *Elpenor*. His *Persians* was performed at the Nemean Games in 205 by the citharode Pylades of Megalopolis. At Cnossos and Priansos, sometime about 170–150, an envoy from Teos called Menecles, as both cities recorded appreciatively in similar inscriptions, entertained his official hosts with several recitals to the kithara of 'the works of Timotheus and Polyidus and of our own (Cretan) ancient poets'; the Cnossians add 'as befitted a man of culture'.[109] The youth of Arcadia at this period

are trained from infancy to sing the traditional hymns and paeans with which they honour the local heroes and gods of each area; and later they learn the

[104] Inscription in *Jahreshefte des Österreichischen archäologischen Instituts* 7 (1904), 92; cf. M. P. Nilsson, *Geschichte der griechischen Religion*, ii² (Munich, 1961), 363 f.

[105] Anon. *Aetna* 296, Petron. *Sat.* 36. 6.

[106] See the 2nd-c. mosaics from Nennig (Rhineland) and Zlitis (Libya) in J. Perrot, *L'Orgue de ses origines hellénistiques à la fin du XIIIᵉ siècle*, 105–9 and pl. i–ii; also the bronze vase from Rheims in the Gréau collection, H. Degering, *Die Orgel*, 74 and pl. iv. 1. The two organists shown in the Zlitis mosaic are women. There is other iconographic and epigraphic evidence for female organists; see Perrot, op. cit. 267.

[107] Sen. *QNat.* 2. 6. 5.

[108] On the Roman taste for massive sonorities cf. Sen. *Ep.* 84. 10 (choirs larger than audiences used to be, singing in unison with a massed wind and string band); S.H.A. *Carinus* 19. 2 (100 trumpeters or horn-players or *pythaulae* or *choraulae*).

[109] *IG* 2². 3055; Plut. *Phil.* 11. 2, Paus. 8. 50. 3; *Inscriptiones Creticae* i pp. 66 no. 11 and 280 no. 1.

nomoi of Philoxenus and Timotheus, and dance them most zealously each year for the Dionysiac auletes in the theatres.[110]

The Stoic Diogenes of Seleucia refers to a composition by Crexus that his readers may be expected to have heard, and he is able to compare Philoxenus' style of dithyramb with Pindar's.[111] Nero's performing repertory included a *Niobe* and a *Nauplius*, which may well have been Timotheus' *nomoi* with those titles.[112] In the following century C. Aelius Themison was still singing Timotheus, though now to new music.[113] And at the Great Didymeia at Miletus in the third century one Aurelius Hierocles defeated 'the Timotheasts and Hegesiasts', who seem to be citharodes and orators in the styles of Timotheus and Hegesias respectively.[114]

Does this continued popularity of leading representatives of the New Music imply that Hellenistic composers went on writing in broadly the same manner? The evidence of the surviving fragments of their music suggests that they may have done so for some time, but that other currents eventually came to the fore.

The various dramatic fragments from papyri of the mid-third to early second century BC[115] are all too short to yield much information, and we do not know whether the texts in them are contemporary or older. But as far as they go, they present a fairly consistent picture of music characterized by modulation between chromatic and diatonic and between conjunct and disjunct tetrachords. In the Vienna fragments there are key-changes marked by explicit signatures where there was a progression between one section of the music and another. We also find a certain amount of chromaticism in the modern sense, exharmonic notes a semitone or perhaps a quarter-tone away from a regular scale degree, or dividing the interval between adjacent degrees. Not all the fragments show agreement of melody with word accent, which implies that some of them

---

[110] Polyb. 4. 20. 8–9. Either he is using *nomoi* loosely to cover both *nomoi* and dithyrambs of these composers, or their citharodic works were actually performed as dithyrambs. This may well be possible, as the two genres had evidently converged a good deal.

[111] Above, pp. 359, 364.

[112] Suet. *Ner.* 21. 2, 39. 3. For the *Nauplius* cf. also Crinagoras, *GP* 1778; Lucillius, *Anth. Pal.* 11. 185.

[113] Above, p. 378.

[114] A. Rehm, *Didyma*, ii: Die Inschriften (Berlin, 1958), no. 181. 5; K. Latte, *Eranos* 53 (1955), 75f. = *Kleine Schriften*, 593f.

[115] Ch. 10, catalogue nos. 7–10. I leave aside the two Euripides fragments. In the following paragraphs I summarize the detailed observations made in Chs. 6, 7, and 10.

were strophic. But in other respects their melodic style seems to have the features we should expect from followers of the New Music.

The Delphic paeans provide clearer evidence, being precisely dated and more extensively preserved. They use a large number of different notes (up to fifteen) and have a wide compass. The free astrophic form is employed, with much use of melodic means to enhance the expressive value of the words. There is alternation between diatonic and chromatic, with some passages in the old pentatonic manner, and some semitonal chromaticism. There is modal progression from section to section by means of conjunct–disjunct switches, much as reconstructed for Philoxenus' *Mysians* (p. 365). What there is not is metrical variety, though rhythmic monotony is avoided by freely alternating the various equivalent forms of paeonic foot (p. 142). Both composers speak of 'shimmering melodies', *aiola melea*, a phrase that suggests a link with the ideology of the New Music.[116] We cannot, of course, determine how far the melodic style of these works diverged from that of Timotheus or Philoxenus. But we certainly have the impression that no major transformation had overcome music between their time and the late second century BC.

There is then a gap in our evidence of more than a century, perhaps a century and a half; of the Mylasa inscription (**14**), which falls within this period, too little remains to be useful. When further texts become available, under the early Empire, it appears that a change has taken place. The style is less ambitious, there is less harmonic elaboration. The music is fully diatonic, though exharmonic ornament is used in places, and sometimes modulation between two scale-systems. Whereas the Hellenistic and earlier pieces are regularly in the E or A mode, so that Mesē functioned as the main tonal centre, the later ones are usually in the E, G, or C modes; and instead of the old tetrachordal structure there sometimes appears a clear sense of the major or minor triad ($c'-e'-g'$ or $a-c'-e'$) and of the importance of the interval of the third.

We know of one composer of this post-Hellenistic era, and one only, whose works achieved wide recognition. This was the Cretan-born citharode Mesomedes. He was a freedman of Hadrian, and apparently enjoyed an imperial salary, which (if we believe a somewhat unreliable source) the cost-cutting Pius reduced but did not

---

[116] Cf. Telestes, *PMG* 805 c. 2, 806. 3; also Soph. *Ichneutai* 327, Eur. *Ion* 499.

terminate. Caracalla honoured him with a cenotaph; Eusebius recorded his *floruit* (AD 141) in his date-tables; Dio Cassius identifies him as 'the man who wrote the citharodic nomes'; Synesius, the cultured Christian Neoplatonist from Cyrene, about AD 400, quotes from his hymn to Nemesis as something that 'we sing to the lyre'; and some of his music was transmitted into the Middle Ages in association with later musical treatises.[117] Why it enjoyed such prestige it is hard for us to comprehend, since the surviving specimens of it strike us as limited and uninspired in comparison with the Delphic paeans, whose composers' names left no echo. Mesomedes relies to some extent on melodic clichés. There is no true modulation (though there are shifts of tonal centre), perhaps no exharmonic ornament, and no perceptible correlation of melody to meaning.

Some other texts from the period, such as the Oslo and Michigan papyri (**30–3**), show us that a more florid style was in existence, usable at least for settings of dramatic scenes, characterized by more division of syllables between notes and decorative treatment of mythological names.[118] This continues through the third century and is seen in its most developed state in the Christian hymn from Oxyrhynchus (**51**). The Timothean style, although it too might have been described by its critics as florid or over-ornate, had little in common with this later one, where, beneath the melismatic embellishments, stood a single plain diatonic scale. The New Music was by now finally dead and forgotten.

The Christian hymn is perhaps the latest composition preserved in the ancient musical notation. The notation apparently fell into disuse not long afterwards (p. 272), and this signals the end of the old professionalism. By the sixth century Olympiodorus could write that no remnant of the Hellenic music was preserved: 'we hear only the rumour of it, and know nothing.'[119]

Of course the Greeks never stopped singing. Traditions of popular music must have continued, and there was the music of the Church. There are no doubt connections to be traced from the Hellenic music of the Roman period to the music of Byzantium. But

---

[117] *Suda* iii. 367. 8; S.H.A. *Pius* 7. 8; Dio Cass. 77. 13. 7; Euseb. *Chron.* Ol. 230. 4; Synesius, *Epist.* 95.
[118] See pp. 202 f.
[119] Ap. David, *Prolegomena Philosophiae* (*Commentaria in Aristotelem Graeca*, xviii. 2) p. 64. 34, quoting *Il.* 2. 486.

they will have to be traced across a wider and deeper gap in our evidence than any of the gaps we have negotiated in the foregoing survey, and on its brink I halt.

EPILOGUE

Greece between Europe and Asia

Greece occupies a unique position at the interface of two continents. Such is the layout of seas and lands that no other country of Europe is so exposed to the warm breath of Asia. 'Europe' and 'Asia' in this context are no empty cartographic labels, but weighty shorthand terms: they stand for two great cultural arenas, not coextensive with the Europe and Asia of atlases but conveniently designated by these names.

Behind Classical Greece on the European side, to the north and west, lay lands dominated by other branches of the great Indo-European family of peoples: Thracians, Illyrians, Celts, Italians, and beyond them others again, Scythians, Balto-Slavs, Germans. While by no means sharing a uniform culture, these peoples all to a greater or lesser degree retained elements of a common patrimony of language and, in some cases at least, of customs, social organization, poetic tradition, mythology, and religion.

Across the sea, to the south and east, Greece looked out towards a concatenation of old established urban civilizations, Egyptian, Phoenician, Syrian and Assyrian, and others stretching away to the sunrise. Within this zone that reached from north Africa across much of southern Asia, cultural influences had radiated eastwards and westwards from the centre, from Mesopotamia and Syria, since the earliest times.

The Greeks came out of a relatively unsophisticated Indo-European background, but their developing culture was to a considerable degree moulded in the second millennium by pre-existing 'Aegean' culture, and both then and later by contacts with the peoples of the east. This is undoubtedly a factor of high importance in relation to ancient Greek music. But how high? Was Curt Sachs, for example, justified in his view of Greek music as belonging wholly to the oriental sphere?[1] Does the balance shift in the course of time? These

'Griechische Musik und der Orient', *Musica* 12 (1958), 518–21.

last few pages will be devoted to a gingerly consideration of these questions.[2]

In respect of instruments the Greeks' indebtedness to Aegean and west Asiatic culture is clear. They may have brought the panpipe and the cowhorn from their previous homelands,[3] but their two principal instruments, the lyre and the paired oboe, came from the East, as did various others that appeared in the course of the historical period, the harp, the lute, the bagpipe. Some, like the drum, the cymbals, and the hornpipe, remained more or less confined to certain cults of Asiatic provenance. This shows that the Greeks did not accept indiscriminately whatever came into their ken. The instruments that they did accept whole-heartedly they made their own: the lyre and the auloi took on distinctively Greek forms, and were developed and improved in ways peculiar to Greece and those who learned from Greece.

The rhythms of ancient Greek music can to some extent be accounted for as Indo-European inheritance, as can the general principle of basing rhythm on the organization of syllabic quantities. We cannot identify any of their rhythms as Asiatic on the strength of foreign evidence, even if an association of the ionic rhythm with certain Asiatic cults and its use initially by East Greek poets (Sappho, Alcaeus, Anacreon; cf. its name 'ionic') may suggest that this rhythm was at home in Anatolia.[4] The paeonic rhythm in quintuple time appears alien to Indo-European tradition, and as the ancients associated it with Crete, it may have been of Minoan origin.[5] The highly distinctive dochmiac rhythm, which makes its appearance suddenly in Aeschylus and has modern Balkan parallels, may also have been taken over from some neighbour people. But in the absence of documentary evidence for rhythms used by non-Greek peoples in the Aegean area, we are groping in the dark.[6]

---

[2] 'Gin'gerlÿ (-nj-) *adv. & a.* with or showing extreme caution so as to avoid making a noise or injuring oneself or what is touched or trodden on' (*Concise Oxford Dictionary*).

[3] It is to be remembered, however, that the earlier Greek panpipe has the 'Aegean' rectangular form, giving way later to the 'European' stepped form (cf. p. 111).

[4] Cf. my *Greek Metre*, 124.

[5] Cf. above, p. 141; *Greek Metre*, 55. Gevaert, ii. 344 n. 2, observing that quintuple rhythm is found with the Turks, Finns, and Basques, diagnosed it as non-Indo-European. However, it has become endemic in eastern Europe regardless of racial distinctions, cf. p. 140 n. 31.

[6] The metre of the Lydian verse inscriptions, which I have elucidated in *Kadmos* 11 (1972), 165–75, does not appear to be relevant to anything in Greek music.

The simple recurring strophe of two to four lines and well-defined shape is another Indo-European feature, not characteristic of Near Eastern texts, and it has remained typical of European song.[7] The singing style that we have identified as normal in ancient Greece—loud, clear, without vocal constriction or artificial mannerism, with a solo singer or a chorus in well-blended unison—again corresponds to something widely found in Europe, to what Lomax has termed the Old European style. It stands in contrast to a tense, strident, ornamented style characteristic of the 'Old High Culture' areas of Asia.[8] That something like this opposition may have existed in Antiquity is suggested by the reference to the 'thin voice' in which the common-east-Mediterranean *Linos* song was sung.[9]

The adoption of an oriental manner of delivery in a specific ritual context where it was traditional is analogous to the use in certain cults, in particular the worship of the Great Mother, of oriental instruments that were not used in Greek music generally. Beside these two phenomena we can set a third: the use of antiphonal or responsorial song in certain cults and ritual settings that are, or may well be, either oriental or pre-Hellenic ('Aegean') in origin. A solo singer leads off, and a chorus answers, either with ritual cries or with more articulate lines of song. The *Linos* is one example; others may be found in the early dithyramb and paean, in dirges and wedding songs, and in the cult of Adonis.[10] It is an arrangement employed from ancient times in Jewish liturgy (and hence by the Christian Church), and almost certainly throughout the Near East.[11]

The typology of scales and melodies is also relevant to the question of Greek music's wider affinities. The standard scale-types of Archaic Greece seem to have been based on a trichord, or two trichords, of pentatonic structure, each containing a major third and a semitone. It is very likely that diatonic music was also known, perhaps more in northern and western parts of Greece than else-

---

[7] Cf. *Glotta* 51 (1973), 184; A. Lomax, *Folk Song Style and Culture*, 333 f.; Nettl, *FTM* 39–42.

[8] A. Lomax, *American Anthropologist* 61 (1959), 927–54 and as above; Nettl, *FTM* 47–9.

[9] See p. 45. The Egyptian and Assyrian representations of singers pressing or beating their larynxes to elicit a tremolo or glottal shake (p. 46 n. 43) are further evidence of the persistence of an oriental singing technique from Antiquity to modern times.   [10] Cf. pp. 339 f.

[11] In modern times it is characteristic of black Africa from Nubia southwards, and consequently of some of the music of black cultures in the Americas. Cf. C. Sachs, *The Rise of Music in the Ancient World*, 92–5; Nettl, *FTM* 115, 140 f., 226, 228.

where;[12] and the emergence of the chromatic genus in the fifth century points to an alternative form of pentatonic, with minor thirds and no semitones (until the lesser interval was divided).[13] The latter, anhemitonic type of pentatonic is much more widespread in the world than the other. It is a common feature of European folk song; but it is also familiar in other areas. It is attested for the ancient Near East (besides diatonic scales) by the vital statistics of certain surviving Egyptian wind instruments, by the score of a Hurrian hymn from about 1400 BC found at Ugarit, and by some of the oldest Hebrew melodies, which are argued, from agreements between widely separated communities, to pre-date the Babylonian Exile.[14] For the older Greek pentatonic system with major thirds, the best parallels are found in the Far East, in India, Mongolia, Tibet, China, Cambodia, Indonesia, Korea, and Japan. As in Greece, the major third usually occupies the upper part of the trichord, with a semitone step below it, and where the scale contains more than one such trichord, they may be either conjunct or separated by a disjunctive tone. Thus we get scales such as *e f a b c′ e′* (west Java, Japan), *e f a bb d′* (Bali), or *d e f a bb d′* (Japan), all of which would be quite at home in ancient Greece.[15] On a monogenetic hypothesis one might suppose that Greece and Japan represent the extremities of a very ancient major-third-trichord belt extending across southern Asia, its continuity broken by a later preference, over most of the area concerned, for the more even division into tone + minor third. In support of such a theory, which was adumbrated by Sachs, it can be pointed out that in China and Java, as in Greece, there is evidence for the encroachment of the minor-third upon the major-third type, and that major-third scales are also to be found among the Moroccan Berbers.[16] The theory would imply that the enharmonic trichord of Archaic Greek music—or perhaps we should say of south and east

---

[12] Cf. p. 165 for the prevalence of diatonic music among central and west Greek tribes.   [13] Cf. p. 164.

[14] See Sachs, op. cit. 73, and *Musik des Altertums* 32; A. Z. Idelsohn, *Jewish Music in its Historical Development* (New York, 1929); A. Sendrey, *Music in Ancient Israel* (London, 1969); Nettl, *FTM* 44; for the Hurrian hymn, my forthcoming study, 'The Babylonian Musical Notation', in *Music and Letters* (1993/4).

[15] Sachs, *The Rise of Music in the Ancient World*, 125–30; L. Picken in E. Wellesz (ed.), *Ancient and Oriental Music*, 130, 139, 141, 144–6, 152, 159, 161, 165–7, 174–6, 178.

[16] Sachs, op. cit. 126f.; Picken, op. cit. 130, 166f. I cannot discover the basis for Sachs's statement, repeated in several of his works and echoed by other writers, that Josephus speaks of the Egyptian harp as being 'enharmonic'.

Greek music—was an old Aegean substrate element. As it appears also in the modes called Phrygian and Lydian, it would seem to have been established in western Anatolia too.

A related matter is the structural importance of the fourth in Greek music and musical thinking. This again associates Greece with a vast zone stretching from north Africa across southern Asia to the Far East, and disjoins it from the greater part of Europe.[17] It is true that our evidence does not suffice for *ancient* Europe, and the existence of quartal melody in Scotland and Ireland might be interpreted as a marginal survival from an originally much larger quartal zone. But in this case one would have to leave open the possibility that quartal music belonged to a pre-Indo-European stratum, and that the general domination of the third in Europe reflects the music of the western Indo-Europeans.

We have seen that in later Antiquity Greek music became fully diatonic and also less tetrachordal, more addicted to the third as the mid-step of the fifth. These developments brought it more into line with what we see as the European norm. The change from the rectangular 'Aegean' panpipe to the stepped European type, though a detail of minor significance in itself, might be a straw in the same wind. To what extent the growing impingement of the Roman world on the Greek may have been a factor in these changes is a matter for speculation. It seems unnecessary to invoke it to account for the triumph of diatonicism, at any rate; the old enharmonic was already in retreat in Aristoxenus' time, and there is a universal tendency for the empty thirds of pentatonic scales to be filled in.

Another development of the Roman period was the increasing use of ornament in melody, something often regarded as typically oriental. But again there is no reason to ascribe it to anything other than internal evolution in Greek musical sensibilities. The elaborate ornamentation that we associate with eastern music was probably a later growth in the Arabic-Persian sphere, where Byzantine influence may have had a part to play.

In Greek music, as in other aspects of early Greek culture, we are faced with the complex product of Indo-European inheritance, Aegean and oriental environment, and Hellenic art and craft. It is our duty and delight to investigate all three of these elements; but the last, to which we have given most attention, was undoubtedly the most potent.

[17] See p. 163.

SELECT BIBLIOGRAPHY

GENERAL

Bibliographies, critical surveys

BUCHHOLTZ, H., *Bursians Jahresbericht über die Fortschritte der Klassischen Altertumswissenschaft* 11 (1877), 1–33.

VELKE, W., ibid. 15 (1878), 149–70.

GUHRAUER, H., ibid. 28 (1881), 168–82, and 44 (1885), 1–35.

VON JAN, C., ibid. 104 (1900), 1–75.

GRAF, E., ibid. 118 (1903), 212–35.

ABERT, H., ibid. 144 (1909), 1–74, and 193 (1922), 1–59.

FELLERER, G., ibid. 246 (1935).

WINNINGTON-INGRAM, R. P., *Lustrum* 3 (1958), 1–56, 259f.

MATHIESEN, T. J., *A Bibliography of Sources for the Study of Ancient Greek Music* (Hackensack, NJ, 1974).

—— *Ancient Greek Music Theory: A Catalogue Raisonné of Manuscripts* (*Répertoire international des sources musicales*, B xi, Munich 1988).

Annual bibliographies under the relevant heading in *L'Année philologique*.

Ethnomusicology

ENGEL, C., *An Introduction to the Study of National Music* (London, 1866).

KUNST, J., *Ethno-musicology*, 3rd edn. (The Hague, 1959).

SACHS, C., *The Wellsprings of Music* (The Hague, 1962).

MERRIAM, A. P., *The Anthropology of Music* (Northwestern University Press, 1964).

NETTL, B., *Theory and Method in Ethnomusicology* (Glencoe and London, 1964).

—— *Folk and Traditional Music of the Western Continents*, 2nd edn. (Englewood Cliffs, NJ, 1973).

LOMAX, A., *Folk Song Style and Culture* (Washington, DC, 1968).

WIORA, W., *Ergebnisse und Aufgaben vergleichender Musikforschung* (Darmstadt, 1975).

Music in antiquity

GEVAERT, F. A., *Histoire et théorie de la musique de l'antiquité*, 2 vols. (Ghent, 1875–81).

WESTPHAL, R., *Die Musik des griechischen Alterthumes* (Leipzig, 1883).

—— *Griechische Harmonik und Melopoeie*, 3rd edn. (= A. Rossbach and R. Westphal, *Theorie der musischen Künste der Hellenen*, ii) (Leipzig, 1886).

REISCH, E., *De musicis Graecorum certaminibus capita quattuor* (Vienna, 1885).

LALOY, L., *Aristoxène de Tarente, disciple d'Aristote, et la musique de l'antiquité* (Paris, 1904).

SACHS, C., *Musik des Altertums* (Breslau, 1924).

REINACH, T., *La Musique grecque* (Paris, 1926).

MOUNTFORD, J. F., 'Greek music in the papyri and inscriptions', in *New Chapters in Greek Literature*, ed. J. U. Powell and E. A. Barber, 2nd ser. (Oxford, 1929), 146–83.

QUASTEN, J., *Musik und Gesang in den Kulten der heidnischen Antike und christlichen Frühzeit* (*Liturgiegeschichtliche Quellen und Forschungen*, xxv, Münster, 1930).

VETTER, W., 'Musik', 'Musikunterricht', *RE* xvi (1931), 823–84.

SACHS, C., *The Rise of Music in the Ancient World East and West* (New York, 1943).

WEGNER, M., *Das Musikleben der Griechen* (Berlin, 1949).

BEHN, F., *Musikleben im Altertum und frühen Mittelalter* (Stuttgart, 1954).

VETTER, W., 'Griechenland. Antike', *MGG* v (1956), 839–65.

HENDERSON, I., 'Ancient Greek Music', in *Ancient and Oriental Music* (*New Oxford History of Music*, i), ed. E. Wellesz (London, 1957), 336–403.

DEL GRANDE, C., *La metrica greca* (from *Enciclopedia classica*, v, Turin, 1960), 401–76, 'Cenni sulla musica greca'.

PÖHLMANN, E., *Griechische Musikfragmente: Ein Weg zur altgriechischen Musik* (Nuremberg, 1960).

WEGNER, M., *Griechenland* (*Musikgeschichte in Bildern*, ii. 4, Leipzig, 1963).

PÖHLMANN, E., *Denkmäler altgriechischer Musik*, Nuremberg, 1970.

MOUNTFORD, J. F., and WINNINGTON-INGRAM, R. P., 'Music', *Oxford Classical Dictionary*, 2nd edn. (Oxford, 1970), 705–13.

HENDERSON, I., and WULSTAN, D., 'Ancient Greek Music', in *Music from the Middle Ages to the Renaissance* (*A History of Western Music*, i), ed. F. W. Sternfeld (London, 1973), 27–58.

NEUBECKER, A. J., *Altgriechische Musik* (Darmstadt, 1977).

MICHAELIDES, S., *The Music of Ancient Greece: An Encyclopedia* (London, 1978).

CHAILLEY, J., *La Musique grecque antique* (Paris, 1979).

WINNINGTON-INGRAM, R. P., 'Greece. I. Ancient', *NG* vii (1980), 659–72.

BARKER, A., *Greek Musical Writings*, 2 vols. (Cambridge, 1984–9).

COMOTTI, G., *Music in Greek and Roman Culture* (Baltimore and London, 1989).

RIETHMÜLLER, A., and ZAMINER, F. (eds.), *Musik im Altertum* (*Neues Handbuch der Musikwissenschaft*, i, Laaber, 1989).

TEXTS AND SOURCES

Collections

PÖHLMANN, E., *Denkmäler altgriechischer Musik* (Nuremberg, 1970). Corpus of musical documents known up to 1970; for more recent items (and a couple overlooked by Pöhlmann) see Ch. 10, nos. 1, 4–6, 10–11, 14, 34–9, 45–50.

JANUS (VON JAN), C., *Musici scriptores Graeci: Aristoteles, Euclides, Nicomachus, Bacchius, Gaudentius, Alypius* (Leipzig, 1895). 'Euclides' includes Cleonides.

ZANONCELLI, L., *La manualistica musicale greca* (Milan, 1990). Jan's text of the *Musici* (above, omitting Aristotle) plus Italian translation and commentary.

RITOÓK, Zs., *Források az ókori görög zeneesztétika történetéhez* (Budapest, 1982). A collection of excerpts from ancient authors on the philosophy and aesthetics of music (Greek and Hungarian).

BARKER, A., *Greek Musical Writings*, 2 vols. (Cambridge, 1984–9). Annotated translations of ps.-Plutarch, Aristoxenus, Euclid, Nicomachus, Ptolemy, Aristides Quintilianus, and numerous excerpts from Plato, Aristotle, Athenaeus, and other authors.

Individual authors

ALCIDAMAS (?), *Against the harmonikoi*. *PHib*. 13. *The Hibeh Papyri*, Part I, ed. B. P. Grenfell and A. S. Hunt, London, 1906, 45–8; translated in Barker, *GMW*, i. 183–5; improved text in *ZPE*, 92 (1992), 16–23.

ANONYMUS BELLERMANNI. Najock, D., *Drei anonyme griechische Traktate über die Musik. Eine kommentierte Neuausgabe des Bellermannschen Anonymus* (Kassel, 1972).

—— Najock, D. (ed.), *Anonyma de musica scripta Bellermanniana* (Leipzig (Bibl. Teubn.), 1975).

ARISTIDES QUINTILIANUS, *De musica libri tres*, ed. R. P. Winnington-Ingram (Leipzig (Bibl. Teubn.), 1963).

—— Translation in Barker, *GMW* ii. 392–535.

ARISTOTLE (Ps.-), *Problems*. Text of musical portions in Jan's *Musici*; translation of most in Barker, *GMW* i. 190–204; ii. 85–97.

—— Gevaert, F., and Vollgraff, J. C., *Problèmes musicaux d'Aristote*. Texte grec avec traduction française, notes philologiques, commentaire musical et appendice (Ghent, 1903).

394 *Select Bibliography*

ARISTOXENUS. Macran, H. S., *The Harmonics of Aristoxenus* (Oxford, 1902).
—— Da Rios, R., *Aristoxeni elementa harmonica* (Rome, 1954).
—— Barker, *GMW* ii. 119–84.
—— *Elementa Rhythmica*. The fragment of Book II and the additional evidence for Aristoxenian rhythmic theory. Texts edited with introduction, translation, and commentary by Lionel Pearson (Oxford, 1990).
—— Fragments of other works: Wehrli, F., *Aristoxenos* (*Die Schule des Aristoteles*, 2), 2nd edn. (Basle, 1967).
ATHENAEUS, *Dipnosophistarum libri xv*, ed. G. Kaibel, 3 vols. (Leipzig (Bibl. Teubn.), 1887–90).
—— *Deipnosophistae*, ed. and trans. B. Gulick, 7 vols. (Cambridge, Mass. (Loeb Classical Library), 1950).
—— Extracts in Barker, *GMW* i. 258–303.
BOETHIUS, *De institutione musica libri quinque*, ed. G. Friedlein (Leipzig, 1867).
BRYENNIUS, MANUEL, *Harmonica*, ed. G. H. Jonker (Groningen, 1970).
CLEONIDES. Translation in O. Strunk, *Source Readings in Music History* (New York, 1950), 34–46.
EUCLID, *Sectio Canonis*. Barker, *GMW* ii. 190–208.
NICOMACHUS. Barker, *GMW* ii. 245–69.
PHILODEMUS, *De Muziek*, met Vertaling en Commentaar door D. A. van Krevelen (Amsterdam, 1939).
—— Rispoli, G. M., *Il primo libro del Peri Mousikes di Filodemo*. Estratto dal Volume I delle *Ricerche sui Papiri Ercolanesi* (*c.* 1969).
—— *Über die Musik, Viertes Buch*, ed. and trans. A. J. Neubecker (*La Scuola di Epicuro*, 4, Naples, 1986).
(Ps.-)PLUTARCH, *De musica*. Weil, H., and Reinach, T., *Plutarque, De la musique*, Édition critique et explicative (Paris, 1900).
—— Lasserre, F., *Plutarque, De la musique*, Texte, traduction, commentaire (Olten and Lausanne, 1954).
—— Einarson, B., and De Lacy, P. H., *Plutarch, Moralia*, xiv (Cambridge, Mass. (Loeb Classical Library), 1967), 344–455.
—— Barker, *GMW* i. 205–57.
PORPHYRY. Düring, I., *Porphyrios' Kommentar zur Harmonielehre des Ptolemaios* (*Göteborgs Högskolas Årsskrift*, 38.2) (Gothenburg, 1932).
PSELLUS, *De tragoedia*. Browning, R., in Γέρας: *Studies presented to G. Thomson* (Prague, 1963), 67–81.
PTOLEMY. Düring, I., *Die Harmonielehre des Klaudios Ptolemaios* (*Göteborgs Högskolas Årsskrift*, 36.1, Gothenburg, 1930).
—— Düring, I., *Ptolemaios und Porphyrios über die Musik* (*Göteborgs Högskolas Årsskrift*, 40.1, Gothenburg, 1934).
—— Barker, *GMW* ii. 270–391.

SEXTUS EMPIRICUS, *Adversus mathematicos*, ed. J. Mau (Leipzig (Bibl. Teubn.), 1954).
— *Against the Musicians*, Bury, R. G., *Sextus Empiricus*, iv (Cambridge, Mass. (Loeb Classical Library), 1961), 372–405.
THEO SMYRNAEUS, *Expositio rerum mathematicarum ad legendum Platonem utilium*, ed. E. Hiller (Leipzig (Bibl. Teubn.), 1878).

INSTRUMENTS

General

SACHS, C., *The History of Musical Instruments* (New York, 1940).
WEGNER, M., *Die Musikinstrumente des alten Orients* (Münster, 1950).
BAINES, A. (ed.), *Musical Instruments Through the Ages* (Harmondsworth, 1961).
AIGN, B., *Die Musikinstrumente des ägäischen Raumes bis um 700 vor Christus* (Frankfurt am Main, 1963).
RIMMER, JOAN, *Ancient Musical Instruments of Western Asia in the British Museum* (London, 1969).
PAQUETTE, D., *L'Instrument de musique dans la céramique de la Grèce antique* (Paris, 1984).

Stringed instruments

VON JAN, C., *De fidibus Graecorum* (Berlin, 1859).
— *Die griechischen Saiteninstrumente*, Programm des Gymnasiums Saargemünd (Leipzig, 1882).
REINACH, T., 'Lyra', Dar.–Sag. iii. 1437–51.
ABERT, H., 'Saiteninstrumente', *RE* iA (1920), 1760–7.
— 'Lyra', *RE* xiii (1927), 2479–89.
HERBIG, R., 'Griechische Harfen', *MDAI*(A) 54 (1929), 164–93.
HUCHZERMEYER, H., *Aulos und Kithara in der griechischen Musik bis zum Ausgang der klassischen Zeit* (Emsdetten, 1931).
HIGGINS, R. A., and WINNINGTON-INGRAM, R. P., 'Lute-players in Greek Art', *JHS* 85 (1965), 62–71.
ROBERTS, HELEN D., *Ancient Greek Stringed Instruments 700–200 BC*, Diss. (Reading, 1974).
— 'The Technique of Playing Ancient Greek Instruments of the Lyre Type', in *Music and Civilization* (*British Museum Yearbook*, 4), ed. T. C. Mitchell (1980), 43–76.
— 'Reconstructing the Greek Tortoise-Shell Lyre', *World Archaeology* 12 (1981), 303–12.
MAAS, MARTHA, and SNYDER, JANE McI., *Stringed Instruments of Ancient Greece* (New Haven and London, 1989).

Wind instruments

HOWARD, A. A., 'The Aulos or Tibia', *Harv. Stud.* 4 (1893), 1–63.

SOUTHGATE, T. L., 'Ancient Flutes from Egypt', *JHS* 35 (1915), 12–21.

VON JAN, C., 'Aulos 4', *RE* ii (1896), 2416–22.

REINACH, T., 'Syrinx', Dar.–Sag. iv (1911), 1596–1600.

—— 'Tibia', Dar.–Sag. v (1919), 300–32.

—— 'Tuba', Dar.–Sag. v (1919), 522–8.

HUCHZERMEYER, H., as above.

SCHLESINGER, KATHLEEN, *The Greek Aulos* (London, 1939).

BODLEY, N. B., 'The Auloi of Meroë', *AJArch.* 50 (1946), 217–40.

BAINES, A., *Bagpipes* (Oxford (Pitt Rivers Museum), 1960; revised edn. 1979).

LANDELS, J. G., 'The Brauron Aulos', *BSA* 58 (1963), 116–19.

—— 'Fragments of Auloi found in the Athenian Agora', *Hesp.* 33 (1964), 392–400.

PERROT, J., *L'Orgue de ses origines hellénistiques à la fin du XIIIe siècle* (Paris, 1965).

BECKER, H., *Zur Entwicklungsgeschichte der antiken und mittelalterlichen Rohrblattinstrumente* (Hamburg, 1966).

BAINES, A., *Woodwind Instruments and their History*, 3rd edn. (London, 1967).

LANDELS, J. G., 'A Newly Discovered Aulos', *BSA* 63 (1968), 231–8.

LETTERS, R. J., 'The Scales of Some Surviving Auloi', *CQ* 19 (1969), 266–8.

MASARAKI, D. W., 'Ein Aulos der Sammlung Karapanos', *MDAI*(A) 89 (1974), 105–21.

BAINES, A., *Brass Instruments* (London, 1976).

BÉLIS, ANNIE, 'Auloi grecs du Louvre', *BCH* 108 (1984), 111–22.

—— 'Fragments d'auloi', *L'Antre corycien*, ii (*BCH* Supp. ix, 1984), 176–81.

HAAS, G., *Die Syrinx in der griechischen Bildkunst* (*Wiener musikwissenschaftliche Beiträge*, 11) (Vienna, 1985).

BÉLIS, ANNIE, 'La Phorbéia', *BCH* 110 (1986), 205–18.

—— 'L'Aulos phrygien', *Rev. Arch.* (1986), 21–40.

—— 'Charnières ou auloi?', *Rev. Arch.* (1988), 109–18.

RHYTHM

CAESAR, J., *Die Grundzüge der griechischen Rhythmik im Anschluss an Aristides Quintilianus* (Marburg, 1861).

WESTPHAL, R., *Griechische Rhythmik*, 3rd edn. (= A. Rossbach and R. Westphal, *Theorie der musischen Künste der Hellenen*, i) (Leipzig, 1885).

GEORGIADES, T., *Der griechische Rhythmus: Musik, Reigen, Vers und Sprache* (Hamburg, 1949).

SACHS, C., *Rhythm and Tempo* (New York, 1953).

GEORGIADES, T., *Greek Music, Verse, and Dance* (New York, 1956).

—— *Musik und Rhythmus bei den Griechen* (Hamburg, 1958).

WEST, M. L., *Greek Metre* (Oxford, 1982).

PEARSON, L., *Aristoxenus, Elementa Rhythmica* (Oxford, 1990).

SCALES AND MODES

FORTLAGE, K., *Das musikalische System der Griechen in seiner Urgestalt* (Leipzig, 1847).

BELLERMANN, J. F., *Die Tonleitern und Musiknoten der Griechen* (Berlin, 1847).

MONRO, D. B., *The Modes of Ancient Greek Music* (Oxford, 1894).

MOUNTFORD, J. F., 'The Musical Scales of Plato's Republic', *CQ* 17 (1923), 125–36.

WINNINGTON-INGRAM, R. P., 'The Spondeion Scale', *CQ* 22 (1928), 83–91.

—— 'Aristoxenus and the Intervals of Greek Music', *CQ* 26 (1932), 195–208.

—— *Mode in Ancient Greek Music* (Cambridge, 1936).

GOMBOSI, O., *Die Tonarten und Stimmungen der antiken Musik* (Copenhagen, 1939).

HENDERSON, I., 'The Growth of the Greek ἁρμονίαι', *CQ* 36 (1942), 94–103.

SHIRLAW, M., 'The Music and Tone Systems of Ancient Greece', *Music Review* 4 (1943), 14–27.

—— [same title], *Music and Letters* 32 (1951), 131–9.

WINNINGTON-INGRAM, R. P., 'The Pentatonic Tuning of the Greek Lyre: A Theory Examined', *CQ* 6 (1956), 169–86.

CHAILLEY, J., 'Le Mythe des modes grecs', *Acta Musicologica* 28 (1956), 137–63.

—— *L'Imbroglio des modes* (Paris, 1960).

VOGEL, M., *Die Enharmonik der Griechen*, 2 vols. (Düsseldorf, 1963).

WEST, M. L., 'The Singing of Homer and the Modes of Early Greek Music', *JHS* 101 (1981), 113–29.

SOLOMON, J., 'Towards a History of Tonoi', *Journal of Musicology* 3 (1984), 242–51.

ČERNÝ, M. K., 'Zur Problematik der altgriechischen "Tonarten"', *Eirene* 25 (1988), 87–103.

ANCIENT THEORY

AMSEL, G., *De vi atque indole rhythmorum quid veteres iudicaverint* (Breslau, 1887).

ABERT, H., *Die Lehre vom Ethos in der griechischen Musik* (Leipzig, 1899).

BOYANCÉ, P., *Le Culte des Muses chez les philosophes grecs* (Paris, 1937).

VAN DER WAERDEN, B. L., 'Die Harmonielehre der Pythagoreer', *Hermes* 78 (1943), 163–99.

VETTER, W., 'Ethos', *MGG* iii (1954), 1581–91.

NEUBECKER, A. J., *Die Bewertung der Musik bei Stoikern und Epikureern. Eine Analyse von Philodems Schrift De Musica* (Berlin, 1956).

MOUTSOPOULOS, E., *La Musique dans l'œuvre de Platon* (Paris, 1959).

RICHTER, L., *Zur Wissenschaftslehre von der Musik bei Platon und Aristoteles* (Berlin, 1961).

LIPPMAN, E. A., *Musical Thought in Ancient Greece* (New York, 1964).

ANDERSON, W. D., *Ethos and Education in Greek Music* (Cambridge, Mass., 1966).

ZOLTAI, D., *Ethos und Affekt: Geschichte der philosophischen Musikästhetik von den Anfängen bis zu Hegel* (Berlin and Budapest, 1970).

BURKERT, W., *Lore and Science in Ancient Pythagoreanism* (Cambridge, Mass., 1972).

NOTATION

BELLERMANN, J. F., as above under Scales and Modes.

SACHS, C., 'Die griechische Instrumentalnotenschrift', 'Die griechische Gesangsnotenschrift', *Zeitschrift für Musikwissenschaft* 6 (1923/4), 289–301 and 7 (1924/5), 1–5.

BARBOUR, J. M., 'The Principles of Greek Notation', *Journal of the American Musicological Society* 13 (1960), 1–17.

BATAILLE, A., 'Remarques sur les deux notations mélodiques de l'ancienne musique grecque', *Recherches de papyrologie* 1 (1961), 5–20.

POTIRON, H., 'La Notation grecque au temps d'Aristoxène', *Revue de musicologie* 50 (1964), 222–5.

CHAILLEY, J., 'Nouvelles remarques sur les deux notations musicales grecques', *Recherches de papyrologie* 4 (1967), 201–16.

WINNINGTON-INGRAM, R. P., 'The First Notational Diagram of Aristides Quintilianus', *Philol.* 117 (1973), 243–9.

—— 'Two Studies in Greek Musical Notation', *Philol.* 122 (1978), 237–48.

MUSIC AT PARTICULAR PERIODS

Down to the seventh century

WEGNER, M., *Musik und Tanz* (*Archaeologia Homerica*, U) (Göttingen, 1968).

Drama

BETHE, E., 'Die griechische Tragödie und die Musik', *Neue Jahrb.* 10 (1907), 81–95.

KRANZ, W., *Stasimon* (Berlin, 1933).

MARX, F., 'Musik in der griechischen Tragödie', *Rh. Mus.* 82 (1933), 230–46.

PICKARD-CAMBRIDGE, A. W., *The Dramatic Festivals of Athens*, 2nd edn. revised by J. Gould and D. M. Lewis (Oxford, 1968).

RICHTER, L., 'Musikalische Aspekte der attischen Tragödienchöre', *Beiträge zur Musikwissenschaft* 14 (1972), 247–98.

PINTACUDA, M., *La Musica nella tragedia greca* (Cefalù, 1978).

—— *Interpretazioni musicali sul teatro di Aristofane* (Palermo, 1982).

RICHTER, L., 'Die Musik der griechischen Tragödie und ihre Wandlungen unter veränderten historischen Bedingungen', in *Die griechische Tragödie in ihrer gesellschaftlichen Funktion*, ed. H. Kuch (Berlin, 1983), 115–39.

GALY, J. H., 'La Musique dans la comédie grecque des v et iv siècles', *Annales de la Faculté des Lettres de Nice* 50 (1985), 77–94.

The New Music

VON WILAMOWITZ-MOELLENDORFF, U., *Timotheos. Die Perser* (Leipzig, 1903).

SCHÖNEWOLF, H., *Der jungattische Dithyrambos*, Diss. (Giessen, 1938).

DÜRING, I., 'Studies in Musical Terminology in Fifth Century Literature', *Eranos* 43 (1945), 176–97.

RICHTER, L., 'Die Neue Musik der griechischen Antike', *Archiv für Musikwissenschaft* 25 (1968), 1–18, 134–47.

RESTANI, D., 'Il *Chirone* di Ferecrate e la "nuova" musica greca', *Rivista italiana di musicologia* 18 (1983), 139–92.

Hellenistic

GUARDUCCI, M., 'Poeti vaganti e conferenzieri dell'età ellenistica', *Atti della Reale Accademia Nazionale dei Lincei*, Classe di scienze morali, storiche e filologiche, serie 6, 2 (1927–9), 629–65.

POLAND, F., 'Technitai', *RE* VA (1934), 2473–558.

FLEISCHAUER, G., *Die Musikergenossenschaften im hellenistisch-römischen Altertum*, Diss. (Halle, 1959).

SIFAKIS, G. M., *Studies in the History of Hellenistic Drama* (London, 1967).

PICKARD-CAMBRIDGE, A. W., as above under Drama.

Index